Microsoft® *Getting Started with* Office XP

Microsoft®

Getting Started with Office XP

Robert T. Grauer
University of Miami

Maryann Barber
University of Miami

PRENTICE HALL *Upper Saddle River, New Jersey 07458*

Senior Acquisitions Editor: David Alexander
VP/Publisher: Natalie Anderson
Managing Editor: Melissa Whitaker
Assistant Editor: Kerri Limpert
Editorial Assistant: Maryann Broadnax
Technical Editor: Cecil Yarbrough
Media Project Manager: Cathleen Profitko
Marketing Assistant: Jason Smith
Production Manager: Gail Steier de Acevedo
Project Manager: Lynne Breitfeller
Production Editor: Greg Hubit
Associate Director, Manufacturing: Vincent Scelta
Manufacturing Buyer: Lynne Breitfeller
Design Manager: Pat Smythe
Interior Design: Jill Yutkowitz
Cover Design: Blair Brown
Cover Illustration: Marjorie Dressler
Composition: GTS
Printer/Binder: Banta Menasha

10 9 8 7 6 5 4 3 2 1
ISBN 0-13-034250-5

Prentice Hall

To Marion —
my wife, my lover, and my best friend

Robert Grauer

To Frank —
for giving me the encouragement, love, and the space

Maryann Barber

CONTENTS

MICROSOFT® EXCEL 2002

1

INTRODUCTION TO MICROSOFT EXCEL: WHAT IS A SPREADSHEET? 1

MICROSOFT® ACCESS 2002

1

INTRODUCTION TO MICROSOFT ACCESS: WHAT IS A DATABASE? 1

MICROSOFT® POWERPOINT® 2002

1

INTRODUCTION TO POWERPOINT: PRESENTATIONS MADE EASY 1

THE INTERNET AND WORLD WIDE WEB: WELCOME TO CYBERSPACE

Getting Started: Essential Computing Concepts

Index

PREFACE

ABOUT THIS SERIES........

Continuing a tradition of excellence, Prentice Hall is proud to announce the latest update in Microsoft Office texts: the new Exploring Microsoft Office XP series by Robert T. Grauer and Maryann Barber.

The hands-on approach and conceptual framework of this comprehensive series helps students master all aspects of the Microsoft Office XP software, while providing the background necessary to transfer and use these skills in their personal and professional lives.

WHAT'S NEW IN THE EXPLORING OFFICE SERIES FOR XP

The entire Exploring Office series has been revised to include the new features found in the Office XP Suite, which contains Word 2002, Excel 2002, Access 2002, PowerPoint 2002, Publisher 2000, FrontPage 2002, and Outlook 2002.

In addition, this revision includes fully revised end-of-chapter material that provides an extensive review of concepts and techniques discussed in the chapter. Many of these exercises feature the World Wide Web and application integration.

Building on the success of the Web site provided for previous editions of this series, Exploring Office XP will introduce the MyPHLIP Companion Web site, a site customized for each instructor that includes on-line, interactive study guides, data file downloads, current news feeds, additional case studies and exercises, and other helpful information. Start out at www.prenhall.com/grauer to explore these resources!

Organization of the Exploring Office Series for XP

The new Exploring Microsoft Office XP series includes four combined Office XP texts from which to choose:

- ***Volume I*** is MOUS certified in each of the major applications in the Office suite (Word, Excel, Access, and PowerPoint). Three additional modules (Essential Computer Concepts, Essentials of Windows, and Essentials of the Internet) are also included.
- ***Volume II*** picks up where Volume I left off, covering the advanced topics for the individual applications. A VBA primer has been added.
- The ***Brief Microsoft Office XP*** edition provides less coverage of the individual applications than Volume I (a total of 8 chapters as opposed to 14). The supplementary modules (Windows, Internet, and Concepts) are not included.
- A new volume, ***Getting Started with Office XP***, contains the first chapter from each application (Word, Excel, Access, and PowerPoint), plus three additional modules: Essentials of Windows, Essentials of the Internet, and Essential Computer Concepts.

Individual texts for Word 2002, Excel 2002, Access 2002, and PowerPoint 2002 provide complete coverage of the application and are MOUS certified. For shorter courses, we have created brief versions of the Exploring texts that give students a four-chapter introduction to each application. Each of these volumes is MOUS certified at the Core level.

To complete the full coverage of this series, custom modules on Microsoft Outlook 2002, Microsoft FrontPage 2002, Microsoft Publisher 2002, and a generic introduction to Microsoft Windows are also available.

The Microsoft Office User Specialist (MOUS) program is globally recognized as the standard for demonstrating desktop skills with the Microsoft Office suite of business productivity applications (Microsoft Word, Microsoft Excel, Microsoft PowerPoint, Microsoft Access, and Microsoft Outlook). With a MOUS certification, thousands of people have demonstrated increased productivity and have proved their ability to utilize the advanced functionality of these Microsoft applications.

By encouraging individuals to develop advanced skills with Microsoft's leading business desktop software, the MOUS program helps fill the demand for qualified, knowledgeable people in the modern workplace. At the same time, MOUS helps satisfy an organization's need for a qualitative assessment of employee skills.

Customize the Exploring Office Series with Prentice Hall's Right PHit Binding Program

The Exploring Office XP series is part of the Right PHit Custom Binding Program, enabling instructors to create their own texts by selecting modules from Office XP Volume I, Volume II, Outlook, FrontPage, and Publisher to suit the needs of a specific course. An instructor could, for example, create a custom text consisting of the core modules in Word and Excel, coupled with the brief modules for Access and PowerPoint, and a brief introduction to computer concepts.

Instructors can also take advantage of Prentice Hall's Value Pack program to shrinkwrap multiple texts together at substantial savings to the student. A value pack is ideal in courses that require complete coverage of multiple applications.

The **Instructor's CD** that accompanies the Exploring Office series contains:

- Student data disks
- Solutions to all exercises and problems
- PowerPoint lectures
- Instructor's manuals in Word format enable the instructor to annotate portions of the instructor manual for distribution to the class
- A Windows-based test manager and the associated test bank in Word format

Prentice Hall's New MyPHLIP Companion Web site at www.prenhall.com/grauer offers current events, exercises, and downloadable supplements. This site also includes an on-line study guide containing true/false, multiple-choice, and essay questions.

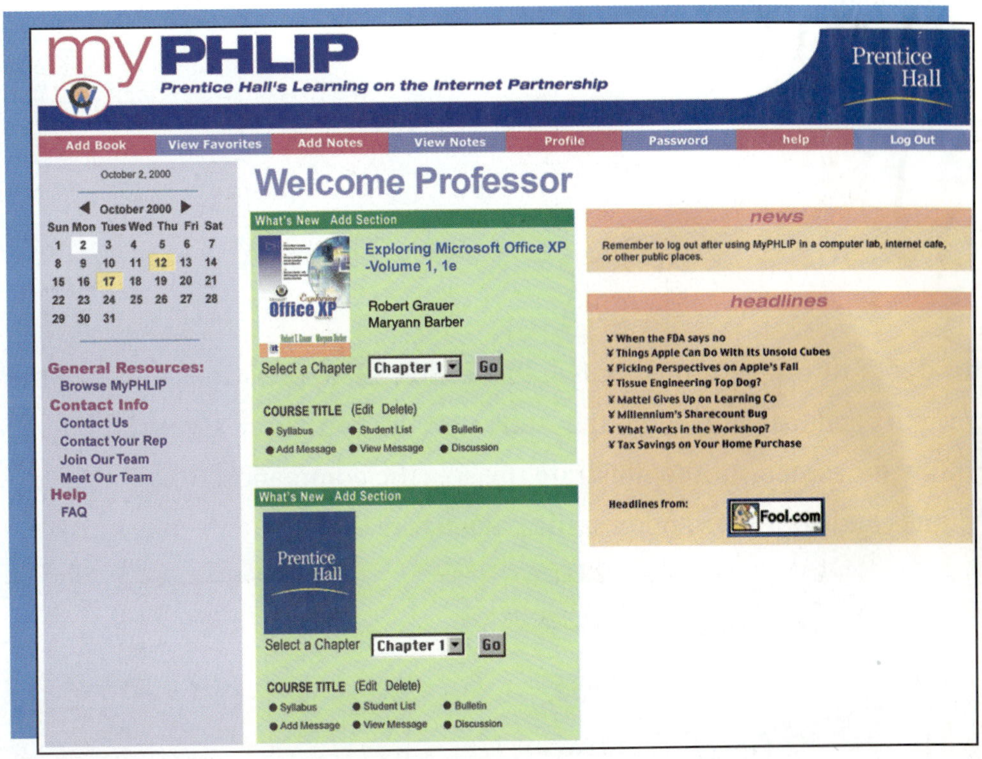

WebCT www.prenhall.com/webct

GOLD LEVEL CUSTOMER SUPPORT available exclusively to adopters of Prentice Hall courses is provided free-of-charge upon adoption and provides you with priority assistance, training discounts, and dedicated technical support.

Blackboard www.prenhall.com/blackboard

Prentice Hall's abundant on-line content, combined with Blackboard's popular tools and interface, result in robust Web-based courses that are easy to implement, manage, and use—taking your courses to new heights in student interaction and learning.

CourseCompass www.coursecompass.com

CourseCompass is a dynamic, interactive on-line course management tool powered by Blackboard. This exciting product allows you to teach with marketing-leading Pearson Education content in an easy-to-use customizable format.

Exploring Microsoft Office XP assumes no prior knowledge of the operating system. A 64-page section introduces the reader to the Essentials of Windows and provides an overview of the operating system. Students are shown the necessary file-management operations to use Microsoft Office successfully.

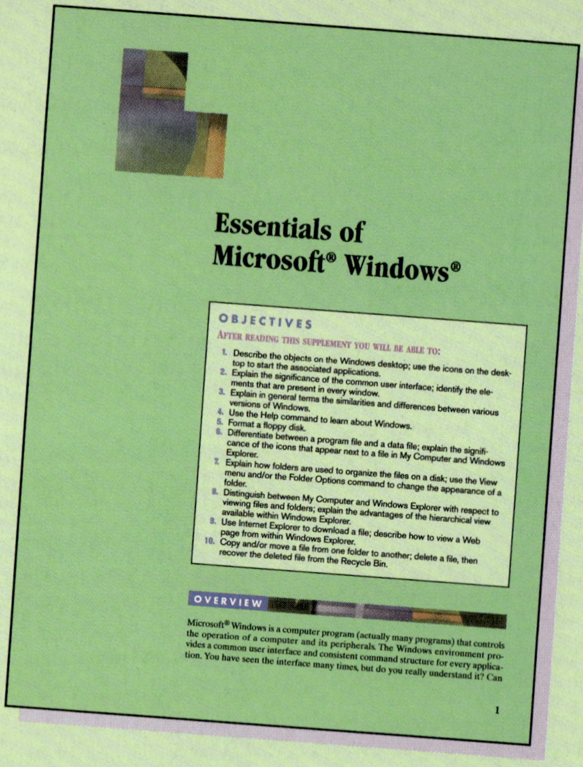

Essentials of Microsoft® Windows®

OBJECTIVES

AFTER READING THIS SUPPLEMENT YOU WILL BE ABLE TO:

1. Describe the objects on the Windows desktop; use the icons on the desktop to start the associated applications.
2. Explain the significance of the common user interface; identify the elements that are present in every window.
3. Explain in general terms the similarities and differences between various versions of Windows.
4. Use the Help command to learn about Windows.
5. Format a floppy disk.
6. Differentiate between a program file and a data file; explain the significance of the icons that appear next to a file in My Computer and Windows Explorer.
7. Explain how folders are used to organize the files on a disk; use the View menu and/or the Folder Options command to change the appearance of a folder.
8. Distinguish between My Computer and Windows Explorer with respect to viewing files and folders; explain the advantages of the hierarchical view available within Windows Explorer.
9. Use Internet Explorer to download a file; describe how to view a Web page from within Windows Explorer.
10. Copy and/or move a file from one folder to another; delete a file, then recover the deleted file from the Recycle Bin.

OVERVIEW

Microsoft® Windows is a computer program (actually many programs) that controls the operation of a computer and its peripherals. The Windows environment provides a common user interface and consistent command structure for every application. You have seen the interface many times, but do you really understand it? Can

1

In-depth tutorials throughout all the Office XP applications enhance the conceptual introduction to each task and guide the student at the computer. Every step in every exercise has a full-color screen shot to illustrate the specific commands. Boxed tips provide alternative techniques and shortcuts and/or anticipate errors that students may make.

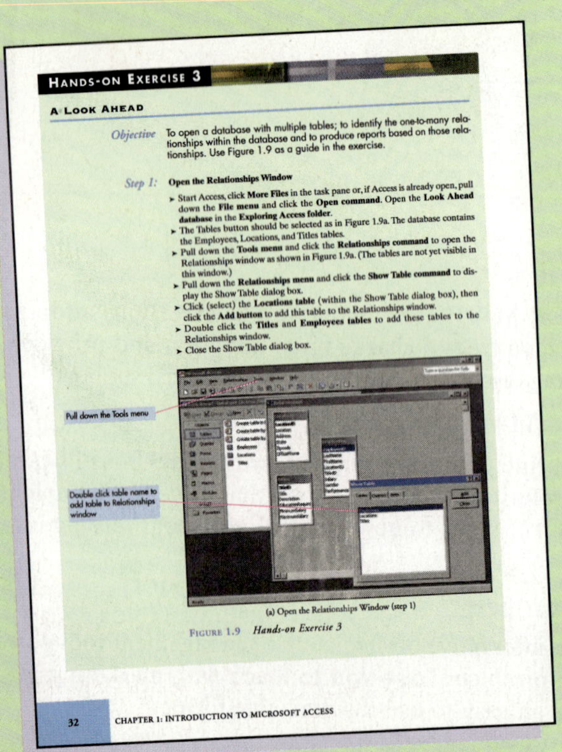

HANDS-ON EXERCISE 3

A LOOK AHEAD

Objective To open a database with multiple tables; to identify the one-to-many relationships within the database and to produce reports based on those relationships. Use Figure 1.9 as a guide in the exercise.

Step 1: **Open the Relationships Window**

- Start Access, click **More Files** in the task pane or, if Access is already open, pull down the **File menu** and click the **Open command**. Open the **Look Ahead database** in the **Exploring Access folder**.
- The Tables button should be selected as in Figure 1.9a. The database contains the Employees, Locations, and Titles tables.
- Pull down the **Tools menu** and click the **Relationships command** to open the Relationships window as shown in Figure 1.9a. (The tables are not yet visible in this window.)
- Pull down the **Relationships menu** and click the **Show Table command** to display the Show Table dialog box.
- Click (select) the **Locations table** (within the Show Table dialog box), then click the **Add button** to add this table to the Relationships window.
- Double click the **Titles** and **Employees tables** to add these tables to the Relationships window.
- Close the Show Table dialog box.

(a) Open the Relationships Window (step 1)

FIGURE 1.9 *Hands-on Exercise 3*

32 CHAPTER 1: INTRODUCTION TO MICROSOFT ACCESS

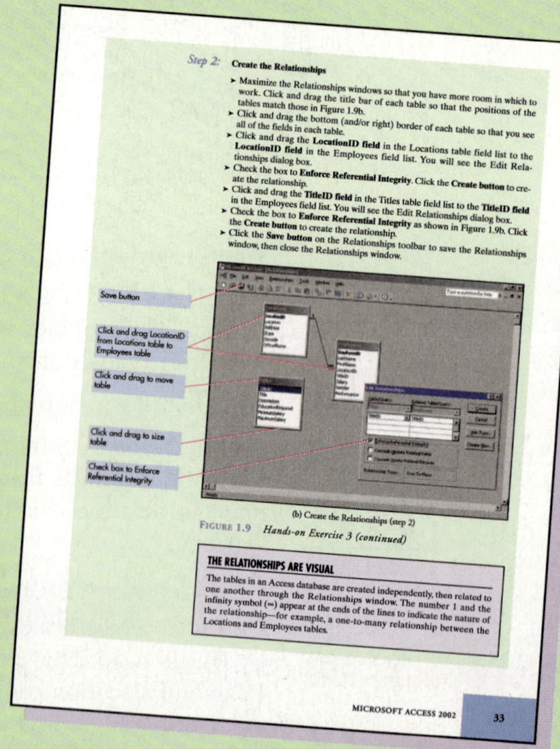

Step 2: **Create the Relationships**

- Maximize the Relationships windows so that you have more room in which to work. Click and drag the title bar of each table so that the positions of the tables match those in Figure 1.9b.
- Click and drag the bottom (and/or right) border of each table so that you see all of the fields in each table.
- Click and drag the **LocationID field** in the Locations table field list to the **LocationID field** in the Employees field list. You will see the Edit Relationships dialog box.
- Check the box to **Enforce Referential Integrity**. Click the **Create button** to create the relationship.
- Click and drag the **TitleID field** in the Titles table field list to the **TitleID field** in the Employees field list. You will see the Edit Relationships dialog box.
- Check the box to **Enforce Referential Integrity** as shown in Figure 1.9b. Click the **Create button** to create the relationship.
- Click the **Save button** on the Relationships toolbar to save the Relationships window, then close the Relationships window.

(b) Create the Relationships (step 2)

FIGURE 1.9 *Hands-on Exercise 3 (continued)*

THE RELATIONSHIPS ARE VISUAL

The tables in an Access database are created independently, then related to one another through the Relationships window. The number 1 and the infinity symbol (∞) appear at the ends of the lines to indicate the nature of the relationship—for example, a one-to-many relationship between the Locations and Employees tables.

MICROSOFT ACCESS 2002 33

The authors have created an entirely new set of end-of-chapter exercises for every chapter in all of the applications. These new exercises have been written to provide the utmost in flexibility, variety, and difficulty.

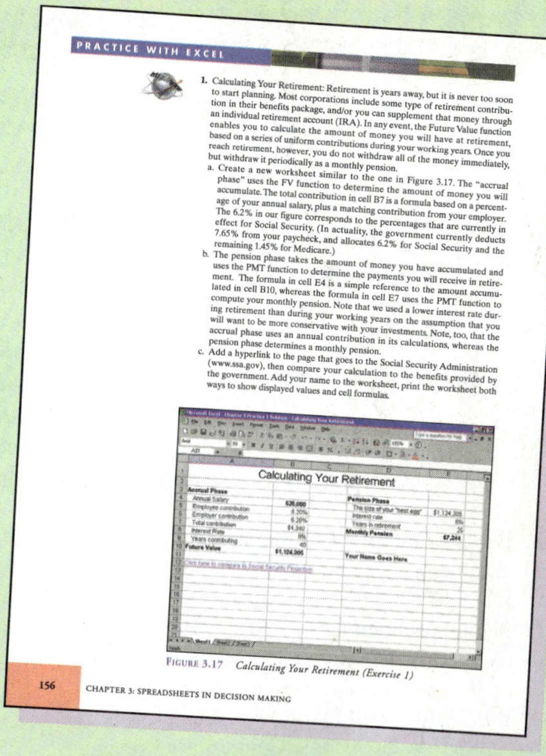
PRACTICE WITH EXCEL

1. Calculating Your Retirement: Retirement is years away, but it is never too soon to start planning. Most corporations include some type of retirement contribution in their benefits package, and/or you can supplement that money through an individual retirement account (IRA). In any event, the Future Value function enables you to calculate the amount of money you will have at retirement, based on a series of uniform contributions during your working years. Once you reach retirement, however, you do not withdraw all of the money immediately, but withdraw it periodically as a monthly pension.
   a. Create a new worksheet similar to the one in Figure 3.17. The "accrual phase" uses the FV function to determine the amount of money you will accumulate. The total contribution in cell B7 is a formula based on a percentage of your annual salary, plus a matching contribution from your employer. The 6.2% in our figure corresponds to the percentages that are currently in effect for Social Security. (In actuality, the government currently deducts 7.65% from your paycheck, and allocates 6.2% for Social Security and the remaining 1.45% for Medicare.)
   b. The pension phase takes the amount of money you have accumulated and uses the PMT function to determine the payments you will receive in retirement. The formula in cell E4 is a simple reference to the amount accumulated in cell B10, whereas the formula in cell E7 uses the PMT function to compute your monthly pension. Note that we used a lower interest rate during retirement than during your working years on the assumption that you will want to be more conservative with your investments. Note, too, that the accrual phase uses an annual contribution in its calculations, whereas the pension phase determines a monthly pension.
   c. Add a hyperlink to the page that goes to the Social Security Administration (www.ssa.gov), then compare your calculation to the benefits provided by the government. Add your name to the worksheet, print the worksheet both ways to show displayed values and cell formulas.

FIGURE 3.17 *Calculating Your Retirement (Exercise 1)*

156 CHAPTER 3: SPREADSHEETS IN DECISION MAKING

Web-based Practice exercises and On Your Own exercises are marked by an icon in the margin and allow further exploration and practice via the World Wide Web.

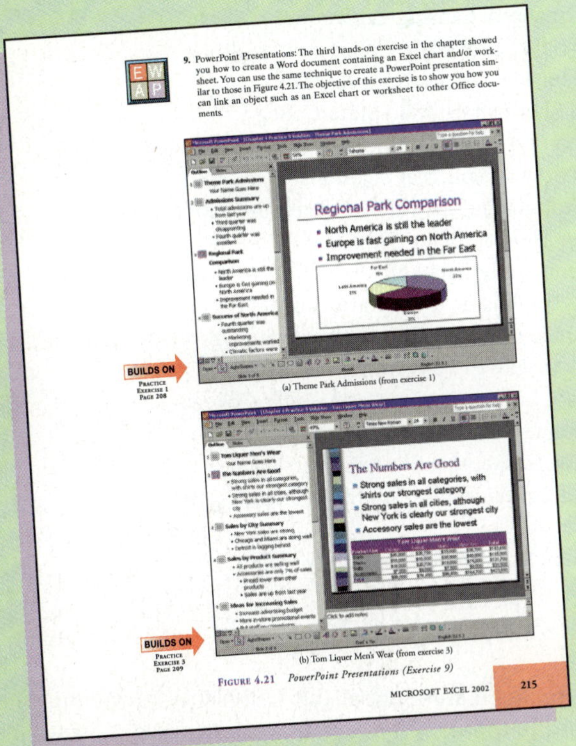
9. PowerPoint Presentations: The third hands-on exercise in the chapter showed you how to create a Word document containing an Excel chart and/or worksheet. You can use the same technique to create a PowerPoint presentation similar to those in Figure 4.21. The objective of this exercise is to show you how you can link an object such as an Excel chart or worksheet to other Office documents.

(a) Theme Park Admissions (from exercise 1)

(b) Tom Liquer Men's Wear (from exercise 3)

FIGURE 4.21 *PowerPoint Presentations (Exercise 9)*

MICROSOFT EXCEL 2002 215

Integration Exercises are marked by an icon in the margin. These exercises take advantage of the Microsoft Office Suite's power to use multiple applications in one document, spreadsheet, or presentation.

Builds On Exercises require students to use selected application files as the starting point in later exercises, thereby introducing new information to students only as needed.

The end-of-chapter material includes multiple-choice questions for self-evaluation plus additional "on your own" exercises to encourage the reader to further explore the application.

ACKNOWLEDGMENTS

We want to thank the many individuals who have helped to bring this project to fruition. David Alexander, senior editor at Prentice Hall, has provided new leadership in extending the series to Office XP. Cathi Profitko did an absolutely incredible job on our Web site. Melissa Whitaker coordinated the myriad details of production and the certification process. Greg Christofferson was instrumental in the acquisition of supporting software. Lynne Breitfeller was the project manager and manufacturing buyer. Greg Hubit has been masterful as the external production editor for every book in the series. Cecil Yarbrough did an outstanding job in checking the manuscript for technical accuracy. Chuck Cox did his usual fine work as copyeditor. Kerri Limpert was the supplements editor. Cindy Stevens, Tom McKenzie, and Michael Olmstead wrote the instructor manuals. Patricia Smythe developed the innovative and attractive design. We also want to acknowledge our reviewers who, through their comments and constructive criticism, greatly improved the series.

Lynne Band, Middlesex Community College
Don Belle, Central Piedmont Community College
Stuart P. Brian, Holy Family College
Carl M. Briggs, Indiana University School of Business
Kimberly Chambers, Scottsdale Community College
Alok Charturvedi, Purdue University
Jerry Chin, Southwest Missouri State University
Dean Combellick, Scottsdale Community College
Cody Copeland, Johnson County Community College
Larry S. Corman, Fort Lewis College
Janis Cox, Tri-County Technical College
Martin Crossland, Southwest Missouri State University
Paul E. Daurelle, Western Piedmont Community College
Carolyn DiLeo, Westchester Community College
Judy Dolan, Palomar College
David Douglas, University of Arkansas
Carlotta Eaton, Radford University
Judith M. Fitspatrick, Gulf Coast Community College
James Franck, College of St. Scholastica
Raymond Frost, Central Connecticut State University
Midge Gerber, Southwestern Oklahoma State University
James Gips, Boston College
Vernon Griffin, Austin Community College
Ranette Halverson, Midwestern State University
Michael Hassett, Fort Hays State University
Mike Hearn, Community College of Philadelphia
Wanda D. Heller, Seminole Community College
Bonnie Homan, San Francisco State University
Ernie Ivey, Polk Community College
Mike Kelly, Community College of Rhode Island
Jane King, Everett Community College
Rose M. Laird, Northern Virginia Community College
John Lesson, University of Central Florida
David B. Meinert, Southwest Missouri State University
Alan Moltz, Naugatuck Valley Technical Community College
Kim Montney, Kellogg Community College
Bill Morse, DeVry Institute of Technology
Kevin Pauli, University of Nebraska
Mary McKenry Percival, University of Miami
Delores Pusins, Hillsborough Community College
Gale E. Rand, College Misericordia
Judith Rice, Santa Fe Community College
David Rinehard, Lansing Community College
Marilyn Salas, Scottsdale Community College
John Shepherd, Duquesne University
Barbara Sherman, Buffalo State College
Robert Spear, Prince George's Community College
Michael Stewardson, San Jacinto College—North
Helen Stoloff, Hudson Valley Community College
Margaret Thomas, Ohio University
Mike Thomas, Indiana University School of Business
Suzanne Tomlinson, Iowa State University
Karen Tracey, Central Connecticut State University
Antonio Vargas, El Paso Community College
Sally Visci, Lorain County Community College
David Weiner, University of San Francisco
Connie Wells, Georgia State University
Wallace John Whistance-Smith, Ryerson Polytechnic University
Jack Zeller, Kirkwood Community College

A final word of thanks to the unnamed students at the University of Miami, who make it all worthwhile. Most of all, thanks to you, our readers, for choosing this book. Please feel free to contact us with any comments and suggestions.

Robert T. Grauer
rgrauer@miami.edu
www.bus.miami.edu/~rgrauer
www.prenhall.com/grauer

Maryann Barber
mbarber@miami.edu
www.bus.miami.edu/~mbarber

Essentials of Microsoft® Windows®

OBJECTIVES

AFTER READING THIS SUPPLEMENT YOU WILL BE ABLE TO:

1. Describe the objects on the Windows desktop; use the icons on the desktop to start the associated applications.
2. Explain the significance of the common user interface; identify the elements that are present in every window.
3. Explain in general terms the similarities and differences between various versions of Windows.
4. Use the Help command to learn about Windows.
5. Format a floppy disk.
6. Differentiate between a program file and a data file; explain the significance of the icons that appear next to a file in My Computer and Windows Explorer.
7. Explain how folders are used to organize the files on a disk; use the View menu and/or the Folder Options command to change the appearance of a folder.
8. Distinguish between My Computer and Windows Explorer with respect to viewing files and folders; explain the advantages of the hierarchical view available within Windows Explorer.
9. Use Internet Explorer to download a file; describe how to view a Web page from within Windows Explorer.
10. Copy and/or move a file from one folder to another; delete a file, then recover the deleted file from the Recycle Bin.

OVERVIEW

Microsoft® Windows is a computer program (actually many programs) that controls the operation of a computer and its peripherals. The Windows environment provides a common user interface and consistent command structure for every application. You have seen the interface many times, but do you really understand it? Can you move and copy files with confidence? Do you know how to back up the Excel spreadsheets, Access databases, and other Office documents that you work so hard to create? If not, now is the time to learn. This section is written for you, the computer novice, and it assumes no previous knowledge.

We begin with an introduction to the Windows desktop, the graphical user interface that enables you to work in intuitive fashion by pointing at icons and clicking the mouse. We identify the basic components of a window and describe how to execute commands and supply information through different elements in a dialog box. We introduce you to My Computer, an icon on the Windows desktop, and show you how to use My Computer to access the various components of your system. We also describe how to access the Help command.

The supplement concentrates, however, on disk and file management. We present the basic definitions of a file and a folder, then describe how to use My Computer to look for a specific file or folder. We introduce Windows Explorer, which provides a more efficient way of finding data on your system, then show you how to move or copy a file from one folder to another. We discuss other basic operations, such as renaming and deleting a file. We also describe how to recover a deleted file (if necessary) from the Recycle Bin.

There are also four hands-on exercises, which enable you to apply the conceptual discussion in the text at the computer. The exercises refer to a set of practice files (data disk) that we have created for you. You can obtain these files from our Web site (www.prenhall.com/grauer) or from a local area network if your professor has downloaded the files for you.

THE DESKTOP

Windows 95 was the first of the so-called "modern Windows" and was followed by Windows NT, Windows 98, Windows 2000, Windows Me (Millennium edition), and most recently, by Windows XP. Each of these systems is still in use. Windows 98 and its successor, Windows Me, are geared for the home user and provide extensive support for games and peripheral devices. Windows NT, and its successor Windows 2000, are aimed at the business user and provide increased security and reliability. Windows XP is the successor to all current breeds of Windows. It has a slightly different look, but maintains the conventions of its various predecessors. Hence we have called this module "Essentials of Microsoft Windows" and refer to Windows in a generic sense. (The screens were taken from Windows 2000 Professional, but could just as easily have been taken from other versions of the operating system.)

All versions of Windows create a working environment for your computer that parallels the working environment at home or in an office. You work at a desk. Windows operations take place on the ***desktop*** as shown in Figure 1. There are physical objects on a desk such as folders, a dictionary, a calculator, or a phone. The computer equivalents of those objects appear as icons (pictorial symbols) on the desktop. Each object on a real desk has attributes (properties) such as size, weight, and color. In similar fashion, Windows assigns properties to every object on its desktop. And just as you can move the objects on a real desk, you can rearrange the objects on the Windows desktop.

Figure 1a displays the typical desktop that appears when Windows is installed on a new computer. It has only a few objects and is similar to the desk in a new office, just after you move in. This desktop might have been taken from any of five systems—Windows 95, Windows NT, Windows 98, Windows 2000, or Windows Me—and is sometimes called "Classic Windows." The icons on this desktop are opened by double clicking. (It is possible to display an alternate desktop with underlined icons that are opened by single clicking, but that option is rarely used.) Figure 1b shows the new Windows XP desktop as it might appear on a home computer, where individual accounts are established for different users.

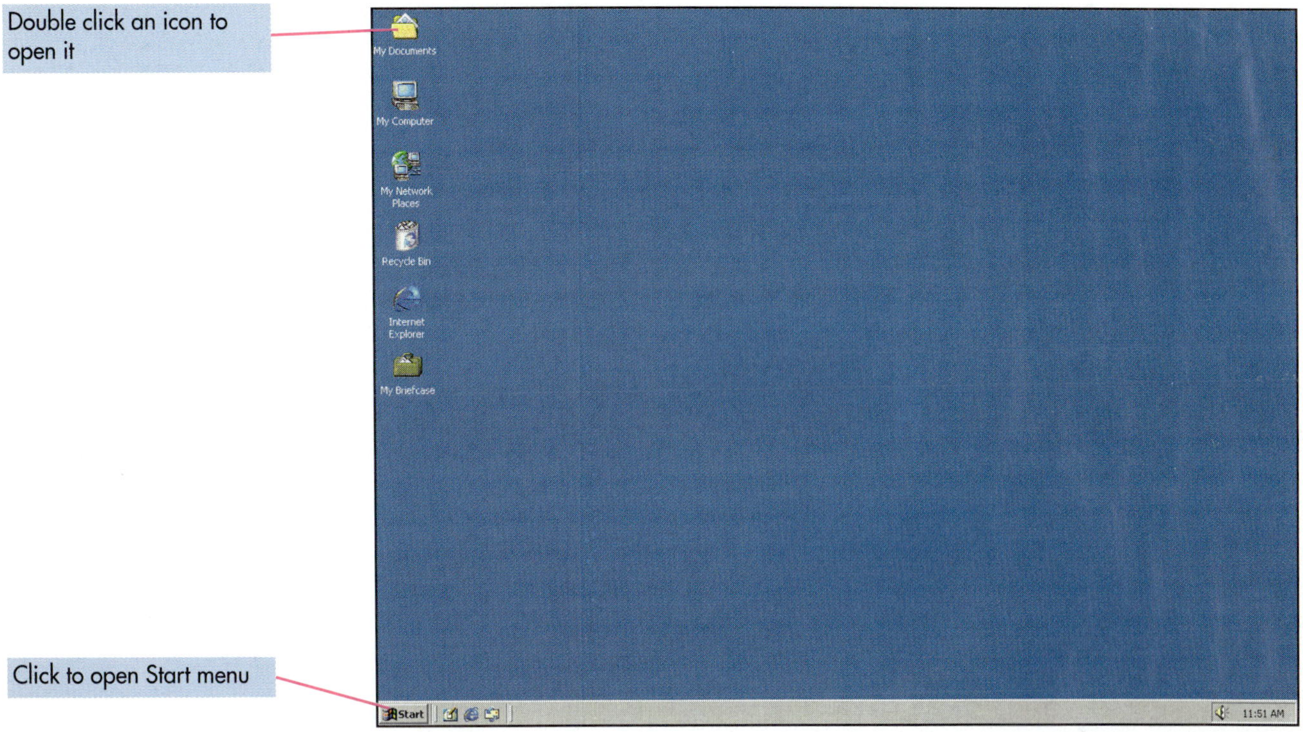

(a) Windows 95, Windows NT, Windows 98, Windows Me, and Windows 2000

(b) Windows XP

FIGURE 1 *The Different Faces of Windows*

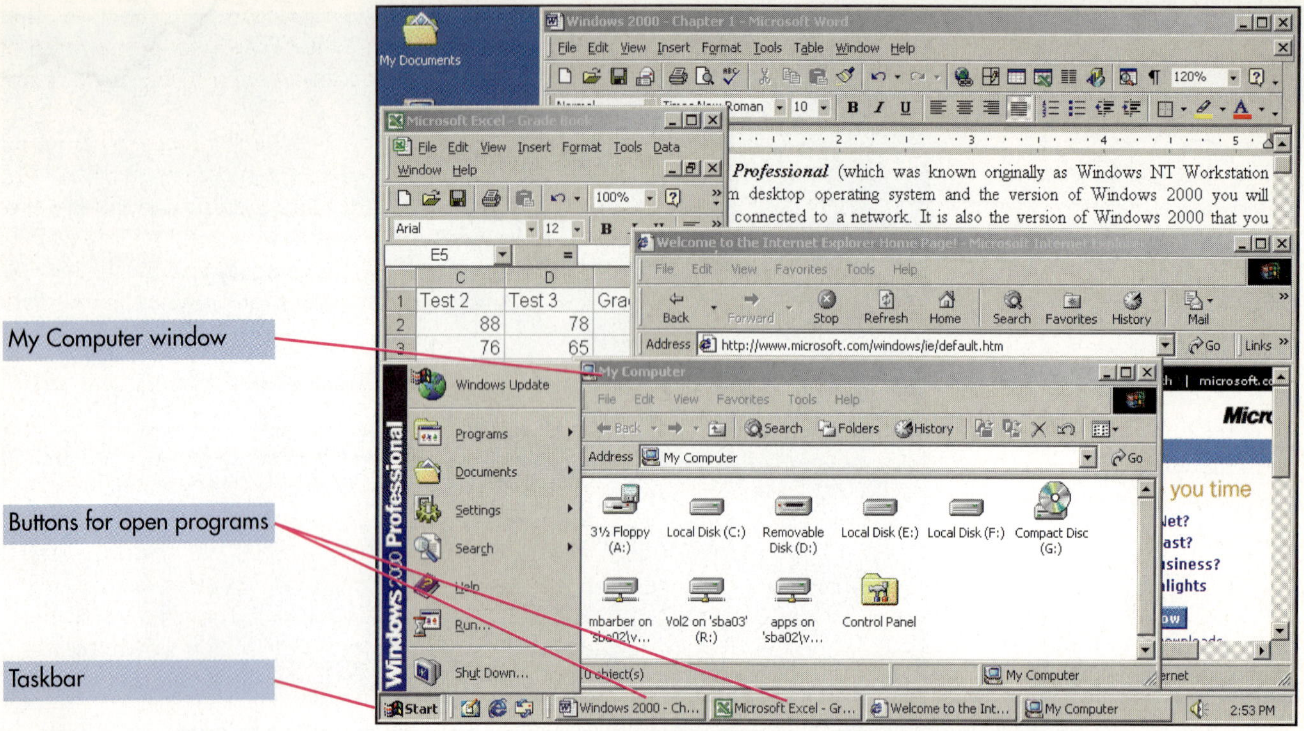

(c) A Working Desktop (all versions of Windows)

FIGURE 1 *The Different Faces of Windows (continued)*

Do not be concerned if your desktop is different from ours. Your real desk is arranged differently from those of your friends, just as your Windows desktop will also be different. Moreover, you are likely to work on different systems—at school, at work, or at home, and thus it is important that you recognize the common functionality that is present on all desktops. The ***Start button***, as its name suggests, is where you begin. Click the Start button and you see a menu that lets you start any program installed on your computer.

Look now at Figure 1c, which displays an entirely different desktop, one with four open windows that is similar to a desk in the middle of a working day. Each window in Figure 1c displays a program that is currently in use. The ability to run several programs at the same time is known as ***multitasking***, and it is a major benefit of the Windows environment. Multitasking enables you to run a word processor in one window, create a spreadsheet in a second window, surf the Internet in a third window, play a game in a fourth window, and so on. You can work in a program as long as you want, then change to a different program by clicking its window.

You can also change from one program to another by using the taskbar at the bottom of the desktop. The ***taskbar*** contains a button for each open program, and it enables you to switch back and forth between those programs by clicking the appropriate button. The taskbar in Figure 1a does not contain any buttons (other than the Start button) since there are no open applications. The taskbar in Figure 1c, however, contains four additional buttons, one for each open window.

The icons on the desktop are used to access programs or other functions. The ***My Computer*** icon is the most basic. It enables you to view the devices on your system, including the drives on a local area network to which you have direct access. Open My Computer in either Figure 1a or 1b, for example, and you see the objects in the My Computer window of Figure 1c. The contents of My Computer depend on the hardware of the specific computer system. Our system, for example, has one floppy drive, three local (hard or fixed) disks, a removable disk (an Iomega Zip drive), a CD-ROM, and access to various network drives. The My Computer window also contains the Control Panel folder that provides access to functions that control other elements of your computing environment. (These capabilities are not used by beginners, are generally "off limits" in a lab environment, and thus are not discussed further.)

The other icons on the desktop are also noteworthy. The ***My Documents*** folder is a convenient place in which to store the documents you create. ***My Network Places*** extends the view of your computer to include the other local area networks (if any) that your computer can access, provided you have a valid username and password. The ***Recycle Bin*** enables you to restore a file that was previously deleted. The Internet Explorer icon starts ***Internet Explorer***, the Web browser that is built into the Windows operating system.

THE DOJ (DEPARTMENT OF JUSTICE) VERSUS MICROSOFT

A simple icon is at the heart of the multibillion dollar lawsuit brought by 19 states against Microsoft. In short, Microsoft is accused of integrating its Internet Explorer browser into the Windows operating system with the goal of dominating the market and eliminating the competition. Is Internet Explorer built into every current version of Microsoft Windows? Yes. Can Netscape Navigator run without difficulty under every current version of Microsoft Windows? The answer is also yes. As of this writing the eventual outcome of the case against Microsoft has yet to be determined.

THE COMMON USER INTERFACE

All Windows applications share a ***common user interface*** and possess a consistent command structure. This means that every Windows application works essentially the same way, which provides a sense of familiarity from one application to the next. In other words, once you learn the basic concepts and techniques in one application, you can apply that knowledge to every other application. Consider, for example, Figure 2, which shows open windows for My Computer and My Network Places, and labels the essential elements in each.

The contents of the two windows are different, but each window has the same essential elements. The ***title bar*** appears at the top of each window and displays the name of the window, My Computer and My Network Places in Figure 2a and 2b, respectively. The icon at the extreme left of the title bar identifies the window and also provides access to a control menu with operations relevant to the window such as moving it or sizing it. The ***minimize button*** shrinks the window to a button on the taskbar, but leaves the window in memory. The ***maximize button*** enlarges the window so that it takes up the entire desktop. The ***restore button*** (not shown in either figure) appears instead of the maximize button after a window has been maximized, and restores the window to its previous size. The ***close button*** closes the window and removes it from memory and the desktop.

The ***menu bar*** appears immediately below the title bar and provides access to ***pull-down menus***. One or more ***toolbars*** appear below the menu bar and let you execute a command by clicking a button as opposed to pulling down a menu. The ***status bar*** at the bottom of the window displays information about the window as a whole or about a selected object within a window.

A vertical (or horizontal) ***scroll bar*** appears at the right (or bottom) border of a window when its contents arc not completely visible and provides access to the unseen areas. A scroll bar does not appear in Figure 2a since all of the objects in the window are visible at the same time. A vertical scroll bar is found in Figure 2b, however, since there are other objects in the window.

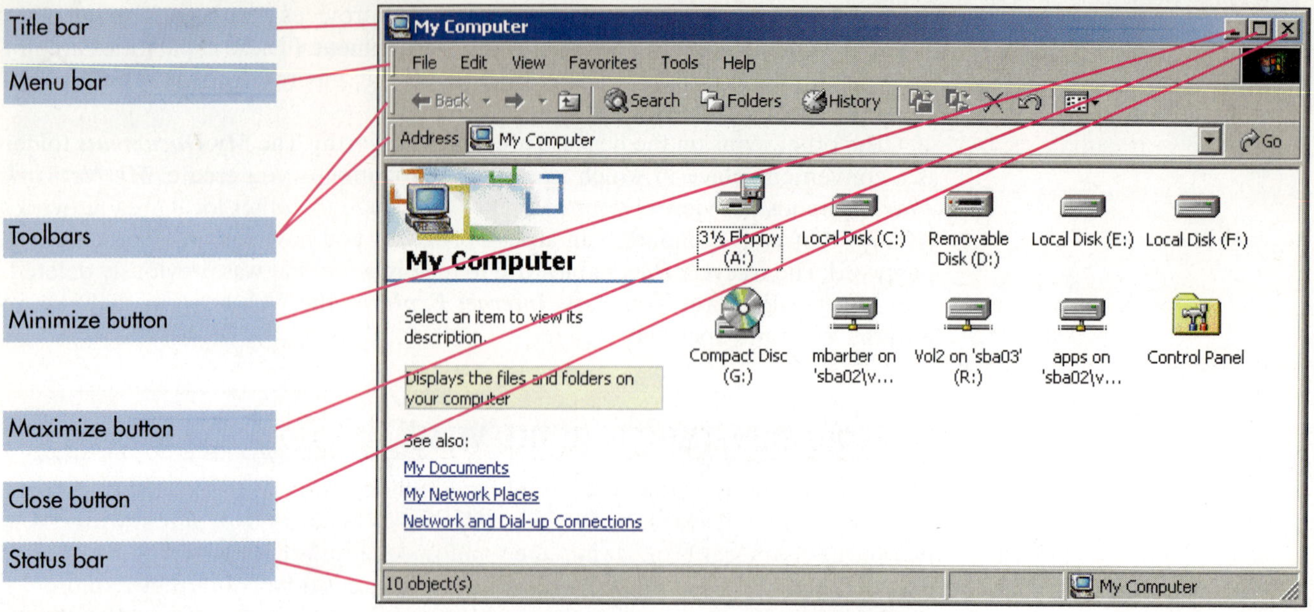

(a) My Computer

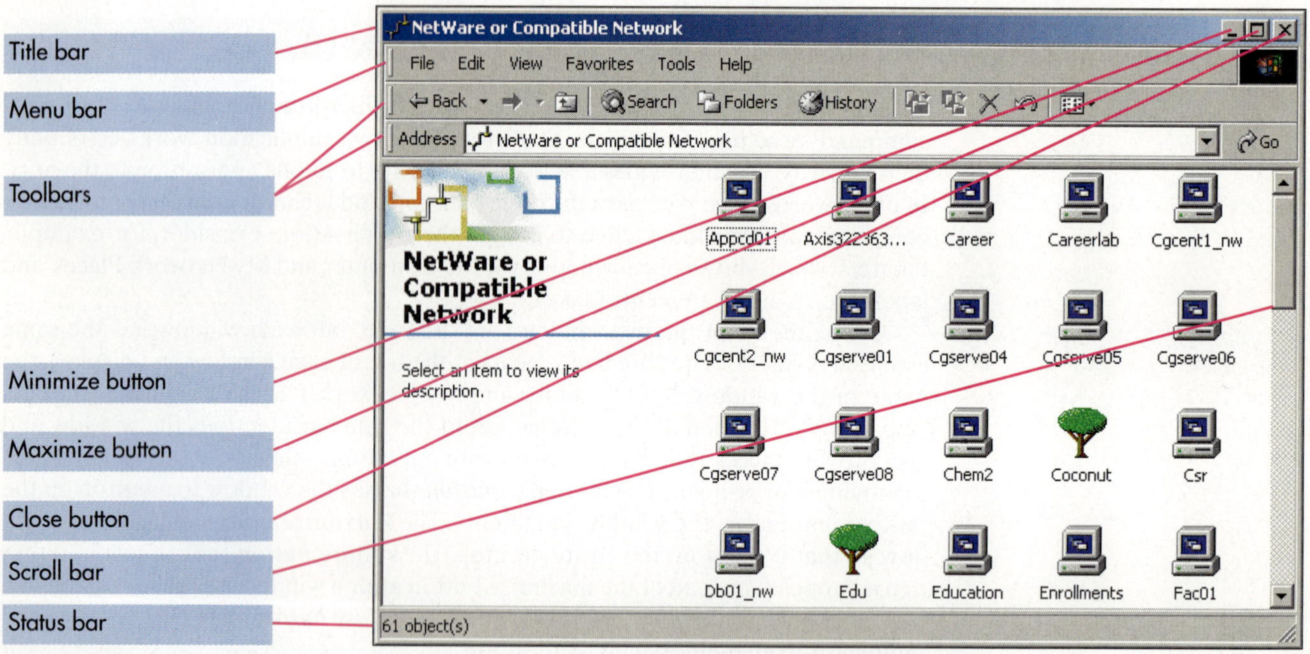

(b) My Network Places

FIGURE 2 *Anatomy of a Window*

Moving and Sizing a Window

A window can be sized or moved on the desktop through appropriate actions with the mouse. To ***size a window***, point to any border (the mouse pointer changes to a double arrow), then drag the border in the direction you want to go—inward to shrink the window or outward to enlarge it. You can also drag a corner (instead of a border) to change both dimensions at the same time. To ***move a window*** while retaining its current size, click and drag the title bar to a new position on the desktop.

Pull-Down Menus

The menu bar provides access to ***pull-down menus*** that enable you to execute commands within an application (program). A pull-down menu is accessed by clicking the menu name or by pressing the Alt key plus the underlined letter in the menu name; for example, press Alt+V to pull down the View menu. (You may have to press the Alt key in order to see the underlines.) Three pull-down menus associated with My Computer are shown in Figure 3.

Commands within a menu are executed by clicking the command or by typing the underlined letter. Alternatively, you can bypass the menu entirely if you know the equivalent keystrokes shown to the right of the command in the menu (e.g., Ctrl+X, Ctrl+C, or Ctrl+V to cut, copy, or paste as shown within the Edit menu). A dimmed command (e.g., the Paste command in the Edit menu) means the command is not currently executable; some additional action has to be taken for the command to become available.

An ellipsis (. . .) following a command indicates that additional information is required to execute the command; for example, selection of the Format command in the File menu requires the user to specify additional information about the format-

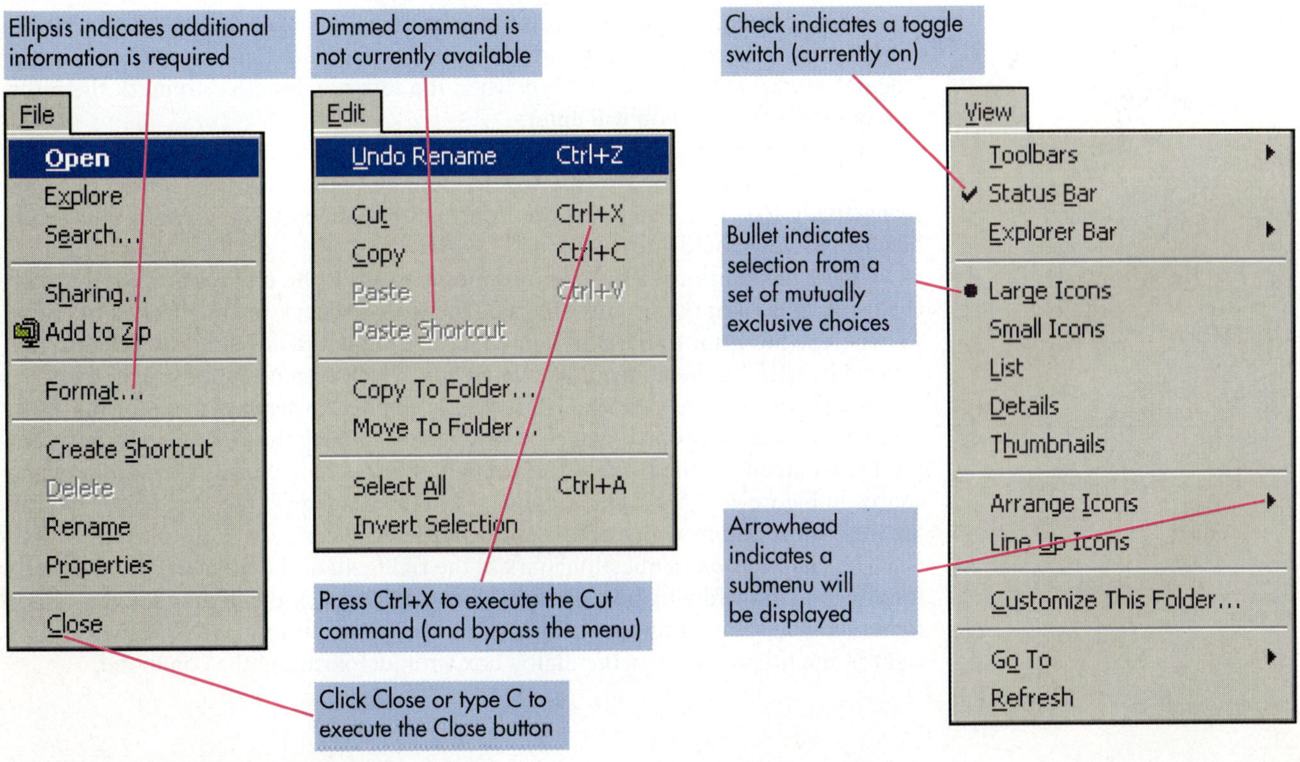

FIGURE 3 *Pull-Down Menus*

ting process. This information is entered into a dialog box (discussed in the next section), which appears immediately after the command has been selected.

A check next to a command indicates a toggle switch, whereby the command is either on or off. There is a check next to the Status Bar command in the View menu of Figure 3, which means the command is in effect (and thus the status bar will be displayed). Click the Status Bar command and the check disappears, which suppresses the display of the status bar. Click the command a second time and the check reappears, as does the status bar in the associated window.

A bullet next to an item (e.g., Large Icons in Figure 3) indicates a selection from a set of mutually exclusive choices. Click another option within the group (e.g., Small Icons) and the bullet will disappear from the previous selection (Large Icons) and appear next to the new selection (Small Icons).

An arrowhead after a command (e.g., the Arrange Icons command in the View menu) indicates that a submenu (also known as a cascaded menu) will be displayed with additional menu options.

Dialog Boxes

A ***dialog box*** appears when additional information is necessary to execute a command. Click the Print command in Internet Explorer, for example, and you are presented with the Print dialog box in Figure 4, requesting information about precisely what to print and how. The information is entered into the dialog box in different ways, depending on the type of information that is required. The tabs at the top of the dialog box provide access to different sets of options. The General and Paper tabs are selected in Figures 4a and 4b, respectively.

Option (Radio) buttons indicate mutually exclusive choices, one of which must be chosen, such as the page range in Figure 4a. You can print all pages, the selection (highlighted text), the current page, or a specific set of pages (such as pages 1–4), but you can choose one and only one option. Click a button to select an option, which automatically deselects the previously selected option.

A ***text box*** enters specific information such as the pages that will be printed in conjunction with selecting the radio button for pages. A flashing vertical bar (an I-beam) appears within the text box when the text box is active, to mark the insertion point for the text you will enter.

A ***spin button*** is another way to enter specific information such as the number of copies. Click the Up or Down arrow to increase or decrease the number of pages, respectively. You can also enter the information explicitly by typing it into a spin box, just as you would a text box.

Check boxes are used instead of option buttons if the choices are not mutually exclusive or if an option is not required. The Collate check box is checked in Figure 4a, whereas the Print to file box is not checked. Individual options are selected and cleared by clicking the appropriate check box, which toggles the box on and off.

A ***list box*** such as the Size is list box in Figure 4b displays some or all of the available choices, any one of which is selected by clicking the desired item. Just click the Down arrow on the list box to display the associated choices such as the paper source in Figure 4b. (A scroll bar appears within an open list box if all of the choices are not visible and provides access to the hidden choices.)

The ***Help button*** (a question mark at the right end of the title bar) provides help for any item in the dialog box. Click the button, then click the item in the dialog box for which you want additional information. The Close button (the X at the extreme right of the title bar) closes the dialog box without executing the command.

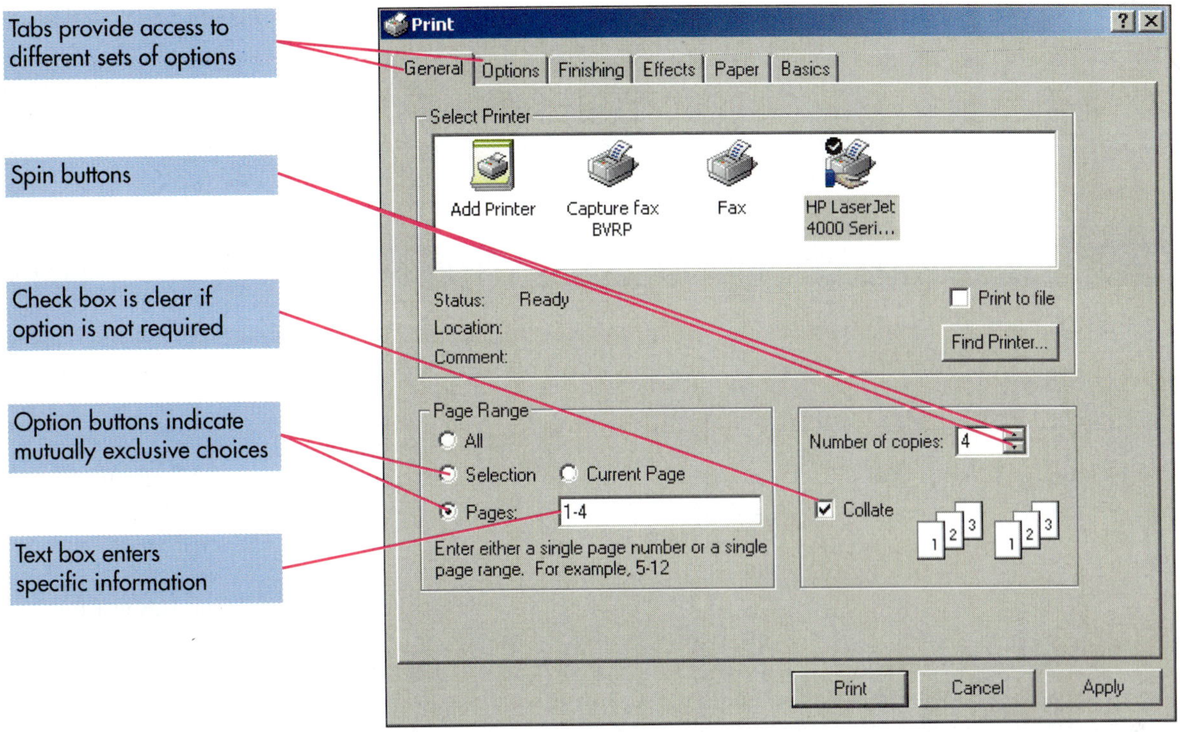

(a) General Tab

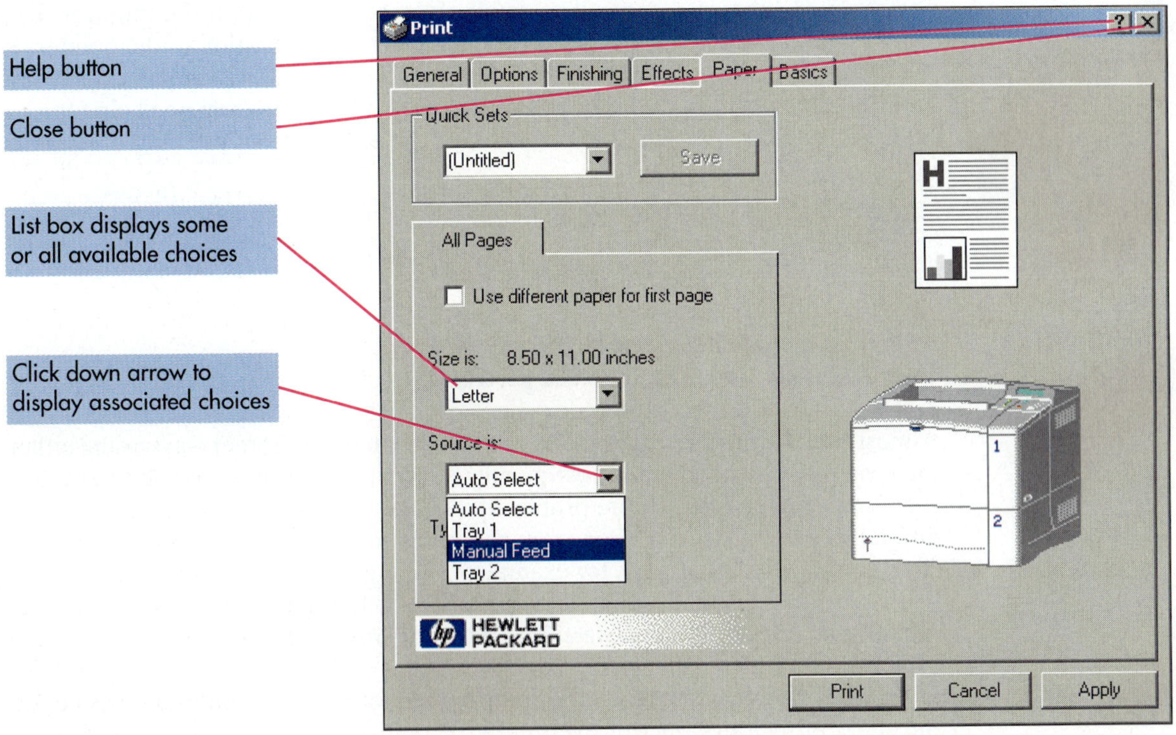

(b) Paper Tab

FIGURE 4 *Dialog Boxes*

All dialog boxes also contain one or more ***command buttons***, the function of which is generally apparent from the button's name. The Print button, in Figure 4a, for example, initiates the printing process. The Cancel button does just the opposite, and ignores (cancels) any changes made to the settings, then closes the dialog box without further action. An ellipsis (three dots) on a command button indicates that additional information will be required if the button is selected.

THE MOUSE

The mouse is indispensable to Windows and is referenced continually in the hands-on exercises throughout the text. There are five basic operations with which you must become familiar:

- To ***point*** to an object, move the mouse pointer onto the object.
- To ***click*** an object, point to it, then press and release the left mouse button.
- To ***right click*** an object, point to the object, then press and release the right mouse button. Right clicking an object displays a context-sensitive menu with commands that pertain to the object.
- To ***double click*** an object, point to it and then quickly click the left button twice in succession.
- To ***drag*** an object, move the pointer to the object, then press and hold the left button while you move the mouse to a new position.

You may also encounter a mouse with a wheel between the left and right buttons that lets you scroll through a document by rotating the wheel forward or backward. The action of the wheel, however, may change, depending on the application in use. In any event, the mouse is a pointing device—move the mouse on your desk and the mouse pointer, typically a small arrowhead, moves on the monitor. The mouse pointer assumes different shapes according to the location of the pointer or the nature of the current action. You will see a double arrow when you change the size of a window, an I-beam as you insert text, a hand to jump from one help topic to the next, or a circle with a line through it to indicate that an attempted action is invalid.

The mouse pointer will also change to an hourglass to indicate Windows is processing your command, and that no further commands may be issued until the action is completed. The more powerful your computer, the less frequently the hourglass will appear.

The Mouse versus the Keyboard

Almost every command in Windows can be executed in different ways, using either the mouse or the keyboard. Most people start with the mouse and add keyboard shortcuts as they become more proficient. There is no right or wrong technique, just different techniques, and the one you choose depends entirely on personal preference in a specific situation. If, for example, your hands are already on the keyboard, it is faster to use the keyboard equivalent. Other times, your hand will be on the mouse and that will be the fastest way. Toolbars provide still other ways to execute common commands.

In the beginning, you may wonder why there are so many different ways to do the same thing, but you will eventually recognize the many options as part of Windows' charm. It is not necessary to memorize anything, nor should you even try; just be flexible and willing to experiment. The more you practice, the faster all of this will become second nature to you.

THE HELP COMMAND

All versions of Windows include extensive documentation with detailed information about virtually every function in Windows. It is accessed through the ***Help command*** on the Start menu, which provides different ways to search for information.

The ***Contents tab*** in Figure 5a is analogous to the table of contents in an ordinary book. The topics are listed in the left pane and the information for the selected topic is displayed in the right pane. The list of topics can be displayed in varying amounts of detail, by opening and closing the various book icons that appear. (The size of the left pane can be increased or decreased by dragging the border between the left and right pane in the appropriate direction.)

A closed book such as "Troubleshooting and Maintenance" indicates the presence of subtopics, which are displayed by opening (clicking) the book. An open book, on the other hand, such as "Internet, E-mail, and Communications," already displays its subtopics. Each subtopic is shown with one of two icons—a question mark to indicate "how to" information, or an open book to indicate conceptual information. Either way, you can click any subtopic in the left pane to view its contents in the right pane. Underlined entries in the right pane (e.g., Related Topics) indicate a hyperlink, which in turn displays additional information. Note, too, that you can print the information in the right pane by pulling down the Options menu and selecting the Print command.

The ***Index tab*** in Figure 5b is analogous to the index of an ordinary book. You enter the first several letters of the topic to look up, such as "floppy disk," choose a topic from the resulting list, and then click the Display button to view the information in the right pane. The underlined entries in the right pane represent hyperlinks, which you can click to display additional topics. And, as in the Contents window, you can print the information in the right pane by pulling down the Options menu and selecting the Print command.

The ***Search tab*** (not shown in Figure 5) displays a more extensive listing of entries than does the Index tab. It lets you enter a specific word or phrase and then it returns every topic containing that word or phrase.

The ***Favorites tab*** enables you to save the information within specified help topics as bookmarks, in order to return to those topics at a later date, as explained in the following hands-on exercise.

FORMATTING A FLOPPY DISK

You will soon begin to work on the computer, which means that you will be using various applications to create different types of documents. Each document is saved in its own file and stored on disk, either on a local disk (e.g., drive C) if you have your own computer, or on a floppy disk (drive A) if you are working in a computer lab at school.

All disks have to be formatted before they can hold data. The formatting process divides a disk into concentric circles called tracks, and then further divides each track into sectors. You don't have to worry about formatting a hard disk, as that is done at the factory prior to the machine being sold. You typically don't even have to format a floppy disk, since most floppies today are already formatted when you buy them. Nevertheless, it is very easy to format a floppy disk and it is a worthwhile exercise. Be aware, however, that formatting erases any data that was previously on a disk, so be careful not to format a disk with important data (e.g., one containing today's homework assignment). Formatting is accomplished through the ***Format command***. The process is straightforward, as you will see in the hands-on exercise that follows.

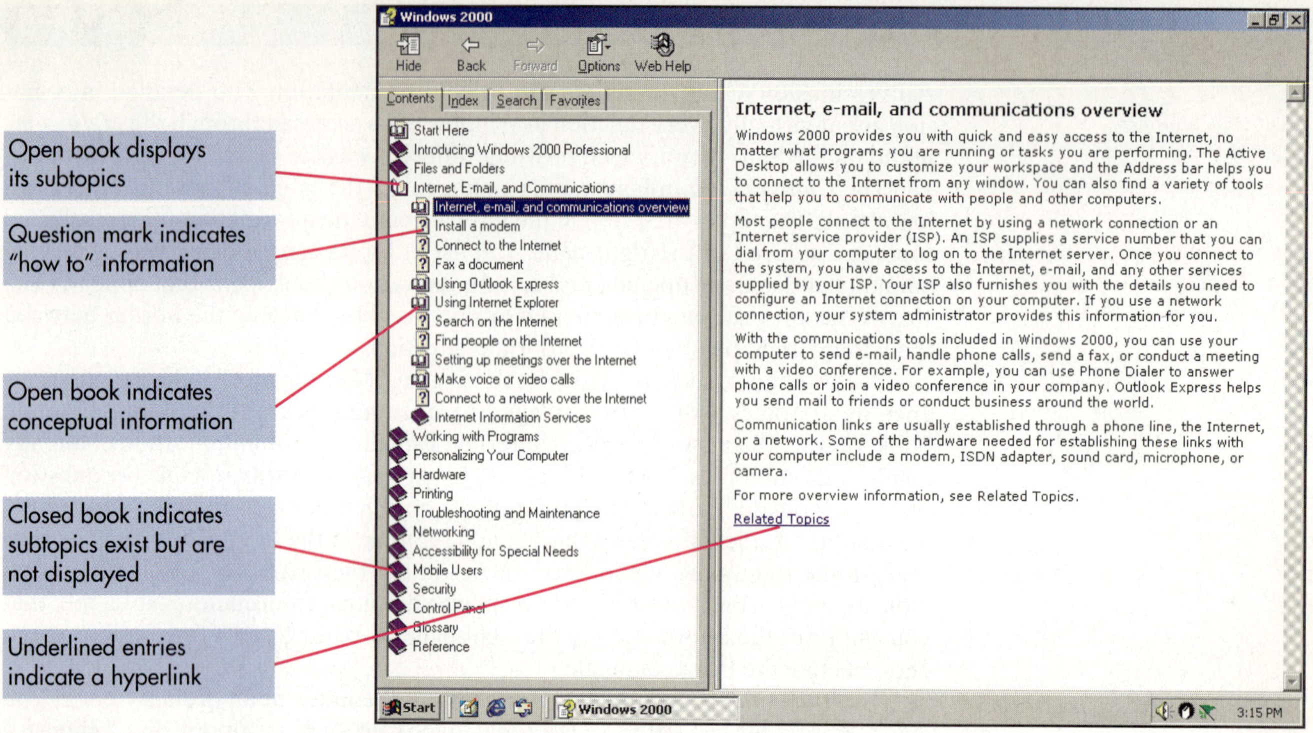

(a) Contents Tab

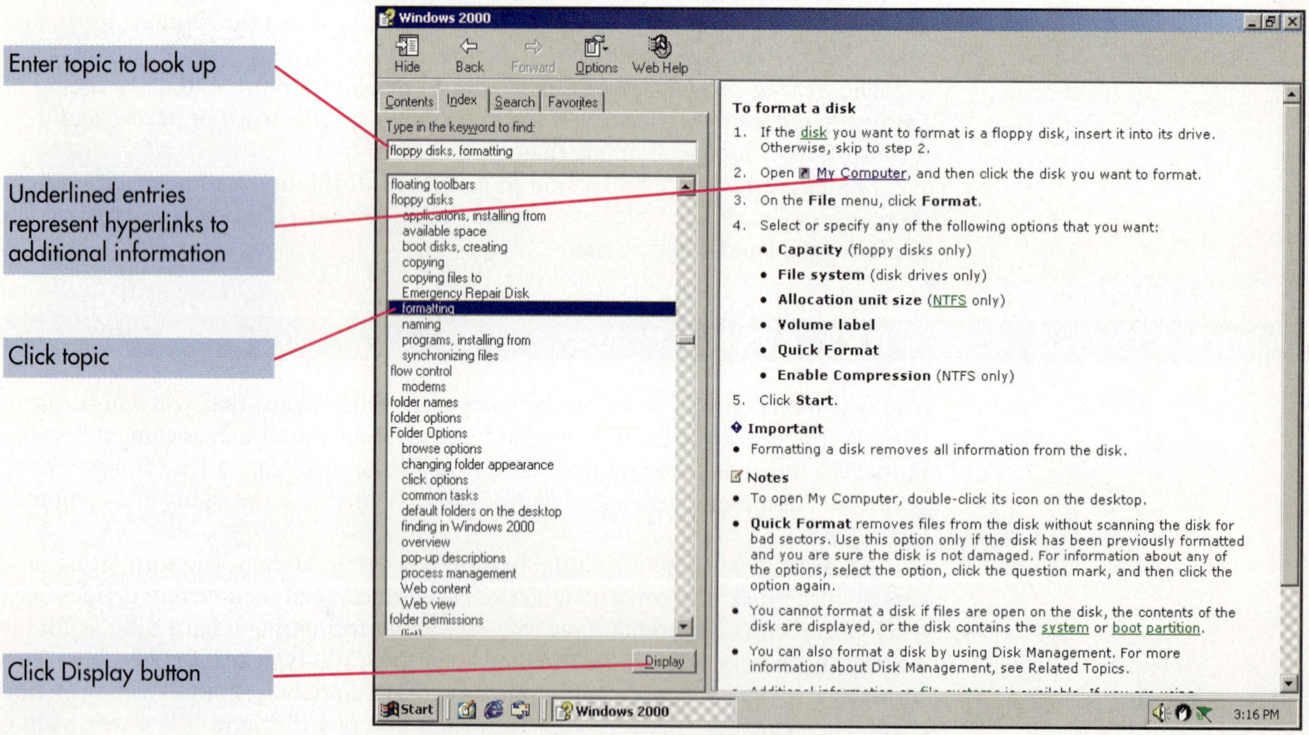

(b) Index Tab

FIGURE 5 *The Help Command*

HANDS-ON EXERCISE 1

WELCOME TO WINDOWS

Objective To turn on the computer, start Windows, and open My Computer; to move and size a window; to format a floppy disk and use the Help command. Use Figure 6 as a guide in the exercise.

Step 1: **Open My Computer**

- Start the computer by turning on the various switches appropriate to your system. Your system will take a minute or so to boot up, after which you may be asked for a **user name** and **password**.
- Enter this information, after which you should see the desktop in Figure 6a. It does not matter if you are using a different version of Windows.
- Close the Getting Started with Windows 2000 window if it appears. Do not be concerned if your desktop differs from ours.
- The way in which you open My Computer (single or double clicking) depends on the options in effect as described in step 2. Either way, however, you can **right click** the **My Computer icon** to display a context-sensitive menu, then click the **Open command**.
- The My Computer window will open on your desktop, but the contents of your window and/or its size and position will be different from ours. You are ready to go to work.

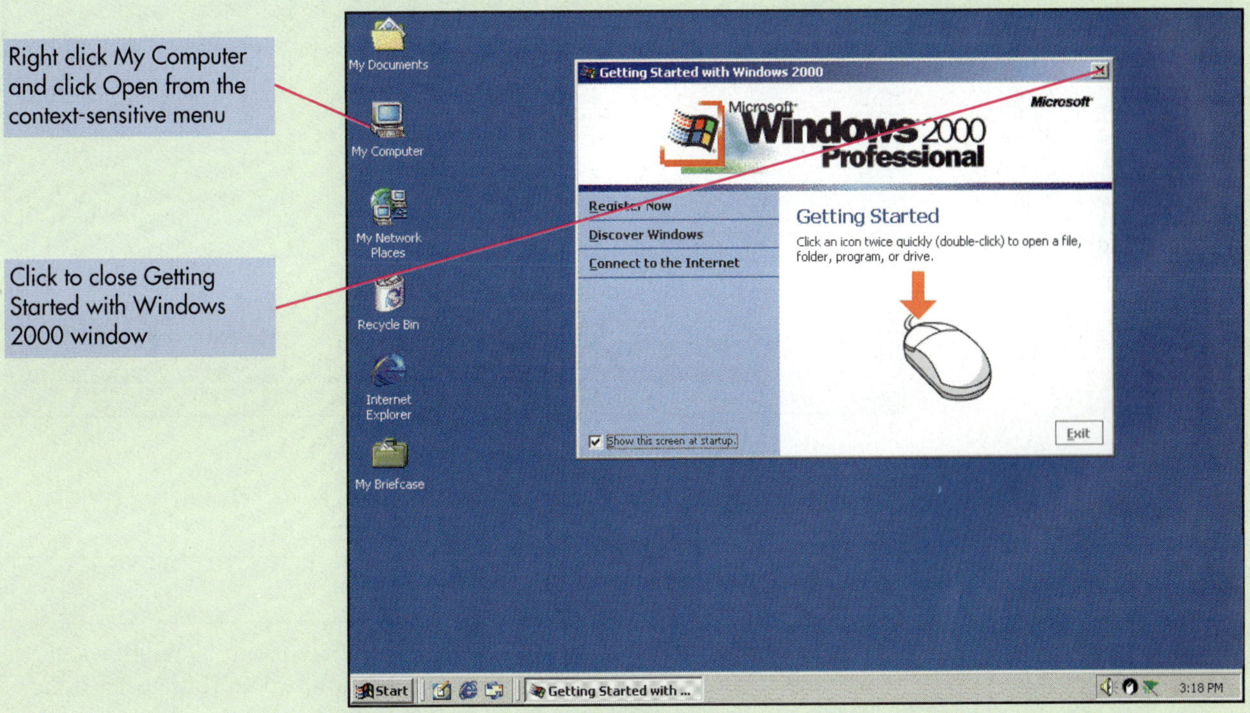

(a) Open My Computer (step 1)

FIGURE 6 *Hands-on Exercise 1*

Step 2: Set the Folder Options

- ➤ Pull down the **Tools menu** and click the **Folder Options command** to display the Folder Options dialog box. Click the **General tab**, then set the options as shown in Figure 6b. (Your network administrator may have disabled this command, in which case you will use the default settings.)
  - The Active desktop enables you to display Web content directly on the desktop. We suggest that you disable this option initially.
  - Enabling Web content in folders displays the template at the left side of the window. The Windows classic option does not contain this information.
  - Opening each successive folder within the same window saves space on the desktop as you browse the system. We discuss this in detail later on.
  - The choice between clicking underlined items and double clicking an icon (without the underline) is personal. We prefer to double click.
- ➤ Click **OK** to accept the settings and close the Folder Options dialog box. The My Computer window on your desktop should be similar to ours.

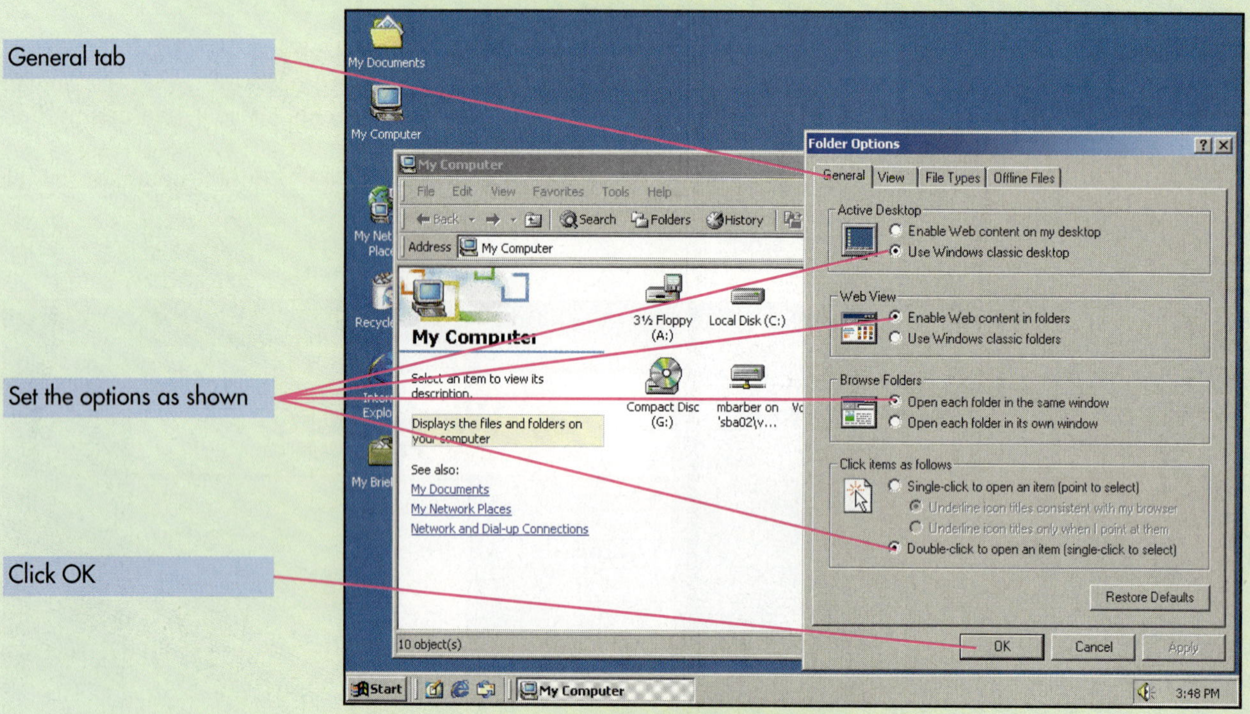

(b) Set the Folder Options (step 2)

FIGURE 6 *Hands-on Exercise 1 (continued)*

IT'S DIFFERENT IN WINDOWS 98

The Folder Options command is under the View menu in Windows 98, whereas it is found in the Tools menu in Windows 2000. Thus, to go from clicking to double clicking in Windows 98, pull down the View menu, click Folder Options, click the General tab, then choose Web style or Classic style, respectively. The procedure to display Web content in a folder is also different in Windows 98; you need to pull down the View menu and toggle the As Web Page command on.

Step 3: Move and Size a Window

- If necessary, pull down the **View menu** and click **Large Icons** so that your My Computer window more closely resembles the window in Figure 6c.
- Move and size the My Computer window on your desktop to match the display in Figure 6c.
  - To change the width or height of the window, click and drag a border (the mouse pointer changes to a double arrow) in the direction you want to go.
  - To change the width and height at the same time, click and drag a corner rather than a border.
  - To change the position of the window, click and drag the title bar.
- Click the **minimize button** to shrink the My Computer window to a button on the taskbar. My Computer is still active in memory, however. Click the **My Computer button** on the taskbar to reopen the window.
- Click the **maximize button** so that the My Computer window expands to fill the entire screen. Click the **restore button** (which replaces the maximize button and is not shown in Figure 6c) to return the window to its previous size.

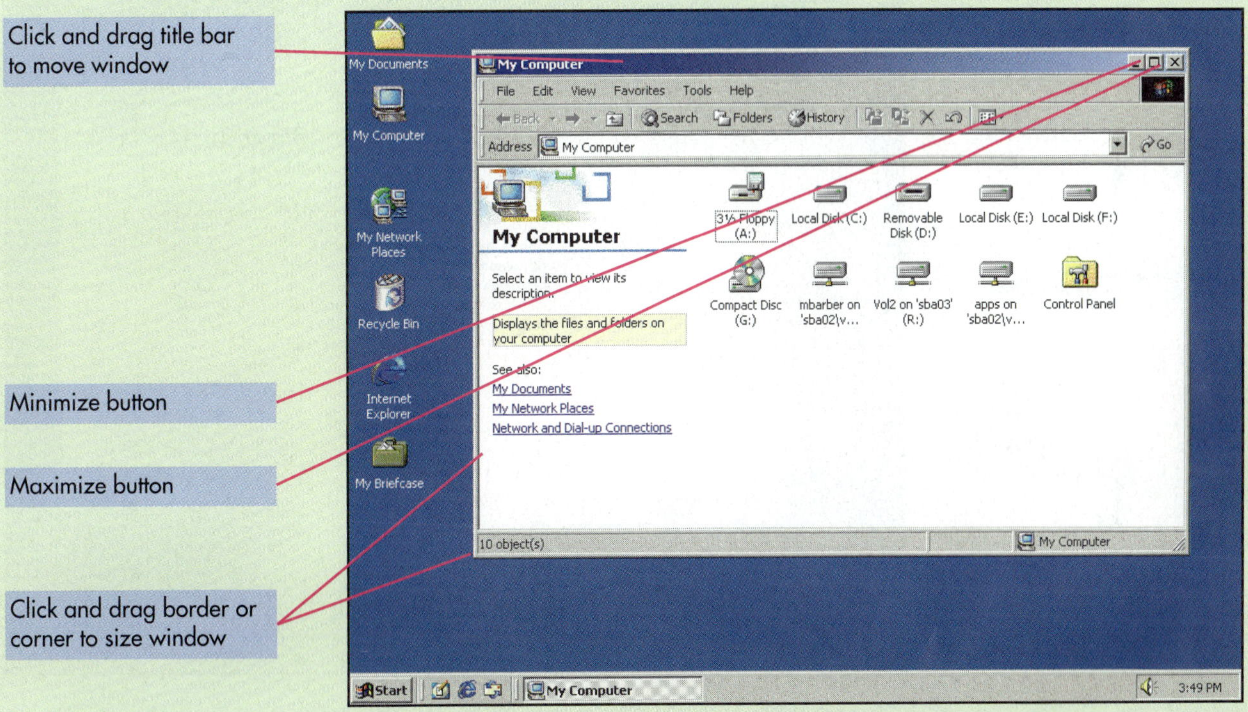

(c) Move and Size a Window (step 3)

FIGURE 6 *Hands-on Exercise 1 (continued)*

MINIMIZING VERSUS CLOSING AN APPLICATION

Minimizing an application leaves the application open in memory and available at the click of the taskbar button. Closing it, however, removes the application from memory, which also causes it to disappear from the taskbar. The advantage of minimizing an application is that you can return to the application immediately. The disadvantage is that leaving too many applications open simultaneously may degrade performance.

Step 4: Use the Pull-Down Menus

➤ Pull down the **View menu**, then click the **Toolbars command** to display a cascaded menu as shown in Figure 6d. If necessary, check the commands for the **Standard Buttons** and **Address Bar**, and clear the commands for Links and Radio.

➤ Pull down the **View menu** to make or verify the following selections. (You have to pull down the View menu each time you make an additional change.)

- The **Status Bar command** should be checked. The Status Bar command functions as a toggle switch. Click the command and the status bar is displayed; click the command a second time and the status bar disappears.)
- Click the **Details command** to change to this view. Notice that the different views are grouped within the menu and that only one view at a time can be selected.

➤ Pull down the **View menu** once again, click (or point to) the **Explorer Bar command**, and verify that none of the options is checked.

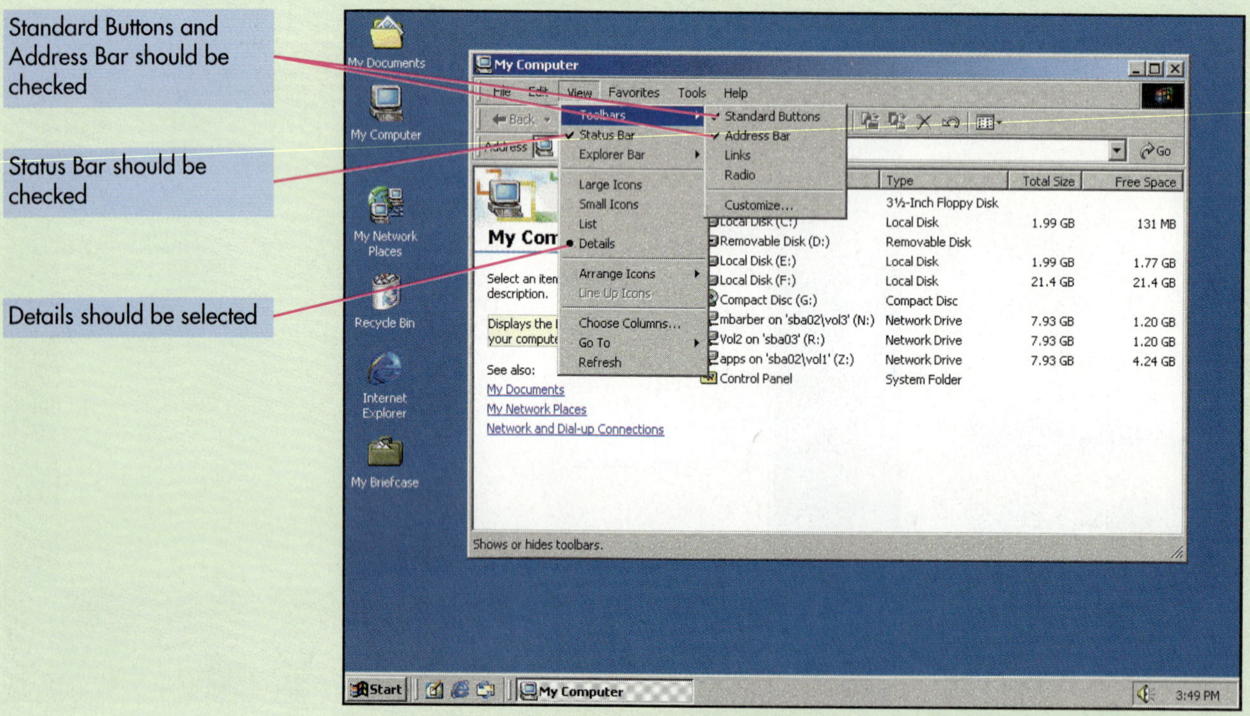

(d) Use the Pull-Down Menus (step 4)

FIGURE 6 *Hands-on Exercise 1 (continued)*

DESIGNATING THE DEVICES ON A SYSTEM

The first (usually only) floppy drive is always designated as drive A. (A second floppy drive, if it were present, would be drive B.) The first hard (local) disk on a system is always drive C, whether or not there are one or two floppy drives. Additional local drives, if any, a Zip (removable storage) drive, a network drive, and/or the CD-ROM are labeled from D on.

Step 5: **Format a Floppy Disk**

- Place a floppy disk in drive A. Select (click) drive A, then pull down the **File menu** and click the **Format command** to display the dialog box in Figure 6e.
  - Set the **Capacity** to match the floppy disk you purchased (1.44MB for a high-density disk and 720KB for a double-density disk).
  - Click the **Volume label text box** if it's empty or click and drag over the existing label. Enter a new label (containing up to 11 characters).
  - You can check the **Quick Format box** if the disk has been previously formatted, as a convenient way to erase the contents of the disk.
- Click the **Start button**, then click **OK** after you have read the warning. The formatting process erases anything that is on the disk, so be sure that you do not need anything on the disk you are about to format.
- Click **OK** after the formatting is complete. Close the Format dialog box, then save the formatted disk for use with various exercises later in the text.
- Close the My Computer window.

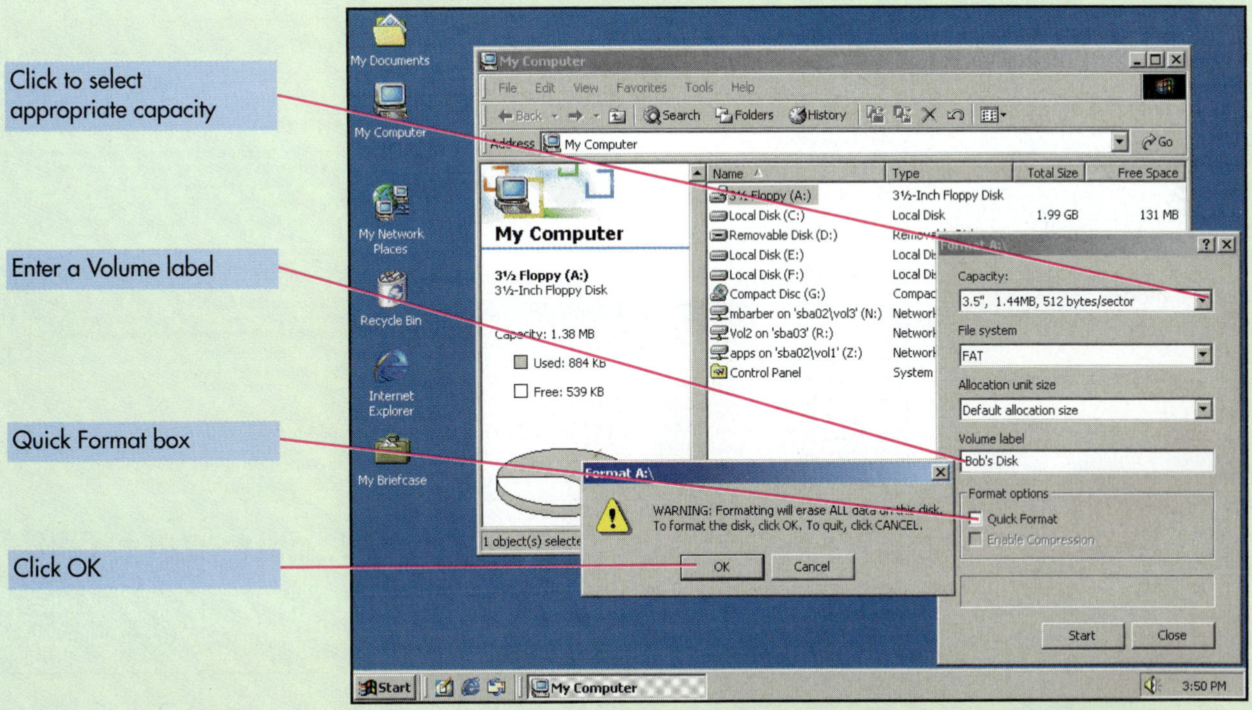

(e) Format a Floppy Disk (step 5)

FIGURE 6 *Hands-on Exercise 1 (continued)*

THE HELP BUTTON

The Help button (a question mark) appears in the title bar of almost every dialog box. Click the question mark, then click the item you want information about (which then appears in a pop-up window). To print the contents of the pop-up window, click the right mouse button inside the window, and click Print Topic. Click outside the pop-up window to close the window and continue working.

Step 6: The Help Command

- Click the **Start button** on the taskbar, then click the **Help command** to display the Help window in Figure 6f. Maximize the Help window.
- Click the **Contents tab**, then click a closed book such as **Hardware** to open the book and display the associated topics. Click any one of the displayed topics such as **Hardware overview** in Figure 6f.
- Pull down the **Options menu** and click the **Print command** to display the Print Topics dialog box. Click the option button to print the selected topic, click **OK**, then click the **Print button** in the resulting dialog box.
- Click the **Index tab**, type **format** (the first several letters in "Formatting disks," the topic you are searching for). Double click this topic within the list of index items. Pull down the **Options menu** and click the **Print command** to print this information as well.
- Submit the printed information to your instructor. Close the Help window.

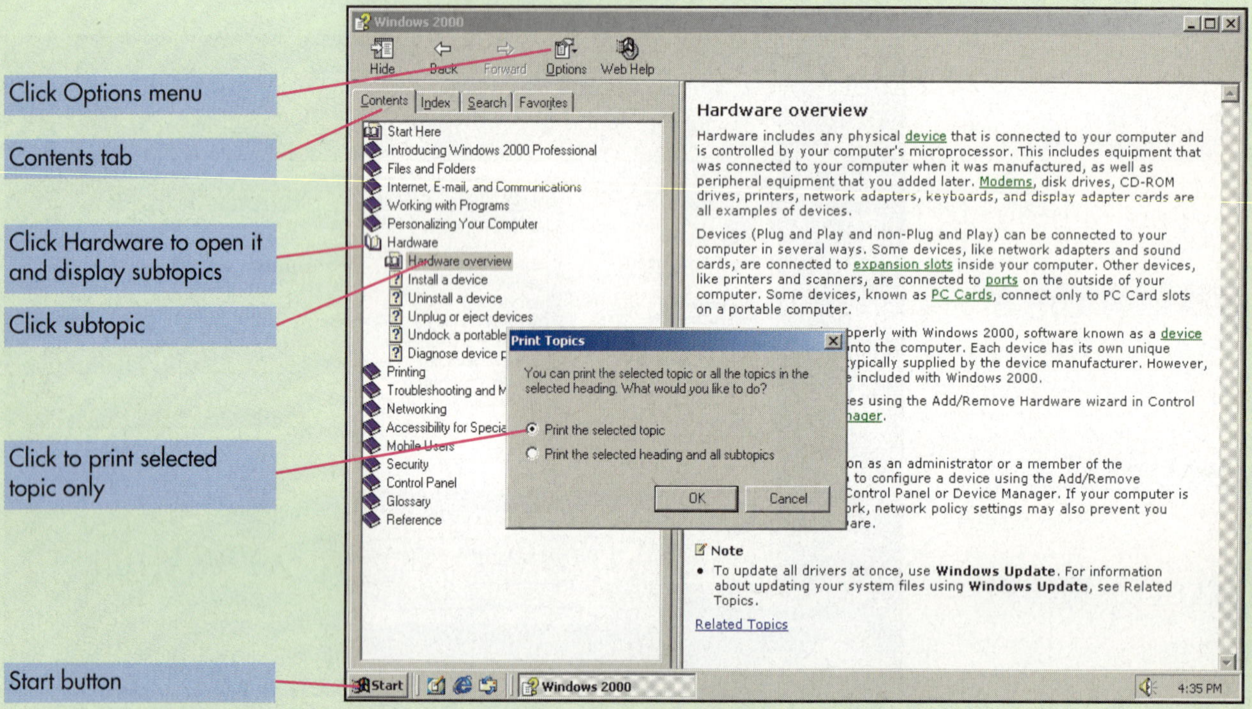

(f) The Help Command (step 6)

FIGURE 6 *Hands-on Exercise 1 (continued)*

THE FAVORITES TAB

Do you find yourself continually searching for the same Help topic? If so, you can make life a little easier by adding the topic to a list of favorite Help topics. Start Help, then use the Contents, Index, or Search tabs to locate the desired topic. Now click the Favorites tab in the Help window, then click the Add button to add the topic. You can return to the topic at any time by clicking the Favorites tab, then double clicking the bookmark to display the information.

Step 7: **Shut Down the Computer**

- It is very important that you shut down your computer properly as opposed to just turning off the power. This enables Windows to properly close all of its system files and to save any changes that were made during the session.
- Click the **Start button**, click the **Shut Down command** to display the Shut Down Windows dialog box in Figure 6g. Click the **drop-down arrow** to display the desired option:
  - Logging off ends your session, but leaves the computer running at full power. This is the typical option you select in a laboratory setting.
  - Shutting down the computer ends the session and also closes Windows so that you can safely turn the power off. (Some computers will automatically turn the power off for you if this option is selected.)
  - Restarting the computer ends your sessions, then closes and restarts Windows to begin a new session.
- Welcome to Windows 2000!

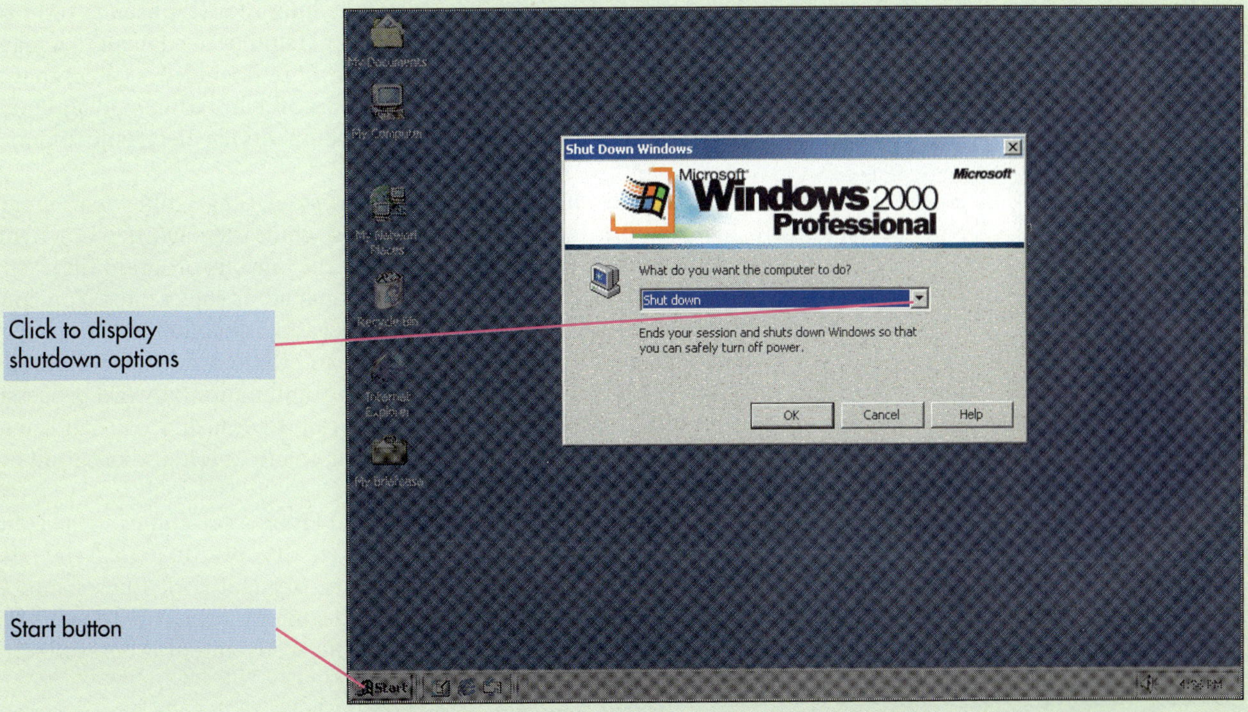

(g) Shut Down the Computer (step 7)

FIGURE 6 *Hands-on Exercise 1 (continued)*

THE TASK MANAGER

The Start button is the normal way to exit Windows. Occasionally, however, an application may "hang"—in which case you want to close the problem application but leave Windows open. Press Ctrl+Alt+Del to display the Windows Security dialog box, then click the Task Manager command button. Click the Applications tab, select the problem application, and click the End Task button.

FILES AND FOLDERS

A ***file*** is a set of instructions or data that has been given a name and stored on disk. There are two basic types of files, ***program files*** and ***data files***. Microsoft Word and Microsoft Excel are examples of program files. The documents and workbooks created by these programs are examples of data files.

A ***program file*** is an executable file because it contains instructions that tell the computer what to do. A ***data file*** is not executable and can be used only in conjunction with a specific program. As a typical student, you execute (run) program files, then you use those programs to create and/or modify the associated data files.

Every file has a ***file name*** that identifies it to the operating system. The file name may contain up to 255 characters and may include spaces. (File names cannot contain the following characters: \, /, :, *, ?, ", <, >, or |. We suggest that you try to keep file names simple and restrict yourself to the use of letters, numbers, and spaces.) Long file names permit descriptive entries such as *Term Paper for Western Civilization* (as distinct from a more cryptic *TPWCIV* that was required under MS-DOS and Windows 3.1).

Files are stored in ***folders*** to better organize the hundreds (thousands, or tens of thousands) of files on a hard disk. A Windows folder is similar in concept to a manila folder in a filing cabinet into which you put one or more documents (files) that are somehow related to each other. An office worker stores his or her documents in manila folders. In Windows, you store your files (documents) in electronic folders on disk.

Folders are the keys to the Windows storage system. Some folders are created automatically; for example, the installation of a program such as Microsoft Office automatically creates one or more folders to hold the various program files. Other folders are created by the user to hold the documents he or she creates. You could, for example, create one folder for your word processing documents and a second folder for your spreadsheets. Alternatively, you can create a folder to hold all of your work for a specific class, which may contain a combination of word processing documents and spreadsheets. The choice is entirely up to you, and you can use any system that makes sense to you. Anything at all can go into a folder—program files, data files, even other folders.

Figure 7 displays the contents of a hypothetical Homework folder with six documents. Figure 7a enables Web content, and so we see the colorful logo at the left of the folder, together with links to My Documents, My Network Places, and My Computer. Figure 7b is displayed without the Web content, primarily to gain space within the window. The display or suppression of the Web content is determined by a setting in the Folder Options command.

Figures 7a and 7b are displayed in different views. Figure 7a uses the ***Large Icons view***, whereas Figure 7b is displayed in the ***Details view***, which shows additional information for each file. (Other possible views include Small Icons, List, and Thumbnail.) The file icon, whether large or small, indicates the ***file type*** or application that was used to create the file. The History of Computers file, for example, is a Microsoft Word document. The Grade Book is a Microsoft Excel workbook.

Regardless of the view and options in effect, the name of the folder (Homework) appears in the title bar next to the icon of an open folder. The minimize, maximize, and Close buttons appear at the right of the title bar. A menu bar with six pull-down menus appears below the title bar. The Standard Buttons toolbar appears below the menu, and the Address Bar (indicating the drive and folder) appears below the toolbar. A status bar appears at the bottom of both windows, indicating that the Homework folder contains six objects (documents) and that the total file size is 525KB.

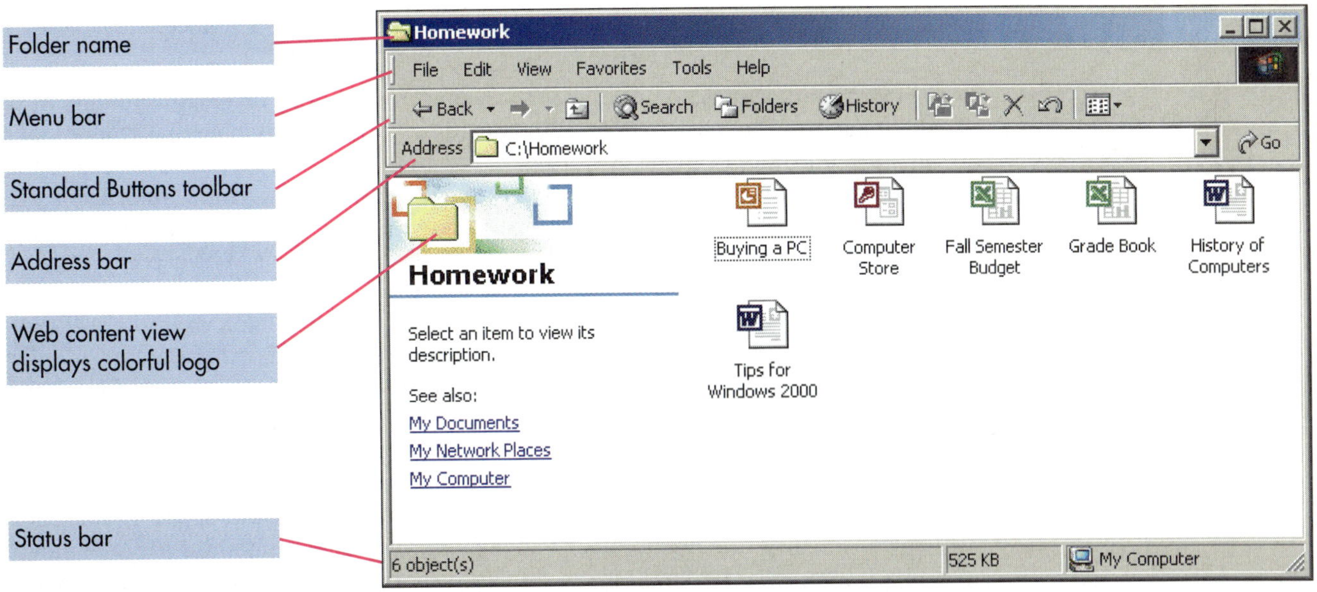

(a) Large Icons View with Web Content Enabled

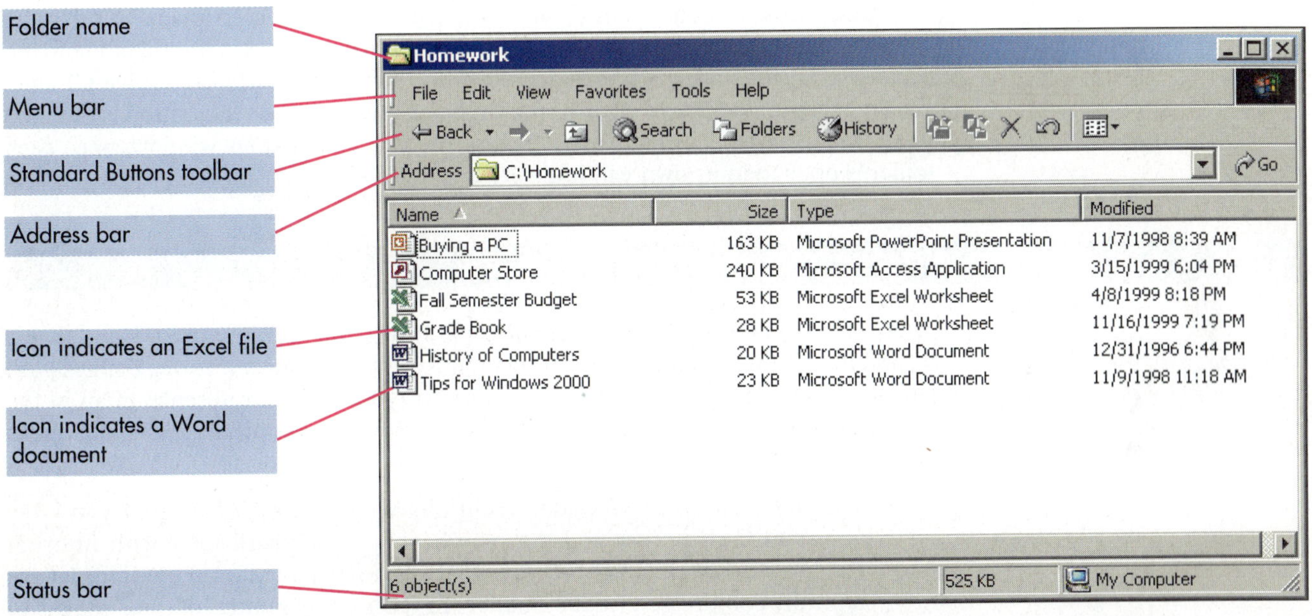

(b) Details View without Web Content

FIGURE 7 *The Homework Folder*

CHANGE THE VIEW

Look closely at the address bar in Figures 7a and 7b to see that both figures display the Homework folder on drive C, although the figures are very different in appearance. Figure 7a displays Web content to provide direct links to three other folders, and the contents of the Homework folder are displayed in the Large Icons view to save space. Figure 7b suppresses the Web content and uses the Details view to provide the maximum amount of information for each file in the Homework folder. You are free to choose whichever options you prefer.

MY COMPUTER

My Computer enables you to browse through the various drives and folders on a system in order to locate a document and go to work. Let's assume that you're looking for a document called "History of Computers" that you saved previously in the Homework folder on drive C. To get to this document, you would open My Computer, from where you would open drive C, open the Homework folder, and then open the document. It's a straightforward process that can be accomplished in two different ways, as shown in Figure 8.

The difference between the two figures is whether each drive or folder is opened in its own window, as shown in Figure 8a, or whether the same window is used for every folder, as in Figure 8b. (This is another option that is set through the Folder Options command.) In Figure 8a you begin by double clicking the My Computer icon on the desktop to open the My Computer window, which in turn displays the devices on your system. Next, you double click the icon for drive C to open a second window that displays the folders on drive C. From there, you double click the icon for the Homework folder to open a third window containing the documents in the Homework folder. Once in the Homework folder, you can double click the icon of an existing document, which starts the associated application and opens the document.

The process is identical in Figure 8b except that each object opens in the same window. The Back arrow on the Standard Buttons toolbar is meaningful in Figure 8b because you can click the button to return to the previous window (drive C), then click it again to go back to My Computer. Note, however, that the button is dimmed in all three windows in Figure 8a because there is no previous window, since each folder is opened in its own window.

THE EXPLORING OFFICE PRACTICE FILES

There is only one way to master the file operations inherent in Windows and that is to practice at the computer. To do so requires that you have a series of files with which to work. We have created these files for you, and we reference them in the next several hands-on exercises. Your instructor will make these files available to you in a variety of ways:

- The files can be downloaded from our Web site, assuming that you have access to the Internet and that you have a basic proficiency with Internet Explorer. Software and other files that are downloaded from the Internet are typically compressed (made smaller) to reduce the amount of time it takes to transmit the file. In essence, you will download a ***compressed file*** (which may contain multiple individual files) from our Web site and then uncompress the file onto a local drive as described in the next hands-on exercise.
- The files might be on a network drive, in which case you can use My Computer (or Windows Explorer, which is discussed later in the chapter) to copy the files from the network drive to a floppy disk. The procedure to do this is described in the third hands-on exercise.
- There may be an actual "data disk" in the computer lab. Go to the lab with a floppy disk, then use the Copy Disk command (on the File menu of My Computer) to duplicate the data disk and create a copy for yourself.

It doesn't matter how you obtain the practice files, only that you are able to do so. Indeed, you may want to try different techniques in order to gain additional practice with Windows.

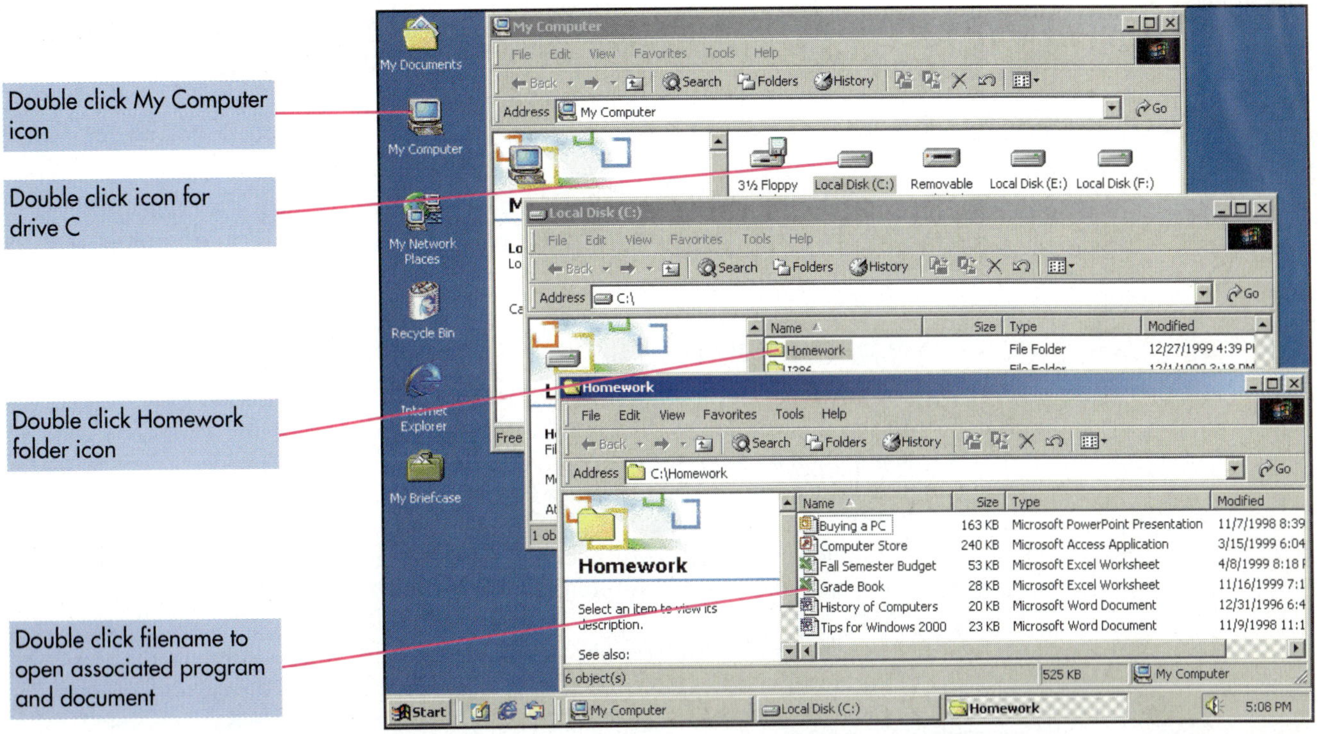

(a) Multiple Windows

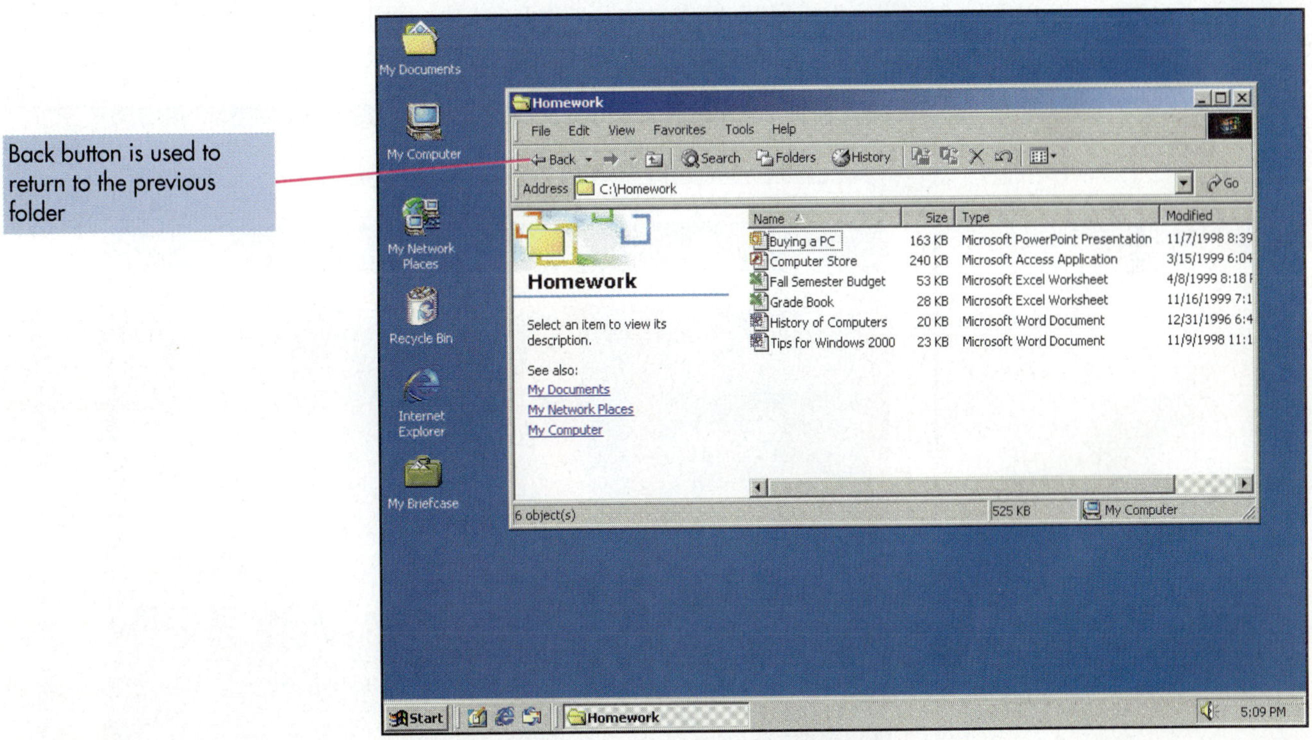

(b) One Window

FIGURE 8 *Browsing My Computer*

HANDS-ON EXERCISE 2

THE PRACTICE FILES VIA THE WEB

Objective To download a file from the Web. The exercise requires a formatted floppy disk and access to the Internet. Use Figure 9 as a guide in the exercise.

Step 1: **Start Internet Explorer**

- Start Internet Explorer, perhaps by double clicking the **Internet Explorer icon** on the desktop, or by clicking the **Start button**, clicking the **Programs command**, then locating the command to start the program. If necessary, click the **maximize button** so that Internet Explorer takes the entire desktop.
- Enter the address of the site you want to visit:
  - Pull down the **File menu**, click the **Open command** to display the Open dialog box, and enter **www.prenhall.com/grauer** (the http:// is assumed). Click **OK**.
  - *Or,* click in the **Address bar** below the toolbar, which automatically selects the current address (so that whatever you type replaces the current address). Enter the address of the site you want to visit, **www.prenhall.com/grauer** (the http:// is assumed). Press **enter**.
- You should see the *Exploring Office Series* home page as shown in Figure 9a. Click the book for **Office XP**, which takes you to the Office XP home page.
- Click the **Student Resources link** (at the top of the window) to go to the Student Resources page.

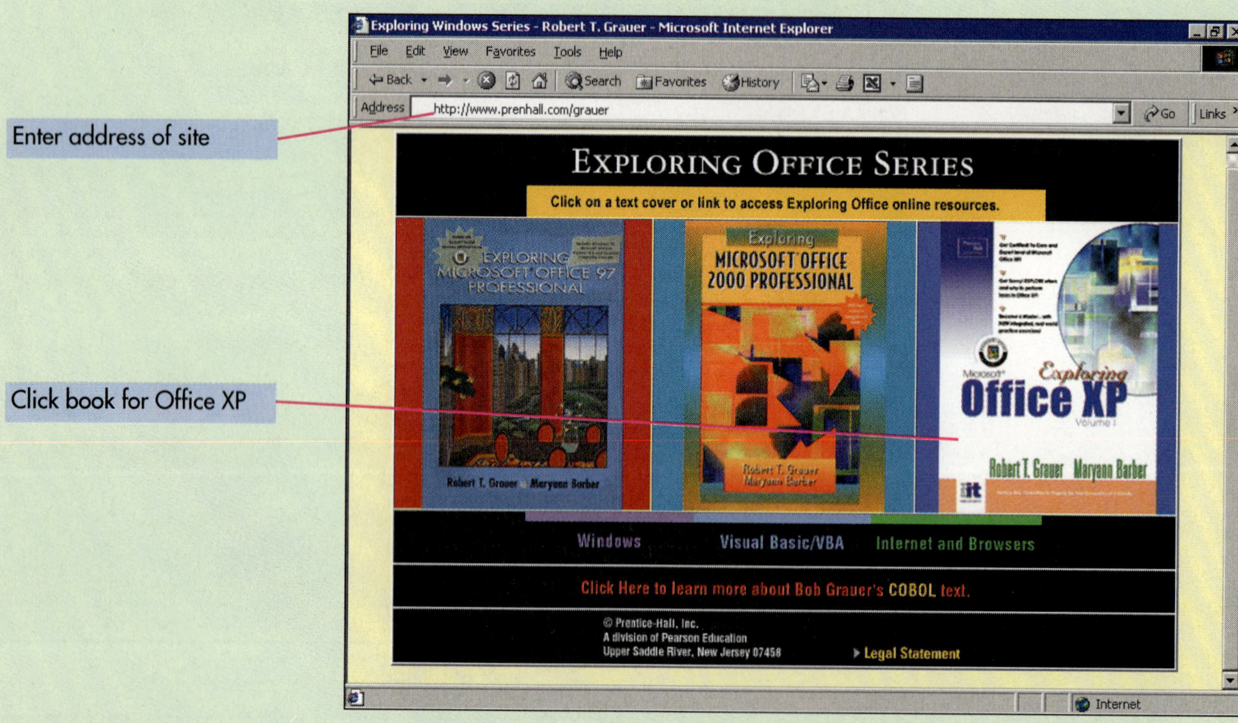

(a) Start Internet Explorer (step 1)

FIGURE 9 *Hands-on Exercise 2*

Step 2: **Download the Practice Files**

- Click the link to **Student Data Disk** (in the left frame), then scroll down the page until you can see **Essentials of Microsoft Windows**.
- Click the indicated link to download the practice files. The Save As dialog box is not yet visible.
- You will see the File Download dialog box asking what you want to do. The option button to save this program to disk is selected. Click **OK**. The Save As dialog box appears as shown in Figure 9b.
- Place a formatted floppy disk in drive A, click the **drop-down arrow** on the Save in list box, and select (click) **drive A**. Click **Save** to begin downloading the file.
- The File Download window will reappear on your screen and show you the status of the downloading operation. If necessary, click **OK** when you see the dialog box indicating that the download is complete.
- Close Internet Explorer.

Click link to Student Resources

Click to select drive A

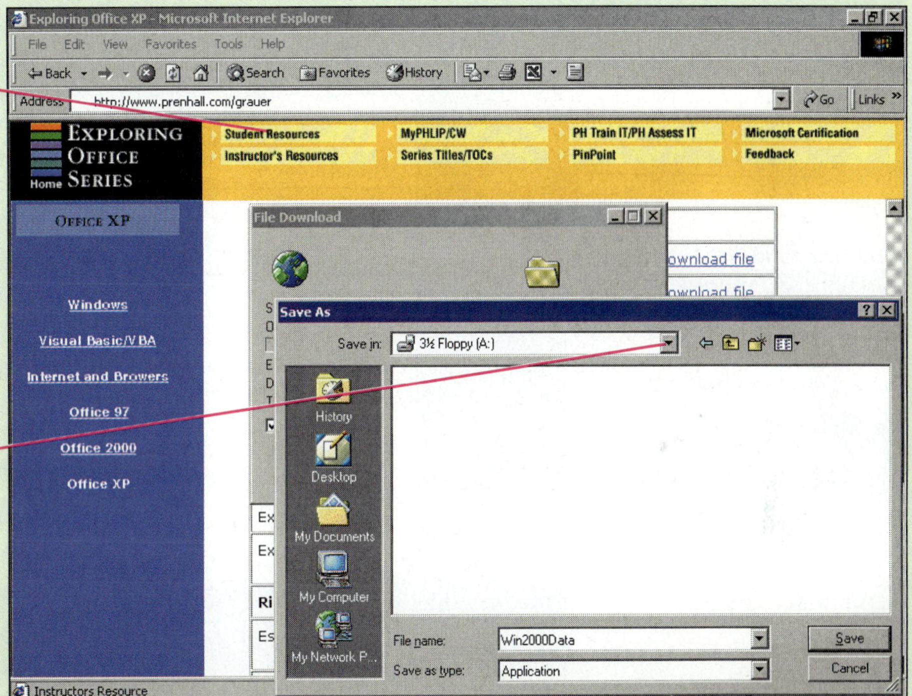

(b) Download the Practice Files (step 2)

FIGURE 9 *Hands-on Exercise 2 (continued)*

REMEMBER THE LOCATION

It's easy to download a file from the Web. The only tricky part, if any, is remembering where you have saved the file. This exercise is written for a laboratory setting, and thus we specified drive A as the destination, so that you will have the file on a floppy disk at the end of the exercise. If you have your own computer, however, it's faster to save the file to the desktop or in a temporary folder on drive C. Just remember where you save the file so that you can access it after it has been downloaded.

Step 3: Open My Computer

- Double click the My Computer icon on the desktop to open My Computer. If necessary, customize My Computer to match Figure 9c.
  - Pull down the **View menu** and change to the **Details view**.
  - Pull down the **View menu** a second time, click (or point to) the **Toolbars command**, then check the **Standard buttons** and **Address Bar** toolbars.
- Pull down the **Tools menu** and click the **Folder Options command** to verify the settings in effect so that your window matches ours. Be sure to **Enable Web content in folders** (in the Web View area), to **Open each folder in the same window** (in the Browse Folders area), and **Double Click to open an item** (in the Click Items area).
- Click the icon for **drive A** to select it. The description of drive A appears at the left of the window.
- Double click the icon for **drive A** to open this drive. The contents of the My Computer window are replaced by the contents of drive A.

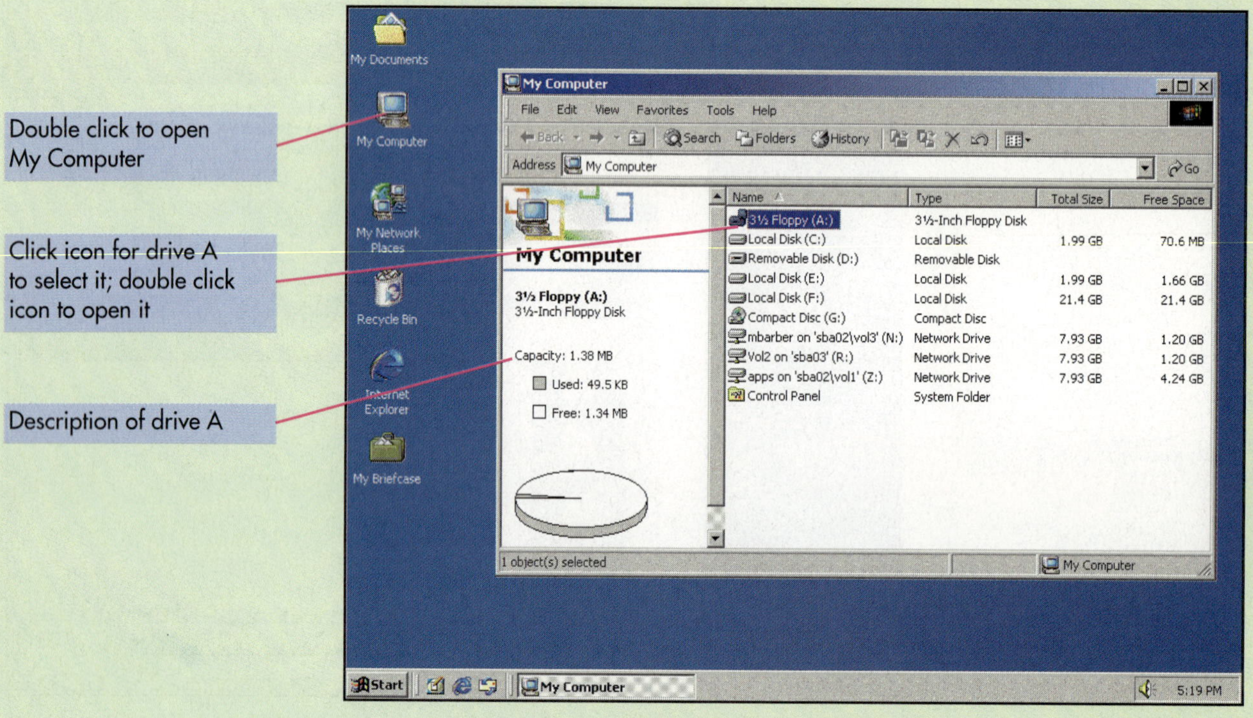

(c) Open My Computer (step 3)

FIGURE 9 *Hands-on Exercise 2 (continued)*

THE RIGHT MOUSE BUTTON

Point to any object on the Windows desktop or within an application window, then click the right mouse button to see a context-sensitive menu with commands pertaining to that object. You could, for example, right click the icon for drive A, then select the Open command from the resulting menu. The right mouse button is one of the most powerful Windows shortcuts and one of its best-kept secrets. Use it!

Step 4: **Install the Practice Files**

- You should see the contents of drive A as shown in Figure 9d. (If your desktop displays two windows rather than one, it is because you did not set the folder options correctly. Pull down the **Tools menu**, click the **Folder Options command**, and choose the option to **Open each folder in the same window**.)
- Double click the **Win2000data file** to install the data disk. You will see a dialog box thanking you for selecting the *Exploring Windows* series. Click **OK**.
  - Check that the Unzip To Folder text box specifies **A:** to extract the files to the floppy disk. (You may enter a different drive and/or folder.)
  - Click the **Unzip button** to extract the practice files and copy them onto the designated drive. Click **OK** after you see the message indicating that the files have been unzipped successfully. Close the WinZip dialog box.
- The practice files have been extracted to drive A and should appear in the Drive A window. If you do not see the files, pull down the **View menu** and click the **Refresh command.**

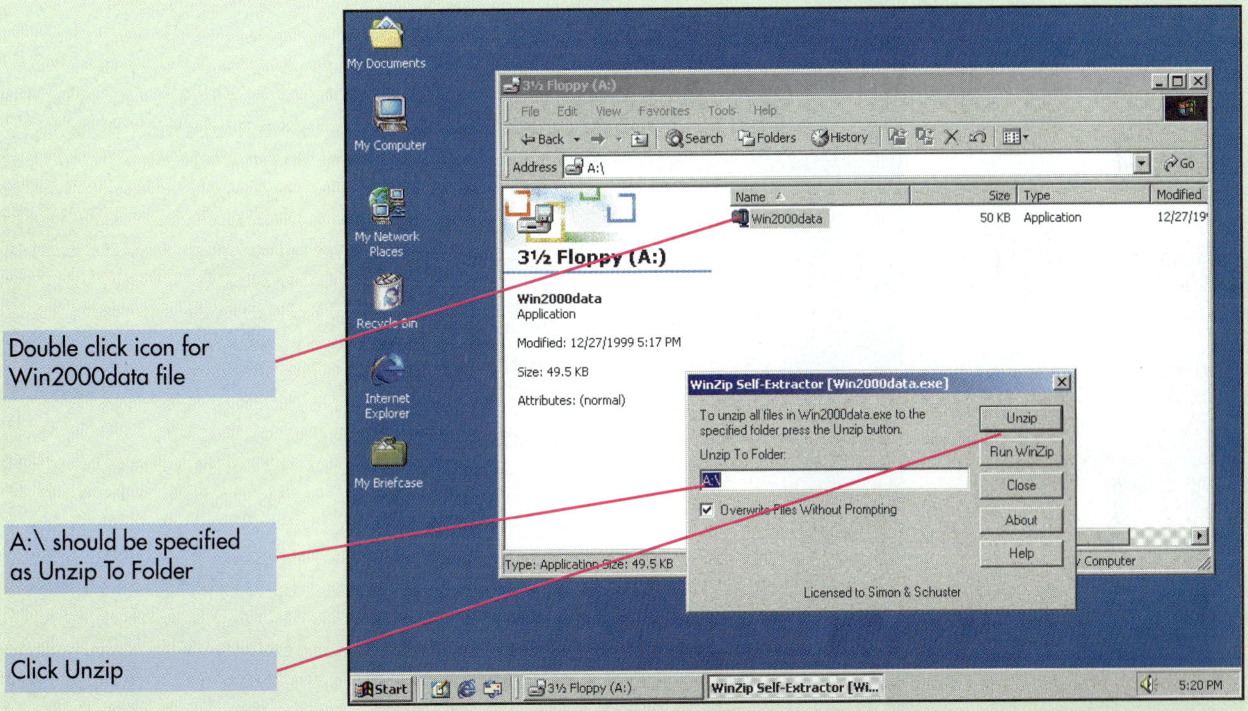

(d) Install the Practice Files (step 4)

FIGURE 9 *Hands-on Exercise 2 (continued)*

DOWNLOADING A FILE

Software and other files are typically compressed to reduce the amount of storage space the files require on disk and/or the time it takes to download the files. In essence, you download a compressed file (which may contain multiple individual files), then you uncompress (expand) the file on your local drive in order to access the individual files. After the file has been expanded, it is no longer needed and can be deleted.

Step 5: **Delete the Compressed File**

- If necessary, pull down the **View menu** and click **Details** to change to the Details view in Figure 9e. (If you do not see the descriptive information about drive A at the left of the window, pull down the **Tools menu**, click the **Folder Options command**, and click the option button to **Enable Web content in folders**.)
- You should see a total of six files in the Drive A window. Five of these are the practice files on the data disk. The sixth file is the original file that you downloaded earlier. This file is no longer necessary, since it has been already been expanded.
- Select (click) the **Win2000data file**. Pull down the **File menu** and click the **Delete command**, or click the **Delete button** on the toolbar. Pause for a moment to be sure you want to delete this file, then click **Yes** when asked to confirm the deletion as shown in Figure 9e.
- The Win2000Data file is permanently deleted from drive A. (Items deleted from a floppy disk or network drive are not sent to the Recycle Bin, and cannot be recovered.)

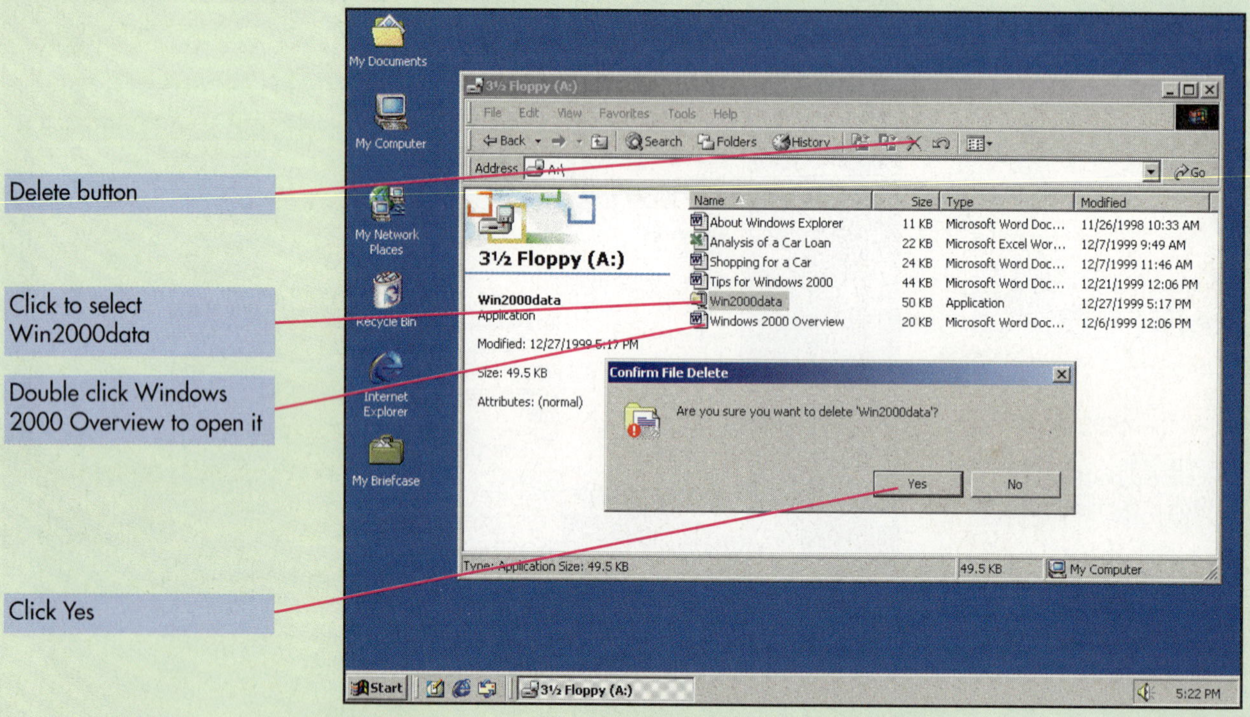

(e) Delete the Compressed File (step 5)

FIGURE 9 *Hands-on Exercise 2 (continued)*

SORT BY NAME, DATE, FILE TYPE, OR SIZE

Files can be displayed in ascending or descending sequence by name, date modified, file type, or size by clicking the appropriate column heading. Click Size, for example, to display files in the order of their size. Click the column heading a second time to reverse the sequence; that is, to switch from ascending to descending, and vice versa.

Step 6: **Modify a Document**

- Double click the **Windows 2000 Overview** document from within My Computer to open the document as shown in Figure 9f. (The document will open in the WordPad accessory if Microsoft Word is not installed on your machine.) If necessary, maximize the window for Microsoft Word.
- If necessary, click inside the document window, then press **Ctrl+End** to move to the end of the document. Add the sentence shown in Figure 9h followed by your name.
- Pull down the **File menu**, click **Print**, then click **OK** to print the document and prove to your instructor that you did the exercise.
- Pull down the **File menu** and click **Exit** to close the application. Click **Yes** when prompted to save the file.

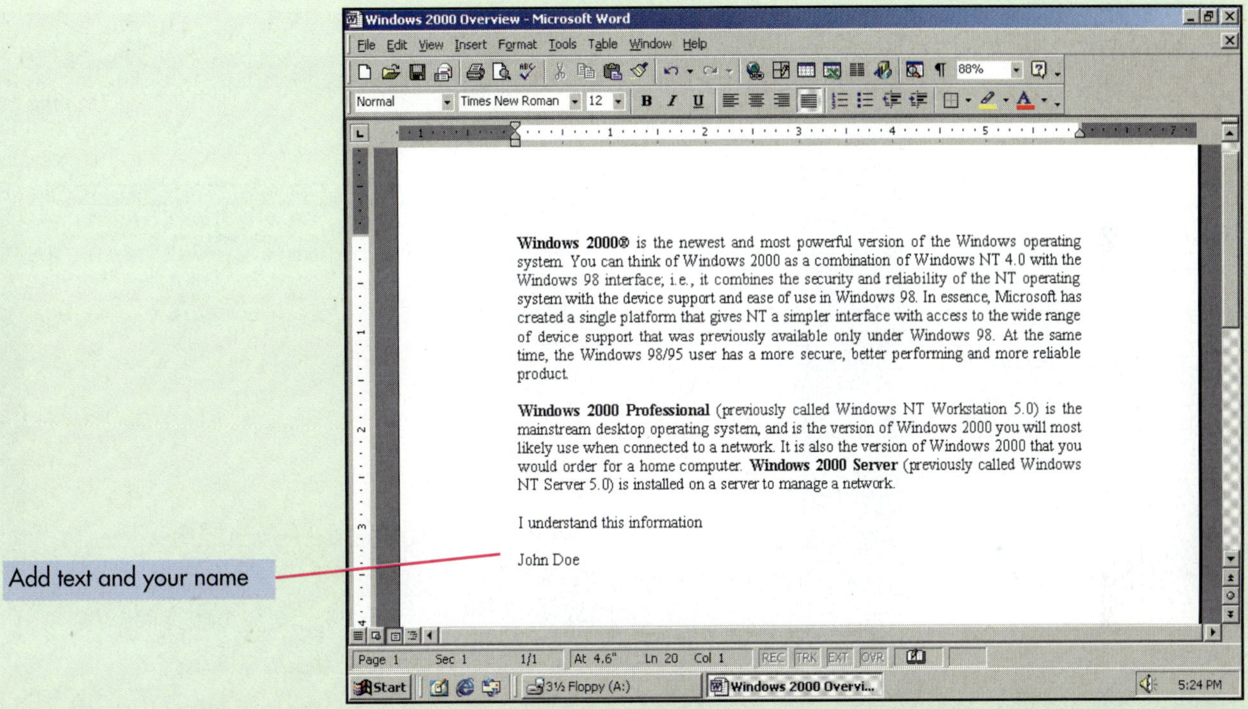

(f) Modify a Document (step 6)

FIGURE 9 *Hands-on Exercise 2 (continued)*

THE DOCUMENT, NOT THE APPLICATION

All versions of Windows are document oriented, meaning that you are able to think in terms of the document rather than the application that created it. You can still open a document in traditional fashion by starting the application that created the document, then using the File Open command in that program to retrieve the document. It's often easier, however, to open the document from within My Computer (or Windows Explorer) by double clicking its icon. Windows then starts the application and opens the data file. In other words, you can open a document without explicitly starting the application.

Step 7: **Check Your Work**

- You should be back in the My Computer window as shown in Figure 9g. If necessary, click the **Views button** to change to the Details view.
- Look closely at the date and time that is displayed next to the Windows 2000 Overview document. It should show today's date and the current time (give or take a minute) since that is when the document was last modified.
- Look closely and see that Figure 9g also contains a sixth document, called "Backup of Windows 2000 Overview". This is a backup copy of the original document that will be created automatically by Microsoft Word if the appropriate options are in effect. (See the boxed tip below.)
- Exit Windows or, alternatively, continue with steps 8 and 9 to return to our Web site and explore additional resources.

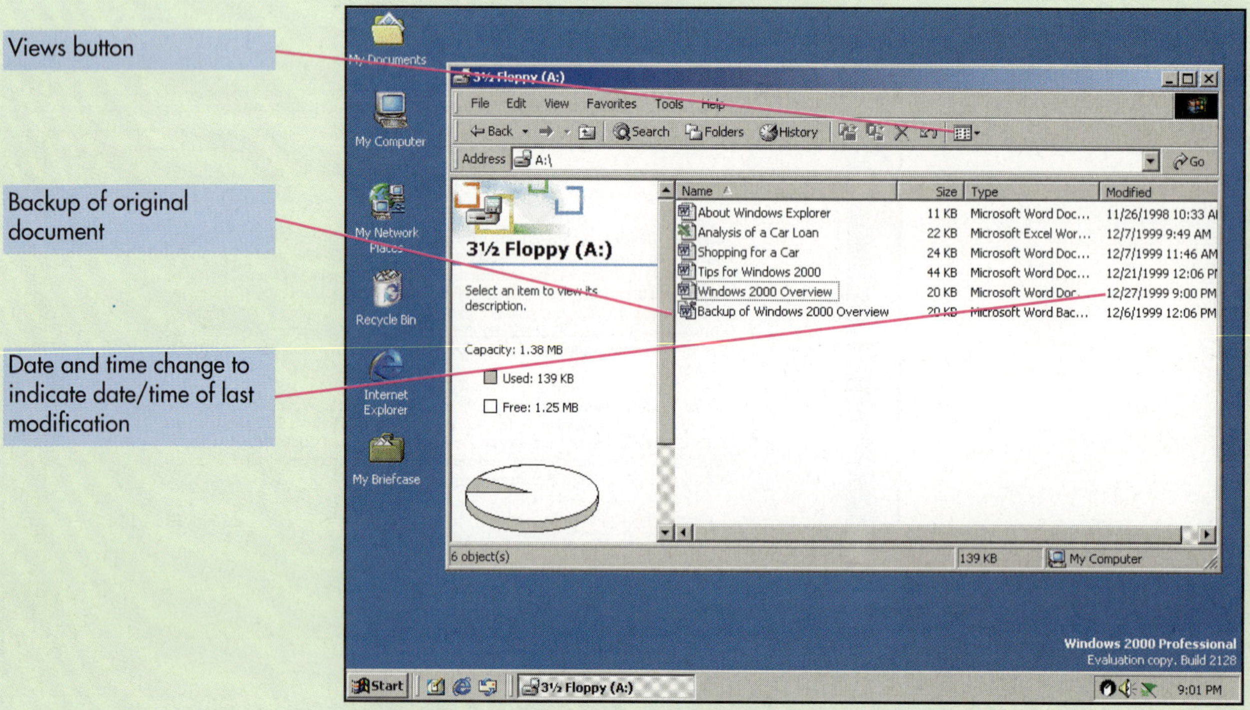

(g) Check Your Work (step 7)

FIGURE 9 *Hands-on Exercise 2 (continued)*

USE WORD TO CREATE A BACKUP COPY

Microsoft Word enables you to automatically create a backup copy of a document in conjunction with the Save command. The next time you are in Microsoft Word, pull down the Tools menu, click the Options command, click the Save tab, then check the box to always create a backup copy. Every time you save a file from this point on, the previously saved version is renamed "Backup of document," and the document in memory is saved as the current version. The disk will contain the two most recent versions of the document, enabling you to retrieve the previous version if necessary.

Step 8: **Download the PowerPoint Lecture**

- Restart Internet Explorer and connect to **www.prenhall.com/grauer**. Click the book for **Office XP**, click the link to **Student Resources**, then choose **PowerPoint Lectures** to display the screen in Figure 9h.
- Click the down arrow until you can click the link to the PowerPoint slides for **Essentials of Windows**. The File Download dialog box will appear with the option to save the file to disk selected by default. Click **OK**.
- Click the **drop-down arrow** on the Save in list box, and select **drive A**. Be sure that the floppy disk is still in drive A, then click **Save** to begin downloading the file. Click **OK** when you see the dialog box indicating that the download is complete.
- Click the taskbar button to return to the **My Computer window** for drive A. You should see all of the files that were previously on the floppy disk plus the file you just downloaded.
- Double click the **Win2000ppt file**, then follow the onscreen instructions to unzip the file to drive A.

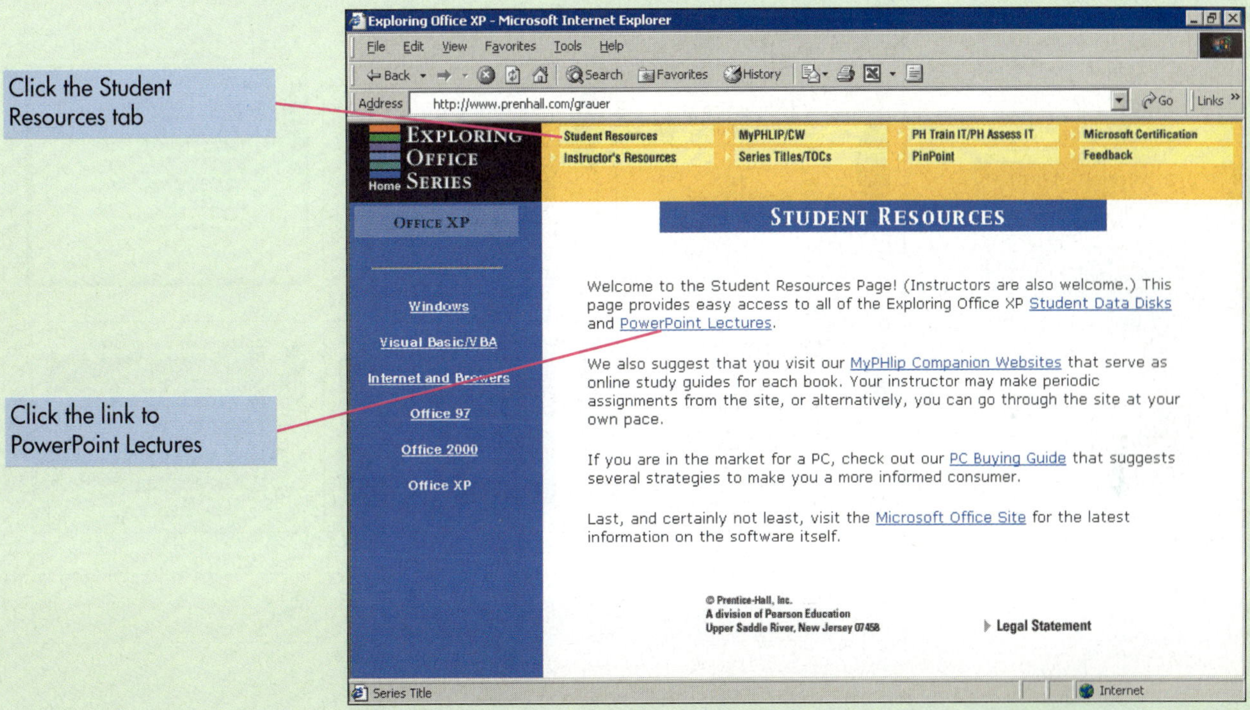

(h) Download the PowerPoint Lecture (step 8)

FIGURE 9 *Hands-on Exercise 2 (continued)*

THE MyPHLIP WEB SITE

The MyPHLIP (Prentice Hall Learning on the Internet Partnership) Web site is another resource that is available for the Exploring Office series. Click the MyPHLIP tab at the top of the screen, which takes you to www.prenhall.com/myphlip, where you will register and select the text you are using. See exercise 3 at the end of the chapter.

Step 9: **Show Time**

- Drive A should now contain a PowerPoint file in addition to the self-extracting file. (Pull down the **View menu** and click the **Refresh command** if you do not see the PowerPoint file.)
- Double click the PowerPoint file to open the presentation, then click the button to Enable Macros (if prompted). You should see the PowerPoint presentation in Figure 9i. (You must have PowerPoint installed on your computer in order to view the presentation.)
- Pull down the **View menu** and click **Slide Show** to begin the presentation, which is intended to review the material in this supplement. Click the left mouse button (or press the **PgDn key**) to move to the next slide.
- Click the left mouse button continually to move from one slide to the next. Close PowerPoint at the end of the presentation.
- Exit Windows if you do not want to continue with the next exercise at this time.

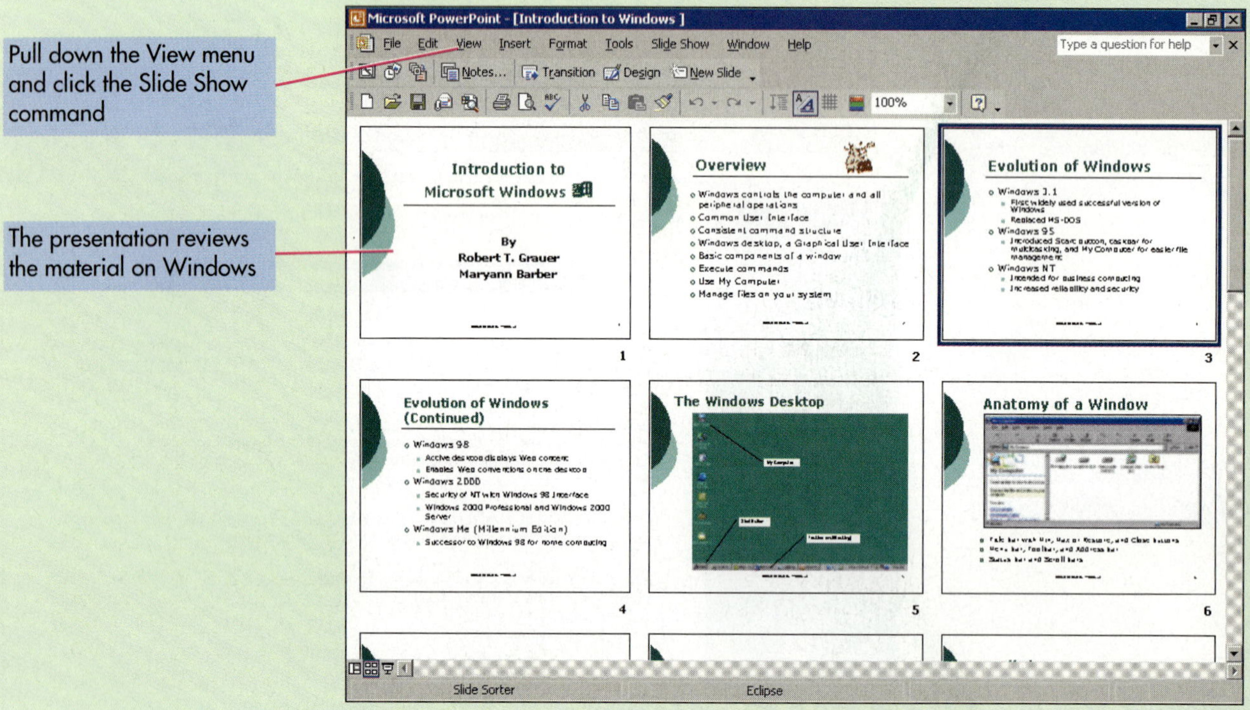

(i) Show Time (step 9)

FIGURE 9 *Hands-on Exercise 2 (continued)*

MISSING POWERPOINT—WHICH VERSION OF OFFICE DO YOU HAVE?

You may have installed Microsoft Office on your computer, but you may not have PowerPoint. That is because Microsoft has created several different versions of Microsoft Office, each with a different set of applications. Unfortunately, PowerPoint is not included in every configuration and may be missing from the suite that is shipped most frequently with new computers.

Windows has two different programs to manage the files and folders on a system, My Computer and Windows Explorer. My Computer is intuitive, but less efficient, as you have to open each folder in succession. Windows Explorer is more sophisticated, as it provides a hierarchical view of the entire system in a single window. A beginner might prefer My Computer, whereas a more experienced user will most likely opt for Windows Explorer.

Assume, for example, that you are taking four classes this semester, and that you are using the computer in each course. You've created a separate folder to hold the work for each class and have stored the contents of all four folders on a single floppy disk. Assume further that you need to retrieve your third English assignment so that you can modify the assignment, then submit the revised version to your instructor. Figure 10 illustrates how Windows Explorer could be used to locate your assignment.

The Explorer window in Figure 10a is divided into two panes. The left pane contains a tree diagram (or hierarchical view) of the entire system showing all drives and, optionally, the folders in each drive. The right pane shows the contents of the active drive or folder. Only one object (a drive or folder) can be active in the left pane, and its contents are displayed automatically in the right pane.

Look carefully at the icon for the English folder in the left pane of Figure 10a. The folder is open, whereas the icon for every other folder is closed. The open folder indicates that the English folder is the active folder. (The name of the active folder also appears in the title bar of Windows Explorer and in the Address bar.) The contents of the active folder (three Word documents in this example) are displayed in the right pane. The right pane is displayed in Details view, but could just as easily have been displayed in another view (e.g., Large Icons).

As indicated, only one folder can be open (active) at a time in the left pane. Thus, to see the contents of a different folder such as Accounting, you would open (click on) the Accounting folder, which automatically closes the English folder. The contents of the Accounting folder would then appear in the right pane. You should organize your folders in ways that make sense to you, such as a separate folder for every class you are taking. You can also create folders within folders; for example, a correspondence folder may contain two folders of its own, one for business correspondence and one for personal letters.

Windows Explorer can also be used to display a Web page, as shown in Figure 10b. All you do is click the icon for Internet Explorer in the left pane to start the program and display its default home page. Alternatively, you can click in the Address bar and enter the address of any Web page directly; for example, click in the Address bar and type www.microsoft.com to display the home page for Microsoft. Once you are browsing pages on the Web, it's convenient to close the left pane so that the page takes the complete window. You can reopen the Folders window by pulling down the View menu, clicking the Explorer Bar command, and toggling Folders on.

THE SMART TOOLBAR

The toolbar in Windows Explorer recognizes whether you are viewing a Web page or a set of files and folders, and changes accordingly. The icons that are displayed when viewing a Web page are identical to those in Internet Explorer and include the Search, Favorites, and History buttons. The buttons that are displayed when viewing a file or folder include the Undo, Delete, and Views buttons that are used in file management.

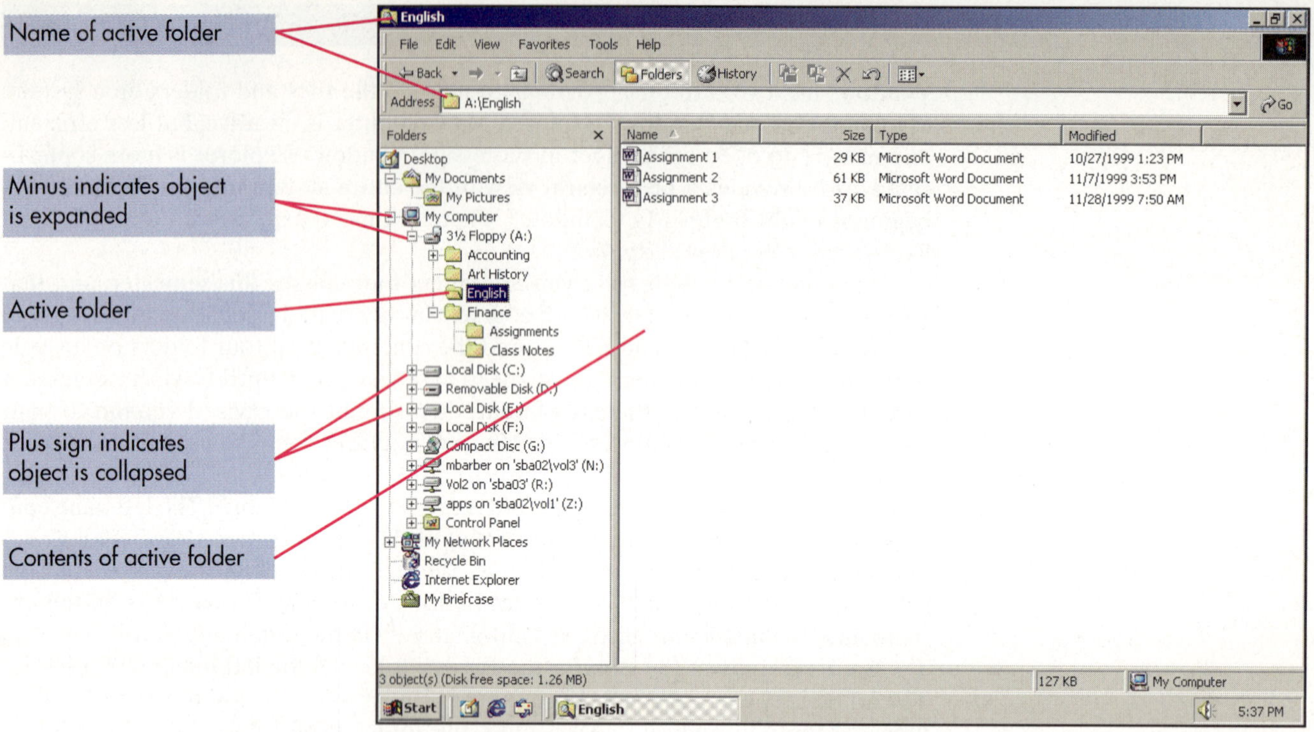

(a) Drive A

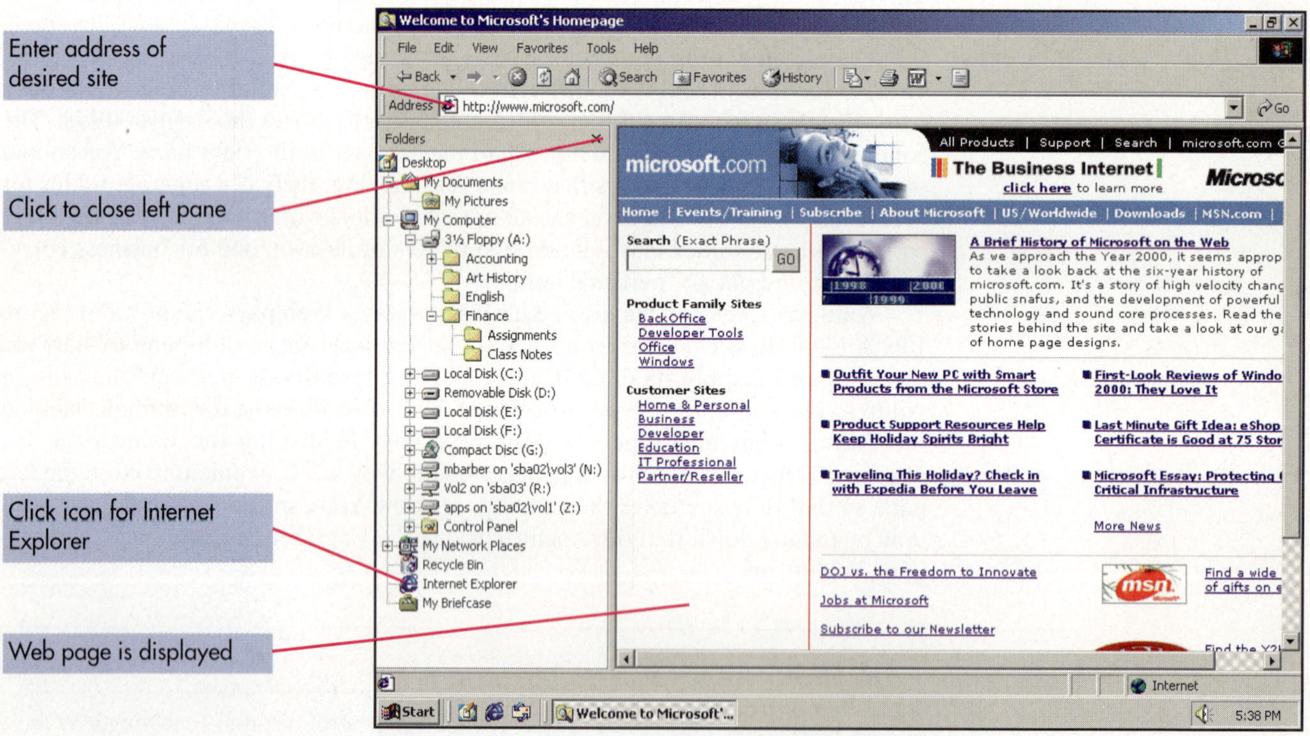

(b) A Web Page

FIGURE 10 *Windows Explorer*

Expanding and Collapsing a Drive or Folder

The tree diagram in Windows Explorer displays the devices on your system in hierarchical fashion. The desktop is always at the top of the hierarchy, and it contains icons such as My Computer, the Recycle Bin, Internet Explorer, and My Network Places. My Computer in turn contains the various drives that are accessible from your system, each of which contains folders, which in turn contain documents and/or additional folders. Each object may be expanded or collapsed by clicking the plus or minus sign, respectively. Click either sign to toggle to the other. Clicking a plus sign, for example, expands the drive, then displays a minus sign next to the drive to indicate that its subordinates are visible.

Look closely at the icon next to My Computer in either Figure 10a or 10b. It is a minus sign (as opposed to a plus sign) and it indicates that My Computer has been expanded to show the devices on the system. There is also a minus sign next to the icon for drive A to indicate that it too has been expanded to show the folders on the disk. Note, however, the plus sign next to drives C and D, indicating that these parts of the tree are currently collapsed and thus their subordinates (in this case, folders) are not visible.

Any folder may contain additional folders, and thus individual folders may also be expanded or collapsed. The minus sign next to the Finance folder, for example, indicates that the folder has been expanded and contains two additional folders, for Assignments and Class Notes, respectively. The plus sign next to the Accounting folder, however, indicates the opposite; that is, the folder is collapsed and its subordinate folders are not currently visible. A folder with neither a plus nor a minus sign, such as Art History, does not contain additional folders and cannot be expanded or collapsed.

The hierarchical view within Windows Explorer, and the ability to expand and collapse the various folders on a system, enables you to quickly locate a specific file or folder. If, for example, you want to see the contents of the Art History folder, you click its icon in the left pane, which automatically changes the display in the right pane to show the documents in that folder. Thus, Windows Explorer is ideal for moving or copying files from one folder or drive to another. You simply select (open) the folder that contains the files, use the scroll bar in the left pane (if necessary) so that the destination folder is visible, then click and drag the files from the right pane to the destination folder.

The Folder Options command functions identically in Windows Explorer and in My Computer. You can decide whether you want to single or double click the icons and/or whether to display Web content within a folder. You can also use the View menu to select the most appropriate view. Our preferences are to double click the icons, to omit Web content, and to use the Details view.

CONVERGENCE OF THE EXPLORERS

Windows Explorer and Internet Explorer are separate programs, but each includes some functionality of the other. You can use Windows Explorer to display a Web page by clicking the Internet Explorer icon within the tree structure in the left pane. Conversely, you can use Internet Explorer to display a local drive, document, or folder. Start Internet Explorer in the usual fashion, click in the Address bar, then enter the appropriate address, such as C:\ to display the contents of drive C.

Hands-on Exercise 3

The Practice Files via a Local Area Network

Objective To use Windows Explorer to copy the practice files from a network drive to a floppy disk. The exercise requires a formatted floppy disk and access to a local area network. Use Figure 11 as a guide in the exercise.

Step 1: **Start Windows Explorer**

- Click the **Start Button**, click **Programs**, click **Accessories**, then click **Windows Explorer**. Click the **maximize button** so that Windows Explorer takes the entire desktop as shown in Figure 11a. Do not be concerned if your desktop is different from ours.
- Make or verify the following selections using the **View menu**. You have to pull down the View menu each time you choose a different command.
  - The **Standard buttons** and **Address bar** toolbars should be selected.
  - The **Status Bar command** should be checked.
  - The **Details view** should be selected.
- Click (select) the **Desktop icon** in the left pane to display the contents of the desktop in the right pane. Your desktop may have different icons from ours, but your screen should almost match Figure 11a. We set additional options in the next step.

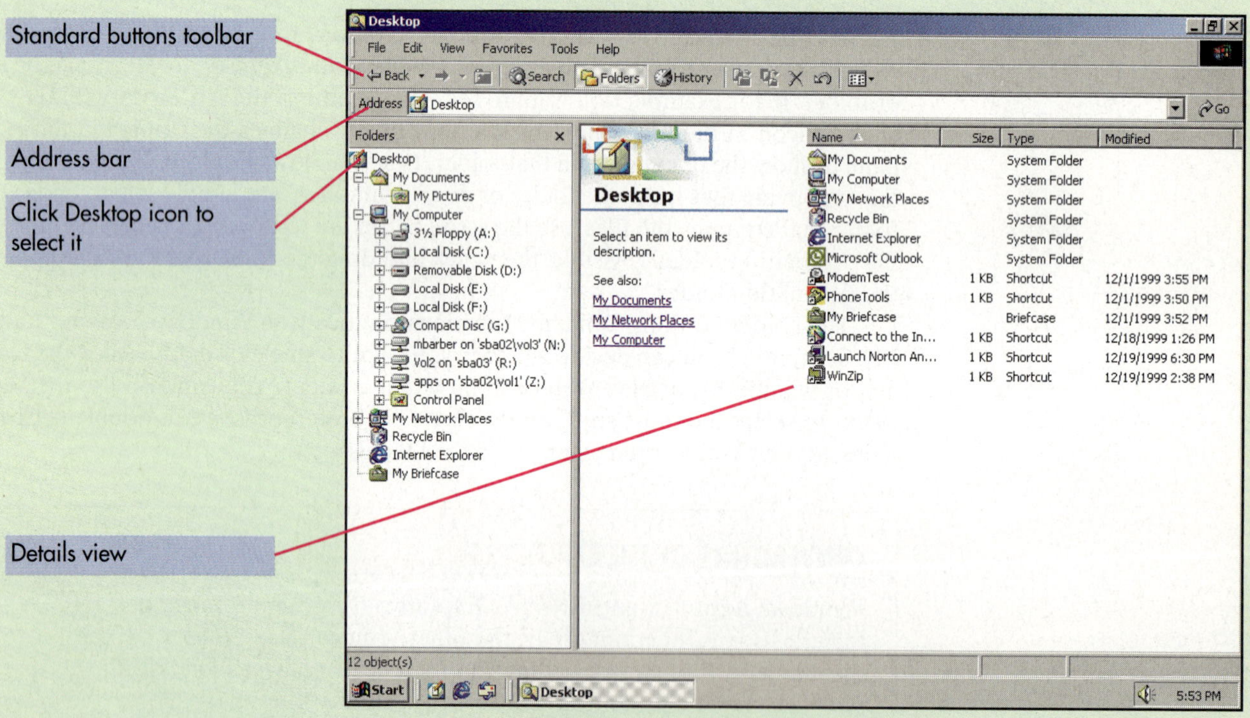

(a) Start Windows Explorer (step 1)

FIGURE 11 *Hands-on Exercise 3*

Step 2: **Change the Folder Options**

- Click the **minus** (or the **plus**) **sign** next to My Computer to collapse (or expand) My Computer and hide (or display) the objects it contains. Toggle the signs back and forth a few times for practice. End with a minus sign next to My Computer as shown in Figure 11b.
- Place a newly formatted floppy disk in drive A. Click the drive icon next to drive A to select the drive and display its contents in the right pane. The disk does not contain any files since zero bytes are used.
- Displaying Web content at the left of a folder (as is done in Figure 11b) is fine when a drive or folder does not contain a large number of files. It is generally a waste of space, however, and so we want to change the folder options.
- Pull down the **Tools menu** and click the **Folder Options command** to display the Folder Options dialog box in Figure 11a. Click the option to **Use Windows classic folders**. Click **OK**.

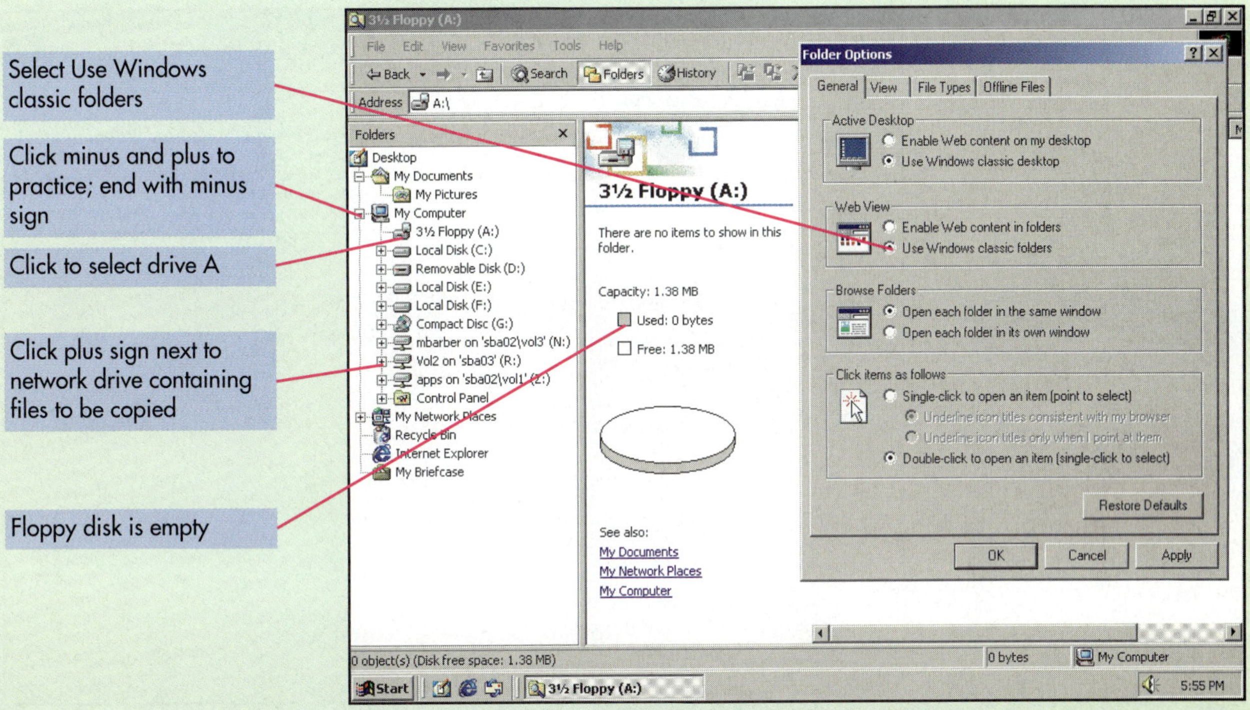

(b) Change the Folder Options (step 2)

FIGURE 11 *Hands-on Exercise 3 (continued)*

THE PLUS AND MINUS SIGN

Any drive, be it local or on the network, may be expanded or collapsed to display or hide its folders. A minus sign indicates that the drive has been expanded and that its folders are visible. A plus sign indicates the reverse; that is, the device is collapsed and its folders are not visible. Click either sign to toggle to the other. Clicking a plus sign, for example, expands the drive, then displays a minus sign next to the drive to indicate that the folders are visible. Clicking a minus sign has the reverse effect.

Step 3: **Select the Network Drive**

- Click the **plus sign** for the network drive that contains the files you are to copy (e.g., drive **R** in Figure 11c). Select (click) the **Exploring Windows 2000 folder** to open this folder.
- You may need to expand other folders on the network drive (such as the Datadisk folder on our network) as per instructions from your professor. Note the following:
  - The Exploring Windows 2000 folder is highlighted in the left pane, its icon is an open folder, and its contents are displayed in the right pane.
  - The status bar indicates that the folder contains five objects and the total file size is 119KB.
- Click the icon next to any other folder to select the folder, which in turn deselects the Exploring Windows 2000 folder. (Only one folder in the left pane is active at a time.) Reselect (click) the **Exploring Windows 2000 folder**.

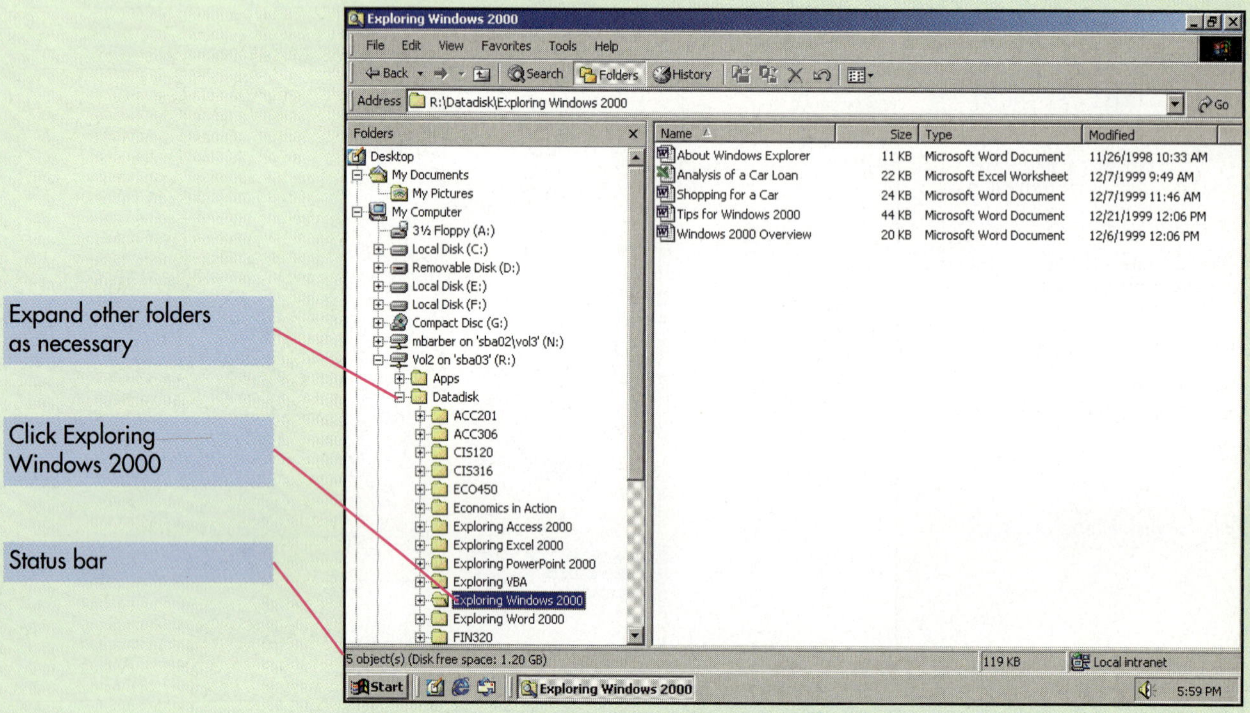

(c) Select the Network Drive (step 3)

FIGURE 11 *Hands-on Exercise 3 (continued)*

CUSTOMIZE WINDOWS EXPLORER

Increase or decrease the size of the left pane within Windows Explorer by dragging the vertical line separating the left and right panes in the appropriate direction. You can also drag the right border of the various column headings (Name, Size, Type, and Modified) in the right pane to increase or decrease the width of the column. And best of all, you can click any column heading to display the contents of the selected folder in sequence by that column. Click the heading a second time and the sequence changes from ascending to descending and vice versa.

Step 4: Copy the Individual Files

- Select (click) the file called **About Windows Explorer**, which highlights the file as shown in Figure 11d. Click and drag the selected file in the right pane to the **drive A icon** in the left pane:
  - You will see the ⃠ symbol as you drag the file until you reach a suitable destination (e.g., until you point to the icon for drive A). The ⃠ symbol will change to a plus sign when the icon for drive A is highlighted, indicating that the file can be copied successfully.
  - Release the mouse to complete the copy operation. You will see a pop-up window, which indicates the status of the copy operation.
- Select (click) the file **Tips for Windows 2000**, which automatically deselects the previously selected file. Copy the selected file to drive A by dragging its icon from the right pane to the drive A icon in the left pane.
- Copy the three remaining files to drive A as well. Select (click) drive **A** in the left pane, which in turn displays the contents of the floppy disk in the right pane. You should see the five files you have copied to drive A.

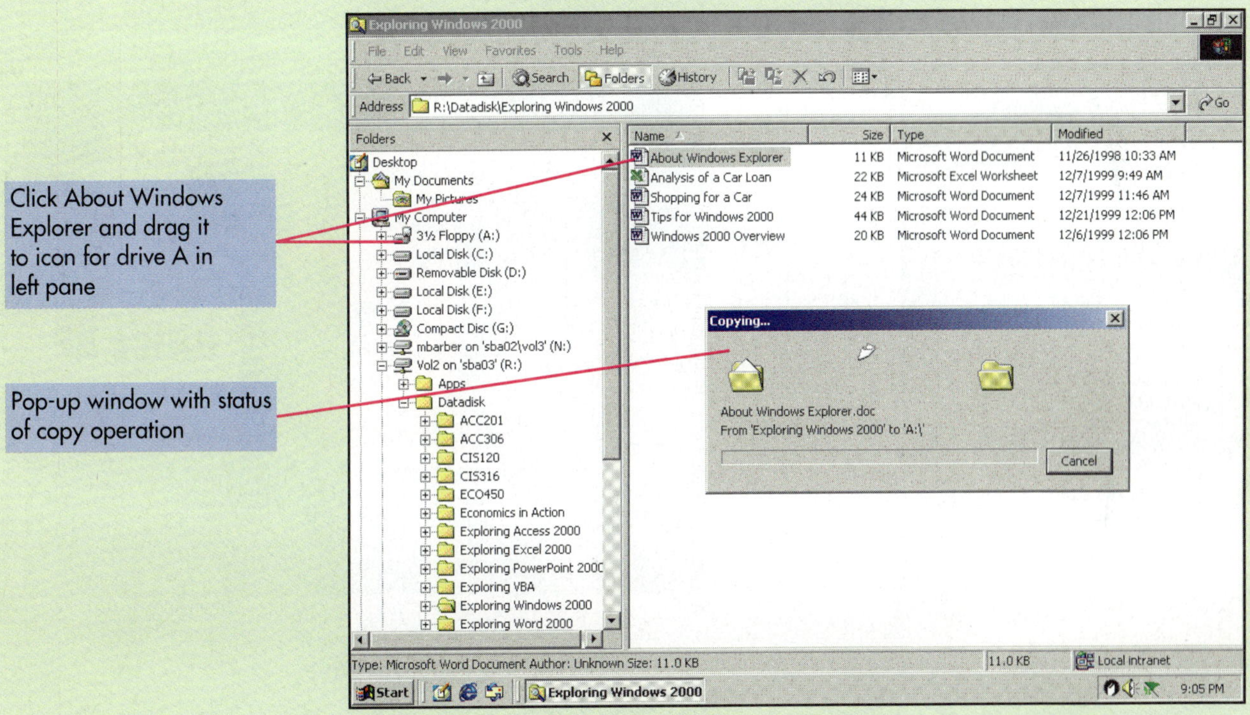

(d) Copy the Individual Files (step 4)

FIGURE 11 *Hands-on Exercise 3 (continued)*

SELECT MULTIPLE FILES

Selecting one file automatically deselects the previously selected file. You can, however, select multiple files by clicking the first file, then pressing and holding the Ctrl key as you click each additional file. Use the Shift key to select multiple files that are adjacent to one another by clicking the first file, then pressing and holding the Shift key as you click the last file.

Step 5: **Display a Web Page**

- This step requires an Internet connection. Click the **minus sign** next to the network drive to collapse that drive. Click the **minus sign** next to any other expanded drive so that the left pane is similar to Figure 11e.
- Click the **Internet Explorer icon** to start Internet Explorer and display the starting page for your configuration. The page you see will be different from ours, but you can click in the Address bar near the top of the window to enter the address of any Web site.
- Look closely at the icons on the toolbar, which have changed to reflect the tools associated with viewing a Web page. Click the **Back button** to return to drive A, the previously displayed item in Windows Explorer. The icons on the toolbar return to those associated with a folder.
- Close Windows Explorer. Shut down the computer if you do not want to continue with the next exercise at this time.

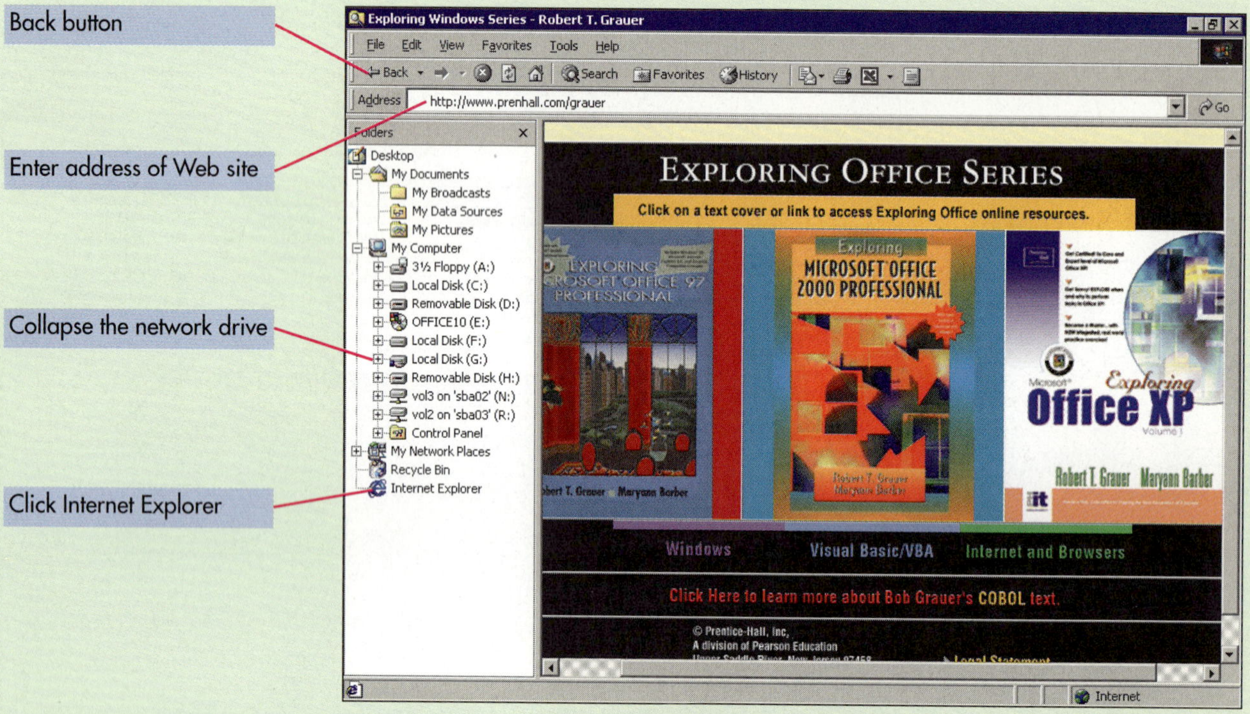

(e) Display a Web Page (step 5)

FIGURE 11 *Hands-on Exercise 3 (continued)*

> **SERVER NOT RESPONDING**
>
> Two things have to occur in order for Internet Explorer to display the requested document—it must locate the server on which the document is stored, and it must be able to connect to that computer. If you see a message similar to "Server too busy or not responding", it implies that Internet Explorer has located the server but was unable to connect because the site is busy or is temporarily down. Try to connect again, in a minute or so, or later in the day.

As you grow to depend on the computer, you will create a variety of files using applications such as Microsoft Word or Excel. Learning how to manage those files is one of the most important skills you can acquire. The previous hands-on exercises provided you with a set of files with which to practice. That way, when you have your own files you will be comfortable executing the various file management commands you will need on a daily basis. This section describes the basic file operations you will need, then presents another hands-on exercise in which you apply those commands.

Moving and Copying a File

The essence of file management is to move and copy a file or folder from one location to another. This can be done in different ways, most easily by clicking and dragging the file icon from the source drive or folder to the destination drive or folder, within Windows Explorer. There is one subtlety, however, in that the result of dragging a file (i.e., whether the file is moved or copied) depends on whether the source and destination are on the same or different drives. Dragging a file from one folder to another folder on the same drive moves the file. Dragging a file to a folder on a different drive copies the file. The same rules apply to dragging a folder, where the folder and every file in it are moved or copied as per the rules for an individual file.

This process is not as arbitrary as it may seem. Windows assumes that if you drag an object (a file or folder) to a different drive (e.g., from drive C to drive A), you want the object to appear in both places. Hence, the default action when you click and drag an object to a different drive is to copy the object. You can, however, override the default and move the object by pressing and holding the Shift key as you drag.

Windows also assumes that you do not want two copies of an object on the same drive, as that would result in wasted disk space. Thus, the default action when you click and drag an object to a different folder on the same drive is to move the object. You can override the default and copy the object by pressing and holding the Ctrl key as you drag. It's not as complicated as it sounds, and you get a chance to practice in the hands-on exercise, which follows shortly.

Deleting a File

The ***Delete command*** deletes (erases) a file from a disk. The command can be executed in different ways, most easily by selecting a file, then pressing the Del key. It's also comforting to know that you can usually recover a deleted file, because the file is not (initially) removed from the disk, but moved instead to the Recycle Bin, from where it can be restored to its original location. Unfortunately, files deleted from a floppy disk are not put in the Recycle Bin and hence cannot be recovered.

The ***Recycle Bin*** is a special folder that contains all files that were previously deleted from any hard disk on your system. Think of the Recycle Bin as similar to the wastebasket in your room. You throw out (delete) a report by tossing it into a wastebasket. The report is gone (deleted) from your desk, but you can still get it back by taking it out of the wastebasket as long as the basket wasn't emptied. The Recycle Bin works the same way. Files are not deleted from the hard disk per se, but moved instead to the Recycle Bin from where they can be restored to their original location.

The Recycle Bin will eventually run out of space, in which case the files that have been in the Recycle Bin the longest are permanently deleted to make room for additional files. Accordingly, once a file is removed from the Recycle Bin it can no longer be restored, as it has been physically deleted from the hard disk. Note, too, that the protection afforded by the Recycle Bin does not extend to files deleted from a floppy disk. Such files can be recovered, but only through utility programs outside of Windows 2000.

Renaming a File

Every file or folder is assigned a name at the time it is created, but you may want to change that name at some point in the future. Point to a file or a folder, click the right mouse button to display a menu with commands pertaining to the object, then click the ***Rename command***. The name of the file or folder will be highlighted with the insertion point (a flashing vertical line) positioned at the end of the name. Enter a new name to replace the selected name, or click anywhere within the name to change the insertion point and edit the name.

Backup

It's not a question of if it will happen, but when—hard disks die, files are lost, or viruses may infect a system. It has happened to us and it will happen to you, but you can prepare for the inevitable by creating adequate backup *before* the problem occurs. The essence of a ***backup strategy*** is to decide which files to back up, how often to do the backup, and where to keep the backup. Once you decide on a strategy, follow it, and follow it faithfully!

Our strategy is very simple—back up what you can't afford to lose, do so on a daily basis, and store the backup away from your computer. You need not copy every file, every day. Instead, copy just the files that changed during the current session. Realize, too, that it is much more important to back up your data files than your program files. You can always reinstall the application from the original disks or CD, or if necessary, go to the vendor for another copy of an application. You, however, are the only one who has a copy of your term paper.

Write Protection

A floppy disk is normally ***write-enabled*** (the square hole is covered with the movable tab) so that you can change the contents of the disk. Thus, you can create (save) new files to a write-enabled disk and/or edit or delete existing files. Occasionally, however, you may want to ***write-protect*** a floppy disk (by sliding the tab to expose the square hole) so that its contents cannot be modified. This is typically done with a backup disk where you want to prevent the accidental deletion of a file and/or the threat of virus infection.

Our Next Exercise

Our next exercise begins with the floppy disk containing the five practice files in drive A. We ask you to create two folders on drive A (step 1) and to move the various files into these folders (step 2). Next, you copy a folder from drive A to the My Documents folder (step 3), modify one of the files in the My Documents folder (step 4), then copy the modified file back to drive A (step 5). We ask you to delete a file in step 6, then recover it from the Recycle Bin in step 7. We also show you how to write-protect a floppy disk in step 8. Let's get started.

Hands-on Exercise 4

File Management

Objective Use Windows Explorer to move, copy, and delete a file; recover a deleted file from the Recycle Bin; write-protect a floppy disk. Use Figure 12 as a guide in the exercise.

Step 1: Create a New Folder

- Start Windows Explorer, maximize its window, and if necessary, change to **Details view**. Place the floppy disk from Exercise 2 or 3 in drive A.
- Select (click) the icon for **drive A** in the left pane of the Explorer window. Drive A should contain the files shown in Figure 12a.
- You will create two folders on drive A, using two different techniques:
  - Point to a blank area anywhere in the **right pane**, click the **right mouse button** to display a context-sensitive menu, click (or point to) the **New command**, then click **Folder** as the type of object to create.
  - The icon for a new folder will appear with the name of the folder (New Folder) highlighted. Type **John Doe's Documents** (use your own name) to change the name of the folder. Press **Enter**.
  - Click the icon for **drive A** in the left pane. Pull down the **File menu**, click (or point to) the **New command**, and click **Folder** as the type of object to create. Type **Automobile** to change the name of the folder. Press **Enter**. The right pane should now contain five documents and two folders.
- Pull down the **View menu**. Click the **Arrange icons command**, then click the **By Name command** to display the folders in alphabetical order.

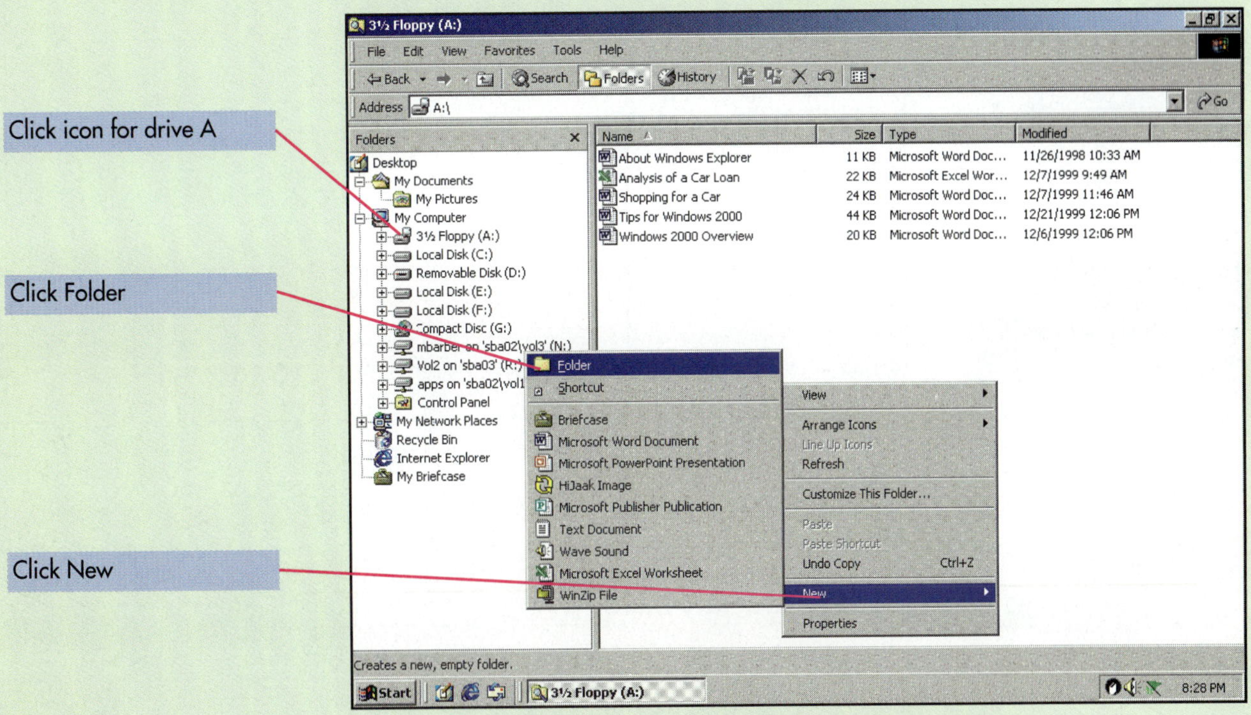

(a) Create a New Folder (step 1)

FIGURE 12 *Hands-on Exercise 4*

Step 2: **Move a File**

- Click the **plus sign** next to drive A to expand the drive as shown in Figure 12b. Note the following:
  - The left pane shows that drive A is selected. The right pane displays the contents of drive A (the selected object in the left pane).
  - There is a minus sign next to the icon for drive A in the left pane, indicating that it has been expanded and that its folders are visible. Thus, the folder names also appear under drive A in the left pane.
- Click and drag the icon for the file **About Windows Explorer** from the right pane, to the **John Doe's Documents folder** in the left pane, to move the file into that folder.
- Click and drag the **Tips for Windows 2000** and **Windows 2000 Overview** documents to the **John Doe's Documents folder** in similar fashion.
- Click the **John Doe's Documents folder** in the left pane to select the folder and display its contents in the right pane. You should see the three files that were just moved.
- Click the icon for **Drive A** in the left pane, then click and drag the remaining files, **Analysis of a Car** and **Shopping for a Car**, to the **Automobile folder**.

Expand drive A

Click and drag icon for About Windows Explorer to John Doe's Documents in left pane

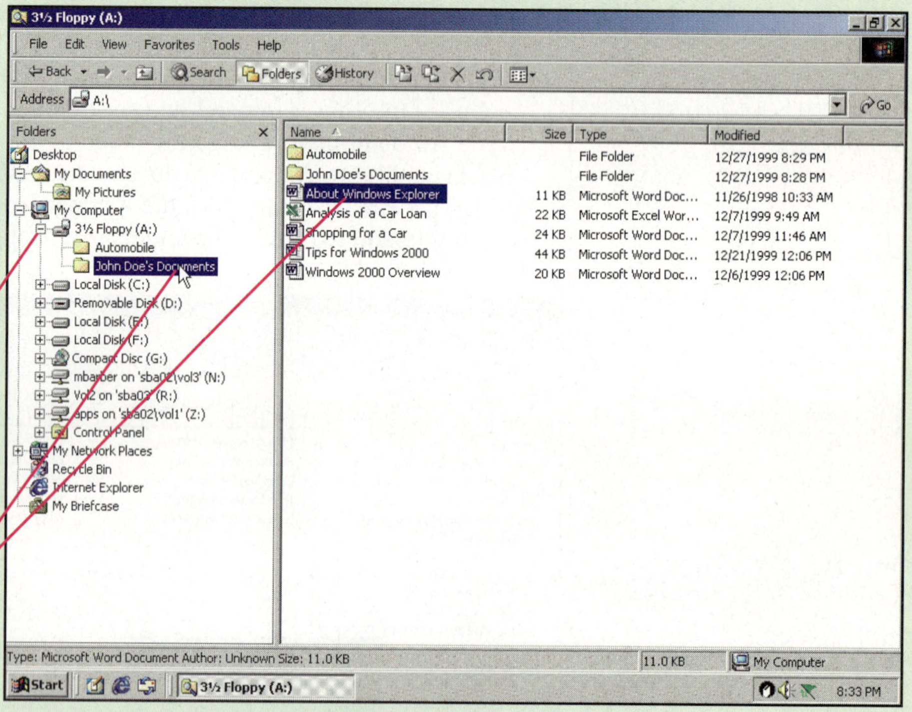

(b) Move a File (step 2)

FIGURE 12 *Hands-on Exercise 4*

RIGHT CLICK AND DRAG

Click and drag with the right mouse button to display a shortcut menu asking whether you want to copy or move the file. This simple tip can save you from making a careless (and potentially serious) error. Use it!

Step 3: Copy a Folder

- Point to **John Doe's Documents folder** in either pane, click the **right mouse button**, and drag the folder to the **My Documents folder** in the left pane, then release the mouse to display a shortcut menu. Click the **Copy Here command.**
  - You may see a Copy files message box as the individual files within John Doe's folder are copied to the My Documents folder.
  - If you see the Confirm Folder Replace dialog box, it means that you already copied the files or a previous student used the same folder when he or she did this exercise. Click the **Yes to All button** so that your files replace the previous versions in the My Documents folder.
- Click the **My Documents folder** in the left pane. Pull down the **View menu** and click the **Refresh command** (or press the **F5 key**) so that the tree structure shows the newly copied folder. (Please remember to delete John Doe's Documents folder at the end of the exercise.)

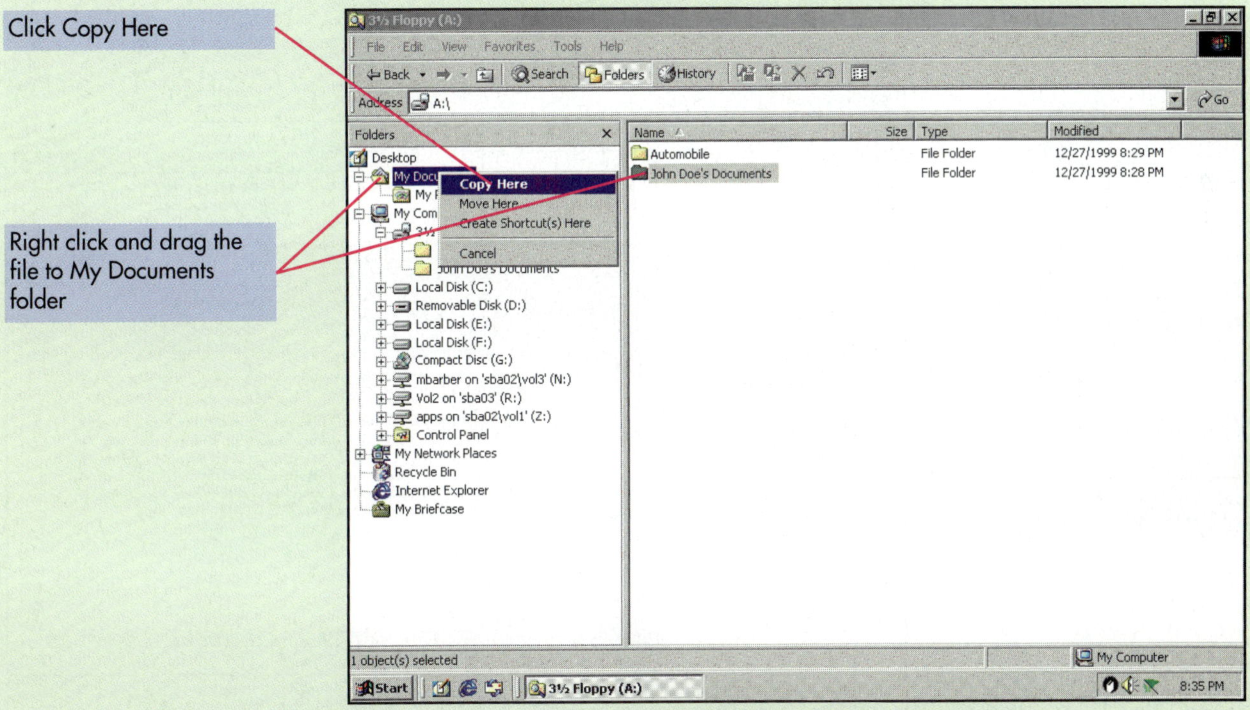

(c) Copy a Folder (step 3)

FIGURE 12 *Hands-on Exercise 4 (continued)*

THE MY DOCUMENTS FOLDER

The My Documents folder is created by default with the installation of Microsoft Windows. There is no requirement that you store your documents in this folder, but it is convenient, especially for beginners who may lack the confidence to create their own folders. The My Documents folder is also helpful in a laboratory environment where the network administrator may prevent you from modifying the desktop and/or from creating your own folders on drive C, in which case you will have to use the My Documents folder.

Step 4: **Modify a Document**

- Click **John Doe's Documents folder** within the My Documents folder to make it the active folder and to display its contents in the right pane. Change to the **Details view**.
- Double click the **About Windows Explorer** document to start Word and open the document. Do not be concerned if the size and/or position of the Microsoft Word window are different from ours.
- If necessary, click inside the document window, then press **Ctrl+End** to move to the end of the document. Add the sentence shown in Figure 12d.
- Pull down the **File menu** and click **Save** to save the modified file (or click the **Save button** on the Standard toolbar). Pull down the **File menu** and click **Exit**.
- Pull down the **View menu** in Windows Explorer and click **Refresh** (or press the **F5 key**) to update the contents of the right pane. The date and time associated with the About Windows Explorer file has been changed to indicate that the file has just been modified.

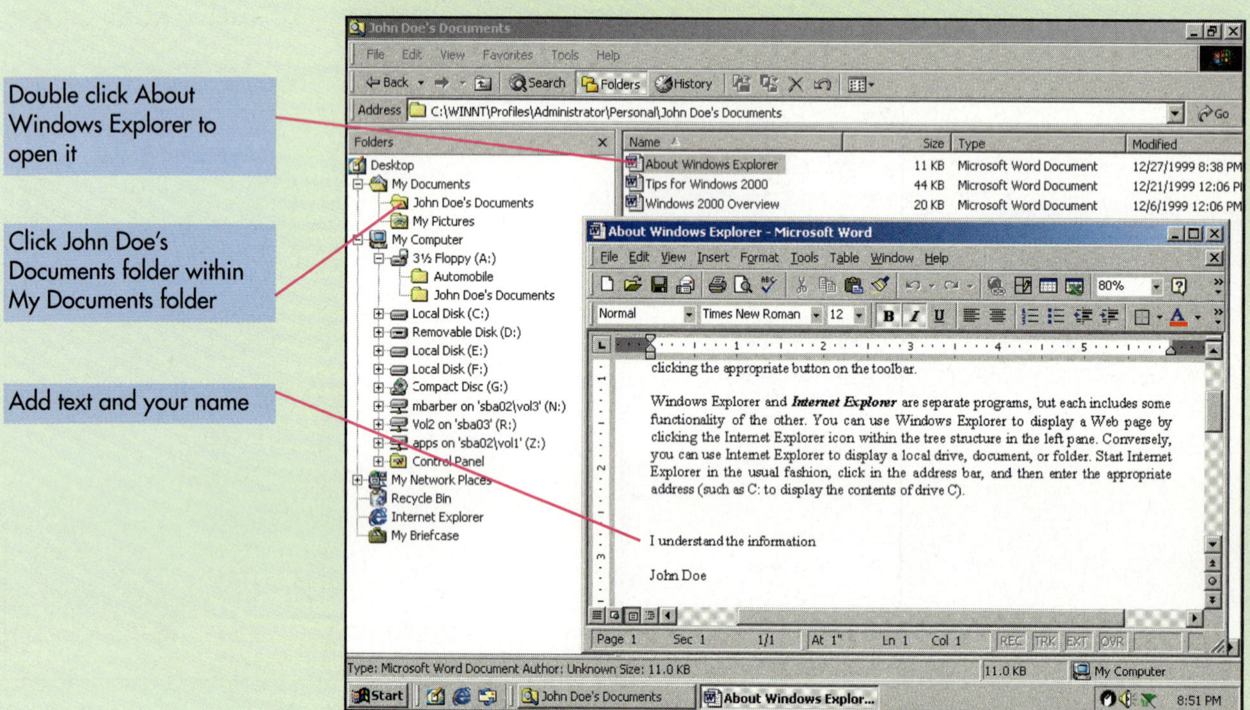

(d) Modify a Document (step 4)

FIGURE 12 *Hands-on Exercise 4 (continued)*

KEYBOARD SHORTCUTS

Ctrl+B, Ctrl+I, and Ctrl+U are shortcuts to boldface, italicize, and underline, respectively. Ctrl+X (the X is supposed to remind you of a pair of scissors), Ctrl+C, and Ctrl+V correspond to Cut, Copy, and Paste, respectively. Ctrl+Home and Ctrl+End move to the beginning or end of a document. These shortcuts are not unique to Microsoft Word, but are recognized in virtually every Windows application. See practice exercise 11 at the end of the chapter.

Step 5: Copy (Back Up) a File

- Verify that **John Doe's folder** within My Documents is the active folder, as denoted by the open folder icon. Click and drag the icon for the **About Windows Explorer** file from the right pane to John Doe's Documents folder on **Drive A** in the left pane.
- You will see the message in Figure 12e, indicating that the folder (on drive A) already contains a file called About Windows Explorer and asking whether you want to replace the existing file. Click **Yes** because you want to replace the previous version of the file on drive A with the updated version from the My Documents folder.
- You have just backed up the file; in other words, you have created a copy of the file on the disk in drive A. Thus, you can use the floppy disk to restore the file in the My Documents folder should anything happen to it.

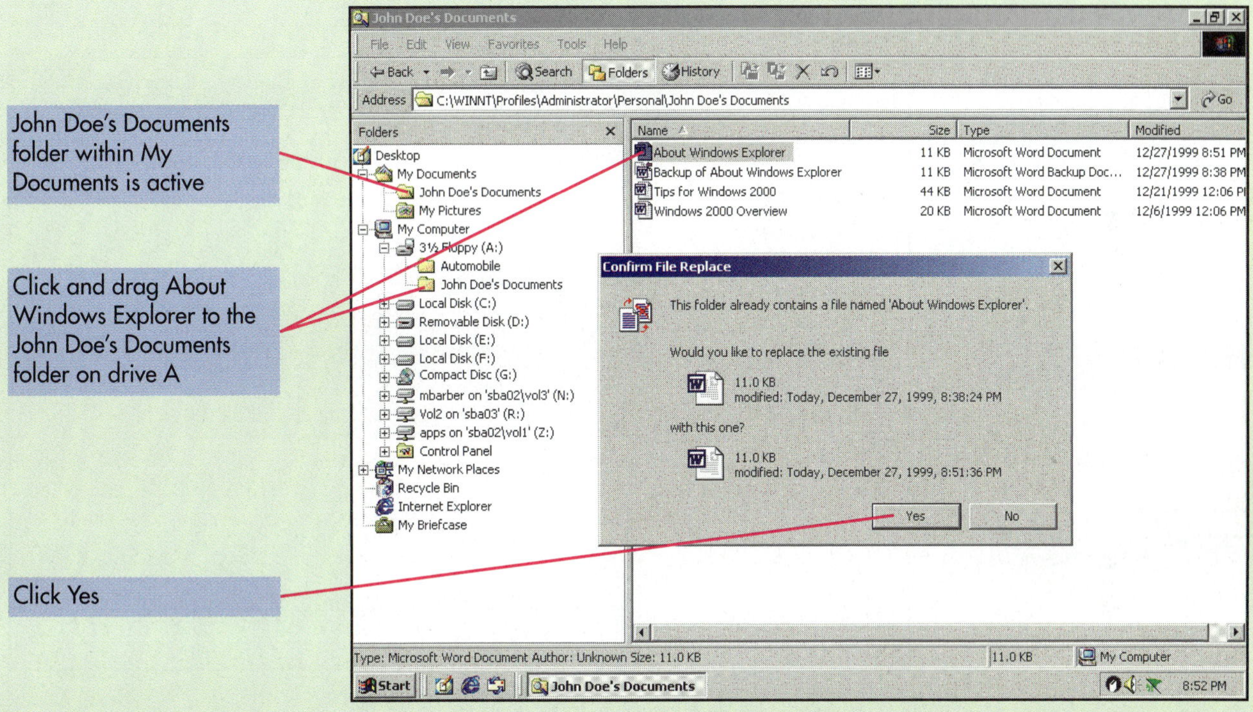

(e) Copy (Back Up) a File (step 5)

FIGURE 12 *Hands-on Exercise 4 (continued)*

FILE EXTENSIONS

Long-time DOS users remember a three-character extension at the end of a file name to indicate the file type; for example, DOC or XLS to indicate a Word document or Excel workbook, respectively. The extensions are displayed or hidden according to a setting in the Folder Options command. Pull down the Tools menu, click the Folder Options command to display the Folder Options dialog box, click the View tab, then check (or clear) the box to hide (or show) file extensions for known file types. Click OK to accept the setting and exit the dialog box.

Step 6: **Delete a Folder**

- Select (click) **John Doe's Documents folder** within the My Documents folder in the left pane. Pull down the **File menu** and click **Delete** (or press the **Del key**).
- You will see the dialog box in Figure 12f asking whether you are sure you want to delete the folder (i.e., send the folder and its contents to the Recycle Bin). Note the recycle logo within the box, which implies that you will be able to restore the file.
- Click **Yes** to delete the folder. The folder disappears from drive C. Pull down the **Edit menu**. Click **Undo Delete**. The deletion is cancelled and the folder reappears in the left pane. If you don't see the folder, pull down the **View menu** and click the **Refresh command**.

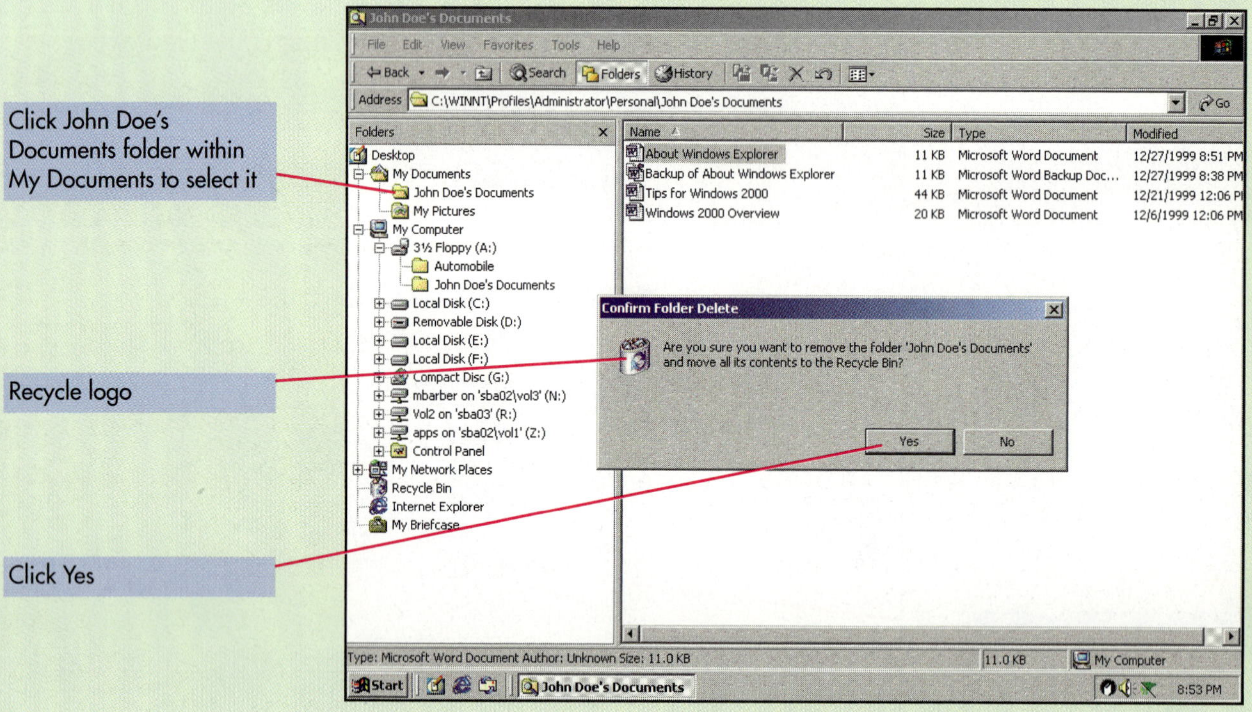

(f) Delete a Folder (step 6)

FIGURE 12 *Hands-on Exercise 4 (continued)*

THE UNDO COMMAND

The Undo command is present not only in application programs such as Word or Excel, but in Windows Explorer as well. You can use the Undo command to undelete a file provided you execute the command immediately (within a few commands) after the Delete command. To execute the Undo command, right-click anywhere in the right pane to display a shortcut menu, then select the Undo action. You can also pull down the Edit menu and click Undo to reverse (undo) the last command. Some operations cannot be undone (in which case the command will be dimmed), but Undo is always worth a try.

Step 7: The Recycle Bin

- Select John Doe's Documents folder within the My Documents folder in the left pane. Select (click) the **About Windows Explorer** file in the right pane. Press the **Del key**, then click **Yes**.
- Click the **Down arrow** in the vertical scroll bar in the left pane until you see the icon for the **Recycle Bin**. Click the icon to make the Recycle Bin the active folder and display its contents in the right pane.
- You will see a different set of files from those displayed in Figure 12g. Pull down the **View menu**, click (or point to) **Arrange icons**, then click **By Delete Date** to display the files in this sequence.
- Click in the **right pane**. Press **Ctrl+End** or scroll to the bottom of the window. Point to the **About Windows Explorer** file, click the **right mouse button** to display the shortcut menu in Figure 12g, then click **Restore**.
- The file disappears from the Recycle bin because it has been returned to John Doe's Documents folder.

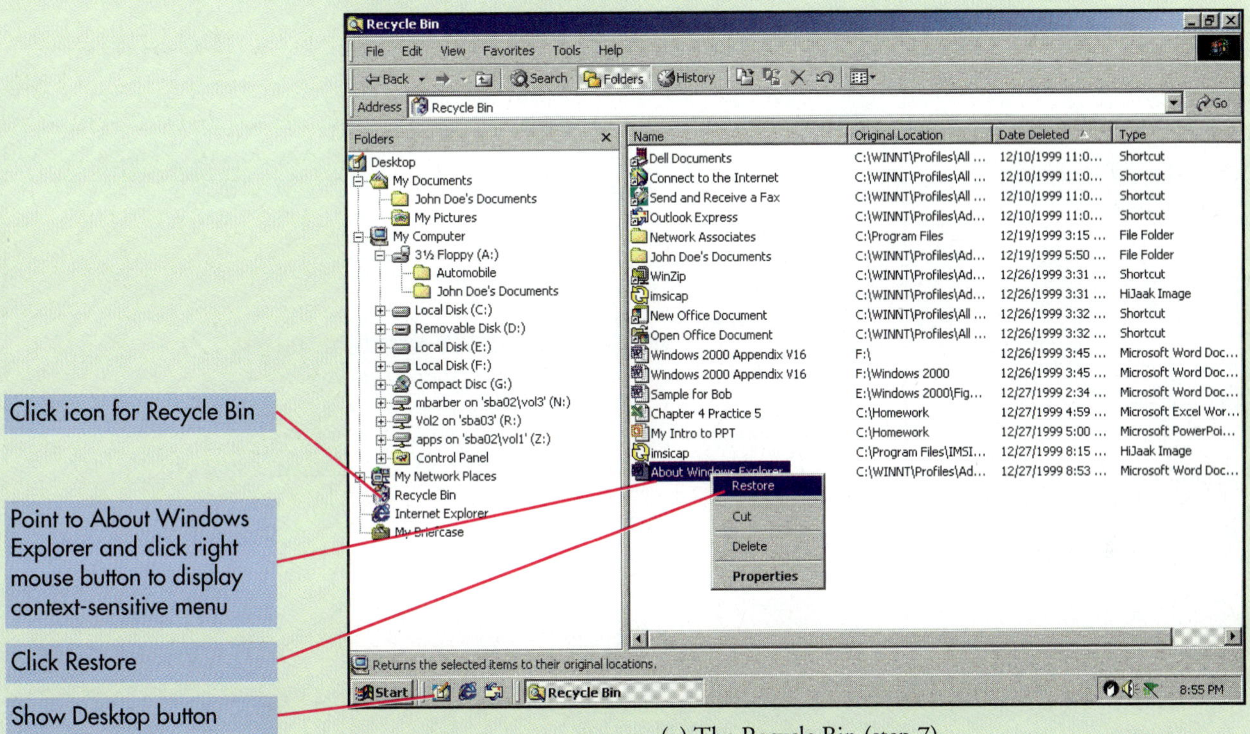

(g) The Recycle Bin (step 7)

FIGURE 12 *Hands-on Exercise 4 (continued)*

THE SHOW DESKTOP BUTTON

The Show Desktop button on the taskbar enables you to minimize all open windows with a single click. The button functions as a toggle switch. Click it once and all windows are minimized. Click it a second time and the open windows are restored to their positions on the desktop. If you do not see the Show Desktop button, right click a blank area of the taskbar to display a context-sensitive menu, click Toolbars, then check the Quick Launch toolbar.

Step 8: **Write-Protect a Floppy Disk**

- Remove the floppy disk from drive A, then move the built-in tab on the disk so that the square hole on the disk is open. Return the disk to the drive.
- If necessary, expand drive A in the left pane, select the **Automobile folder**, select the **Analysis of a Car Loan document** in the right pane, then press the **Del key**. Click **Yes** when asked whether to delete the file.
- You will see the message in Figure 12h indicating that the file cannot be deleted because the disk has been write-protected. Click **OK**. Remove the write-protection by moving the built-in tab to cover the square hole.
- Repeat the procedure to delete the **Analysis of a Car Loan document**. Click **Yes** in response to the confirmation message asking whether you want to delete the file.
- The file disappears from the right pane, indicating it has been deleted. The **Automobile folder** on drive A should contain only one file.
- Delete **John Doe's Documents folder** from My Documents as a courtesy to the next student. Exit Windows Explorer. Shut down the computer.

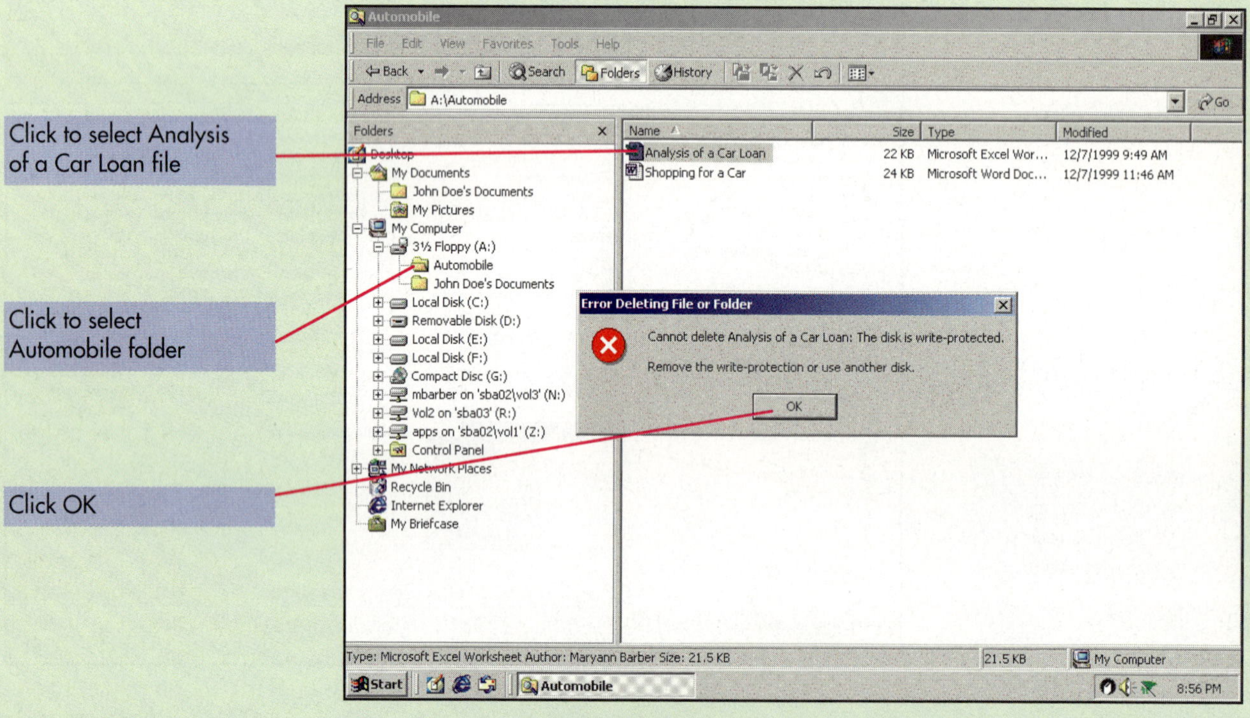

(h) Write-Protect a Floppy Disk (step 8)

FIGURE 12 *Hands-on Exercise 4 (continued)*

BACK UP IMPORTANT FILES

We cannot overemphasize the importance of adequate backup and urge you to copy your data files to floppy disks and store those disks away from your computer. You might also want to write-protect your backup disks so that you cannot accidentally erase a file. It takes only a few minutes, but you will thank us, when (not if) you lose an important file and don't have to wish you had another copy.

Microsoft Windows controls the operation of a computer and its peripherals. Windows 98 and its successor, Windows Me, are geared for the home user and provide extensive support for games and peripheral devices. Windows NT and its successor, Windows 2000, are aimed at the business user and provide increased security and reliability. Windows XP replaces all current versions of Windows. All versions of Windows follow the same conventions and have the same basic interface.

All Windows operations take place on the desktop. Every window on the desktop contains the same basic elements, which include a title bar, a control-menu box, a minimize button, a maximize or restore button, and a close button. Other elements that may be present include a menu bar, vertical and/or horizontal scroll bars, a status bar, and various toolbars. All windows may be moved and sized. The Help command in the Start menu provides access to detailed information.

Multitasking is a major benefit of the Windows environment as it enables you to run several programs at the same time. The taskbar contains a button for each open program and enables you to switch back and forth between those programs by clicking the appropriate button.

A dialog box supplies information needed to execute a command. Option buttons indicate mutually exclusive choices, one of which must be chosen. Check boxes are used if the choices are not mutually exclusive or if an option is not required. A text box supplies descriptive information. A (drop-down or open) list box displays multiple choices, any of which may be selected. A tabbed dialog box provides access to multiple sets of options.

A floppy disk must be formatted before it can store data. Formatting is accomplished through the Format command within the My Computer window. My Computer enables you to browse the disk drives and other devices attached to your system. The contents of My Computer depend on the specific configuration.

A file is a set of data or set of instructions that has been given a name and stored on disk. There are two basic types of files, program files and data files. A program file is an executable file, whereas a data file can be used only in conjunction with a specific program. Every file has a file name and a file type. The file name can be up to 255 characters in length and may include spaces.

Files are stored in folders to better organize the hundreds (or thousands) of files on a disk. A folder may contain program files, data files, and/or other folders. There are two basic ways to search through the folders on your system, My Computer and Windows Explorer. My Computer is intuitive but less efficient than Windows Explorer, as you have to open each folder in succession. Windows Explorer is more sophisticated, as it provides a hierarchical view of the entire system.

Windows Explorer is divided into two panes. The left pane displays all of the devices and, optionally, the folders on each device. The right pane shows the contents of the active (open) drive or folder. Only one drive or folder can be active in the left pane. Any device, be it local or on the network, may be expanded or collapsed to display or hide its folders. A minus sign indicates that the drive has been expanded and that its folders are visible. A plus sign indicates that the device is collapsed and its folders are not visible.

The result of dragging a file (or folder) from one location to another depends on whether the source and destination folders are on the same or different drives. Dragging the file to a folder on the same drive moves the file. Dragging the file to a folder on a different drive copies the file. It's easier, therefore, to click and drag with the right mouse button to display a context-sensitive menu from which you can select the desired operation.

The Delete command deletes (removes) a file from a disk. If, however, the file was deleted from a local (fixed or hard) disk, it is not really gone, but moved instead to the Recycle Bin from where it can be subsequently recovered.

KEY TERMS

Backup strategy (p. 42)
Check box (p. 8)
Close button (p. 5)
Command button (p. 10)
Common user interface (p. 5)
Compressed file (p. 22)
Contents tab (p. 11)
Copy a file (p. 47)
Data file (p. 20)
Delete a file (p. 41)
Desktop (p. 2)
Details view (p. 20)
Dialog box (p. 8)
Favorites tab (p. 18)
File (p. 20)
Filename (p. 20)
File type (p. 20)
Folder (p. 20)
Folder Options command (p. 14)
Format command (p. 17)
Help command (p. 18)
Index tab (p. 14)
Internet Explorer (p. 40)
List box (p. 8)
Maximize button (p. 5)
Menu bar (p. 5)
Minimize button (p. 5)
Mouse operations (p. 10)
Move a file (p. 44)
Move a window (p. 15)
Multitasking (p. 4)
My Computer (p. 22)
My Documents folder (p. 45)
My Network Places (p. 5)
New command (p. 43)
Option button (p. 8)
Program file (p. 20)
Pull-down menu (p. 7)
Radio button (p. 8)
Recycle Bin (p. 49)
Rename command (p. 42)
Restore a file (p. 5)
Restore button (p. 5)
Scroll bar (p. 5)
Size a window (p. 15)
Spin button (p. 8)
Start button (p. 4)
Status bar (p. 5)
Taskbar (p. 4)
Text box (p. 8)
Task Manager (p. 19)
Title bar (p. 5)
Toolbar (p. 5)
Undo command (p. 48)
Windows 2000 (p. 2)
Windows 95 (p. 2)
Windows 98 (p. 2)
Windows Explorer (p. 33)
Windows Me (p. 2)
Windows NT (p. 2)
Windows XP (p. 2)
Write-enabled (p. 42)
Write-protected (p. 42)

MULTIPLE CHOICE

1. Which versions of the Windows operating system were intended for the home computer?
   (a) Windows NT and Windows 98
   (b) Windows NT and Windows XP
   (c) Windows NT and Windows 2000
   (d) Windows 98 and Windows Me
2. What happens if you click and drag a file from drive C to drive A?
   (a) The file is copied to drive A
   (b) The file is moved to drive A
   (c) A menu appears that allows you to choose between moving and copying
   (d) The file is sent to the recycle bin
3. Which of the following is *not* controlled by the Folder Options command?
   (a) Single or double clicking to open a desktop icon
   (b) The presence or absence of Web content within a folder
   (c) The view (e.g., using large or small icons) within My Computer
   (d) Using one or many windows when browsing My Computer
4. What is the significance of a faded (dimmed) command in a pull-down menu?
   (a) The command is not currently accessible
   (b) A dialog box will appear if the command is selected
   (c) A Help window will appear if the command is selected
   (d) There are no equivalent keystrokes for the particular command
5. Which of the following is true regarding a dialog box?
   (a) Option buttons indicate mutually exclusive choices
   (b) Check boxes imply that multiple options may be selected
   (c) Both (a) and (b)
   (d) Neither (a) nor (b)

6. Which of the following is the first step in sizing a window?
   (a) Point to the title bar
   (b) Pull down the View menu to display the toolbar
   (c) Point to any corner or border
   (d) Pull down the View menu and change to large icons

7. Which of the following is the first step in moving a window?
   (a) Point to the title bar
   (b) Pull down the View menu to display the toolbar
   (c) Point to any corner or border
   (d) Pull down the View menu and change to large icons

8. How do you exit from Windows?
   (a) Click the Start button, then click the Shut Down command
   (b) Right click the Start button, then click the Shut Down command
   (c) Click the End button, then click the Shut Down command
   (d) Right click the End button, then click the Shut Down command

9. Which button appears immediately after a window has been maximized?
   (a) The close button
   (b) The minimize button
   (c) The maximize button
   (d) The restore button

10. What happens to a window that has been minimized?
   (a) The window is still visible but it no longer has a minimize button
   (b) The window shrinks to a button on the taskbar
   (c) The window is closed and the application is removed from memory
   (d) The window is still open but the application is gone from memory

11. What is the significance of three dots next to a command in a pull-down menu?
   (a) The command is not currently accessible
   (b) A dialog box will appear if the command is selected
   (c) A Help window will appear if the command is selected
   (d) There are no equivalent keystrokes for the particular command

12. The Recycle Bin enables you to restore a file that was deleted from:
   (a) Drive A
   (b) Drive C
   (c) Both (a) and (b)
   (d) Neither (a) nor (b)

13. The left pane of Windows Explorer may contain:
   (a) One or more folders with a plus sign
   (b) One or more folders with a minus sign
   (c) Both (a) and (b)
   (d) Neither (a) nor (b)

14. Which of the following was suggested as essential to a backup strategy?
   (a) Back up all program files at the end of every session
   (b) Store backup files at another location
   (c) Both (a) and (b)
   (d) Neither (a) nor (b)

ANSWERS

1. d	**5.** c	**9.** d	**13.** c
2. a	**6.** c	**10.** b	**14.** b
3. c	**7.** a	**11.** b	
4. a	**8.** a	**12.** b	

1. My Computer: The document in Figure 13 is an effective way to show your instructor that you understand the My Computer window, and further that you have basic proficiency in Microsoft Word.
   a. Open My Computer to display the contents of your configuration. Pull down the View menu and switch to the Details view. Size the window as necessary. Press Alt + Print Screen to capture the copy of the My Computer window to the Windows clipboard. (The Print Screen key captures the entire screen. Using the Alt key, however, copies just the current window.)
   b. Click the Start menu, click Programs, then click Microsoft Word.
   c. Pull down the Edit menu. Click the Paste command to copy the contents of the clipboard to the document you are about to create. The My Computer window should be pasted into your document.
   d. Press Ctrl+End to move to the end of your document. Press Enter two or three times to leave blank lines as appropriate. Type a modified form of the memo in Figure 13 so that it conforms to your configuration.
   e. Finish the memo and sign your name. Pull down the File menu, click the Print command, then click OK in the dialog box to print the document.

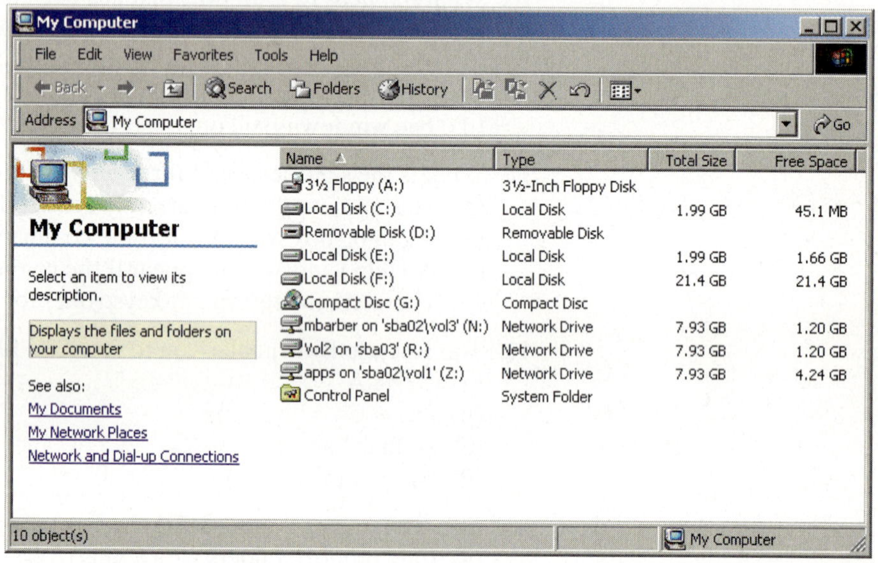

Dear Professor,

Please find the contents of My Computer as it exists on my computer system. I have selected the Folder Options to enable Web content in a folder and to double click an object to open it. I used the View menu to choose the Details view. My system consists of a floppy drive (drive A), three local disks (C, E, and F), a removable disk for backup (drive D), and a CD-ROM drive (drive G). In addition, I have access to three network drives (N, R, and Z).

I enjoyed reading the supplement and look forward to using this information as I learn more about the applications in Microsoft Office.

Sincerely,

Eric Simon

FIGURE 13 *My Computer (exercise 1)*

2. Windows Explorer: Prove to your instructor that you have completed the fourth hands-on exercise by creating a document similar to the one in Figure 14. Use the technique described in the previous problem to capture the screen and paste it into a Word document.

   Compare the documents in Figures 13 and 14 that show My Computer and Windows Explorer, respectively. My Computer is intuitive and preferred by beginners, but it is very limited when compared to Windows Explorer. The latter displays a hierarchical view of your system, showing the selected object in the left pane and the contents of the selected object in the right pane. We urge you, therefore, to become comfortable with Windows Explorer, as that will make you more productive.

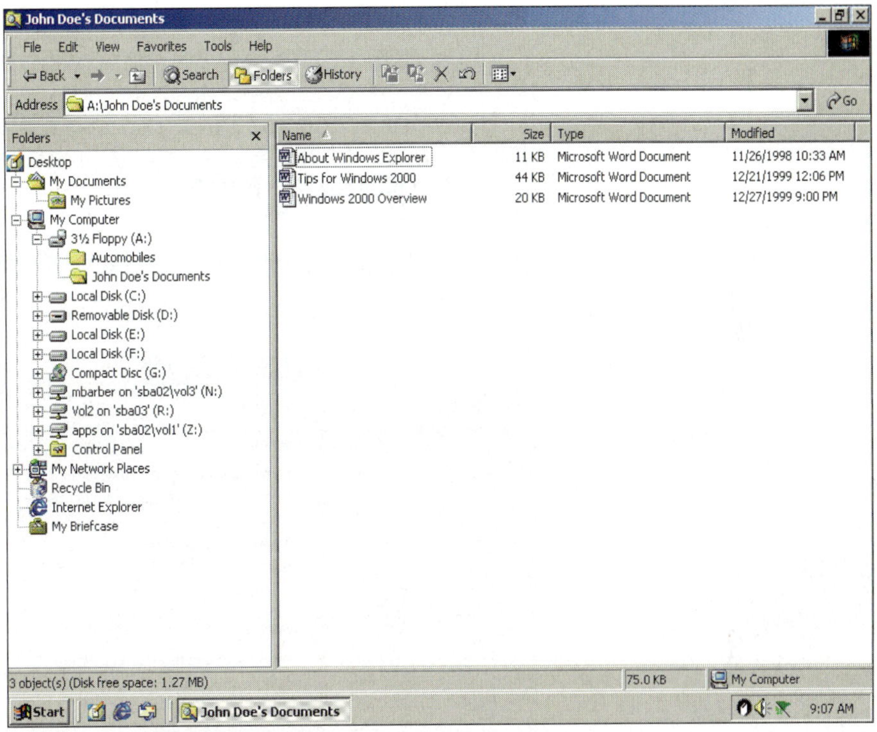

Dear Professor,

This document shows that I have completed the last hands-on exercise and that I have a basic proficiency in Windows Explorer. I can now create a folder and move and copy files with confidence. These skills will become increasingly important as I use various applications throughout the semester.

I also understand the role of the Windows clipboard, an area of memory that is available to every application. I simply press the Print Screen key to capture a screen to the clipboard, and then I use the Paste button to copy the contents of the clipboard into the Word document.

Sincerely,

Alex Rogers

FIGURE 14 *Windows Explorer (exercise 2)*

3. MyPHLIP Web Site: Every text in the *Exploring Office XP* series has a corresponding MyPHLIP (Prentice Hall Learning on the Internet Partnership) Web site, where you will find a variety of student resources as well as online review questions for each chapter. Go to www.prenhall.com/myphlip and follow the instructions. The first time at the site you will be prompted to register by supplying your e-mail address and choosing a password. Next, you choose the discipline (CIS/MIS) and a book (e.g., *Exploring Microsoft Office XP, Volume I*), which in turn will take you to a page similar to Figure 15.

   Your professor will tell you whether he or she has created an online syllabus, in which case you should click the link to find your professor after adding the book. Either way, the next time you return to the site, you will be taken directly to your text. Select any chapter, click "Go", then use the review questions as directed.

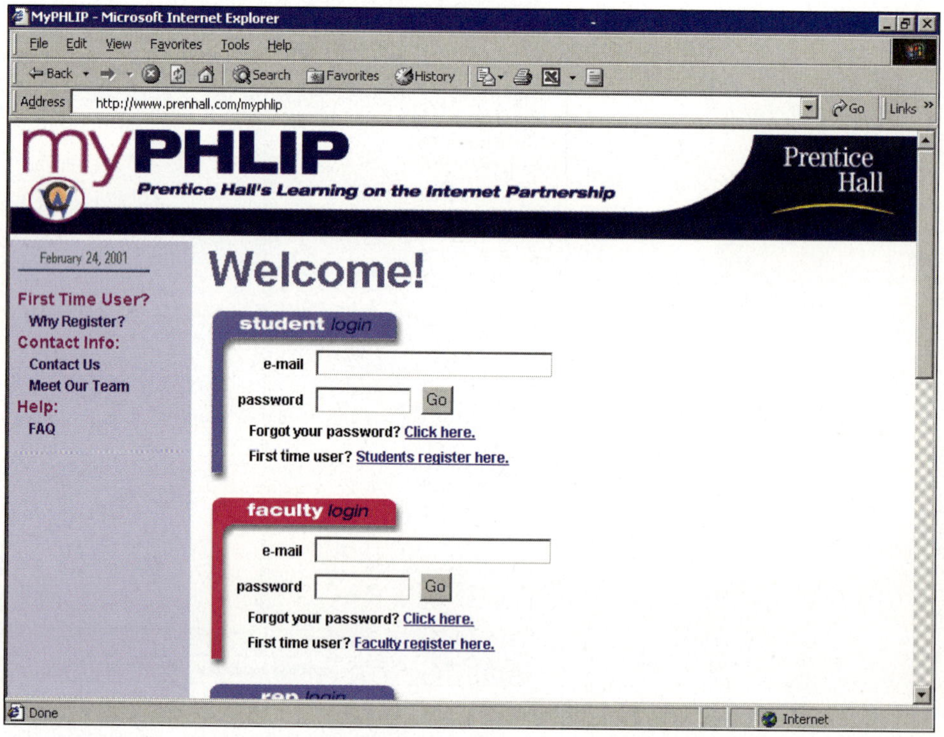

FIGURE 15 *MyPHLIP Web Site (Windows module) (exercise 3)*

4. Organize Your Work: A folder may contain documents, programs, or other folders. The My Classes folder in Figure 16, for example, contains five folders, one folder for each class you are taking this semester. Folders help you to organize your files, and you should become proficient in their use. The best way to practice with folders is on a floppy disk, as was done in Figure 16. Accordingly:
   a. Format a floppy disk or use the floppy disk you have been using throughout the chapter.
   b. Create a Correspondence folder. Create a Business and a Personal folder within the Correspondence folder.
   c. Create a My Courses folder. Within the My Courses folder create a separate folder for each course you are taking.
   d. Use the technique described in problems 1 and 2 to capture the screen in Figure 16 and incorporate it into a document. Add a short paragraph that describes the folders you have created, then submit the document.

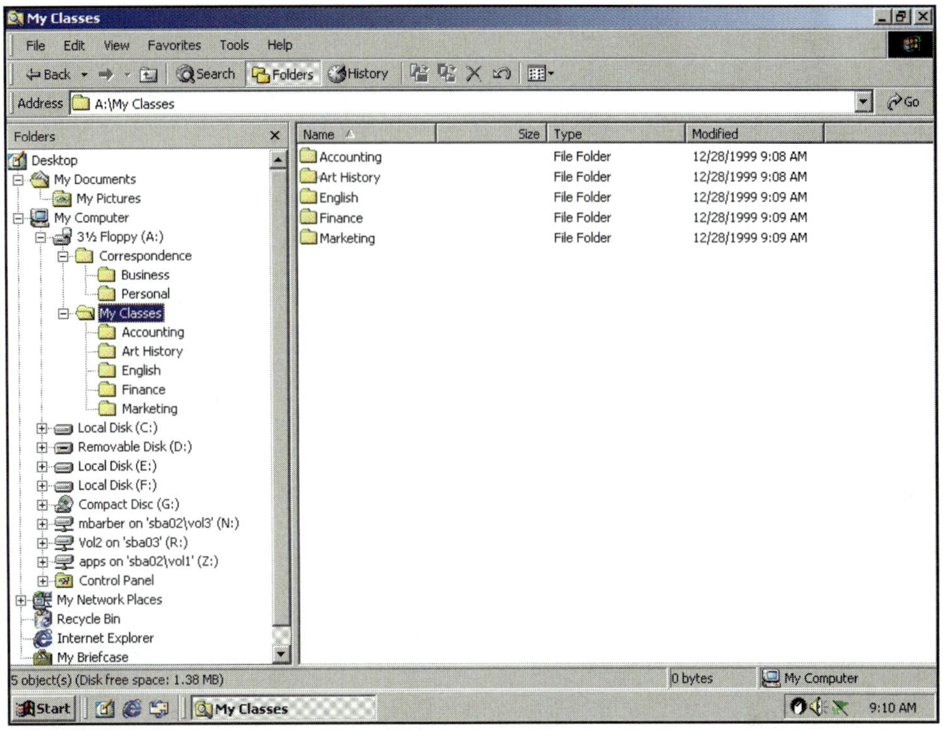

FIGURE 16 *Organize Your Work (exercise 4)*

5. The Windows Web Site: The Web is the best source for information on any application. Go to the Windows home page (www.microsoft.com/windows) as shown in Figure 17, then write a short note to your instructor summarizing the contents of that page and the associated links. Similar pages exist for all Microsoft applications such as www.microsoft.com/office for Microsoft Office.

6. Implement a Screen Saver: A screen saver is a delightful way to personalize your computer and a good way to practice with Microsoft Windows. This is typically not something you can do in a laboratory setting, but it is well worth doing on your own machine. Point to a blank area of the desktop, click the right mouse button to display a context-sensitive menu, then click the Properties command to open the Display Properties dialog box in Figure 18. Click the Screen Saver tab, click the Down arrow in the Screen Saver list box, and select Marquee Display. Click the Settings command button, enter the text and other options for your message, then click OK to close the Options dialog box. Click OK a second time to close the Display Properties dialog box.

7. The Active Desktop: The Active Desktop displays Web content directly on the desktop, then updates the information automatically according to a predefined schedule. You can, for example, display a stock ticker or scoreboard similar to what you see on television. You will need your own machine and an Internet connection to do this exercise, as it is unlikely that the network administrator will let you modify the desktop:
   a. Right click the Windows desktop, click Properties to show the Display Properties dialog box, then click the Web tab. Check the box to show Web content on the Active desktop.
   b. Click the New button, then click the Visit Gallery command button to go to the Active Desktop Gallery in Figure 19 on page 59. Choose any category, then follow the onscreen instructions to display the item on your desktop. We suggest you start with the stock ticker or sports scoreboard.
   c. Summarize your opinion of the active desktop in a short note to your instructor. Did the feature work as advertised? Is the information useful to you?

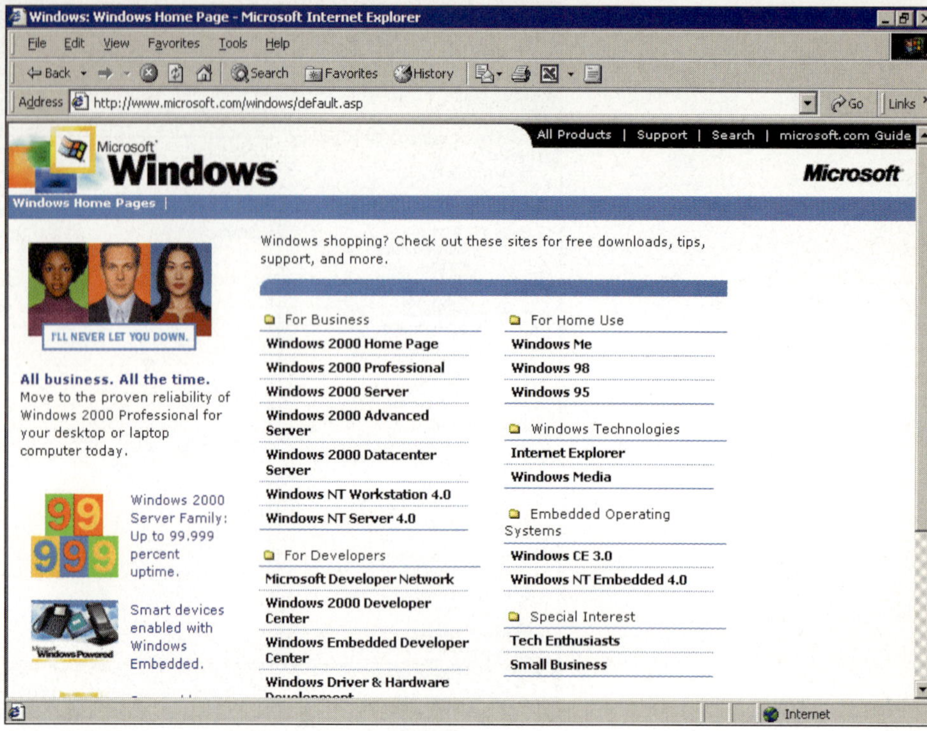

FIGURE 17 *The Windows Web Site (exercise 5)*

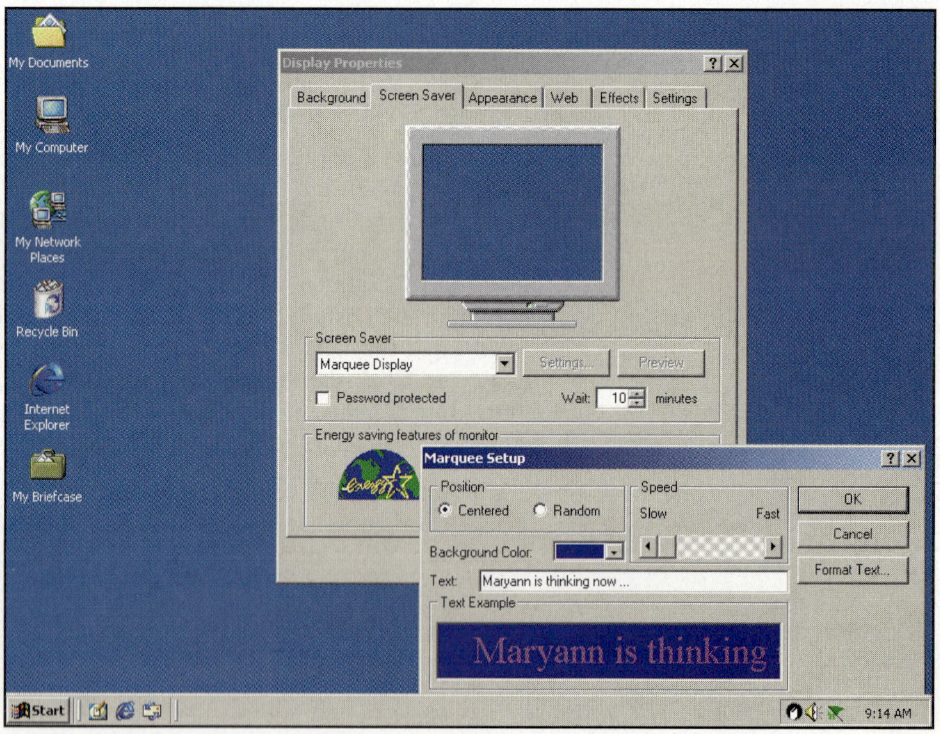

FIGURE 18 *Implement a Screen Saver (exercise 6)*

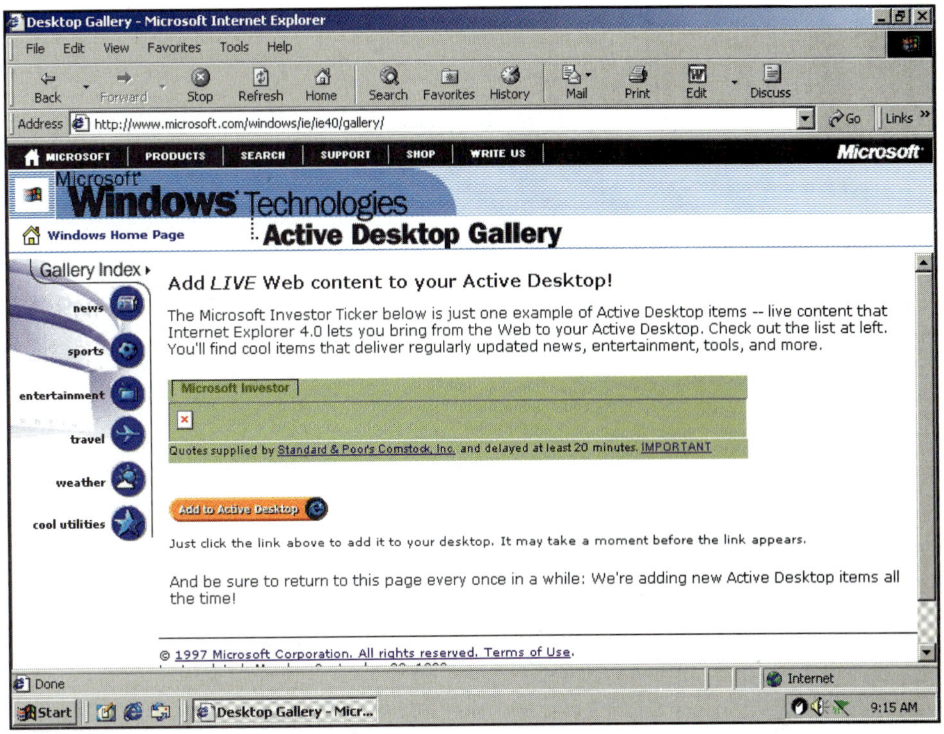

FIGURE 19 *The Active Desktop (exercise 7)*

8. The Control Panel: The Control Panel enables you to change the hardware or software settings on your system. You will not have access to the Control Panel in a lab environment, but you will need it at home if you change your configuration, perhaps by installing a new program. Click the Start button, click Settings, then select Control Panel to display the Control Panel window. Click the down arrow on the Views button to change to the Details view as shown in Figure 20. (The Control Panel can also be opened from My Computer.)

   Write a short report (two or three paragraphs is sufficient) that describes some of the capabilities within Control Panel. *Be careful about making changes, however, and be sure you understand the nature of the new settings before you accept any of the changes.*

9. Users and Passwords: Windows 2000 enables multiple users to log onto the same machine, each with his or her own user name and password. The desktop settings for each user are stored individually, so that all users have their own desktop. The administrator and default user is created when Windows 2000 is first installed, but new users can be added or removed at any time. Once again you will need your own machine:
   a. Click the Start button, click Settings, then click Control Panel to open the Control Panel window as shown in Figure 21. The Control Panel is a special folder that allows you to modify the hardware and/or software settings on your computer.
   b. Double click the Users and Passwords icon to display the dialog box in Figure 20. *Be very careful about removing a user or changing a password, because you might inadvertently deny yourself access to your computer.*
   c. Summarize the capabilities within the users and passwords dialog box in a short note to your instructor. Can you see how these principles apply to the network you use at school or work?

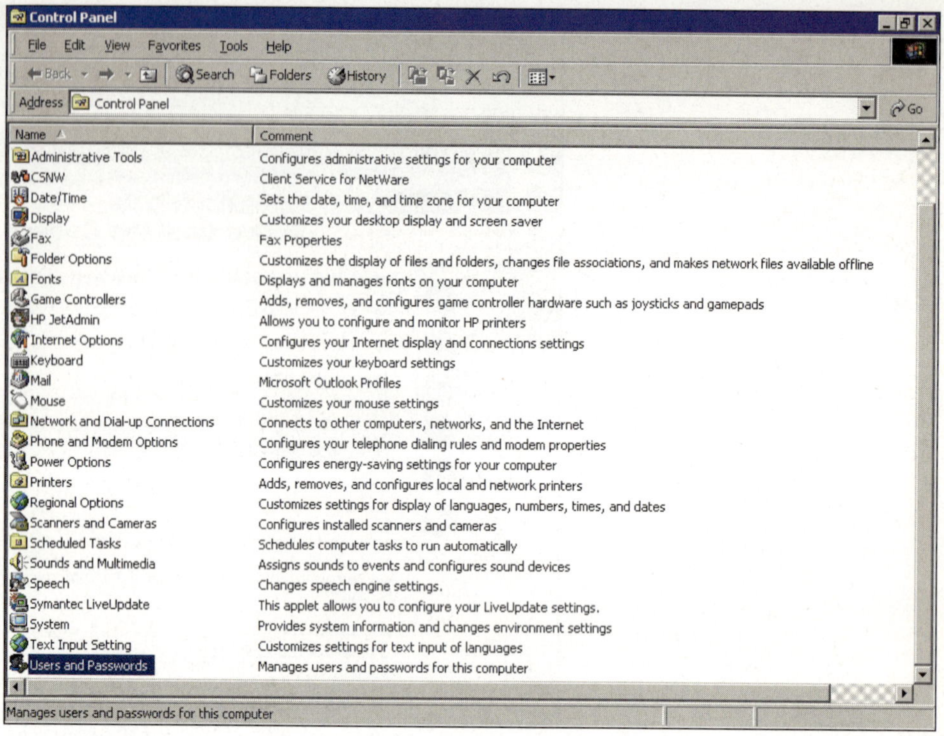

FIGURE 20 *The Control Panel (exercise 8)*

FIGURE 21 *Users and Passwords (exercise 9)*

10. The Fonts Folder: The Fonts folder within the Control Panel displays the names of the fonts available on a system and enables you to obtain a printed sample of any specific font. Click the Start button, click (or point to) the Settings command, click (or point to) Control Panel, then double click the Fonts icon to open the Fonts folder and display the fonts on your system.
    a. Double click any font to open a Fonts window as shown in Figure 22, then click the Print button to print a sample of the selected font.
    b. Open a different font. Print a sample page of this font as well.
    c. Locate the Wingdings font and print this page. Do you see any symbols you recognize? How do you insert these symbols into a document?
    d. How many fonts are there in your fonts Folder? Do some fonts appear to be redundant with others? How much storage space does a typical font require? Write the answers to these questions in a short paragraph.
    e. Start Word. Create a title page containing your name, class, date, and the title of this assignment (My Favorite Fonts). Center the title. Use boldface or italics as you see fit. Be sure to use a suitable type size.
    f. Staple the various pages together (the title page, the three font samples, and the answers to the questions in part d). Submit the assignment to your instructor.

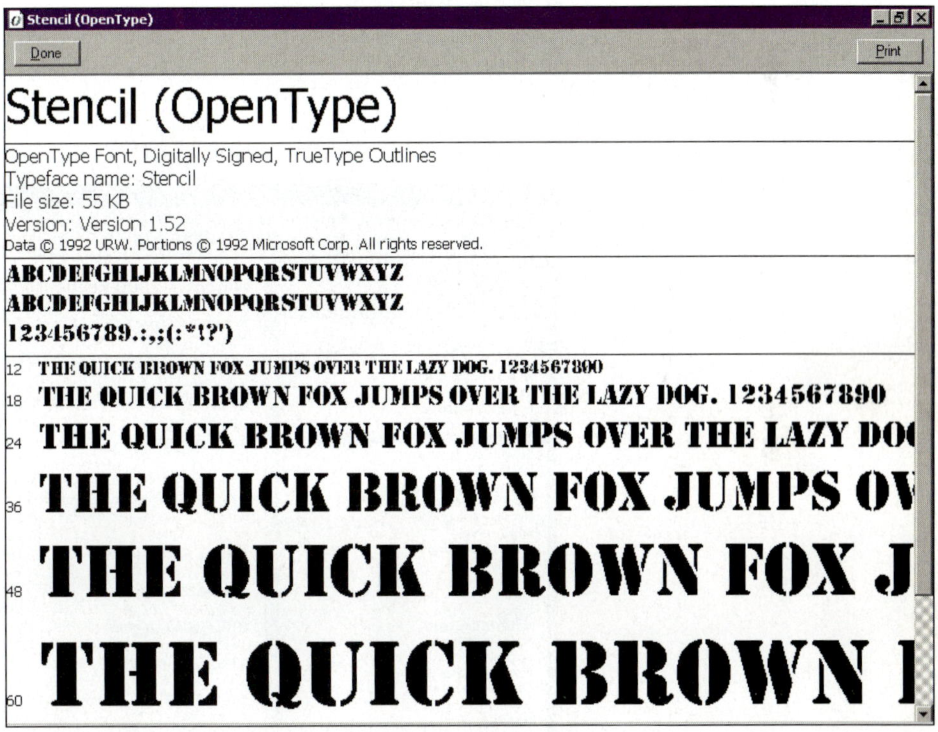

FIGURE 22 *The Fonts Folder (exercise 10)*

11. Keyboard Shortcuts: Microsoft Windows is a graphical user interface in which users "point and click" to execute commands. As you gain proficiency, however, you will find yourself gravitating toward various keyboard shortcuts as shown in Figures 23a and 23b. There is absolutely no need to memorize these shortcuts, nor should you even try. A few, however, have special appeal and everyone has his or her favorite. Use the Help menu to display this information, pick your three favorite shortcuts, and submit them to your instructor. Compare your selections with those of your classmates.

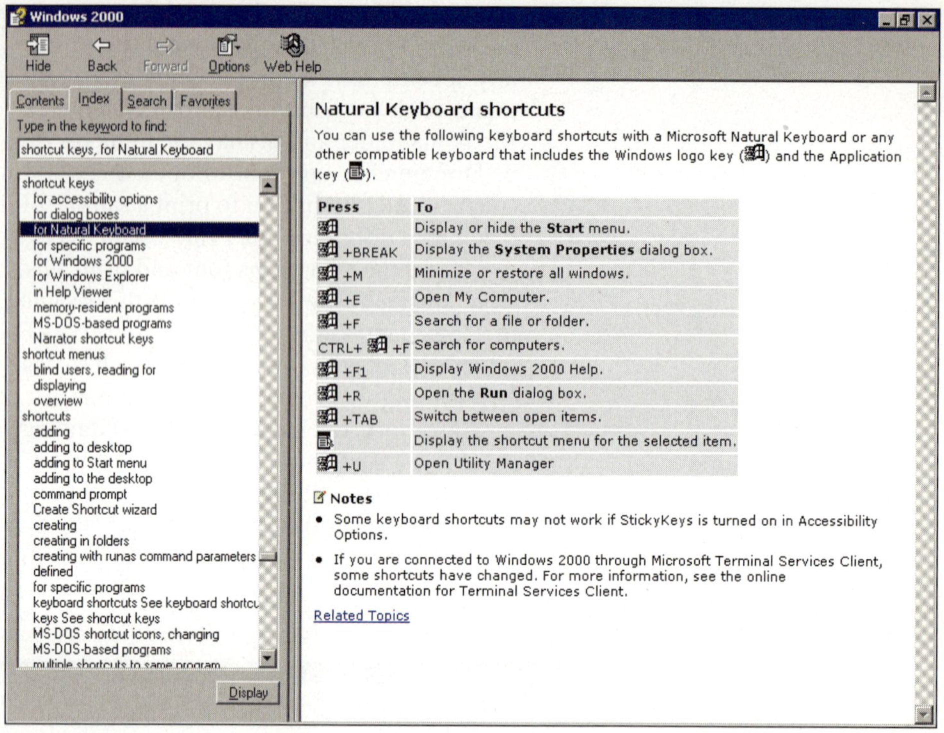

(a)

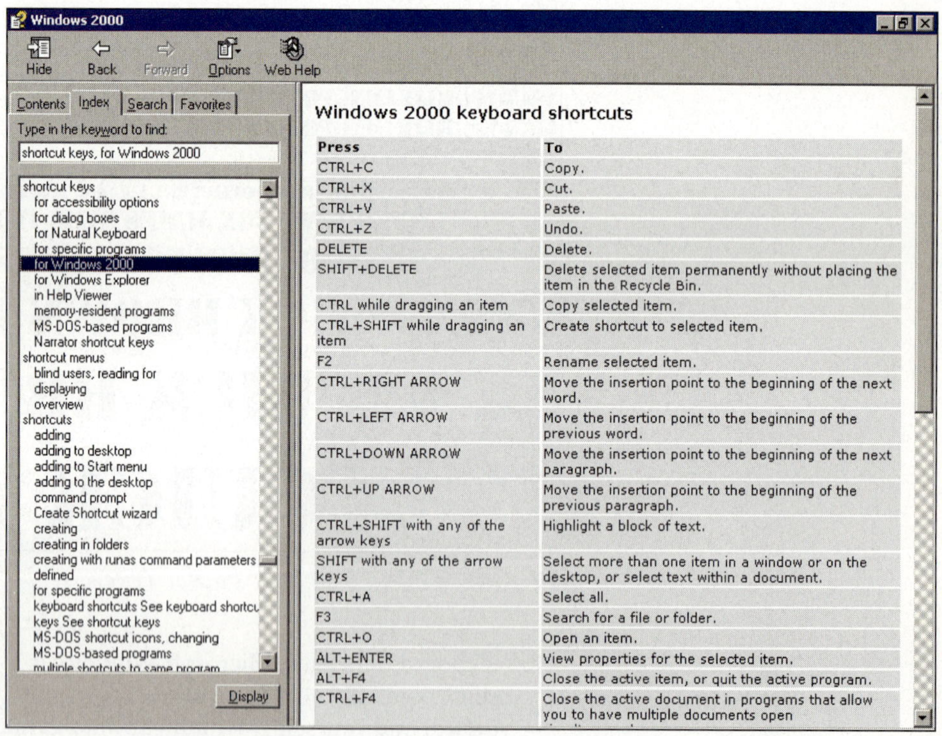

(b)

FIGURE 23 *Shortcut Keys for Natural Keyboard (Exercise 11)*

Planning for Disaster

Do you have a backup strategy? Do you even know what a backup strategy is? You had better learn, because sooner or later you will wish you had one. You will erase a file, be unable to read from a floppy disk, or worse yet suffer a hardware failure in which you are unable to access the hard drive. The problem always seems to occur the night before an assignment is due. The ultimate disaster is the disappearance of your computer, by theft or natural disaster. Describe, in 250 words or less, the backup strategy you plan to implement in conjunction with your work in this class.

Your First Consultant's Job

Go to a real installation such as a doctor's or attorney's office, the company where you work, or the computer lab at school. Determine the backup procedures that are in effect, then write a one-page report indicating whether the policy is adequate and, if necessary, offering suggestions for improvement. Your report should be addressed to the individual in charge of the business, and it should cover all aspects of the backup strategy; that is, which files are backed up and how often, and what software is used for the backup operation. Use appropriate emphasis (for example, bold italics) to identify any potential problems. This is a professional document (it is your first consultant's job), and its appearance should be perfect in every way.

File Compression

You've learned your lesson and have come to appreciate the importance of backing up all of your data files. The problem is that you work with large documents that exceed the 1.44MB capacity of a floppy disk. Accordingly, you might want to consider the acquisition of a file compression program to facilitate copying large documents to a floppy disk in order to transport your documents to and from school, home, or work. (A Zip file is different from a Zip drive. The latter is a hardware device, similar in concept to a large floppy disk, with a capacity of 100MB or 250MB.)

You can download an evaluation copy of the popular WinZip program at www.winzip.com. Investigate the subject of file compression and submit a summary of your findings to your instructor.

The Threat of Virus Infection

A computer virus is an actively infectious program that attaches itself to other programs and alters the way a computer works. Some viruses do nothing more than display an annoying message at an inopportune time. Most, however, are more harmful, and in the worst case, erase all files on the disk. Use your favorite search engine to research the subject of computer viruses in order to answer the following questions. When is a computer subject to infection by a virus? What precautions does your school or university take against the threat of virus infection in its computer lab? What precautions, if any, do you take at home? Can you feel confident that your machine will not be infected if you faithfully use a state-of-the-art antivirus program that was purchased in January 2001?

The Briefcase

It is becoming increasingly common for people to work on more than one machine. Students, for example, may alternate between machines at school and home. In similar fashion, an office worker may use a desktop and a laptop, or have a machine at work and at home. In every instance, you need to transfer files back and forth between the two machines. This can be done using the Copy command from within Windows Explorer. It can also be done via the Briefcase folder. Your instructor has asked you to look into the latter capability and to prepare a brief report describing its use. Do you recommend the Briefcase over a simple Copy command?

Cut, Copy, and Paste

The Cut, Copy, and Paste commands are used in conjunction with one another to move and copy data within a document, or from one Windows document to another. The commands can also be executed from within My Computer or Windows Explorer to move and copy files. You can use the standard Windows shortcuts of Ctrl+X, Ctrl+C, and Ctrl+V to cut, copy, and paste, respectively. You can also click the corresponding icons on the Standard Buttons toolbar within Windows Explorer or My Computer.

Experiment with this technique, then write a short note to your instructor that summarizes the various ways in which files can be moved or copied within Windows 2000.

Register Now

It is good practice to register every program you purchase, so that the vendor can notify you of new releases and/or other pertinent information. Windows provides an online capability whereby you can register via modem. To register your copy of Windows, click the Start button, click Programs, click Accessories, click Welcome to Windows, then click the Registration Wizard. Follow the directions that are displayed on the screen. (Registering a program does carry the risk of having unwanted sales messages sent to you by e-mail. At the Web site, look for a check box in which you choose whether to receive unsolicited e-mail.) You can do this exercise only if you are working on your own computer.

CHAPTER 1

Microsoft® Word 2002: What Will Word Processing Do for Me?

OBJECTIVES

AFTER READING THIS CHAPTER YOU WILL BE ABLE TO:

1. Define word wrap; differentiate between a hard and a soft return.
2. Distinguish between the insert and overtype modes.
3. Describe the elements on the Microsoft Word screen.
4. Create, save, retrieve, edit, and print a simple document.
5. Check a document for spelling; describe the function of the custom dictionary.
6. Describe the AutoCorrect and AutoText features; explain how either feature can be used to create a personal shorthand.
7. Use the thesaurus to look up synonyms and antonyms.
8. Explain the objectives and limitations of the grammar check; customize the grammar check for business or casual writing.
9. Differentiate between the Save and Save As commands; describe various backup options that can be selected.

OVERVIEW

Have you ever produced what you thought was the perfect term paper only to discover that you omitted a sentence or misspelled a word, or that the paper was three pages too short or one page too long? Wouldn't it be nice to make the necessary changes, and then be able to reprint the entire paper with the touch of a key? Welcome to the world of word processing, where you are no longer stuck with having to retype anything. Instead, you retrieve your work from disk, display it on the monitor and revise it as necessary, then print it at any time, in draft or final form.

This chapter provides a broad-based introduction to word processing in general and Microsoft Word in particular. We begin by presenting (or perhaps reviewing) the essential concepts of a word processor, then show you how these concepts are implemented in Word. We show you how to create a document, how to save it on disk, then retrieve the document you just created. We introduce you to the spell check and thesaurus, two essential tools in any word processor. We also present the grammar check as a convenient way of finding a variety of errors but remind you there is no substitute for carefully proofreading the final document.

THE BASICS OF WORD PROCESSING

All word processors adhere to certain basic concepts that must be understood if you are to use the programs effectively. The next several pages introduce ideas that are applicable to any word processor (and which you may already know). We follow the conceptual material with a hands-on exercise that enables you to apply what you have learned.

The Insertion Point

The ***insertion point*** is a flashing vertical line that marks the place where text will be entered. The insertion point is always at the beginning of a new document, but it can be moved anywhere within an existing document. If, for example, you wanted to add text to the end of a document, you would move the insertion point to the end of the document, then begin typing.

Word Wrap

A newcomer to word processing has one major transition to make from a typewriter, and it is an absolutely critical adjustment. Whereas a typist returns the carriage at the end of every line, just the opposite is true of a word processor. One types continually *without* pressing the enter key at the end of a line because the word processor automatically wraps text from one line to the next. This concept is known as ***word wrap*** and is illustrated in Figure 1.1.

The word *primitive* does not fit on the current line in Figure 1.1a, and is automatically shifted to the next line, *without* the user having to press the enter key. The user continues to enter the document, with additional words being wrapped to subsequent lines as necessary. The only time you use the enter key is at the end of a paragraph, or when you want the insertion point to move to the next line and the end of the current line doesn't reach the right margin.

Word wrap is closely associated with another concept, that of hard and soft returns. A ***hard return*** is created by the user when he or she presses the enter key at the end of a paragraph; a ***soft return*** is created by the word processor as it wraps text from one line to the next. The locations of the soft returns change automatically as a document is edited (e.g., as text is inserted or deleted, or as margins or fonts are changed). The locations of the hard returns can be changed only by the user, who must intentionally insert or delete each hard return.

There are two hard returns in Figure 1.1b, one at the end of each paragraph. There are also six soft returns in the first paragraph (one at the end of every line except the last) and three soft returns in the second paragraph. Now suppose the margins in the document are made smaller (that is, the line is made longer) as shown in Figure 1.1c. The number of soft returns drops to four and two (in the first and second paragraphs, respectively) as more text fits on a line and fewer lines are needed. The revised document still contains the two original hard returns, one at the end of each paragraph.

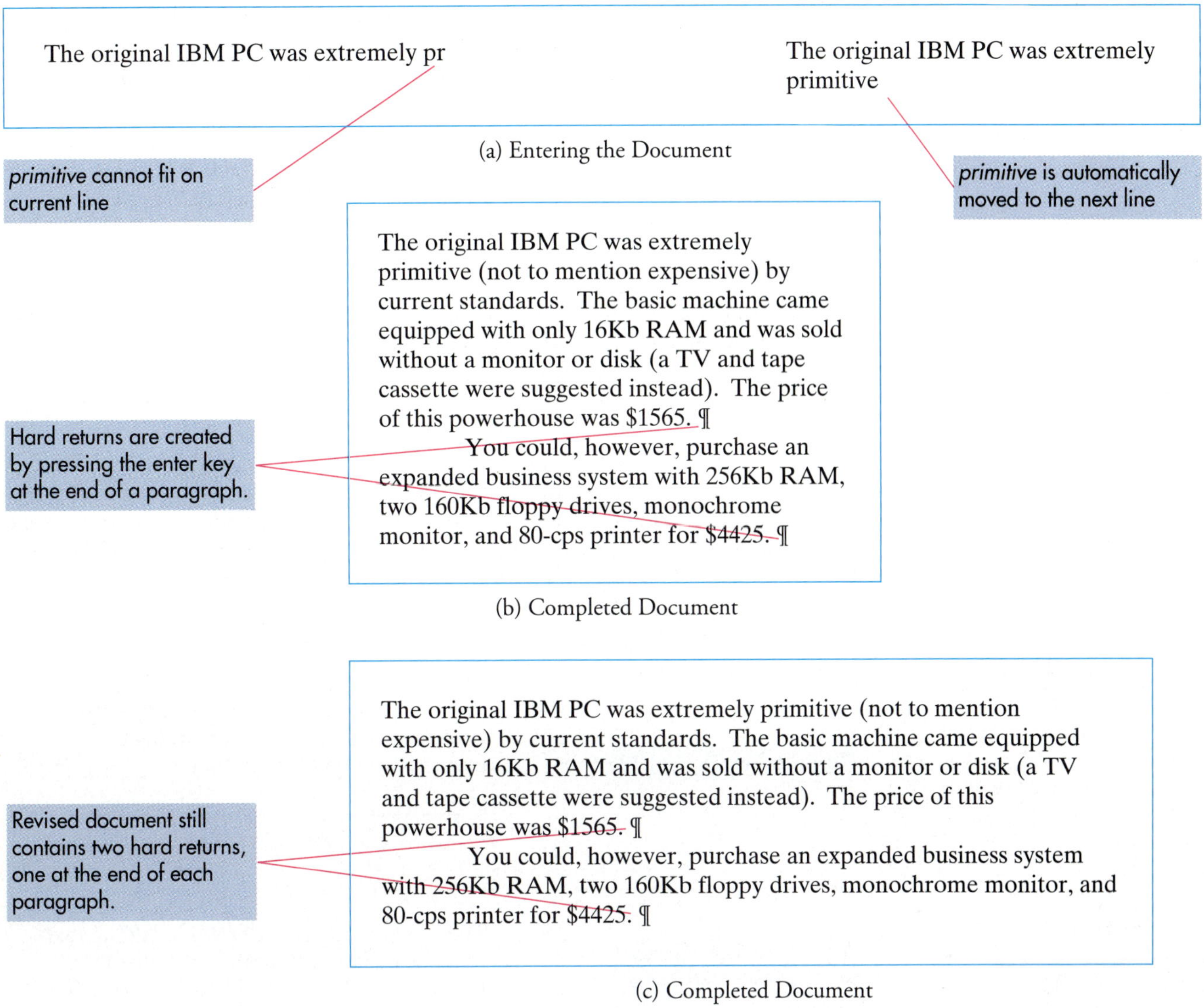

FIGURE 1.1 *Word Wrap*

Toggle Switches

Suppose you sat down at the keyboard and typed an entire sentence without pressing the Shift key; the sentence would be in all lowercase letters. Then you pressed the Caps Lock key and retyped the sentence, again without pressing the Shift key. This time the sentence would be in all uppercase letters. You could repeat the process as often as you like. Each time you pressed the Caps Lock key, the sentence would switch from lowercase to uppercase and vice versa.

The point of this exercise is to introduce the concept of a ***toggle switch***, a device that causes the computer to alternate between two states. The Caps Lock key is an example of a toggle switch. Each time you press it, newly typed text will change from uppercase to lowercase and back again. We will see several other examples of toggle switches as we proceed in our discussion of word processing.

Insert versus Overtype

Microsoft Word is always in one of two modes, ***insert*** or ***overtype***, and uses a toggle switch (the Ins key) to alternate between the two. Press the Ins key once and you switch from insert to overtype. Press the Ins key a second time and you go from overtype back to insert. Text that is entered into a document during the insert mode moves existing text to the right to accommodate the characters being added. Text entered from the overtype mode replaces (overtypes) existing text. Regardless of which mode you are in, text is always entered or replaced immediately to the right of the insertion point.

The insert mode is best when you enter text for the first time, but either mode can be used to make corrections. The insert mode is the better choice when the correction requires you to add new text; the overtype mode is easier when you are substituting one or more character(s) for another. The difference is illustrated in Figure 1.2.

Figure 1.2a displays the text as it was originally entered, with two misspellings. The letters *se* have been omitted from the word *insert,* and an *x* has been erroneously typed instead of an *r* in the word *overtype.* The insert mode is used in Figure 1.2b to add the missing letters, which in turn moves the rest of the line to the right. The overtype mode is used in Figure 1.2c to replace the *x* with an *r.*

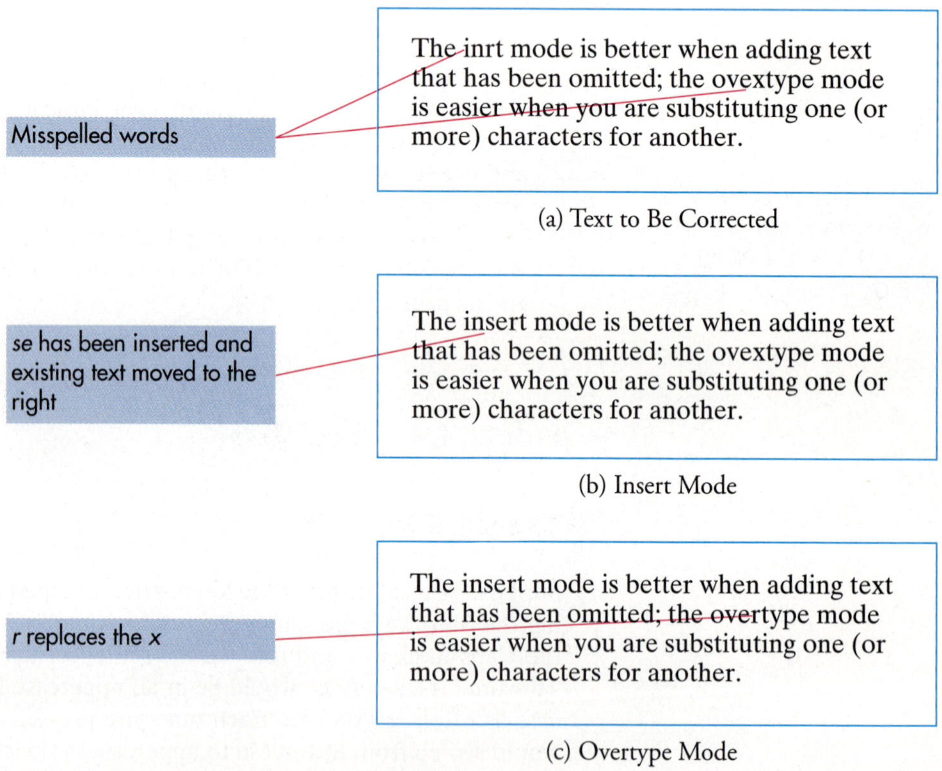

FIGURE 1.2 *Insert and Overtype Modes*

Deleting Text

The Backspace and Del keys delete one character immediately to the left or right of the insertion point, respectively. The choice between them depends on when you need to erase a character(s). The Backspace key is easier if you want to delete a character immediately after typing it. The Del key is preferable during subsequent editing.

You can delete several characters at one time by selecting (dragging the mouse over) the characters to be deleted, then pressing the Del key. And finally, you can delete and replace text in one operation by selecting the text to be replaced and then typing the new text in its place.

LEARN TO TYPE

The ultimate limitation of any word processor is the speed at which you enter data; hence the ability to type quickly is invaluable. Learning how to type is easy, especially with the availability of computer-based typing programs. As little as a half hour a day for a couple of weeks will have you up to speed, and if you do any significant amount of writing at all, the investment will pay off many times.

INTRODUCTION TO MICROSOFT WORD

We used Microsoft Word to write this book, as can be inferred from the screen in Figure 1.3. Your screen will be different from ours in many ways. You will not have the same document nor is it likely that you will customize Word in exactly the same way. You should, however, be able to recognize the basic elements that are found in the Microsoft Word window that is open on the desktop.

There are actually two open windows in Figure 1.3—an application window for Microsoft Word and a document window for the specific document on which you are working. The application window has its own Minimize, Maximize (or Restore) and Close buttons. The document window has only a Close button. There is, however, only one title bar that appears at the top of the application window and it reflects the application (Microsoft Word) as well as the document name (Word Chapter 1). A menu bar appears immediately below the title bar. Vertical and horizontal scroll bars appear at the right and bottom of the document window. The Windows taskbar appears at the bottom of the screen and shows the open applications.

Microsoft Word is also part of the Microsoft Office suite of applications, and thus shares additional features with Excel, Access, and PowerPoint, that are also part of the Office suite. ***Toolbars*** provide immediate access to common commands and appear immediately below the menu bar. The toolbars can be displayed or hidden using the Toolbars command in the ***View menu***.

The ***Standard toolbar*** contains buttons corresponding to the most basic commands in Word—for example, opening a file or printing a document. The icon on the button is intended to be indicative of its function (e.g., a printer to indicate the Print command). You can also point to the button to display a ***ScreenTip*** showing the name of the button. The ***Formatting toolbar*** appears under the Standard toolbar and provides access to such common formatting operations as boldface, italics, or underlining.

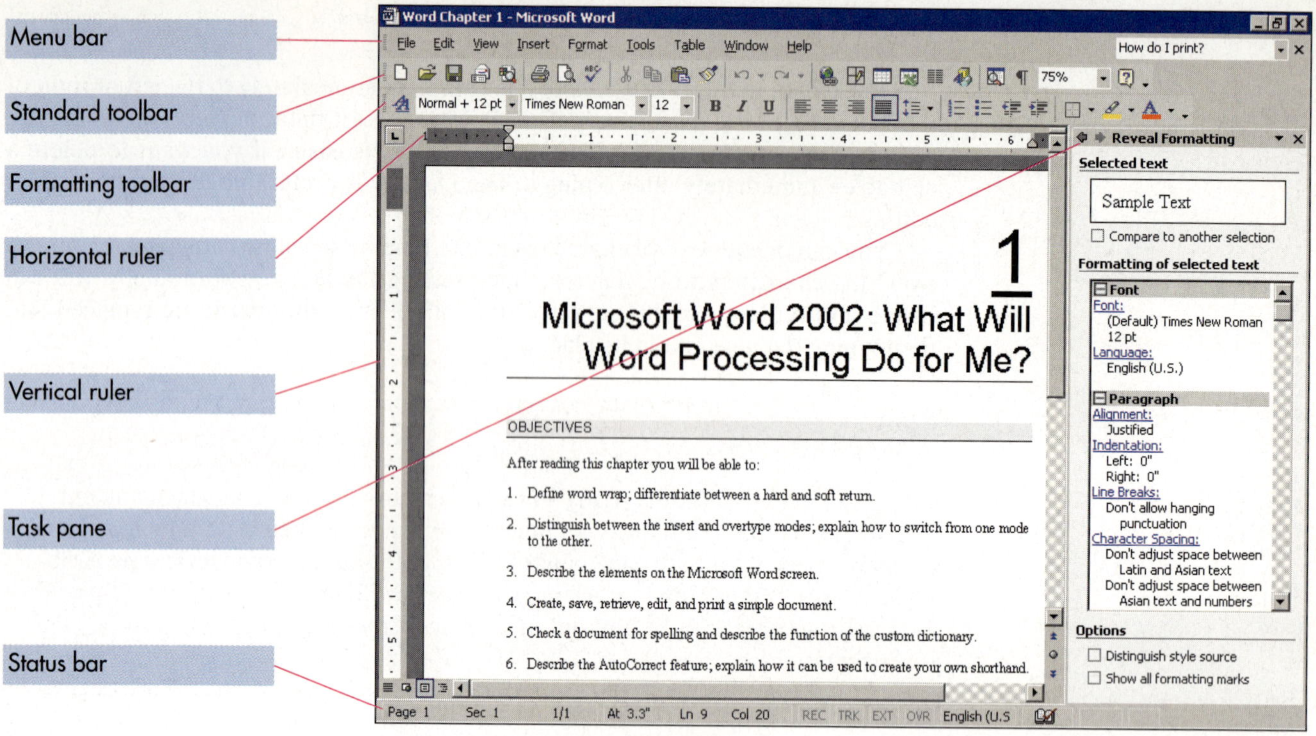

FIGURE 1.3 *Microsoft Word*

The toolbars may appear overwhelming at first, but there is absolutely no need to memorize what the individual buttons do. That will come with time. We suggest, however, that you will have a better appreciation for the various buttons if you consider them in groups, according to their general function, as shown in Figure 1.4a. Note, too, that many of the commands in the pull-down menus are displayed with an image that corresponds to a button on a toolbar.

The ***horizontal ruler*** is displayed underneath the toolbars and enables you to change margins, tabs, and/or indents for all or part of a document. A ***vertical ruler*** shows the vertical position of text on the page and can be used to change the top or bottom margins.

The ***status bar*** at the bottom of the document window displays the location of the insertion point (or information about the command being executed). The status bar also shows the status (settings) of various indicators—for example, OVR to show that Word is in the overtype, as opposed to the insert, mode.

THE TASK PANE

All applications in Office XP provide access to a ***task pane*** that facilitates the execution of subsequent commands. (Microsoft refers to the suite as Office XP, but designates the individual applications as version 2002.) The task pane serves many functions. It can be used to display the formatting properties of selected text, open an existing document, or search for appropriate clip art. The task pane will open automatically in response to certain commands. It can also be toggled open or closed through the Task pane command in the View menu. The task pane is discussed in more detail throughout the chapter.

Starts a new document, opens an existing document, saves the document in memory

E-mails the document or opens the task pane to initiate a search for documents containing the specified text

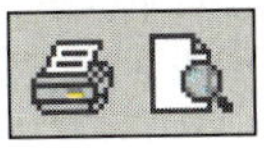

Prints the document or previews the document prior to printing

Checks the spelling and grammar of the document

Cuts or copies the selected text; pastes the contents of the Windows clipboard; copies the formatting of the selected text

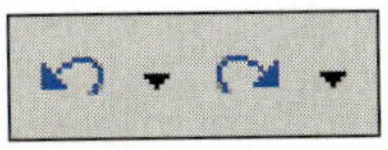

Undoes or redoes a previously executed command

Inserts a hyperlink

Draws a table; inserts a table; inserts an Excel worksheet; creates columns; toggles the display of the Drawing toolbar on and off

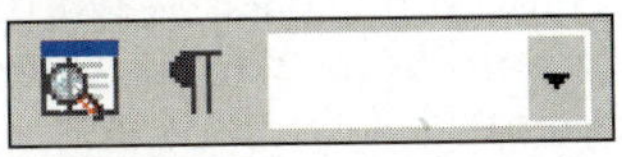

Toggles the Document map on and off; toggles the nonprinting characters on and off; changes the zoom percentage

Displays the Office Assistant

(a) Standard Toolbar

Applies a specific style to the selected text

Changes the typeface or changes the type size

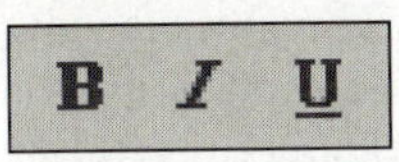

Toggles boldface, italics, or underline on and off

Aligns left, center, right, or full; controls the line spacing

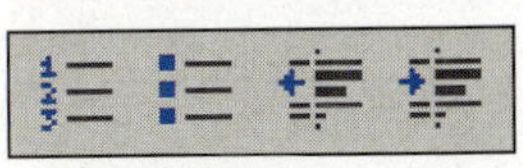

Creates a numbered or bulleted list; decreases or increases the indent

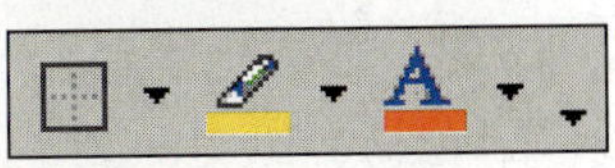

Creates a border, applies highlighting to the selected text, or applies color to the selected text

(b) Formatting Toolbar

FIGURE 1.4 *Toolbars*

The ***File Menu*** is a critically important menu in virtually every Windows application. It contains the Save and Open commands to save a document on disk, then subsequently retrieve (open) that document at a later time. The File Menu also contains the ***Print command*** to print a document, the ***Close command*** to close the current document but continue working in the application, and the ***Exit command*** to quit the application altogether.

The ***Save command*** copies the document that you are working on (i.e., the document that is currently in memory) to disk. The command functions differently the first time it is executed for a new document, in that it displays the Save As dialog box as shown in Figure 1.5a. The dialog box requires you to specify the name of the document, the drive (and an optional folder) in which the document is stored, and its file type. All subsequent executions of the command will save the document under the assigned name, each time replacing the previously saved version with the new version.

The ***file name*** (e.g., My First Document) can contain up to 255 characters including spaces, commas, and/or periods. (Periods are discouraged, however, since they are too easily confused with DOS extensions.) The Save In list box is used to select the drive (which is not visible in Figure 1.5a) and the optional folder (e.g., Exploring Word). The ***Places bar*** provides a shortcut to any of its folders without having to search through the Save In list box. Click the Desktop icon, for example, and the file is saved automatically on the Windows desktop. The ***file type*** defaults to a Word 2002 document. You can, however, choose a different format such as Word 95 to maintain compatibility with earlier versions of Microsoft Word. You can also save any Word document as a Web page (or HTML document).

The ***Open command*** is the opposite of the Save command as it brings a copy of an existing document into memory, enabling you to work with that document. The Open command displays the Open dialog box in which you specify the file name, the drive (and optionally the folder) that contains the file, and the file type. Microsoft Word will then list all files of that type on the designated drive (and folder), enabling you to open the file you want. The Save and Open commands work in conjunction with one another. The Save As dialog box in Figure 1.5a, for example, saves the file My First Document in the Exploring Word folder. The Open dialog box in Figure 1.5b loads that file into memory so that you can work with the file, after which you can save the revised file for use at a later time.

The toolbars in the Save As and Open dialog boxes have several buttons in common that facilitate the execution of either command. The Views button lets you display the files in either dialog box in one of four different views. The Details view (in Figure 1.5a) shows the file size as well as the date and time a file was last modified. The Preview view (in Figure 1.5b) shows the beginning of a document, without having to open the document. The List view displays only the file names, and thus lets you see more files at one time. The Properties view shows information about the document, including the date of creation and number of revisions.

SORT BY NAME, DATE, OR FILE SIZE

The files in the Save As and Open dialog boxes can be displayed in ascending or descending sequence by name, date modified, or size. Change to the Details view, then click the heading of the desired column; for example, click the Modified column to list the files according to the date they were last changed. Click the column heading a second time to reverse the sequence.

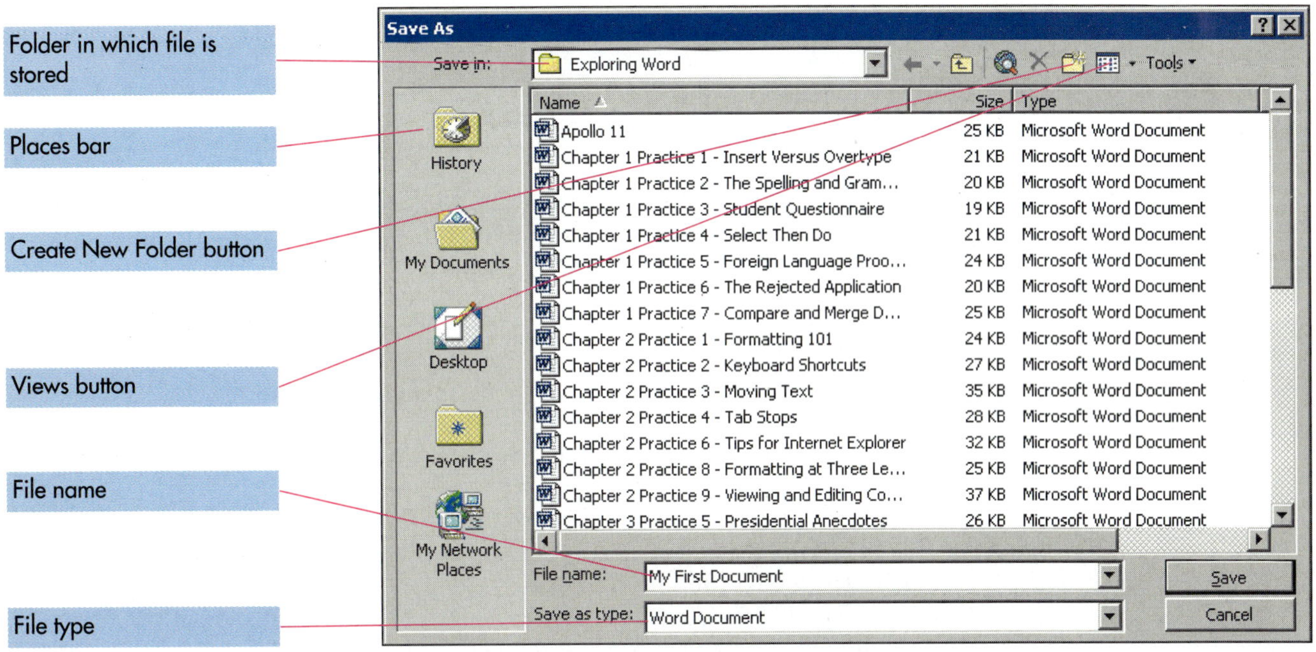

(a) Save As Dialog Box (details view)

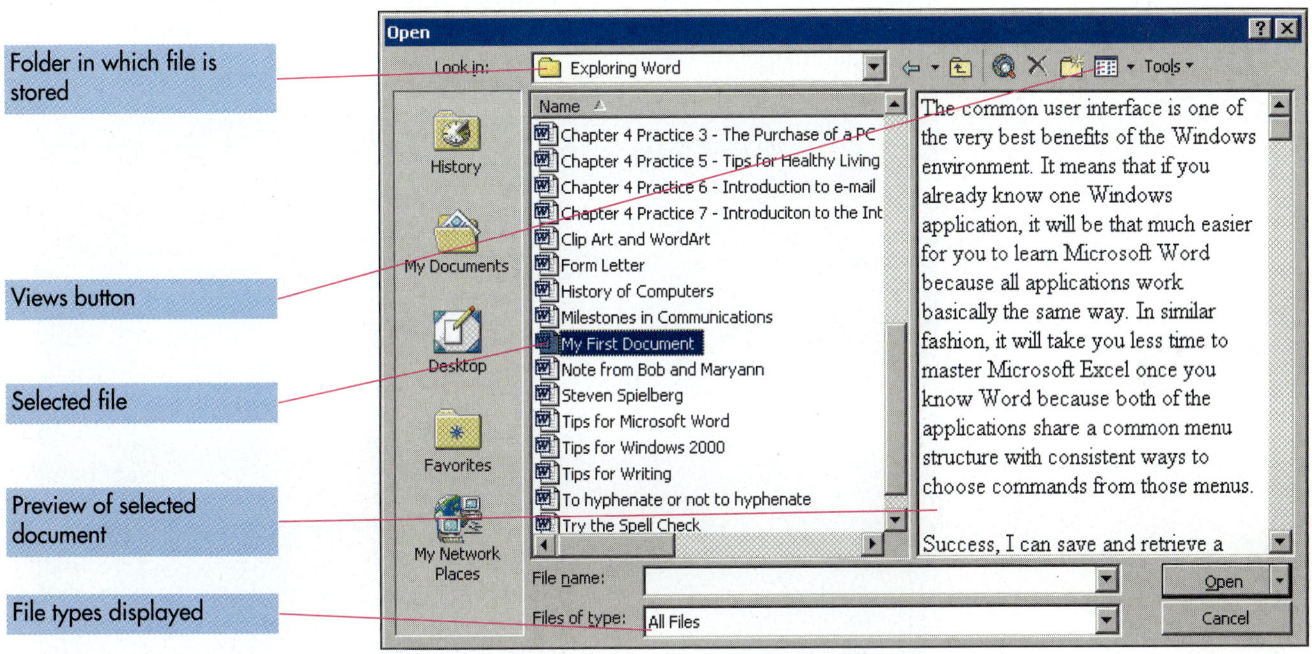

(b) Open Dialog Box (details view)

FIGURE 1.5 *The Save and Open Commands*

LEARNING BY DOING

Every chapter contains a series of hands-on exercises that enable you to apply what you learn at the computer. The exercises in this chapter are linked to one another in that you create a simple document in exercise one, then open and edit that document in exercise two. The ability to save and open a document is critical, and you do not want to spend an inordinate amount of time entering text unless you are confident in your ability to retrieve it later.

Hands-on Exercise 1

My First Document

Objective To start Microsoft Word in order to create, save, and print a simple document; to execute commands via the toolbar or from pull-down menus. Use Figure 1.6 as a guide in doing the exercise.

Step 1: **The Windows Desktop**

- Turn on the computer and all of its peripherals. The floppy drive should be empty prior to starting your machine. This ensures that the system starts from the hard disk, which contains the Windows files, as opposed to a floppy disk, which does not.
- Your system will take a minute or so to get started, after which you should see the Windows desktop in Figure 1.6a. Do not be concerned if the appearance of your desktop is different from ours.
- You may see a Welcome to Windows dialog box with command buttons to take a tour of the operating system. If so, click the appropriate button(s) or close the dialog box.
- You should be familiar with basic file management and very comfortable moving and copying files from one folder to another. If not, you may want to review this material.

Start button

(a) The Windows Desktop (step 1)

FIGURE 1.6 *Hands-on Exercise 1*

Step 2: **Obtain the Practice Files**

➤ We have created a series of practice files (also called a "data disk") for you to use throughout the text. Your instructor will make these files available to you in a variety of ways:

- The files may be on a network drive, in which case you use Windows Explorer to copy the files from the network to a floppy disk.
- There may be an actual "data disk" that you are to check out from the lab in order to use the Copy Disk command to duplicate the disk.

➤ You can also download the files from our Web site provided you have an Internet connection. Start Internet Explorer, then go to the Exploring Windows home page at **www.prenhall.com/grauer**.

- Click the book for **Office XP**, which takes you to the Office XP home page. Click the **Student Resources tab** (at the top of the window) to go to the Student Resources page as shown in Figure 1.6b.
- Click the link to **Student Data Disk** (in the left frame), then scroll down the page until you can select Word 2002. Click the link to download the student data disk.
- You will see the File Download dialog box asking what you want to do. The option button to save this program to disk is selected. Click **OK**. The Save As dialog box appears.
- Click the ***down arrow*** in the Save In list box to enter the drive and folder where you want to save the file. It's best to save the file to the Windows desktop or to a temporary folder on drive C.
- Double click the file after it has been downloaded to your PC, then follow the onscreen instructions.

➤ Check with your instructor for additional information.

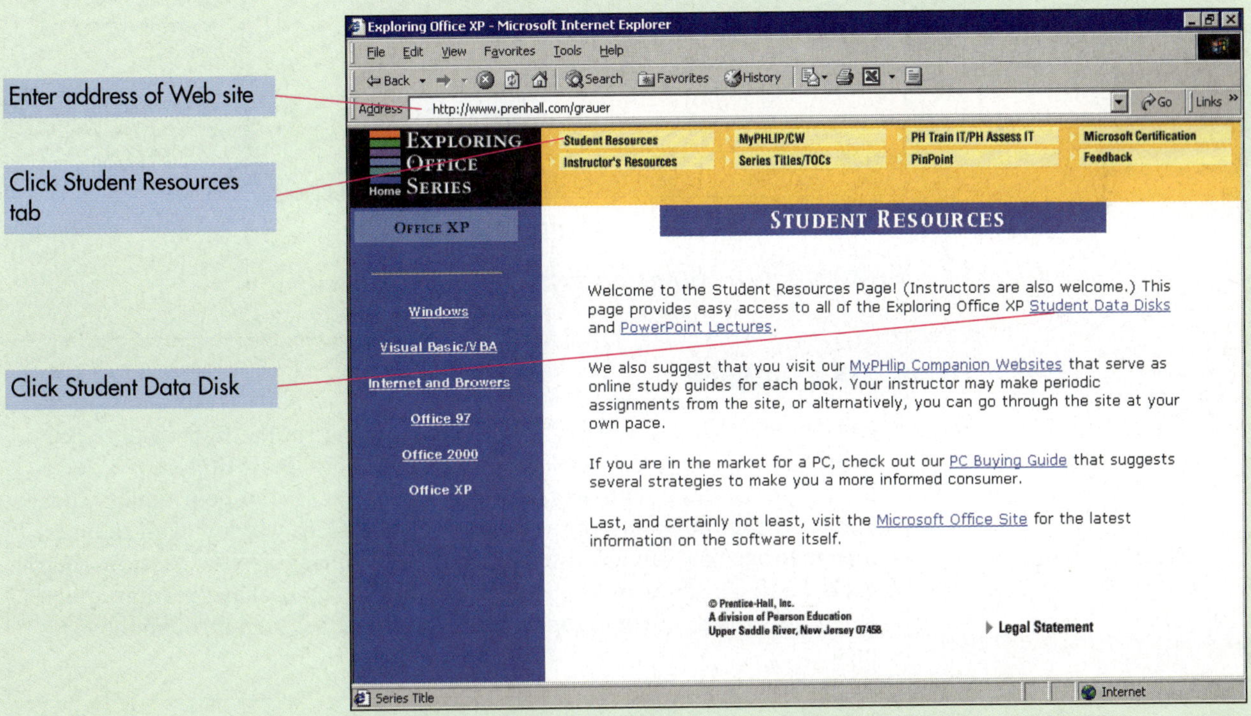

(b) Obtain the Practice Files (step 2)

FIGURE 1.6 *Hands-on Exercise 1 (continued)*

Step 3: **Start Microsoft Word**

- ➤ Click the **Start button** to display the Start menu. Click (or point to) the Programs menu, then click **Microsoft Word 2002** to start the program.
- ➤ You should see a blank document within the Word application window. (Click the **New Blank document** button on the Standard toolbar if you do not see a document.) Close the task pane if it is open.
- ➤ Click and drag the Office Assistant out of the way. (The Assistant is illustrated in step six of this exercise.)
- ➤ Do not be concerned if your screen is different from ours as we include a troubleshooting section immediately following the exercise.

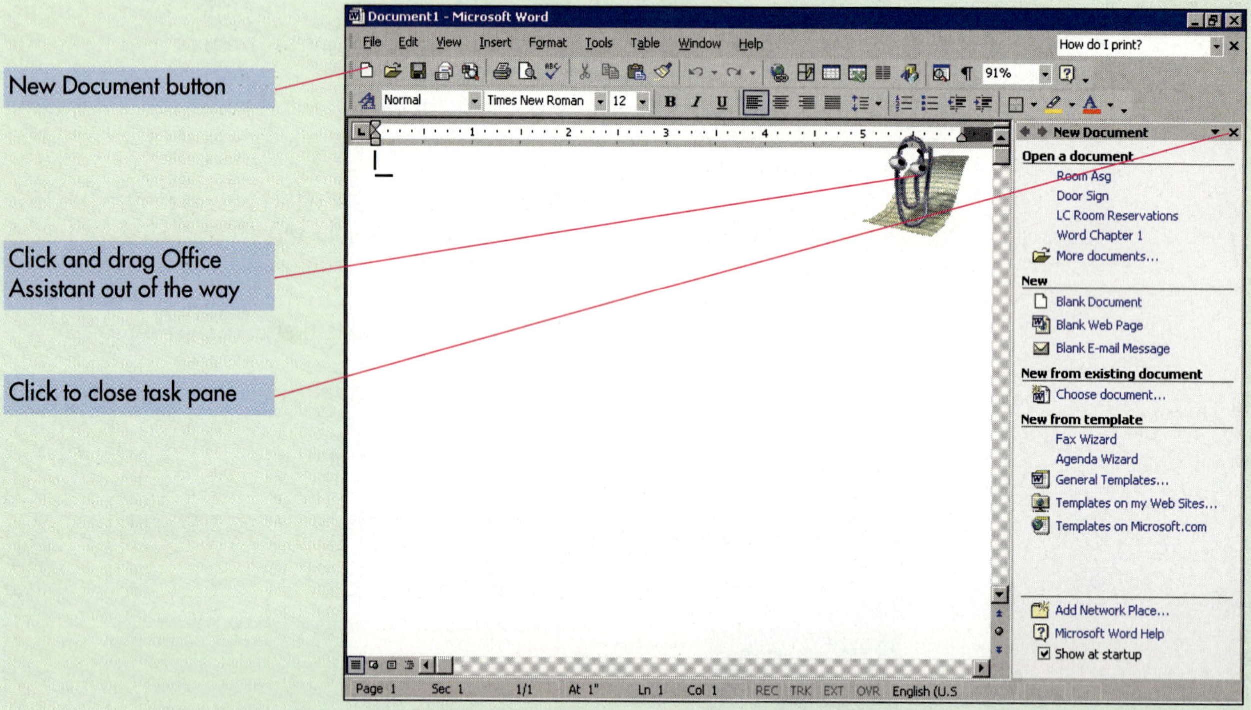

(c) Start Microsoft Word (step 3)

FIGURE 1.6 *Hands-on Exercise 1 (continued)*

ASK A QUESTION

Click in the "Ask a Question" list box that appears at the right of the document window, enter the text of a question such as "How do I save a document?", press enter, and Word returns a list of potential help topics. Click any topic that appears promising to open the Help window with detailed information. You can ask multiple questions during a Word session, then click the down arrow in the list box to return to an earlier question, which will return you to the help topics. You can also access help through the Help menu.

Step 4: **Create the Document**

- Create the document in Figure 1.6d. Type just as you would on a typewriter with one exception; do *not* press the enter key at the end of a line because Word will automatically wrap text from one line to the next.
- Press the **enter key** at the end of the paragraph.
- You may see a red or green wavy line to indicate spelling or grammatical errors, respectively. Both features are discussed later in the chapter.
- Point to the red wavy line (if any), click the **right mouse button** to display a list of suggested corrections, then click (select) the appropriate substitution.
- Ignore the green wavy line (if any).

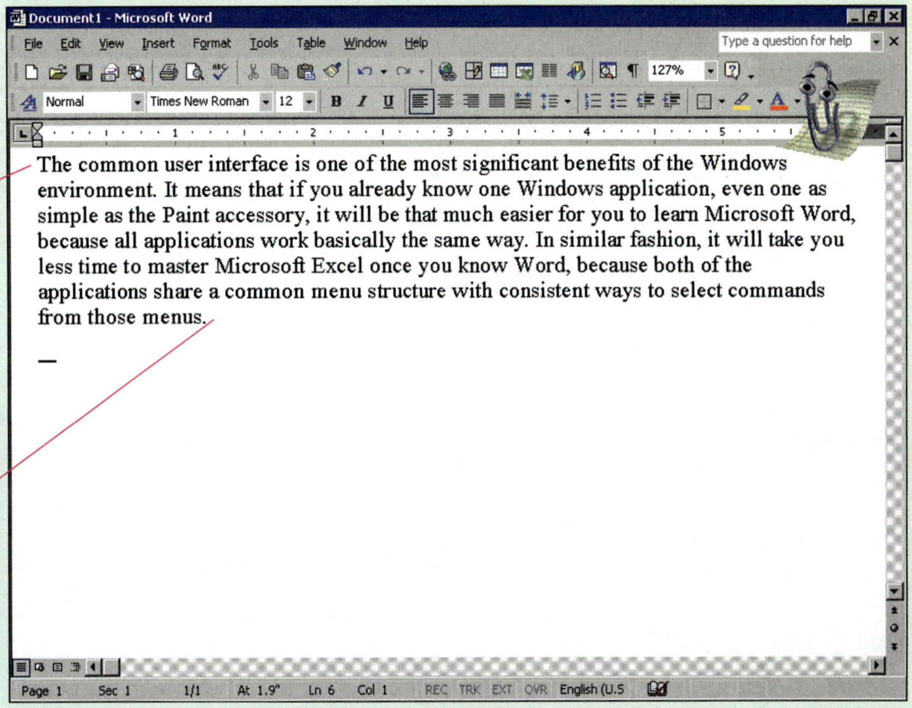

(d) Create the Document (step 4)

FIGURE 1.6 *Hands-on Exercise 1 (continued)*

SEPARATE THE TOOLBARS

You may see the Standard and Formatting toolbars displayed on one row to save space within the application window. If so, we suggest that you separate the toolbars, so that you see all of the buttons on each. Click the Toolbar Options down arrow that appears at the end of any visible toolbar to display toolbar options, then click the option to show the buttons on two rows. Click the down arrow a second time to show the buttons on one row if you want to return to the other configuration.

Step 5: Save the Document

- Pull down the **File menu** and click **Save** (or click the **Save button** on the Standard toolbar). You should see the Save As dialog box in Figure 1.6e.
- If necessary, click the **drop-down arrow** on the View button and select the **Details view**, so that the display on your monitor matches our figure. (The title bar shows Document1 because the file has not yet been saved.)
- To save the file:
  - Click the **drop-down arrow** on the Save In list box.
  - Click the appropriate drive, e.g., drive C or drive A, depending on whether or not you installed the data disk on your hard drive.
  - Double click the **Exploring Word folder**, to make it the active folder (the folder in which you will save the document).
  - Click and drag over the default entry in the File name text box. Type **My First Document** as the name of your document. (A DOC extension will be added automatically when the file is saved to indicate that this is a Word document.)
  - Click **Save** or press the **enter key**. The title bar changes to reflect the new document name (My First Document).
- Add your name at the end of the document, then click the **Save button** on the Standard toolbar to save the document with the revision.
- This time the Save As dialog box does not appear, since Word already knows the name of the document.

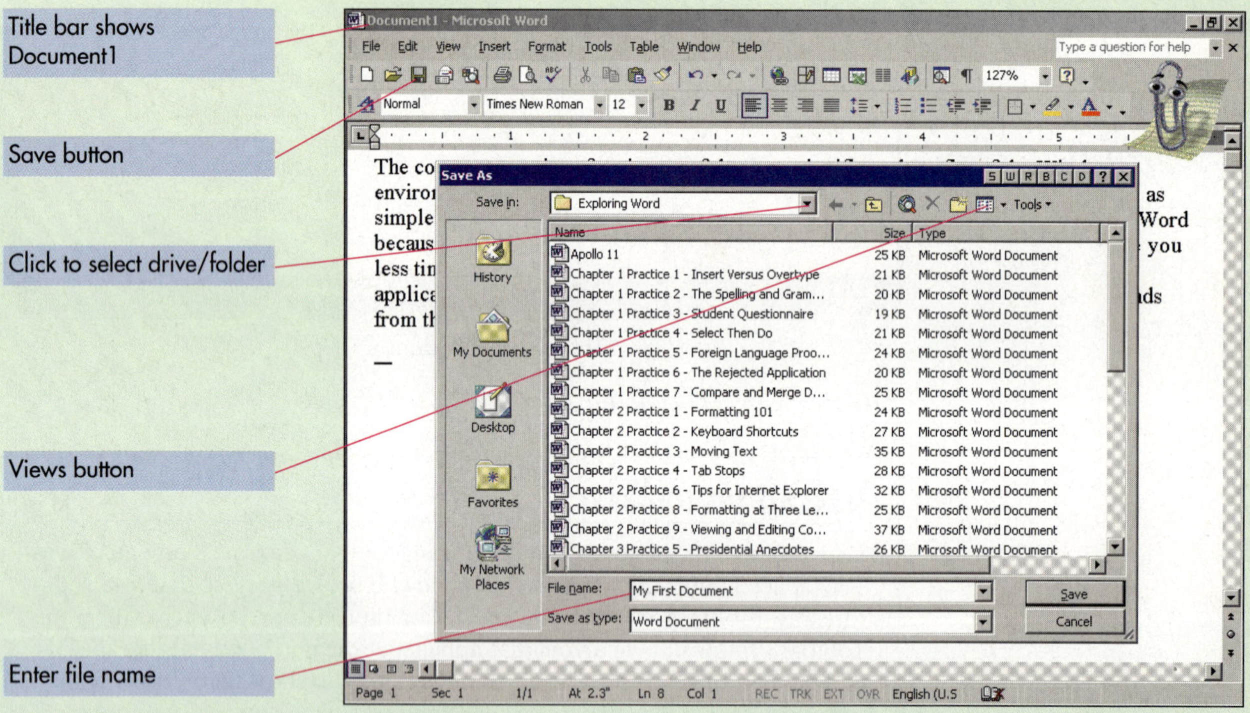

(e) Save the Document (step 5)

FIGURE 1.6 *Hands-on Exercise 1 (continued)*

Step 6: **The Office Assistant**

- If necessary, pull down the **Help menu** and click the command to **Show the Office Assistant**. You may see a different character than the one we have selected.
- Click the **Assistant**, enter the question, **How do I print?** as shown in Figure 1.6f, then click the **Search button** to look for the answer. The size of the Assistant's balloon expands as the Assistant suggests several topics that may be appropriate.
- Click the topic, **Print a document**, which in turn displays a Help window that contains links to various topics, each with detailed information. Click the **Office Assistant** to hide the balloon (or drag the Assistant out of the way).
- Click any of the links in the Help window to read the information. You can print the contents of any topic by clicking the **Print button** in the Help window. Close the Help window when you are finished.

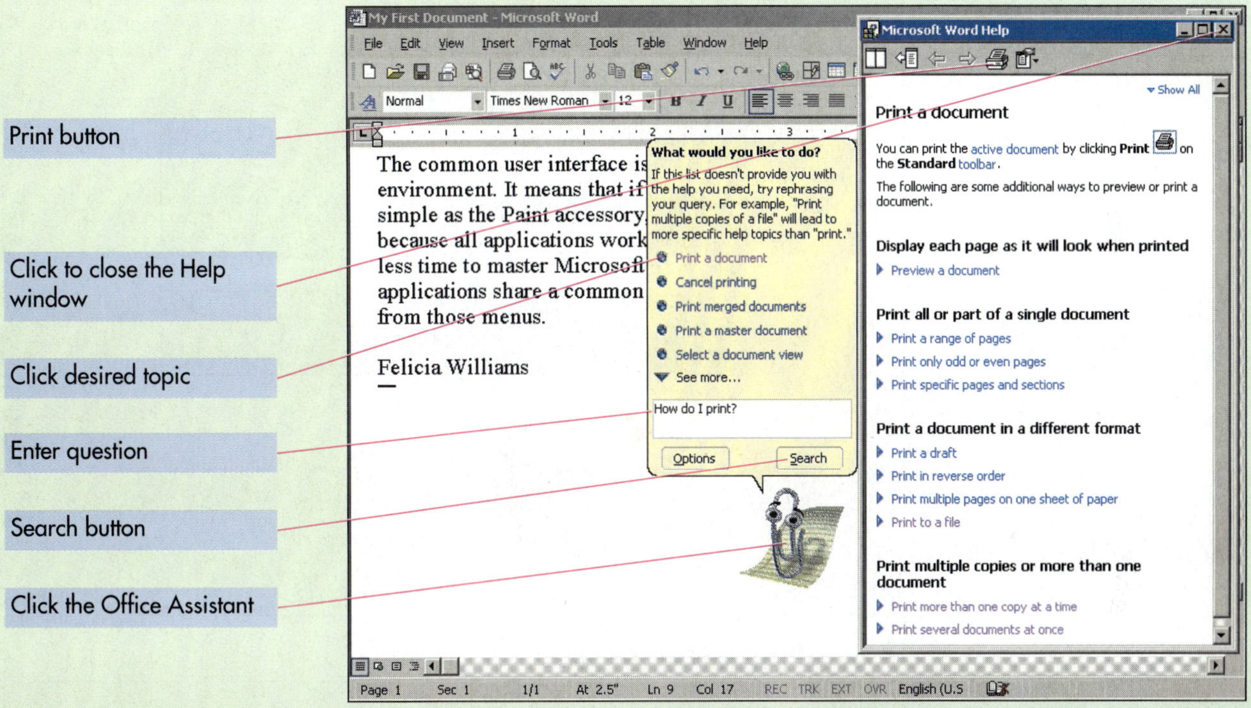

(f) The Office Assistant (step 6)

FIGURE 1.6 *Hands-on Exercise 1 (continued)*

TIP OF THE DAY

You can set the Office Assistant to greet you with a "tip of the day" each time you start Word. Click the Microsoft Word Help button (or press the F1 key) to display the Assistant, then click the Options button to display the Office Assistant dialog box. Click the Options tab, then check the Show the Tip of the Day at Startup box and click OK. The next time you start Microsoft Word, you will be greeted by the Assistant, who will offer you the tip of the day.

Step 7: **Print the Document**

- ➤ You can print the document in one of two ways:
  - Pull down the **File menu**. Click **Print** to display the dialog box of Figure 1.6g. Click the **OK command button** to print the document.
  - Click the **Print button** on the Standard toolbar to print the document immediately without displaying the Print dialog box.
- ➤ Submit this document to your instructor.

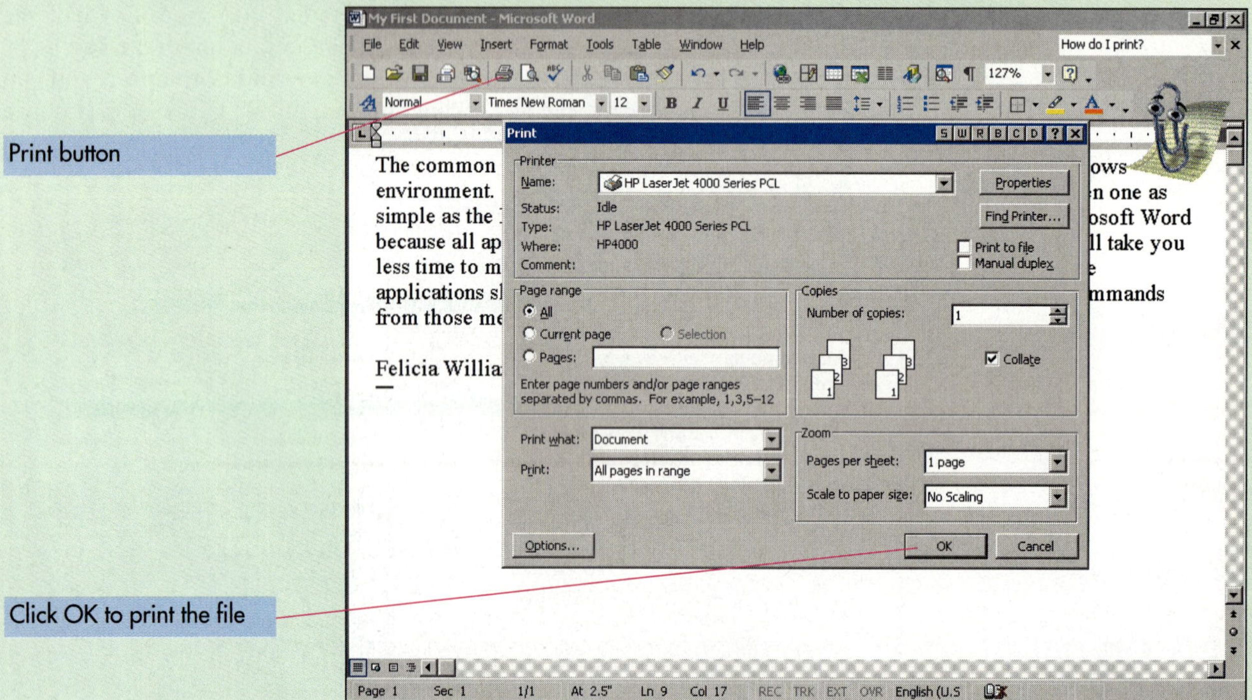

(g) Print the Document (step 7)

FIGURE 1.6 *Hands-on Exercise 1 (continued)*

ABOUT MICROSOFT WORD

Pull down the Help menu and click About Microsoft Word to display the specific version number and other licensing information, including the product ID. This help screen also contains two very useful command buttons, System Information and Technical Support. The first button displays information about the hardware installed on your system, including the amount of memory and available space on the hard drive. The Technical Support button describes various ways to obtain technical assistance.

Step 8: **Close the Document**

- ➤ Pull down the **File menu**. Click **Close** to close this document but remain in Word. (If you don't see the Close command, click the **double arrow** at the bottom of the menu.) Click **Yes** if prompted to save the document.
- ➤ Pull down the **File menu** a second time. Click **Exit** to close Word if you do not want to continue with the next exercise at this time.

We trust that you completed the hands-on exercise without difficulty, and that you were able to create, save, and print the document in the exercise. There is, however, considerable flexibility in the way you do the exercise in that you can display different toolbars and menus, and/or execute commands in a variety of ways. This section describes various ways in which you can customize Microsoft Word, and in so doing, will help you to troubleshoot future exercises.

Figure 1.7 displays two different views of the same document. Your screen may not match either figure, and indeed, there is no requirement that it should. You should, however, be aware of different options so that you can develop preferences of your own. Consider:

- Figure 1.7a uses short menus (note the double arrow at the bottom of the menu to display additional commands) and a shared row for the Standard and Formatting toolbars. Figure 1.7b displays the full menu and displays the toolbars on separate rows. We prefer the latter settings, which are set through the Customize command in the Tools menu.
- Figure 1.7a shows the Office Assistant (but drags it out of the way), whereas Figure 1.7b hides it. We find the Assistant distracting, and display it only when necessary by pressing the F1 key. You can also use the appropriate option in the Help menu to hide or show the Assistant, and/or you can right click the Assistant to hide it.
- Figure 1.7a shows the document with the task pane open, whereas the task pane is closed in Figure 1.7b. The task pane serves a variety of functions as you will see throughout the text. These include opening a document, inserting clip art, creating a mail merge, or displaying the formatting properties of selected text.
- Figure 1.7a displays the document in the ***Normal view*** whereas Figure 1.7b uses the ***Print Layout view***. The Normal view is simpler, but the Print Layout view more closely resembles the printed page as it displays top and bottom margins, headers and footers, graphic elements in their exact position, a vertical ruler, and other elements not seen in the Normal view.
- Figure 1.7a displays the ¶ and other nonprinting symbols, whereas they are hidden in Figure 1.7b. We prefer the cleaner screen without the symbols, but on occasion display the symbols if there is a problem in formatting a document. The ***Show/Hide ¶ button*** toggles the symbols on or off.
- Figure 1.7b displays an additional toolbar, the Drawing toolbar, at the bottom of the screen. Microsoft Word has more than 20 toolbars that are suppressed or displayed through the Toolbars command in the View menu. Note, too, that you can change the position of any visible toolbar by dragging its move handle (the parallel lines) at the left of the toolbar.

THE MOUSE VERSUS THE KEYBOARD

Almost every command in Microsoft Office can be executed in different ways, using either the mouse or the keyboard. Most people start with the mouse and add keyboard shortcuts as they become more proficient. There is no right or wrong technique, just different techniques, and the one you choose depends entirely on personal preference in a specific situation. If, for example, your hands are already on the keyboard, it is faster to use the keyboard. Other times, your hand will be on the mouse and that will be the fastest way.

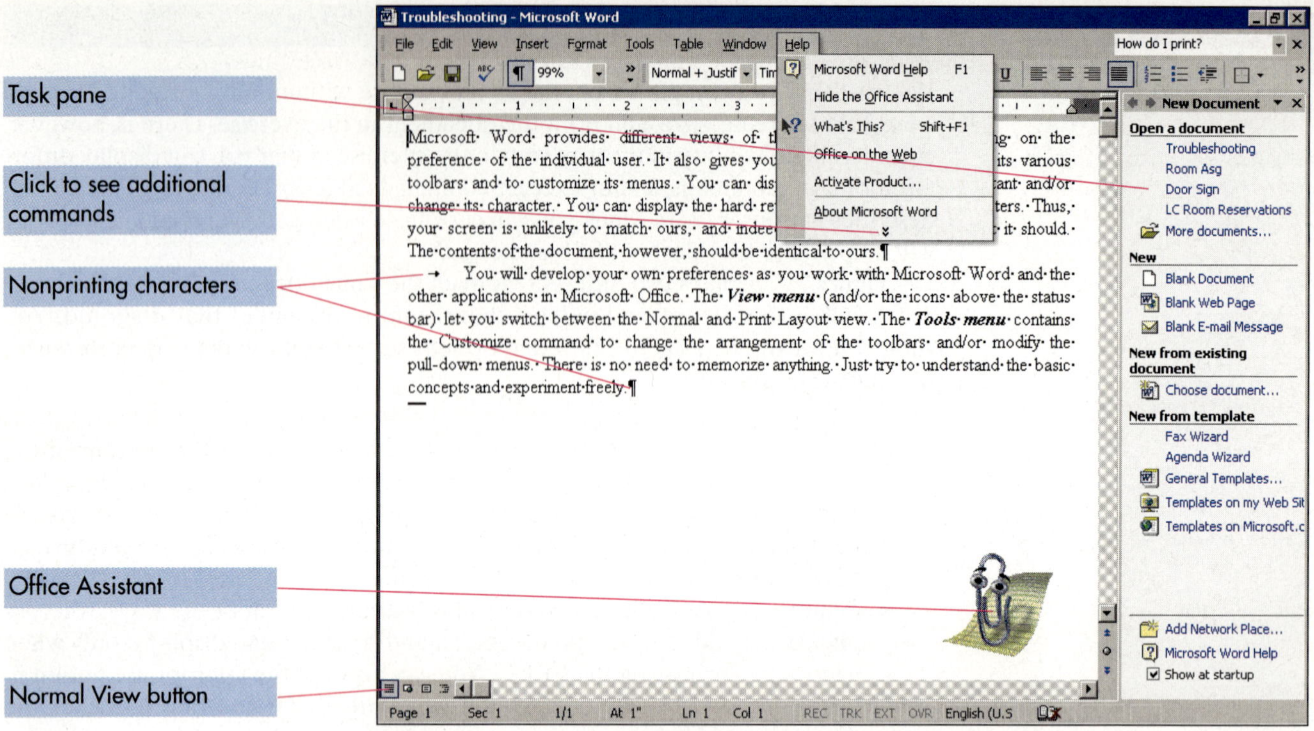

(a) Normal View

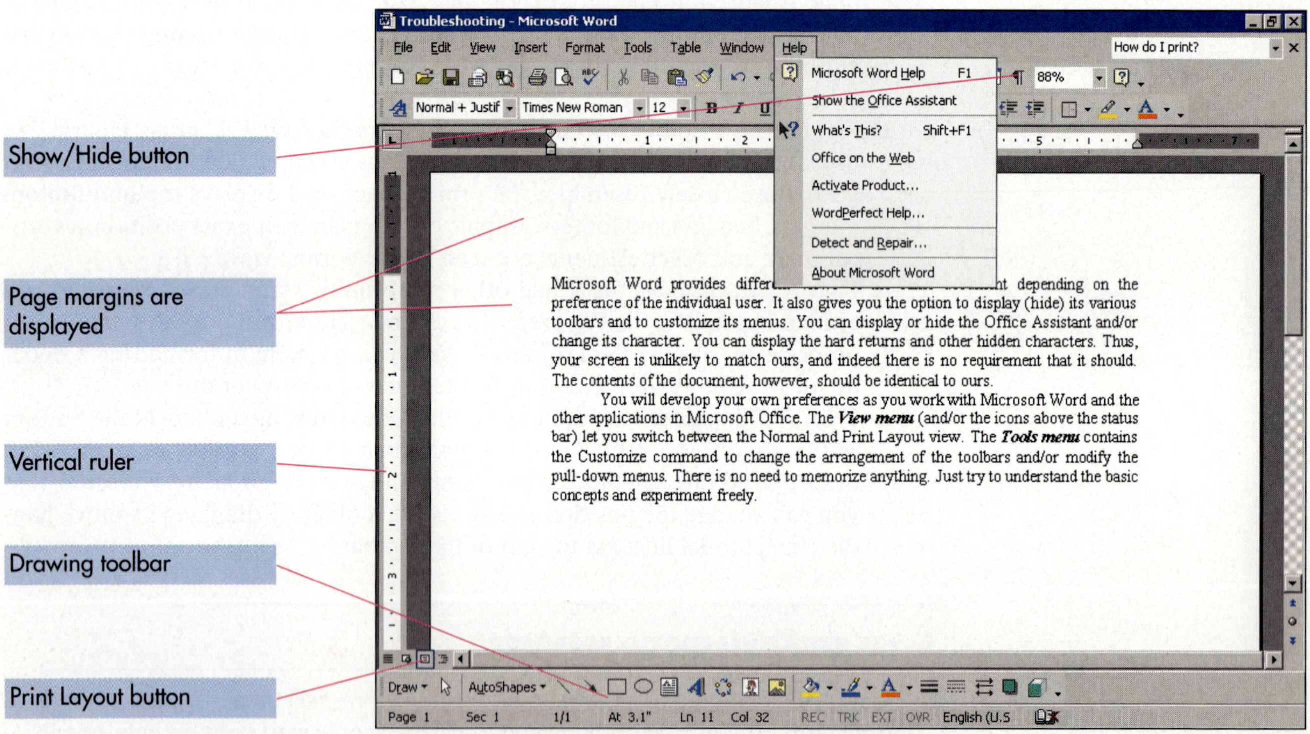

(b) Print Layout View

FIGURE 1.7 *Troubleshooting*

HANDS-ON EXERCISE 2

MODIFYING AN EXISTING DOCUMENT

Objective To open an existing document, revise it, and save the revision; to use the Undo, Redo, and Help commands. Use Figure 1.8 as a guide in doing the exercise.

Step 1: **Open an Existing Document**

- Start Word. Click and drag the Assistant out of the way if it appears. Close the task pane if it is open because we want you to practice locating a document within the Open dialog box.
- Pull down the **File menu** and click the **Open command** (or click the **Open button** on the Standard toolbar). You should see an Open dialog box similar to Figure 1.8a.
- If necessary, click the **drop-down arrow** on the Views button and change to the Details view. Click and drag the vertical border between columns to increase (decrease) the size of a column.
- Click the **drop-down arrow** on the Look in list box. Select (click) the drive that contains the Exploring Windows folder. Double click the folder to open it.
- Click the **down arrow** on the vertical scroll bar until you can select **My First Document** from the previous exercise.
- Double click the document (or click the **Open button** within the dialog box). Your document should appear on the screen.

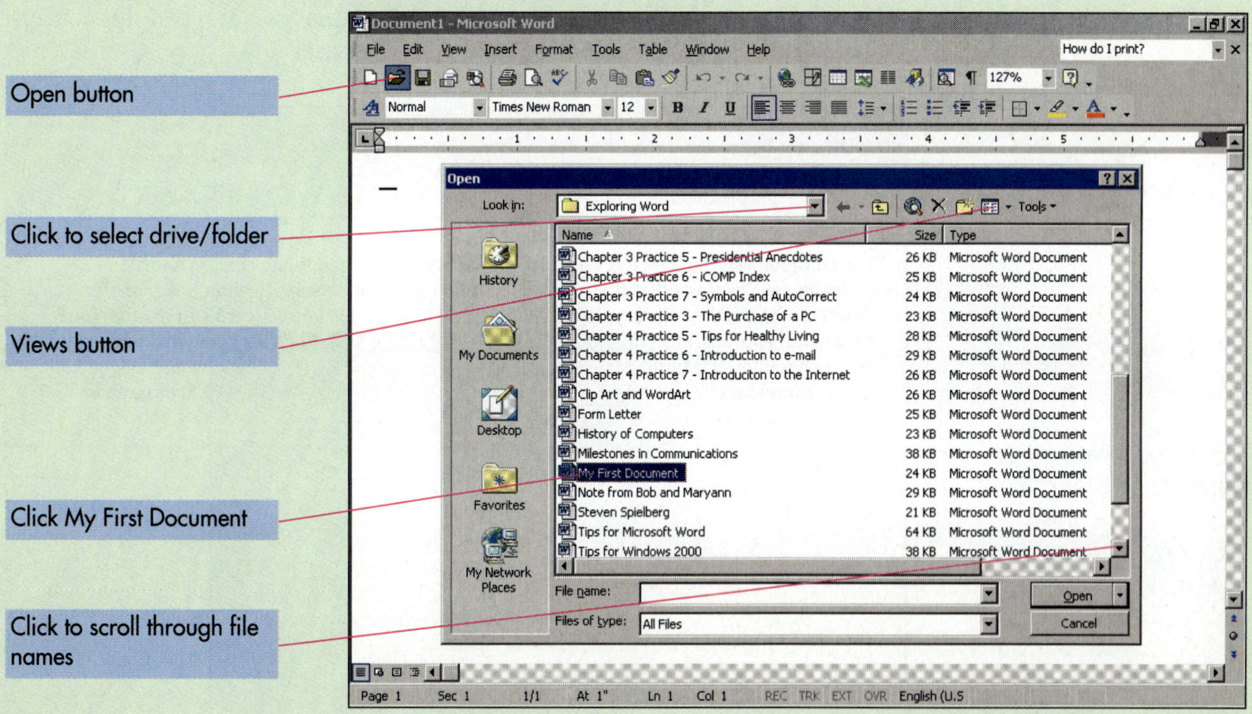

(a) Open an Existing Document (step 1)

FIGURE 1.8 *Hands-on Exercise 2*

Step 2: **Troubleshooting**

➤ Modify the settings within Word so that the document on your screen matches Figure 1.8b.

- To separate the Standard and Formatting toolbars, pull down the **Tools menu**, click **Customize**, click the **Options tab**, then check the box that indicates the Standard and Formatting toolbars should be displayed on two rows. Click the **Close button**.
- To display the complete menus, pull down the **Tools menu**, click **Customize**, click the **Options tab**, then check the box to always show full menus. Click the **Close Button**.
- To change to the Normal view, pull down the **View menu** and click **Normal** (or click the **Normal View button** at the bottom of the window).
- To change the amount of text that is visible on the screen, click the **drop-down arrow** on the **Zoom box** on the Standard toolbar and select **Page Width**.
- To display (hide) the ruler, pull down the **View menu** and toggle the **Ruler command** on or off. End with the ruler on. (If you don't see the Ruler command, click the **double arrow** at the bottom of the menu, or use the **Options command** in the Tools menu to display the complete menus.)
- To show or hide the Office Assistant, pull down the **Help menu** and click the appropriate command.
- Pull down the **View menu** and click the **Toolbars command** to display or hide additional toolbars.

➤ Click the **Show/Hide ¶ button** to display or hide the hard returns as you see fit. The button functions as a toggle switch.

➤ There may still be subtle differences between your screen and ours, depending on the resolution of your monitor. These variations, if any, need not concern you as long as you are able to complete the exercise.

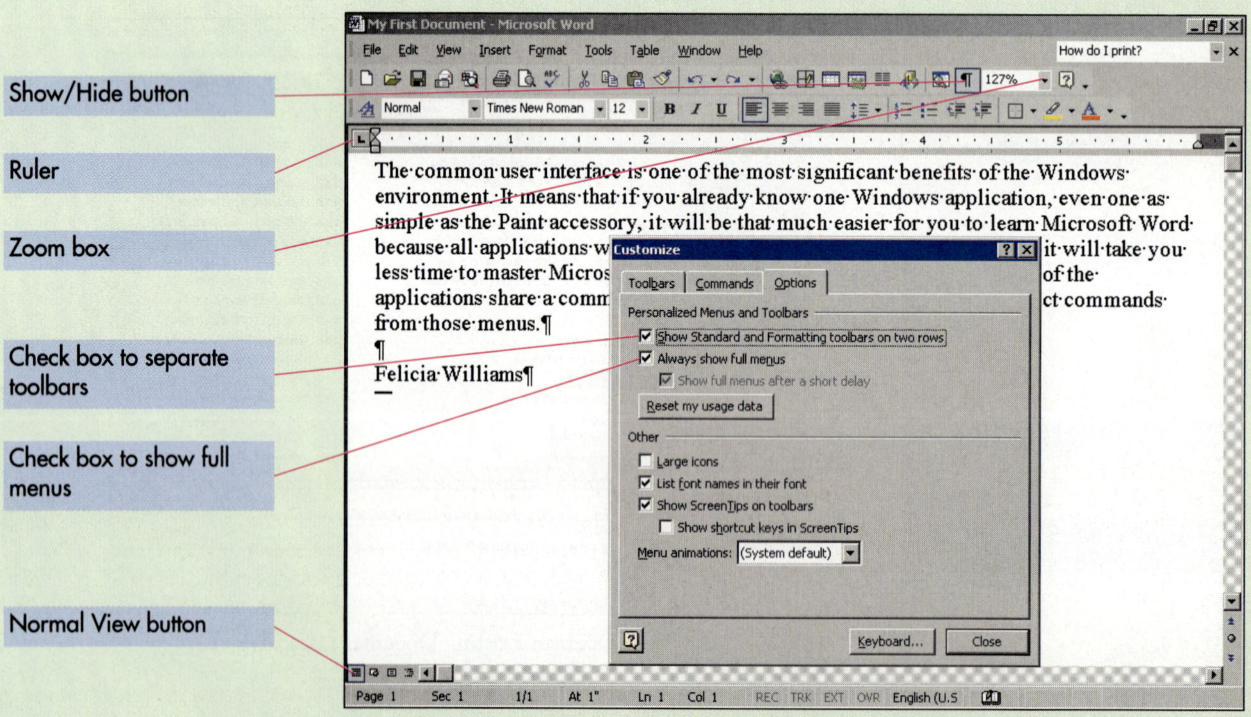

(b) Troubleshooting (step 2)

FIGURE 1.8 *Hands-on Exercise 2 (continued)*

Step 3: **Modify the Document**

- Press **Ctrl+End** to move to the end of the document. Press the **up arrow key** once or twice until the insertion point is on a blank line above your name. If necessary, press the **enter key** once (or twice) to add additional blank line(s).
- Add the sentence, **Success, I can save and retrieve a document!**, as shown in Figure 1.8c.
- Make the following additional modifications to practice editing:
  - Change the phrase *most significant* to **very best**.
  - Change *Paint accessory* to **game of Solitaire**.
  - Change the word *select* to **choose**.
- Use the **Ins key** to switch between insert and overtype modes as necessary. (You can also double click the **OVR indicator** on the status bar to toggle between the insert and overtype modes.)
- Pull down the **File menu** and click **Save**, or click the **Save button**.

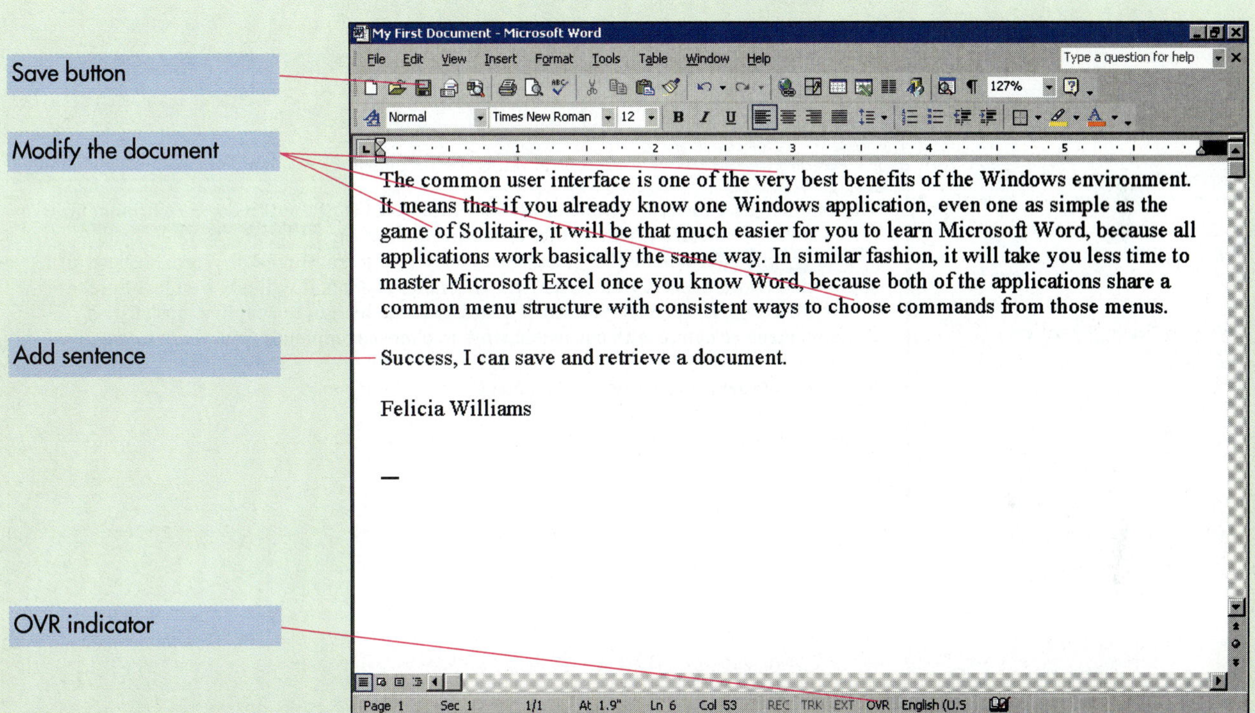

(c) Modify the Document (step 3)

FIGURE 1.8 *Hands-on Exercise 2 (continued)*

MOVING WITHIN A DOCUMENT

Press Ctrl+Home and Ctrl+End to move to the beginning and end of a document, respectively. You can also press the Home or End key to move to the beginning or end of a line. These shortcuts work not just in Word, but in any other Office application, and are worth remembering as they allow your hands to remain on the keyboard as you type.

Step 4: Deleting Text

- Press and hold the left mouse button as you drag the mouse over the phrase, **even one as simple as the game of Solitaire**, as shown in Figure 1.8d.
- Press the **Del** key to delete the selected text from the document. Pull down the **Edit menu** and click the **Undo command** (or click the **Undo button** on the Standard toolbar) to reverse (undo) the last command. The deleted text should be returned to your document.
- Pull down the **Edit menu** a second time and click the **Redo command** (or click the **Redo button**) to repeat the Delete command.
- Try this simple experiment. Click the **Undo button** repeatedly to undo the commands one at a time, until you have effectively canceled the entire session. Now click the **Redo command** repeatedly, one command at a time, until you have put the entire document back together.
- Click the **Save button** on the Standard toolbar to save the revised document a final time.

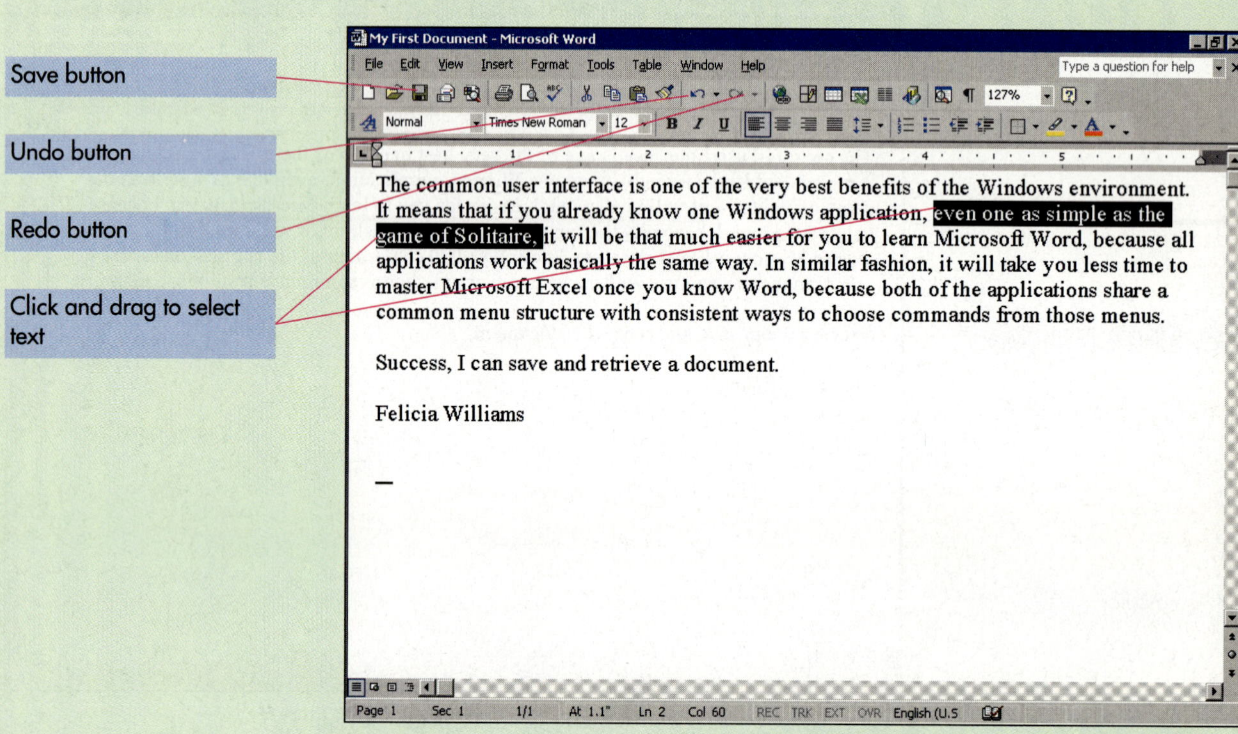

(d) Deleting Text (step 4)

FIGURE 1.8 *Hands-on Exercise 2 (continued)*

> **THE UNDO AND REDO COMMANDS**
>
> Click the drop-down arrow next to the Undo button to display a list of your previous actions, then click the action you want to undo, which also undoes all of the preceding commands. Undoing the fifth command in the list, for example, will also undo the preceding four commands. The Redo command works in reverse and cancels the last Undo command.

Step 5: **E-mail Your Document**

- You should check with your professor before attempting this step.
- Click the **E-mail button** on the Standard toolbar to display a screen similar to Figure 1.8e. The text of your document is entered automatically into the body of the e-mail message.
- Enter your professor's e-mail address in the To text box. The document title is automatically entered in the Subject line. Press the **Tab key** to move to the Introduction line. Type a short note above the inserted document to your professor, then click the **Send a Copy button** to mail the message.
- The e-mail window closes and you are back in Microsoft Word. The introductory text has been added to the document. Pull down the **File menu**. Click **Close** to close the document (there is no need to save the document).
- Pull down the **File menu**. Click **Exit** if you do not want to continue with the next exercise at this time.

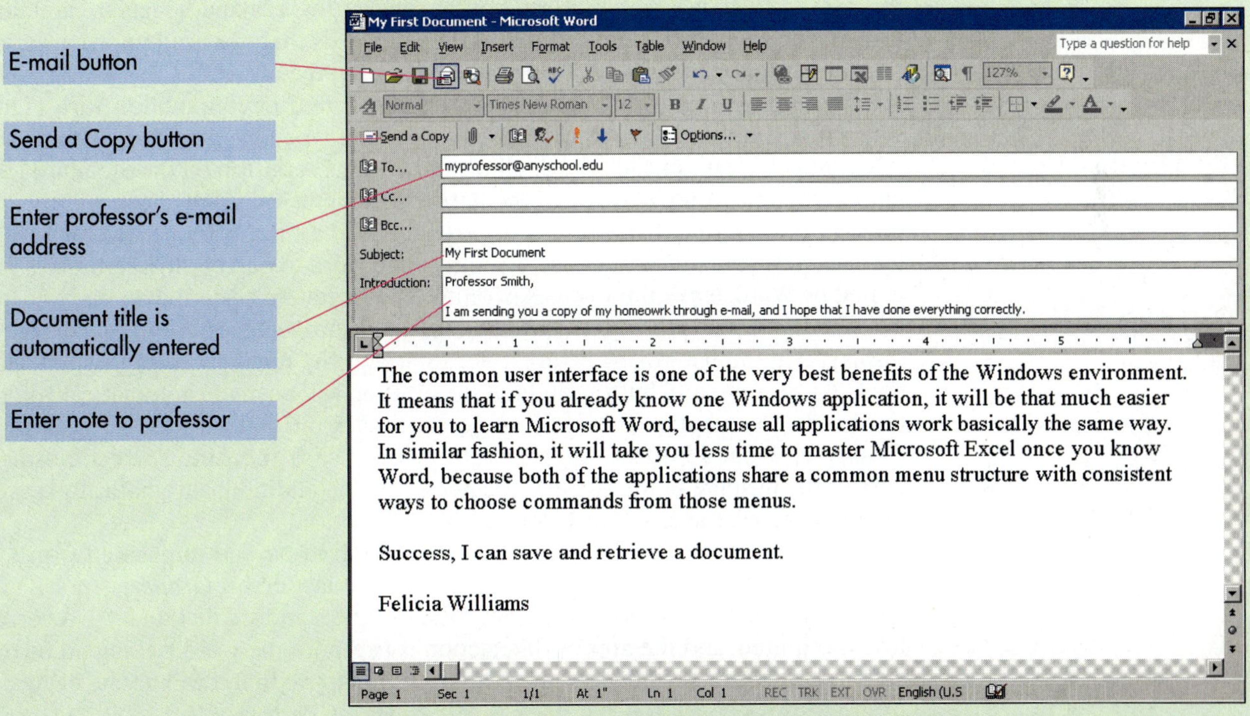

(e) E-mail Your Document (step 5)

FIGURE 1.8 *Hands-on Exercise 2 (continued)*

DOCUMENT PROPERTIES

Prove to your instructor how hard you've worked by printing various statistics about your document, including the number of revisions and the total editing time. Pull down the File menu, click the Print command to display the Print dialog box, click the drop-down arrow in the Print What list box, select Document properties, then click OK. You can view the information (without printing) by pulling down the File menu, clicking the Properties command, then selecting the Statistics tab.

There is simply no excuse to misspell a word, since the ***spell check*** is an integral part of Microsoft Word. (The spell check is also available for every other application in the Microsoft Office.) Spelling errors make your work look sloppy and discourage the reader before he or she has read what you had to say. They can cost you a job, a grade, a lucrative contract, or an award you deserve.

The spell check can be set to automatically check a document as text is entered, or it can be called explicitly by clicking the Spelling and Grammar button on the Standard toolbar. The spell check compares each word in a document to the entries in a built-in dictionary, then flags any word that is in the document, but not in the built-in dictionary, as an error.

The dictionary included with Microsoft Office is limited to standard English and does not include many proper names, acronyms, abbreviations, or specialized terms, and hence, the use of any such item is considered a misspelling. You can, however, add such words to a ***custom dictionary*** so that they will not be flagged in the future. The spell check will inform you of repeated words and irregular capitalization. It cannot, however, flag properly spelled words that are used improperly, and thus cannot tell you that *Two be or knot to be* is not the answer.

The capabilities of the spell check are illustrated in conjunction with Figure 1.9a. Microsoft Word will indicate the errors as you type by underlining them in red. Alternatively, you can click the Spelling and Grammar button on the Standard toolbar at any time to move through the entire document. The spell check will then go through the document and return the errors one at a time, offering several options for each mistake. You can change the misspelled word to one of the alternatives suggested by Word, leave the word as is, or add the word to a custom dictionary.

The first error is the word *embarassing,* with Word's suggestion(s) for correction displayed in the list box in Figure 1.9b. To accept the highlighted suggestion, click the Change command button, and the substitution will be made automatically in the document. To accept an alternative suggestion, click the desired word, then click the Change command button. Alternatively, you can click the AutoCorrect button to correct the mistake in the current document, and, in addition, automatically correct the same mistake in any future document.

The spell check detects both irregular capitalization and duplicated words, as shown in Figures 1.9c and 1.9d, respectively. The last error, *Grauer*, is not a misspelling per se, but a proper noun not found in the standard dictionary. No correction is required, and the appropriate action is to ignore the word (taking no further action)—or better yet, add it to the custom dictionary so that it will not be flagged in future sessions.

A spell check will catch embarassing mistakes, iRregular capitalization, and duplicate words words. It will also flag proper nouns, for example Robert Grauer, but you can add these terms to a custom dictionary. It will not notice properly spelled words that are used incorrectly; for example, too bee or knot to be is not the answer.

(a) The Text

FIGURE 1.9 *The Spell Check*

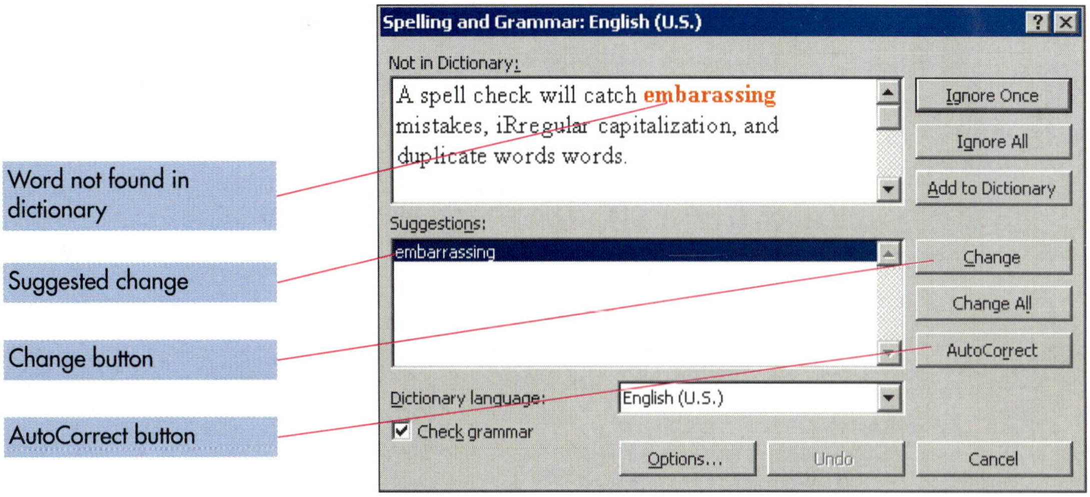

(b) Ordinary Misspelling

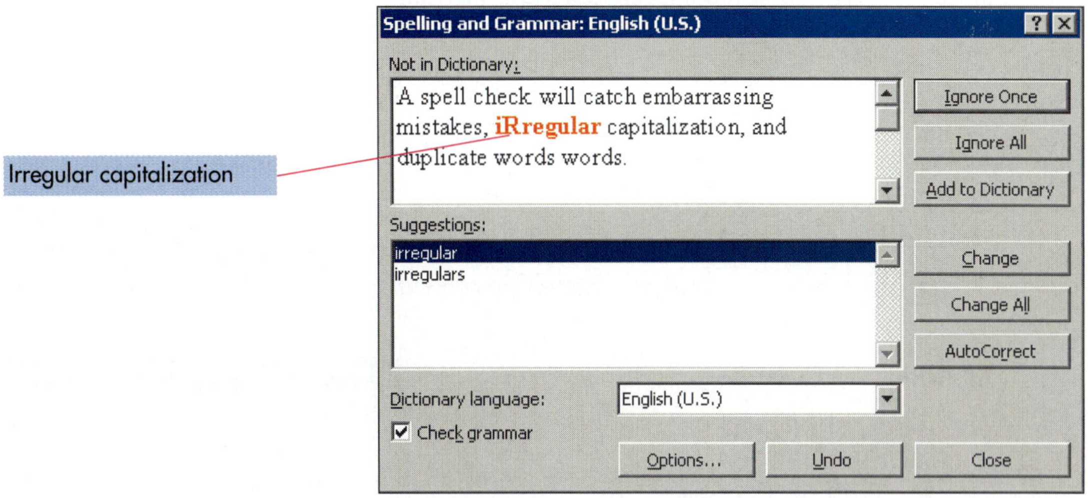

(c) Irregular Capitalization

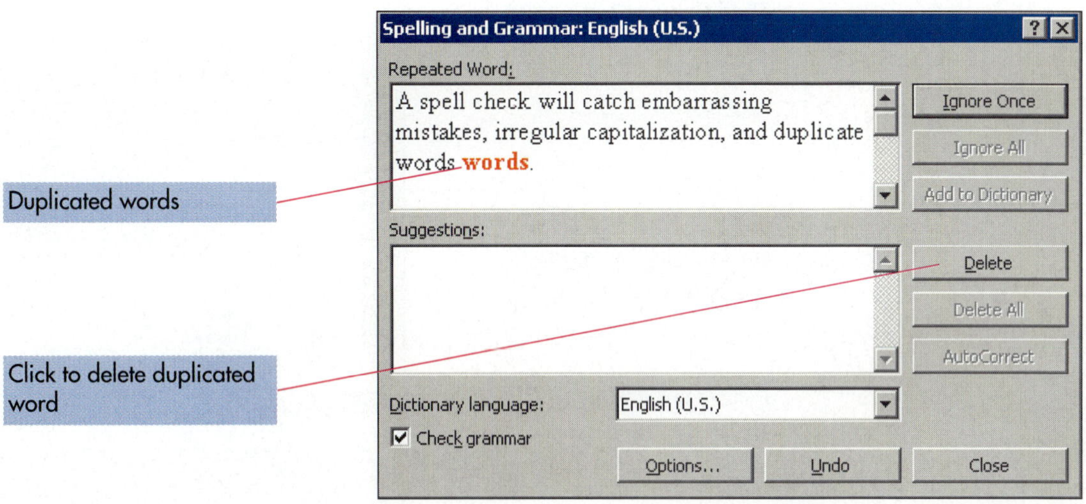

(d) Duplicated Word

FIGURE 1.9 *The Spell Check (continued)*

AutoCorrect and AutoText

The ***AutoCorrect*** feature corrects mistakes as they are made without any effort on your part. It makes you a better typist. If, for example, you typed *teh* instead of *the,* Word would change the spelling without even telling you. Word will also change *adn* to *and, i* to *I,* and occurence to occur*r*ence. All of this is accomplished through a predefined table of common mistakes that Word uses to make substitutions whenever it encounters an entry in the table. You can add additional items to the table to include the frequent errors you make. You can also use the feature to define your own shorthand—for example, cis for Computer Information Systems as shown in Figure 1.10a.

The AutoCorrect feature will also correct mistakes in capitalization; for example, it will capitalize the first letter in a sentence, recognize that MIami should be Miami, and capitalize the days of the week. It's even smart enough to correct the accidental use of the Caps Lock key, and it will toggle the key off!

The ***AutoText*** feature is similar in concept to AutoCorrect in that both substitute a predefined item for a specific character string. The difference is that the substitution occurs automatically with the AutoCorrect entry, whereas you have to take deliberate action for the AutoText substitution to take place. AutoText entries can also include significantly more text, formatting, and even clip art.

Microsoft Word includes a host of predefined AutoText entries. And as with the AutoCorrect feature, you can define additional entries of your own. (You may, however, not be able to do this in a computer lab environment.) The entry in Figure 1.10b is named "signature" and once created, it is available to all Word documents. To insert an AutoText entry into a new document, just type the first several letters in the AutoText name (signature in our example), then press the enter key when Word displays a ScreenTip containing the text of the entry.

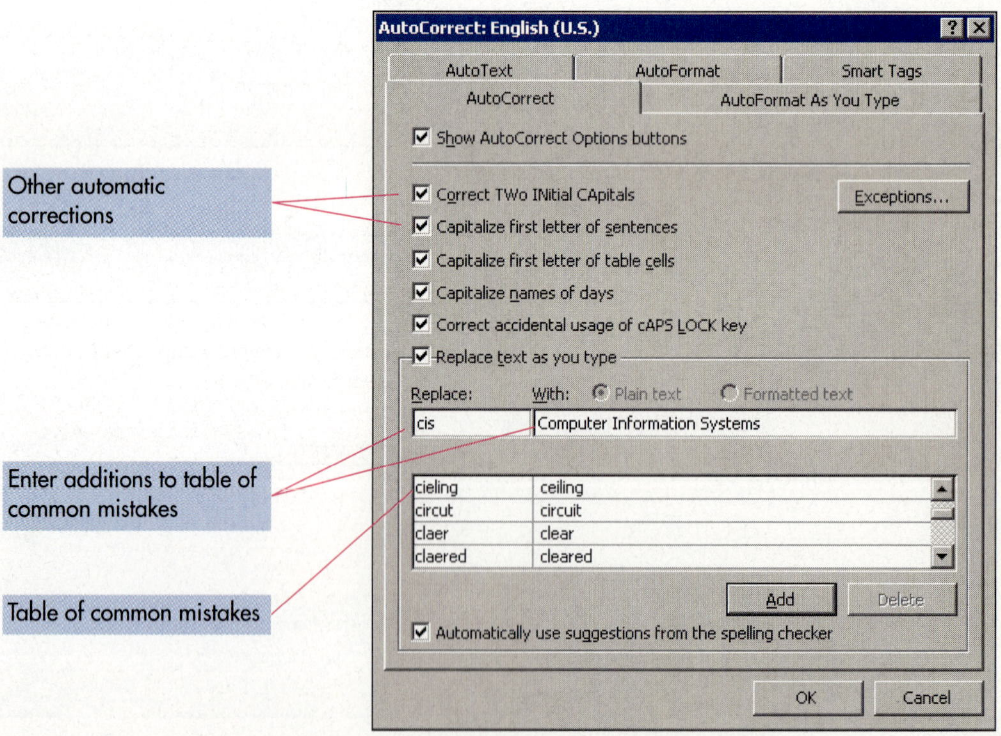

(a) AutoCorrect

FIGURE 1.10 *AutoCorrect and AutoText*

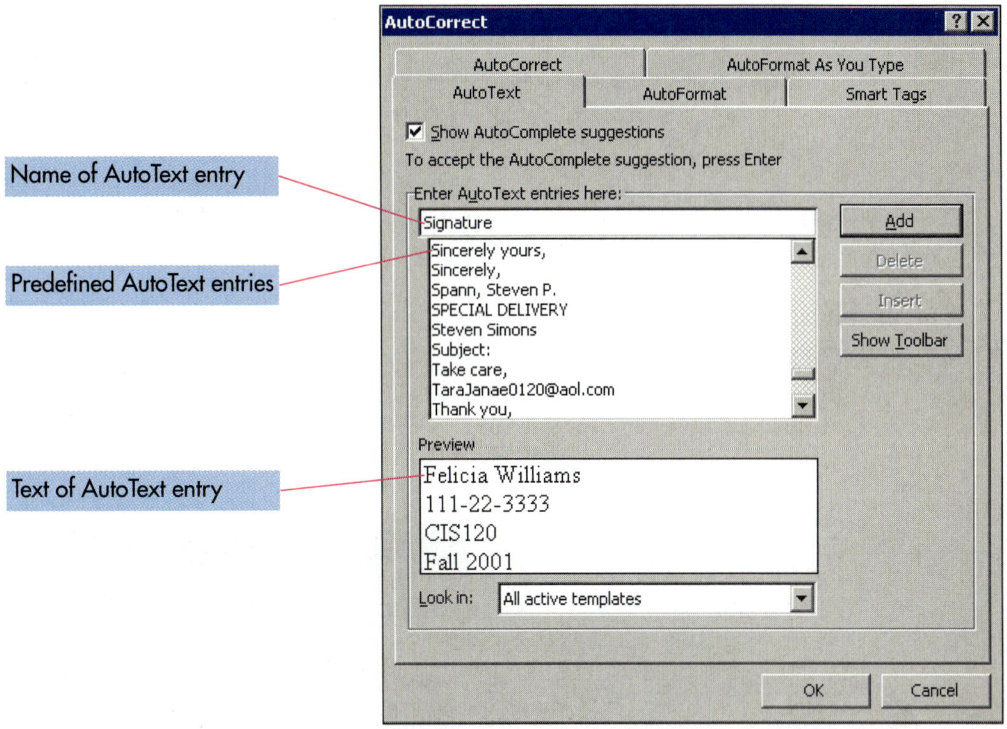

(b) AutoText

FIGURE 1.10 *AutoCorrect and AutoText (continued)*

THESAURUS

The ***thesaurus*** helps you to avoid repetition and polish your writing. The thesaurus is called from the Language command in the Tools menu. You position the cursor at the appropriate word within the document, then invoke the thesaurus and follow your instincts. The thesaurus recognizes multiple meanings and forms of a word (for example, adjective, noun, and verb) as in Figure 1.11a. Click a meaning, then double click a synonym to produce additional choices as in Figure 1.11b. You can explore further alternatives by selecting a synonym or antonym and clicking the Look Up button. We show antonyms in Figure 1.11c.

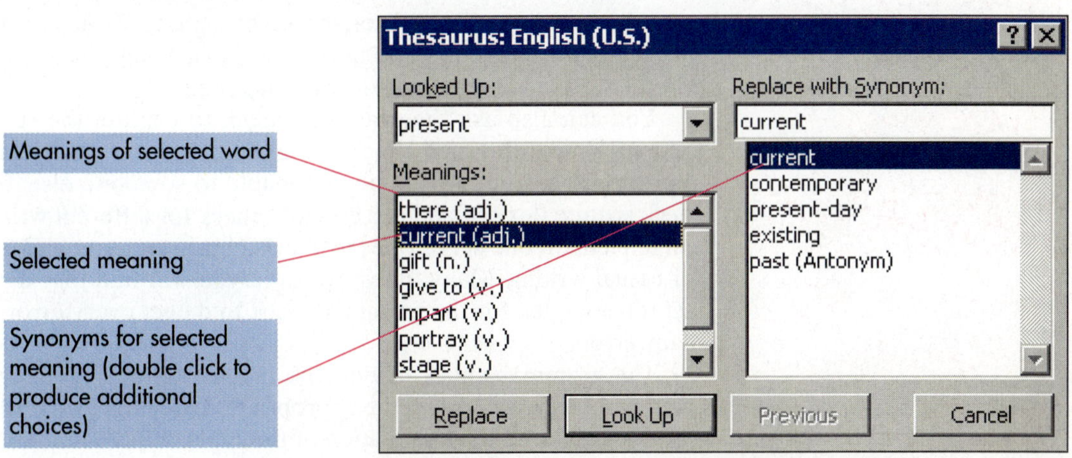

(a) Initial Word

FIGURE 1.11 *The Thesaurus*

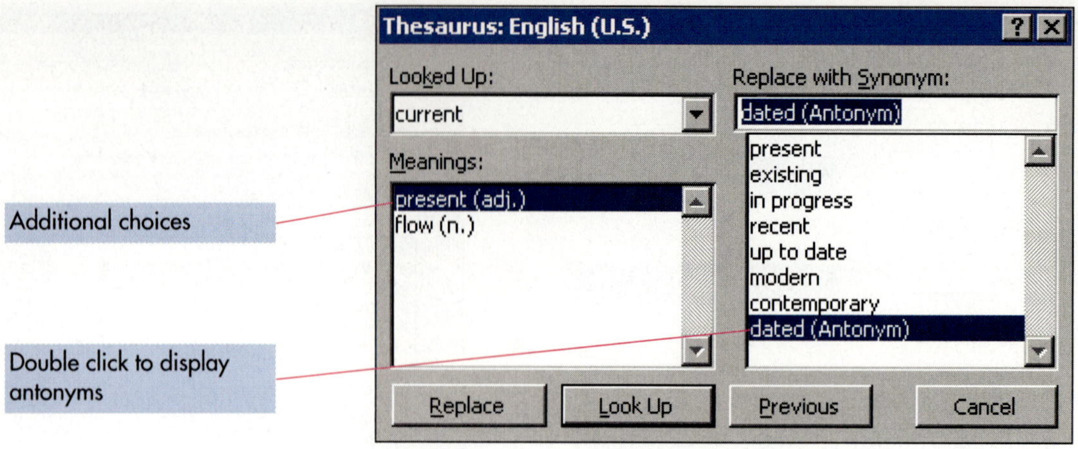

(b) Additional Choices

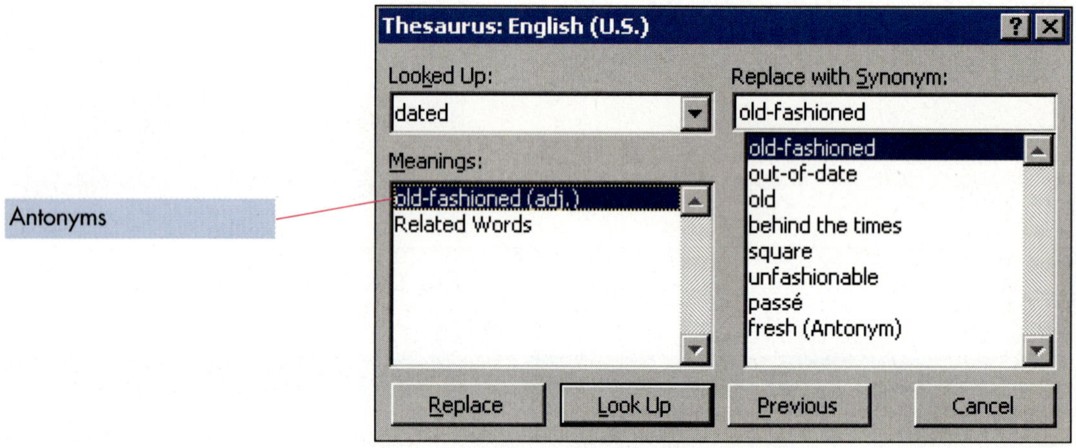

(c) Antonyms

FIGURE 1.11 *The Thesaurus (continued)*

GRAMMAR CHECK

The ***grammar check*** attempts to catch mistakes in punctuation, writing style, and word usage by comparing strings of text within a document to a series of predefined rules. As with the spell check, errors are brought to the screen, where you can accept the suggested correction and make the replacement automatically, or more often, edit the selected text and make your own changes.

You can also ask the grammar check to explain the rule it is attempting to enforce. Unlike the spell check, the grammar check is subjective, and what seems appropriate to you may be objectionable to someone else. Indeed, the grammar check is quite flexible, and can be set to check for different writing styles; that is, you can implement one set of rules to check a business letter and a different set of rules for casual writing. Many times, however, you will find that the English language is just too complex for the grammar check to detect every error, although it will find many errors.

The grammar check caught the inconsistency between subject and verb in Figure 1.12a and suggested the appropriate correction (am instead of are). In Figure 1.12b, it suggested the elimination of the superfluous comma. These examples show the grammar check at its best, but it is often more subjective and less capable. It missed the error "no perfect" in Figure 1.12c (although it did catch "to" instead of "too"). Suffice it to say, that there is no substitute for carefully proofreading every document.

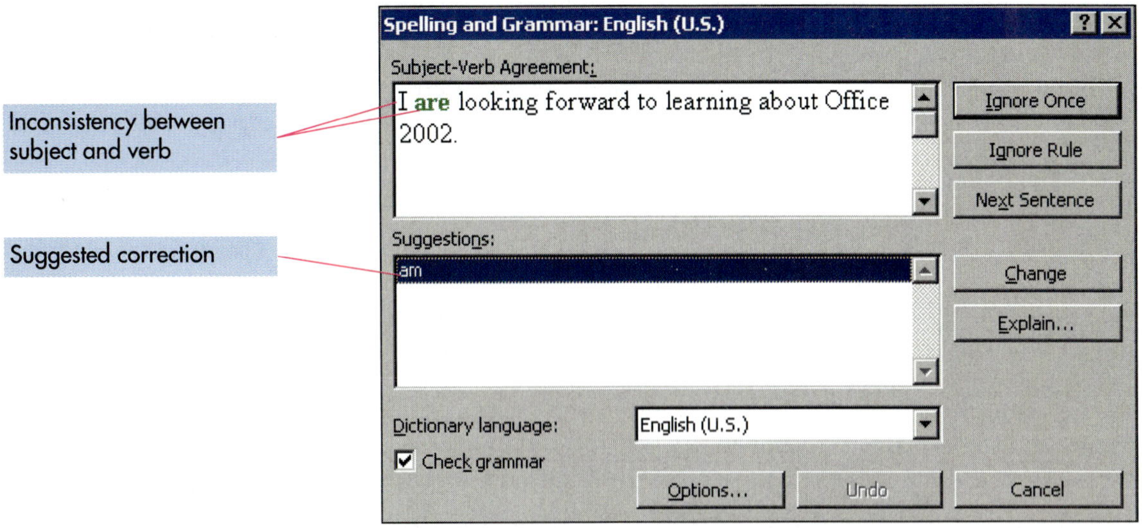

(a) Inconsistent Verb

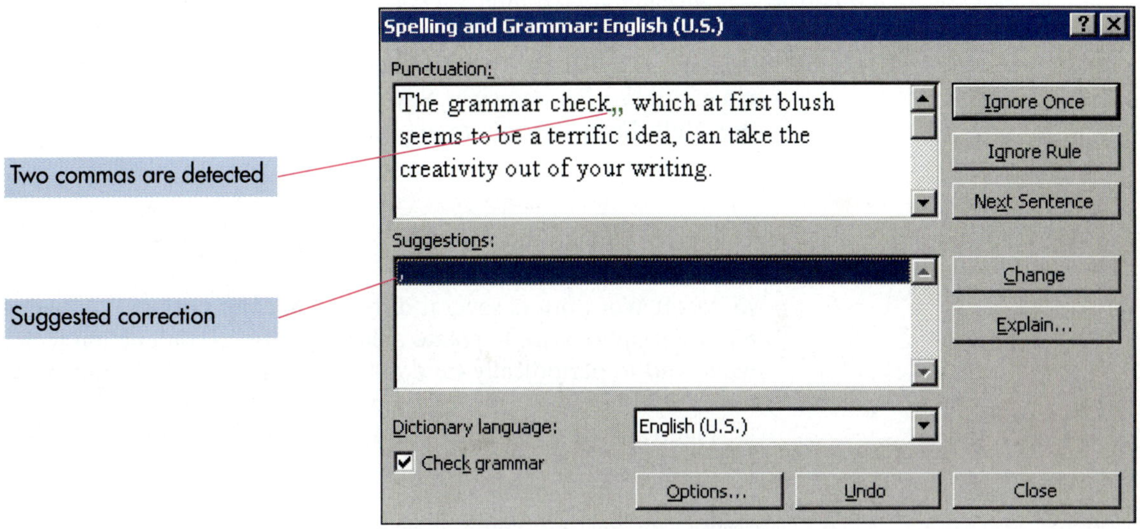

(b) Doubled Punctuation

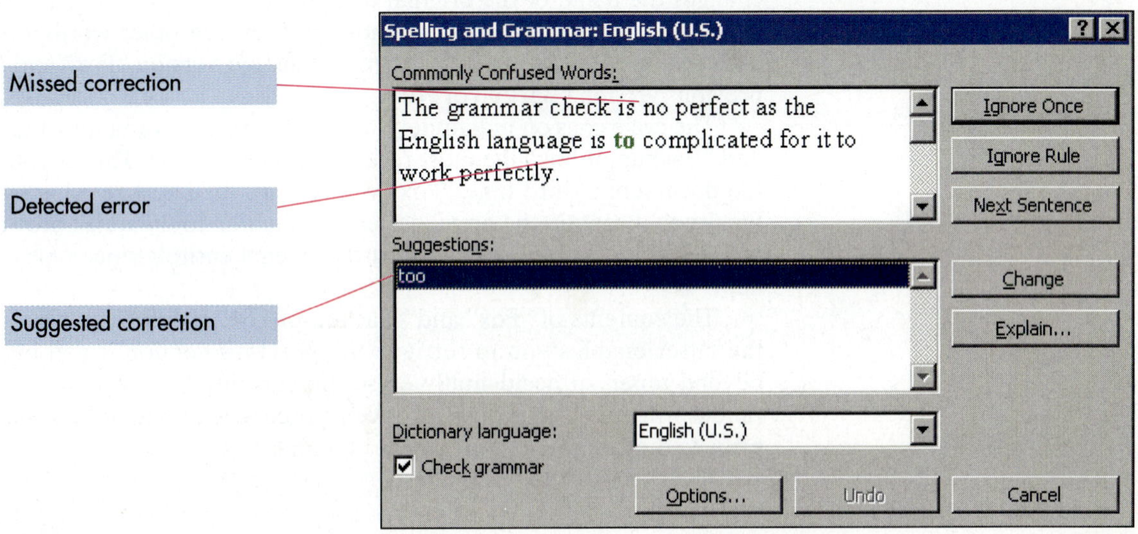

(c) Limitations

FIGURE 1.12 *The Grammar Check*

The Save command was used in the first two exercises. The Save As command will be introduced in the next exercise as a very useful alternative. We also introduce you to different backup options. We believe that now, when you are first starting to learn about word processing, is the time to develop good working habits.

You already know that the Save command copies the document currently being edited (the document in memory) to disk. The initial execution of the command requires you to assign a file name and to specify the drive and folder in which the file is to be stored. All subsequent executions of the Save command save the document under the original name, replacing the previously saved version with the new one.

The ***Save As command*** saves another copy of a document under a different name (and/or a different file type), and is useful when you want to retain a copy of the original document. The Save As command provides you with two copies of a document. The original document is kept on disk under its original name. A copy of the document is saved on disk under a new name and remains in memory. All subsequent editing is done on the new document.

We cannot overemphasize the importance of periodically saving a document, so that if something does go wrong, you won't lose all of your work. Nothing is more frustrating than to lose two hours of effort, due to an unexpected program crash or to a temporary loss of power. Save your work frequently, at least once every 15 minutes. Pull down the File menu and click Save, or click the Save button on the Standard toolbar. Do it!

Backup Options

Microsoft Word offers several different ***backup*** options. We believe the two most important options are to create a backup copy in conjunction with every save command, and to periodically (and automatically) save a document. Both options are implemented in step 3 in the next hands-on exercise.

Figure 1.13 illustrates the option to create a backup copy of the document every time a Save command is executed. Assume, for example, that you have created the simple document, *The fox jumped over the fence* and saved it under the name "Fox". Assume further that you edit the document to read, *The quick brown fox jumped over the fence,* and that you saved it a second time. The second save command changes the name of the original document from "Fox" to "Backup of Fox", then saves the current contents of memory as "Fox". In other words, the disk now contains two versions of the document: the current version "Fox" and the most recent previous version "Backup of Fox".

The cycle goes on indefinitely, with "Fox" always containing the current version, and "Backup of Fox" the most recent previous version. Thus if you revise and save the document a third time, "Fox" will contain the latest revision while "Backup of Fox" would contain the previous version alluding to the quick brown fox. The original (first) version of the document disappears entirely since only two versions are kept.

The contents of "Fox" and "Backup of Fox" are different, but the existence of the latter enables you to retrieve the previous version if you inadvertently edit beyond repair or accidentally erase the current "Fox" version. Should this occur (and it will), you can always retrieve its predecessor and at least salvage your work prior to the last save operation.

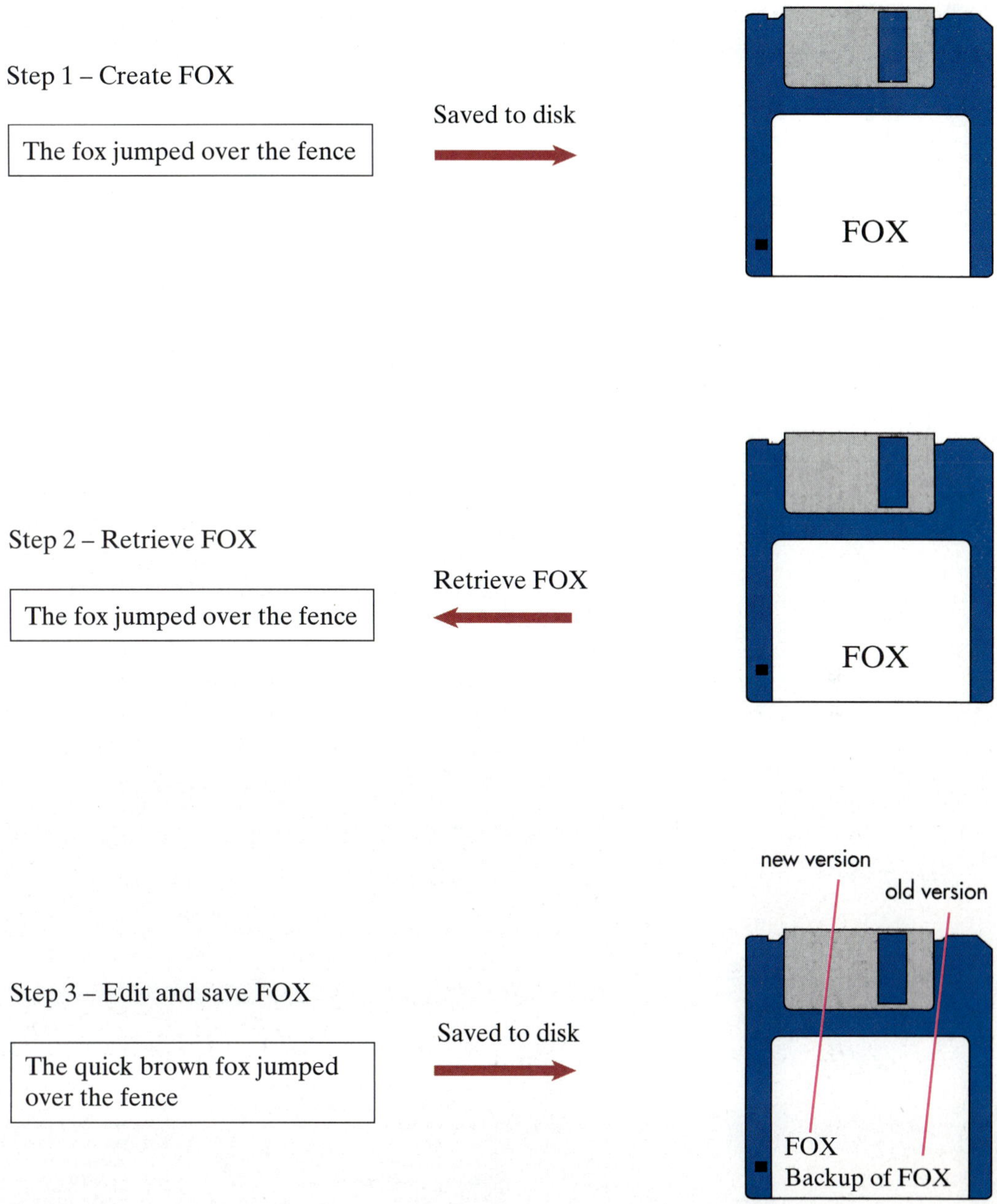

FIGURE 1.13 *Backup Procedures*

COMPARE AND MERGE DOCUMENTS

The Compare and Merge Documents command lets you compare the content of two documents to one another in order to see the differences between those documents. It is very useful if you have lost track of different versions of a document and/or if you are working with others. You can also use the command to see how well you did the hands-on exercises. The command highlights the differences in the documents and then it gives you the option to accept or reject changes. See exercise 7 at the end of the chapter.

HANDS-ON EXERCISE 3

THE SPELL CHECK, THESAURUS, AND GRAMMAR CHECK

Objective To open an existing document, check it for spelling, then use the Save As command to save the document under a different file name. Use Figure 1.14 as a guide in the exercise.

Step 1: **Preview a Document**

- Start Microsoft Word. Pull down the **Help menu**. Click the command to **Hide** the **Office Assistant**.
- If necessary, pull down the **View menu** and click the command to open the **Task pane**. Click the link to **More documents** in the task pane or pull down the **File menu** and click **Open** (or click the **Open button** on the Standard toolbar). You should see a dialog box similar to the one in Figure 1.14a.
- Select the appropriate drive, drive C or drive A, depending on the location of your data. Double click the **Exploring Word folder** to make it the active folder (the folder from which you will open the document).
- Scroll in the Name list box until you can select (click) the **Try the Spell Check** document. Click the **drop-down arrow** on the **Views button** and click **Preview** to preview the document as shown in Figure 1.14a.
- Click the **Open command button** to open the file. Your document should appear on the screen.

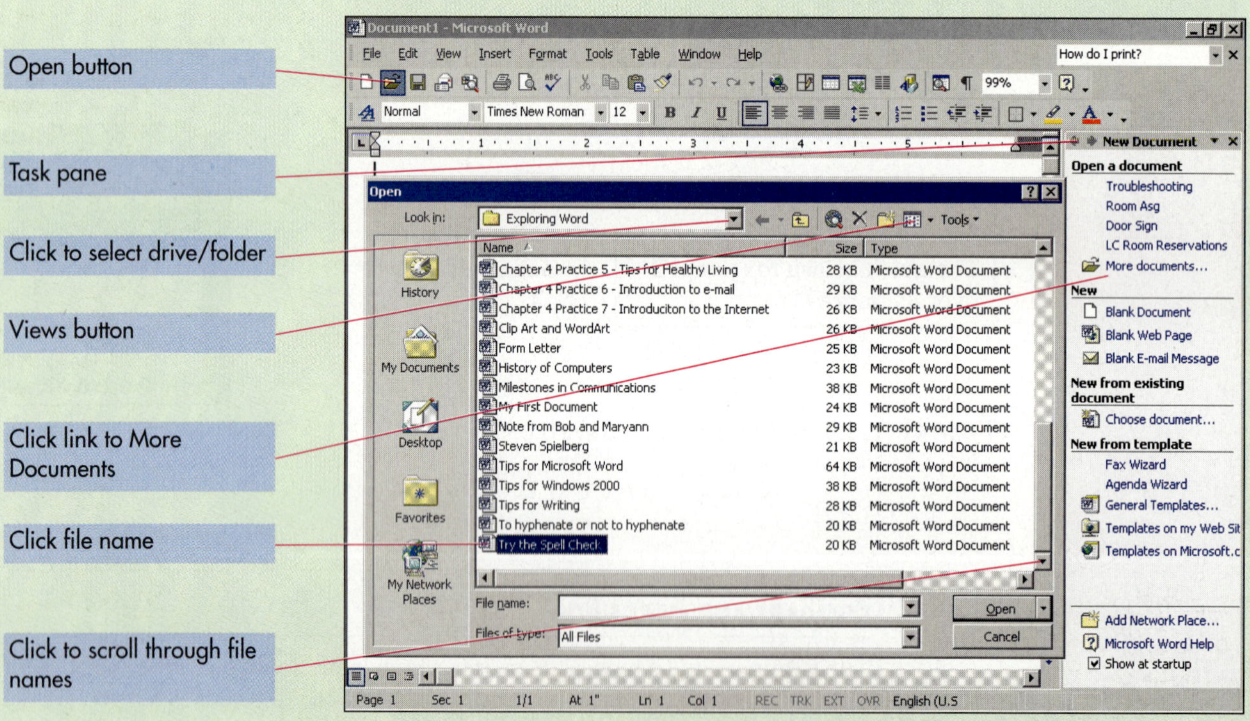

(a) Preview a Document (step 1)

FIGURE 1.14 *Hands-on Exercise 3*

Step 2: **The Save As Command**

- Pull down the **File menu**. Click **Save As** to produce the dialog box in Figure 1.14b.
- Enter **Modified Spell Check** as the name of the new document. (A file name may contain up to 255 characters, and blanks are permitted.) Click the **Save command button**.
- There are now two identical copies of the file on disk: Try the Spell Check, which we supplied, and Modified Spell Check, which you just created.
- The title bar shows the latter name (Modified Spell Check) as it is the document in memory. All subsequent changes will be made to this document.

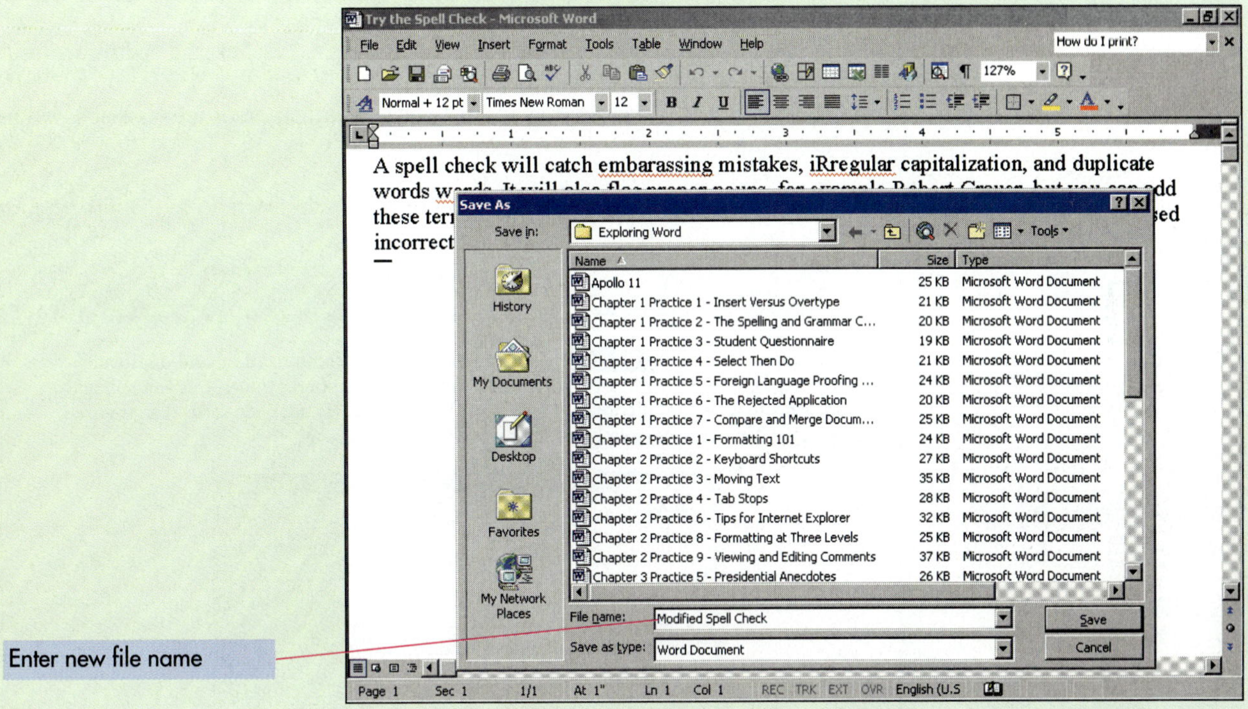

(b) The Save As Command (step 2)

FIGURE 1.14 *Hands-on Exercise 3 (continued)*

THE WORD COUNT TOOLBAR

How close are you to completing the 500-word paper that your professor assigned? Pull down the Tools menu and click the Word Count command to display a dialog box that shows the number of pages, words, paragraphs, and characters in your document. There is also a command button to display the Word Count toolbar so that it remains on the screen throughout the session. Click the Recount button on the toolbar at any time to see the current statistics for your document.

Step 3: The Spell Check

- If necessary, press **Ctrl+Home** to move to the beginning of the document. Click the **Spelling and Grammar button** on the Standard toolbar to check the document.
- "Embarassing" is flagged as the first misspelling as shown in Figure 1.14c. Click the **Change button** to accept the suggested spelling.
- "iRregular" is flagged as an example of irregular capitalization. Click the **Change button** to accept the suggested correction.
- Continue checking the document, which displays misspellings and other irregularities one at a time. Click the appropriate command button as each mistake is found.
  - Click the **Delete button** to remove the duplicated word.
  - Click the **Ignore Once button** to accept Grauer (or click the **Add button** to add Grauer to the custom dictionary).
- The last sentence is flagged because of a grammatical error and is discussed in the next step.

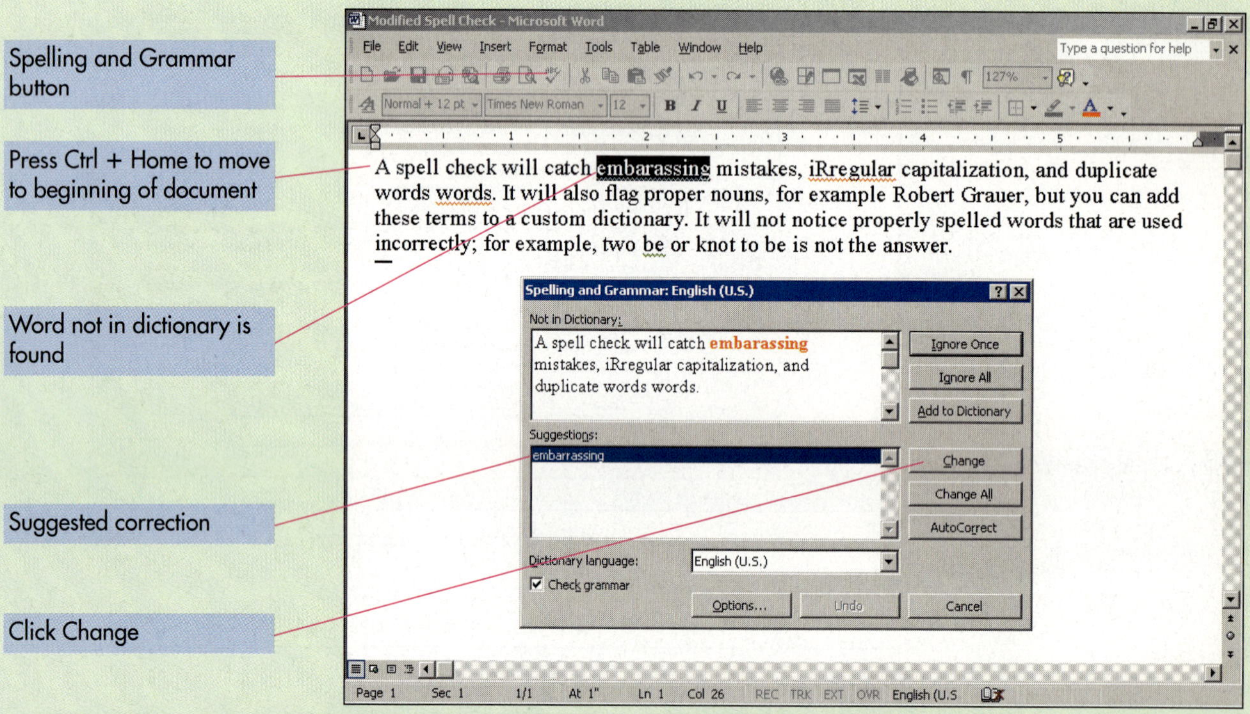

(c) The Spell Check (step 3)

FIGURE 1.14 *Hands-on Exercise 3 (continued)*

AUTOMATIC SPELLING AND GRAMMAR CHECKING

Red and green wavy lines may appear throughout a document to indicate spelling and grammatical errors, respectively. Point to any underlined word, then click the right mouse button to display a context-sensitive help menu with suggested corrections. To enable (disable) these options, pull down the Tools menu, click the Options command, click the Spelling and Grammar tab, and check (clear) the options to check spelling (or grammar) as you type.

Step 4: **The Grammar Check**

- The last phrase, "Two be or knot to be is not the answer", should be flagged as an error, as shown in Figure 1.14d. If this is not the case:
  - Pull down the **Tools menu**, click **Options**, then click the **Spelling and Grammar tab**.
  - Check the box to **Check Grammar with Spelling**, then click the button to **Recheck document**. Click **Yes** when told that the spelling and grammar check will be reset, then click **OK** to close the Options dialog box.
  - Press **Ctrl+Home** to return to the beginning of the document, then click the **Spelling and Grammar button** to recheck the document.
- The Grammar Check suggests substituting "are" for "be", which is not what you want. Click in the preview box and make the necessary corrections. Change "two" to "to" and "knot" to "not". Click **Change**.
- Click **OK** when you see the dialog box indicating that the spelling and grammar check is complete. Enter any additional grammatical changes manually. Save the document.

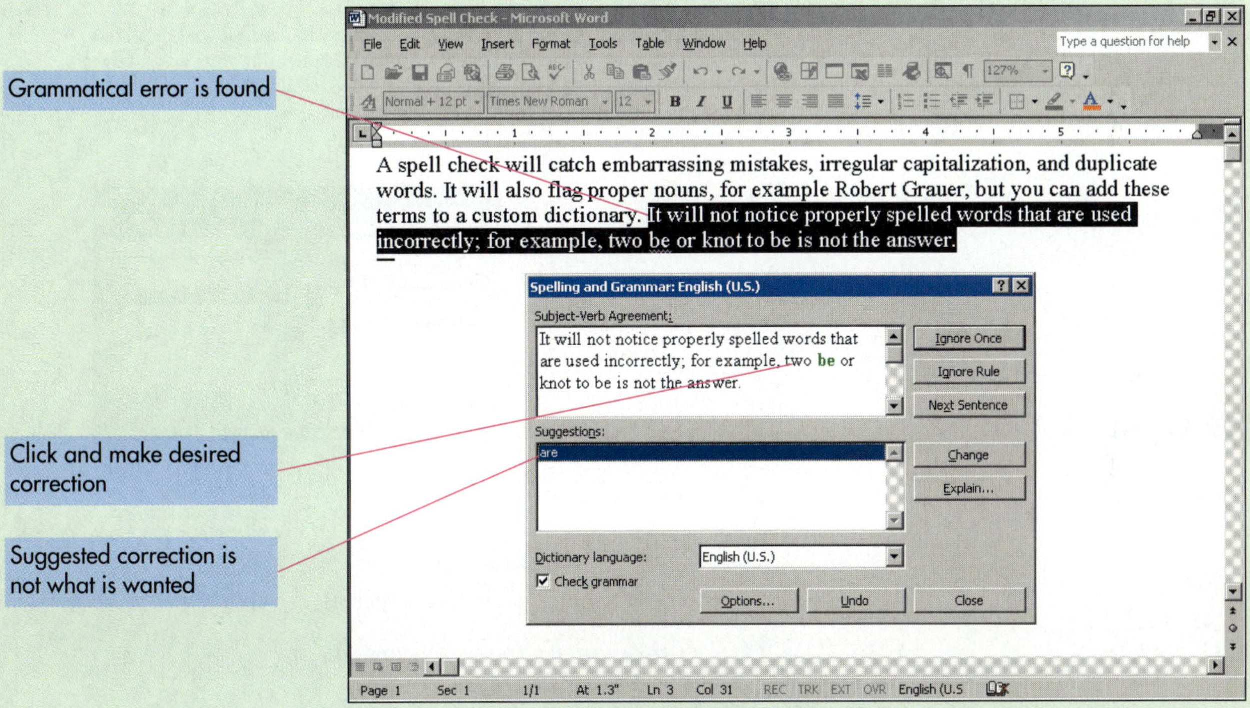

(d) The Grammar Check (step 4)

FIGURE 1.14 *Hands-on Exercise 3 (continued)*

CHECK SPELLING ONLY

The grammar check is invoked by default in conjunction with the spell check. You can, however, check the spelling of a document without checking its grammar. Pull down the Tools menu, click Options to display the Options dialog box, then click the Spelling and Grammar tab. Clear the box to check grammar with spelling, then click OK to accept the change and close the dialog box.

Step 5: The Thesaurus

- Select the word **flag**, which appears toward the beginning of your document.
- Pull down the **Tools menu**, click **Language**, then click **Thesaurus** to display the associated dialog box as shown in Figure 1.14e.
- Choose the proper form of the word; that is, you want to find synonyms for the word "flag" when it is used as a verb as opposed to its use as a noun.
- Select **identify** from the list of synonyms, then click the **Replace button** to make the change automatically.
- Right click the word **incorrectly** (which appears in the last sentence) to display a context-sensitive menu, click **synonyms**, then choose **inaccurately** to make the substitution into the document.
- Save the document.

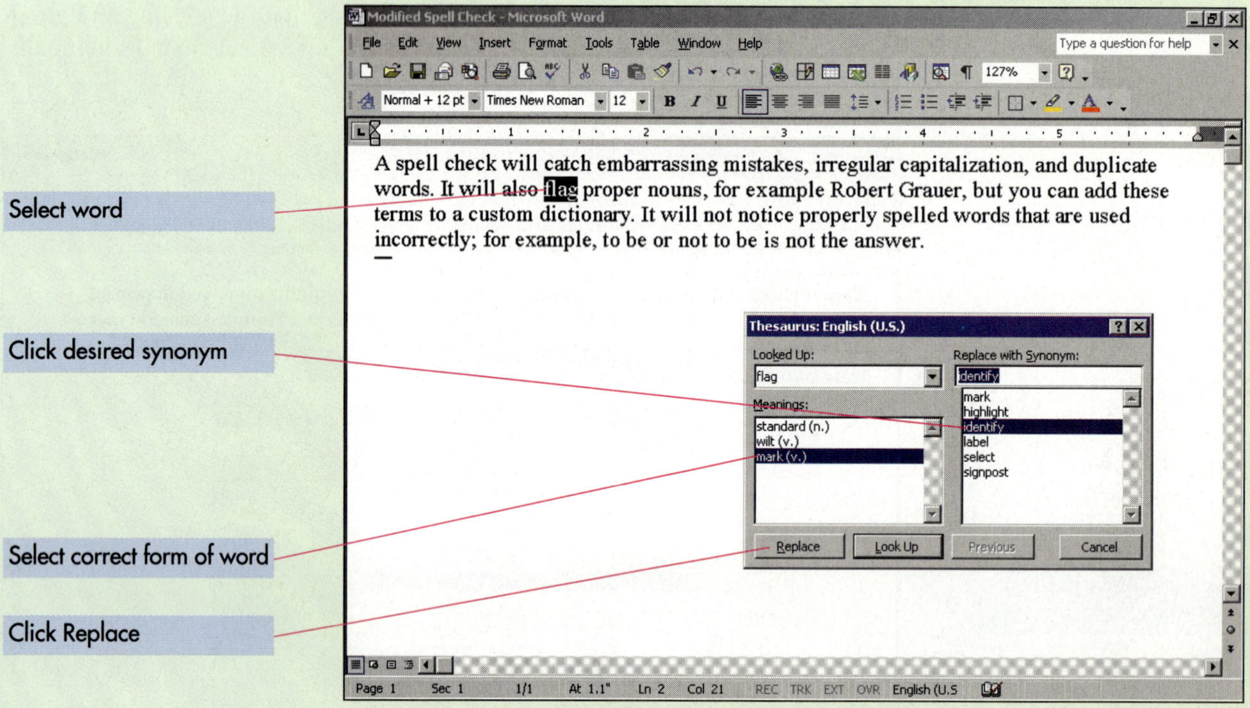

(e) The Thesaurus (step 5)

FIGURE 1.14 *Hands-on Exercise 3 (continued)*

> ### FOREIGN LANGUAGE PROOFING TOOLS
>
> The English version of Microsoft Word supports the spelling, grammar, and thesaurus features in more than 80 foreign languages. Support for Spanish and French is built in at no additional cost, whereas you will have to pay an additional fee for other languages. Just pull down the Tools menu and click the Select Language command to change to a different language. You can even check multiple languages within the same document. See practice exercise 5 at the end of the chapter.

Step 6: **AutoCorrect**

- Press **Ctrl+End** to move to the end of the document. Press the **enter key** twice.
- Type the *misspelled* phrase, **Teh AutoCorrect feature corrects common spelling mistakes**. Word will automatically change "Teh" to "The".
- Press the **Home key** to return to the beginning of the line, where you will notice a blue line, under the "T", indicating that an automatic correction has taken place. Point to the blue line, then click the **down arrow** to display the AutoCorrect options.
- Click the command to **Control AutoCorrect options**, which in turn displays the dialog box in Figure 1.14f. Click the **AutoCorrect tab**, then click the **down arrow** on the scroll bar to view the list of corrections. Close the dialog box.
- Add the sentence, **The feature also changes special symbols such as :) to ☺ to indicate I understand my work**. (You will have to use the AutoCorrect options to change the first ☺ back to the :) within the sentence.)

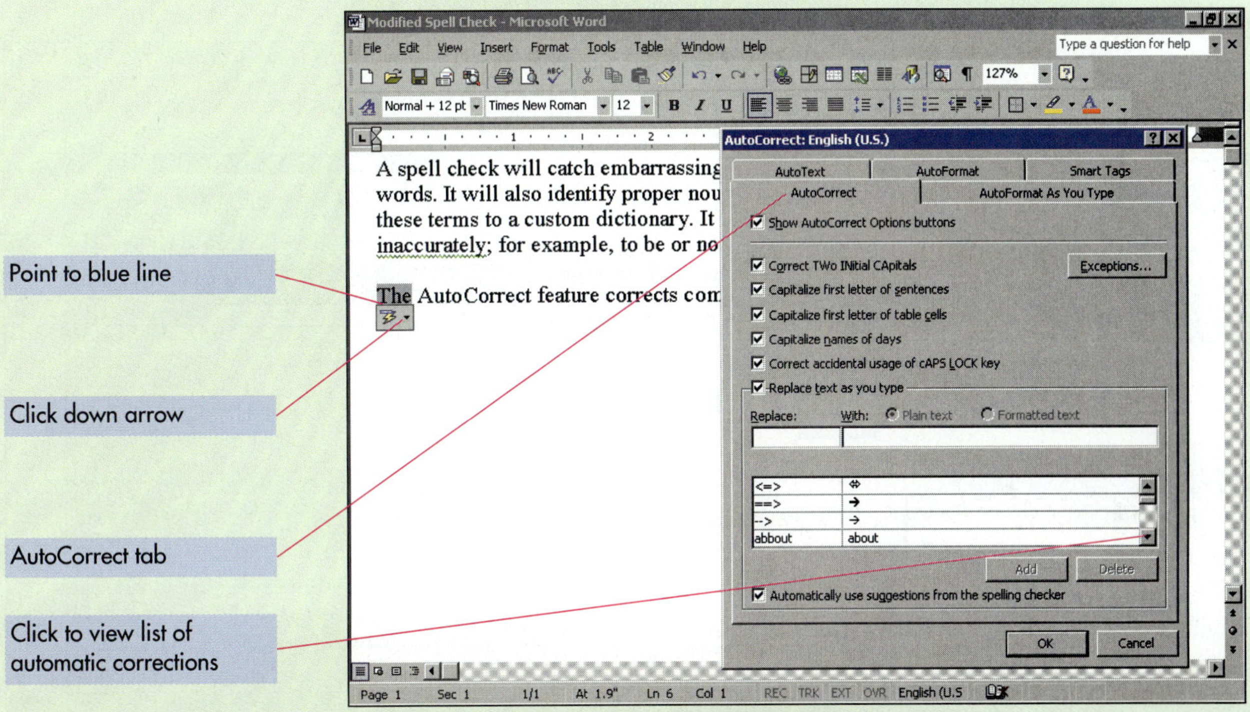

(f) AutoCorrect (step 6)

FIGURE 1.14 *Hands-on Exercise 3 (continued)*

> **CREATE YOUR OWN SHORTHAND**
>
> Use AutoCorrect to expand abbreviations such as "usa" for United States of America. Pull down the Tools menu, click AutoCorrect Options, type the abbreviation in the Replace text box and the expanded entry in the With text box. Click the Add command button, then click OK to exit the dialog box and return to the document. The next time you type usa in a document, it will automatically be expanded to United States of America.

Step 7: Create an AutoText Entry

- Press **Ctrl+End** to move to the end of the document. Press the **enter key** twice. Enter your name and class.
- Click and drag to select the information you just entered. Pull down the **Insert menu**, select the **AutoText command**, then select **AutoText** to display the AutoCorrect dialog box in Figure 1.14g.
- Your name (Felicia Williams in our example) is suggested automatically as the name of the AutoText entry. Click the **Add button**.
- To test the entry, you can delete your name and other information, then use the AutoText feature. Your name and other information should still be highlighted. Press the **Del key** to delete the information.
- Type the first few letters of your name and watch the screen as you do. You should see a ScreenTip containing your name and other information. Press the **enter key** or the **F3 key** when you see the ScreenTip.
- Save the document. Print the document for your instructor. Exit Word.

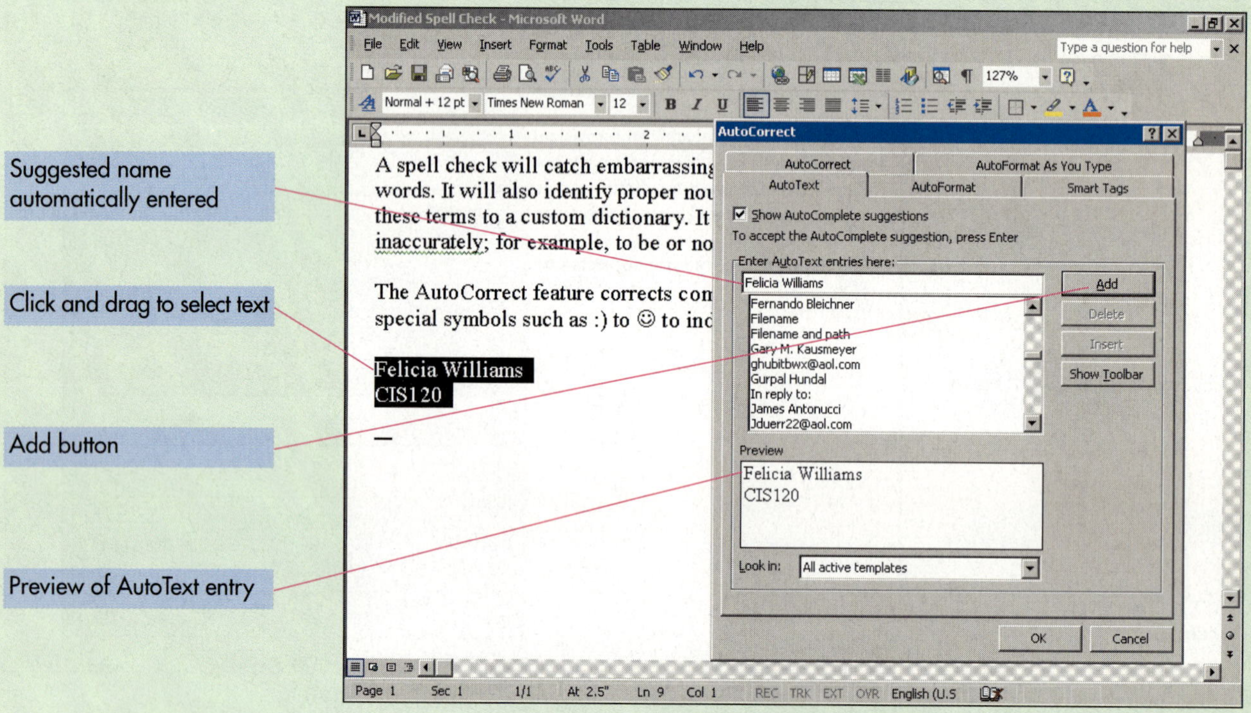

(g) Create an AutoText Entry (step 7)

FIGURE 1.14 *Hands-on Exercise 3 (continued)*

THE AUTOTEXT TOOLBAR

Point to any visible toolbar, click the right mouse button to display a context-sensitive menu, then click AutoText to display the AutoText toolbar. The AutoText toolbar groups the various AutoText entries into categories, making it easier to select the proper entry. Click the down arrow on the All Entries button to display the various categories, click a category, then select the entry you want to insert into the document.

SUMMARY

The chapter provided a broad-based introduction to word processing in general and to Microsoft Word in particular. Help is available from many sources. You can use the Help menu or the Office Assistant as you can in any Office application. You can also go to the Microsoft Web site to obtain more recent, and often more detailed, information.

Microsoft Word is always in one of two modes, insert or overtype; the choice between the two depends on the desired editing. The insertion point marks the place within a document where text is added or replaced.

The enter key is pressed at the end of a paragraph, but not at the end of a line because Word automatically wraps text from one line to the next. A hard return is created by the user when he or she presses the enter key; a soft return is created by Word as it wraps text and begins a new line.

The Save and Open commands work in conjunction with one another. The Save command copies the document in memory to disk under its existing name. The Open command retrieves a previously saved document. The Save As command saves the document under a different name and is useful when you want to retain a copy of the current document prior to all changes.

A spell check compares the words in a document to those in a standard and/or custom dictionary and offers suggestions to correct the mistakes it finds. It will detect misspellings, duplicated phrases, and/or irregular capitalization, but will not flag properly spelled words that are used incorrectly. Foreign-language proofing tools for French and Spanish are built into the English version of Microsoft Word 2002.

The AutoCorrect feature corrects predefined spelling errors and/or mistakes in capitalization, automatically, as the words are entered. The AutoText feature is similar in concept except that it can contain longer entries that include formatting and clip art. Either feature can be used to create a personal shorthand to expand abbreviations as they are typed.

The thesaurus suggests synonyms and/or antonyms. It can also recognize multiple forms of a word (noun, verb, and adjective) and offer suggestions for each. The grammar check searches for mistakes in punctuation, writing style, and word usage by comparing strings of text within a document to a series of predefined rules.

KEY TERMS

AutoCorrect (p. 26)
AutoText (p. 26)
Backup (p. 30)
Close command (p. 8)
Custom dictionary (p. 24)
Exit command (p. 8)
File menu (p. 8)
File name (p. 8)
File type (p. 8)
Formatting toolbar (p. 5)
Grammar check (p. 28)
Hard return (p. 2)
Horizontal ruler (p. 6)
Insert mode (p. 4)
Insertion point (p. 2)
Normal view (p. 17)
Office Assistant (p. 12)
Open command (p. 8)
Overtype mode (p. 4)
Places Bar (p. 8)
Print command (p. 8)
Print Layout view (p. 17)
Save As command (p. 30)
Save command (p. 8)
ScreenTip (p. 5)
Show/Hide ¶ button (p. 17)
Soft return (p. 2)
Spell check (p. 24)
Standard toolbar (p. 5)
Status bar (p. 6)
Task pane (p. 6)
Thesaurus (p. 27)
Toggle switch (p. 3)
Toolbar (p. 5)
Undo command (p. 22)
Vertical ruler (p. 6)
View menu (p. 20)
Word wrap (p. 2)

MULTIPLE CHOICE

1. When entering text within a document, the enter key is normally pressed at the end of every:
   (a) Line
   (b) Sentence
   (c) Paragraph
   (d) All of the above

2. Which menu contains the commands to save the current document, or to open a previously saved document?
   (a) The Tools menu
   (b) The File menu
   (c) The View menu
   (d) The Edit menu

3. How do you execute the Print command?
   (a) Click the Print button on the standard toolbar
   (b) Pull down the File menu, then click the Print command
   (c) Use the appropriate keyboard shortcut
   (d) All of the above

4. The Open command:
   (a) Brings a document from disk into memory
   (b) Brings a document from disk into memory, then erases the document on disk
   (c) Stores the document in memory on disk
   (d) Stores the document in memory on disk, then erases the document from memory

5. The Save command:
   (a) Brings a document from disk into memory
   (b) Brings a document from disk into memory, then erases the document on disk
   (c) Stores the document in memory on disk
   (d) Stores the document in memory on disk, then erases the document from memory

6. What is the easiest way to change the phrase, *revenues, profits, gross margin,* to read *revenues, profits, and gross margin*?
   (a) Use the insert mode, position the cursor before the *g* in *gross,* then type the word *and* followed by a space
   (b) Use the insert mode, position the cursor after the *g* in *gross,* then type the word *and* followed by a space
   (c) Use the overtype mode, position the cursor before the *g* in *gross,* then type the word *and* followed by a space
   (d) Use the overtype mode, position the cursor after the *g* in *gross,* then type the word *and* followed by a space

7. A document has been entered into Word with a given set of margins, which are subsequently changed. What can you say about the number of hard and soft returns before and after the change in margins?
   (a) The number of hard returns is the same, but the number and/or position of the soft returns is different
   (b) The number of soft returns is the same, but the number and/or position of the hard returns is different
   (c) The number and position of both hard and soft returns is unchanged
   (d) The number and position of both hard and soft returns is different

8. Which of the following will be detected by the spell check?
   (a) Duplicate words
   (b) Irregular capitalization
   (c) Both (a) and (b)
   (d) Neither (a) nor (b)

9. Which of the following is likely to be found in a custom dictionary?
   (a) Proper names
   (b) Words related to the user's particular application
   (c) Acronyms created by the user for his or her application
   (d) All of the above

10. Ted and Sally both use Word. Both have written a letter to Dr. Joel Stutz and have run a spell check on their respective documents. Ted's program flags *Stutz* as a misspelling, whereas Sally's accepts it as written. Why?
    (a) The situation is impossible; that is, if they use identical word processing programs they should get identical results
    (b) Ted has added *Stutz* to his custom dictionary
    (c) Sally has added *Stutz* to her custom dictionary
    (d) All of the above reasons are equally likely as a cause of the problem

11. The spell check will do all of the following *except:*
    (a) Flag properly spelled words used incorrectly
    (b) Identify misspelled words
    (c) Accept (as correctly spelled) words found in the custom dictionary
    (d) Suggest alternatives to misspellings it identifies

12. The AutoCorrect feature will:
    (a) Correct errors in capitalization as they occur during typing
    (b) Expand user-defined abbreviations as the entries are typed
    (c) Both (a) and (b)
    (d) Neither (a) nor (b)

13. When does the Save As dialog box appear?
    (a) The first time a file is saved using either the Save or Save As commands
    (b) Every time a file is saved
    (c) Both (a) and (b)
    (d) Neither (a) nor (b)

14. Which of the following is true about the thesaurus?
    (a) It recognizes different forms of a word; for example, a noun and a verb
    (b) It provides antonyms as well as synonyms
    (c) Both (a) and (b)
    (d) Neither (a) nor (b)

15. The grammar check:
    (a) Implements different rules for casual and business writing
    (b) Will detect all subtleties in the English language
    (c) Is always run in conjunction with a spell check
    (d) All of the above

ANSWERS

1. c	**6.** a	**11.** a
2. b	**7.** a	**12.** c
3. d	**8.** c	**13.** a
4. a	**9.** d	**14.** c
5. c	**10.** c	**15.** a

1. Insert versus Overtype: Open the *Chapter 1 Practice 1* document that is shown in Figure 1.15 and make the following changes.
   a. Enter your instructor's name and your name in the To and From lines, respectively.
   b. Change "better" to "preferable" in the third line of the first paragraph.
   c. Delete the word "then" from the last line in the first paragraph.
   d. Click at the end of the first paragraph, and add the sentence, "The insert mode adds characters at the insertion point while moving existing text to the right in order to make room for the new text."
   e. Delete the last paragraph, which describes how to delete text. Create a new paragraph in its place with the following text: "There are two other keys that function as toggle switches of which you should be aware. The Caps Lock key toggles between upper- and lowercase letters. The Num Lock key alternates between typing numbers and using the arrow keys."
   f. Print the revised document for your instructor.
   g. Create a cover sheet for the assignment with your name, your instructor's name, today's date, and the assignment number.

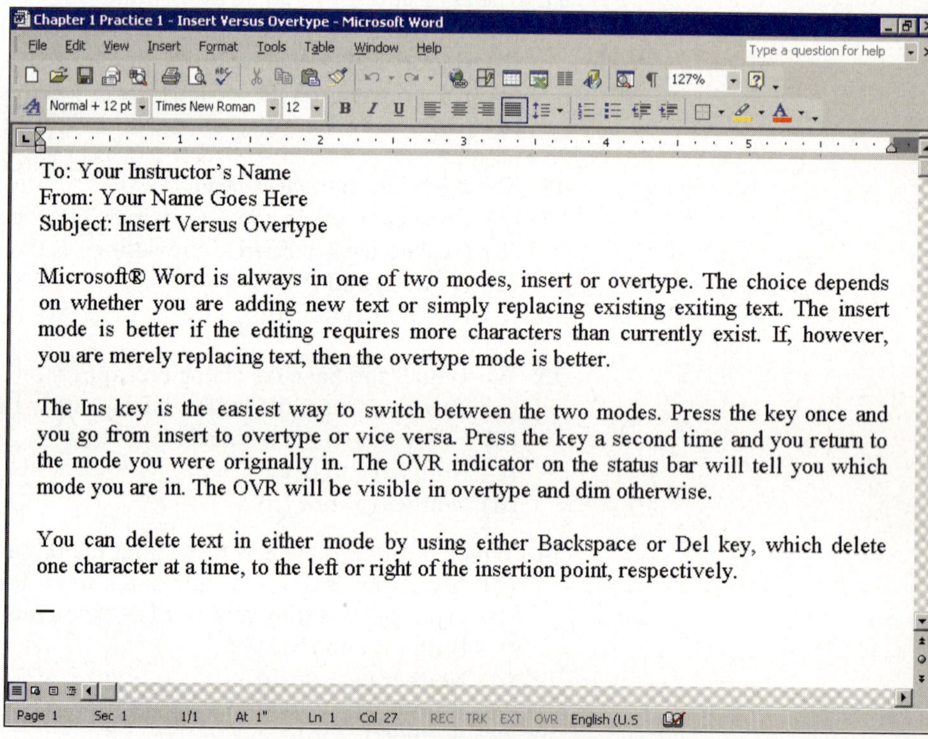

FIGURE 1.15 *Insert versus Overtype (Exercise 1)*

2. The Spelling and Grammar Check: Open the *Chapter 1 Practice* 2 document that is displayed in Figure 1.16, then run the spelling and grammar check to correct the various errors that are contained in the original document. Print this version of the corrected document for your instructor.

   Read the corrected document carefully and make any other necessary corrections. You should find several additional errors because the English language is very complicated and it is virtually impossible to correct every error automatically. Print this version of the document as well. Add a cover page and submit both versions of the corrected document to your instructor.

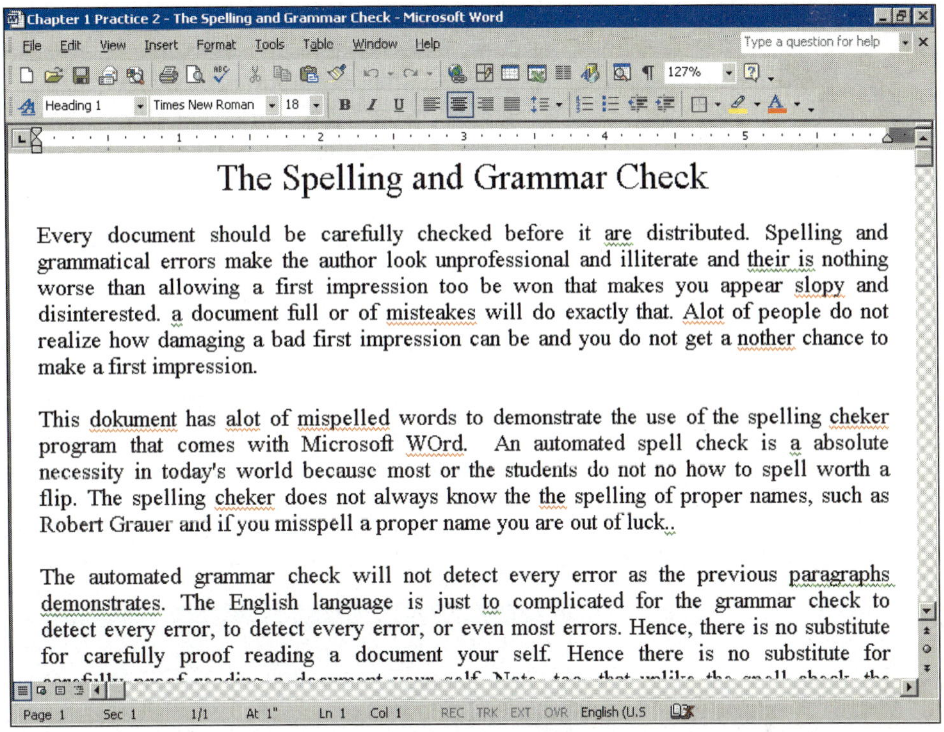

FIGURE 1.16 *The Spelling and Grammar Check (Exercise 2)*

3. Student Questionnaire: Use the partially completed document in *Chapter 1 Practice 3* to describe your background. If there is time in the class, your instructor can have you exchange assignments with another student. There are many variations on this "icebreaker," and the assignment will let you gain practice with Microsoft Word.

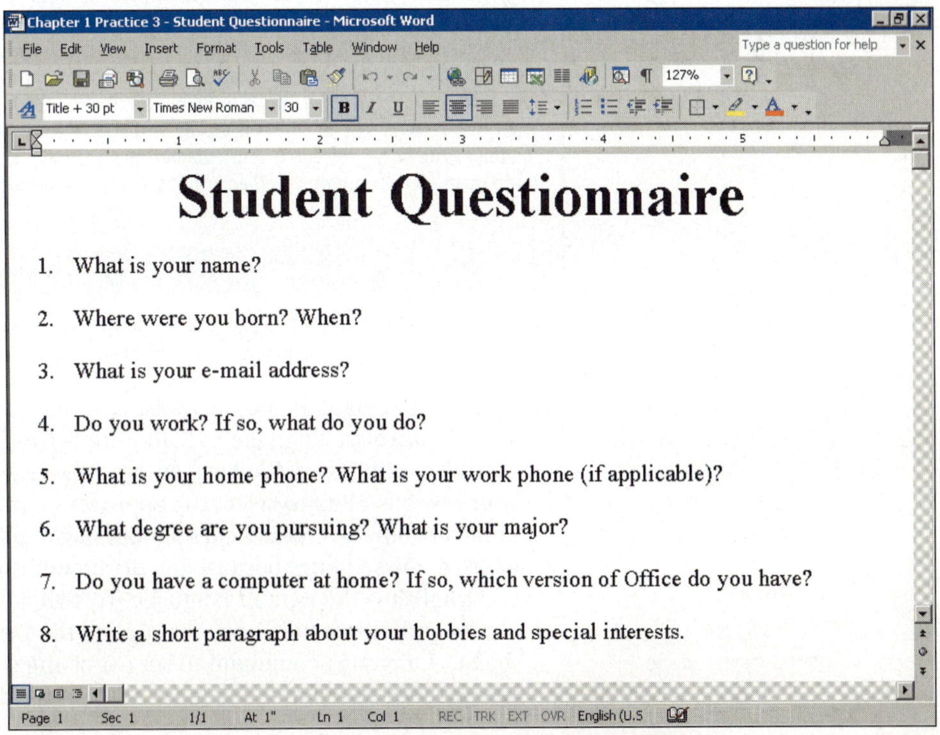

FIGURE 1.17 *Student Questionnaire (Exercise 3)*

4. Select-Then-Do: Formatting is not covered in this chapter, but it is very easy to apply basic formatting to a document, especially if you have used another application in Microsoft Office. Many formatting operations are implemented in the context of "select-then-do" as described in the document in Figure 1.18. You select the text that you want to format, then you execute the appropriate formatting command, most easily by clicking the appropriate button on the Formatting toolbar. The function of each button should be apparent from its icon, but you can simply point to a button to display a ScreenTip that is indicative of its function.

   An unformatted version of the document in Figure 1.18 is found in the *Chapter 1 Practice 4* document in the Exploring Word folder. Open the document, then format it to match the completed document in the figure. The title of the document is centered in 22-point Arial, whereas the rest of the document is set in 12-point Times New Roman. Boldface, italicize, and highlight the text as indicated in the actual document. A color font is also indicated, but do not be concerned if you do not have a color printer. Add your name to the bottom of the completed document, then print the document for your instructor.

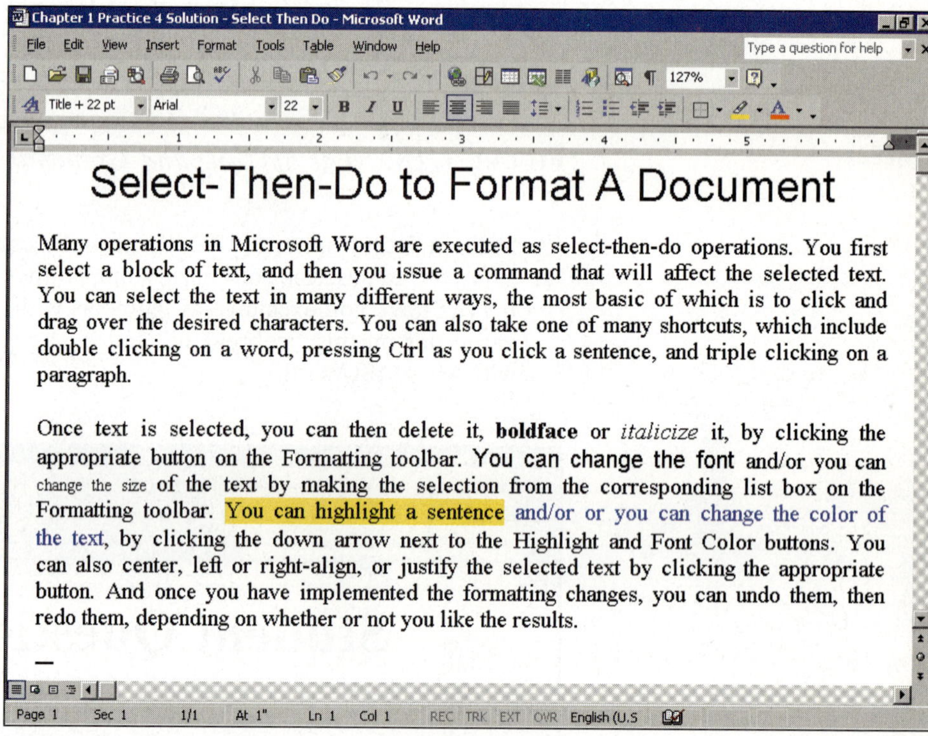

FIGURE 1.18 *Select-Then-Do (Exercise 4)*

5. Foreign Language Proofing Tools: Use the document in Figure 1.19 to practice with the foreign language proofing tools for French and Spanish that are built into Microsoft Word. We have entered the text of the document for you, but it is your responsibility to select the appropriate proofing tool for the different parts of the document. Open the document in *Chapter 1 Practice 5*, which will indicate multiple misspellings because the document is using the English spell check.

   English is the default language. To switch to a different language, select the phrase, pull down the Tools menu, click the Language command, and then click the Set Language command to set (or change) the language in effect. Add your name to the completed document and print it for your instructor.

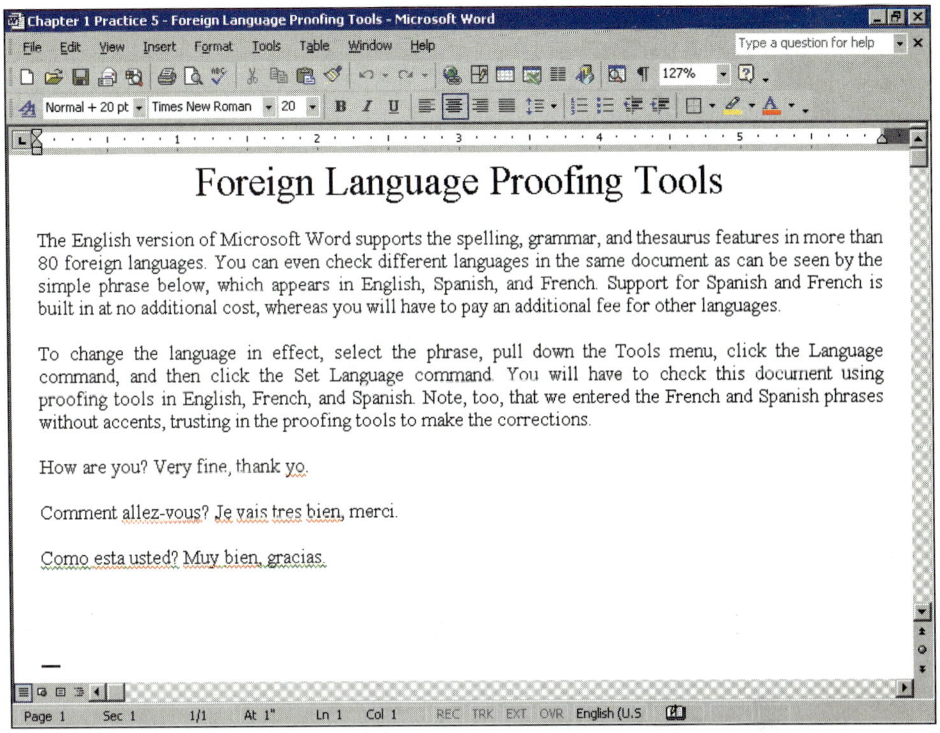
Foreign Language Proofing Tools

The English version of Microsoft Word supports the spelling, grammar, and thesaurus features in more than 80 foreign languages. You can even check different languages in the same document as can be seen by the simple phrase below, which appears in English, Spanish, and French. Support for Spanish and French is built in at no additional cost, whereas you will have to pay an additional fee for other languages.

To change the language in effect, select the phrase, pull down the Tools menu, click the Language command, and then click the Set Language command. You will have to check this document using proofing tools in English, French, and Spanish. Note, too, that we entered the French and Spanish phrases without accents, trusting in the proofing tools to make the corrections.

How are you? Very fine, thank yo.

Comment allez-vous? Je vais tres bien, merci.

Como esta usted? Muy bien, gracias.

FIGURE 1.19 *Foreign Language Proofing Tools (Exercise 5)*

6. The Rejected Job Applicant: The individual who wrote the letter in Figure 1.20 has been rejected for every job for which he has applied. He is a good friend and you want to help. Open the document in *Chapter 1 Practice 6* and correct the obvious spelling errors. Read the document carefully and make any additional corrections that you think appropriate. Sign your name and print the corrected letter.

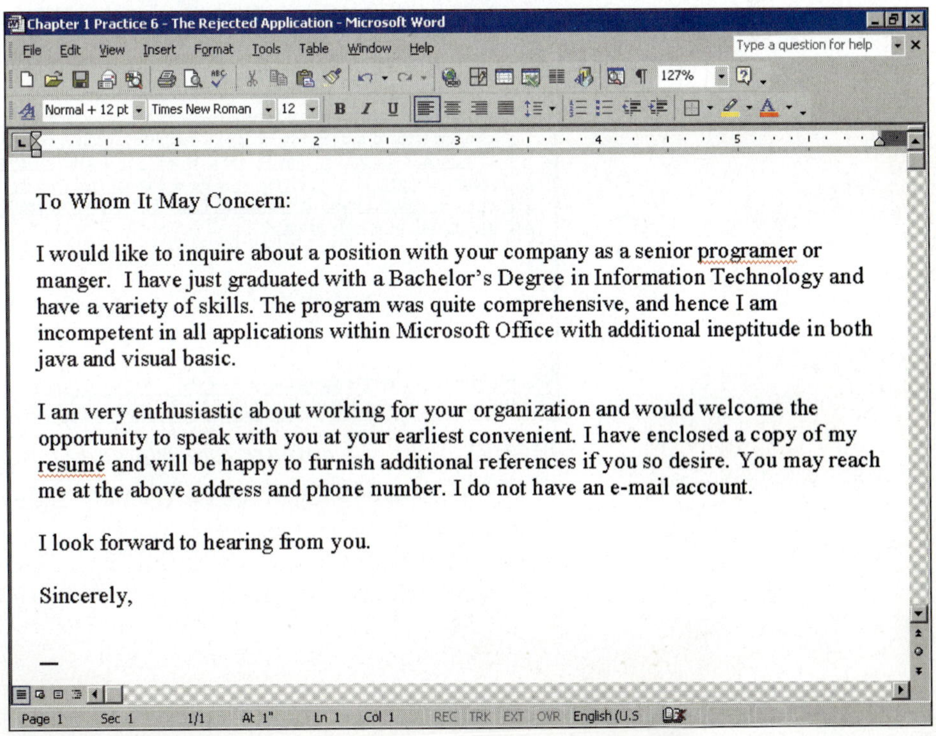
To Whom It May Concern:

I would like to inquire about a position with your company as a senior programer or manger. I have just graduated with a Bachelor's Degree in Information Technology and have a variety of skills. The program was quite comprehensive, and hence I am incompetent in all applications within Microsoft Office with additional ineptitude in both java and visual basic.

I am very enthusiastic about working for your organization and would welcome the opportunity to speak with you at your earliest convenient. I have enclosed a copy of my resumé and will be happy to furnish additional references if you so desire. You may reach me at the above address and phone number. I do not have an e-mail account.

I look forward to hearing from you.

Sincerely,

FIGURE 1.20 *The Rejected Job Applicant (Exercise 6)*

BUILDS ON

HANDS-ON EXERCISE 2, PAGES 19–23

7. Compare and Merge Documents: The Compare and Merge Documents command lets you compare two documents in order to see the changes between those documents. You can use the command to see how well you completed the first two hands-on exercises. Proceed as follows:
   a. Open the completed *Chapter 1 Practice 7* document in the Exploring Word folder. This document contains a paragraph from the hands-on exercise followed by a paragraph that describes the Compare and Merge Documents command.
   b. Pull down the Tools menu and click the Compare and Merge Documents command to display the associated dialog box and select *My First Document* (the document you created).
   c. Check the box for Legal Blackline (to display a thin black line in the left margin showing where the changes occur), then click the Compare button. The two documents are merged together as shown in Figure 1.21. Click the Print button to print the merged documents for your instructor.
   d. Accept or reject the changes as you see fit. Use the Help command to learn more about merging documents and tracking changes.
   e. Summarize your thoughts about these commands in a short note to your instructor. Compare your findings to those of your classmates.
   f. Learn how to insert comments into a document that contain suggestions for improving the document. What happens if different users insert comments into the same document?

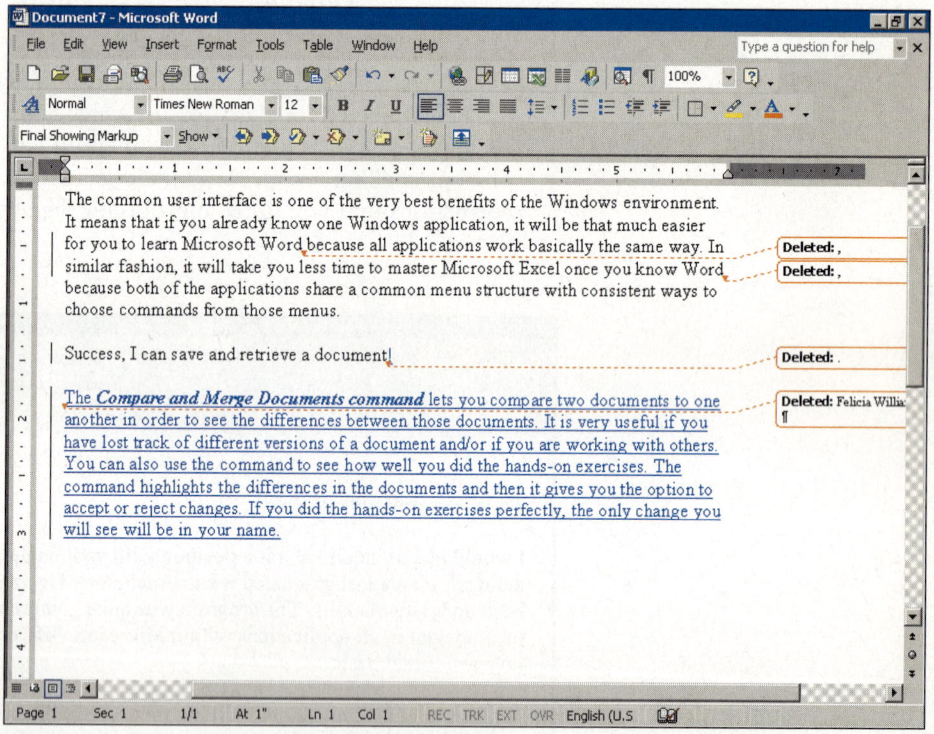

FIGURE 1.21 *Compare and Merge Documents (Exercise 7)*

Acronym Finder

Do you know what the acronym, PCMCIA stands for? Some might say it stands for "People Can't Memorize Computer Industry Acronyms", although the real meaning is "Personal Computer Memory Card International Association", which refers to the PC cards that are used with notebook computers. Use your favorite Internet search engine to locate a site that publishes lists of acronyms. Select five computer-related terms and create a short document with the acronym and its meaning. Select a second list of any five acronyms that appeal to you. Print the document and submit it to your instructor.

The Reference Desk

The Reference Desk, at www.refdesk.com, contains a treasure trove of information for the writer. You will find access to several online dictionaries, encyclopedias, and other references. Go to the site and select five links that you think will be of interest to you as a writer. Create a short document that contains the name of the site, its Web address, and a brief description of the information that is found at the site. Print the document and submit it to your instructor.

Planning for Disaster

Do you have a backup strategy? Do you even know what a backup strategy is? You should learn, because sooner or later you will wish you had one. You will erase a file, be unable to read from a floppy disk, or worse yet suffer a hardware failure in which you are unable to access the hard drive. The problem always seems to occur the night before an assignment is due. The ultimate disaster is the disappearance of your computer, by theft or natural disaster (e.g., Hurricane Andrew). Describe in 250 words or less the backup strategy you plan to implement in conjunction with your work in this class.

A Letter Home

You really like this course and want very much to have your own computer, but you're strapped for cash and have decided to ask your parents for help. Write a one-page letter describing the advantages of having your own system and how it will help you in school. Tell your parents what the system will cost, and that you can save money by buying through the mail. Describe the configuration you intend to buy (don't forget to include the price of software) and then provide prices from at least three different companies. Cut out the advertisements and include them in your letter. Bring your material to class and compare your research with that of your classmates.

Computer Magazines

A subscription to a computer magazine should be given serious consideration if you intend to stay abreast in a rapidly changing field. The reviews on new products are especially helpful, and you will appreciate the advertisements should you need to buy. Go to the library or a newsstand and obtain a magazine that appeals to you, then write a brief review of the magazine for class. Devote at least one paragraph to an article or other item you found useful.

A Junior Year Abroad

How lucky can you get? You are spending the second half of your junior year in Paris. The problem is you will have to submit your work in French, and the English version of Microsoft Word won't do. Is there a foreign-language version available? What about the dictionary and thesaurus? How do you enter the accented characters, which occur so frequently? You are leaving in two months, so you'd better get busy. What are your options? *Bon voyage!*

Changing Menus and Toolbars

Office XP enables you to display a series of short menus that contain only basic commands. The additional commands are made visible by clicking the double arrow that appears at the bottom of the menu. New commands are added to the menu as they are used, and conversely, other commands are removed if they are not used. A similar strategy is followed for the Standard and Formatting toolbars that are displayed on a single row, and thus do not show all of the buttons at one time. The intent is to simplify Office XP for the new user by limiting the number of commands that are visible. The consequence, however, is that the individual is not exposed to new commands, and hence may not use Office to its full potential. Which set of menus do you prefer? How do you switch from one set to the other?

CHAPTER 1

Introduction to Microsoft® Excel: What Is a Spreadsheet?

OBJECTIVES

AFTER READING THIS CHAPTER YOU WILL BE ABLE TO:

1. Describe a spreadsheet and suggest several potential applications; explain how the rows and columns of a spreadsheet are identified.
2. Distinguish between a formula and a constant; explain the use of a predefined function within a formula.
3. Open an Excel workbook; insert and delete rows and columns of a worksheet; save and print the modified worksheet.
4. Describe the three-dimensional nature of an Excel workbook; distinguish between a workbook and a worksheet.
5. Print a worksheet to show either the displayed values or the cell contents; use the Page Setup command to modify the appearance of the printed worksheet.
6. Copy and/or move cells within a worksheet; differentiate between relative, absolute, and mixed references.
7. Format a worksheet to include boldface, italics, shading, and borders; change the font and/or alignment of a selected entry.

OVERVIEW

The spreadsheet is the PC application that is used most frequently by business managers and executives. This chapter provides a broad-based introduction to spreadsheets in general and to Microsoft Excel in particular. A spreadsheet (also called a worksheet) is stored within a workbook, which in turn may contain multiple worksheets. The chapter discusses how the rows and columns of a spreadsheet are labeled and the difference between a formula and a constant.

All of the illustrations in this chapter are set in the context of a professor's grade book that computes the semester averages for his or her students. You will learn how students can be inserted or removed from the worksheet and how changing a student's grade automatically recalculates the dependent values in the worksheet. We also show you how to create a new workbook, how to move and copy formulas within the worksheet, and how to format the worksheet.

The hands-on exercises in the chapter enable you to apply all of the material at the computer, and are indispensable to the learn-by-doing philosophy we follow throughout the text. As you do the exercises, you may recognize many commands from other Office applications, all of which share a common user interface and consistent command structure.

INTRODUCTION TO SPREADSHEETS

A ***spreadsheet*** is the computerized equivalent of an accountant's ledger. As with the ledger, it consists of a grid of rows and columns that enables you to organize data in a readily understandable format. Figures 1.1a and 1.1b show the same information displayed in ledger and spreadsheet format, respectively.

"What is the big deal?" you might ask. The big deal is that after you change an entry (or entries), the spreadsheet will, automatically and almost instantly, recompute all of the formulas. Consider, for example, the profit projection spreadsheet shown in Figure 1.1b. As the spreadsheet is presently constructed, the unit price is \$20 and the projected sales are 1,200 units, producing gross sales of \$24,000 (\$20/unit × 1,200 units). The projected expenses are \$19,200, which yields a profit of \$4,800 (\$24,000 − \$19,200). If the unit price is increased to \$22 per unit, the spreadsheet recomputes the formulas, adjusting the values of gross sales and net profit. The modified spreadsheet of Figure 1.1c appears automatically.

With a calculator and bottle of correction fluid or a good eraser, the same changes could also be made to the ledger. But imagine a ledger with hundreds of entries and the time that would be required to make the necessary changes to the ledger by hand. The same spreadsheet will be recomputed automatically by the computer. And the computer will not make mistakes. Herein lie the advantages of a spreadsheet—the ability to make changes, and to have the computer carry out the recalculation faster and more accurately than could be accomplished manually.

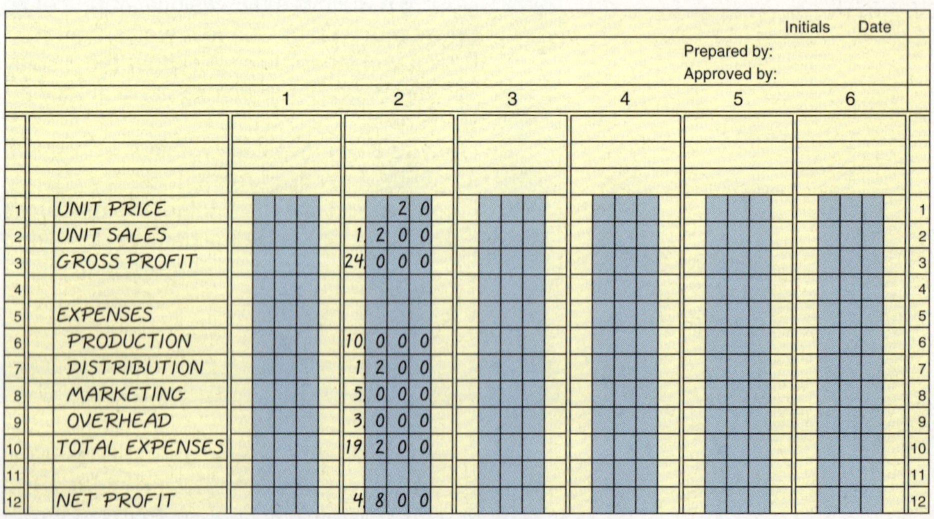

(a) The Accountant's Ledger

FIGURE 1.1 *The Accountant's Ledger*

Unit price is increased to $22

Formulas recompute automatically

	A	B
1	Profit Projection	
2		
3	Unit Price	$20
4	Unit Sales	1,200
5	Gross Sales	$24,000
6		
7	Expenses	
8	Production	$10,000
9	Distribution	$1,200
10	Marketing	$5,000
11	Overhead	$3,000
12	Total Expenses	$19,200
13		
14	Net Profit	$4,800

(b) Original Spreadsheet

	A	B
1	Profit Projection	
2		
3	Unit Price	$22
4	Unit Sales	1,200
5	Gross Sales	$26,400
6		
7	Expenses	
8	Production	$10,000
9	Distribution	$1,200
10	Marketing	$5,000
11	Overhead	$3,000
12	Total Expenses	$19,200
13		
14	Net Profit	$7,200

(c) Modified Spreadsheet

FIGURE 1.1 *The Accountant's Ledger (continued)*

The Professor's Grade Book

A second example of a spreadsheet, one with which you can easily identify, is that of a professor's grade book. The grades are recorded by hand in a notebook, which is nothing more than a different kind of accountant's ledger. Figure 1.2 contains both manual and spreadsheet versions of a grade book.

Figure 1.2a shows a handwritten grade book as it has been done since the days of the little red schoolhouse. For the sake of simplicity, only five students are shown, each with three grades. The professor has computed class averages for each exam, as well as a semester average for every student. The final counts *twice* as much as either test; for example, Adams's average is equal to (100+90+81+81)/4 = 88. This is the professor's grading scheme and it is incorporated into the manual grade book and equivalent spreadsheet.

Figure 1.2b shows the grade book as it might appear in a spreadsheet, and is essentially unchanged from Figure 1.2a. Walker's grade on the final exam in Figure 1.2b is 90, giving him a semester average of 85 and producing a class average on the final of 75.2 as well. Now consider Figure 1.2c, in which the grade on Walker's final has been changed to 100, causing Walker's semester average to change from 85 to 90, and the class average on the final to go from 75.2 to 77.2. As with the profit projection, a change to any entry within the grade book automatically recalculates all other dependent formulas as well. Hence, when Walker's final exam was regraded, all dependent formulas (the class average for the final as well as Walker's semester average) were recomputed.

As simple as the idea of a spreadsheet may seem, it provided the first major reason for managers to have a personal computer on their desks. Essentially, anything that can be done with a pencil, a pad of paper, and a calculator can be done faster and far more accurately with a spreadsheet. The spreadsheet, like the personal computer, has become an integral part of every type of business. Indeed, it is hard to imagine that these calculations were ever done by hand. The spreadsheet has become an integral part of corporate culture.

Final counts twice so average is computed as (100 + 90 + 81 + 81)/4

	TEST 1	TEST 2	FINAL	AVERAGE
ADAMS	100	90	81	88
BAKER	90	76	87	85
GLASSMAN	90	78	78	81
MOLDOF	60	60	40	50
WALKER	80	80	90	85
CLASS AVERAGE	84.0	76.8	75.2	
NOTE: FINAL COUNTS DOUBLE				

(a) The Professor's Grade Book

Walker's original grade is 90

	A	B	C	D	E
1	Student	Test 1	Test 2	Final	Average
2					
3	Adams	100	90	81	88.0
4	Baker	90	76	87	85.0
5	Glassman	90	78	78	81.0
6	Moldof	60	60	40	50.0
7	Walker	80	80	90	85.0
8					
9	Class Average	84.0	76.8	75.2	

(b) Original Grades

Grade on Walker's final is changed to 100

Formulas recompute automatically

	A	B	C	D	E
1	Student	Test 1	Test 2	Final	Average
2					
3	Adams	100	90	81	88.0
4	Baker	90	76	87	85.0
5	Glassman	90	78	78	81.0
6	Moldof	60	60	40	50.0
7	Walker	80	80	100	90.0
8					
9	Class Average	84.0	76.8	77.2	

(c) Modified Spreadsheet

FIGURE 1.2 *The Professor's Grade Book*

Row and Column Headings

A spreadsheet is divided into rows and columns, with each row and column assigned a heading. Rows are given numeric headings ranging from 1 to 65,536 (the maximum number of rows allowed). Columns are assigned alphabetic headings from column A to Z, then continue from AA to AZ and then from BA to BZ and so on, until the last of 256 columns (column IV) is reached.

The intersection of a row and column forms a ***cell***, with the number of cells in a spreadsheet equal to the number of rows times the number of columns. The professor's grade book in Figure 1.2, for example, has 5 columns labeled A through E, 9 rows numbered from 1 to 9, and a total of 45 cells. Each cell has a unique ***cell reference***; for example, the cell at the intersection of column A and row 9 is known as cell A9. The column heading always precedes the row heading in the cell reference.

Formulas and Constants

Figure 1.3 is an alternate view of the professor's grade book that shows the cell contents rather than the computed values. Cell E3, for example, does not contain the number 88 (Adams's average for the semester), but rather the formula to compute the average from the exam grades. Indeed, it is the existence of the formula that lets you change the value of any cell containing a grade for Adams (cells B3, C3, or D3), and have the computed average in cell E3 change automatically.

To create a spreadsheet, one goes from cell to cell and enters either a constant or a formula. A ***constant*** is an entry that does not change. It may be a number, such as a student's grade on an exam, or it may be descriptive text (a label), such as a student's name. A ***formula*** is a combination of numeric constants, cell references, arithmetic operators, and/or functions (described below) that displays the result of a calculation. You can ***edit*** (change) the contents of a cell by returning to the cell and reentering the constant or formula.

A formula always begins with an equal sign. Consider, for example, the formula in cell E3, =(B3+C3+2*D3)/4, which computes Adams's semester average. The formula is built in accordance with the professor's rules for computing a student's semester average, which counts the final twice as much as the other tests. Excel uses symbols +, −, *, /, and ^ to indicate addition, subtraction, multiplication, division, and exponentiation, respectively, and follows the normal rules of arithmetic precedence. Any expression in parentheses is evaluated first, then within an expression exponentiation is performed first, followed by multiplication or division in left to right order, then finally addition or subtraction.

The formula in cell E3 takes the grade on the first exam (in cell B3), plus the grade on the second exam (in cell C3), plus two times the grade on the final (in cell D3), and divides the result by four. Thus, should any of the exam grades change, the semester average (a formula whose results depend on the individual exam grades) will also change. This, in essence, is the basic principle behind the spreadsheet and explains why, when one number changes, various other numbers throughout the spreadsheet change as well.

A formula may also include a ***function***, or predefined computational task, such as the AVERAGE function in cells B9, C9, and D9. The function in cell B9, for example, =AVERAGE(B3:B7), is interpreted to mean the average of all cells starting at cell B3 and ending at cell B7 and is equivalent to the formula =(B3+B4+B5+B6+B7)/5. You can appreciate that functions are often easier to use than the corresponding formulas, especially with larger spreadsheets (and classes with many students). Excel contains a wide variety of functions that help you to create very powerful spreadsheets. Financial functions, for example, enable you to calculate the interest payments on a car loan or home mortgage.

Constant (entry that does not change)

Function (predefined computational task)

Formula (displays the result of a calculation)

	A	B	C	D	E
1	Student	Test 1	Test 2	Final	Average
2					
3	Adams	100	90	81	=(B3+C3+2*D3)/4
4	Baker	90	76	87	=(D4+C4+2*D4)/4
5	Glassman	90	78	78	=(B5+C5+2*D5)/4
6	Moldof	60	60	40	=(B6+C6+2*D6)/4
7	Walker	80	80	90	=(B7+C7+2*D7)/4
8					
9	Class Average	=AVERAGE(B3:B7)	=AVERAGE(C3:C7)	=AVERAGE(D3:D7)	

FIGURE 1.3 *The Professor's Grade Book (cell formulas)*

Figure 1.4 displays the professor's grade book as it is implemented in Microsoft Excel. Microsoft Excel is a Windows application, and thus shares the common user interface with which you are familiar. (It's even easier to learn Excel if you already know another Office application such as Microsoft Word.) You should recognize, therefore, that the desktop in Figure 1.4 has two open windows—an application window for Microsoft Excel and a document window for the workbook, which is currently open.

Each window has its own Minimize, Maximize (or Restore), and Close buttons. Both windows have been maximized and thus the title bars have been merged into a single title bar that appears at the top of the application window. The title bar reflects the application (Microsoft Excel) as well as the name of the workbook (Grade Book) on which you are working. A menu bar appears immediately below the title bar. Two toolbars, which are discussed in depth on page 8, appear below the menu bar. Vertical and horizontal scroll bars appear at the right and bottom of the document window. The Windows taskbar appears at the bottom of the screen and shows the open applications. The Ask a Question list box appears to the right of the menu bar and provides instant access to the Help facility.

The terminology is important, and we distinguish between spreadsheet, worksheet, and workbook. Excel refers to a spreadsheet as a ***worksheet***. Spreadsheet is a generic term; *workbook* and *worksheet* are unique to Excel. An Excel ***workbook*** contains one or more worksheets. The professor's grades for this class are contained in the CIS120 worksheet within the Grade Book workbook. This workbook also contains additional worksheets (CIS223 and CIS316) as indicated by the worksheet tabs at the bottom of the window. These worksheets contain the professor's grades for other courses that he or she is teaching this semester.

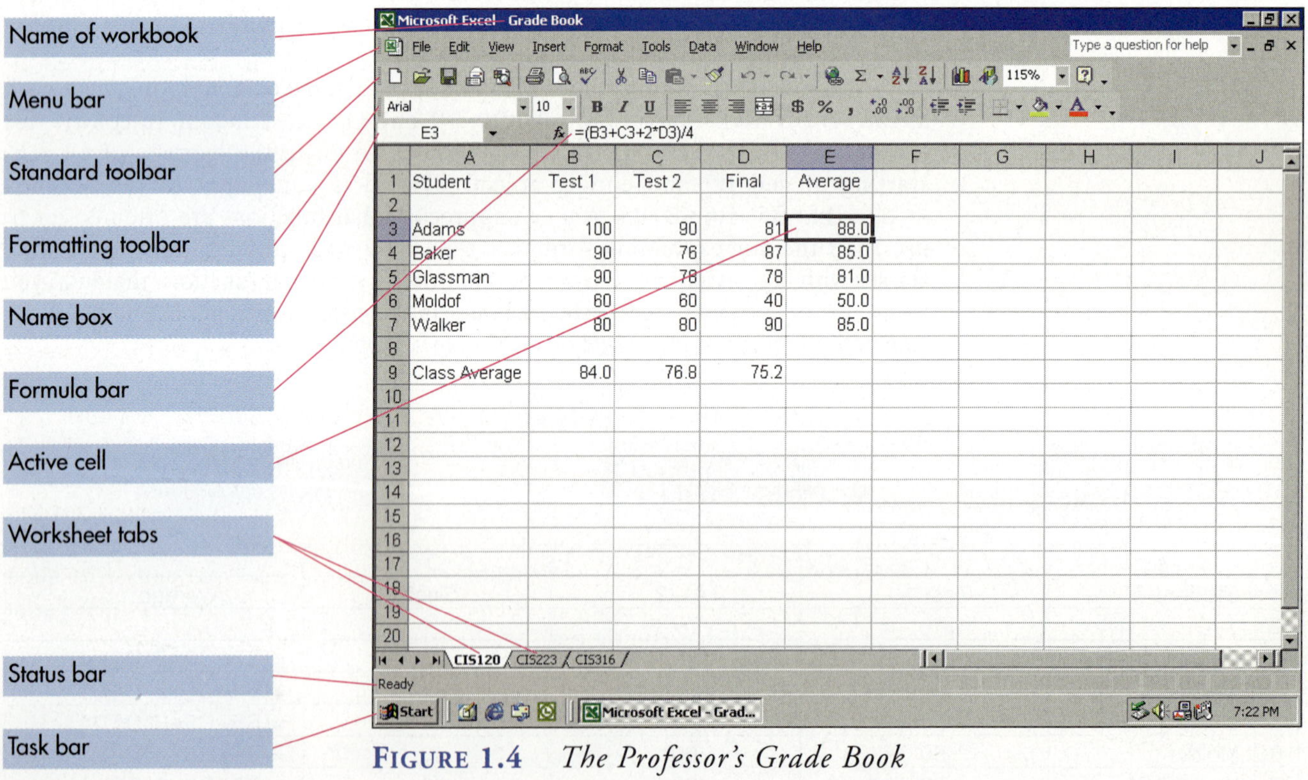

FIGURE 1.4 *The Professor's Grade Book*

Figure 1.4 resembles the grade book shown earlier, but it includes several other elements that enable you to create and/or edit the worksheet. The heavy border around cell E3 indicates that it (cell E3) is the ***active cell***. Any entry made at this time is made into the active cell, and any commands that are executed affect the contents of the active cell. The active cell can be changed by clicking a different cell, or by using the arrow keys to move to a different cell.

The displayed value in cell E3 is 88.0, but as indicated earlier, the cell contains a formula to compute the semester average rather than the number itself. The contents of the active cell, =(B3+C3+2*D3)/4, are displayed in the ***formula bar*** near the top of the worksheet. The cell reference for the active cell, cell E3 in Figure 1.4, appears in the ***Name box*** at the left of the formula bar.

The ***status bar*** at the bottom of the worksheet keeps you informed of what is happening as you work within Excel. It displays information about a selected command or an operation in progress.

THE EXCEL WORKBOOK

An Excel workbook is the electronic equivalent of the three-ring binder. A workbook contains one or more worksheets (or chart sheets), each of which is identified by a tab at the bottom of the workbook. The worksheets in a workbook are normally related to one another; for example, each worksheet may contain the sales for a specific division within a company. The advantage of a workbook is that all of its worksheets are stored in a single file, which is accessed as a unit.

Toolbars

Excel provides several different ways to accomplish the same task. Commands may be accessed from a pull-down menu, from a shortcut menu (which is displayed by pointing to an object and clicking the right mouse button), and/or through keyboard equivalents. Commands can also be executed from one of many ***toolbars*** that appear immediately below the menu bar. The Standard and Formatting toolbars are displayed by default. The toolbars appear initially on the same line, but can be separated as described in the hands-on exercise that follows.

The ***Standard toolbar*** contains buttons corresponding to the most basic commands in Excel—for example, opening and closing a workbook, printing a workbook, and so on. The icon on the button is intended to be indicative of its function (e.g., a printer to indicate the Print command). You can also point to the button to display a ***ScreenTip*** showing the name of the button.

The ***Formatting toolbar*** appears under the Standard toolbar, and provides access to common formatting operations such as boldface, italics, or underlining. It also enables you to change the alignment of entries within a cell and/or change the font or color. The easiest way to master the toolbars is to view the buttons in groups according to their general function, as shown in Figure 1.5.

The toolbars may appear overwhelming at first, but there is absolutely no need to memorize what the individual buttons do. That will come with time. Indeed, if you use another office application such as Microsoft Word, you may already recognize many of the buttons on the Standard and Formatting toolbars. Note, too, that many of the commands in the pull-down menus are displayed with an image that corresponds to a button on a toolbar.

Opens a new workbook; opens an existing workbook; saves a workbook; sends a workbook via e-mail; or executes a search

Prints the workbook; previews the workbook prior to printing; checks the spelling

Cuts or copies the selecton to the clipboard; pastes the clipboard contents; copies the formatting of the selected cells

Undoes or redoes a previously executed command

Inserts a hyperlink; sums the suggested range; performs an ascending or descending sort

Starts the Chart Wizard; displays the Drawing toolbar

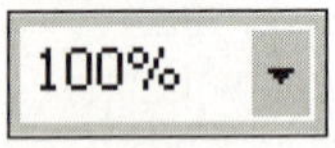

Changes the magnification

Displays the Office Assistant

(a) The Standard Toolbar

Changes the font or point size

Toggles boldface, italics, and underline on and off

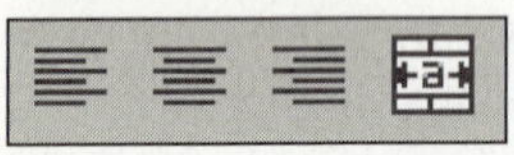

Aligns left, center, right; merges cells and centers

Applies accounting, percentage, or comma formatting; increases or decreases the number of decimals

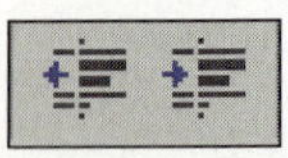

Decreases or increases the indent

Applies a border format; applies a background color; applies a font color

(b) The Formatting Toolbar

FIGURE 1.5 *Toolbars*

THE FILE MENU

The ***File menu*** is a critically important menu in virtually every Windows application. It contains the Save and Open commands to save a workbook on disk, then subsequently retrieve (open) that workbook at a later time. The File menu also contains the ***Print command*** to print a workbook, the ***Close command*** to close the current workbook but continue working in the application, and the ***Exit command*** to quit the application altogether.

The ***Save command*** copies the workbook that you are working on (i.e., the workbook that is currently in memory) to disk. The command functions differently the first time it is executed for a new workbook, in that it displays the Save As dialog box as shown in Figure 1.6a. The dialog box requires you to specify the name of the workbook, the drive (and an optional folder) in which the workbook is to be stored, and its file type. All subsequent executions of the command save the workbook under the assigned name, replacing the previously saved version with the new version.

The ***file name*** (e.g., My First Spreadsheet) can contain up to 255 characters including spaces, commas, and/or periods. (Periods are discouraged, however, since they are too easily confused with DOS extensions.) The Save In list box is used to select the drive (which is not visible in Figure 1.6a) and the optional folder (e.g., Exploring Excel). The ***Places bar*** provides shortcuts to any of its folders without having to search through the Save In list box. Click the Desktop icon, for example, and the file is saved on the Windows desktop. You can also use the Favorites folder, which is accessible from every application in Office XP.

The ***file type*** defaults to an Excel 2002 workbook. You can, however, choose a different format to maintain compatibility with earlier versions of Microsoft Excel. You can also save any Excel workbook as a Web page or HTML document.

The ***Save As command*** saves a copy of an existing workbook under a different name, and/or a different file type, and is useful when you want to retain a copy of the original workbook. The Save As command results in two copies of the workbook. The original workbook is kept on disk under the original name. A copy of the workbook is saved on disk under the new name and remains in memory.

The ***Open command*** is the opposite of the Save command as it brings a copy of an existing workbook into memory, enabling you to work with that workbook. The Open command displays the Open dialog box in which you specify the file name, the drive (and optionally the folder) that contains the file, and the file type. Microsoft Excel will then list all files of that type on the designated drive (and folder), enabling you to open the file you want.

The Save and Open commands work in conjunction with one another. The Save As dialog box in Figure 1.6a, for example, saves the file My First Spreadsheet in the Exploring Excel folder. The Open dialog box in Figure 1.6b loads that file into memory so that you can work with the file, after which you can save the revised file for use at a later time.

The toolbars in the Save As and Open dialog boxes have several buttons in common that facilitate the execution of either command. The Views button lets you display the files in one of four different views. The Details view shows the file size as well as the date and time a file was last modified. The Preview view shows the beginning of a workbook, without having to open the workbook. The List view displays only the file names, and thus lets you see more files at one time. The Properties view shows information about the workbook including the date of creation and number of revisions.

Other buttons provide limited file management without having to go to My Computer or Windows Explorer. You can, for example, delete a file, create a new folder, or start your Web browser from either dialog box. The Tools button provides access to additional commands that are well worth exploring.

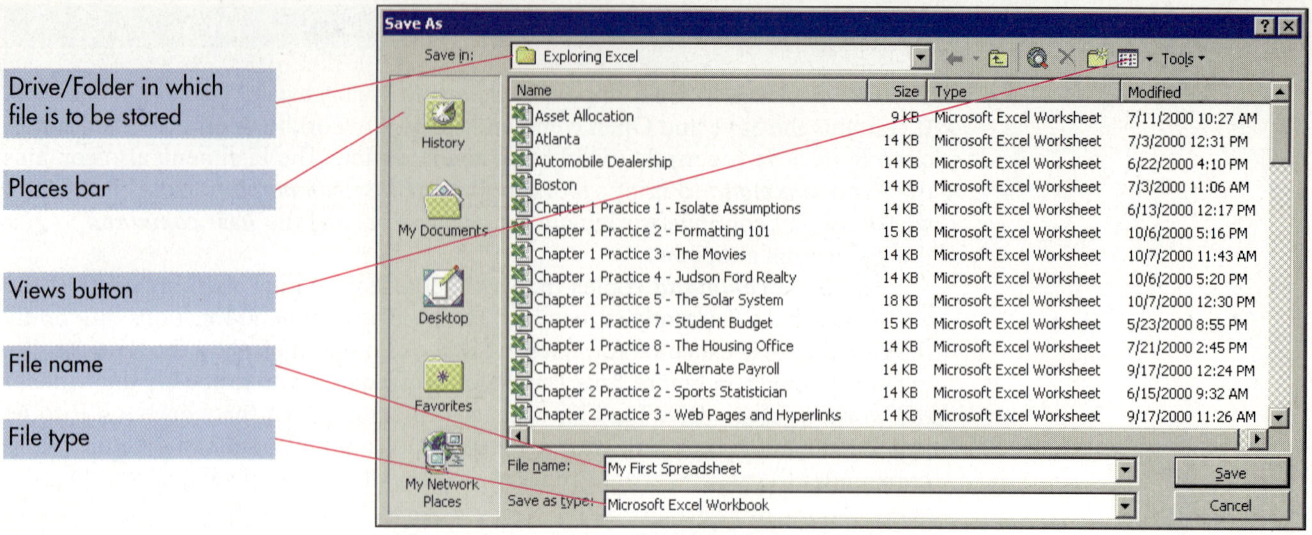

(a) Save As Dialog Box (Details View)

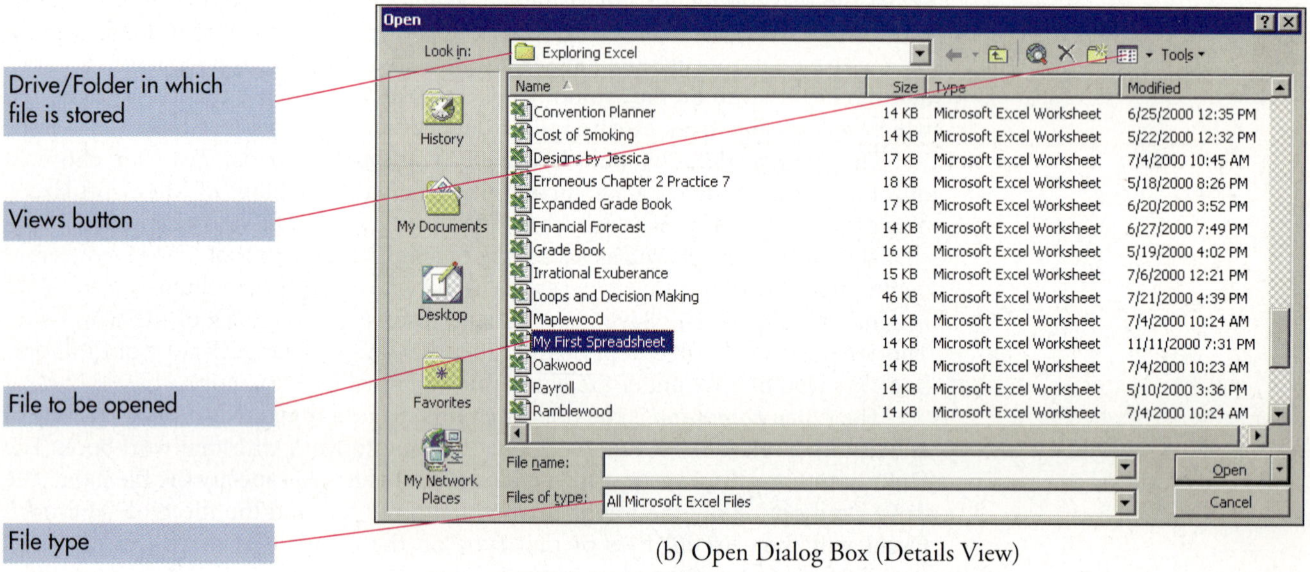

(b) Open Dialog Box (Details View)

FIGURE 1.6 *The Save and Open Commands*

SORT BY NAME, DATE, OR FILE SIZE

The files in the Save As and Open dialog boxes can be displayed in ascending or descending sequence by name, date modified, or size. Change to the Details view, then click the heading of the desired column; for example, click the Modified column to list the files according to the date they were last changed. Click the column heading a second time to reverse the sequence—that is, to switch from ascending to descending, and vice versa.

Hands-on Exercise 1

Introduction to Microsoft Excel

Objective To start Microsoft Excel; to open, modify, and print an existing workbook. Use Figure 1.7 as a guide in the exercise.

Step 1: **Welcome to Windows**

- Turn on the computer and all of its peripherals. The floppy drive should be empty prior to starting your machine. This ensures that the system starts by reading from the hard disk, which contains the Windows files, as opposed to a floppy disk, which does not.
- Your system will take a minute or so to get started, after which you should see the desktop in Figure 1.7a. Do not be concerned if the appearance of your desktop is different from ours.
- You may also see a Welcome to Windows dialog box with commands to take a tour of the operating system. If so, click the appropriate button(s) or close the dialog box.
- You should be familiar with basic file management and very comfortable moving and copying files from one folder to another. If not, you may want to review the material in the Essentials of Windows section of this text.
- You are ready to download the practice files you will need for the hands-on exercises that appear throughout the text.

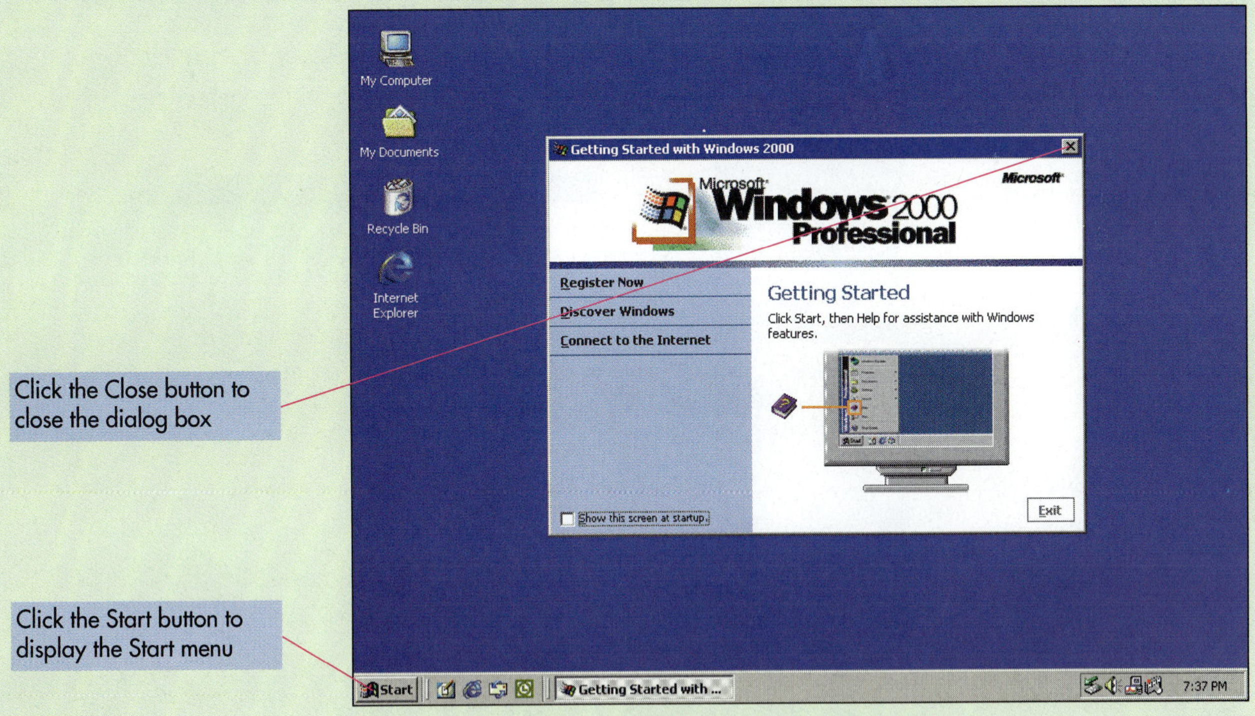

(a) Welcome to Windows (step 1)

Figure 1.7 *Hands-on Exercise 1*

Step 2: **Obtain the Practice Files**

- We have created a series of practice files (also called a "data disk") for you to use throughout the text. The files may be on a network drive, in which case you use Windows Explorer to copy the files from the network to a floppy disk.
- You can also download the files from our Website provided you have an Internet connection. Start Internet Explorer, then go to the Exploring Windows Series home page at **www.prenhall.com/grauer**.
  - Click the book for **Office XP**, which takes you to the Office XP home page. Click the **Student Resources tab** (at the top of the window) to go to the Student Resources page as shown in Figure 1.7b.
  - Click the link to **Student Data Disk** (in the left frame), then scroll down the page until you can select Excel 2002. Choose **Exploring Excel 2002** if you have the individual Excel text. Choose **Excel 2002 Volume I** if you are using *Exploring Microsoft Office Volume I*. Click the link to download the file.
  - You will see the File Download dialog box asking what you want to do. The option button to save this program to disk is selected. Click **OK**. The Save As dialog box appears.
  - Click the down arrow in the Save In list box to select the drive and folder where you want to save the file. It's best to save the file to the Windows desktop or to a temporary folder on drive C.
  - Double click the file after it has been downloaded to your PC, then follow the onscreen instructions.
- Check with your instructor for additional information.

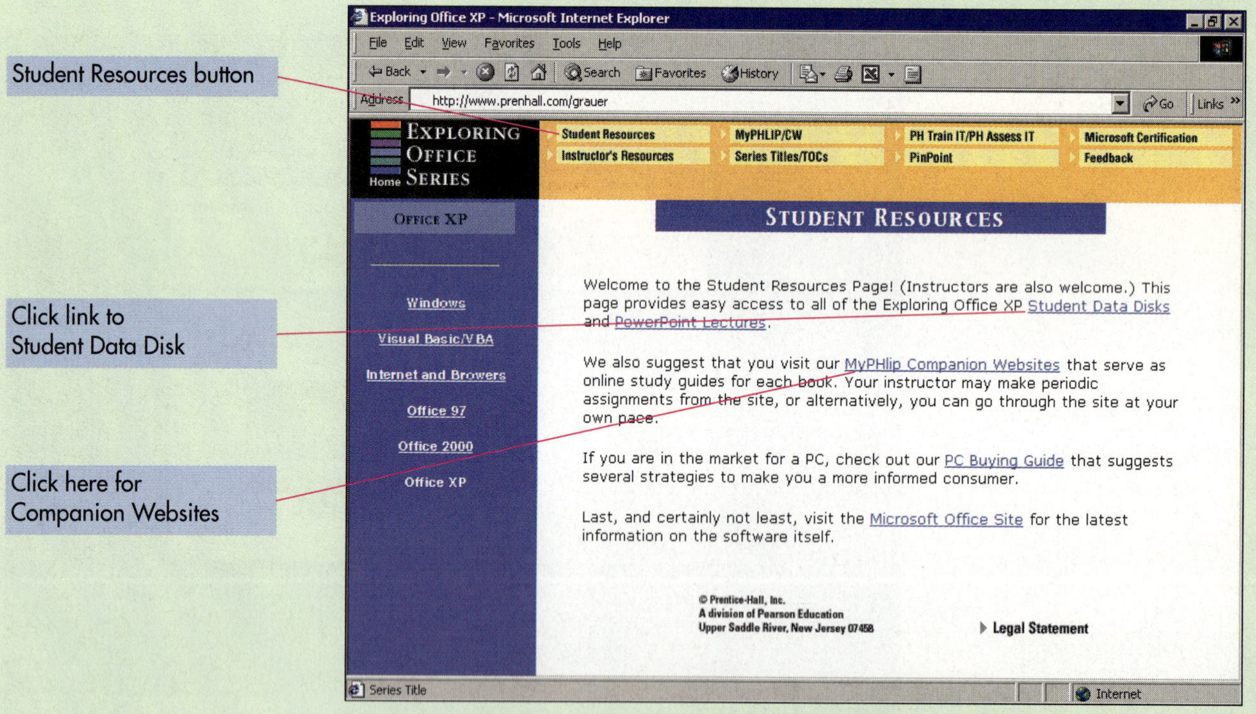

(b) Obtain the Practice Files (step 2)

FIGURE 1.7 *Hands-on Exercise 1 (continued)*

Step 3: **Start Excel**

- Click the **Start button** to display the Start menu. Click (or point to) the **Programs menu**, then click **Microsoft Excel** to start the program. Close the task pane if it is open.
- Click and drag the Office Assistant out of the way. (The Office Assistant is illustrated in step 8 of this exercise.)
- If necessary, click the **Maximize button** in the application window so that Excel takes the entire desktop as shown in Figure 1.7c. Click the **Maximize button** in the document window (if necessary) so that the document window is as large as possible.

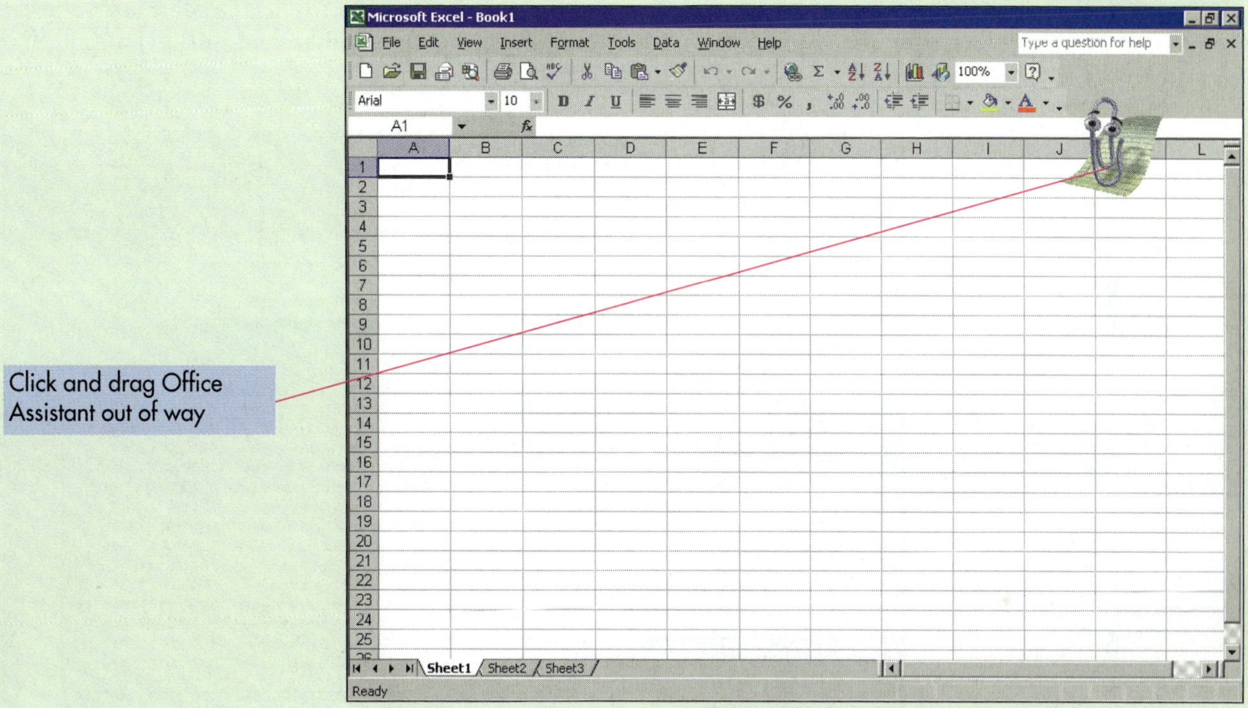

(c) Start Excel (step 3)

FIGURE 1.7 *Hands-on Exercise 1 (continued)*

ABOUT THE ASSISTANT

The Assistant is very powerful and hence you want to experiment with various ways to use it. To ask a question, click the Assistant's icon to toggle its balloon on or off. To change the way in which the Assistant works, click the Options button within the balloon and experiment with the various check boxes to see their effects. If you find the Assistant distracting, click and drag the character out of the way or hide it altogether by pulling down the Help menu and clicking the Hide the Office Assistant command. Pull down the Help menu and click the Show the Office Assistant command to return the Assistant to the desktop.

Step 4: **Open the Workbook**

- Pull down the **File menu** and click **Open** (or click the **Open button** on the Standard toolbar). You should see a dialog box similar to the one in Figure 1.7d.
- Click the **drop-down arrow** on the Views button, then click **Details** to change to the Details view. Click and drag the vertical border between two columns to increase (or decrease) the size of a column.
- Click the **drop-down arrow** on the Look In list box. Click the appropriate drive, drive C or drive A, depending on the location of your data. Double click the **Exploring Excel folder** to make it the active folder (the folder from which you will retrieve and into which you will save the workbook).
- Click the **down scroll arrow** if necessary in order to click **Grade Book** to select the professor's grade book. Click the **Open command button** to open the workbook and begin the exercise.

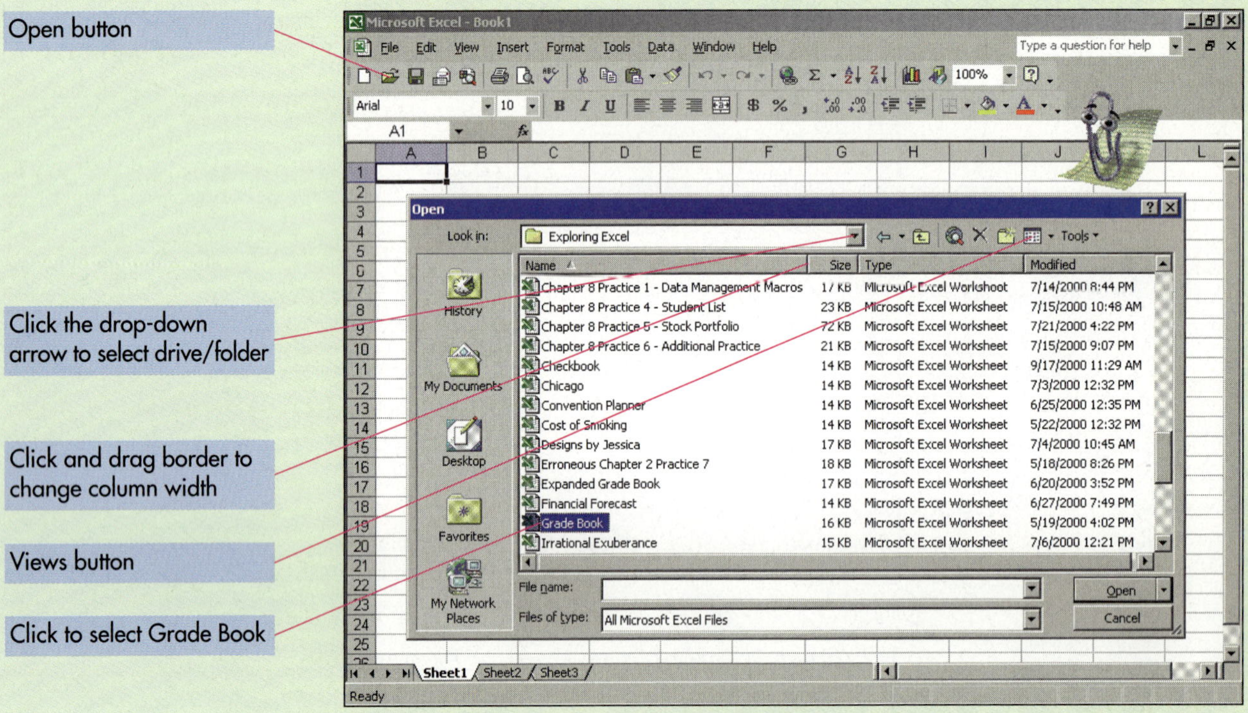

(d) Open the Workbook (step 4)

FIGURE 1.7 *Hands-on Exercise 1 (continued)*

SEPARATE THE TOOLBARS

You may see the Standard and Formatting toolbars displayed on one row to save space within the application window. If so, we suggest that you separate the toolbars, so that you see all of the buttons on each. Click the down arrow at the end of any visible toolbar to display toolbar options, then click the option to show the buttons on two rows. Click the down arrow a second time to show the buttons on one row if you prefer this configuration.

Step 5: **The Save As Command**

- Pull down the **File menu**. Click **Save As** to display the dialog box shown in Figure 1.7e.
- Enter **Finished Grade Book** as the name of the new workbook. (A file name may contain up to 255 characters. Spaces and commas are allowed in the file name.)
- Click the **Save button**. Press the **Esc key** or click the **Close button** if you see a Properties dialog box.
- There are now two identical copies of the file on disk: "Grade Book" and "Finished Grade Book," which you just created. The title bar shows the latter name, which is the workbook currently in memory.
- You will work with "Finished Grade Book," but can always return to the original "Grade Book" if necessary.

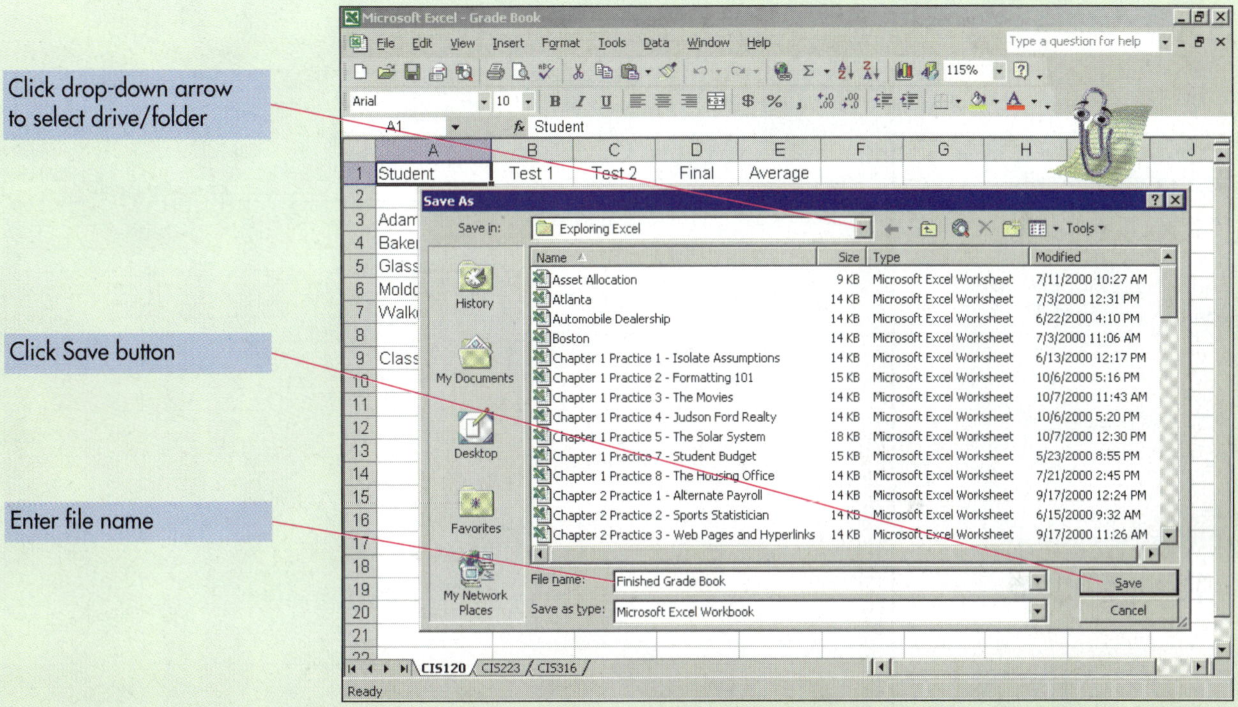

(e) Save As Command (step 5)

FIGURE 1.7 *Hands-on Exercise 1 (continued)*

QUIT WITHOUT SAVING

There will be times when you do not want to save the changes to a workbook—for example, when you have edited it beyond recognition and wish you had never started. The Undo command, useful as it is, reverses only the last operation and is of no use if you need to cancel all changes. Pull down the File menu and click the Close command, then click No in response to the message asking whether to save the changes. Pull down the File menu, click the file's name at the bottom of the menu to reopen the file, then begin all over.

Step 6: **The Active Cell, Formula Bar, and Worksheet Tabs**

- You should see the workbook in Figure 1.7f. Click in **cell B3**, the cell containing Adams's grade on the first test. Cell B3 is now the active cell and is surrounded by a heavy border. The Name box indicates that cell B3 is the active cell, and its contents are displayed in the formula bar.
- Click in **cell B4** (or press the **down arrow key**) to make it the active cell. The Name box indicates cell B4 while the formula bar indicates a grade of 90.
- Click in **cell E3**, the cell containing the formula to compute Adams's semester average; the worksheet displays the computed average of 88.0, but the formula bar displays the formula, =(B3+C3+2*D3)/4, to compute that average based on the test grades.
- Click the **CIS223 tab** to view a different worksheet within the same workbook. This worksheet contains the grades for a different class.
- Click the **CIS316 tab** to view this worksheet. Click the **CIS120 tab** to return to this worksheet and continue with the exercise.

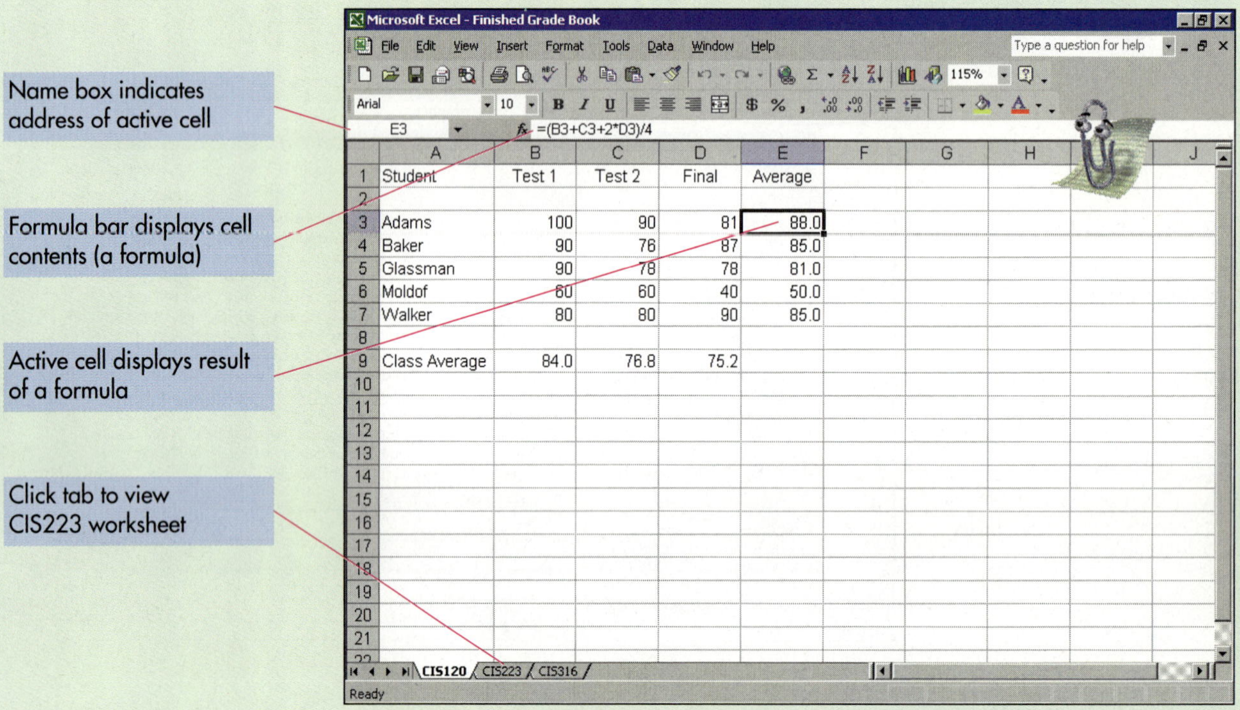

(f) The Active Cell, Formula Bar, and Worksheet Tabs (step 6)

FIGURE 1.7 *Hands-on Exercise 1 (continued)*

THE MENUS MAY CHANGE

Office XP gives you the option of displaying short menus (ending in a double arrow to show additional commands) as opposed to complete menus with all commands. We prefer the complete menus because that is the way you learn an application, but the settings may be different on your system. Pull down the Tools menu, click the Customize command to display the Customize dialog box, click the Options tab, and clear the box that menus show recently used commands first.

Step 7: **Experiment (What If?)**

- Click in **cell C4**, the cell containing Baker's grade on the second test. Enter a corrected value of **86** (instead of the previous entry of 76). Press **enter** (or click in another cell).
- The effects of this change ripple through the worksheet, automatically changing the computed value for Baker's average in cell E4 to 87.5. The class average on the second test in cell C9 changes to 78.8.
- Change Walker's grade on the final from 90 to **100**. Press **enter** (or click in another cell). Walker's average in cell E7 changes to 90.0, while the class average in cell D9 changes to 77.2.
- Your worksheet should match Figure 1.7g. Save the workbook.

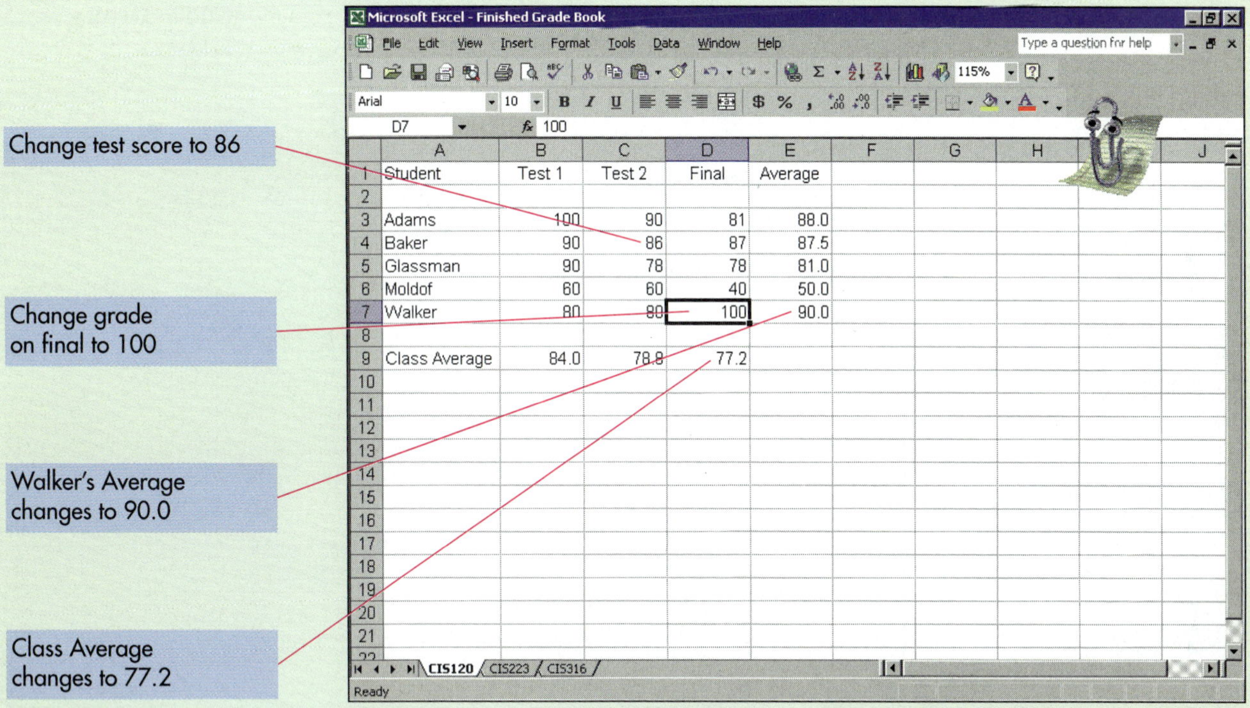

(g) Experiment (What If?) (step 7)

FIGURE 1.7 *Hands-on Exercise 1 (continued)*

THE UNDO AND REDO COMMANDS

The Undo Command lets you undo the last several changes to a workbook. Click the down arrow next to the Undo button on the Standard toolbar to display a reverse-order list of your previous commands, then click the command you want to undo, which also cancels all of the preceding commands. Undoing the fifth command in the list, for example, will also undo the preceding four commands. The Redo command redoes (reverses) the last command that was undone. It, too, displays a reverse-order list of commands, so that redoing the fifth command in the list will also redo the preceding four commands.

Step 8: **The Office Assistant**

- If necessary, pull down the **Help menu** and click the command to **Show the Office Assistant**. You may see a different character than the one we have selected. Click the Assistant, then enter the question, **How do I use the Office Assistant?** as shown in Figure 1.7h.
- Click the **Search button** in the Assistant's balloon to look for the answer. The size of the Assistant's balloon expands as the Assistant suggests several topics that may be appropriate.
- Select (click) any topic, which in turn displays a Help window with multiple links associated with the topic you selected.
- Read the displayed information and explore Help, then close the Help window when you are finished.
- Pull down the **File menu** and click **Exit** to close Excel if you do not wish to continue with the next exercise at this time. Save the workbook if you are prompted.

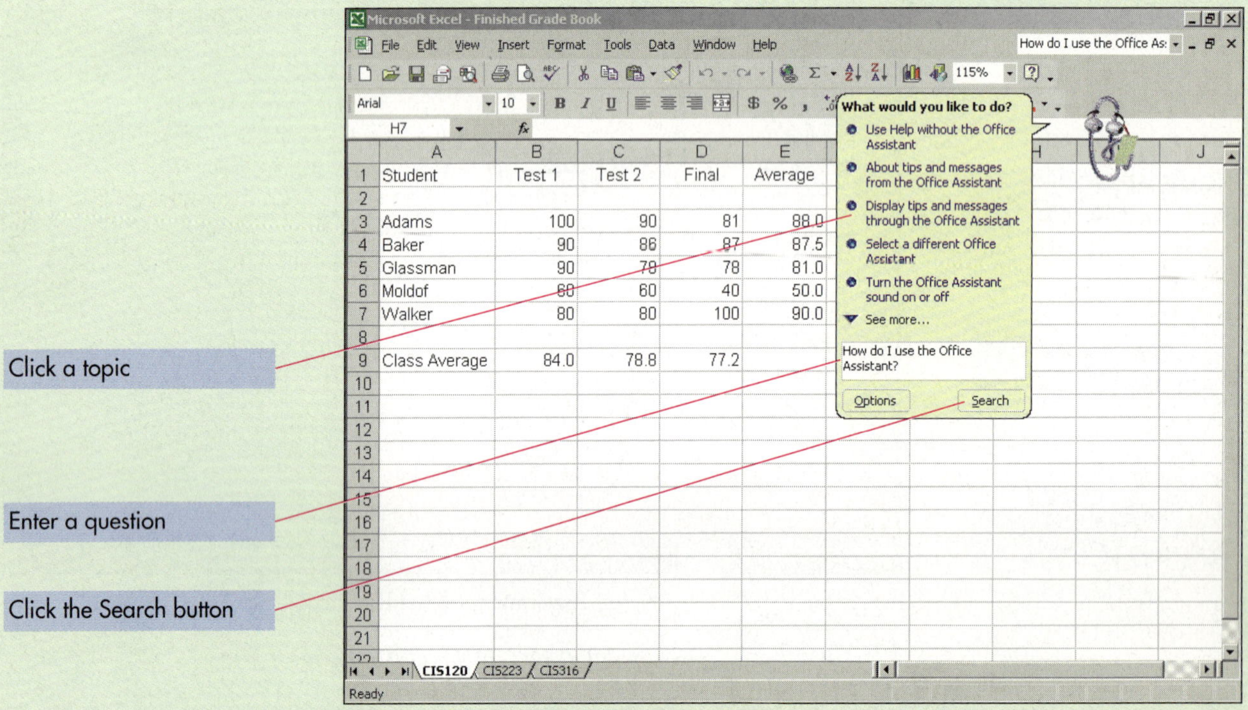

(h) The Office Assistant (step 8)

FIGURE 1.7 *Hands-on Exercise 1 (continued)*

ABOUT MICROSOFT EXCEL

Pull down the Help menu and click About Microsoft Excel to display the specific release number as well as other licensing information, including the Product ID. This Help screen also contains two very useful command buttons, System Info and Technical Support. The first button displays information about the hardware installed on your system, including the amount of memory and available space on the hard drive. The Technical Support button provides information on obtaining technical assistance.

We trust that you completed the hands-on exercise without difficulty and that you are more confident in your ability than when you first began. The exercise was not complicated, but it did accomplish several objectives and set the stage for a second exercise, which follows shortly.

Consider now Figure 1.8, which contains a modified version of the professor's grade book. Figure 1.8a shows the grade book at the end of the first hands-on exercise and reflects the changes made to the grades for Baker and Walker. Figure 1.8b shows the worksheet as it will appear at the end of the second exercise. Several changes bear mention:

1. One student has dropped the class and two other students have been added. Moldof appeared in the original worksheet in Figure 1.8a, but has somehow managed to withdraw; Coulter and Courier did not appear in the original grade book but have been added to the worksheet in Figure 1.8b.
2. A new column containing the students' majors has been added.

The implementation of these changes is accomplished through a combination of the ***Insert command*** (to add individual cells, rows, or columns) and/or the ***Delete command*** (to remove individual cells, rows, or columns). Execution of either command automatically adjusts the cell references in existing formulas to reflect the insertion or deletion of the various cells. The Insert and Delete commands can also be used to insert or delete a worksheet. The professor could, for example, add a new sheet to a workbook to include grades for another class and/or delete a worksheet for a class that was no longer taught. We focus initially, however, on the insertion and deletion of rows and columns within a worksheet.

Moldof will be dropped from class

	A	B	C	D	E
1	Student	Test 1	Test 2	Final	Average
2					
3	Adams	100	90	81	88.0
4	Baker	90	86	87	87.5
5	Glassman	90	78	78	81.0
6	Moldof	60	60	40	50.0
7	Walker	80	80	100	90.0
8					
9	Class Average	84.0	78.8	77.2	

(a) After Hands-on Exercise 1

A new column has been added (Major)

Two new students have been added

Moldof has been deleted

	A	B	C	D	E	F
1	Student	Major	Test 1	Test 2	Final	Average
2						
3	Adams	CIS	100	90	81	88.0
4	Baker	MKT	90	86	87	87.5
5	Coulter	ACC	85	95	100	95.0
6	Courier	FIN	75	75	85	80.0
7	Glassman	CIS	90	78	78	81.0
8	Walker	CIS	80	80	100	90.0
9						
10	Class Average		86.7	84.0	88.5	

(b) After Hands-on Exercise 2

FIGURE 1.8 *The Modified Grade Book*

Figure 1.9 displays the cell formulas in the professor's grade book and corresponds to the worksheets in Figure 1.8. The "before" and "after" worksheets reflect the insertion of a new column containing the students' majors, the addition of two new students, Coulter and Courier, and the deletion of an existing student, Moldof.

Let us consider the formula to compute Adams's semester average, which is contained in cell E3 of the original grade book, but in cell F3 in the modified grade book. The formula in Figure 1.9a referenced cells B3, C3, and D3 (the grades on test 1, test 2, and the final). The corresponding formula in Figure 1.9b reflects the fact that a new column has been inserted, and references cells C3, D3, and E3. The change in the formula is made automatically by Excel, without any action on the part of the user other than to insert the new column. The formulas for all other students have been adjusted in similar fashion.

Some students (all students below Baker) have had a further adjustment to reflect the addition of the new students through insertion of new rows in the worksheet. Glassman, for example, appeared in row 5 of the original worksheet, but appears in row 7 of the revised worksheet. Hence the formula to compute Glassman's semester average now references the grades in row 7, rather than in row 5 as in the original worksheet.

Finally, the formulas to compute the class averages have also been adjusted. These formulas appeared in row 9 of Figure 1.9a and averaged the grades in rows 3 through 7. The revised worksheet has a net increase of one student, which automatically moves these formulas to row 10, where the formulas are adjusted to average the grades in rows 3 through 8.

Formula references grades in B3, C3, and D3

Function references grades in rows 3–7

	A	B	C	D	E
1	Student	Test1	Test2	Final	Average
2					
3	Adams	100	90	81	=(B3+C3+2*D3)/4
4	Baker	90	86	87	=(B4+C4+2*D4)/4
5	Glassman	90	78	78	=(B5+C5+2*D5)/4
6	Moldof	60	60	40	=(B6+C6+2*D6)/4
7	Walker	80	80	100	=(B7+C7+2*D7)/4
8					
9	Class Average	=AVERAGE(B3:B7)	=AVERAGE(C3:C7)	=AVERAGE(D3:D7)	

(a) Before

	A	B	C	D	E	F
1	Student	Major	Test1	Test2	Final	Average
2						
3	Adams	CIS	100	90	81	=(C3+D3+2*E3)/4
4	Baker	MKT	90	86	87	=(C4+D4+2*E4)/4
5	Coulter	ACC	85	95	100	=(C5+D5+2*E5)/4
6	Courier	FIN	75	75	85	=(C6+D6+2*E6)/4
7	Glassman	CIS	90	78	78	=(C7+D7+2*E7)/4
8	Walker	CIS	80	80	100	=(C8+D8+2*E8)/4
9						
10	Class Average		=AVERAGE(C3:C8)	=AVERAGE(D3:D8)	=AVERAGE(E3:E8)	

Function changes to reference grades in rows 3–8 (due to addition of 2 new students and deletion of 1)

Formula changes to reference grades in C3, D3, and E3 due to addition of new column

(b) After

FIGURE 1.9 *The Insert and Delete Commands*

The ***Page Setup command*** gives you complete control of the printed worksheet as illustrated in Figure 1.10. Many of the options may not appear important now, but you will appreciate them as you develop larger and more complicated worksheets later in the text.

The Page tab in Figure 1.10 determines the orientation and scaling of the printed page. ***Portrait orientation*** (8½ × 11) prints vertically down the page. ***Landscape orientation*** (11 × 8½) prints horizontally across the page and is used when the worksheet is too wide to fit on a portrait page. The option buttons indicate mutually exclusive items, one of which *must* be selected; that is, a worksheet must be printed in either portrait or landscape orientation. Option buttons are also used to choose the scaling factor. You can reduce (enlarge) the output by a designated scaling factor, or you can force the output to fit on a specified number of pages. The latter option is typically used to force a worksheet to fit on a single page.

The Margins tab not only controls the margins, but will also center the worksheet horizontally and/or vertically. The Margins tab also determines the distance of the header and footer from the edge of the page.

The Header/Footer tab lets you create a header (and/or footer) that appears at the top (and/or bottom) of every page. The pull-down list boxes let you choose from several preformatted entries, or alternatively, you can click the appropriate command button to customize either entry.

The Sheet tab offers several additional options. The Gridlines option prints lines to separate the cells within the worksheet. The Row and Column Headings option displays the column letters and row numbers. Both options should be selected for most worksheets. Information about the additional entries can be obtained by clicking the Help button.

The Print Preview command button is available from all four tabs within the Page Setup dialog box. The command shows you how the worksheet will appear when printed and saves you from having to rely on trial and error.

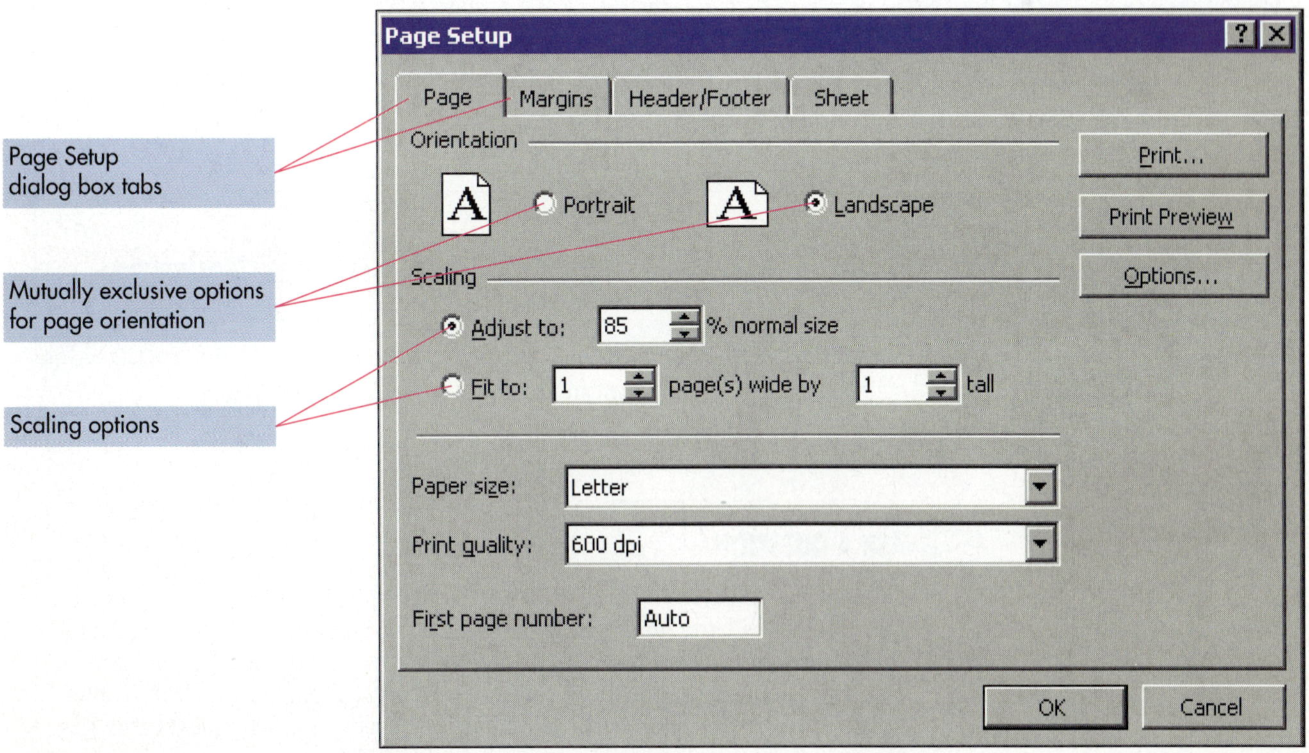

FIGURE 1.10 *The Page Setup Command*

Hands-on Exercise 2

Modifying a Worksheet

Objective To open an existing workbook; to insert and delete rows and columns in a worksheet; to print cell formulas and displayed values; to use the Page Setup command. Use Figure 1.11 as a guide.

Step 1: Open an Existing Workbook

- Start Excel. If necessary, pull down the **View menu** and click the **Task Pane command** to display the task pane as shown in Figure 1.11a. You should see the Finished Grade Book from the previous exercise since the most recently used workbooks are listed automatically.
- Click the link to the **Finished Grade Book workbook**. (Click the link to **More Workbooks** if the workbook is not listed to display the Open dialog box where you can select the drive and folder to locate your workbook.)
- The task pane closes automatically after the workbook has been opened.

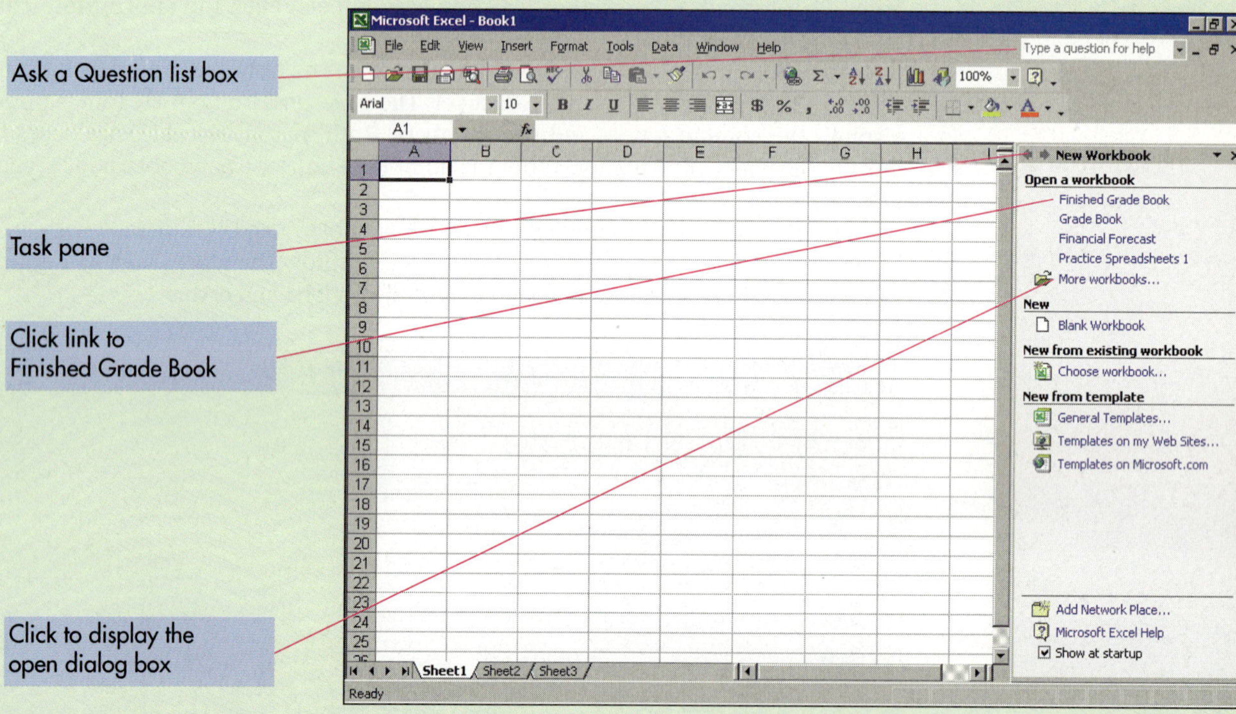

(a) Open an Existing Workbook (step 1)

FIGURE 1.11 *Hands-on Exercise 2*

> **ASK A QUESTION**
>
> Click in the "Ask a Question" list box to the right of the menu bar, type a question, press enter, and Excel returns a list of Help topics. Click any topic that appears promising to open the Help window with detailed information. You can ask multiple questions during an Excel session, then click the down arrow in the list box to return to an earlier question, which will return you to the Help topics.

Step 2: Delete a Row

- Click any cell in **row 6** (the row you will delete). Pull down the **Edit menu**. Click **Delete** to display the dialog box in Figure 1.11b. Click **Entire row**. Click **OK** to delete row 6.
- Moldof has disappeared from the grade book, and the class averages (now in row 8) have been updated automatically.
- Pull down the **Edit menu** and click **Undo Delete** (or click the **Undo button** on the Standard toolbar) to reverse the last command.
- The row for Moldof has been put back into the worksheet.
- Click any cell in **row 6**, and this time delete the entire row for good.
- Save the workbook.

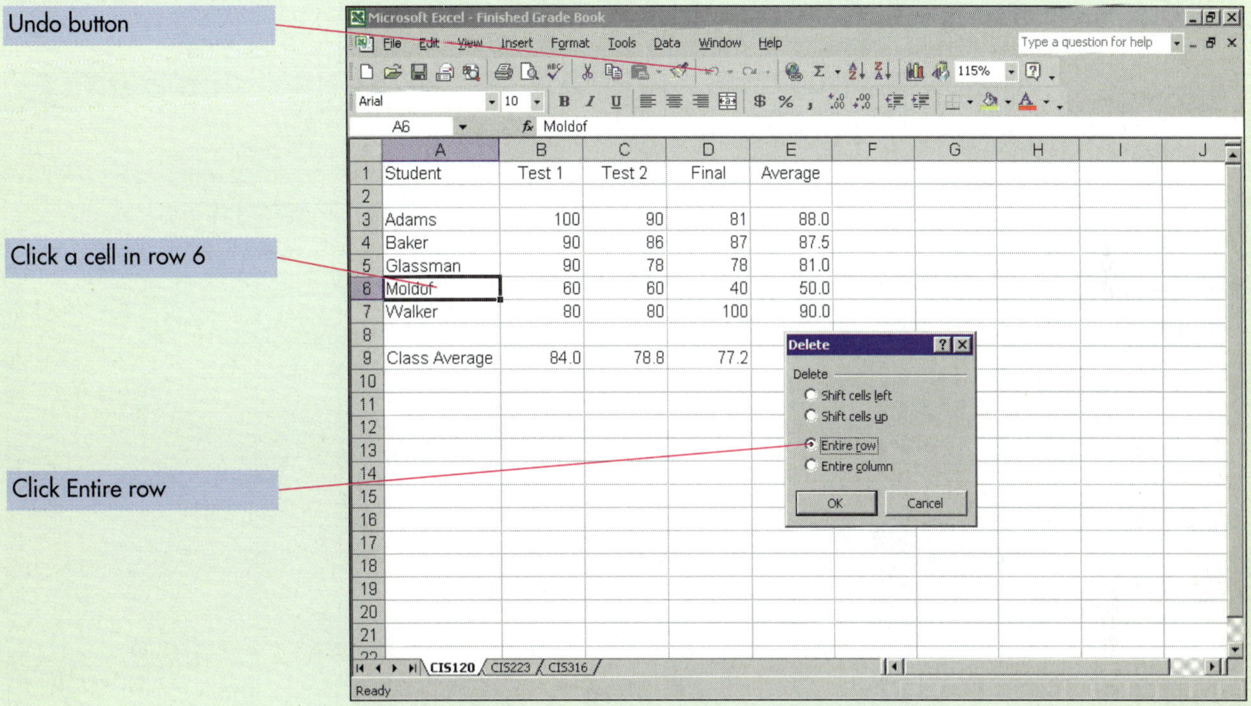

(b) Delete a Row (step 2)

FIGURE 1.11 *Hands-on Exercise 2 (continued)*

INSERT COMMENT COMMAND

You can add a comment, which displays a ScreenTip when you point to the cell, to any cell in a worksheet to explain a formula or other piece of information associated with that cell. Click in the cell that is to hold the comment, pull down the Insert menu, and click Comment to display a box in which you enter the comment. Click outside the box when you have completed the entry. Point to the cell (which should have a tiny red triangle) and you will see the comment you just created.

Step 3: **Insert a Row**

- Click any cell in **row 5** (the row containing Glassman's grades). Pull down the **Insert menu**. Click **Rows** to add a new row above the current row.
- A new row is inserted into the worksheet with the same formatting as in the row above. (Thus, you can ignore the Format Painter button, which allows you to change the formatting.) Row 5 is now blank, and Glassman is now in row 6.
- Enter the data for the new student in row 5 as shown in Figure 1.11c. Click in **cell A5**. Type **Coulter**. Press the **right arrow key** or click in **cell B5**. Enter the test grades of 85, 95, 100 in cells B5, C5, and D5, respectively.
- Enter the formula to compute the semester average, **=(B5+C5+2*D5)/4**. Be sure to begin the formula with an equal sign. Press **enter**.
- Click the **Save button** on the Standard toolbar, or pull down the **File menu** and click **Save** to save the changes made to this point.

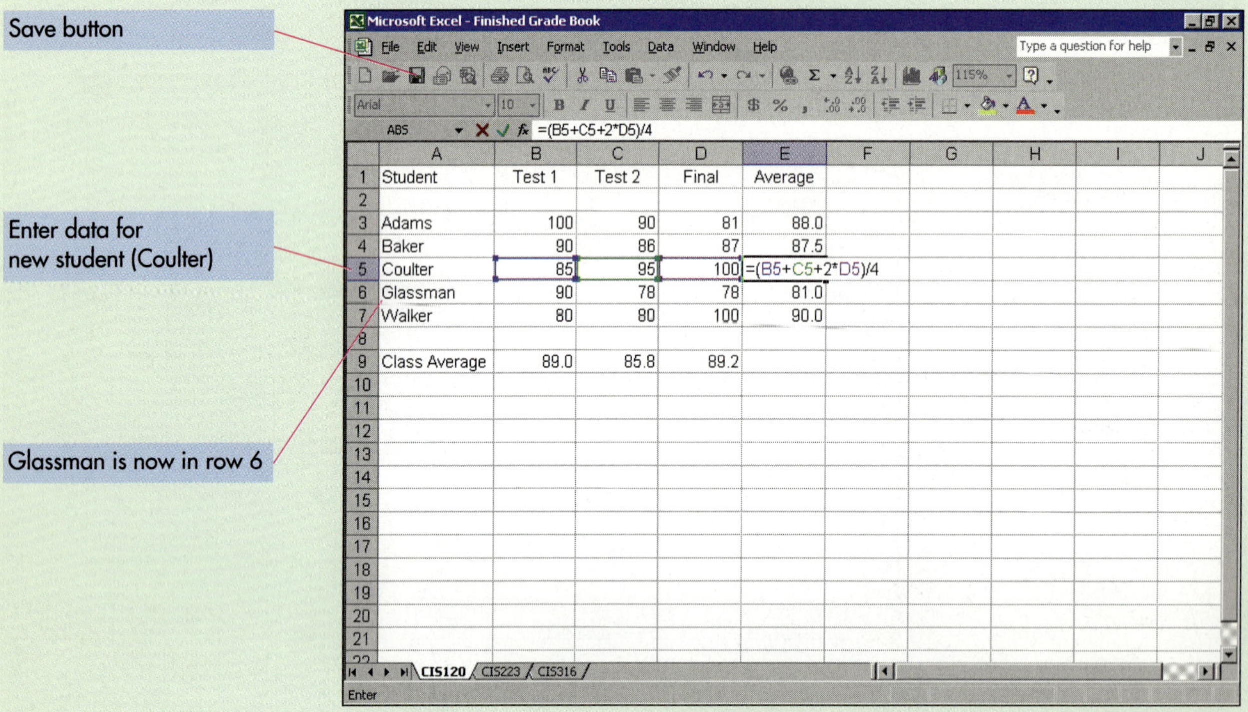

(c) Insert a Row (step 3)

FIGURE 1.11 *Hands-on Exercise 2 (continued)*

CORRECTING MISTAKES

The fastest way to change the contents of an existing cell is to double click in the cell in order to make the changes directly in the cell rather than on the formula bar. Use the mouse or arrow keys to position the insertion point at the point of correction. Press the Ins key to toggle between insert and overtype and/or use the Backspace or Del key to erase a character. Press the Home and End keys to move to the first and last characters in the cell, respectively.

Step 4: **The AutoComplete Feature**

- Point to the row heading for **row 6** (which now contains Glassman's grades), then click the **right mouse button** to select the row and display a shortcut menu. Click **Insert** to insert a new row 6, which moves Glassman to row 7 as shown in Figure 1.11d.
- Click in **cell A6**. Type **C**, the first letter in "Courier," which also happens to be the first letter in "Coulter," a previous entry in column A. If the AutoComplete feature is on (see boxed tip), Coulter's name will be automatically inserted in cell A6 with "oulter" selected.
- Type **ourier** (the remaining letters in "Courier," which replace "oulter."
- Enter Courier's grades in the appropriate cells (75, 75, and 85 in cells B6, C6, and D6, respectively). Click in **cell E6**. Enter the formula to compute the semester average, **=(B6+C6+2*D6)/4**. Press **enter**.

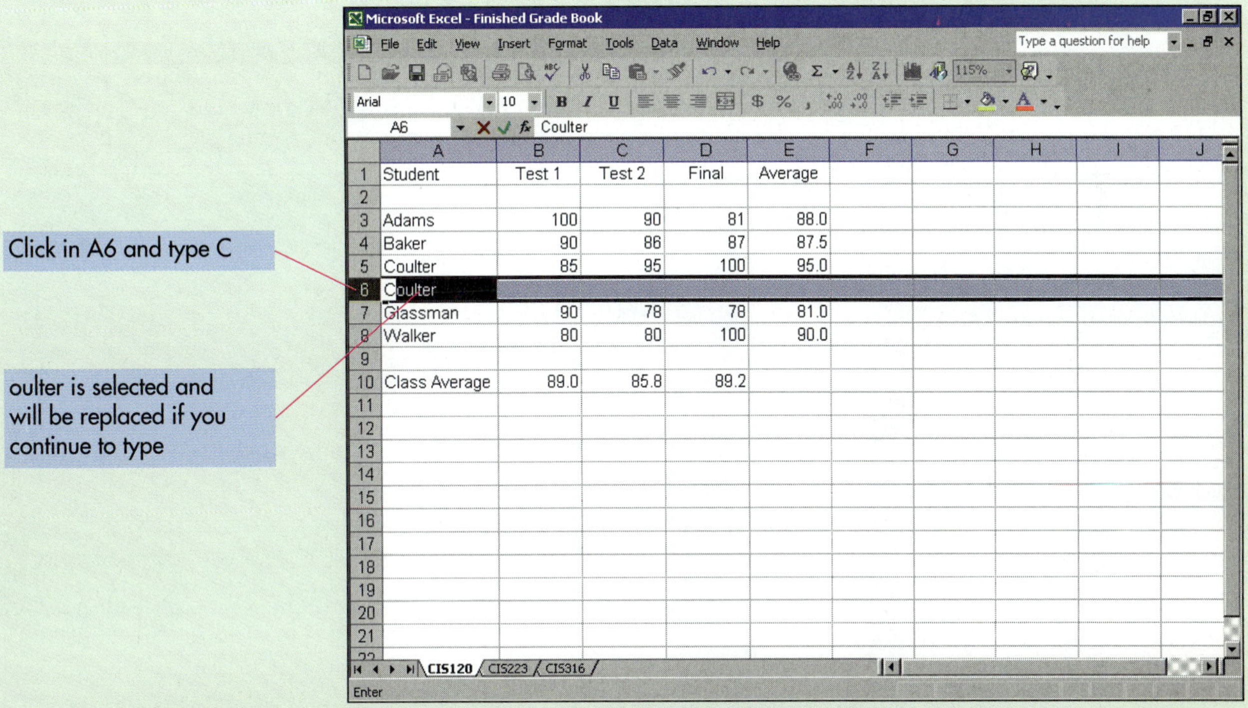

(d) The AutoComplete Feature (step 4)

FIGURE 1.11 *Hands-on Exercise 2 (continued)*

> **AUTOCOMPLETE**
>
> As soon as you begin typing a label into a cell, Excel searches for and (automatically) displays any other label in that column that matches the letters you typed. It's handy if you want to repeat a label, but it can be distracting if you want to enter a different label that just happens to begin with the same letter. To turn the feature on (off), pull down the Tools menu, click Options, then click the Edit tab. Check (clear) the box to enable the AutoComplete feature.

Step 5: **Insert a Column**

- Point to the column heading for column B, then click the **right mouse button** to display a shortcut menu as shown in Figure 1.11e.
- Click **Insert** to insert a new column, which becomes the new column B. All existing columns have been moved to the right.
- Click in **cell B1**. Type **Major**.
- Click in **cell B3**. Enter **CIS** as Adams's major. Press the **down arrow** to move automatically to the major for the next student.
- Type **MKT** in cell B4. Press the **down arrow**. Type **ACC** in cell B5. Press the **down arrow**. Type **FIN** in cell B6.
- Press the **down arrow** to move to cell B7. Type **C** (AutoComplete will automatically enter "IS" to complete the entry). Press the **down arrow** to move to cell B8. Type **C** (the AutoComplete feature again enters "IS"), then press **enter** to complete the entry.

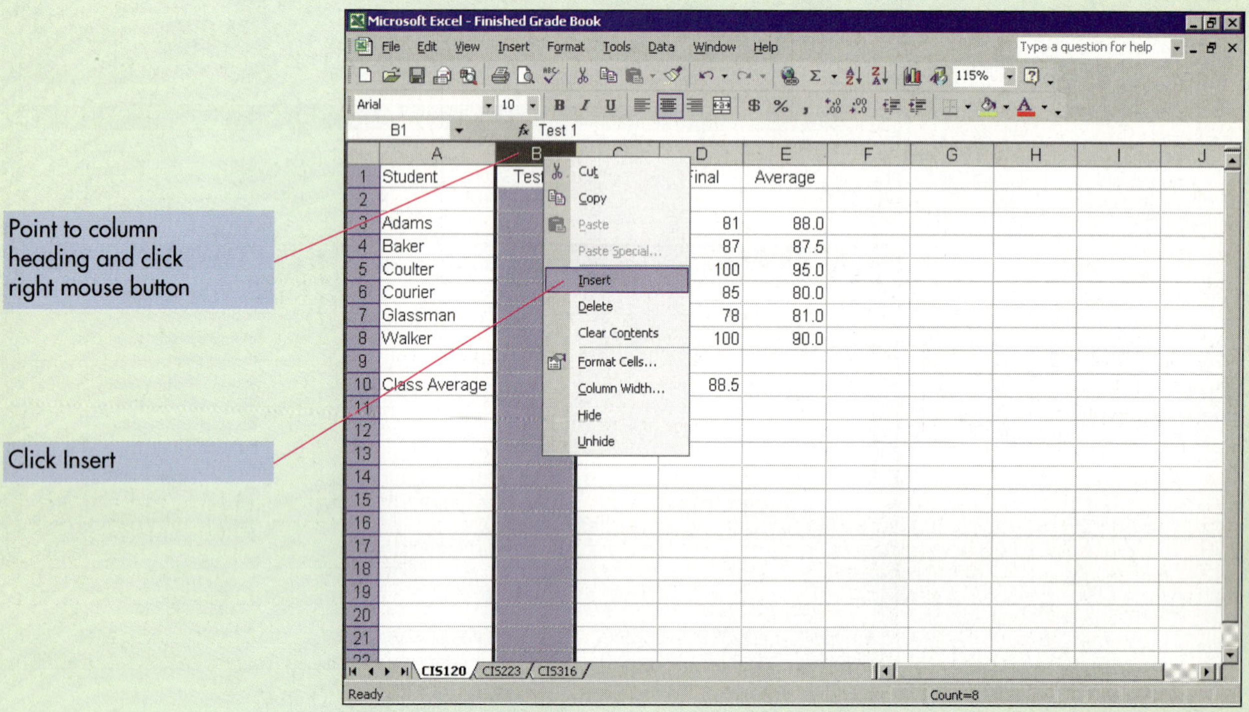

(e) Insert a Column (step 5)

FIGURE 1.11 *Hands-on Exercise 2 (continued)*

INSERTING AND DELETING INDIVIDUAL CELLS

You can insert and/or delete individual cells as opposed to an entire row or column. To insert a cell, click in the cell to the left or above where you want the new cell to go, pull down the Insert menu, then click Cells to display the Insert dialog box. Click the appropriate option button to shift cells right or down and click OK. To delete a cell or cells, select the cell(s), pull down the Edit menu, click the Delete command, then click the option button to shift cells left or up. See practice exercise 2 at the end of the chapter.

Step 6: Display the Cell Formulas

- Pull down the **Tools menu**. Click **Options** to display the Options dialog box. Click the **View tab**. Check the box for **Formulas**. Click **OK**. (You can also press Ctrl+~ to toggle between cell formulas and displayed values.)
- The worksheet should display the cell formulas as shown in Figure 1.11f. If necessary, click the **right scroll arrow** on the horizontal scroll bar until column F, the column containing the formulas to compute the semester averages, comes into view.
- If necessary (i.e., if the formulas are not completely visible), double click the border between the column headings for columns F and G. This increases the width of column F to accommodate the widest entry in that column.

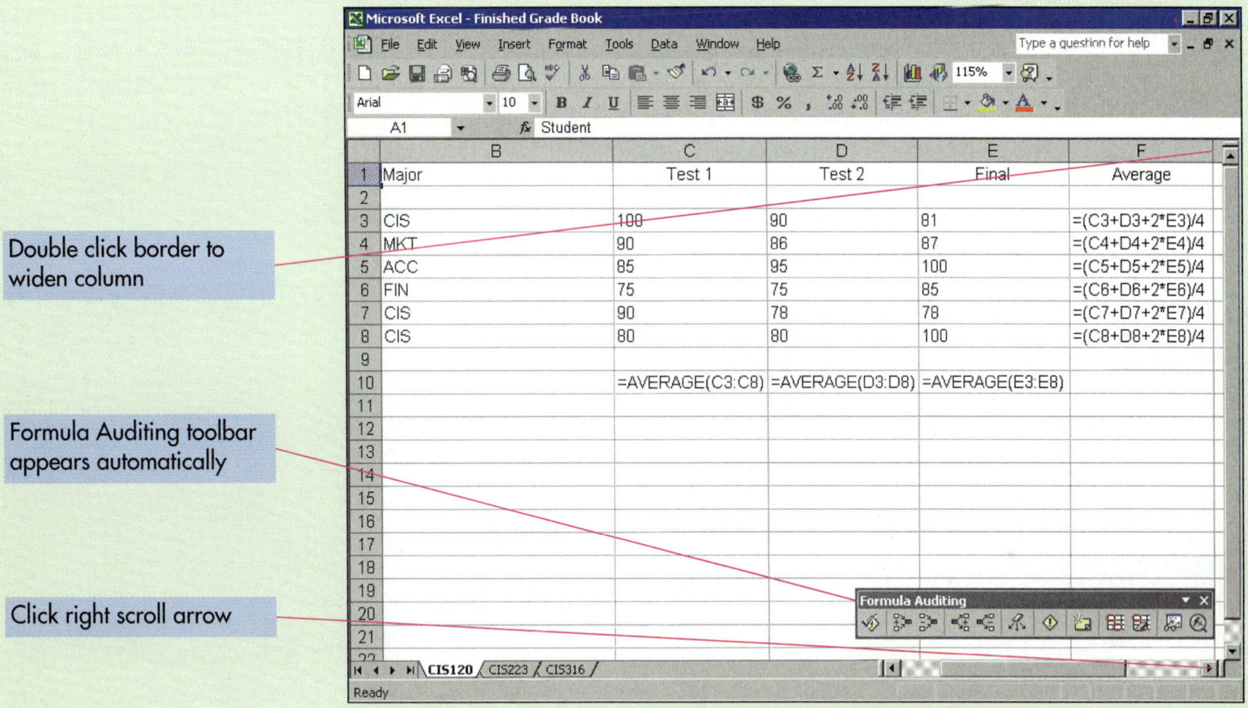

(f) Display the Cell Formulas (step 6)

FIGURE 1.11 *Hands-on Exercise 2 (continued)*

THE FORMULA AUDITING TOOLBAR

The Formula Auditing Toolbar appears automatically any time the display is changed to show cell formulas rather than displayed values. The toolbar is designed to help you detect and correct errors in cell formulas. Click in any cell, then click the Trace Precedents button to show the cells that are used to evaluate the formula in the selected cell. You can also click in any cell and use the Trace Dependents button to show those cells whose formula references the selected cell. Click the Remove All Arrows button to erase the arrows from the display.

Step 7: The Page Setup Command

- Pull down the **File menu**. Click the **Page Setup command** to display the Page Setup dialog box as shown in Figure 1.11g.
  - Click the **Page tab**. Click the **Landscape option button**. Click the option button to **Fit to 1 page**.
  - Click the **Margins tab**. Check the box to center the worksheet horizontally.
  - Click the **Header/Footer tab**. Click the **drop-down arrow** on the Footer list box. Scroll to the top of the list and click **(none)** to remove the footer.
  - Click the **Sheet tab**. Check the boxes to print Row and Column Headings and Gridlines.
- Click **OK** to exit the Page Setup dialog box.
- Save the workbook.

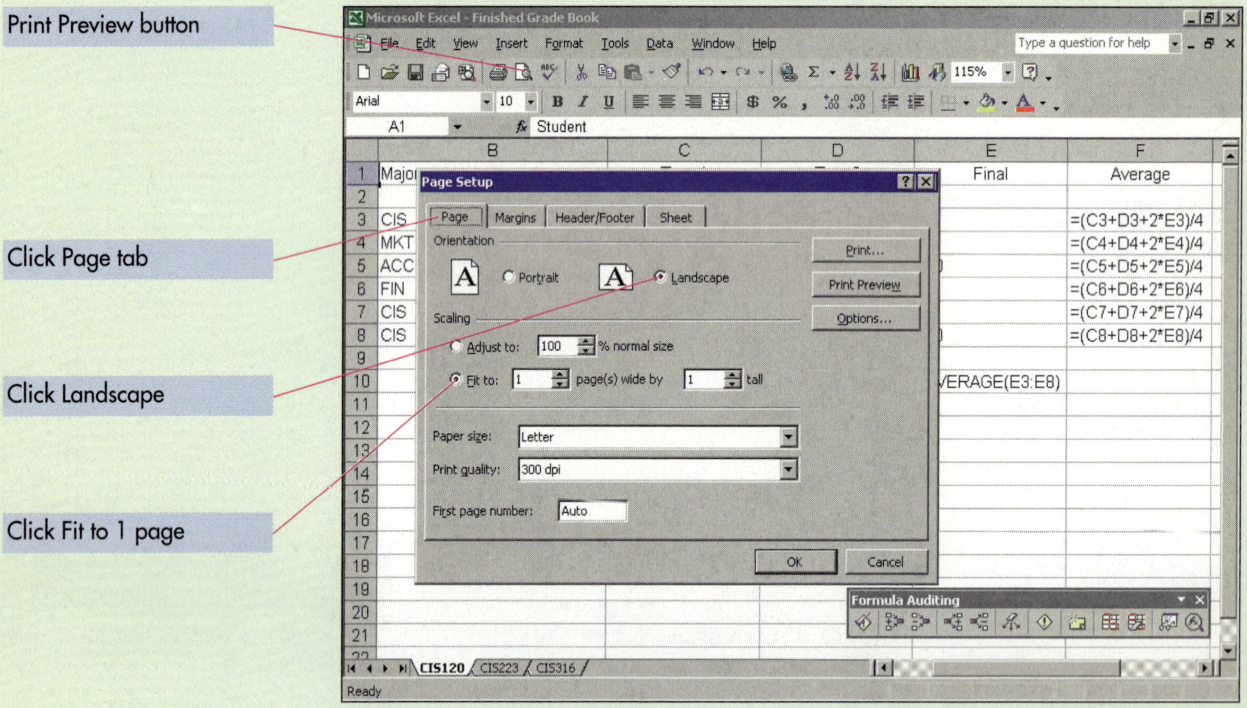

(g) The Page Setup Command (step 7)

FIGURE 1.11 *Hands-on Exercise 2 (continued)*

KEYBOARD SHORTCUTS—THE DIALOG BOX

Press Tab or Shift+Tab to move forward (backward) between fields in a dialog box, or press the Alt key plus the underlined letter to move directly to an option. Use the space bar to toggle check boxes on or off and the up (down) arrow keys to move between options in a list box. Press enter to activate the highlighted command button and Esc to exit the dialog box without accepting the changes. These are universal shortcuts and apply to any Windows application.

Step 8: The Print Preview Command

- Pull down the **File menu** and click **Print Preview** (or click the **Print Preview button** on the Standard toolbar).
- Your monitor should match the display in Figure 1.11h. (The Page Setup dialog box is also accessible from this screen.)
- Click the **Print command button** to display the Print dialog box, then click **OK** to print the worksheet.
- Press **Ctrl+~** to switch to displayed values rather than cell formulas. Click the **Print button** on the Standard toolbar to print the worksheet without displaying the Print dialog box.

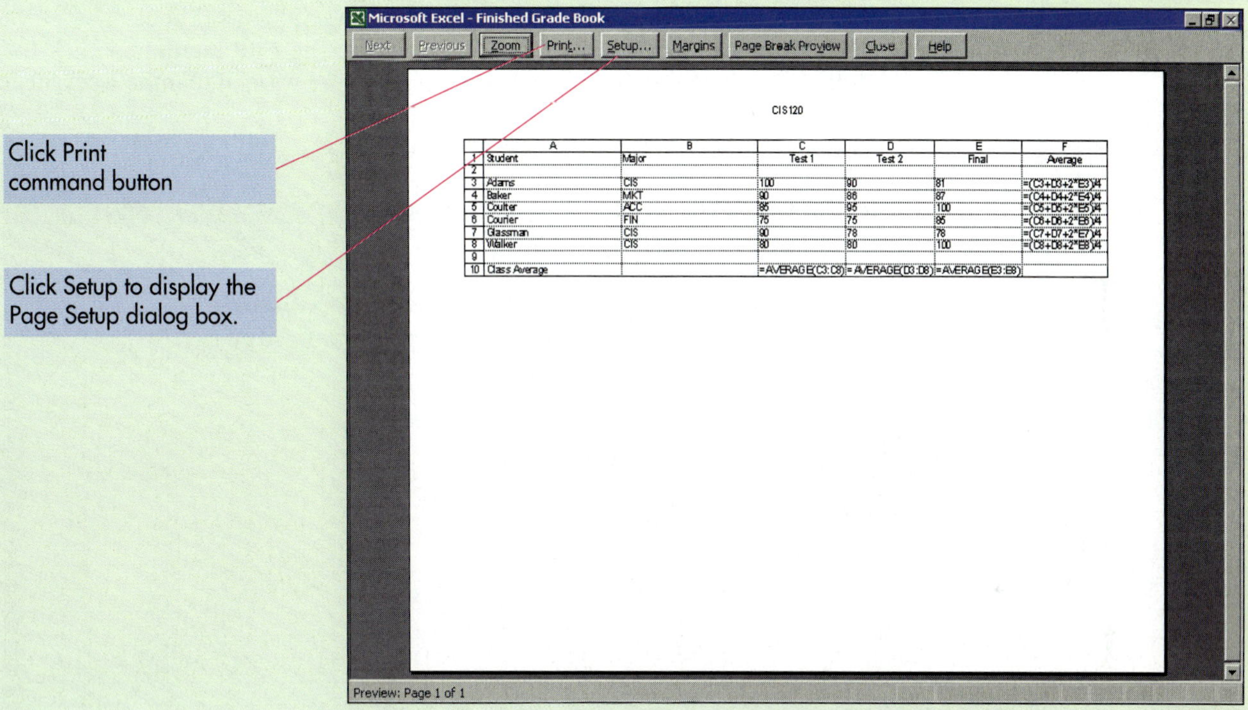

(h) The Print Preview Command (step 8)

FIGURE 1.11 *Hands-on Exercise 2 (continued)*

FIND AND REPLACE

Anyone familiar with a word processor takes the Find and Replace command for granted, but many people are surprised to learn that the same commands are also found in Excel. The commands are found in the Edit menu and provide the same options as in Microsoft Word. You can replace text and/or formatting throughout a worksheet. See practice exercise 4 at the end of the chapter.

Step 9: Insert and Delete a Worksheet

- Pull down the **Insert menu** and click the **Worksheet command** to insert a new worksheet. The worksheet is inserted as Sheet1.
- Click in cell **A1**, type **Student**, and press **enter**. Enter the labels and student data as shown in Figure 1.11i. Enter the formulas to calculate the students' semester averages in column D. (The midterm and final count equally.)
- Enter the formulas in row 7 to compute the class averages on each exam. If necessary, click and drag the column border between columns A and B to widen column A.
- Double click the name of the worksheet (Sheet1) to select the name. Type a new name, **CIS101**, to replace the selected text and press **enter**. If necessary, click and drag the worksheet tab to the beginning of the workbook.
- Click the worksheet tab for **CIS223**. Pull down the **Edit menu** and click the **Delete Sheet command**. Click **Delete** when you are warned that the worksheet will be permanently deleted.
- Save the workbook. Print the new worksheet. Exit Excel.

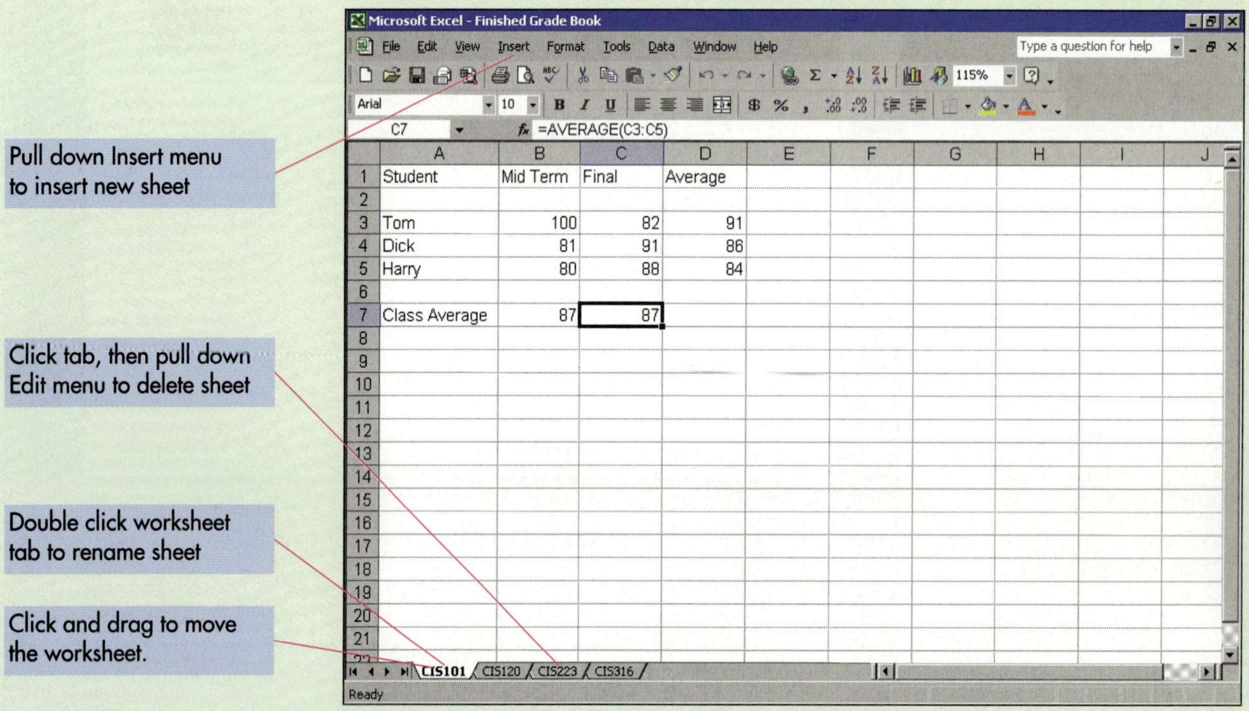

(i) Insert and Delete a Worksheet (step 9)

FIGURE 1.11 *Hands-on Exercise 2 (continued)*

MOVING, COPYING, AND RENAMING WORKSHEETS

The fastest way to move a worksheet is to click and drag the worksheet tab. You can copy a worksheet in similar fashion by pressing and holding the Ctrl key as you drag the worksheet tab. To rename a worksheet, double click its tab to select the current name, type the new name, and press the enter key.

Figure 1.12 contains a much improved version of the professor's grade book. The most *obvious* difference is in the appearance of the worksheet, as a variety of formatting commands have been used to make it more attractive. The exam scores and semester averages are centered under the appropriate headings. The exam weights are formatted with percentages, and all averages are displayed with exactly one decimal point. Boldface and italics are used for emphasis. Shading and borders are used to highlight various areas of the worksheet. The title has been centered over the worksheet and is set in a larger typeface.

The most *significant* differences, however, are that the weight of each exam is indicated within the worksheet, and that the formulas to compute the students' semester averages reference these cells in their calculations. The professor can change the contents of the cells containing the exam weights and see immediately the effect on the student averages.

The isolation of cells whose values are subject to change is one of the most important concepts in the development of a spreadsheet. This technique lets the professor explore alternative grading strategies. He or she may notice, for example, that the class did significantly better on the final than on either of the first two exams. The professor may then decide to give the class a break and increase the weight of the final relative to the other tests. But before the professor says anything to the class, he or she wants to know the effect of increasing the weight of the final to 60%. What if the final should count 70%? The effect of these and other changes can be seen immediately by entering the new exam weights in the appropriate cells at the bottom of the worksheet.

Title is centered in larger font size; it is also in boldface and italics

Formatting includes boldface, shading, and borders

Exam weights are used to calculate the semester average

	A	B	C	D	E
1	***CIS120 - Spring Semester***				
2					
3	**Student**	**Test 1**	**Test 2**	**Final**	**Average**
4	Costa, Frank	70	80	90	82.5
5	Ford, Judd	70	85	80	78.8
6	Grauer, Jessica	90	80	98	91.5
7	Howard, Lauren	80	78	98	88.5
8	Krein, Darren	85	70	95	86.3
9	Moldof, Adam	75	75	80	77.5
10					
11	**Class Averages**	**78.3**	**78.0**	**90.2**	
12					
13	**Exam Weights**	**25%**	**25%**	**50%**	

FIGURE 1.12 *A Better Grade Book*

ISOLATE ASSUMPTIONS

The formulas in a worksheet should always be based on cell references rather than on specific values—for example, B13 or $B$13 rather than .25. The cells containing these values should be clearly labeled and set apart from the rest of the worksheet. You can then vary the inputs (or ***assumptions*** on which the worksheet is based) to see the effect within the worksheet. The chance for error is also minimized because you are changing the contents of a single cell rather than changing the multiple formulas that reference those values.

CELL RANGES

Every command in Excel operates on a rectangular group of cells known as a ***range***. A range may be as small as a single cell or as large as the entire worksheet. It may consist of a row or part of a row, a column or part of a column, or multiple rows and/or columns. The cells within a range are specified by indicating the diagonally opposite corners, typically the upper-left and lower-right corners of the rectangle. Many different ranges could be selected in conjunction with the worksheet of Figure 1.12. The exam weights, for example, are found in the range B13:D13. The students' semester averages are found in the range E4:E9. The student data is contained in the range A4:E9.

The easiest way to select a range is to click and drag—click at the beginning of the range, then press and hold the left mouse button as you drag the mouse to the end of the range where you release the mouse. Once selected, the range is highlighted and its cells will be affected by any subsequent command. The range remains selected until another range is defined or until you click another cell anywhere on the worksheet.

COPY COMMAND

The ***Copy command*** duplicates the contents of a cell, or range of cells, and saves you from having to enter the contents of every cell individually. Figure 1.13 illustrates how the command can be used to duplicate the formula to compute the class average on the different tests. The cell that you are copying from, cell B11, is called the ***source range***. The cells that you are copying to, cells C11 and D11, are the ***destination range***. The formula is not copied exactly, but is adjusted as it is copied, to compute the average for the pertinent test.

The formula to compute the average on the first test was entered in cell B11 as =AVERAGE(B4:B9). The range in the formula references the cell seven rows above the cell containing the formula (i.e., cell B4 is seven rows above cell B11) as well as the cell two rows above the formula (i.e., cell B9). When the formula in cell B11 is copied to C11, it is adjusted so that the cells referenced in the new formula are in the same relative position as those in the original formula; that is, seven and two rows above the formula. The formula in cell C11 becomes =AVERAGE(C4:C9). The formula in cell D11 becomes =AVERAGE(D4:D9).

	A	B	C	D	E
1			CIS120 - Spring Semester		
2					
3	Student	Test 1	Test 2	Final	Average
4	Costa, Frank	70	80	90	=$B$13*B4+$C$13*C4+$D$13*D4
5	Ford, Judd	70	85	80	=$B$13*B5+$C$13*C5+$D$13*D5
6	Grauer, Jessica	90	80	98	=$B$13*B6+$C$13*C6+$D$13*D6
7	Howard, Lauren	80	78	98	=$B$13*B7+$C$13*C7+$D$13*D7
8	Krein, Darren	85	70	95	=$B$13*B8+$C$13*C8+$D$13*D8
9	Moldof, Adam	75	75	80	=$B$13*B9+$C$13*C9+$D$13*D9
10					
11	Class Averages	=AVERAGE(B4:B9)	=AVERAGE(C4:C9)	=AVERAGE(D4:D9)	
12					
13	Exam Weights	25%	25%	50%	

Formula was entered in B11

Relative addresses adjust when formula is copied

Absolute addresses stay the same when formula is copied

Relative addresses adjust when formula is copied

FIGURE 1.13 *The Copy Command*

Figure 1.13 also illustrates how the Copy command is used to copy the formula for a student's semester average, from cell E4 (the source range) to cells E5 through E9 (the destination range). This is slightly more complicated than the previous example because the formula is based on a student's grades, which vary from one student to the next, and on the exam weights, which do not. The cells referring to the student's grades should adjust as the formula is copied, but the addresses referencing the exam weights should not.

The distinction between cell references that remain constant versus cell references that change is made by means of a dollar sign. An ***absolute reference*** remains constant throughout the copy operation and is specified with a dollar sign in front of the column and row designation, for example, $B$13. A ***relative reference***, on the other hand, adjusts during a copy operation and is specified without dollar signs; for example, B4. (A ***mixed reference*** uses a single dollar sign to make the column absolute and the row relative; for example, $A5. Alternatively, you can make the column relative and the row absolute as in A$5.)

Consider, for example, the formula to compute a student's semester average as it appears in cell E4 of Figure 1.13:

=$B$13*B4+$C$13*C4+$D$13*D4

- Final exam grade is in cell D4 and is a *relative reference*
- Weight for final exam is in cell D13 and is an *absolute reference*
- Test 2 grade is in cell C4 and is a *relative reference*
- Weight for test 2 is in cell C13 and is an *absolute reference*
- Test 1 grade is in cell B4 and is a *relative reference*
- Weight for Test 1 is in cell B13 and is an *absolute reference*

The formula in cell E4 uses a combination of relative and absolute addresses to compute the student's semester average. Relative addresses are used for the exam grades (found in cells B4, C4, and D4) and change automatically when the formula is copied to the other rows. Absolute addresses are used for the exam weights (found in cells B13, C13, and D13) and remain constant.

The copy operation is implemented by using the ***clipboard*** common to all Windows applications and a combination of the Copy and Paste commands from the Edit menu. (Office 2002 also supports the Office Clipboard that can hold 24 separate items. All references to the "clipboard" in this chapter, however, are to the Windows clipboard.) The contents of the source range are copied to the clipboard, from where they are pasted to the destination range. The contents of the clipboard are replaced with each subsequent Copy command but are unaffected by the Paste command. Thus, you can execute the Paste command several times in succession to paste the contents of the clipboard to multiple locations.

MIXED REFERENCES

Most spreadsheets can be developed using only absolute or relative references such as $A1$1 or A, respectively. Mixed references, where only the row ($A1) or column (A$1) changes, are more subtle, and thus are typically not used by beginners. Mixed references are necessary in more sophisticated worksheets and add significantly to the power of Excel.

The ***move operation*** is not used in the grade book, but its presentation is essential for the sake of completeness. The move operation transfers the contents of a cell (or range of cells) from one location to another. After the move is completed, the cells where the move originated (that is, the source range) are empty. This is in contrast to the Copy command, where the entries remain in the source range and are duplicated in the destination range.

A simple move operation is depicted in Figure 1.14a, in which the contents of cell A3 are moved to cell C3, with the formula in cell C3 unchanged after the move. In other words, the move operation simply picks up the contents of cell A3 (a formula that adds the values in cells A1 and A2) and puts it down in cell C3. The source range, cell A3, is empty after the move operation has been executed.

Figure 1.14b depicts a situation where the formula itself remains in the same cell, but one of the values it references is moved to a new location; that is, the entry

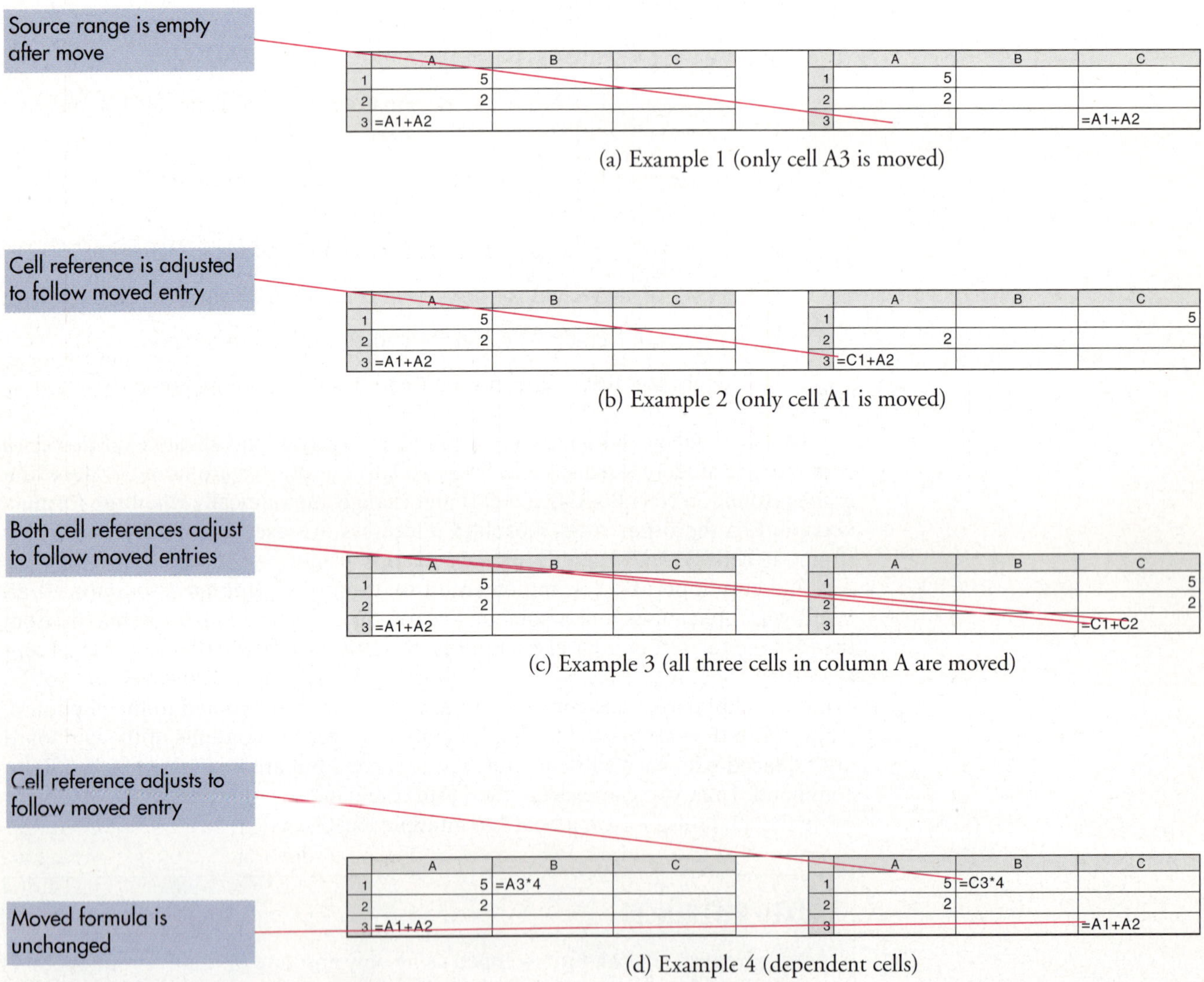

FIGURE 1.14 *The Move Command*

Cell reference adjusts to follow moved entry

	A	B	C
1	5	=$A$3*4	
2	2		
3	=$A$1+$A$2		

	A	B	C
1		=$C$3*4	5
2			2
3			=$C$1+$C$2

Both cell references adjust to follow moved entries

(e) Example 5 (absolute cell addresses)

FIGURE 1.14 *The Move Command (continued)*

in A1 is moved to C1. The formula in cell A3 is adjusted to follow the moved entry to its new location; that is, the formula is now =C1+A2.

The situation is different in Figure 1.14c as the contents of all three cells—A1, A2, and A3—are moved. After the move has taken place, cells C1 and C2 contain the 5 and the 2, respectively, with the formula in cell C3 adjusted to reflect the movement of the contents of cells A1 and A2. Once again the source range (A1:A3) is empty after the move is completed.

Figure 1.14d contains an additional formula in cell B1, which is *dependent* on cell A3, which in turn is moved to cell C3. The formula in cell C3 is unchanged after the move because *only* the formula was moved, *not* the values it referenced. The formula in cell B1 changes because cell B1 refers to an entry (cell A3) that was moved to a new location (cell C3).

Figure 1.14e shows that the specification of an absolute reference has no meaning in a move operation, because the cell addresses are adjusted as necessary to reflect the cells that have been moved. Moving a formula that contains an absolute reference does not adjust the formula. Moving a value that is specified as an absolute reference, however, adjusts the formula to follow the cell to its new location. Thus all of the absolute references in Figure 1.14e are changed to reflect the entries that were moved.

The move operation is a convenient way to improve the appearance of a worksheet after it has been developed. It is subtle in its operation, and we suggest you think twice before moving cell entries because of the complexities involved.

The move operation is implemented by using the Windows clipboard and a combination of the Cut and Paste commands from the Edit menu. The contents of the source range are transferred to the clipboard, from which they are pasted to the destination range. (Executing a Paste command after a Cut command empties the clipboard. This is different from pasting after a Copy command, which does not affect the contents of the clipboard.)

LEARNING BY DOING

As we have already indicated, there are many different ways to accomplish the same task. You can execute commands using a pull-down menu, a shortcut menu, a toolbar, or the keyboard. In the exercise that follows we emphasize pull-down menus (the most basic technique) but suggest various shortcuts as appropriate.

Realize, however, that while the shortcuts are interesting, it is far more important to focus on the underlying concepts in the exercise, rather than specific key strokes or mouse clicks. The professor's grade book was developed to emphasize the difference between relative and absolute cell references. The grade book also illustrates the importance of isolating assumptions so that alternative strategies (e.g., different exam weights) can be considered.

Hands-on Exercise 3

Creating a Workbook

Objective To create a new workbook; to copy formulas containing relative and absolute references. Use Figure 1.15 as a guide in doing the exercise.

Step 1: **Create a New Workbook**

- Click the **Start button**, click (or point to) the **Programs command,** then click **Microsoft Excel** to start the program. If Excel is already open, click the **New button** on the Standard toolbar (or click **Blank Workbook** in the task pane) to open a new workbook.
- Click and drag the Office Assistant out of the way or hide it altogether. (Pull down the **Help menu** and click **Hide the Office Assistant.**)
- If necessary, separate the Standard and Formatting toolbars. Pull down the **View menu**, click **Toolbars**, click **Customize**, and click the **Options tab**. Check the box that indicates the Standard and Formatting toolbars should be displayed on two rows.
- Close the task pane. Click in cell **A1**. Enter the title of the worksheet, **CIS120 - Spring Semester.**
- Enter the column headings in row 3 as in Figure 1.15a. Click in cell **A3** and type **Student**, then press the **right arrow key** to move to cell **B3**. Type **Test 1**.
- Press the **right arrow key** to move to cell **C3**. Type **Test 2**. Enter the words **Final** and **Average** in cells D3 and E3, respectively. Your worksheet should match Figure 1.15a.

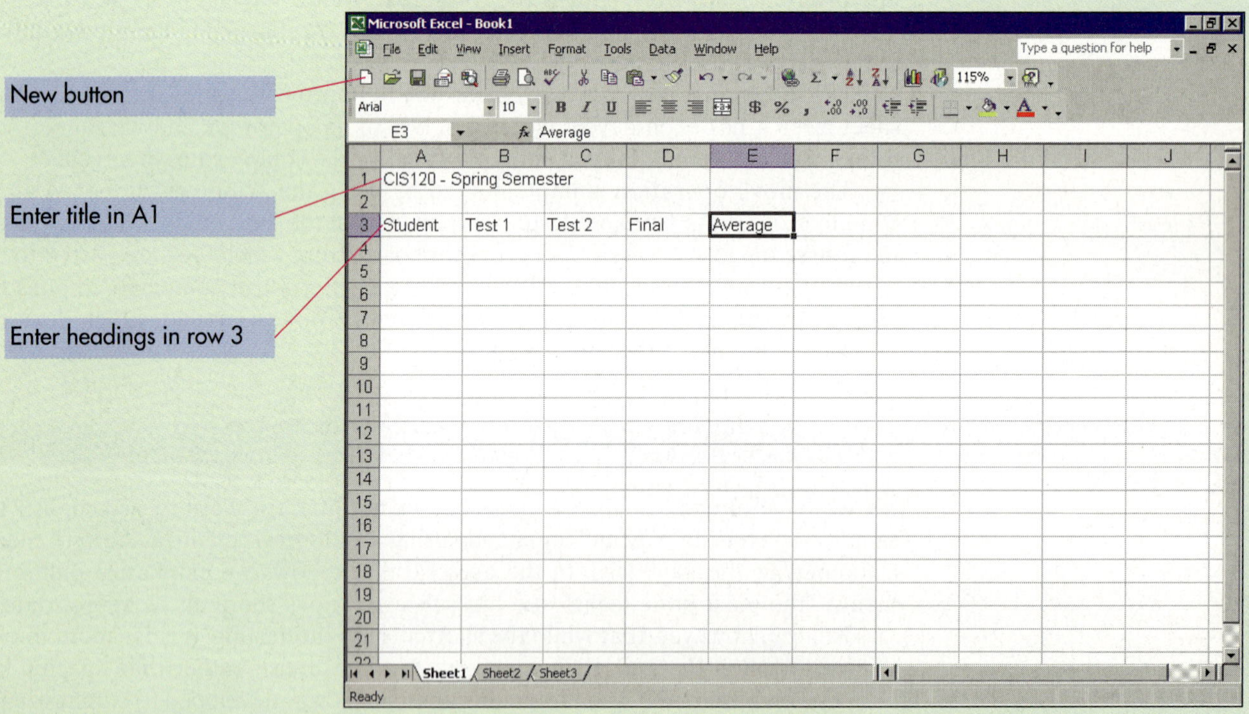

(a) Create a New Workbook (step 1)

FIGURE 1.15 *Hands-on Exercise 3*

Step 2: **Save the Workbook**

- Pull down the **File menu** and click **Save** (or click the **Save button** on the Standard toolbar) to display the Save As dialog box as shown in Figure 1.15b. (The Save As dialog box always appears the first time you save a workbook, so that you can give the workbook a name.)
- Click the **drop-down arrow** on the Save In list box. Click the appropriate drive, drive C or drive A, depending on where you are saving your Excel workbooks.
- Double click the **Exploring Excel folder** to make it the active folder (the folder in which you will save the document).
- Click and drag **Book1** (the default entry) in the File name text box to select it, then type **Better Grade Book** as the name of the workbook. Click **Save** or press the **enter key**. The title bar changes to reflect the name of the workbook.

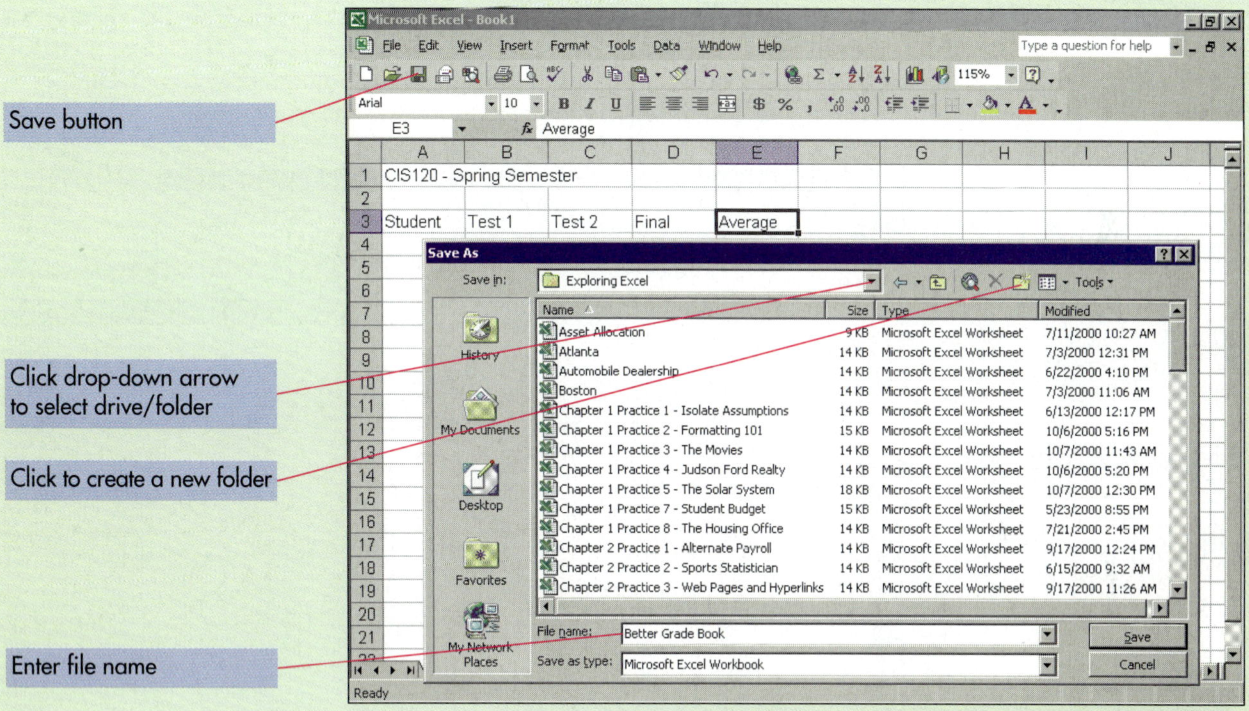

(b) Save the Workbook (step 2)

FIGURE 1.15 *Hands-on Exercise 3 (continued)*

> **CREATE A NEW FOLDER**
>
> Do you work with a large number of different workbooks? If so, it may be useful to store those workbooks in different folders, perhaps one folder for each subject you are taking. Pull down the File menu, click the Save As command to display the Save As dialog box, then click the Create New Folder button to display the associated dialog box. Enter the name of the folder, then click OK. Once the folder has been created, use the Look In box to change to that folder the next time you open that workbook. See practice exercise 7 at the end of the chapter.

Step 3: Enter Student Data and Literal Information

- Click in cell **A4** and type **Costa, Frank**, then enter Frank's grades on the two tests and the final as shown in Figure 1.15c. Do *not* enter Frank's semester average in cell E4 as that will be entered as a formula.
- If necessary, click and drag the border between columns A and B so that you can read Frank Costa's complete name. Check that you entered the data for this student correctly. If you made a mistake, return to the cell and retype the entry.
- Enter the names and grades for the other students in rows 5 through 9. Do *not* enter the student averages.
- Complete the entries in column A by typing **Class Averages** and **Exam Weights** in cells **A11** and **A13**, respectively.
- Enter the exam weights in row 13. Click in cell **B13** and enter **.25**, press the **right arrow key** to move to cell **C13** and enter **.25**, then press the **right arrow key** to move to cell **D13** and enter **.5**. Press **enter**.
- Do *not* be concerned that the exam weights do not appear as percentages as they will be formatted in a later exercise. Save the workbook.

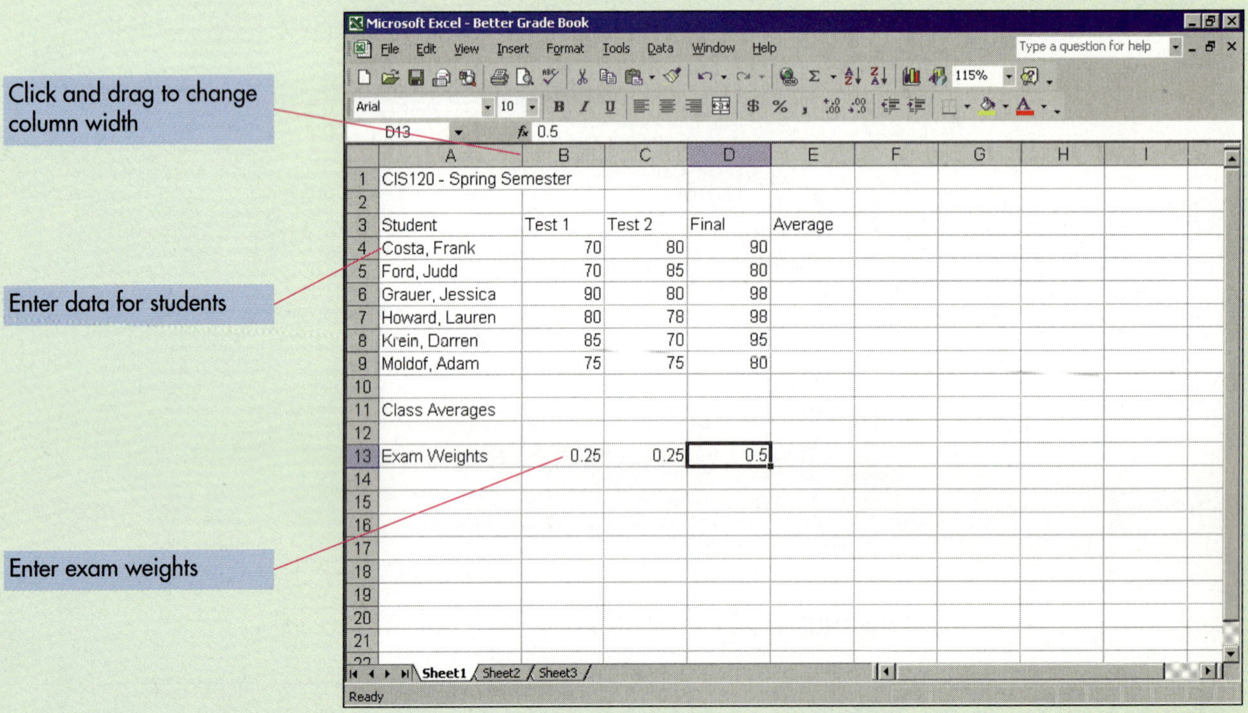

(c) Enter Student Data and Literal Information (step 3)

FIGURE 1.15 *Hands-on Exercise 3 (continued)*

COLUMN WIDTHS AND ROW HEIGHTS

Drag the border between column headings to change the column width; for example, to increase (decrease) the width of column A, drag the border between column headings A and B to the right (left). Double click the right boundary of a column heading to change the column width to accommodate the widest entry in that column. Use the same techniques to change the row heights. See practice exercise 2 at the end of the chapter.

Step 4: Compute the Student Semester Averages

- Click in cell **E4** and type the formula **=$B$13*B4+$C$13*C4+$D$13*D4** to compute the semester average for the first student. Press **enter**. Check that the displayed value in cell E4 is 82.5 as shown in Figure 1.15d.
- Click in cell **E4** to make this the active cell, then click the **Copy button** on the Standard toolbar. A moving border will surround cell E4 indicating that its contents have been copied to the clipboard.
- Click and drag to select cells **E5** through **E9** as the destination range. Click the **Paste button** to copy the contents of the clipboard to the destination range. Ignore the Paste Options button that appears automatically any time the Paste command is executed.
- Press **Esc** to remove the moving border around cell E4. The Paste Options button also disappears.
- Click in cell **E5** and look at the formula. The cells that reference the grades have changed to B5, C5, and D5. The cells that reference the exam weights—$B$13, $C$13, and $D$13—are the same as in cell E4.
- Save the workbook.

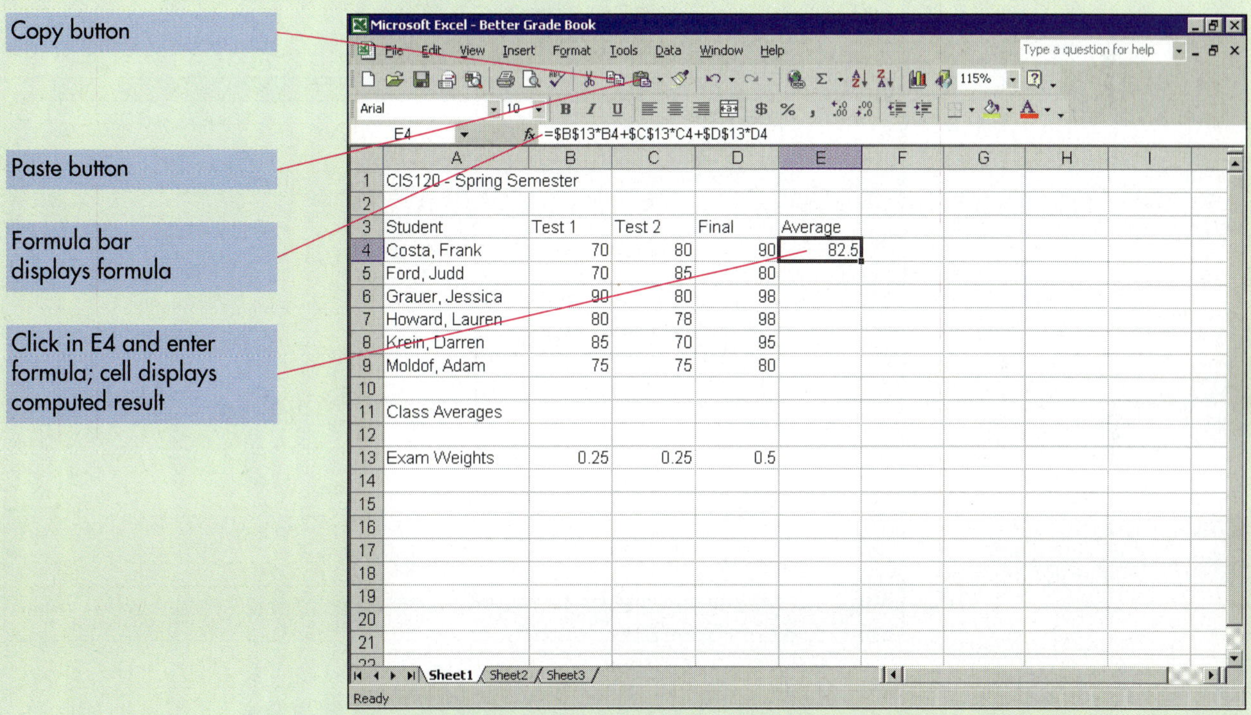

(d) Compute the Student Semester Averages (step 4)

FIGURE 1.15 *Hands-on Exercise 3 (continued)*

THE PASTE OPTIONS BUTTON

The Paste Options button (includes options from the Paste Special command and) provides flexibility when you paste the contents of the clipboard into a worksheet. Press Esc to ignore the options and you automatically paste both the cell formulas and associated formatting. Alternatively, you can click the down arrow to display options to copy values rather than formulas with or without formatting, Formatting is discussed in detail later in the chapter.

Step 5: Compute the Class Averages

- ➤ Click in cell **B11** and type the formula **=AVERAGE(B4:B9)** to compute the class average on the first test. Press the **enter key** when you have completed the formula.
- ➤ Point to cell B11, then click the **right mouse button** to display a context-sensitive menu, then click the **Copy command**. You should see a moving border around cell B11, indicating that the contents of this cell have been copied to the clipboard.
- ➤ Click and drag to select cells **C11** and **D11** as shown in Figure 1.15e. Click the **Paste button** on the standard toolbar to copy the contents of the clipboard to the destination range. Press **Esc** to remove the moving border.
- ➤ Click anywhere in the worksheet to deselect cells C11 through D11. Cells C11 and D11 should contain 78 and 90.16667, the class averages on Test 2 and the Final, respectively. Do not worry about formatting at this time.
- ➤ Save the workbook.

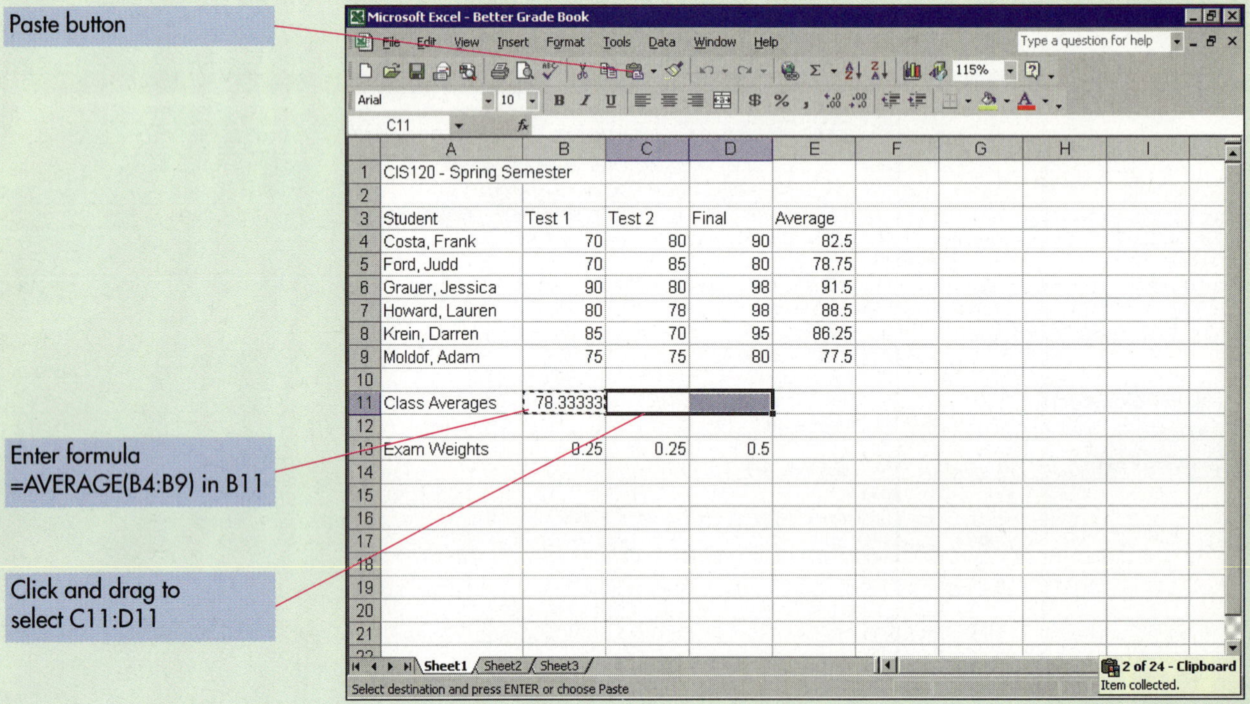

(e) Compute the Class Averages (step 5)

FIGURE 1.15 *Hands-on Exercise 3 (continued)*

TWO DIFFERENT CLIPBOARDS

The Office clipboard holds a total of up to 24 objects from multiple applications, as opposed to the Windows clipboard, which stores only the results of the last Cut or Copy command. Thus, each time you execute a Cut or Copy command, the contents of the Windows clipboard are replaced, whereas the copied object is added to the objects already in the Office clipboard. To display the Office clipboard, open the task pane, click the down arrow and select clipboard. Leave the clipboard open as you execute multiple cut and copy operations to observe what happens.

Step 6: Change the Exam Weights

- Change the entries in cells **B13** and **C13** to **.20** and the entry in cell **D13** to **.60**. The semester average for every student changes automatically; for example, Costa and Moldof change to 84 and 78, respectively, as shown in Figure 1.15f.
- The professor decides this does not make a significant difference and wants to go back to the original weights. Click the **Undo button** three times to reverse the last three actions. You should see .25, .25, and .50 in cells B13, C13, and D13, respectively.
- Click in cell **A15** and type the label **Grading Assistant**. Press **enter**. Type your name in cell **A16**, so that you will get credit for this assignment.
- Save the workbook. You do not need to print the workbook yet, since we will do that at the end of the next exercise, after we have formatted the workbook.
- Exit Excel if you are not ready to begin the next exercise at this time.

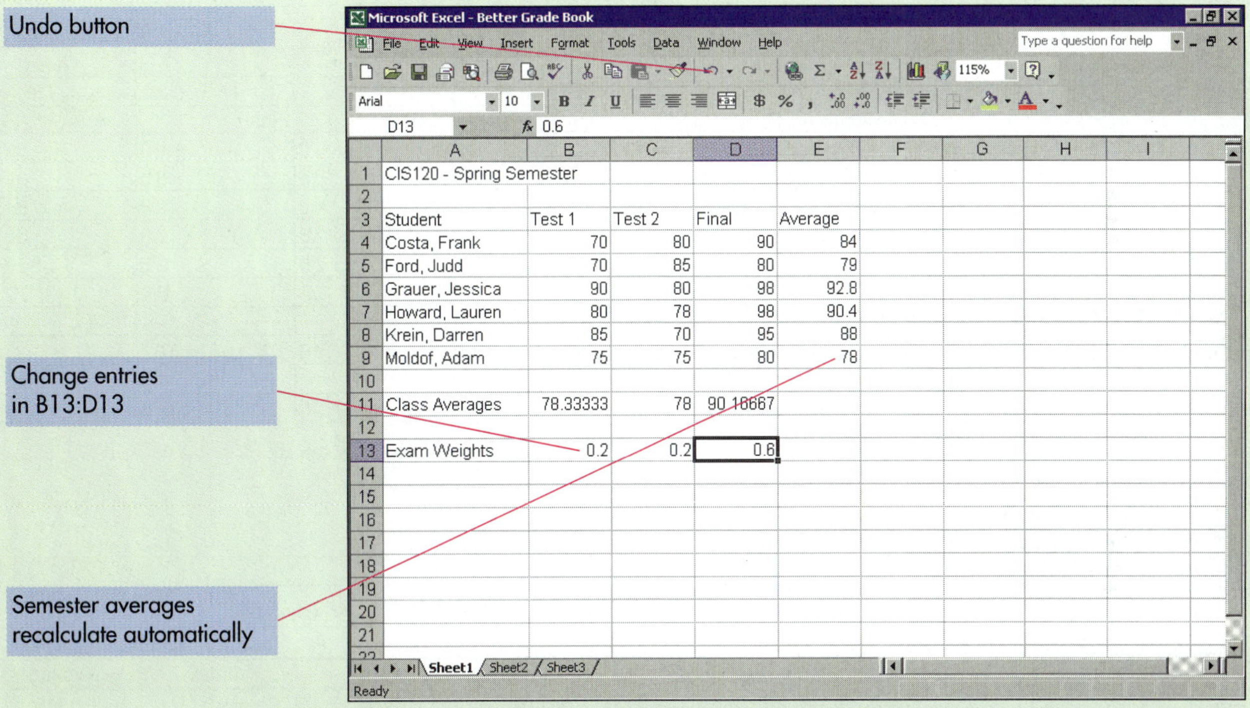

(f) Change the Exam Weights (step 6)

FIGURE 1.15 *Hands-on Exercise 3 (continued)*

CHANGE THE ZOOM SETTING

You can increase or decrease the size of a worksheet as it appears on the monitor by clicking the down arrow on the zoom box and selecting an appropriate percentage. If you are working with a large spreadsheet and cannot see it at one time on the screen, choose a number less than 100%. Conversely, if you find yourself squinting because the numbers are too small, select a percentage larger than 100%. Changing the magnification on the screen does not affect printing; that is, worksheets are always printed at 100% unless you change the scaling within the Page Setup command.

Figure 1.16a shows the grade book as it exists at the end of the third hands-on exercise, without concern for its appearance. Figure 1.16b shows the grade book as it will appear at the end of the next exercise after it has been formatted. The differences between the two are due entirely to formatting. Consider:

- The exam weights are formatted as percentages in Figure 1.16b, as opposed to decimals in Figure 1.16a. The class and semester averages are displayed with a single decimal place in Figure 1.16b.
- Boldface and italics are used for emphasis, as are shading and borders.
- Exam grades and computed averages are centered under their respective headings, as are the exam weights.
- The worksheet title is centered across all five columns.

Class Averages are not uniformly formatted

Percentages are not formatted

	A	B	C	D	E
1	CIS120 - Spring Semester				
2					
3	Student	Test 1	Test 2	Final	Average
4	Costa, Frank	70	80	90	82.5
5	Ford, Judd	70	85	80	78.75
6	Grauer, Jessica	90	80	98	91.5
7	Howard, Lauren	80	78	98	88.5
8	Krein, Darren	85	70	95	86.25
9	Moldof, Adam	75	75	80	77.5
10					
11	Class Averages	78.33333333	78	90.16666667	
12					
13	Exam Weights	0.25	0.25	0.5	

(a) At the End of Hands-on Exercise 3

Title is centered across columns; font is larger and both bold and italics

Shading, borders, and boldface are used for emphasis

Test grades are centered in columns

Uniform number of decimal places

Percent formatting has been applied

	A	B	C	D	E
1	***CIS120 - Spring Semester***				
2					
3	**Student**	**Test 1**	**Test 2**	**Final**	**Average**
4	Costa, Frank	70	80	90	82.5
5	Ford, Judd	70	85	80	78.8
6	Grauer, Jessica	90	80	98	91.5
7	Howard, Lauren	80	78	98	88.5
8	Krein, Darren	85	70	95	86.3
9	Moldof, Adam	75	75	80	77.5
10					
11	**Class Averages**	**78.3**	**78.0**	**90.2**	
12					
13	**Exam Weights**	**25%**	**25%**	**50%**	

(b) At the End of Hands-on Exercise 4

FIGURE 1.16 *Developing the Grade Book*

FORMAT CELLS COMMAND

The ***Format Cells command*** controls the formatting for numbers, alignment, fonts, borders, and patterns (color). Execution of the command produces a tabbed dialog box in which you choose the particular formatting category, then enter the desired options. All formatting is done within the context of ***select-then-do***. You select the cells to which the formatting is to apply, then you execute the Format Cells command (or click the appropriate button on the Formatting toolbar).

Once a format has been assigned to a cell, the formatting remains in the cell and is applied to all subsequent values that are entered into that cell. You can, however, change the formatting by executing a new formatting command. You can also remove the formatting by using the Clear command in the Edit menu. Note, too, that changing the format of a number changes the way the number is displayed, but does not change its value. If, for example, you entered 1.2345 into a cell, but displayed the number as 1.23, the actual value (1.2345) would be used in all calculations involving that cell. The numeric formats are shown in Figure 1.17a and described below.

- ***General format*** is the default format for numeric entries and displays a number according to the way it was originally entered. Numbers are shown as integers (e.g., 123), decimal fractions (e.g., 1.23), or in scientific notation (e.g., 1.23E+10) if the number exceeds 11 digits.
- ***Number format***, which displays a number with or without the 1000 separator (e.g., a comma) and with any number of decimal places. Negative numbers can be displayed with parentheses and/or can be shown in red.
- ***Currency format***, which displays a number with the 1000 separator and an optional dollar sign (which is placed immediately to the left of the number). Negative values can be preceded by a minus sign or displayed with parentheses and/or can be shown in red.
- ***Accounting format***, which displays a number with the 1000 separator, an optional dollar sign (at the left border of the cell, which vertically aligns the dollar signs within a column), negative values in parentheses, and zero values as hyphens.
- ***Date format***, which displays the date in different ways, such as March 4, 2001, 3/4/01, or 4-Mar-01.
- ***Time format***, which displays the time in different formats, such as 10:50 PM or the equivalent 22:50 (24-hour time).
- ***Percentage format***, whereby the number is multiplied by 100 for display purposes only, a percent sign is included, and any number of decimal places can be specified.
- ***Fraction format***, which displays a number as a fraction, and is appropriate when there is no exact decimal equivalent. A fraction is entered into a cell by preceding the fraction with an equal sign—for example, = ⅓.
- ***Scientific format***, which displays a number as a decimal fraction followed by a whole number exponent of 10; for example, the number 12345 would appear as 1.2345E+04. The exponent, +04 in the example, is the number of places the decimal point is moved to the left (or right if the exponent is negative). Very small numbers have negative exponents.
- ***Text format***, which left aligns the entry and is useful for numerical values that have leading zeros and should be treated as text, such as ZIP codes.
- ***Special format***, which displays a number with editing characters, such as hyphens in a Social Security number or parentheses around the area code of a telephone number.
- ***Custom format***, which allows you to develop your own formats.

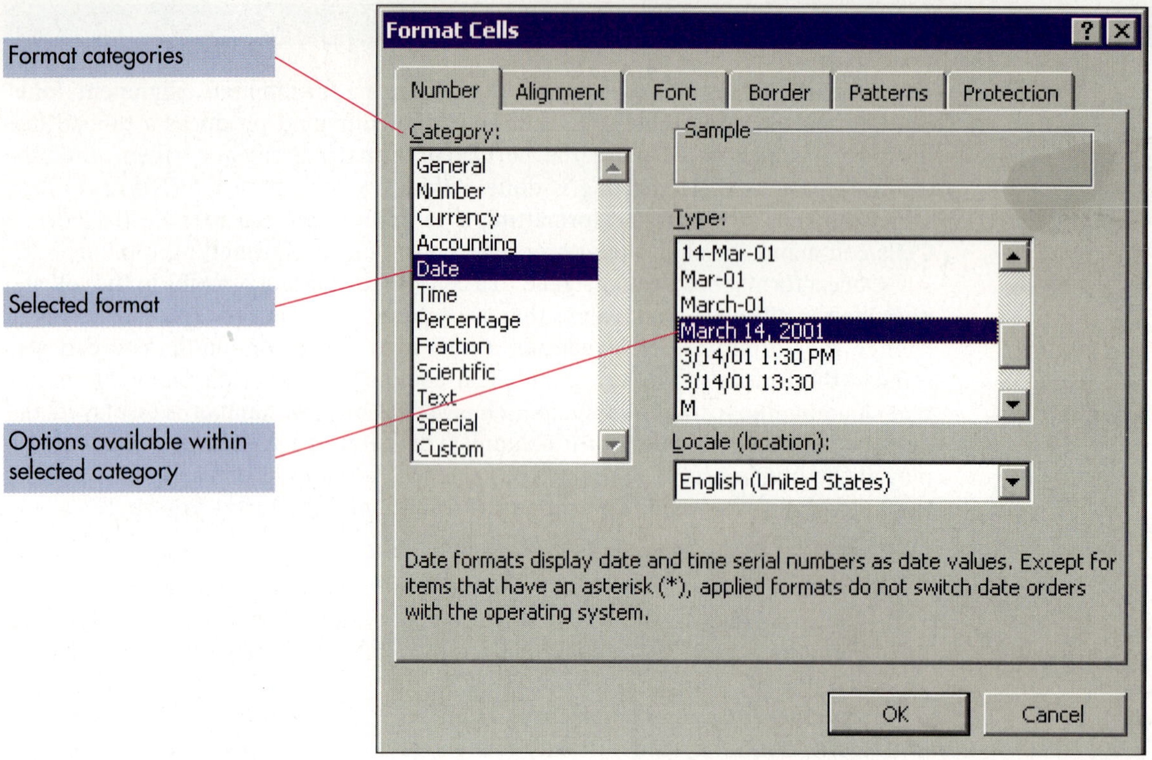

(a) The Number Tab

FIGURE 1.17 *The Format Cells Command*

Alignment

The contents of a cell (whether text or numeric) may be aligned horizontally and/or vertically as indicated by the dialog box of Figure 1.17b. The default horizontal ***alignment*** is general, which left-aligns text and right-aligns date and numbers. You can also center an entry across a range of selected cells (or ***merge cells***), as in the professor's grade book, which centered the title in cell A1 across columns A through E. Clear the box to merge cells if you want to ***split cells*** that have been previously merged. The Fill option duplicates the characters in the cell across the entire width of that cell.

Vertical alignment is important only if the row height is changed and the characters are smaller than the height of the row. Entries may be vertically aligned at the top, center, or bottom (the default) of a cell.

It is also possible to wrap the text within a cell to emulate the word wrap of a word processor. You select multiple cells and merge them together. And finally, you can achieve some interesting effects by rotating text up to 90° in either direction.

Fonts

You can use the same fonts in Excel as you can in any other Windows application. All fonts are WYSIWYG (What You See Is What You Get), meaning that the worksheet you see on the monitor will match the printed worksheet.

Any entry in a worksheet may be displayed in any font, style, or point size as indicated by the dialog box of Figure 1.17c. The example shows Arial, Bold Italic, and 14 points, and corresponds to the selection for the worksheet title in the improved grade book. Special effects, such as subscripts or superscripts, are also possible. You can even select a different color, but you will need a color printer to see the effect on the printed page. The Preview box shows the text as it will appear in the worksheet.

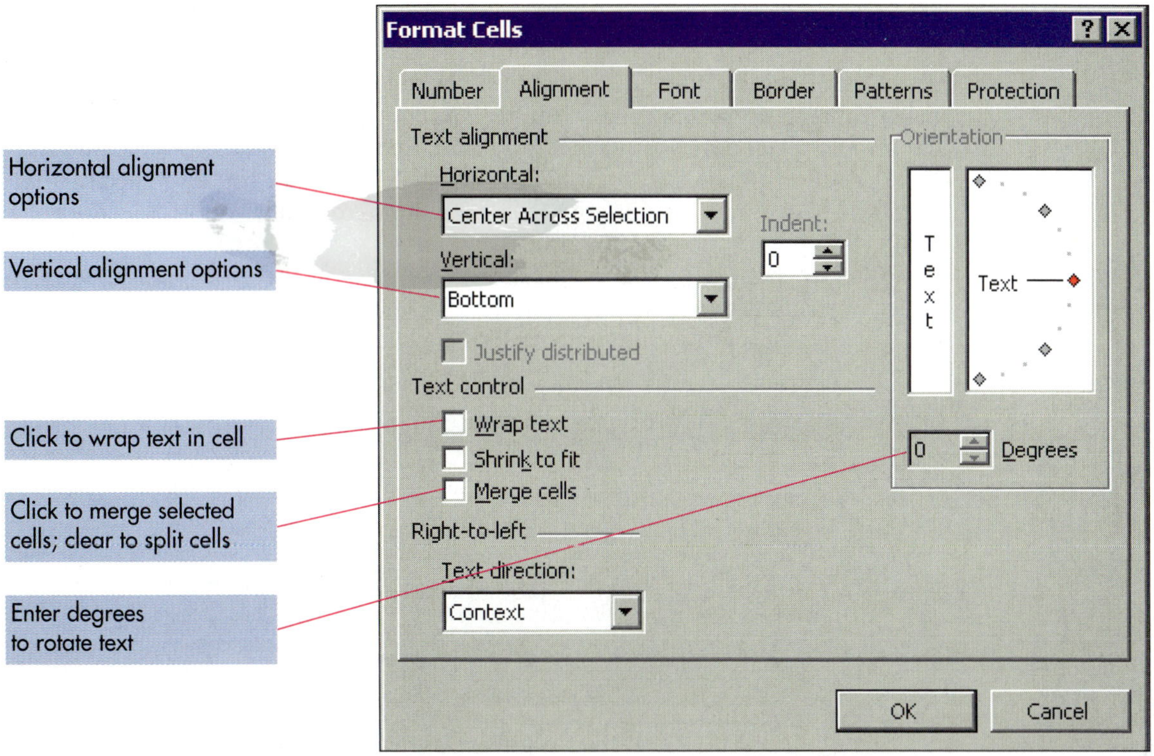

(b) The Alignment Tab

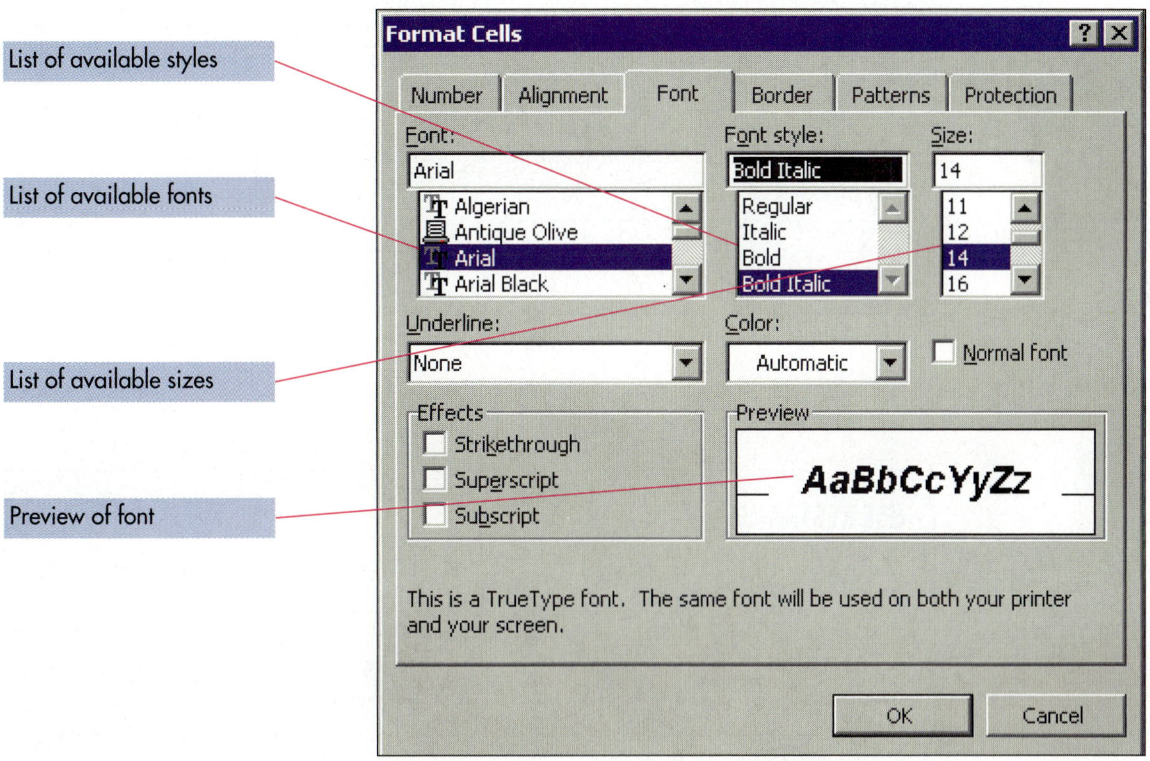

(c) Font Tab

FIGURE 1.17 *The Format Cells Command (continued)*

Borders, Patterns, and Shading

The ***Border tab*** in Figure 1.17d enables you to create a border around a cell (or cells) for additional emphasis. You can outline the entire selection, or you can choose the specific side or sides; for example, thicker lines on the bottom and right sides produce a drop shadow, which is very effective. You can also specify a different line style and/or a different color for the border, but you will need a color printer to see the effect on the printed output.

The ***Patterns tab*** (not shown in the figure) lets you choose a different color in which to shade the cell and further emphasize its contents. The Pattern drop-down list box lets you select an alternate pattern, such as dots or slanted lines.

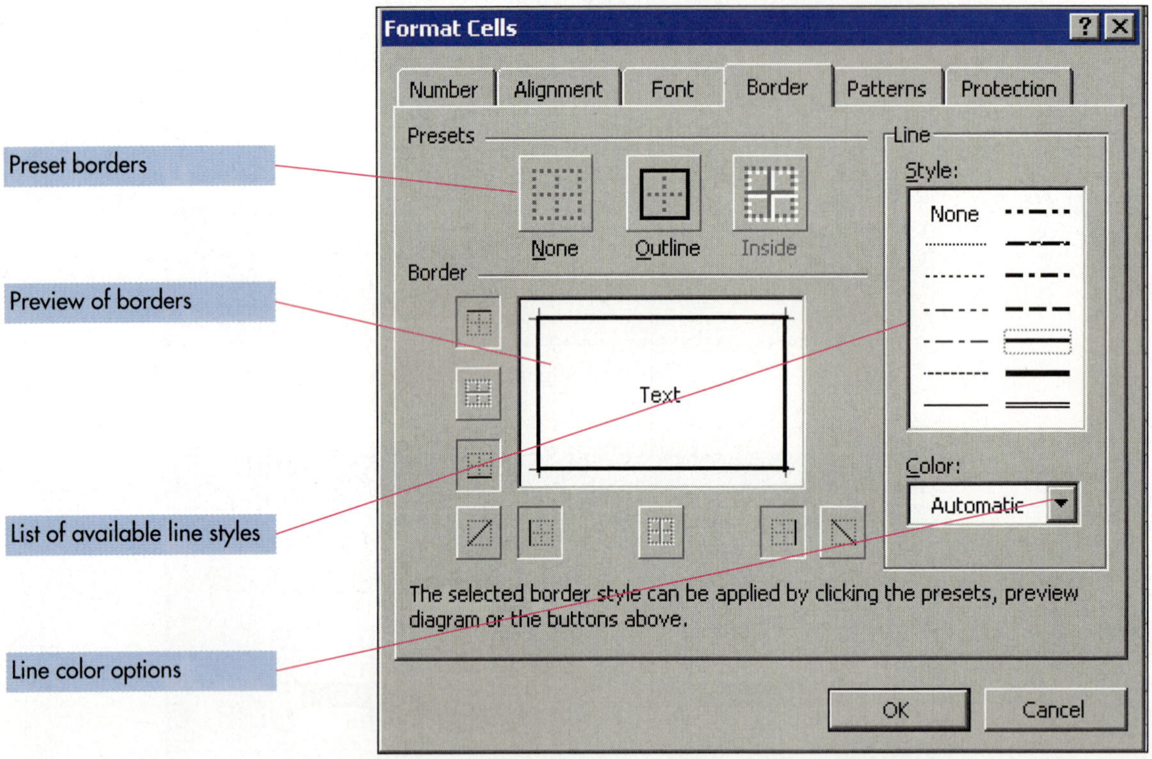

(d) The Border Tab

FIGURE 1.17 *The Format Cells Command (continued)*

USE RESTRAINT

More is not better, especially in the case of too many typefaces and styles, which produce cluttered worksheets that impress no one. Limit yourself to a maximum of two typefaces per worksheet, but choose multiple sizes and/or styles within those typefaces. Use boldface or italics for emphasis, but do so in moderation, because if you emphasize too many elements, the effect is lost.

HANDS-ON EXERCISE 4

FORMATTING A WORKSHEET

Objective To format a worksheet using boldface, italics, shading, and borders; to change the font and/or alignment of a selected entry. Use Figure 1.18 as a guide in the exercise.

Step 1: **Center the Title**

- Open **Better Grade Book** from the previous exercise. Click in cell **A1** to select the cell containing the title of the worksheet. Click the **Bold button** on the Formatting toolbar to boldface the title. Click the **Italics button** to italicize the title.
- Click in cell **A15** and click the **Bold button**. Click the **Bold button** a second time, and the boldface disappears. Click the **Bold button** again, and you are back to boldface. The same is true of the Italics button; that is, the Bold and Italics buttons function as toggle switches.
- Click in cell **A1**. Click the **down arrow** on the Font size list box and change the size to **14** to further accentuate the title.
- Click and drag to select cells **A1** through **E1**, which represents the width of the entire worksheet. Click the **Merge and Center button** on the Formatting toolbar as shown in Figure 1.18a to center the title across the width of your worksheet.
- Save the workbook.

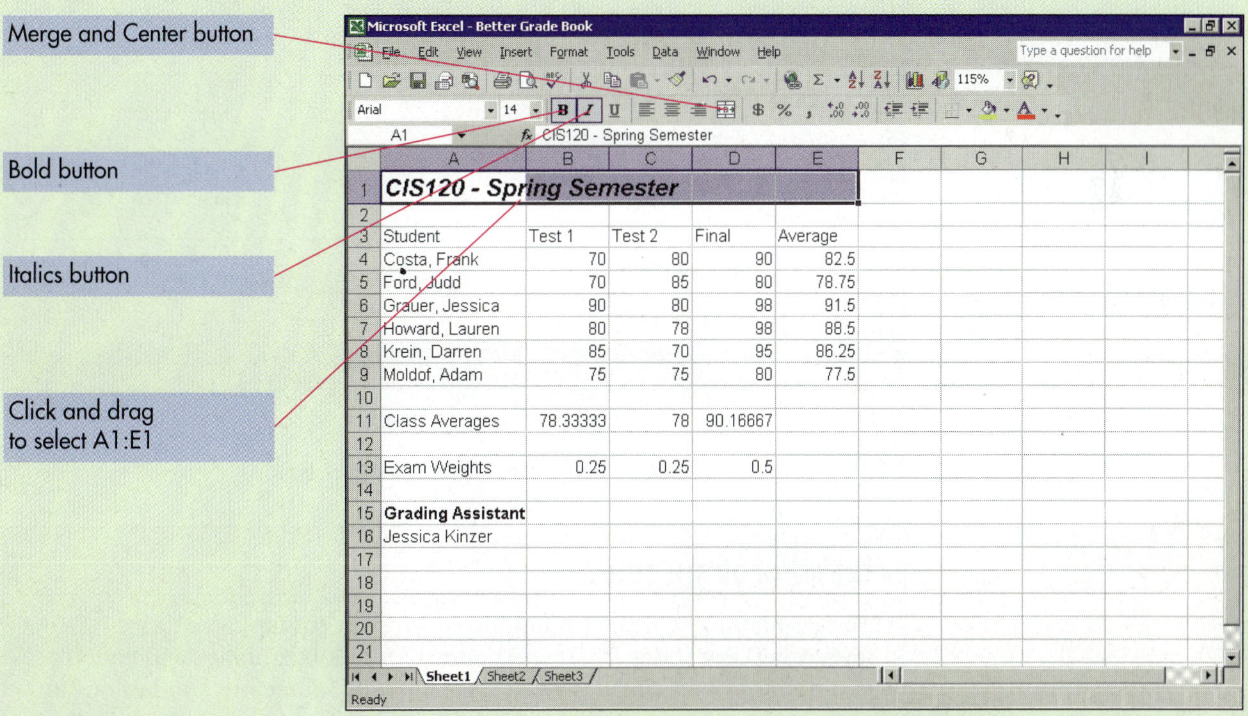

(a) Center the Title (step 1)

FIGURE 1.18 *Hands-on Exercise 4*

Step 2: **Format the Exam Weights**

- Click and drag to select cells **B13** through **D13**. Pull down the **Format menu**, then click the **Cells command** to display the dialog box in Figure 1.18b.
- If necessary, click the **Number tab**. Click **Percentage** in the Category list box. Click the **down spin arrow** in the Decimal Places box to select **zero decimals**, then click **OK**. The exam weights are displayed with percent signs and no decimal places.
- You can also use the buttons on the Formatting toolbar to accomplish the same formatting. First remove the formatting by clicking the **Undo button** on the Standard toolbar to cancel the formatting command.
- Check that cells B13 through D13 are still selected. Click the **Percent Style button** on the Formatting toolbar. (You can also pull down the **Format menu**, click the **Style command**, then choose the **Percent Style** from the Style Name list box.) Once again cells B13 through D13 are displayed in percent.
- Save the workbook.

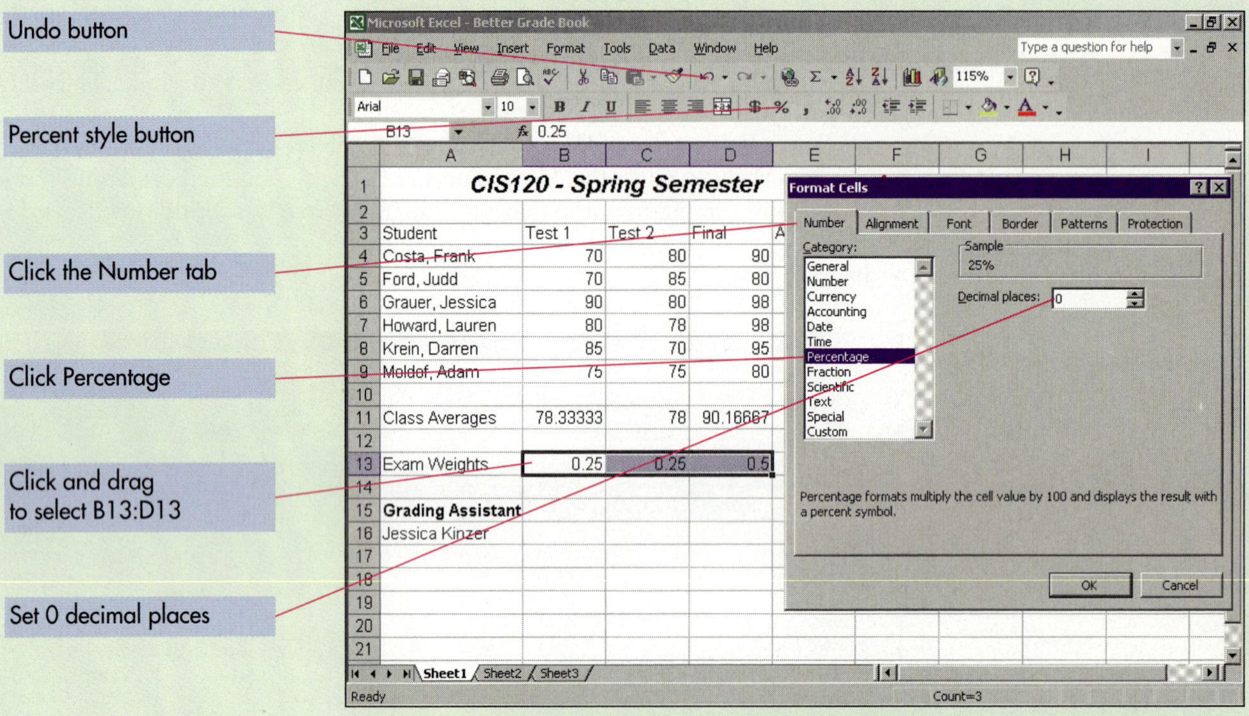

(b) Format the Exam Weights (step 2)

FIGURE 1.18 *Hands-on Exercise 4 (continued)*

THE MENU OR THE TOOLBAR

The Formatting toolbar is often the easiest way to implement a variety of formatting operations. There are buttons for boldface, italics, and underlining (each of which functions as a toggle switch). There are also buttons for alignment (including merge and center), currency, percent, and comma formats, together with buttons to increase or decrease the number of decimal places. You can find various buttons to change the font, point size, color, and borders.

Step 3: **Format the Class Averages**

- Click and drag to select cells **B11 through D11**. Now press and hold the **Ctrl key** as you click and drag to select cells **E4 through E9**. Using the Ctrl key in this way allows you to select noncontiguous (nontouching) cells as shown in Figure 1.18c.
- Format the selected cells using the Formatting toolbar or the Format menu:
  - To use the Format menu, pull down the **Format menu**, click **Cells**, click the **Number tab**, then click **Number** in the Category list box. Click the **down spin arrow** in the Decimal Places text box to reduce the decimal places to one. Click **OK**.
  - To use the Formatting toolbar, click the appropriate button repeatedly to increase or decrease the number of decimal places to one.
- Click and drag to select cells **B3 through E13**. Click the **Center button** to center the numeric data in the worksheet under the respective column headings.
- Save the workbook.

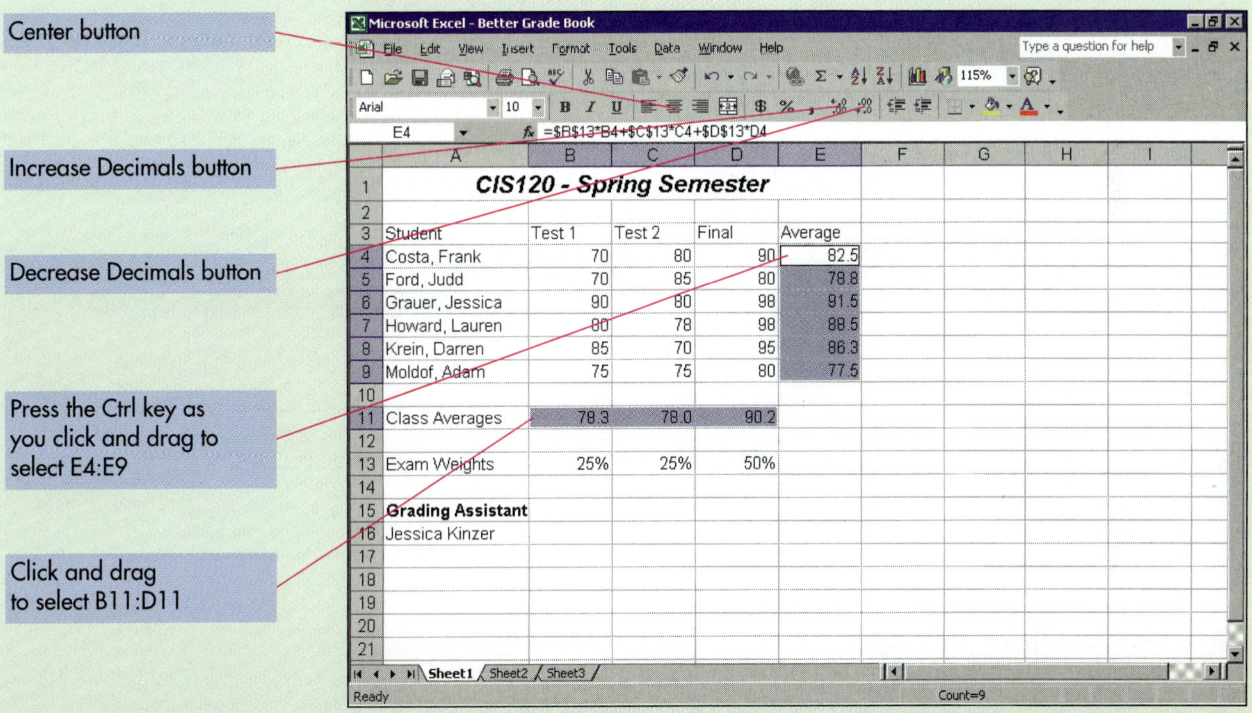

(c) Format the Class Averages (step 3)

FIGURE 1.18 *Hands-on Exercise 4 (continued)*

CLEAR THE FORMATS, BUT KEEP THE CONTENTS

You can clear the formatting in a cell and retain the contents, and/or you can clear contents but retain the formatting. Click and drag over the cell(s) for which the command is to apply, then pull down the Edit menu, click the Clear command, and choose the appropriate option—for example, the option to clear Formats. Click the tiny square immediately below the name box (to the left of the header for column A) to select the entire worksheet, then clear the formats for the worksheet. You can then repeat the steps in this exercise to practice the various formatting commands.

Step 4: **Borders and Color**

- Click and drag to select cells **A3 through E3**. Press and hold the **Ctrl key** as you click and drag to select the range **A11:E11**.
- Continue to press the **Ctrl key** as you click and drag to select cells **A13:E13**. All three cell ranges should be selected, which means that any formatting command you execute will apply to all of the selected cells.
- Pull down the **Format menu** and click **Cells** (or point to any of the selected cells and click the **right mouse button** to display a shortcut menu, then click **Format Cells**). Click the **Border tab** to display the dialog box in Figure 1.18d.
- Choose a line width from the Style section. Click the **Top** and **Bottom** boxes in the Border section. Click **OK** to exit the dialog box.
- Check that all three ranges are still selected (A3:E3, A11:E11, *and* A13:E13). Click the **down arrow** on the **Fill Color button** on the Formatting toolbar. Click **yellow** (or whatever color appeals to you).
- Click the **Bold button** on the Formatting toolbar. Click outside the selected cells to see the effects of the formatting change. Save the workbook.

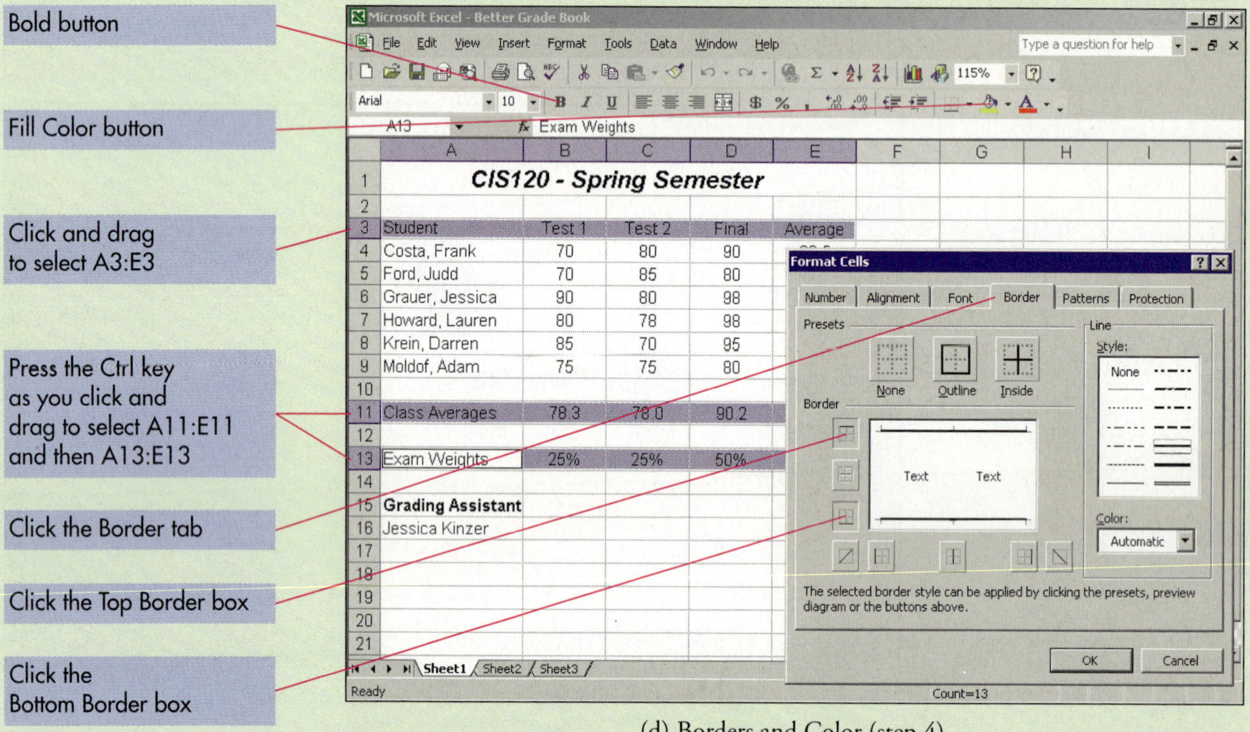

(d) Borders and Color (step 4)

FIGURE 1.18 *Hands-on Exercise 4 (continued)*

USE A PEN TO DRAW THE BORDER

You can draw borders of any thickness or color around the cells in a worksheet using a "pen" as opposed to a menu command. Click the down arrow on the Borders button on the Standard toolbar, then click the Draw Borders command to change the mouse pointer to a pen and simultaneously display the Borders toolbar. Click the Line Color or Line Style buttons to change the appearance of the border, then draw the borders directly in the worksheet. Close the Borders toolbar when you are finished.

Step 5: **The Completed Worksheet**

➤ Check that your worksheet matches ours as shown in Figure 1.18e. Pull down the **File menu**. Click **Page Setup** to display the Page Setup dialog box.
- Click the **Margins tab**. Check the box to center the worksheet horizontally.
- Click the **Sheet tab**. Check the boxes to print Row and Column Headings and Gridlines.
- Click the **Header/Footer tab**. If necessary, click the **drop-down arrow** on the Header list box. Scroll to the top of the list and click **(none)** to remove the header. Click the **drop-down arrow** on the Footer list box. Scroll to the top of the list and click **(none)** to remove the footer. Click **OK**.

➤ Click the **Print Preview button** to preview the worksheet before printing:
- If you are satisfied with the appearance of the worksheet, click the **Print button** within the Preview window, then click **OK** to print the worksheet.
- If you are not satisfied with the appearance of the worksheet, click the **Setup button** within the Preview window to make the necessary changes.

➤ Save the workbook.

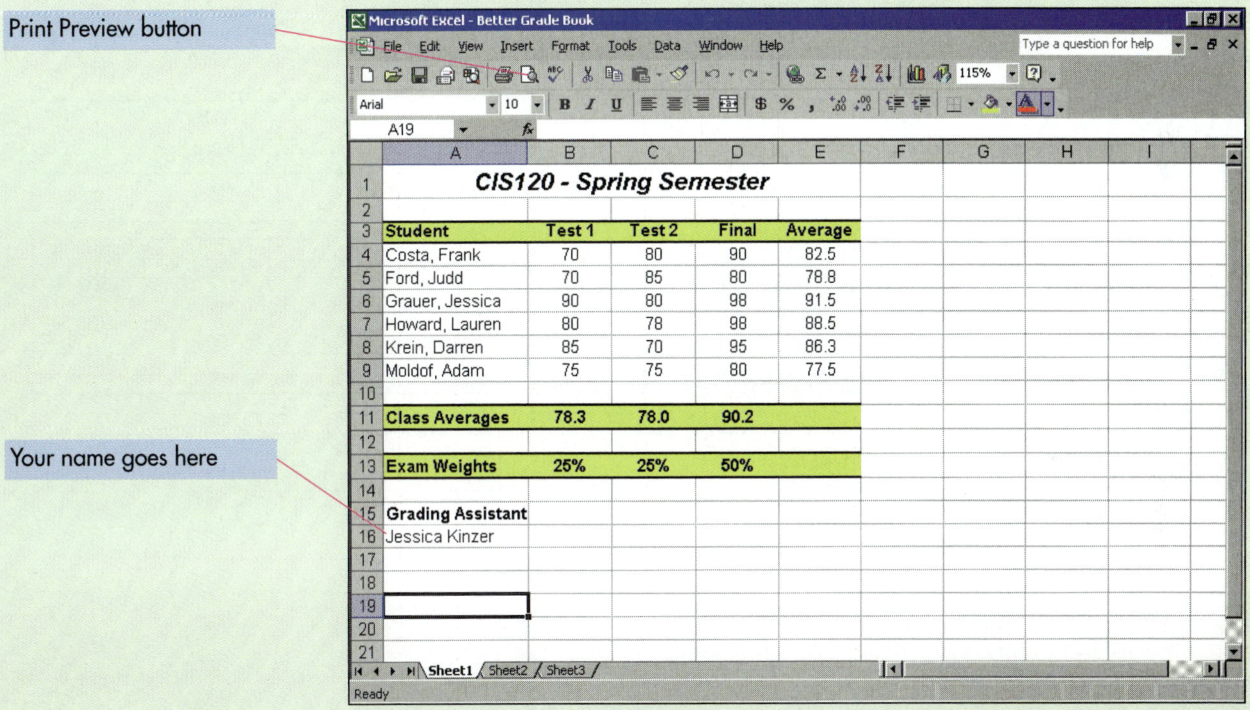

(e) The Completed Worksheet (step 5)

FIGURE 1.18 *Hands-on Exercise 4 (continued)*

FIND-AND-REPLACE FORMATTING

You can use the Find and Replace command to replace formatting as well as text. Pull down the Edit menu and click the Replace command to display the Find and Replace dialog box, then click the options button to display a Format button next to both text boxes. Click the Format button next to the Find text box and specify Bold as the Font style. Click the Format button next to the Replace text box and choose Italic. Now click the Replace All button to replace all bold with Italics. Try this within the grade book. See practice exercise 4 at the end of the chapter.

Step 6: Print the Cell Formulas

- Pull down the **Tools menu**, click **Options**, click the **View tab**, check the box for **Formulas**, then click **OK** (or use the keyboard shortcut **Ctrl+˜**). The worksheet should display the cell formulas.
- If necessary, click the arrow to the right of the horizontal scroll box so that column E, the column containing the cell formulas, comes into view.
- Double click the border between the column headings for columns E and F to increase the width of column E to the widest entry in the column.
- Pull down the **File menu**. Click **Page Setup** to display the Page Setup dialog box. Click the **Page tab**. Click the **Landscape** orientation **button**. Click the option button to **Fit to 1 Page**. Click **OK** to exit the Page Setup dialog box.
- Click the **Print Preview button** to preview the worksheet before printing as shown in Figure 1.18f. Click the **Zoom button** to increase/decrease the size of the worksheet as necessary. If you are not satisfied with the appearance of the worksheet, click the **Setup button** within the Preview window to make the necessary changes. Print the worksheet.
- Pull down the **File menu**. Click **Exit**. Click **No** if prompted to save changes.

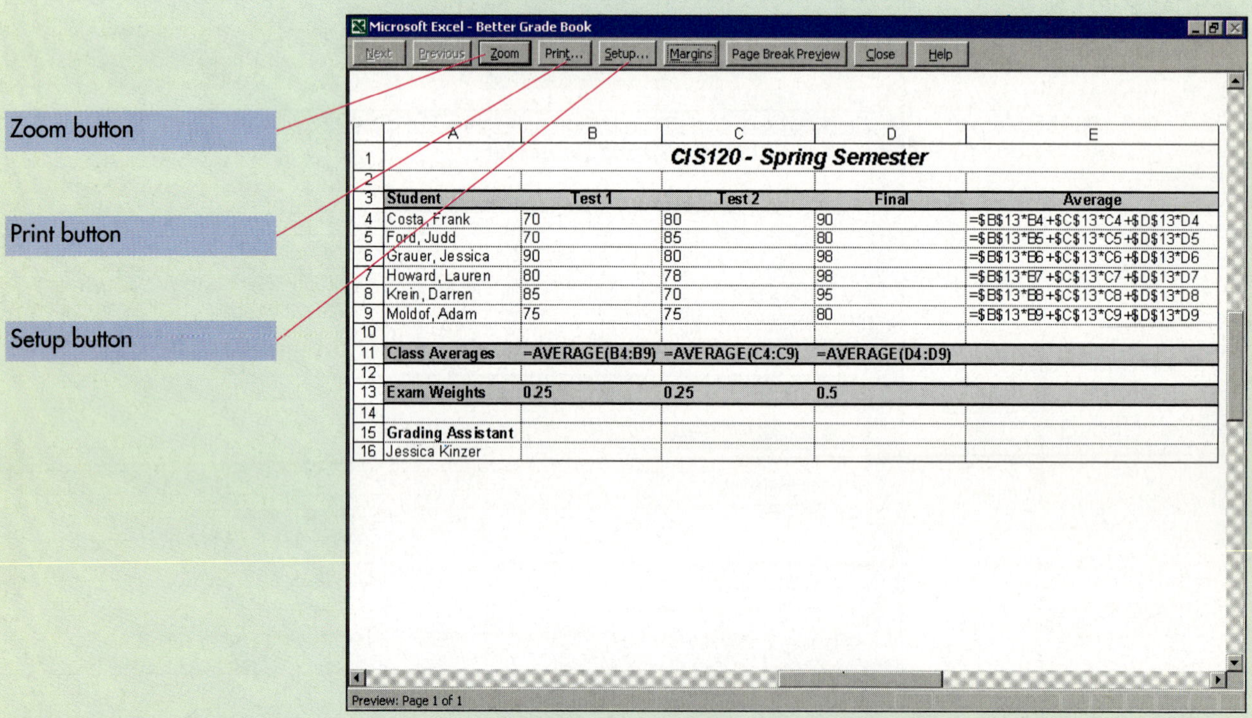

(f) Print the Cell Formulas (step 6)

FIGURE 1.18 *Hands-on Exercise 4 (continued)*

CLICK AND DRAG TO CORRECT A CELL FORMULA

Press Ctrl+˜ to display the cell formulas, then click in any cell that contains a formula. Look closely and you will see that each cell reference in that formula appears in a different color that corresponds to the border color of the referenced cell. To change a cell reference in the formula (e.g., from A4 to B4), drag the color-coded border surrounding cell A4 (the reference you want to change) to cell B4 (the new reference).

SUMMARY

A spreadsheet is the computerized equivalent of an accountant's ledger. It is divided into rows and columns, with each row and column assigned a heading. The intersection of a row and column forms a cell. Spreadsheet is a generic term. Workbook and worksheet are Excel specific. An Excel workbook contains one or more worksheets.

Every cell in a worksheet (spreadsheet) contains either a formula or a constant. A formula begins with an equal sign and is a combination of numeric constants, cell references, arithmetic operators, and/or functions. A constant is an entry that does not change and may be numeric or descriptive text.

The Insert and Delete commands add or remove individual cells, rows, or columns of a worksheet. The commands are also used to insert or delete worksheets within a workbook. The Open command brings a workbook from disk into memory. The Save command copies the workbook in memory to disk.

The Page Setup command provides complete control over the printed page, enabling you to print a worksheet with or without gridlines or row and column headings. The Page Setup command also controls margins, headers and footers, centering the worksheet on a page, and orientation. The Print Preview command shows the worksheet as it will print and should be used prior to printing.

All worksheet commands operate on a cell or group of cells known as a range. A range is selected by dragging the mouse to highlight the range; the range remains selected until another range is selected or you click another cell in the worksheet. Noncontiguous (nonadjacent) ranges may be selected in conjunction with the Ctrl key.

The formulas in a cell or range of cells may be copied or moved anywhere within a worksheet. An absolute reference remains constant throughout a copy operation whereas a relative address is adjusted for the new location. Absolute and relative references have no meaning in a move operation.

Formatting is done within the context of select-then-do; that is, select the cell or range of cells, then execute the appropriate command. The Format Cells command controls the formatting for numbers, alignment, font, borders, and patterns (colors). The Formatting toolbar simplifies the formatting process.

KEY TERMS

Absolute reference (p. 33)
Accounting format (p. 43)
Active cell (p. 7)
Alignment (p. 44)
Assumptions (p. 31)
Border tab (p. 46)
Cell (p. 4)
Cell reference (p. 4)
Clipboard (p. 33)
Close command (p. 9)
Constant (p. 5)
Copy command (p. 32)
Currency format (p. 43)
Custom format (p. 43)
Date format (p. 43)
Delete command (p. 19)
Destination range (p. 32)
Edit (p. 5)
Exit command (p. 9)
File menu (p. 9)
File name (p. 9)
File type (p. 9)
Format Cells command (p. 43)
Formatting toolbar (p. 7)
Formula (p. 5)
Formula bar (p. 7)
Fraction format (p. 43)
Function (p. 5)
General format (p. 43)
Insert command (p. 19)
Landscape orientation (p. 21)
Merge cells (p. 44)
Mixed reference (p. 33)
Move operation (p. 34)
Name box (p. 7)
Number format (p. 43)
Office Assistant (p. 18)
Open command (p. 9)
Page Setup command (p. 21)
Patterns tab (p. 46)
Percentage format (p. 43)
Places bar (p. 9)
Portrait orientation (p. 21)
Print command (p. 9)
Range (p. 32)
Relative reference (p. 33)
Save command (p. 9)
Save As command (p. 9)
Scientific format (p. 43)
Select-then-do (p. 43)
Source range (p. 32)
Special format (p. 43)
Split cells (p. 44)
Spreadsheet (p. 2)
Standard toolbar (p. 7)
Status bar (p. 7)
Task pane (p. 22)
Text format (p. 43)
Time format (p. 43)
Toolbars (p. 7)
Undo command (p. 17)
Workbook (p. 6)
Worksheet (p. 6)

MULTIPLE CHOICE

1. Which of the following is true?
   (a) A worksheet contains one or more workbooks
   (b) A workbook contains one or more worksheets
   (c) A spreadsheet contains one or more worksheets
   (d) A worksheet contains one or more spreadsheets
2. The cell at the intersection of the second column and third row is cell:
   (a) B3
   (b) 3B
   (c) C2
   (d) 2C
3. What is the effect of typing F5+F6 into a cell *without* a beginning equal sign?
   (a) The entry is equivalent to the formula =F5+F6
   (b) The cell will display the contents of cell F5 plus cell F6
   (c) The entry will be treated as a text entry and display F5+F6 in the cell
   (d) The entry will be rejected by Excel which will signal an error message
4. The Open command:
   (a) Brings a workbook from disk into memory
   (b) Brings a workbook from disk into memory, then erases the workbook on disk
   (c) Stores the workbook in memory on disk
   (d) Stores the workbook in memory on disk, then erases the workbook from memory
5. The Save command:
   (a) Brings a workbook from disk into memory
   (b) Brings a workbook from disk into memory, then erases the workbook on disk
   (c) Stores the workbook in memory on disk
   (d) Stores the workbook in memory on disk, then erases the workbook from memory
6. In the absence of parentheses, the order of operation is:
   (a) Exponentiation, addition or subtraction, multiplication or division
   (b) Addition or subtraction, multiplication or division, exponentiation
   (c) Multiplication or division, exponentiation, addition or subtraction
   (d) Exponentiation, multiplication or division, addition or subtraction
7. Cells A1, A2, and A3 contain the values 10, 20, and 40, respectively, what value will be displayed in a cell containing the cell formula =A1/A2*A3+1?
   (a) 1.125
   (b) 21
   (c) 20.125
   (d) Impossible to determine
8. The entry =AVERAGE(A4:A6):
   (a) Is invalid because the cells are not contiguous
   (b) Computes the average of cells A4 and A6
   (c) Computes the average of cells A4, A5, and A6
   (d) None of the above
9. Which of the following was suggested with respect to printing a workbook?
   (a) Print the displayed values only
   (b) Print the cell formulas only
   (c) Print both the displayed values and cell formulas
   (d) Print neither the displayed values nor the cell formulas

10. Which options are mutually exclusive in the Page Setup menu?
    (a) Portrait and landscape orientation
    (b) Cell gridlines and row and column headings
    (c) Left and right margins
    (d) All of the above

11. What is the end result of clicking in a cell, then clicking the Italics button on the Formatting toolbar twice in a row?
    (a) The cell contents are displayed in Italics
    (b) The cell contents are displayed in ordinary (nonitalicized) type
    (c) The cell contents are unchanged and appear exactly as they did prior to clicking the Italics button twice in a row
    (d) Impossible to determine

12. Which of the following best describes the formula used to compute a student's semester average, when the weights of each exam are isolated at the bottom of a spreadsheet?
    (a) The student's individual grades are entered as absolute references and the exam weights are entered as relative references
    (b) The student's individual grades are entered as relative references and the exam weights are entered as absolute references
    (c) All cell references are relative
    (d) All cell references are absolute

13. Cell B11 contains the formula, =SUM (B3:B9). What will the contents of cell C11 be if the formula in cell B11 is copied to cell C11?
    (a) =SUM (C3:C9)
    (b) =SUM (B3:B9)
    (c) =SUM ($B$3:$B$9)
    (d) =SUM ($C$3:$C$9)

14. Cell E6 contains the formula, =B6*$B$12+C6*$C$12+D6*$D$12. What will be the formula in cell E7 if the contents of cell E6 are copied to that cell?
    (a) =B7*$B$12+C7*$C$12+D7*$D$12
    (b) =B7*$B$13+C7*$C$13+D7*$D$13
    (c) =B6*$B$13+C6*$C$13+D6*$D$13
    (d) None of the above

15. A formula containing the reference =D$5 is copied to a cell one column over and two rows down. How will the entry appear in its new location?
    (a) =E5
    (b) =E$5
    (c) =E$6
    (d) =$E5

ANSWERS

1. b	**6.** d	**11.** c
2. a	**7.** b	**12.** b
3. c	**8.** c	**13.** a
4. a	**9.** c	**14.** a
5. c	**10.** a	**15.** b

1. Isolate Assumptions: Figure 1.19 displays a new grade book with a different grading scheme. Students take three exams worth 100 points each, submit a term paper and various homework assignments worth 50 points each, then receive a grade for the semester based on their total points. The maximum points possible is 400. A student's semester average is computed by dividing his or her total points by this number.
   a. Open the partially completed workbook, *Chapter 1 Practice 1*, in the Exploring Excel folder. Click in cell G4 and enter a formula to compute Anderson's total points. Click in cell H4 and enter a formula that will compute Anderson's semester average. Be sure this formula includes an absolute reference to cell B16.
   b. Click and drag to select the formulas in cells G4 and H4, then copy these formulas to cells G5 through H12.
   c. Click in cell B14 and enter a formula that will compute the class average on the first exam. Copy this formula to cells C14 to H14.
   d. Format the worksheet appropriately. (You need not copy our formatting exactly.) Add your name as the grading assistant, then print the worksheet twice, once to show displayed values and once to show the cell formulas. Use landscape printing and be sure that the worksheet fits on one sheet of paper.
   e. The professor is concerned about the grades being too low and wants to introduce a curve. He does this by reducing the point threshold on which the students' semester averages are based. Click in cell B16 and change the threshold to 350, which automatically raises the average of every student.
   f. Print the displayed values that reflect the change in part (e). Can you see the value of isolating the assumptions within a worksheet?
   g. Add a cover page, then submit the complete assignment (four pages in all counting the cover page) to your instructor.

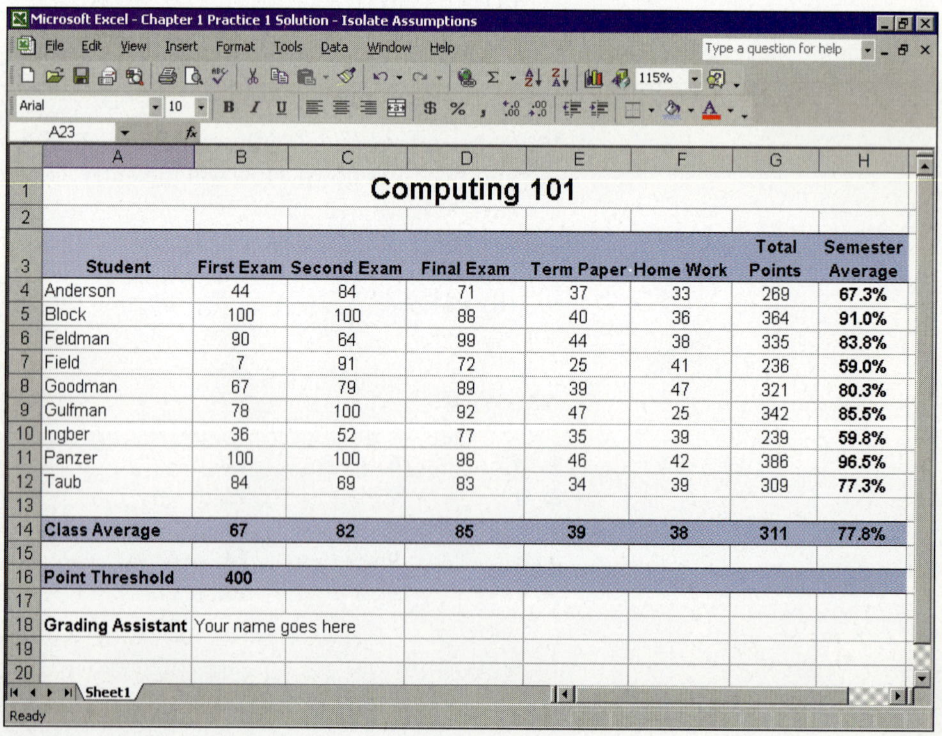

FIGURE 1.19 *Isolate Assumptions (Exercise 1)*

2. Formatting and Cell Movement: Figure 1.20 provides practice with formatting and basic cell operations (inserting and deleting cells, moving cells, splitting and/or merging cells). Open the partially completed *Chapter 1 Practice 2 workbook*, then follow the instructions in the individual cells to create the workbook in Figure 1.20. Cell B3, for example, asks you to italicize the text in green. The formatting is easy, but inserting and deleting cells is a little trickier since it can affect cells that have been merged together. You will find it easier, therefore, if you follow the instructions to split the cells first (cell A14 in the finished workbook), then merge the cells at the end of the exercise. Print the completed workbook for your instructor. Use landscape orientation so that the worksheet fits on one page.

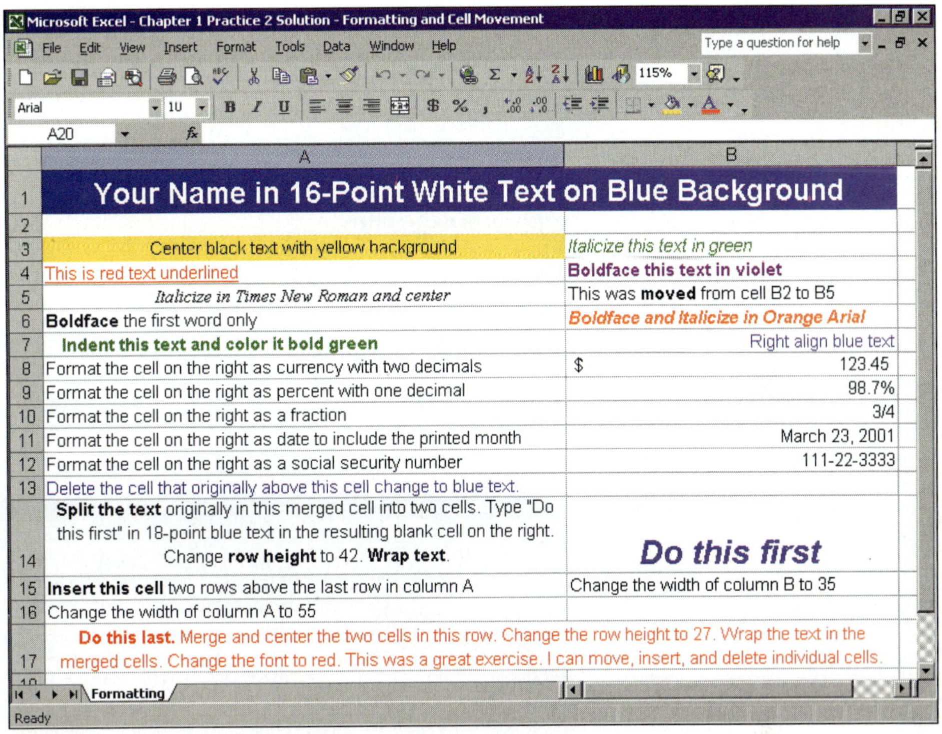

FIGURE 1.20 *Formatting and Cell Movement (Exercise 2)*

3. The Movies: Figure 1.21 displays a spreadsheet that is used to compute the weekly revenue for a chain of movie theatres. Open the partially completed version of this spreadsheet in *Chapter 1 Practice 3*, then proceed as follows:
   a. Click in cell D4 and enter a formula, using a combination of relative and absolute references, to compute the ticket revenues for the first theatre.
   b. Click in cells E4 and F4 to enter the appropriate formulas in these cells for the first theatre. Copy the formulas in cells D4, E4, and F4 to the appropriate rows for the other theatres.
   c. Click in cell B9 and enter the function to compute the total number of evening tickets that were sold. Copy this formula to the appropriate cells in row 9 to compute the other totals.
   d. Format the completed worksheet as appropriate. Print the worksheet twice, once to show the displayed values and once to show the cell contents. Submit both printouts to your instructor as proof you did this exercise.

4. Judson Ford Realty: The worksheet in Figure 1.22 displays the sales for Judson Ford Realty for the month of October. You can open a partially completed version of this worksheet in *Chapter 1 Practice 4*, but it is up to you to complete the worksheet so that it matches Figure 1.22..
   a. The price per square foot is the selling price divided by the square feet.

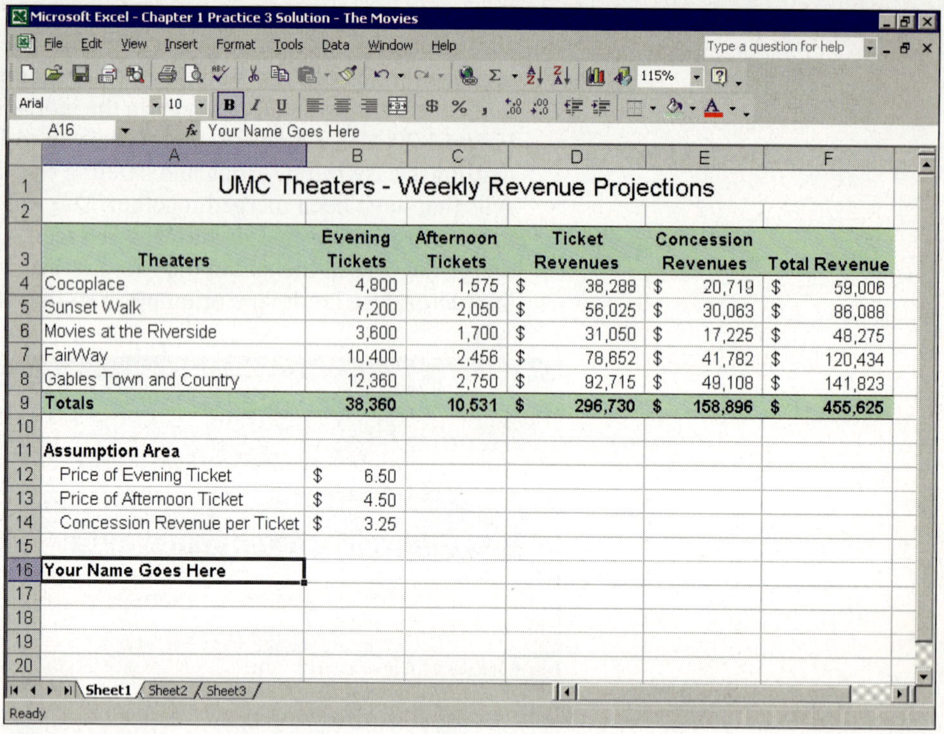

Theaters	Evening Tickets	Afternoon Tickets	Ticket Revenues	Concession Revenues	Total Revenue
UMC Theaters - Weekly Revenue Projections					
Cocoplace	4,800	1,575	$ 38,288	$ 20,719	$ 59,006
Sunset Walk	7,200	2,050	$ 56,025	$ 30,063	$ 86,088
Movies at the Riverside	3,600	1,700	$ 31,050	$ 17,225	$ 48,275
FairWay	10,400	2,456	$ 78,652	$ 41,782	$ 120,434
Gables Town and Country	12,360	2,750	$ 92,715	$ 49,108	$ 141,823
Totals	**38,360**	**10,531**	**$ 296,730**	**$ 158,896**	**$ 455,625**
Assumption Area					
Price of Evening Ticket	$ 6.50				
Price of Afternoon Ticket	$ 4.50				
Concession Revenue per Ticket	$ 3.25				
Your Name Goes Here					

FIGURE 1.21 *The Movies (Exercise 3)*

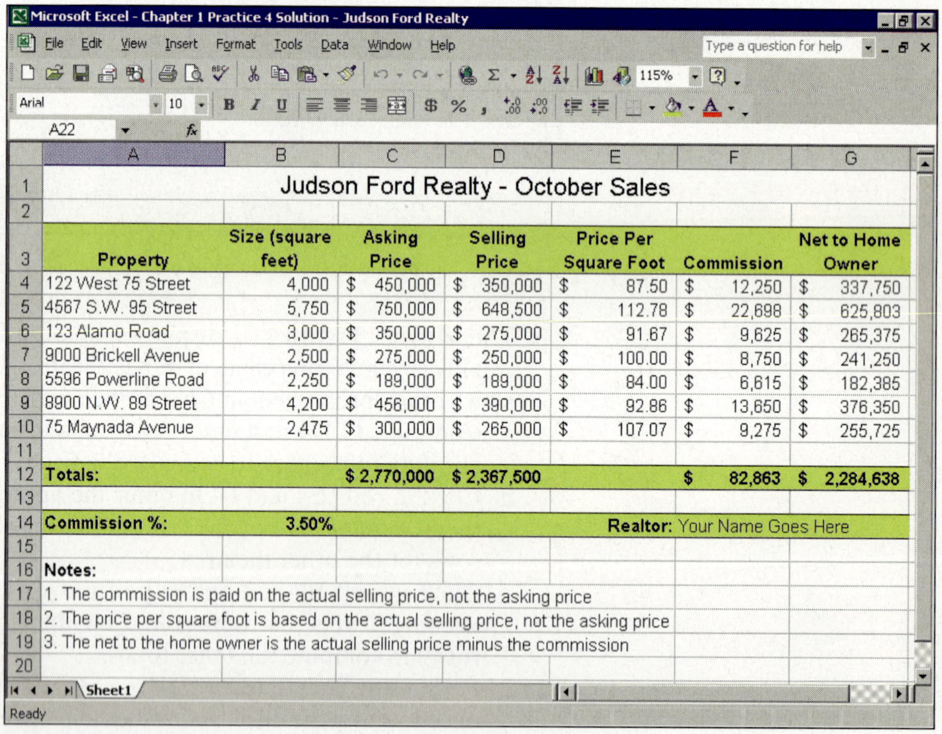

Property	Size (square feet)	Asking Price	Selling Price	Price Per Square Foot	Commission	Net to Home Owner
Judson Ford Realty - October Sales						
122 West 75 Street	4,000	$ 450,000	$ 350,000	$ 87.50	$ 12,250	$ 337,750
4567 S.W. 95 Street	5,750	$ 750,000	$ 648,500	$ 112.78	$ 22,698	$ 625,803
123 Alamo Road	3,000	$ 350,000	$ 275,000	$ 91.67	$ 9,625	$ 265,375
9000 Brickell Avenue	2,500	$ 275,000	$ 250,000	$ 100.00	$ 8,750	$ 241,250
5596 Powerline Road	2,250	$ 189,000	$ 189,000	$ 84.00	$ 6,615	$ 182,385
8900 N.W. 89 Street	4,200	$ 456,000	$ 390,000	$ 92.86	$ 13,650	$ 376,350
75 Maynada Avenue	2,475	$ 300,000	$ 265,000	$ 107.07	$ 9,275	$ 255,725
Totals:		**$ 2,770,000**	**$ 2,367,500**		**$ 82,863**	**$ 2,284,638**
Commission %:	**3.50%**				**Realtor:** Your Name Goes Here	

Notes:
1. The commission is paid on the actual selling price, not the asking price
2. The price per square foot is based on the actual selling price, not the asking price
3. The net to the home owner is the actual selling price minus the commission

FIGURE 1.22 *Judson Ford Realty (Exercise 4)*

b. The realtor's commission is a percentage of the selling price and is based on the commission percentage in cell B14.
c. The net to the homeowner is the selling price minus the commission.
d. Compute the totals for the agency as shown in row 12. Format the worksheet in an appropriate fashion. You need not match our formatting exactly.
e. Use the Find and Replace command to change the text in the various addresses. Change all occurrences of "Str" to "Street", "Rd" to "Road", and "Ave" to "Avenue". You also need to replace the Courier New font with Arial throughout the worksheet.
f. Add your name in cell F14, then print the worksheet to show both displayed values and cell formulas. Create a cover sheet, then submit the assignment to your instructor.

5. The Solar System: The potential uses of a spreadsheet are limited only by your imagination as can be seen by Figure 1.23, which displays a spreadsheet with information about our solar system. Open the partially completed version of the workbook in *Chapter 1 Practice 5*, then complete the worksheet by developing the formulas for the first planet, copying those formulas to the remaining rows in the worksheet, then formatting appropriately.
   a. Click in cell C15 and enter your weight on earth. You can specify your weight in pounds rather than kilograms.
   b. Click in cell C16 and enter the function =Pi() as shown in Figure 1.23. The displayed value for the cell shows the value of Pi to several decimal places.
   c. Click in cell D4 and enter the formula to compute the diameter of the first planet (Mercury). The diameter of a planet is equal to twice its radius.
   d. Click in cell E4 and enter the formula to compute the circumference of a planet. The circumference is equal to the diameter times the constant Pi.
   e. Click in cell F4 and enter the formula to compute the surface area, which is equal to four times Pi times the radius squared.

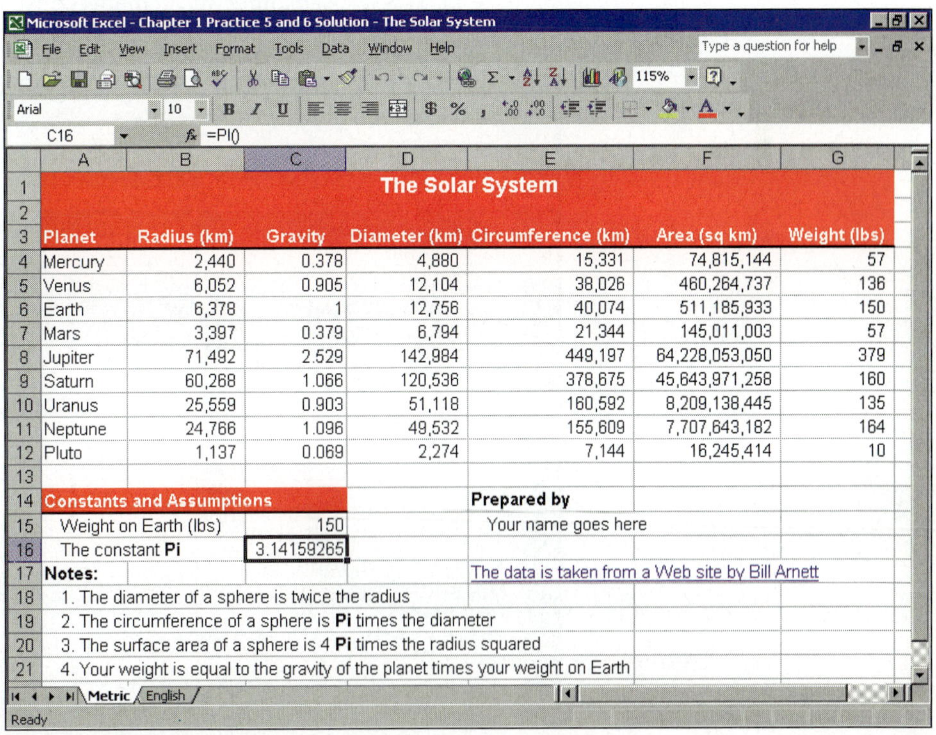

	A	B	C	D	E	F	G
1	The Solar System						
2							
3	Planet	Radius (km)	Gravity	Diameter (km)	Circumference (km)	Area (sq km)	Weight (lbs)
4	Mercury	2,440	0.378	4,880	15,331	74,815,144	57
5	Venus	6,052	0.905	12,104	38,026	460,264,737	136
6	Earth	6,378	1	12,756	40,074	511,185,933	150
7	Mars	3,397	0.379	6,794	21,344	145,011,003	57
8	Jupiter	71,492	2.529	142,984	449,197	64,228,053,050	379
9	Saturn	60,268	1.066	120,536	378,675	45,643,971,258	160
10	Uranus	25,559	0.903	51,118	160,592	8,209,138,445	135
11	Neptune	24,766	1.096	49,532	155,609	7,707,643,182	164
12	Pluto	1,137	0.069	2,274	7,144	16,245,414	10
13							
14	Constants and Assumptions				Prepared by		
15	Weight on Earth (lbs)		150		Your name goes here		
16	The constant **Pi**		3.14159265				
17	**Notes:**				The data is taken from a Web site by Bill Arnett		
18	1. The diameter of a sphere is twice the radius						
19	2. The circumference of a sphere is **Pi** times the diameter						
20	3. The surface area of a sphere is 4 **Pi** times the radius squared						
21	4. Your weight is equal to the gravity of the planet times your weight on Earth						

FIGURE 1.23 *The Solar System (Exercise 5)*

f. Click in cell G4 and enter the formula to compute your weight on Mercury, which is your weight on earth times the relative gravity of Mercury compared to that of earth.

g. Copy the formulas in row 4 to the remainder of the worksheet, then format the worksheet appropriately. You need not copy our formatting exactly. Add your name in cell E16 as indicated.

h. The worksheet contains a hyperlink to a Web site by Bill Arnett, which has additional information about the planets. If you click the hyperlink within Excel your browser will open automatically, and you will be connected to the site, provided you have an Internet connection.

i. Print the worksheet two ways, once with displayed values, and once to show the cell contents. Use landscape orientation and appropriate scaling so that the worksheet fits on a single page.

BUILDS ON
Practice Exercise 5
Page 59

6. Worksheet References: Figure 1.24 displays a second worksheet within the workbook for our solar system from the previous exercise. The worksheet in Figure 1.24 uses the English system (e.g., miles) as opposed to the metric system (kilometers). It's up to you to develop the appropriate conversion.

a. Open the completed workbook from the previous exercise, then click the English tab to display the worksheet in Figure 1.24. The radius of the individual planets is not entered directly into this worksheet, but is calculated from the metric worksheet.

b. Click in cell B4 and enter the formula =Metric!B4*English!$C$17. The names of the worksheets, Metric and English, are followed by exclamation points to indicate which worksheet is to be used. Cell C17 in the English worksheet contains the conversion factor to change kilometers to miles.

c. Copy the formula in cell B4 to the remaining rows in column B. The worksheet references are absolute and will not change when the formula is copied. Cell B4 is a relative reference, however, and will be modified to reflect the appropriate row as the formula is copied. The reference to cell C17, $C$17, is absolute and remains constant throughout.

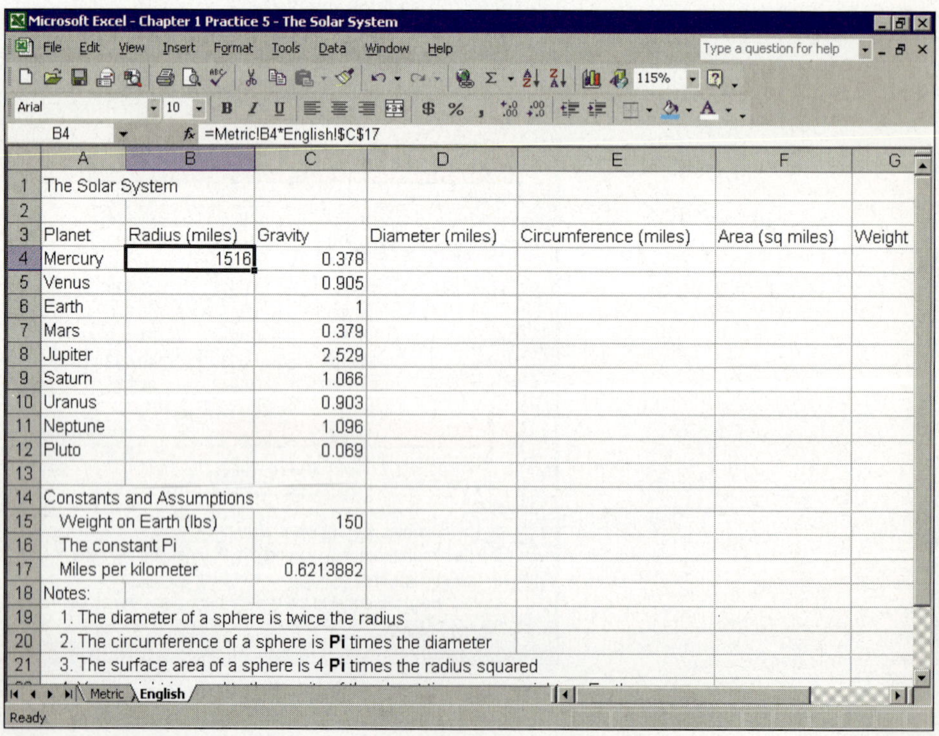

FIGURE 1.24 *Worksheet References (Exercise 6)*

d. Develop the remaining formulas in row 4 using the information from the previous exercise. Copy these formulas to the remaining rows in the worksheet, then format the worksheet appropriately.

e. Print the worksheet twice, once to show displayed values, and once to show cell formulas.

7. Student Budget: Figure 1.25 displays a hypothetical budget for a nine-month academic year. You can use the partially completed version of this worksheet in the *Chapter 1 Practice 7* workbook, or you can create your own. If you use our file, then the totals in your worksheet should correspond exactly to those in Figure 1.25, whereas if you create your own budget, the numbers will differ. In any event, we would like you to show at least one month where you run a deficit. Negative numbers should be formatted to appear in red.

Substitute your name for Maryann's, then complete the worksheet and format it appropriately. Print the worksheet two ways, to show both displayed values and cell formulas, then submit both pages to your instructor. Be sure to use the Page Setup command to specify landscape printing, and appropriate scaling so that the entire worksheet fits on a single page.

Use this exercise to practice your file-mangement skills by saving the solution in a new folder. Complete the exercise, then pull down the File menu and click the Save As command to display the Save As dialog box. Change to the Exploring Excel folder, click the New Folder button on the toolbar, then create a new folder as shown in Figure 1.25.

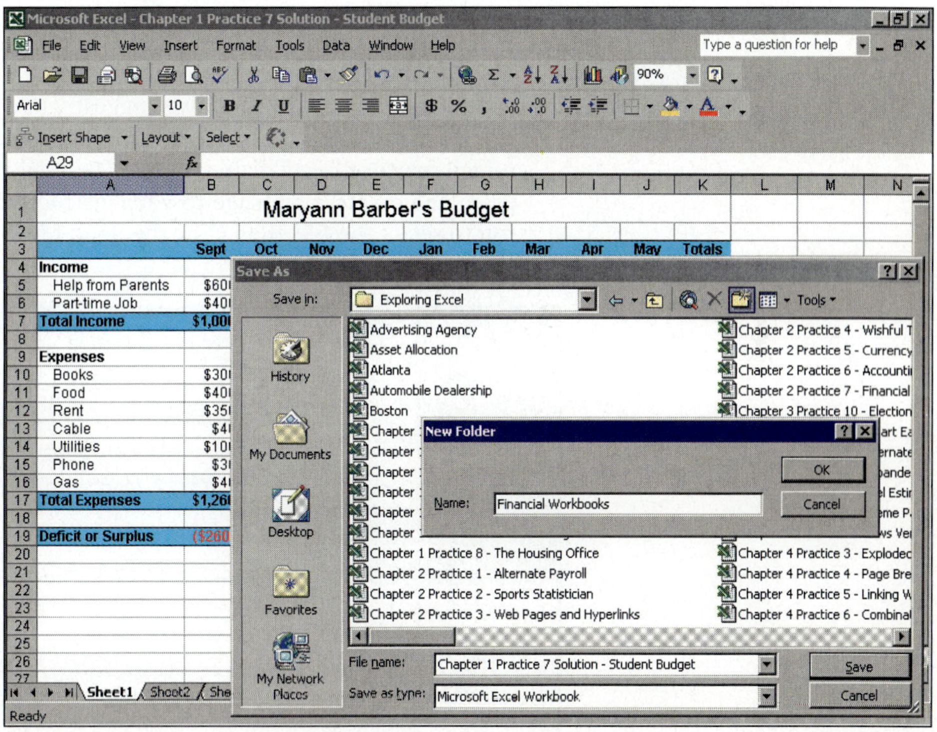

FIGURE 1.25 *Student Budget (Exercise 7)*

8. The Housing Office: Open the partially completed workbook in *Chapter 1 Practice 8*, then complete the workbook to match Figure 1.26. You can modify the formatting, but the displayed values should be the same. Pay special attention to the formula for the meal plan revenue (cell G4 for the first residence hall), which uses a combination of relative and absolute addresses. Note, too, that each double room has two students, each of whom is required to pay for the meal plan. Place your name somewhere in the worksheet, then print the worksheet two ways, to show both displayed values and cell formulas.

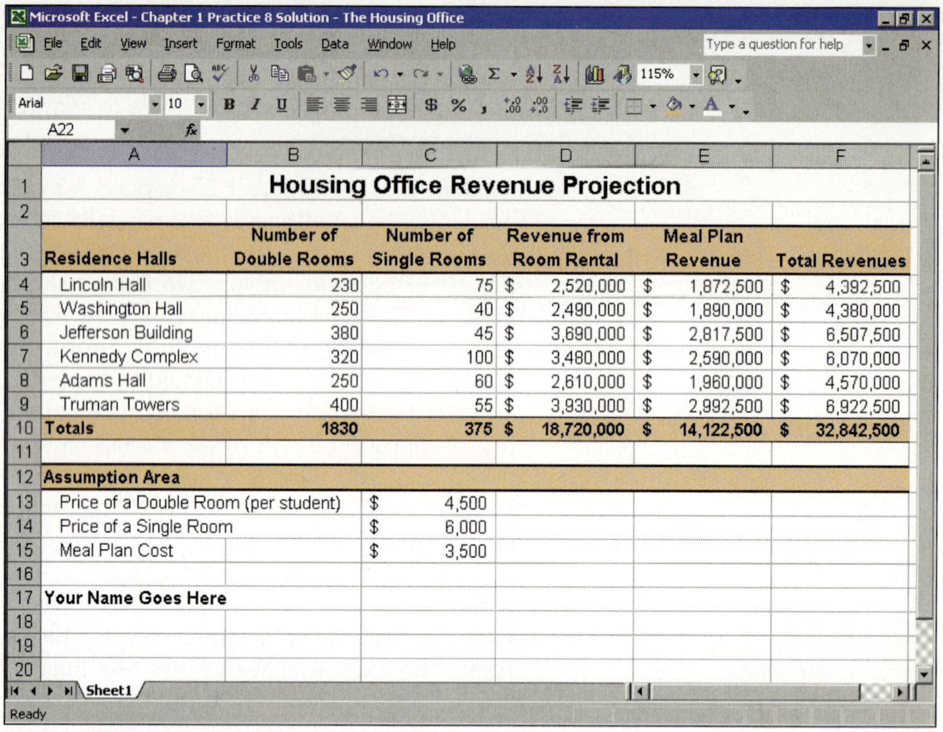

FIGURE 1.26 *The Housing Office (Exercise 8)*

9. E-mail Your Homework: It's easy to send an Excel workbook as an attached file as shown in Figure 1.27, but we suggest you check with your professor first. He or she may prefer that you print the assignment, rather than mail it and/or e-mail may not be available to you. If e-mail is an option, start your e-mail program and create a message to your instructor. Click the Insert (or Attach) button to select the file, then click the Send button to mail the message.

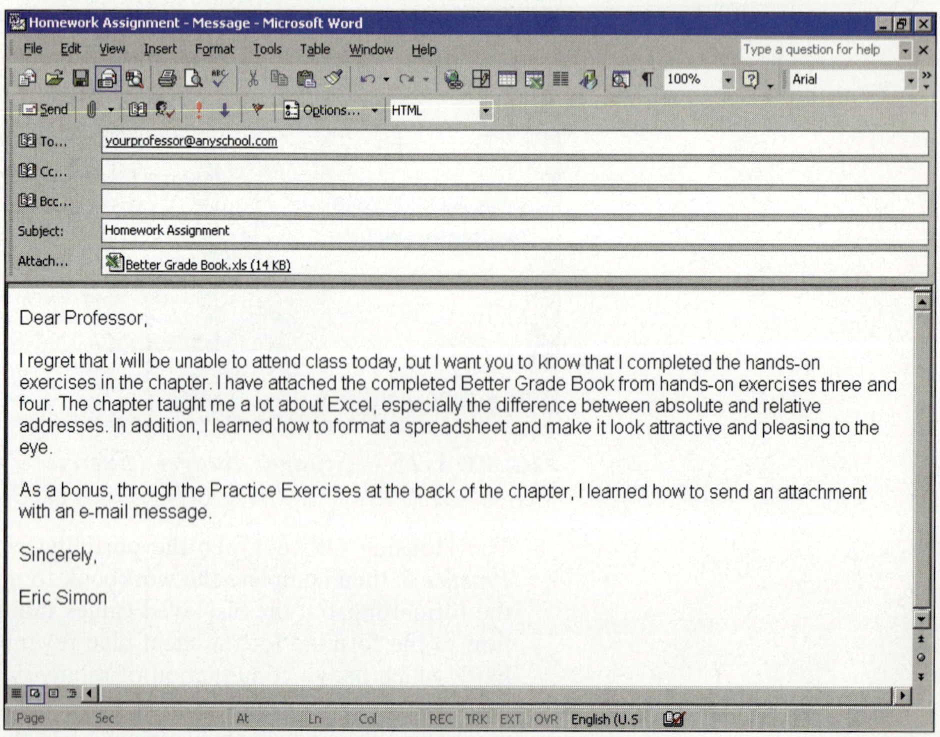

FIGURE 1.27 *E-mail Your Homework (Exercise 9)*

The MyPHLIP Web Site

Every text in the *Exploring Office XP* series has a corresponding MyPHLIP (Prentice Hall Learning on the Internet Partnership) Web site, where you will find a variety of student resources as well as online review questions for each chapter. Go to www.prenhall.com/myphlip and follow the instructions. The first time at the site you will be prompted to register by supplying your e-mail address and choosing a password. Next, you choose the discipline (CIS/MIS) and a book (e.g., *Exploring Microsoft Office XP, Volume I*). Your professor will tell you whether he or she has created an online syllabus, in which case you should click the link to find your professor after adding the book. Either way, the next time you return to the site, you will be taken directly to your text. Select any chapter, click "Go", then use the review questions as directed.

Residential Colleges

Congratulations! You have been recommended for a work-study assignment in the Office of Housing. Your supervisor has collected data on the number of students living in each dorm, and further, has divided that data according to the year in school. Your job is to open the partially completed *Residential Colleges* workbook, and compute the total number of students living in each dorm, as well as the total number of students for each year. In addition, you are to determine the percentage of the dormitory population for year in school.

The Cost of Smoking

Smoking is hazardous to your health as well as your pocketbook. A one-pack-a-day habit, at $3/pack, will cost you more than $1,000 per year. For the same money you could buy 20 concert tickets at $50 each, or more than 700 gallons of gas at $1.50 per gallon. Open the partially completed *Cost of Smoking* workbook and compute the number of various items that you could buy over the course of a year in lieu of cigarettes.

Accuracy Counts

The *Underbid* workbook on the data disk was the last assignment completed by your predecessor prior to his unfortunate dismissal. The worksheet contains a significant error, which caused your company to underbid a contract and assume a subsequent loss of $100,000. As you look for the error, don't be distracted by the attractive formatting. The shading, lines, and other touches are nice, but accuracy is more important than anything else. Write a memo to your instructor describing the nature of the error.

Two Different Clipboards

The Office clipboard is different from the Windows clipboard, but both clipboards share some functionality. Thus, whenever you copy an object to the Windows clipboard, it can also be copied to the Office clipboard, where the last 24 copied objects are retained. This is in contrast to the Windows clipboard, where each copy operation replaces the clipboard in its entirety. Experiment with the Office clipboard from different applications, then summarize your findings in a brief note to your instructor. Explain how the Office clipboard can be accessed from the task pane in Excel and/or an icon that appears on the Windows taskbar.

The Office Assistant

The Office Assistant monitors your work and offers advice throughout a session. You can tell that the Assistant has a suggestion when you see a light bulb on the Office Assistant button on the Standard toolbar or in the Office Assistant window. You can read the suggestions as they occur and/or review them at the end of a session. Redo one or more of the exercises in this chapter, but this time pay attention to the Assistant. Write a brief note to your instructor describing three tips (shortcuts) offered by the Assistant. (You should, however, reset the Assistant before you begin, or else the Assistant will not repeat tips that were offered in a previous session.) Start the Assistant, click the Options button, click the Options tab, then click the button to Reset tips.

Planning for Disaster

This case has nothing to do with spreadsheets per se, but it is perhaps the most important case of all, as it deals with the question of backup. Do you have a backup strategy? Do you even know what a backup strategy is? You had better learn, because sooner or later you will wish you had one. You will erase a file, be unable to read from a floppy disk, or worse yet suffer a hardware failure in which you are unable to access the hard drive. The problem always seems to occur the night before an assignment is due. Describe in 250 words or less the backup strategy you plan to implement in conjunction with your work in this class.

The Threat of Virus Infection

A computer virus is an actively infectious program that attaches itself to other programs and alters the way a computer works. Some viruses do nothing more than display an annoying message at an inopportune time. Most, however, are more harmful, and in the worst case erase all files on the disk. Use your favorite search engine to research the subject of computer viruses in order to answer the following questions: When is a computer subject to infection by a virus? What precautions does your school or university take against the threat of virus infection in its computer lab? What precautions, if any, do you take at home? Can you feel confident that your machine will not be infected if you faithfully use a state-of-the-art antivirus program that was purchased in January 2001?

CHAPTER 1

Introduction to Microsoft® Access: What Is a Database?

OBJECTIVES

AFTER READING THIS CHAPTER YOU WILL BE ABLE TO:

1. Define the terms field, record, table, and database.
2. Describe the Database window and the objects in an Access database.
3. Add, edit, and delete records within a table.
4. Explain the importance of data validation in table maintenance; provide several examples of the way in which it is enforced.
5. Apply a filter (by form or selection) to a table; sort a table on one or more fields.
6. Use the PivotTable and PivotChart views to display information.
7. Identify the one-to-many relationships in a relational database.

OVERVIEW

All businesses and organizations maintain data of one kind or another. Companies store data about their employees. Schools and universities store data about their students and faculties. Magazines and newspapers store data about their subscribers. The list goes on and on, and while each of these examples refers to different types of data, they all operate under the same basic principles of database management.

This chapter introduces you to Microsoft Access, the application in the Microsoft Office suite that performs database management. We describe the objects in an Access database and show you how to add, edit, and delete records of a table. We explain how to obtain information from the database by running reports and queries that have been previously created. We discuss how to display selected records through a filter and how to display those records in different sequences. And finally, we provide a look ahead, by showing how the real power of Access is derived from a relational database that contains multiple tables.

Imagine, if you will, that you are the manager of a college bookstore and that you maintain data for every book in the store. Accordingly, you have recorded the specifics of each book (the title, author, publisher, price, and so on) in a manila folder, and have stored the folders in one drawer of a file cabinet.

One of your major responsibilities is to order books at the beginning of each semester, which in turn requires you to contact the various publishers. You have found it convenient, therefore, to create a second set of folders with data about each publisher—such as the publisher's phone number, address, discount policy, and so on. You also found it necessary to create a third set of folders with data about each order—such as when the order was placed, the status of the order, which books were ordered, how many copies, and so on.

Normal business operations will require you to make repeated trips to the filing cabinet to maintain the accuracy of the data and keep it up to date. You will have to create a new folder whenever a new book is received, whenever you contract with a new publisher, or whenever you place a new order. In similar fashion, you will have to modify the data in an existing folder to reflect changes that occur, such as an increase in the price of a book, a change in a publisher's address, or an update in the status of an order. And, lastly, you will need to remove the folder of any book that is no longer carried by the bookstore, or of any publisher with whom you no longer have contact, or of any order that was canceled.

The preceding discussion describes the bookstore of 40 years ago—before the advent of computers and computerized databases. The bookstore manager of today needs the same information as his or her predecessor. Today's manager, however, has the information readily available, at the touch of a key or the click of a mouse, through the miracle of modern technology.

Information systems have their own vocabulary. A ***field*** is a basic fact (or data element)—such as the name of a book or the telephone number of a publisher. A ***record*** is a set of fields. A ***table*** is a set of records. Every record in a table contains the same fields in the same order. A ***database*** consists of one or more tables. In our example each record in the Books table will contain the identical six fields—ISBN (a unique identifying number for the book), title, author, year of publication, price, and publisher. In similar fashion, every record in the Publishers table will have the same fields for each publisher just as every record in the Orders table has the same fields for each order.

You can think of the file cabinet in the manual system as a database. Each set of folders in the file cabinet corresponds to a table within the database. Thus the bookstore database consists of three separate tables—or books, publishers, and orders. Each table, in turn, consists of multiple records, corresponding to the folders in the file cabinet. The Books table, for example, contains a record for every book title in the store. The Publishers table has a record for each publisher, just as the Orders table has a record for each order.

The real power of Access is derived from a database with multiple tables—such as Books, Publishers, and Orders tables within the Bookstore database. For the time being, however, we focus on a simpler database with only one table so that you can learn the basics of Access. After you are comfortable working with a single table, we will show you how to work with multiple tables and relate them to one another.

GARBAGE IN, GARBAGE OUT

The information produced by a system is only as good as the data on which the information is based. In other words, no system, be it manual or electronic, can produce valid output from invalid input. The phenomenon is described by the acronym "GIGO"—garbage in, garbage out.

Microsoft Access, the fourth major application in the Microsoft Office, is used to create and manage a database such as the one for the college bookstore. Consider now Figure 1.1, which shows how Microsoft Access appears on the desktop. Our discussion assumes a basic familiarity with the Windows operating system and the user interface that is common to all Windows applications. You should recognize, therefore, that the desktop in Figure 1.1 has two open windows—an application window for Microsoft Access and a document (database) window for the database that is currently open.

Each window has its own title bar and Minimize, Maximize (or Restore), and Close buttons. The title bar in the application window contains the name of the application (Microsoft Access). The title bar in the document (database) window contains the name of the database that is currently open (Bookstore). The application window for Access has been maximized to take up the entire desktop, and hence the Restore button is visible. The database window has not been maximized.

A menu bar appears immediately below the application title bar. A toolbar (similar to those in other Office applications) appears below the menu bar and offers alternative ways to execute common commands.

The Database Window

The ***Database window*** displays the various objects in an Access database. There are seven types of objects—tables, queries, forms, reports, pages, macros, and modules. Every database must contain at least one table, and it may contain any or all (or none) of the other objects. Each object type is accessed through the appropriate button within the Database window. In this chapter we concentrate on tables, but we briefly describe the other types of objects as a preview of what you will learn as you read our book.

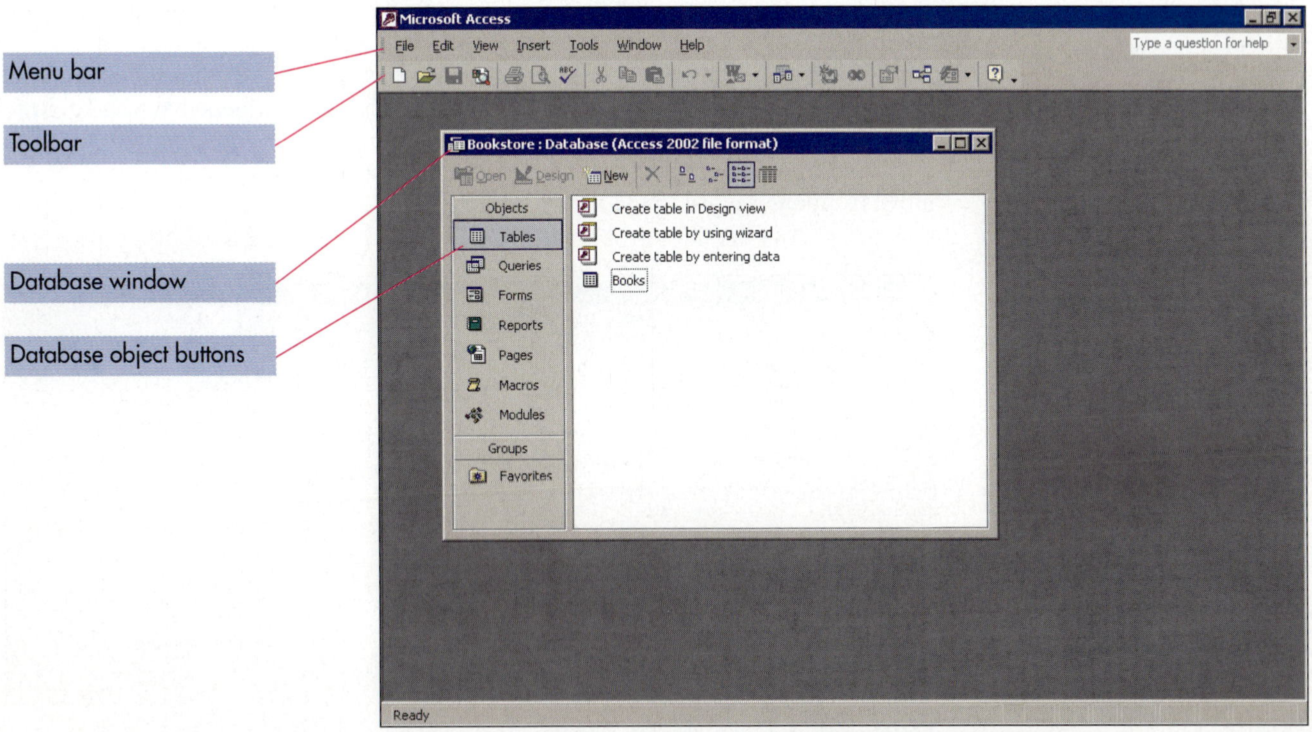

FIGURE 1.1 *The Database Window*

Tables

A ***table*** stores data about a physical entity such as a person, place, or thing, and it is the basic element in any database. A table is made up of records, which in turn are made up of fields. It is similar to an Excel worksheet in appearance, with each record appearing in a separate row. Each field appears in a separate column.

Access provides different ways in which to view a table. The ***Datasheet view*** is where you add, edit, and delete records of a table, and it is the view on which we concentrate throughout the chapter. The ***Design view*** is used to create (and/or modify) the table by specifying the fields it will contain and the associated properties for each field. The field type (for example, text or numeric data) and the field length are examples of field properties.

Access 2002 introduces two additional views that provide a convenient way to display summary information from a table. The ***PivotTable view*** is similar in concept to an Excel pivot table and provides a convenient way to summarize data about groups of records. The ***PivotChart view*** creates a chart from the associated PivotTable view. These views are illustrated later in the chapter.

Figure 1.2 shows the Datasheet view for the Books table in our bookstore. The first row in the table displays the field names. Each additional row contains a record (the data for a specific book). Each column represents a field (one fact about a book). Every record in the table contains the same fields in the same order: ISBN number, Title, Author, Year, List Price, and Publisher.

The ***primary key*** is the field (or combination of fields) that makes each record in a table unique. The ISBN is the primary key in the Books table and it ensures that every record in a table is different from every other record and hence it prevents the occurrence of duplicate records. A primary key is not required but is strongly recommended. There can be only one primary key per table.

The status bar at the bottom of Figure 1.2 indicates that there are 22 records in the table and that you are positioned on record number 13. You can work on only one record at a time. The vertical scroll bar at the right of the window indicates that there are more records in the table than can be seen at one time. The horizontal scroll bar at the bottom of the window indicates that you cannot see an entire record.

The triangle that appears to the left of the record indicates that the data in the current record has been saved. The triangle will change to a pencil as you begin to enter new data, then it will change back to a triangle after you complete the data entry and move to another record, since data is saved automatically as soon as you move from one record to the next.

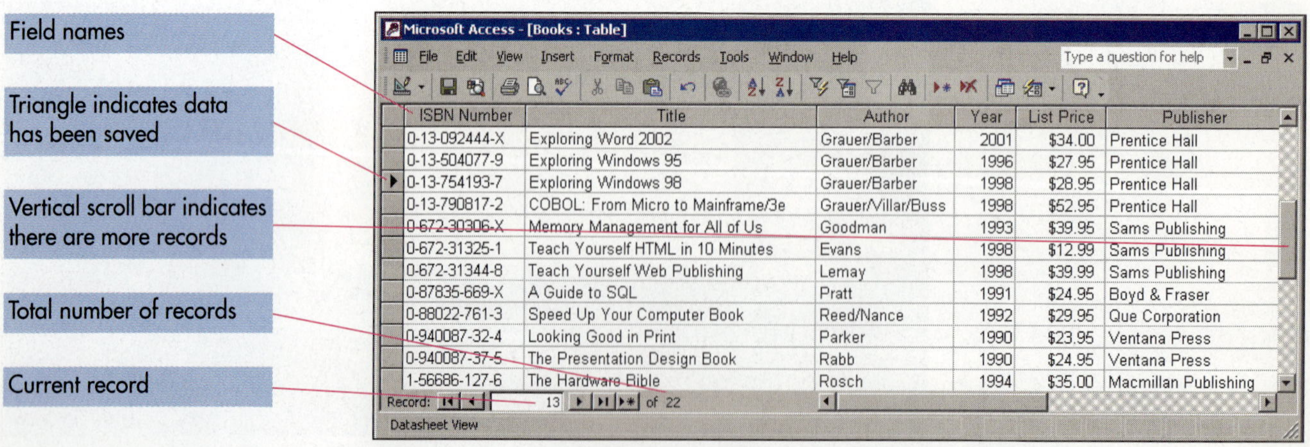

FIGURE 1.2 *An Access Table*

Forms, Queries, and Reports

As previously indicated, an Access database contains different types of objects. A table (or set of tables) is at the heart of any database, since it contains the actual data. The other objects in a database—such as forms, queries, and reports—are based on an underlying table. Figure 1.3a displays a form based on the Books table shown earlier. A ***form*** provides a friendlier interface than does a table and it is easier to use when entering or modifying data. Note, for example, the command buttons in the form to add a new record, or to find or delete an existing record, to print a record, and to close the form. In short, the form provides access to all of the data maintenance operations that are available through a table. The status bar and navigation buttons at the bottom of the form are similar to those that appear at the bottom of a table.

Figure 1.3b displays a query that lists the books for a particular publisher (Prentice Hall in this example). A ***query*** provides information based on the data within an underlying table. The Books table, for example, contains records for many publishers, but the query in Figure 1.3b shows only the books that were published by a specific publisher. The results of the query are similar in appearance to the underlying table, except that the query contains selected records and/or selected fields for those records. The query may also list the records in a different sequence from that of the table. (A query can also be used to add new records and/or modify existing records.)

Figure 1.3c displays a ***report*** that contains the same information as the query in Figure 1.3b. The report, however, provides the information in a more attractive format than the query. Note, too, that a report can be based on either a table or a query. Thus, you could have based the report on the Books table, rather than the query, in which case the report would list every book in the table, as opposed to a limited subset of the records within the table.

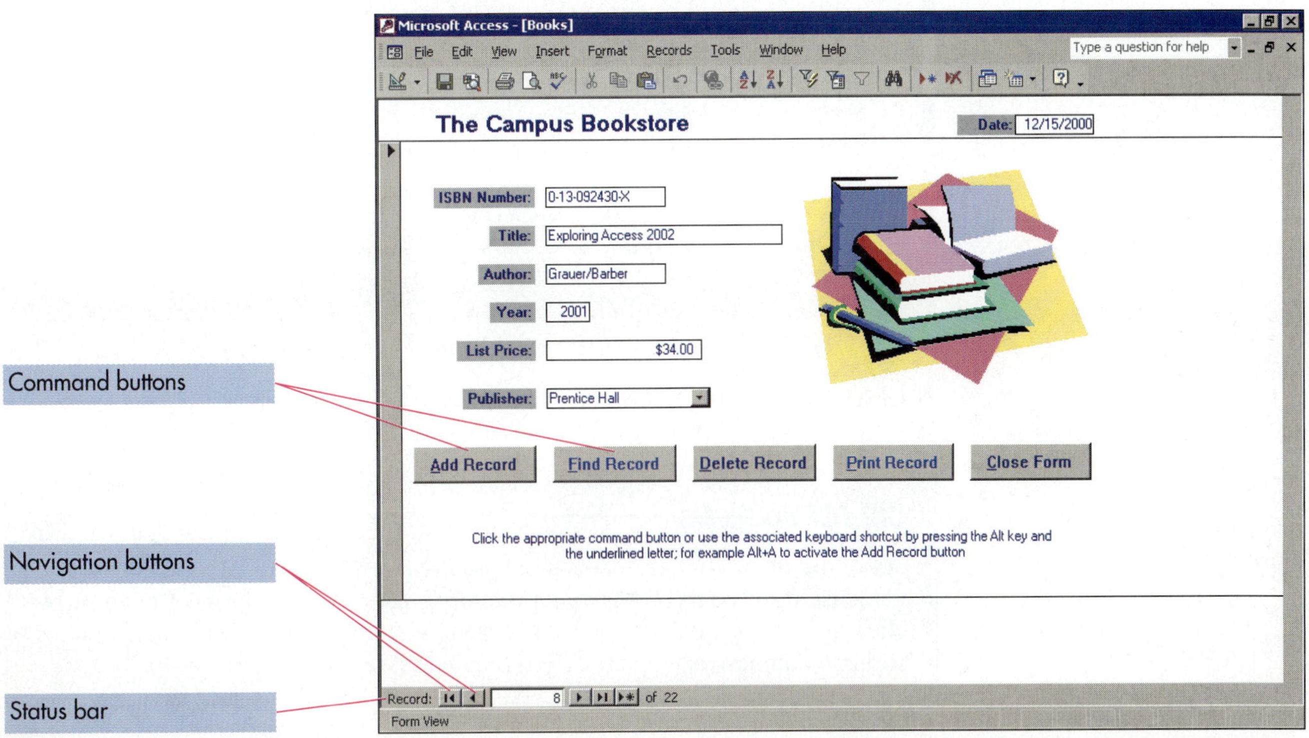

(a) Form

FIGURE 1.3 *Forms, Queries, and Reports*

Displays only books published by Prentice Hall

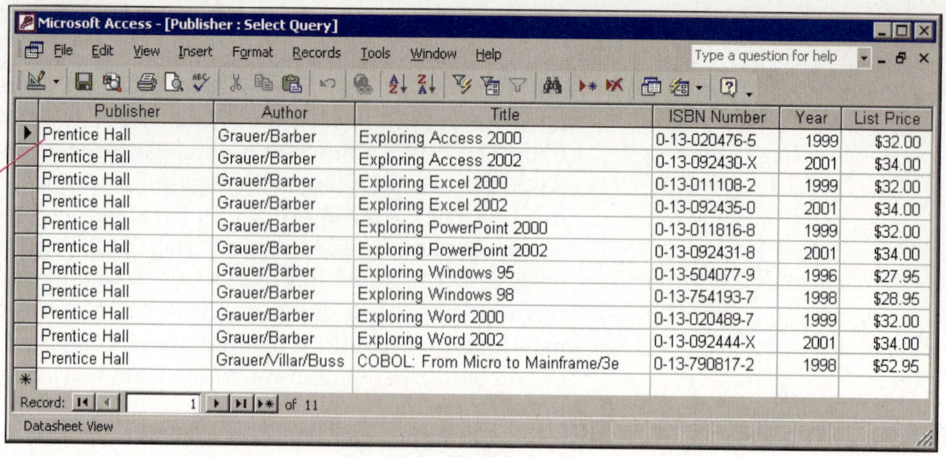

Publisher	Author	Title	ISBN Number	Year	List Price
Prentice Hall	Grauer/Barber	Exploring Access 2000	0-13-020476-5	1999	$32.00
Prentice Hall	Grauer/Barber	Exploring Access 2002	0-13-092430-X	2001	$34.00
Prentice Hall	Grauer/Barber	Exploring Excel 2000	0-13-011108-2	1999	$32.00
Prentice Hall	Grauer/Barber	Exploring Excel 2002	0-13-092435-0	2001	$34.00
Prentice Hall	Grauer/Barber	Exploring PowerPoint 2000	0-13-011816-8	1999	$32.00
Prentice Hall	Grauer/Barber	Exploring PowerPoint 2002	0-13-092431-8	2001	$34.00
Prentice Hall	Grauer/Barber	Exploring Windows 95	0-13-504077-9	1996	$27.95
Prentice Hall	Grauer/Barber	Exploring Windows 98	0-13-754193-7	1998	$28.95
Prentice Hall	Grauer/Barber	Exploring Word 2000	0-13-020489-7	1999	$32.00
Prentice Hall	Grauer/Barber	Exploring Word 2002	0-13-092444-X	2001	$34.00
Prentice Hall	Grauer/Villar/Buss	COBOL: From Micro to Mainframe/3e	0-13-790817-2	1998	$52.95

(b) Query

Report is based on query shown in Figure 1.3b

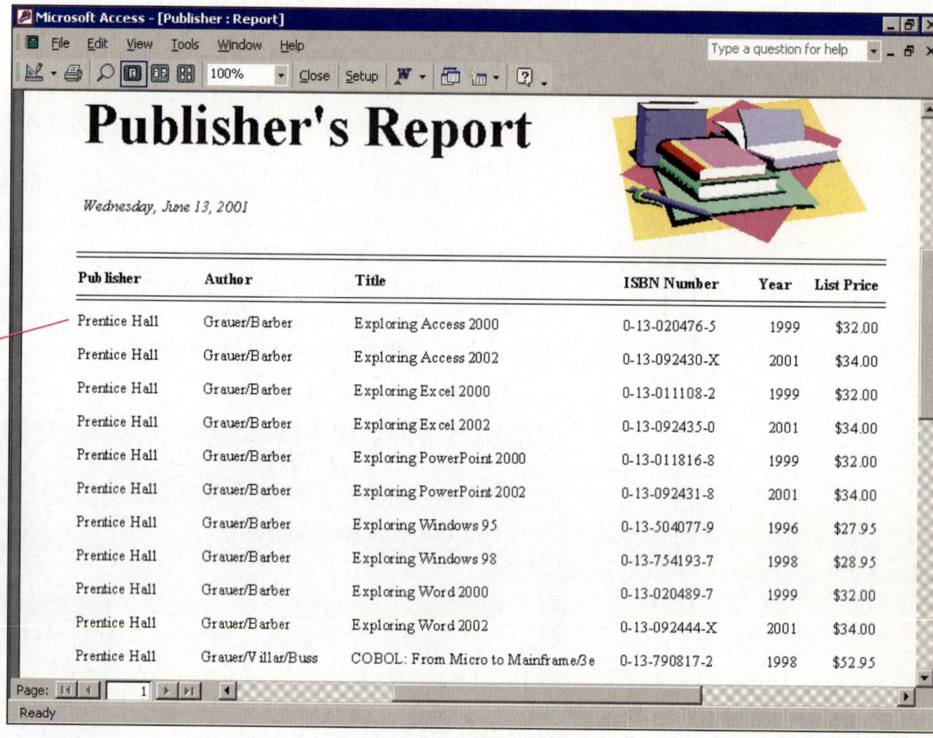

Publisher	Author	Title	ISBN Number	Year	List Price
Prentice Hall	Grauer/Barber	Exploring Access 2000	0-13-020476-5	1999	$32.00
Prentice Hall	Grauer/Barber	Exploring Access 2002	0-13-092430-X	2001	$34.00
Prentice Hall	Grauer/Barber	Exploring Excel 2000	0-13-011108-2	1999	$32.00
Prentice Hall	Grauer/Barber	Exploring Excel 2002	0-13-092435-0	2001	$34.00
Prentice Hall	Grauer/Barber	Exploring PowerPoint 2000	0-13-011816-8	1999	$32.00
Prentice Hall	Grauer/Barber	Exploring PowerPoint 2002	0-13-092431-8	2001	$34.00
Prentice Hall	Grauer/Barber	Exploring Windows 95	0-13-504077-9	1996	$27.95
Prentice Hall	Grauer/Barber	Exploring Windows 98	0-13-754193-7	1998	$28.95
Prentice Hall	Grauer/Barber	Exploring Word 2000	0-13-020489-7	1999	$32.00
Prentice Hall	Grauer/Barber	Exploring Word 2002	0-13-092444-X	2001	$34.00
Prentice Hall	Grauer/Villar/Buss	COBOL: From Micro to Mainframe/3e	0-13-790817-2	1998	$52.95

(c) Report

FIGURE 1.3 *Forms, Queries, and Reports (continued)*

ONE FILE HOLDS ALL

All of the objects in an Access database are stored in a single file on disk. The database itself is opened through the Open command in the File menu or by clicking the Open button on the Database toolbar. The individual objects within a database are opened from the Database window.

HANDS-ON EXERCISE 1

INTRODUCTION TO ACCESS

Objective To open an existing Access database; to add, edit, and delete records within a table in that database; to open forms, queries, and reports within an existing database. Use Figure 1.4 as a guide in the exercise.

Step 1: **Welcome to Windows**

- Turn on the computer and all of its peripherals. The floppy drive should be empty prior to starting your machine.
- Your system will take a minute or so to get started, after which you should see the desktop in Figure 1.4a. Do not be concerned if the appearance of your desktop is different from ours.
- If necessary, click the **Close button** to close the Welcome window and continue with the exercise.

Start button

(a) Welcome to Windows (step 1)

FIGURE 1.4 *Hands-on Exercise 1*

> **WELCOME TO WINDOWS**
>
> All versions of Windows typically greet you with a Welcome window that highlights features in the operating system. The contents of this window depend on the specific version of Windows, but you should have no trouble exploring. If you do not see the Welcome window when you start your machine, click the Start button, click Run, then type "Welcome" (or C:\Windows\Welcome), and press the enter key. Relax and enjoy the show.

Step 2: Obtain the Practice Files

- ➤ We have created a series of practice files (also called a "data disk") for you to use in conjunction with your text. You can also download the files from our Web site provided you have an Internet connection. Start Internet Explorer, then go to the Exploring Windows home page at **www.prenhall.com/grauer**.
  - Click the book for Office XP, which takes you to the Office XP home page. Click the **Student Resources** tab (at the top of the window) to go to the Student Resources page as shown in Figure 1.4b.
  - Click the Link to **Student Data Disk** (in the left frame), then scroll down the page until you can select Access 2002. Click the link to download the student data disk.
  - You will see the File Download dialog box. The option button to save this program to disk is selected. Click OK. The Save As dialog box appears.
  - Click the **down arrow** in the Save In list box to enter the drive and folder where you want to save the file. It's best to save the file to the Windows desktop or to the My Documents folder on drive C.
- ➤ Double click the file after it has been downloaded, then follow the onscreen instructions. Check with your instructor for additional information.

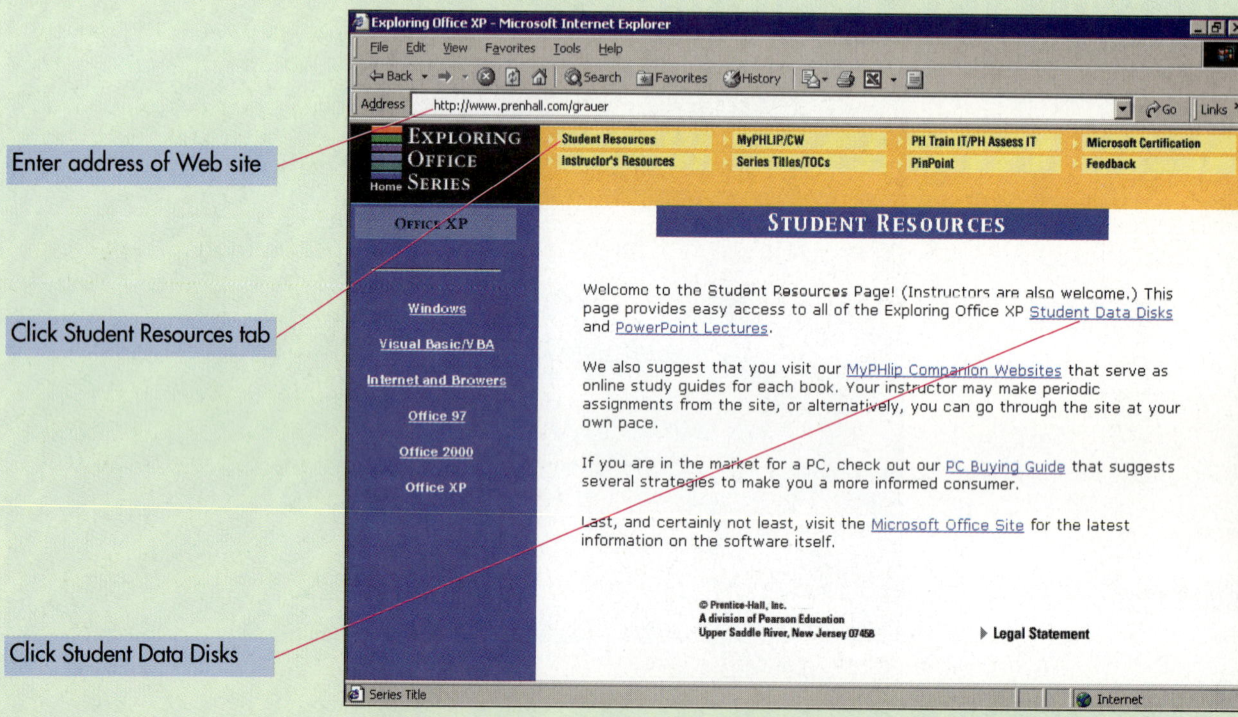

(b) Obtain the Practice Files (step 2)

FIGURE 1.4 *Hands-on Exercise 1 (continued)*

WORK ON DRIVE C

Even in a lab setting, it is preferable to work on the local hard drive, as opposed to a floppy disk. The hard drive is much faster, which is important when working with the large file sizes associated with Access. Work on drive C through the exercise, then use Windows Explorer at the end of the exercise to copy the database to a floppy disk that you can take with you.

Step 3: **Start Microsoft Access**

- Click the **Start button** to display the Start menu. Click (or point to) the **Programs menu**, then click **Microsoft Access** to start the program. Right click the **Office Assistant** if it appears and click the **Hide command**.
- Pull down the **File menu** and click the **Open command** to display the Open dialog box in Figure 1.4c. (Do this even if the task pane is open.)
- Click the **down arrow** on the **Views button**, then click **Details** to change to the Details view.
- Click and drag the vertical border between columns to increase (or decrease) the size of a column.
- Click the **drop-down arrow** on the Look In list box. Click the appropriate drive (drive C is recommended rather than drive A) depending on the location of your data. Double click the **Exploring Access folder**.
- Click the down scroll arrow (if needed) to click the **Bookstore database**. Click the **Open command button** to open the database.

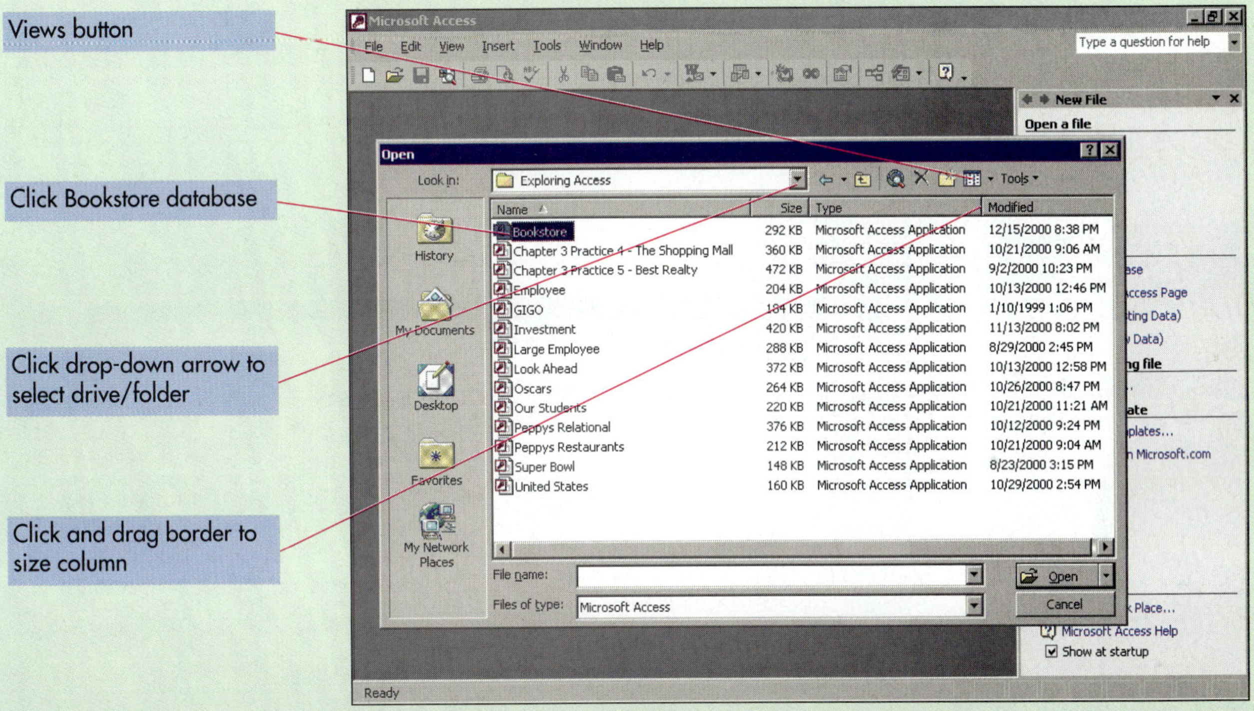

(c) Start Microsoft Access (step 3)

FIGURE 1.4 *Hands-on Exercise 1 (continued)*

FILE FORMATS

The file format for Access 2002 is different than that of Access 2000. The earlier program cannot read the newer format, but Access 2002 can work with files that were created by its predecessor. If you have Access 2002 on your computer, but you know you will be working with individuals who have the earlier program, it is more convenient to leave your files in Access 2000 format. Pull down the Help menu and click About Microsoft Access to display the version number of your software.

Step 4: **Open the Books Table**

- If necessary, click the **Maximize button** in the application window so that Access takes the entire desktop.
- You should see the database window for the Bookstore database with the Tables button already selected. Double click the icon next to Books to open the table as shown in Figure 1.4d.
- Click the **Maximize button** so that the Books table fills the Access window and reduces the clutter on the screen.
- Practice with the navigation buttons above the status bar to move from one record to the next. Click ► or ◄ to move forward to the next record or return to the previous record.
- Click |◄ to move to the first record in the table or ►| to move to the last record in the table.
- Click in any field of the first record. The status indicator at the bottom of the Books table indicates record 1 of 22. The triangle symbol in the record selector indicates that the record has not changed since it was last saved.

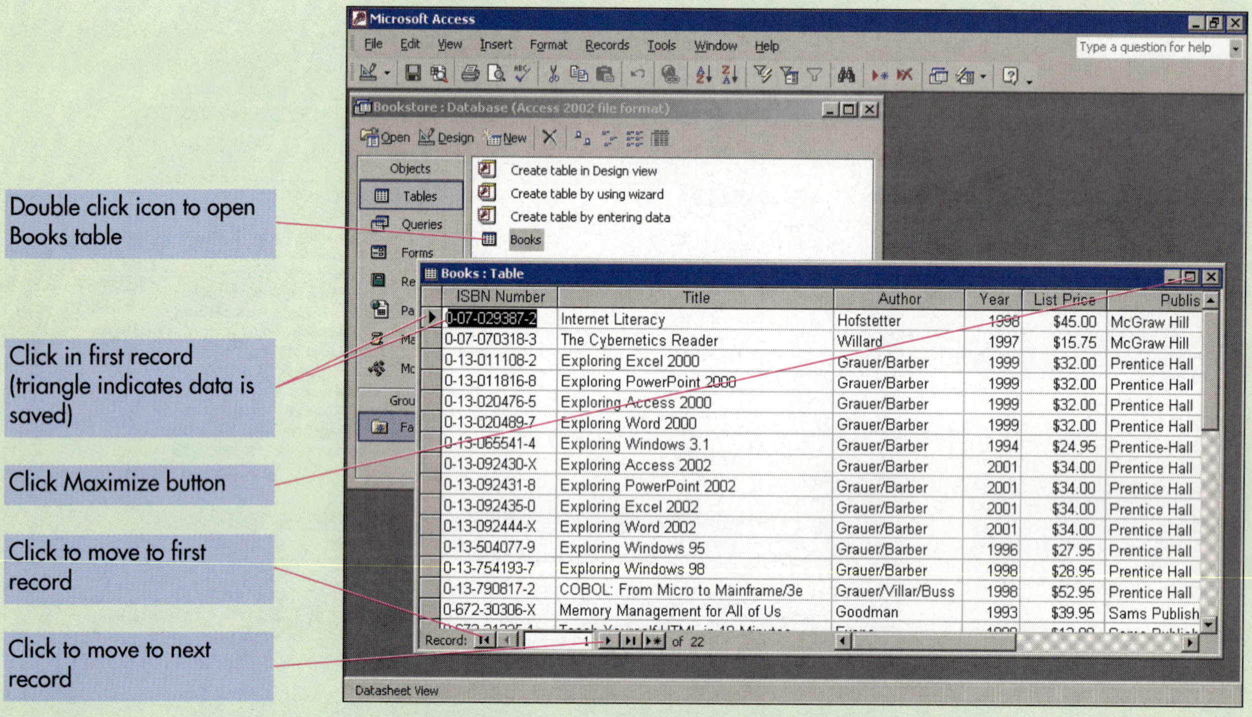

(d) Open the Books Table (step 4)

FIGURE 1.4 *Hands-on Exercise 1 (continued)*

MOVING FROM FIELD TO FIELD

Press the Tab key, the right arrow key, or the enter key to move to the next field in the current record (or the first field in the next record if you are already in the last field of the current record). Press Shift+Tab or the left arrow key to return to the previous field in the current record (or the last field in the previous record if you are already in the first field of the current record). Press Home or End to move to the first or last field, respectively.

Step 5: **Add a New Record**

- Pull down the **Insert menu** and click **New Record** (or click the **New Record button** on the Table Datasheet toolbar). The record selector moves to the last record (record 23). The insertion point is positioned in the first field (ISBN Number).
- Enter data for the new record as shown in Figure 1.4e. The record selector changes to a pencil as soon as you enter the first character in the new record.
- Press **enter** when you have entered the last field for the record. The record has been saved to the database, and the record selector changes to a triangle.
- Add another record. Enter **0-13-034260-2** as the ISBN. The title is **Exploring Microsoft Office XP Volume II** by **Grauer/Barber**. The price is **$54.00**. The book was published by **Prentice Hall** in **2001**. Be sure to press **enter** when you have completed the data entry.
- The status bar should show 24 records.

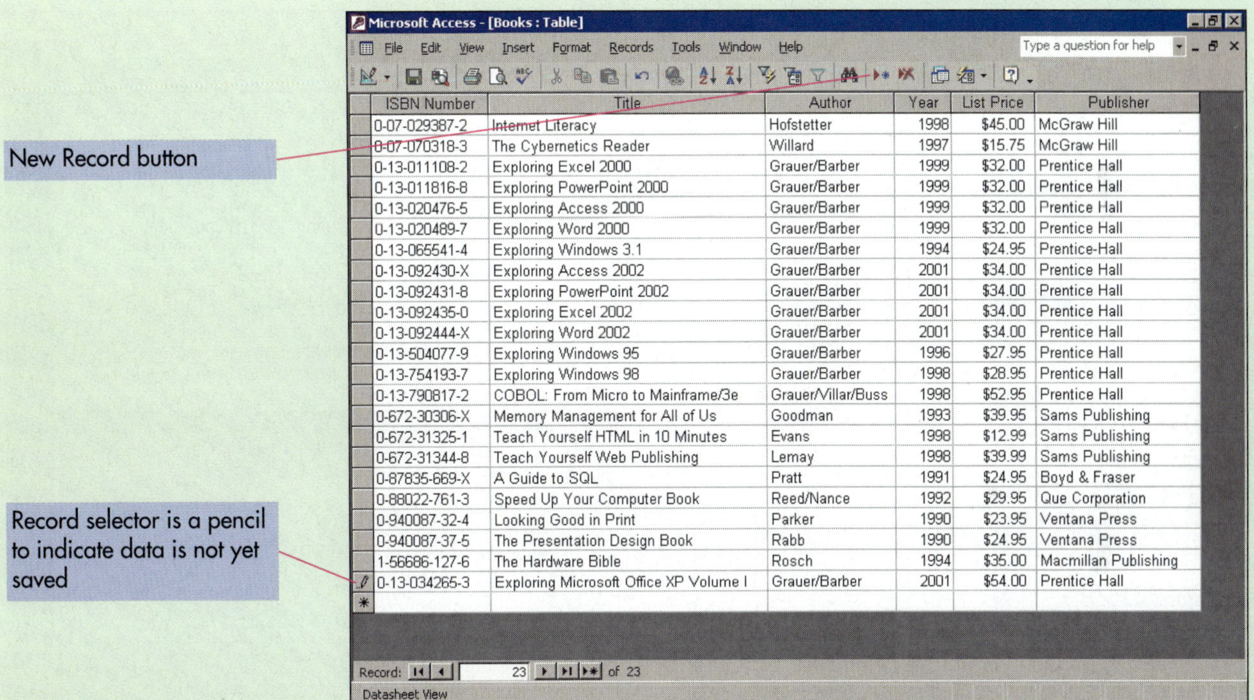

(e) Add a New Record (step 5)

FIGURE 1.4 *Hands-on Exercise 1 (continued)*

> **CREATE YOUR OWN SHORTHAND**
>
> Use the AutoCorrect feature that is common to all Office applications to expand abbreviations such as "PH" for Prentice Hall. Pull down the Tools menu, click AutoCorrect, type the abbreviation in the Replace text box and the expanded entry in the With text box. Click the Add command button, then click OK to exit the dialog box and return to the document. The next time you type PH (in uppercase) as you enter a record, it will be automatically expanded to Prentice Hall.

Step 6: **Edit a Record**

- Press **Ctrl+Home** to move to the first record. Click in the **Title field**, pull down the **Edit menu**, and click **Find** (or click the **Find button** on the toolbar) to display the dialog box in Figure 1.4f.
- Enter **COBOL** in the Find What text box. Check that the other parameters for the Find command match the dialog box in Figure 1.4f. Be sure that the Title field is selected in the Look in list box and Any Part of Field is selected in the Match text box.
- Click the **Find Next command button**. Access moves to record 14, the record containing the designated character string, and selects the matching word in the Title field for that record. Click **Cancel** to close the Find dialog box.
- Press the **tab key** three times to move from the Title field to the Price field (or click directly in the price field). The current price ($52.95) is already selected. Type **$58.95**, then press the **enter key**.

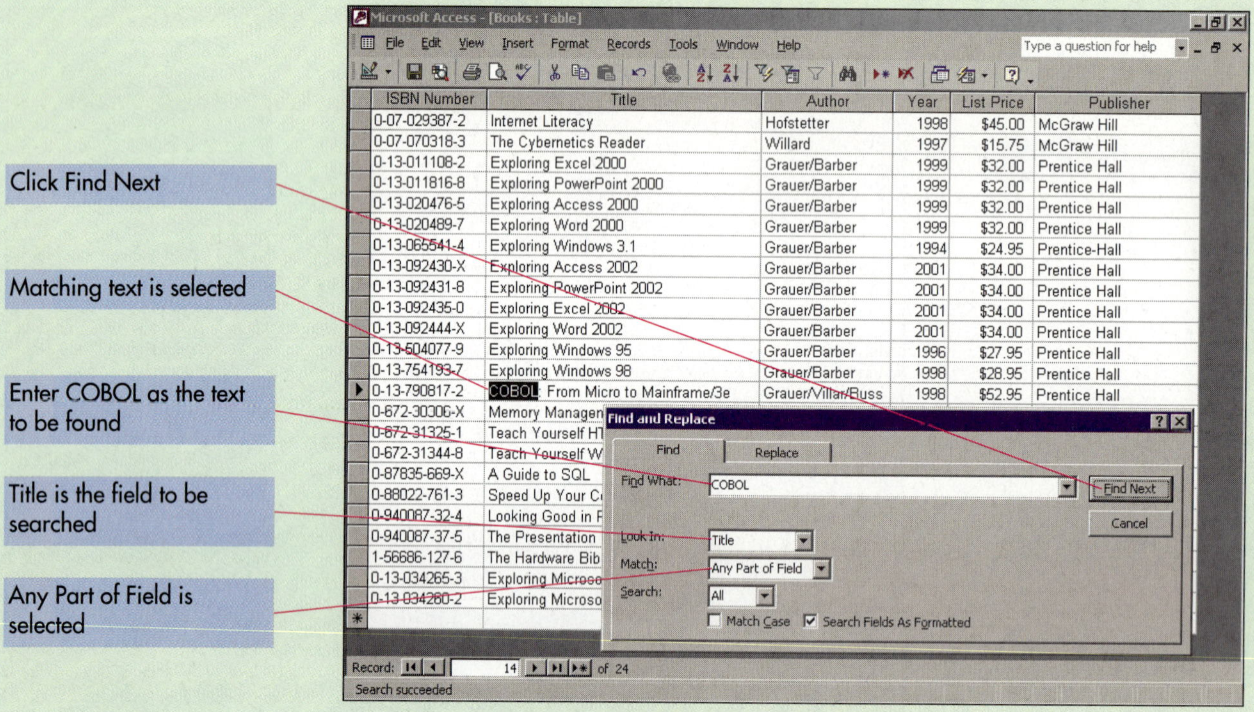

(f) Edit a Record (step 6)

FIGURE 1.4 *Hands-on Exercise 1 (continued)*

USE WHAT YOU KNOW

The Find command is contained in the Edit menu of every Office application, and it is an ideal way to search for specific records within a table. You have the option to search a single field or the entire record, to match all or part of the selected field(s), to move forward or back in a table, and to specify a case-sensitive search. The Replace command can be used to substitute one value for another. Be careful, however, about using the Replace All option for global replacement because unintended replacements are all too common.

Step 7: Delete a Record

- Use the Find command to search for the book **A Guide to SQL**. (You can enter "SQL" in the Find What dialog box, then use the same search parameters as in the previous step.)
- The Find command should return the appropriate record, which is *not visible* in Figure 1.4g. (This is because we have deleted the record to display the dialog box in the figure.)
- Pull down the **Edit menu** and click the **Select Record command** to highlight the entire record. You can also click the record selector (the box immediately to the left of the first field) to select the record without having to use a pull-down menu.
- Press the **Del key** (or click the **Delete Record button** on the toolbar) to delete the record. You will see the dialog box in Figure 1.4g indicating that you are about to delete a record and asking you to confirm the deletion. Click **Yes**.
- Pull down the **Edit menu**. The Undo command is dim, indicating that you cannot undelete a record. Press **Esc** to continue working.

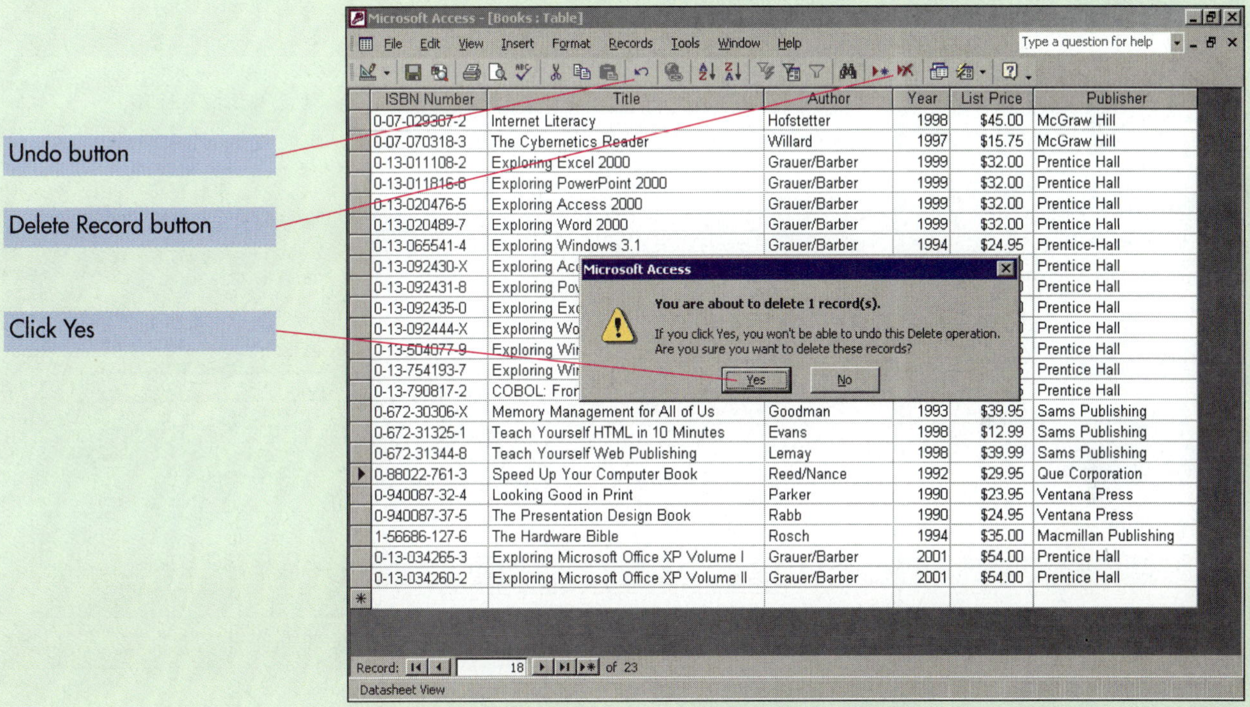

(g) Delete a Record (step 7)

FIGURE 1.4 *Hands-on Exercise 1 (continued)*

THE UNDO COMMAND

The Undo command is common to all Office applications, but it is implemented differently in Access. Word, Excel, and PowerPoint let you undo the last several operations. Access, however, because it saves changes automatically as soon as you move to the next record, lets you undo only the last command that was executed. Even this is limited, because once you delete a record, you cannot undo the deletion; that is, the record is permanently deleted.

Step 8: Print the Table

- Pull down the **File menu** and click the **Print Preview command** to see the table prior to printing. The status bar indicates that you are viewing page one (and further, that there are additional pages).
- Click the **Setup button** on the Print Preview toolbar to display the Page Setup dialog box as shown in Figure 1.4h.
- Click the **Page tab**. Click the **Landscape option button**. Click **OK** to accept the settings and close the dialog box.
- The table should now fit on one page. (If it still does not fit on one page, click the Setup button on the Print Preview toolbar to display the Page Setup dialog box, click the **Margins tab**, and make the margins smaller.)
- Click the **Print button** to print the table. Alternatively, you can pull down the File menu, click **Print** to display the Print dialog box, click the **All options button**, then click **OK**.
- Click **Close** to close the Print Preview window. Close the table.

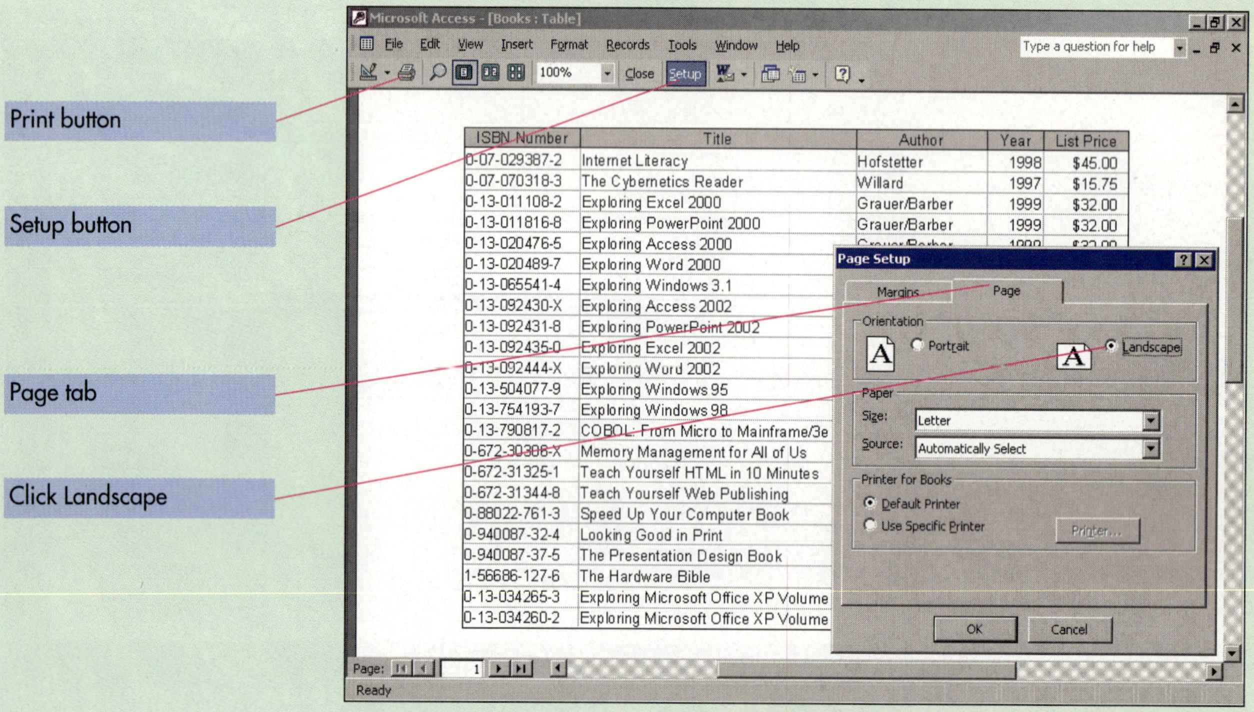

(h) Print the Table (step 8)

FIGURE 1.4 *Hands-on Exercise 1 (continued)*

TIP OF THE DAY

You can set the Office Assistant to greet you with a "tip of the day" each time you start Access. Click the Microsoft Access Help button (or press the F1 key) to display the Assistant, then click the Options button to display the Office Assistant dialog box. Click the Options tab, then check the Show the Tip of the Day at Startup Box and click OK. The next time you start Access, you will be greeted by the Assistant, who will offer you the tip of the day.

Step 9: Open the Books Form

- Click the **Forms button** in the Database window. Double click the **Books form** to open the form, and if necessary, maximize the form so that it takes the entire window.
- Click the **Add Record command button** or use the keyboard shortcut, **Alt+A**. Click in the text box for **ISBN number**, then use the **tab key** to move from field to field as you enter data for the book as shown in Figure 1.4i.
- Enter text in the **Price field** to view the data validation that is built into Access. Click **OK** when you see the error message, then enter the indicated price. Click the **drop-down arrow** on the Publisher's list box to display the available publishers and to select the appropriate one. The use of a combo box ensures that you cannot misspell a publisher's name.
- Click the button to **Print Record** (or press **Alt+P**) to print the form for the record that you just added.
- Close the Books form to return to the Database window.

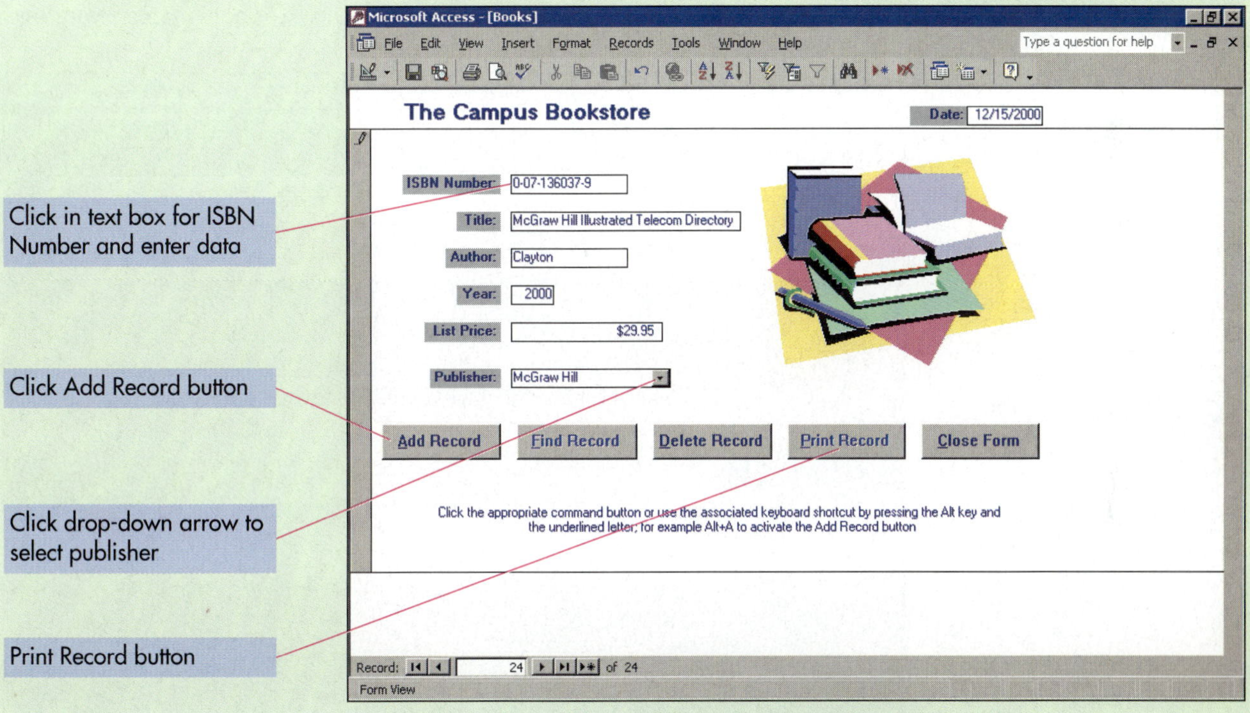

(i) Open the Books Form (step 9)

FIGURE 1.4 *Hands-on Exercise 1 (continued)*

DATA VALIDATION

No system, no matter how sophisticated, can produce valid output from invalid input. Thus, good systems are built to anticipate errors in data entry and to reject those errors prior to saving a record. Access will automatically prevent you from adding records with a duplicate primary key or an invalid field type (such as text data in a numeric field). Other types of validation, such as requiring the author's name, are implemented by the database developer.

Step 10: Run a Query

- ➤ Click the **Queries button** in the Database window. Double click the **Publisher query** to run the query. You will see a dialog box asking you to enter the name of a publisher.
- ➤ Type **McGraw Hill** and press **enter** to see the results of the query, which should contain three books by this publisher. (If you do not see any books, it is because you spelled the publisher incorrectly. Close the query to return to the Database window, then rerun the query.)
- ➤ You can use a query to display information, as was just done, and/or you can modify data in the underlying table. Click in the **Publisher field** for the blank record in the last row (the record selector is an asterisk). Type **McGraw Hill** to begin entering the data for a new record as shown in Figure 1.4j.
- ➤ You can enter data for any publisher within the query, but you must satisfy the requirements for data validation. See what happens if you omit the ISBN number or Author's name, or enter alphabetic data for the year or price. (The missing ISBN is **0-07-561585-1**.)
- ➤ Click the **Close button** to close the query and return to the Database window.

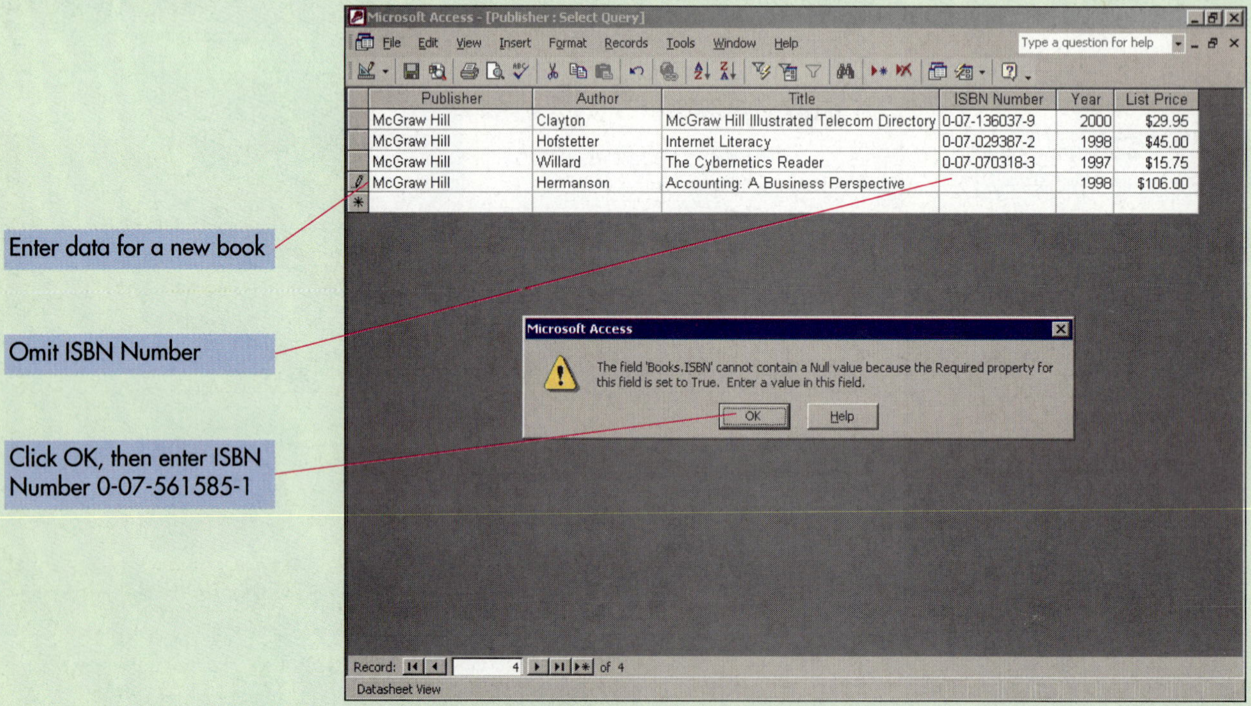

(j) Run a Query (step 10)

FIGURE 1.4 *Hands-on Exercise 1 (continued)*

FORMAT A DATASHEET

Format your tables and/or queries to make the results stand out. Click anywhere in a table or query (in Datasheet view), pull down the Format menu, and click the Datasheet command to display the Format Datasheet dialog box. You can change the style of the table to sunken or raised, change the color of the gridlines or suppress them altogether. The Format command also enables you to change the row height or column width and/or to hide rows and columns. See practice exercise 3 at the end of the chapter.

Step 11: **Open a Report**

- Click the **Reports button** in the Database window to display the available reports. Double click the icon for the **Publisher report**. Type **McGraw Hill** in the Parameter dialog box. Press **enter**.
- Click the **Maximize button** in the Report Window so that the report takes the entire screen as shown in Figure 1.4k.
- Click the **Zoom button** to toggle to 100% so that you can read the report, which should contain four records.
- Two books were in the database initially, one book was entered through a form, and one book was entered through a query. All of the books in the report are published by McGraw Hill, which is consistent with the parameter you entered earlier.
- Click the **Print button** on the Report toolbar. Click the **Close button** to close the Report window.

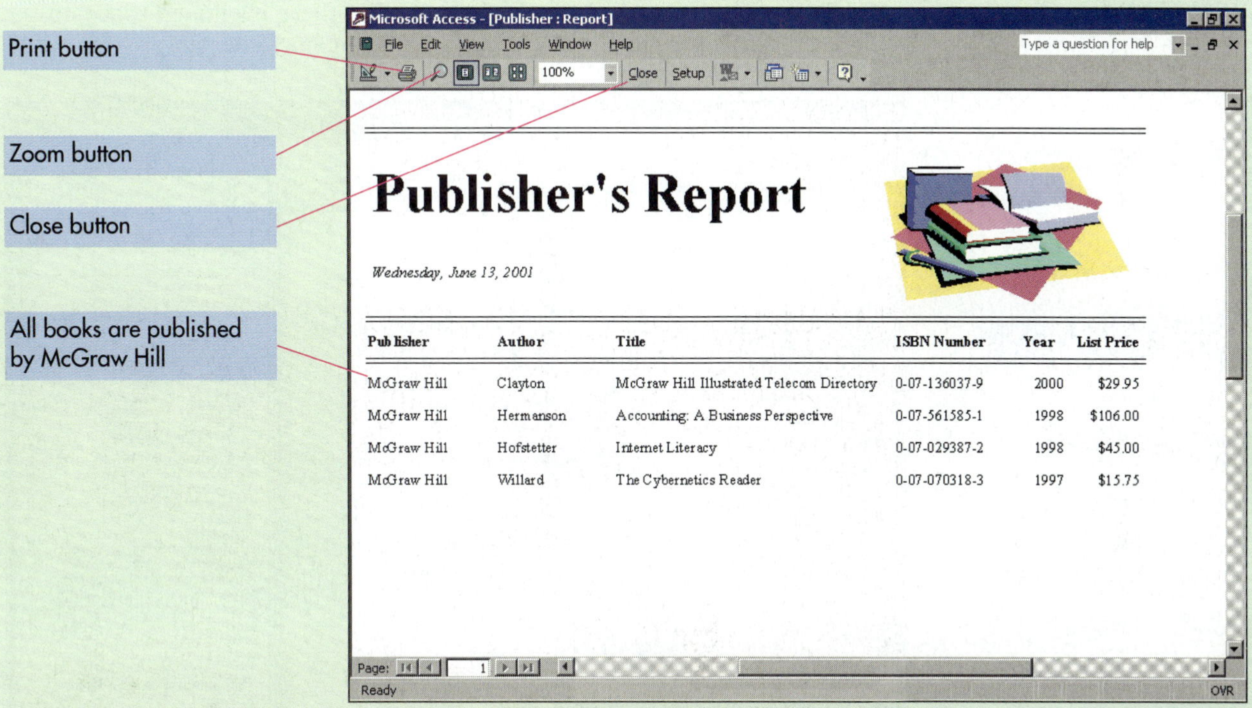

(k) Open a Report (step 11)

FIGURE 1.4 *Hands-on Exercise 1 (continued)*

THE PRINT PREVIEW TOOLBAR

The Print Preview Toolbar is displayed automatically when you preview a report prior to printing. Click the Zoom button to toggle back and forth between fitting the entire page in the window and viewing the report at 100% magnification. Click the one, two, and multiple page buttons, to view different portions of the report in reports that extend over multiple pages. Use the Setup button to change the margins and/or orientation. Click the Close button to exit Print Preview.

Step 12: **The Office Assistant**

- If necessary, pull down the **Help menu** and click the command to **Show the Office Assistant**. Click the **Assistant**, then enter the question, **How do I sort records?** in the balloon.
- Click the **Search button** in the Assistant's balloon to look for the answer.
- Select any topic (we selected **Sort records**), which in turn displays a Help window as shown in Figure 1.4l. Click the Office Assistant to hide the balloon.
- The left pane contains the Contents, Answer Wizard, and Index tabs. Click the **Contents tab**, then double click the various book icons to expand the various help topics. Click the icon next to any topic to display the information.
- Continue to experiment, then close the Help window when you are finished. Right click the **Office Assistant** and click the **Hide command**.
- Pull down the **File menu** and click **Exit** to close Access if you do not want to continue with the next exercise at this time.
- If you are working in a school computer lab, use **Windows Explorer** to copy the Bookstore Database to drive A. (Be sure that there is enough space on the floppy disk.) Delete the file from the My Documents folder.

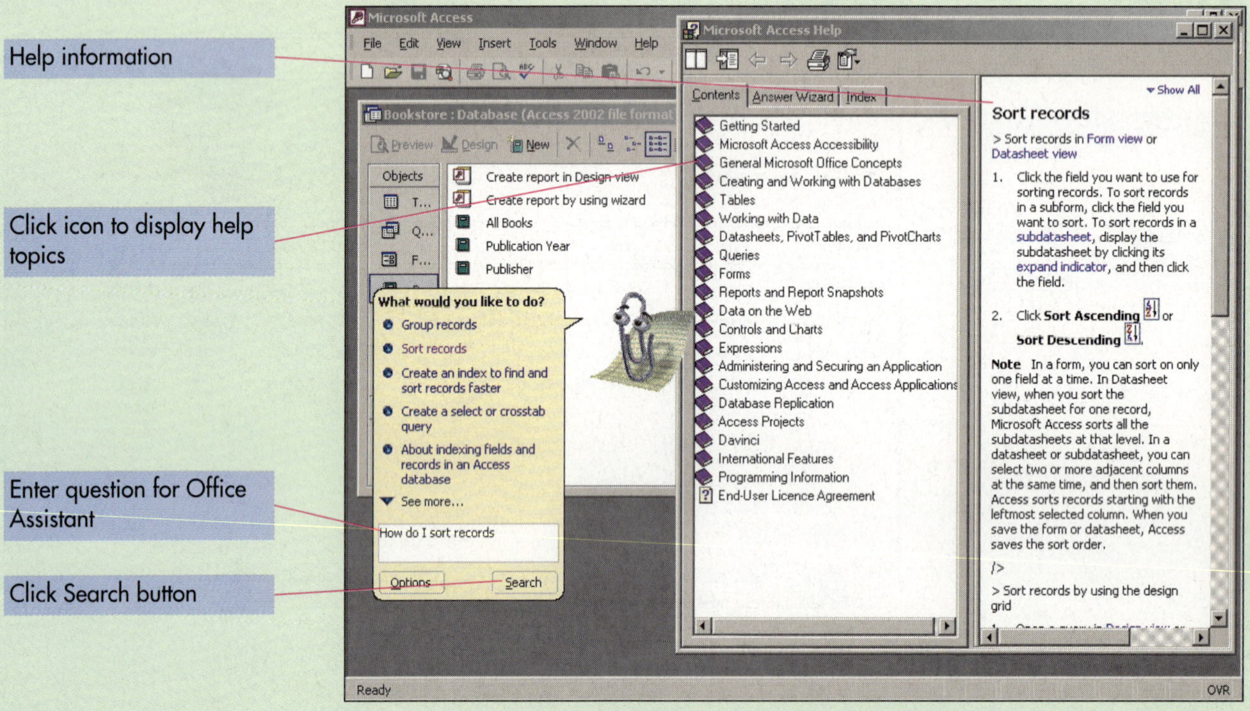

(l) The Office Assistant (step 12)

FIGURE 1.4 *Hands-on Exercise 1 (continued)*

CHOOSE YOUR OWN ASSISTANT

Choose your own personal assistant from one of several available candidates. Press the F1 key to display the Assistant, click the Assistant to display the balloon, click the Options button to display the Office Assistant dialog box, then click the Gallery tab where you choose your character. (The Office XP CD is required in order to select some of the other characters.)

The exercise just completed described how to use an existing report to obtain information from the database. But what if you are in a hurry and don't have the time to create the report? There is a faster way. You can open the table in the Datasheet view, then apply a filter and/or a sort to the table to display selected records in any order. A ***filter*** displays a subset of records from the table according to specified criteria. A ***sort*** lists those records in a specific sequence, such as alphabetically by last name or by EmployeeID. We illustrate both of these concepts in conjunction with Figure 1.5.

Figure 1.5a displays an employee table with 14 records. Each record has 8 fields. The records in the table are displayed in sequence according to the EmployeeID, which is also the primary key (the field or combination of fields that uniquely identifies a record). The status bar indicates that there are 14 records in the table. What if, however, you wanted a partial list of those records, such as employees with a specific title?

Figure 1.5b displays a filtered view of the same table in which we see only the Account Reps. The status bar shows that this is a filtered list, and that there are 8 records that satisfy the criteria. (The employee table still contains the original 14 records, but only 8 records are visible with the filter in effect.) The table has also been sorted so that the selected employees are displayed in alphabetical order, as opposed to EmployeeID order.

Two operations are necessary to go from Figure 1.5a to Figure 1.5b—filtering and sorting. The easiest way to implement a filter is to click in any cell that contains the value of the desired criterion (such as any cell that contains "Account Rep" in the Title field), then click the ***Filter by Selection*** button on the Database toolbar. To sort the table, click in the field on which you want to sequence the records (the LastName field in this example), then click the ***Sort Ascending*** button on the Database toolbar. The ***Sort Descending*** button is appropriate for numeric fields such as salary, if you want to display the records with the highest value listed first.

The operations can be done in any order; that is, you can filter a table to show only selected records, then you can sort the filtered table to display the records in a different order. Conversely, you can sort a table and then apply a filter. It does not matter which operation is performed first, and indeed, you can go back and forth between the two. You can also filter the table further, by applying a second (or third) criterion; for example, click in a cell containing "Good," then click the Filter by Selection button a second time to display the Account Reps with good performance. You can also click the ***Remove Filter*** button at any time to display all of the records in the complete table.

Figure 1.5c illustrates an alternate and more powerful way to apply a filter known as ***Filter by Form***, in which you can select the criteria from a drop-down list, and/or apply multiple criteria simultaneously. However, the real advantage of the Filter by Form command extends beyond these conveniences to two additional capabilities. First, you can specify relationships within a criterion; for example, you can select employees with a salary greater than (or less than) $40,000. Filter by Selection, on the other hand, requires you to specify criteria equal to an existing value. Figure 1.5d displays the filtered table of Chicago employees earning more than $40,000.

A second advantage of the Filter by Form command is that you can specify alternative criteria (such as employees in Chicago *or* employees who are account reps) by clicking the Or tab. (The latter capability is not implemented in Figure 1.5.) Suffice it to say, however, that the availability of the various filter and sort commands enables you to obtain information from a database quickly and easily.

Sequence is EmployeeID (primary key)

Fourteen records in table

Employees : Table

EmployeeID	LastName	FirstName	Location	Title	Salary	Gender	Performance
10000	Milgrom	Pamela	Boston	Manager	$57,500	F	Average
11111	Adams	Jennifer	Atlanta	Trainee	$19,500	F	Average
20000	Johnson	James	Chicago	Account Rep	$47,500	M	Good
22222	Coulter	Tracey	Atlanta	Manager	$100,000	F	Good
30000	Marlin	Billy	Miami	Manager	$125,000	M	Good
33333	Smith	Mark	Chicago	Account Rep	$42,500	M	Average
40000	Manin	Ann	Boston	Account Rep	$49,500	F	Average
44444	Smith	Francine	Atlanta	Account Rep	$65,000	F	Good
50000	Brown	Martin	Atlanta	Trainee	$18,500	M	Poor
55555	Frank	Vernon	Miami	Account Rep	$75,000	M	Good
60000	Rubin	Patricia	Boston	Account Rep	$45,000	F	Average
66666	Charles	Kenneth	Boston	Account Rep	$40,000	M	Poor
70000	Adamson	David	Chicago	Manager	$52,000	M	Poor
77777	Marder	Kelly	Chicago	Account Rep	$38,500	F	Average

Record: 1 of 14

(a) The Employee Table (by EmployeeID)

Sequence is alphabetical order by LastName

Eight records in filtered list

Employees : Table

EmployeeID	LastName	FirstName	Location	Title	Salary	Gender	Performance
66666	Charles	Kenneth	Boston	Account Rep	$40,000	M	Poor
55555	Frank	Vernon	Miami	Account Rep	$75,000	M	Good
20000	Johnson	James	Chicago	Account Rep	$47,500	M	Good
40000	Manin	Ann	Boston	Account Rep	$49,500	F	Average
77777	Marder	Kelly	Chicago	Account Rep	$38,500	F	Average
60000	Rubin	Patricia	Boston	Account Rep	$45,000	F	Average
44444	Smith	Francine	Atlanta	Account Rep	$65,000	F	Good
33333	Smith	Mark	Chicago	Account Rep	$42,500	M	Average

Record: 1 of 8 (Filtered)

(b) Filtered List (Account Reps by last name)

Click drop-down arrow to select criteria

Enter data with relational operator >

Or tab

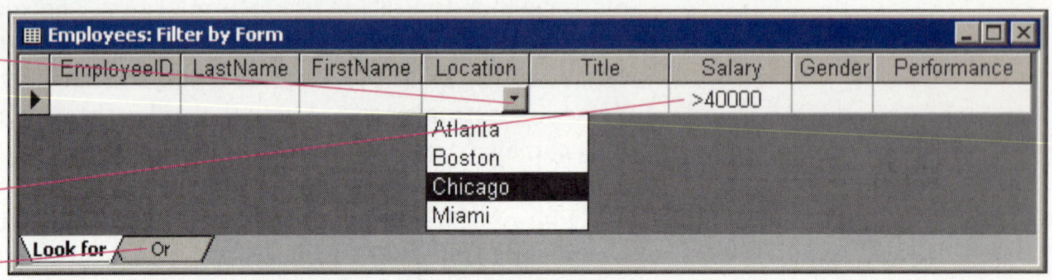

(c) Filter by Form

Three records in filtered list

Employees : Table

EmployeeID	LastName	FirstName	Location	Title	Salary	Gender	Performance
70000	Adamson	David	Chicago	Manager	$52,000	M	Poor
20000	Johnson	James	Chicago	Account Rep	$47,500	M	Good
33333	Smith	Mark	Chicago	Account Rep	$42,500	M	Average

Record: 1 of 3 (Filtered)

(d) Filtered List (Chicago employees earning more than $40,000)

FIGURE 1.5 *Filters and Sorting*

Pivot Tables and Pivot Charts

A database exists to provide information. In essence, you add, edit, and delete records of a table to maintain the data within that table. The data within a specific employee record is of great importance to that employee, but it is less important to the organization as a whole than is information that is gleaned from multiple records. You can obtain information by applying filters to a table and/or by sorting the records within a table. You can also create a pivot table and/or a pivot chart.

A ***pivot table*** computes summary statistics for the records in a table (or query) according to the value of various fields within the table. A ***pivot chart*** provides the same information in graphical form. Pivot tables have been available for several years in Microsoft Excel, although they are a well-kept secret in that many knowledgeable individuals do not know of their existence. The feature is new to Access 2002, but it is an invaluable way to summarize the data within a database.

The PivotTable view in Figure 1.6a displays the average salary for each location-title combination within the Employees table. Account Reps in Atlanta, for example, earn $65,000 on average compared to their counterparts in Boston, who earn $44,833.33, which is roughly comparable to the average salary of all Account Reps of $49,222.22. One can see at a glance, therefore, that the Atlanta employees are compensated at a much higher rate than employees in other locations.

The pivot table is created within the PivotTable view. In essence, all that you do is click and drag a field from the field list to the indicated drop area. The Title, Location, and Gender fields, for example, have been moved to the row, column, and filter areas, respectively. The latter enables you to apply a filter to view summary data for selected records. There is no filter in effect as the table is presently constructed. You could, however, click the down arrow next to the Gender field to display statistics for only the male or only the female employees. The fields in the row and column areas, Title and Location in this example, can be expanded or collapsed to show detail or summary statistics. All of the fields are currently collapsed so that no details are visible. Click any of the plus signs, however, and the associated detail values will be displayed.

A pivot table is very flexible in that you can add or remove fields by dragging the field names on or off the table. You can also switch the orientation (pivot the table) by dragging a field to or from the row, column, or filter area. Further, you can change the means of calculation within the Total or Detail Fields area by switching to the sum, minimum, or maximum value, as opposed to the average value in the present table. And finally, you can change the data in the underlying table, then refresh the pivot table to reflect the changes in the table.

The PivotChart view in Figure 1.6b displays the graphical equivalent of the associated pivot table. Any changes made to the pivot chart are reflected automatically in the pivot table and vice versa. You could, for example, click the down arrow next to the Field button for location, then clear the check box that appears next to Chicago to suppress the values from this location. (The pivot chart would no longer show the Chicago data.) You can also switch the rows and columns within the pivot chart by clicking the corresponding button on the PivotTable/PivotChart toolbar.

DATA VERSUS INFORMATION

Data and information are not synonymous although the terms are often used interchangeably. Data is the raw material and consists of the table (or tables) that comprise a database. Information is the finished product. Data is converted to information by selecting (filtering) records, by sequencing (sorting) the selected records, and/or by summarizing data from multiple records. Decisions within an organization are based on information that is compiled from multiple records, as opposed to raw data.

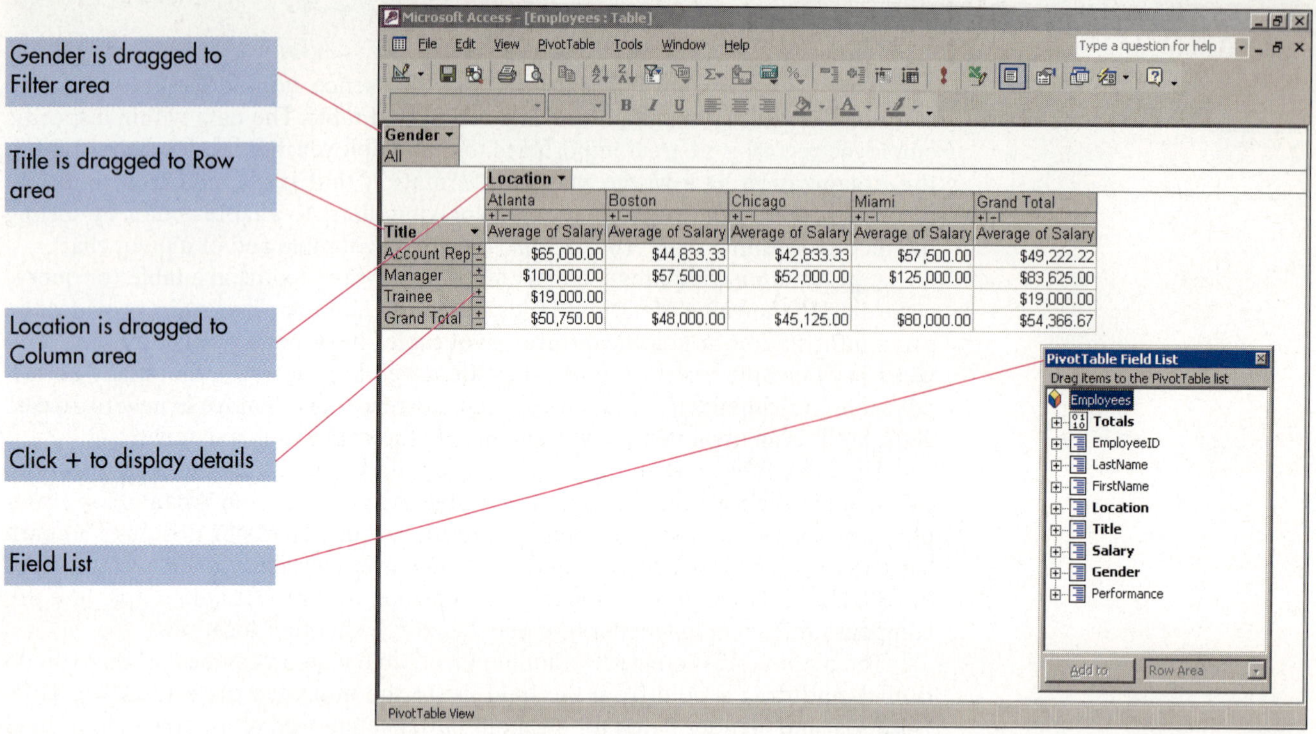

(a) Pivot Table

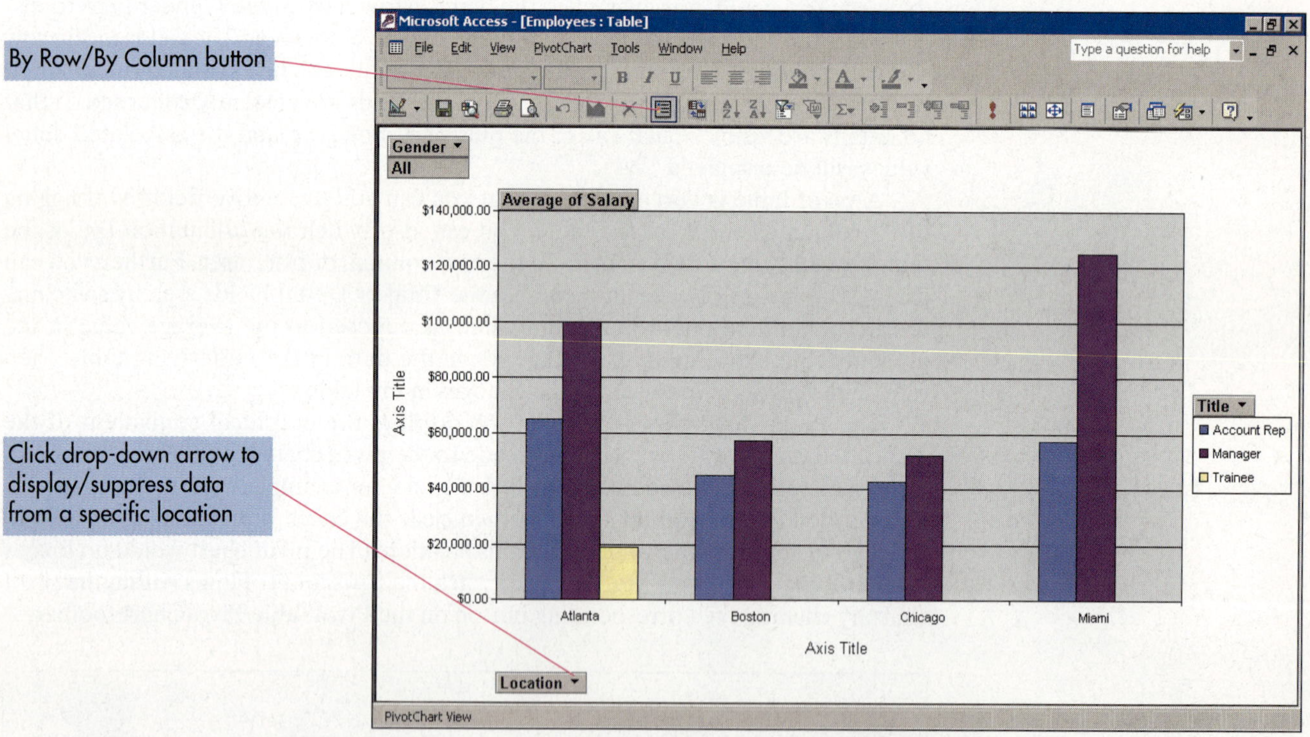

(b) Pivot Chart

FIGURE 1.6 *Pivot Tables and Pivot Charts*

HANDS-ON EXERCISE 2

FILTERS, SORTING, PIVOT TABLES, AND PIVOT CHARTS

Objective To display selected records within a table by applying the Filter by Selection and Filter by Form criteria; to sort the records in a table; to create a pivot table and corresponding chart. Use Figure 1.7 as a guide in the exercise.

Step 1: **Open the Employees Table**

- Start Access as you did in the previous exercise, but this time you will open a different database. Click **More Files** in the task pane or pull down the **File menu** and click the **Open command**. Either way, open the **Employee database** in the **Exploring Access folder**.
- If necessary, click the **Tables button** in the database window, then double click the **Employees table**, as shown in Figure 1.7a.
- Click the **Maximize button** so that the Employees table fills the Access window. If necessary, click the **Maximize button** in the application window so that Access takes the entire desktop.
- Pull down the **Insert menu** and click **New Record** (or click the **New Record button** on either the toolbar or the status bar). The record selector moves to the last record (now record 15).
- Add data for yourself, using 12345 as the EmployeeID, and your first and last name. Assign yourself to the **Miami office** as an **Account Rep** with a salary of **$40,000** and a **Good performance**.
- Press **enter** after you have completed the last field.

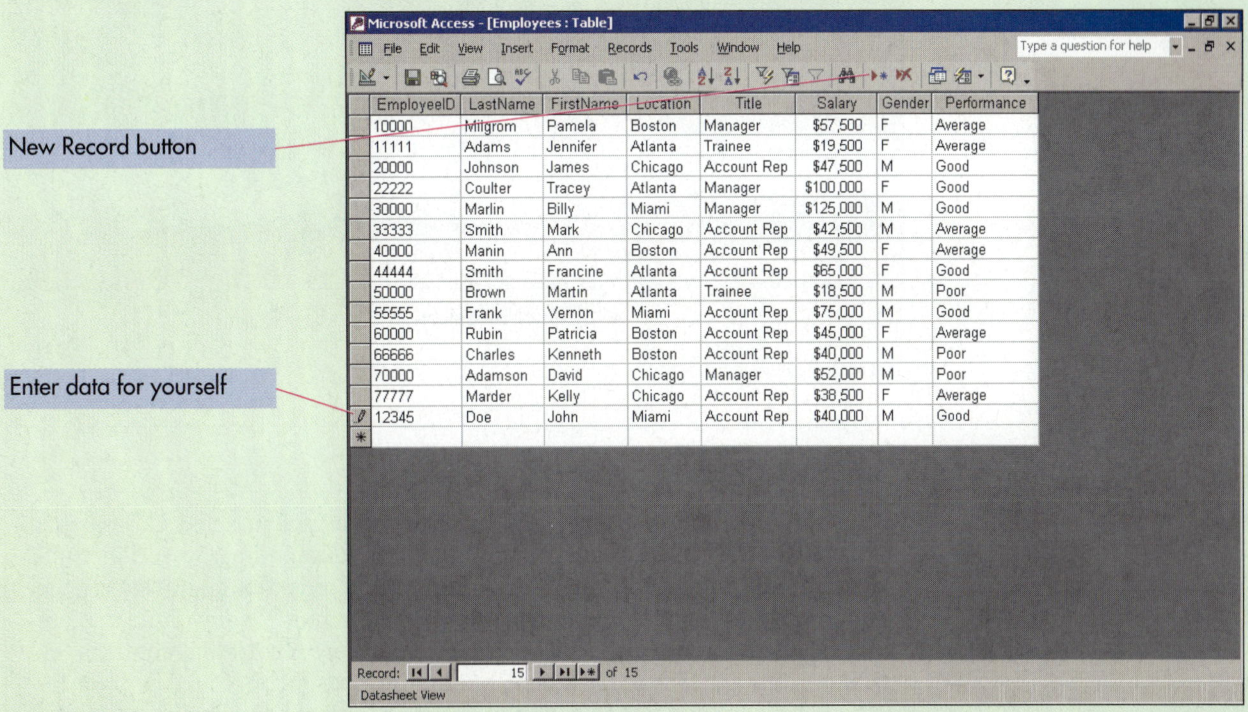

(a) Open the Employees Table (step 1)

FIGURE 1.7 *Hands-on Exercise 2*

Step 2: **Filter by Selection**

- The Employees table should contain 15 records, including the record you added for yourself. Click in the Title field of any record that contains the title **Account Rep**, then click the **Filter by Selection button**.
- You should see 9 employees, all of whom are Account Reps, as shown in Figure 1.7b. The status bar indicates that there are 9 records (as opposed to 15) and that there is a filter condition in effect.
- Click in the performance field of any employee with a good performance (we clicked in the performance field of the first record), then click the **Filter by Selection button** a second time.
- This time you see 4 employees, each of whom is an Account Rep with a performance evaluation of good. The status bar indicates that 4 records satisfy this filter condition.
- Click the **Print button** to print the filtered table.

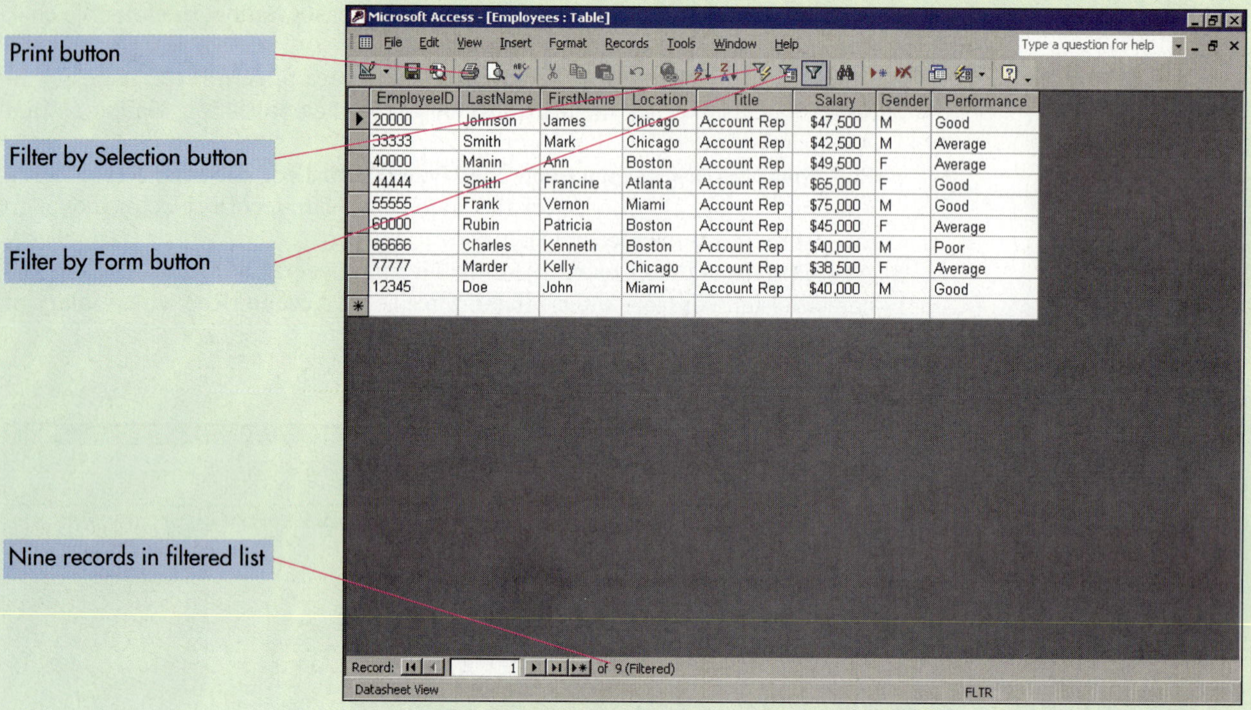

(b) Filter by Selection (step 2)

FIGURE 1.7 *Hands-on Exercise 2 (continued)*

FILTER EXCLUDING SELECTION

The Filter by Selection button on the Database toolbar selects all records that meet the designated criterion. The Filter Excluding Selection command does just the opposite and displays all records that do not satisfy the criterion. First, click the Remove Filter button to remove any filters that are in effect, then click in the appropriate field of any record that contains the value you want to exclude. Pull down the Records menu, click (or point to) the Filter command, then click the Filter Excluding Selection command to display the records that do not meet the criterion.

Step 3: **Filter by Form**

- Click the **Filter by Form button** to display the form in Figure 1.7c where you can enter or remove criteria in any sequence. Each time you click in a field, a drop-down list appears that displays all of the values for the field that occur within the table.
- Click in the columns for Title and Performance to remove the criteria that were entered in the previous step. Select the existing entries and press the **Del key**.
- Click in the cell underneath the Salary field and type **>30000** (as opposed to selecting a specific value). Click in the cell underneath the Location Field and select **Chicago**.
- Click the **Apply Filter button** to display the records that satisfy these criteria. (You should see 4 records.)
- Click the **Print button** to print the table.

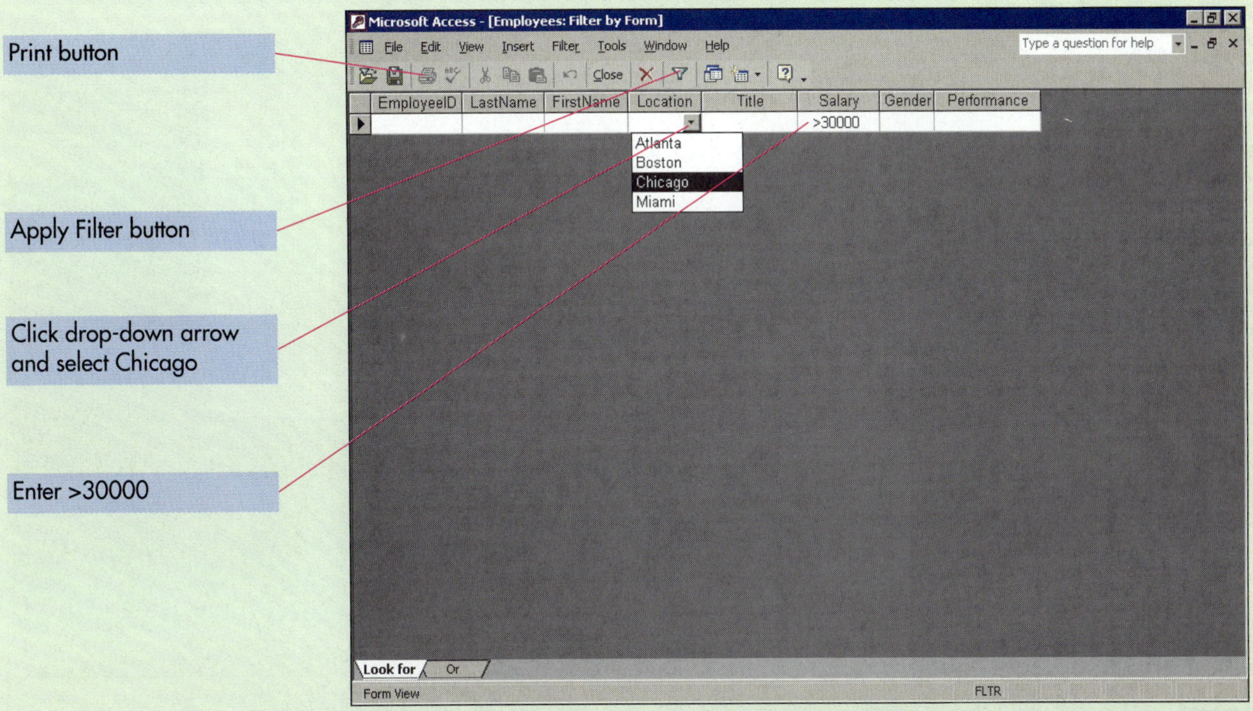

(c) Filter by Form (step 3)

FIGURE 1.7 *Hands-on Exercise 2 (continued)*

FILTER BY FORM VERSUS FILTER BY SELECTION

The Filter by Form command has all of the capabilities of the Filter by Selection command, and provides two additional capabilities. First, you can use relational operators such as >, >=, <, or <=, as opposed to searching for an exact value. Second, you can search for records that meet one of several conditions (the equivalent of an "Or" operation). Enter the first criterion as you normally would, then click the Or tab at the bottom of the window to display a second form in which you enter the alternate criteria. (To delete an alternate criterion, click the associated tab, then click the Delete button on the toolbar.)

Step 4: **Sort the Table**

- Click the **Remove Filter button** to display the complete table of 15 employees.
- Click in the **LastName field** of any record, then click the **Sort Ascending button**. The records are displayed in alphabetical (ascending) order by last name as shown in Figure 1.7d.
- Click in the **Salary field** of any record, then click the **Sort Descending button**. The records are in descending order of salary; that is, the employee with the highest salary is listed first.
- Click in the **Location field** of any record, then click the **Sort Ascending button** to display the records by location, although the employees within a location are not in any specific order.
- You can sort on two fields at the same time provided the fields are next to each other, as described in the next step.

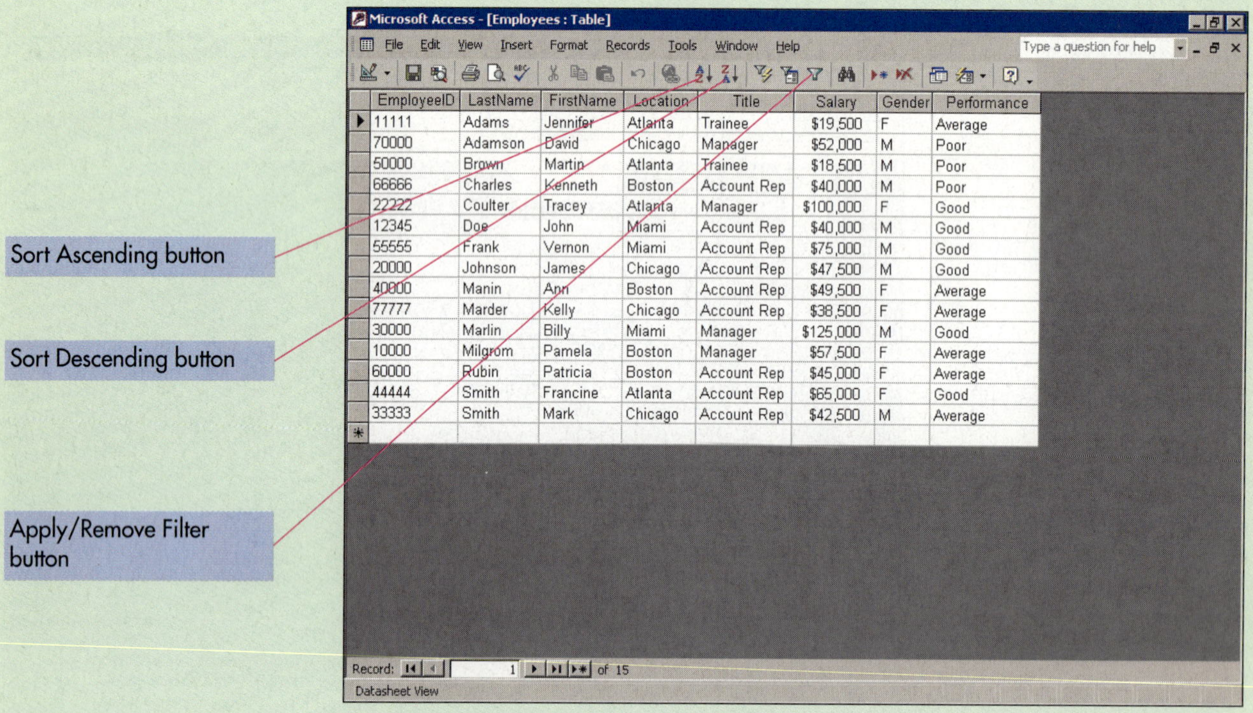

EmployeeID	LastName	FirstName	Location	Title	Salary	Gender	Performance
11111	Adams	Jennifer	Atlanta	Trainee	$19,500	F	Average
70000	Adamson	David	Chicago	Manager	$52,000	M	Poor
50000	Brown	Martin	Atlanta	Trainee	$18,500	M	Poor
66666	Charles	Kenneth	Boston	Account Rep	$40,000	M	Poor
22222	Coulter	Tracey	Atlanta	Manager	$100,000	F	Good
12345	Doe	John	Miami	Account Rep	$40,000	M	Good
55555	Frank	Vernon	Miami	Account Rep	$75,000	M	Good
20000	Johnson	James	Chicago	Account Rep	$47,500	M	Good
40000	Manin	Ann	Boston	Account Rep	$49,500	F	Average
77777	Marder	Kelly	Chicago	Account Rep	$38,500	F	Average
30000	Marlin	Billy	Miami	Manager	$125,000	M	Good
10000	Milgrom	Pamela	Boston	Manager	$57,500	F	Average
60000	Rubin	Patricia	Boston	Account Rep	$45,000	F	Average
44444	Smith	Francine	Atlanta	Account Rep	$65,000	F	Good
33333	Smith	Mark	Chicago	Account Rep	$42,500	M	Average

(d) Sort the Table (step 4)

FIGURE 1.7 *Hands-on Exercise 2 (continued)*

THE SORT OR FILTER—WHICH IS FIRST?

It doesn't matter whether you sort a table and then apply a filter, or filter first and then sort. The operations are cumulative. Thus, once a table has been sorted, any subsequent display of filtered records for that table will be in the specified sequence. Alternatively, you can apply a filter, then sort the filtered table by clicking in the desired field and clicking the appropriate sort button. Remember, too, that all filter commands are cumulative, and hence you must remove the filter to see the original table.

Step 5: **Sort on Two Fields**

- Click the header for the **Location field** to select the entire column. Click and drag the Location header so that the Location field is moved to the left of the LastName field as shown in Figure 1.7e.
- Click anywhere to deselect the column, then click on the **Location header** and click and drag to select both the Location header and the LastName Header.
- Click the **Sort Ascending button**. The records are sorted by location and alphabetically within location. (You could extend the sort to three fields such as Location, LastName, and FirstName using the same technique.)

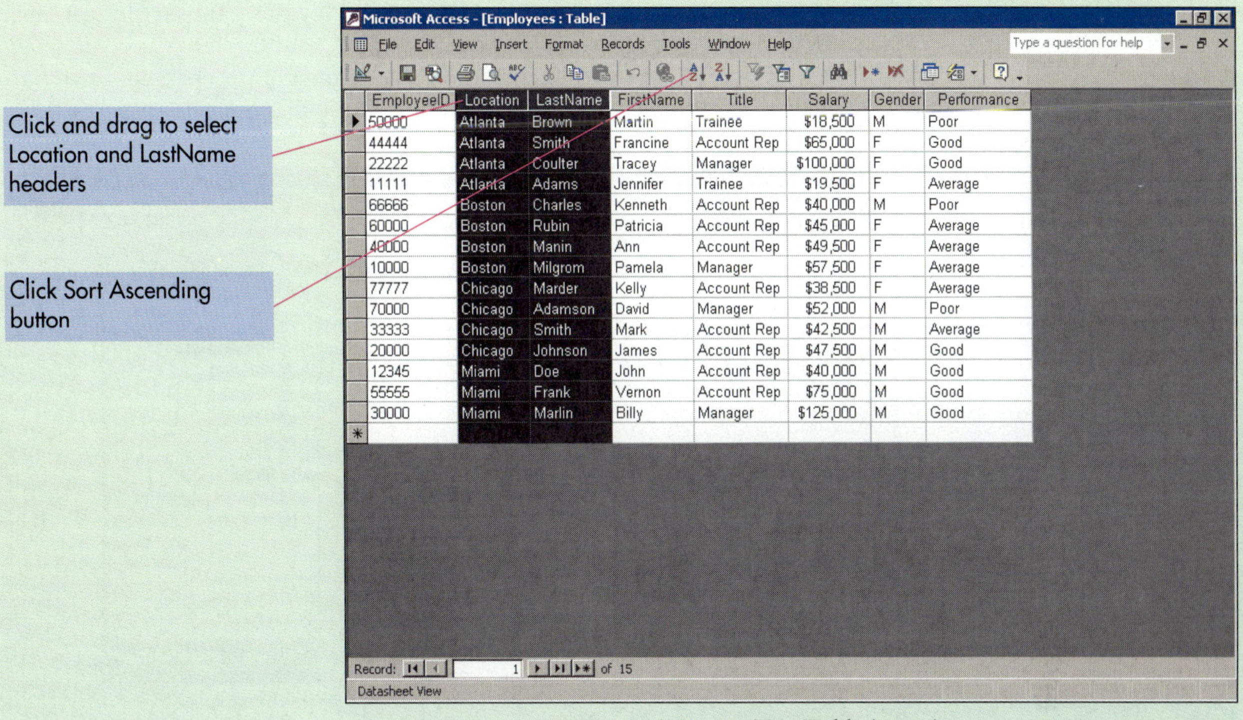

(e) Sort on Two Fields (step 5)

FIGURE 1.7 *Hands-on Exercise 2 (continued)*

REMOVING VERSUS DELETING A FILTER

Removing a filter displays all of the records that are in a table, but it does not delete the filter because the filter is stored permanently with the table. To delete the filter entirely is more complicated than simply removing it. Pull down the Record menu, click Filter, then click the Advanced Filter/Sort command to display a grid containing the criteria for the filter. Clear the Sort and Criteria rows by clicking in any cell containing an entry and deleting that entry, then click the Apply Filter button when all cells are clear to return to the Datasheet view. The Apply Filter button should be dim, indicating that the table does not contain a filter.

Step 6: Create a Pivot Table

- Pull down the **View menu** and select the **PivotTable view** to display an empty pivot table. If necessary, pull down the **View menu** a second time and click the **Field List command** (or click the **Field List button**) on the toolbar to display the field list.
- Click and drag the **Location field** to the row area. Click and drag the **Title field** to the column area as shown in Figure 1.7f.
- Drag the **Salary field** to the **Totals or Detail Fields** drop zone. This should display the individual salaries by location and title.
- Right click on any **Salary column** (do not click the drop-down arrow), select the **AutoCalc command**, then click **Sum** to display the total salaries for each location-title combination.
- Pull down the **File menu** and click the **Print command** (or click the **Print button** on the PivotTable toolbar) to print the pivot table.

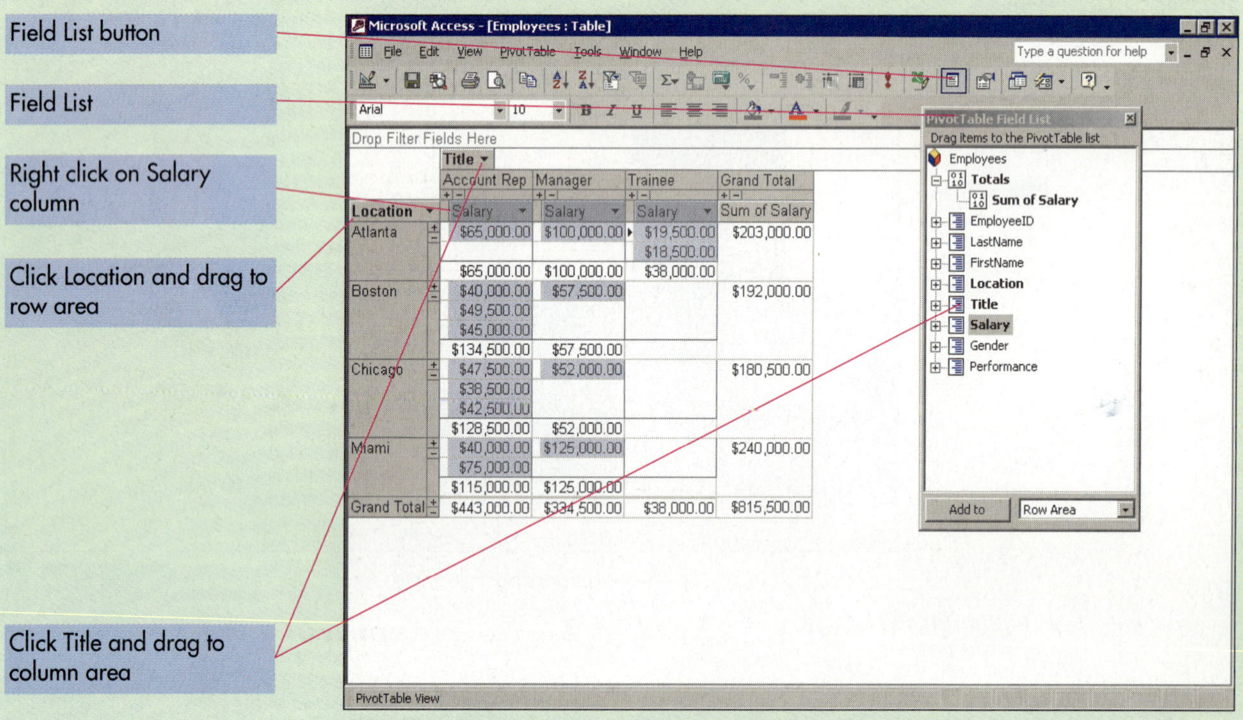

(f) Create a Pivot Table (step 6)

FIGURE 1.7 *Hands-on Exercise 2 (continued)*

THE AUTOCALC FUNCTIONS

Use the AutoCalc menu to display multiple functions (Sum, Count, Min, Max, or Average) within the same table. Each additional function appears in its own column at the right of the pivot table. To delete a function that is no longer needed, display the field list, click the plus sign next to the Totals field that appears within the list, right click the function you want to delete, then click the Delete command.

Step 7: Create a Pivot Chart

- Pull down the **View menu** and select the **PivotChart view** to display the pivot chart in Figure 1.7g. The chart corresponds to the pivot table you just created.
- Pull down the **PivotChart menu** and click the **Show Legend command** to display the legend. The specific titles now appear below the Title button.
- Pull down the **PivotChart menu** and click the **By Row/By Column command** to reverse the rows and columns.
- Click the **View button** and return to the **Datasheet view**. Click the row selector for **David Adamson** (the current Chicago manager, whose performance is poor). Press the **Del key**, then click **Yes** when asked to delete the record.
- Pull down the **View menu** and return to the **PivotChart view**. The column for Chicago in the Manager position has disappeared, since there is no longer an employee in that position in Chicago.
- Pull down the **File menu**, click the **Page Setup command**, click the **Page tab**, then change to **Landscape printing**. Click the **Print button** on the PivotTable toolbar to print the pivot table.
- Click the **Close button** to close the Employee table. Exit Access if you do not want to continue with the next exercise at this time.

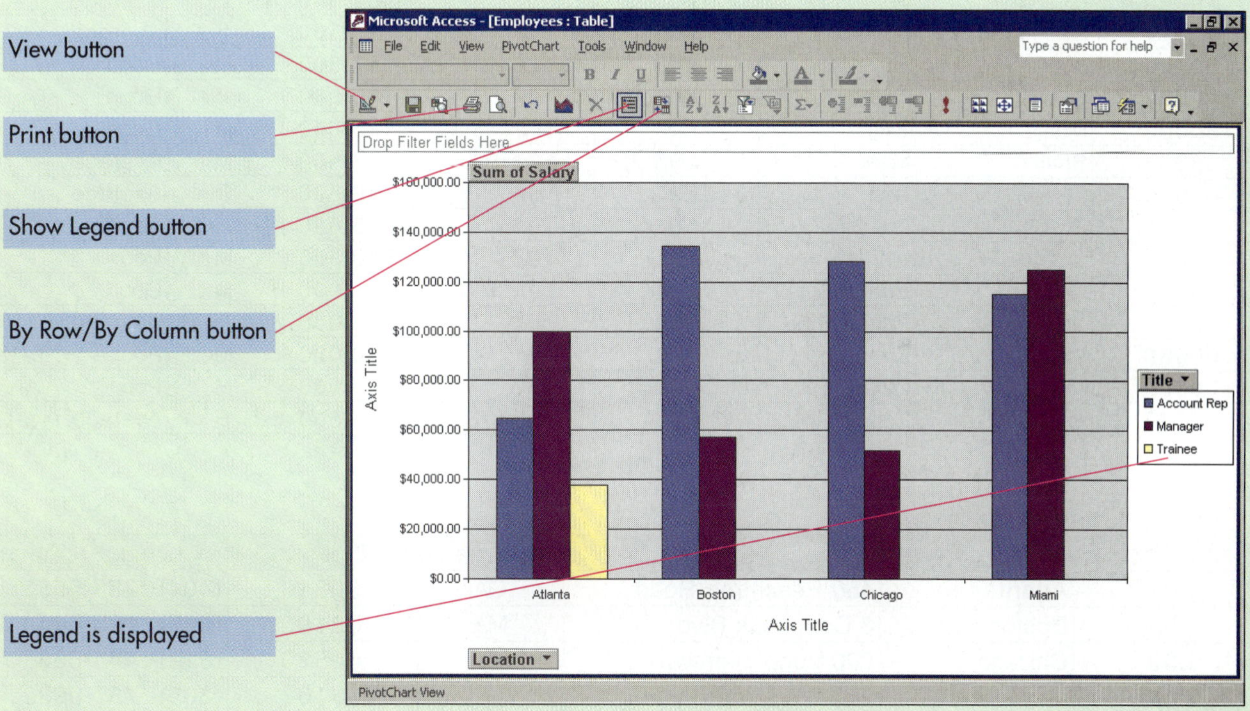

(g) Create a Pivot Chart (step 7)

FIGURE 1.7 *Hands-on Exercise 2 (continued)*

ADD A FILTER

Pull down the View menu and click Field list to display the field list, then click and drag a third field (e.g., Gender) to the Drop Filter Fields area. Click the down arrow next to the new field and select values to display on the chart, such as all men or all women. You can also show selected values in the row and column fields; that is, you can omit a specific location or title.

LOOKING AHEAD: A RELATIONAL DATABASE

The Bookstore and Employee databases are both examples of simple databases in that they each contained only a single table. The real power of Access, however, is derived from multiple tables and the relationships between those tables. This type of database is known as a ***relational database*** and is illustrated in Figure 1.8. This figure expands the original Employee database by adding two tables, for locations and titles, respectively.

The Employees table in Figure 1.8a is the same table we used at the beginning of the previous exercise, except for the substitution of a LocationID and TitleID for the location and title, respectively. The Locations table in Figure 1.8b has all of the fields that pertain to each location: LocationID, Location, Address, State, Zipcode, and Office Phone. One field, the LocationID, appears in both Employees and Locations tables and links the two tables to one another. In similar fashion, the Titles table in Figure 1.8c has the information for each title: the TitleID, Title, Description, Education Required, and Minimum and Maximum Salary. The TitleID appears in both the Employees and Titles tables to link those tables to one another.

EmployeeID	LastName	FirstName	LocationID	TitleID	Salary	Gender	Performance
10000	Milgrom	Pamela	L02	T02	$57,500	F	Average
11111	Adams	Jennifer	L01	T03	$19,500	F	Average
20000	Johnson	James	L03	T01	$47,500	M	Good
22222	Coulter	Tracey	L01	T02	$100,000	F	Good
30000	Marlin	Billy	L04	T02	$125,000	M	Good
33333	Smith	Mark	L03	T01	$42,500	M	Average
40000	Manin	Ann	L02	T01	$49,500	F	Average
44444	Smith	Francine	L01	T01	$65,000	F	Good
50000	Brown	Mark	L01	T03	$18,500	M	Poor
55555	Frank	Vernon	L04	T01	$75,000	M	Good
60000	Rubin	Patricia	L02	T01	$45,000	F	Average
66666	Charles	Kenneth	L02	T01	$40,000	M	Poor
70000	Adamson	David	L03	T02	$52,000	M	Poor
77777	Marder	Kelly	L03	T01	$38,500	F	Average

(a) The Employees Table

LocationID	Location	Address	State	Zipcode	OfficePhone
L01	Atlanta	450 Peachtree Road	GA	30316	(404) 333-5555
L02	Boston	3 Commons Blvd	MA	02190	(617) 123-4444
L03	Chicago	500 Loop Highway	IL	60620	(312) 444-6666
L04	Miami	210 Biscayne Blvd	FL	33103	(305) 787-9999

(b) The Locations Table

TitleID	Title	Description	EducationRequired	MinimumSalary	MaximumSalary
T01	Account Rep	A marketing ...	Four year degree	$25,000	$75,000
T02	Manager	A supervisory ...	Four year degree	$50,000	$150,000
T03	Trainee	An entry-level ...	Two year degree	$18,000	$25,000

(c) The Titles Table

FIGURE 1.8 *A Relational Database*

To obtain information about a specific employee's title or location, you go to the Employee's table, then use the LocationID and TitleID to locate the appropriate records in the Locations and Titles tables, respectively. The tables are color-coded to emphasize the relationships between them. It sounds complicated, but it is really quite simple and very elegant. More importantly, it enables you to obtain detailed information about any employee, location, or title. To show how it works, we will ask a series of questions that require you to look in one or more tables for the answer. Consider:

Query: At which location does Pamela Milgrom work? What is the phone number of her office?
Answer: Pamela works in the Boston office, at 3 Commons Blvd., Boston, MA, 02190. The phone number is (617) 123-4444.

Did you answer the question correctly? You had to search the Employees table for Pamela Milgrom to obtain the LocationID (L02 in this example) corresponding to her office. You then searched the Locations table for this LocationID to obtain the address and phone number for that location. The process required you to use both the Locations and Employees tables, which are linked to one another through a ***one-to-many relationship***. One location can have many employees, but a specific employee can work at only one location. Let's try another question:

Query: Which employees are managers?
Answer: There are four managers: Pamela Milgrom, Tracey Coulter, Billy Marlin, and David Adamson.

The answer to this question is based on the one-to-many relationship that exists between titles and employees. One title can have many employees, but a given employee has only one title. To answer the query, you search the Titles table for "manager" to determine its TitleID (T02). You then go to the Employees table and select those records that have this value in the TitleID field.

The design of a relational database enables us to extract information from multiple tables in a single query. Equally important, it simplifies the way data is changed in that modifications are made in only one place. Consider:

Query: Which employees work in the Boston office? What is their phone number?
Answer: There are four employees in Boston: Pamela Milgrom, Ann Manin, Patricia Rubin, and Kenneth Charles, each with the same number (617 123-4444).

Once again, we draw on the one-to-many relationship between locations and employees. Thus, we begin in the Locations table where we search for "Boston" to determine its LocationID (L02) and phone number (617 123-4444). Then we go to the Employees table to select those records with this value in the LocationID field.

Query: What change(s) are necessary to accommodate a new telephone number for the Boston office?
Answer: Only one change is necessary. One would open the Locations table, locate the record for Boston, and change the phone number.

This query illustrates the ease with which changes are made to a relational database. There are four employees in Boston, but each employee record contains the LocationID (L02), rather than the actual information for the Boston office. Thus, changing the contents of the appropriate record in the Locations table automatically changes the information for the employees in that location.

HANDS-ON EXERCISE 3

A LOOK AHEAD

Objective To open a database with multiple tables; to identify the one-to-many relationships within the database and to produce reports based on those relationships. Use Figure 1.9 as a guide in the exercise.

Step 1: **Open the Relationships Window**

- Start Access, click **More Files** in the task pane or, if Access is already open, pull down the **File menu** and click the **Open command**. Open the **Look Ahead database** in the **Exploring Access folder**.
- The Tables button should be selected as in Figure 1.9a. The database contains the Employees, Locations, and Titles tables.
- Pull down the **Tools menu** and click the **Relationships command** to open the Relationships window as shown in Figure 1.9a. (The tables are not yet visible in this window.)
- Pull down the **Relationships menu** and click the **Show Table command** to display the Show Table dialog box.
- Click (select) the **Locations table** (within the Show Table dialog box), then click the **Add button** to add this table to the Relationships window.
- Double click the **Titles** and **Employees tables** to add these tables to the Relationships window.
- Close the Show Table dialog box.

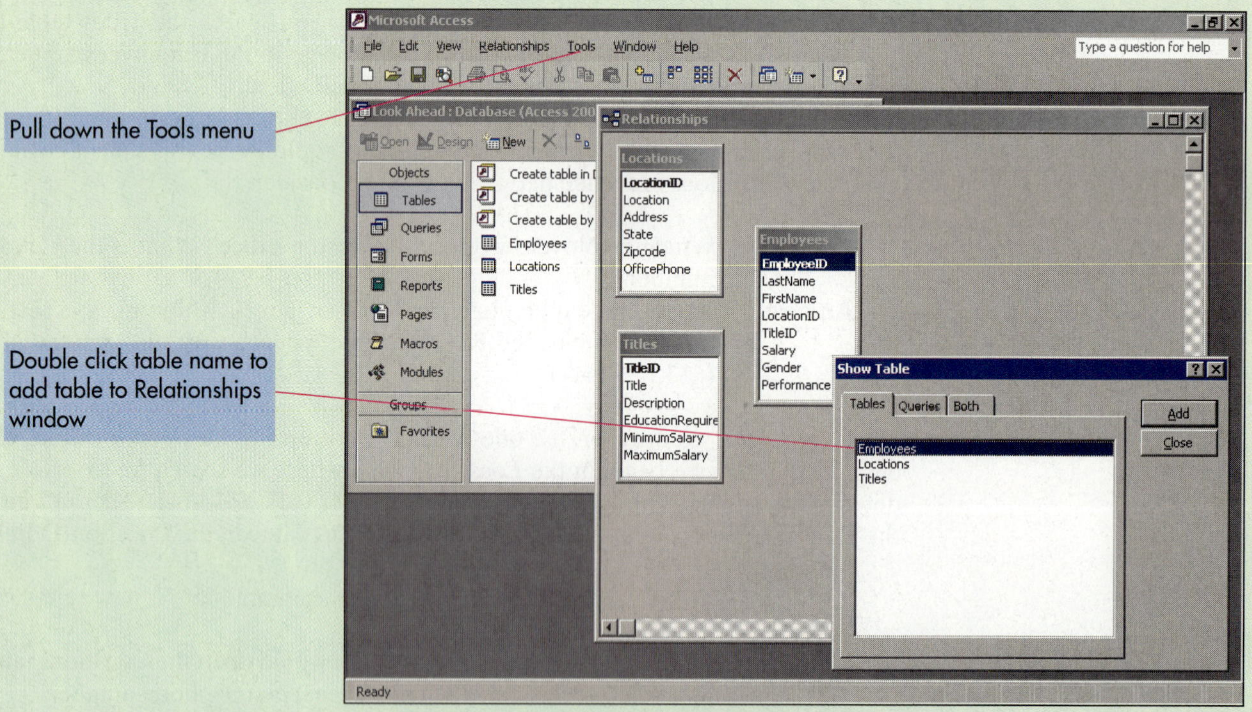

(a) Open the Relationships Window (step 1)

FIGURE 1.9 *Hands-on Exercise 3*

Step 2: **Create the Relationships**

- Maximize the Relationships windows so that you have more room in which to work. Click and drag the title bar of each table so that the positions of the tables match those in Figure 1.9b.
- Click and drag the bottom (and/or right) border of each table so that you see all of the fields in each table.
- Click and drag the **LocationID field** in the Locations table field list to the **LocationID field** in the Employees field list. You will see the Edit Relationships dialog box.
- Check the box to **Enforce Referential Integrity**. Click the **Create button** to create the relationship.
- Click and drag the **TitleID field** in the Titles table field list to the **TitleID field** in the Employees field list. You will see the Edit Relationships dialog box.
- Check the box to **Enforce Referential Integrity** as shown in Figure 1.9b. Click the **Create button** to create the relationship.
- Click the **Save button** on the Relationships toolbar to save the Relationships window, then close the Relationships window.

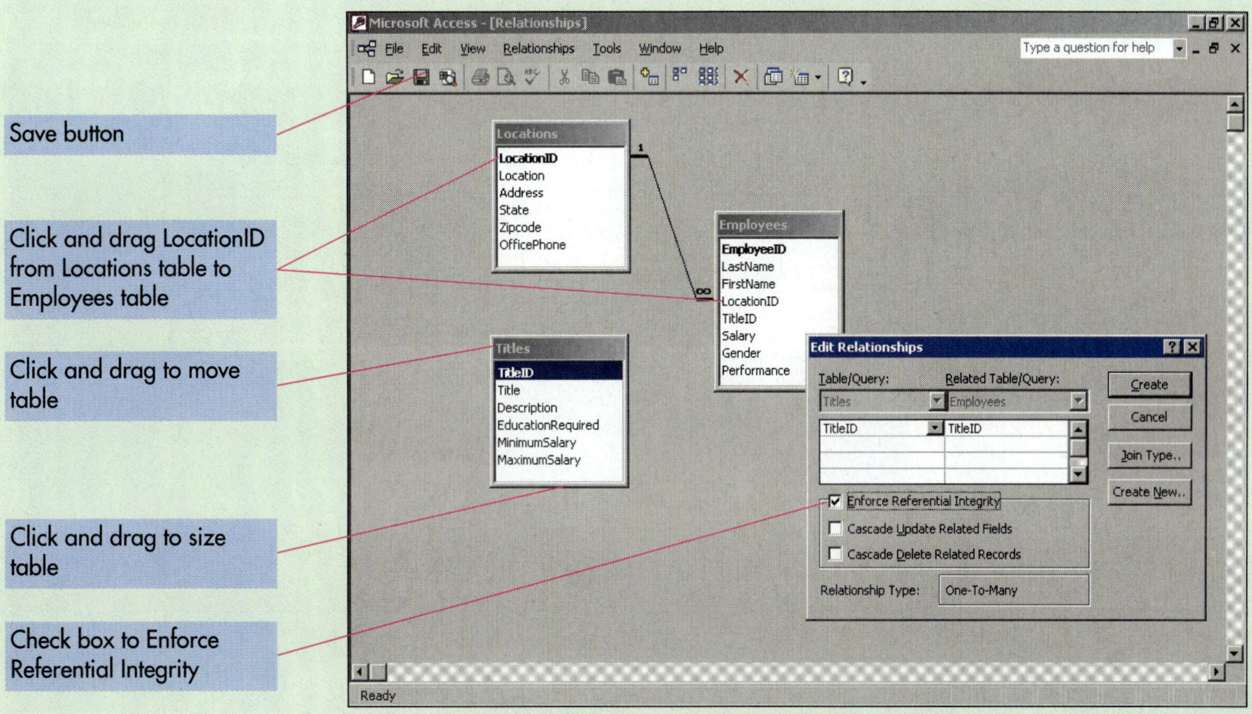

(b) Create the Relationships (step 2)

FIGURE 1.9 *Hands-on Exercise 3 (continued)*

THE RELATIONSHIPS ARE VISUAL

The tables in an Access database are created independently, then related to one another through the Relationships window. The number 1 and the infinity symbol (∞) appear at the ends of the lines to indicate the nature of the relationship—for example, a one-to-many relationship between the Locations and Employees tables.

Step 3: Referential Integrity

- Double click the **Employees table** to open the table. Maximize the window. Pull down the **Insert** menu and click the **New Record command** (or click the **New Record button**) on the Table Datasheet toolbar.
- Enter data for yourself, using 12345 as the EmployeeID, and your first and last name as shown in Figure 1.9c. Enter an invalid LocationID (e.g., **L44**), then complete the record as shown in the figure.
- Press the **enter key** when you have completed the data entry, then click **OK** when you see the error message. Access prevents you from entering a location that does not exist.
- Click in the **LocationID field** and enter **L04**, the LocationID for Miami. Press the **down arrow key** to move to the next record, which automatically saves the current record.
- Close the Employees table.

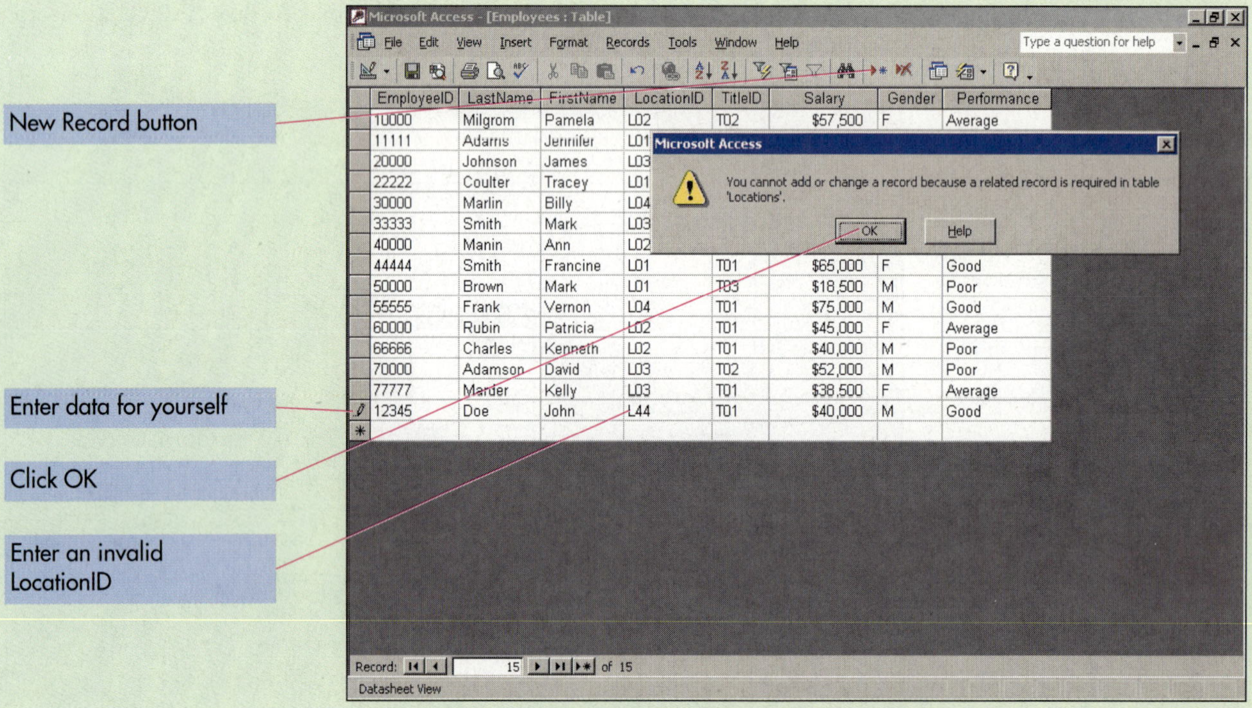

(c) Referential Integrity (step 3)

FIGURE 1.9 *Hands-on Exercise 3 (continued)*

REFERENTIAL INTEGRITY

The tables in a database must be consistent with one another, a concept known as referential integrity. Thus, Access automatically implements certain types of data validation to prevent such errors from occurring. You cannot, for example, enter a record in the Employees table that contains an invalid value for either the LocationID or the TitleID. Nor can you delete a record in the Locations or Titles table if it has related records in the Employees table.

Step 4: Simplified Data Entry

- Click the **Forms button** in the Database window, then double click the **Employees Form** to open this form as shown in Figure 1.9d. Click the **Add Record button**, then click in the text box for the EmployeeID.
- Enter the data for **Bob Grauer** one field at a time, pressing the **Tab key** to move from one field to the next. Click the **down arrow** when you come to the location field to display the available locations, then select (click) **Miami**.
- Press the **Tab key** to move to the Title field, click the **down arrow** and choose **Account Rep**.
- Complete the data for Bob's record by entering **$150,000**, **M**, and **Excellent** in the Salary, Gender, and Performance fields, respectively.
- Click the **Close Form button** when you have finished entering the data.

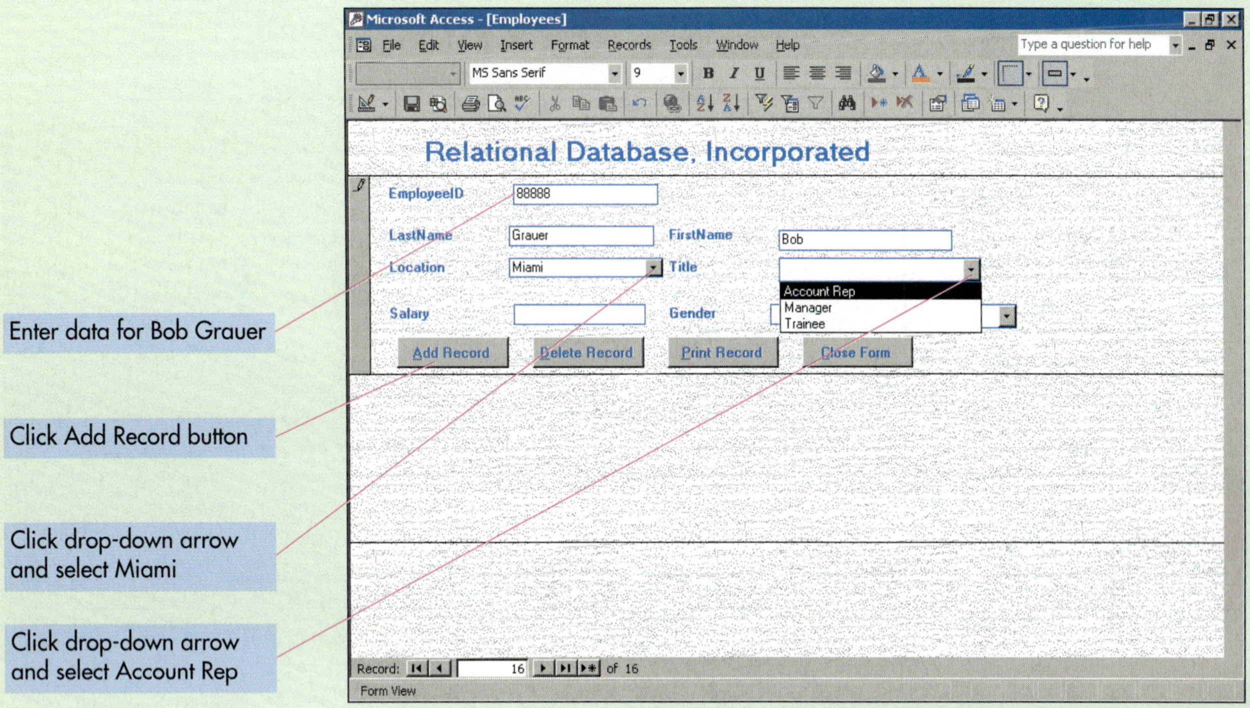

(d) Simplified Data Entry (step 4)

FIGURE 1.9 *Hands-on Exercise 3 (continued)*

SIMPLIFIED DATA ENTRY

The success of any system depends on the accuracy of its data as well as its ease of use. Both objectives are met through a well-designed form that guides the user through the process of data entry and simultaneously rejects invalid responses. The drop-down list boxes for the Location, Title, and Performance fields ensure that the user can enter only valid values in these fields. Data entry is also simplified in these fields in that you can enter just the first letter of a field, then press the Tab key to move to the next field. The command buttons at the bottom of the form provide easy access to basic commands.

Step 5: **View the Employee Master List**

- Click the **Reports button** in the Database window. Double click the **Employee Master List** report to open the report as shown in figure 1.9e. Click and drag the horizontal and/or vertical scroll bars to view the report.
- This report lists selected fields for all employees in the database. Note that the two new employees, you and Bob Grauer, appear in alphabetical order. Both employees are in the Miami Office.
- Click the **Print button** to print the report.
- Close the Report window.

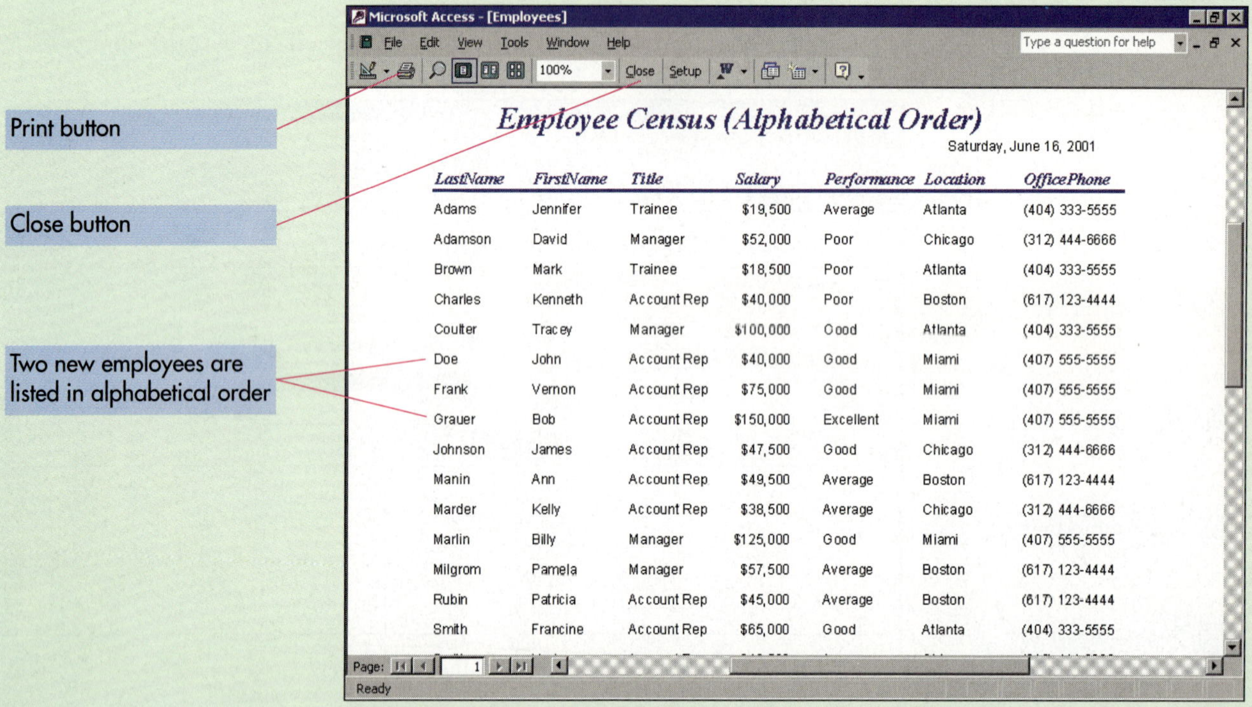

(e) View the Employee Master List (step 5)

FIGURE 1.9 *Hands-on Exercise 3 (continued)*

> **ASK A QUESTION**
>
> Click in the "Ask a Question" list box that appears at the right of the document window, enter the text of a question such as "How do I print a report?", press enter, and Access returns a list of potential Help topics. Click any topic that appears promising to open the Help window with detailed information. You can ask multiple questions during an Access session, then click the down arrow in the list box to return to an earlier question, which will return you to the Help topics. Help can also be accessed via the Help menu.

Step 6: **Change the Locations Table**

- Click the **Tables button** in the Database window, then double click the **Locations table** to open this table as shown in figure 1.9f. Maximize the window if necessary.
- Click the **plus sign** next to location L04 (Miami) to view the employees in this office. The plus sign changes to a minus sign as the employee records for this location are shown.
- Your name appears in this list as does Bob Grauer's. Click the **minus sign** and the list of related records disappears.
- Click and drag to select **Miami** (the current value in the Location field). Type **Orlando** and press the **Tab key**. Enter the corresponding values for the other field: **1000 Kirkman Road**, **FL**, **32801**, and **(407) 555-5555** for the address, state, zip code, and office phone, respectively.
- Close the **Locations table**. You have moved the Miami Office to Orlando.

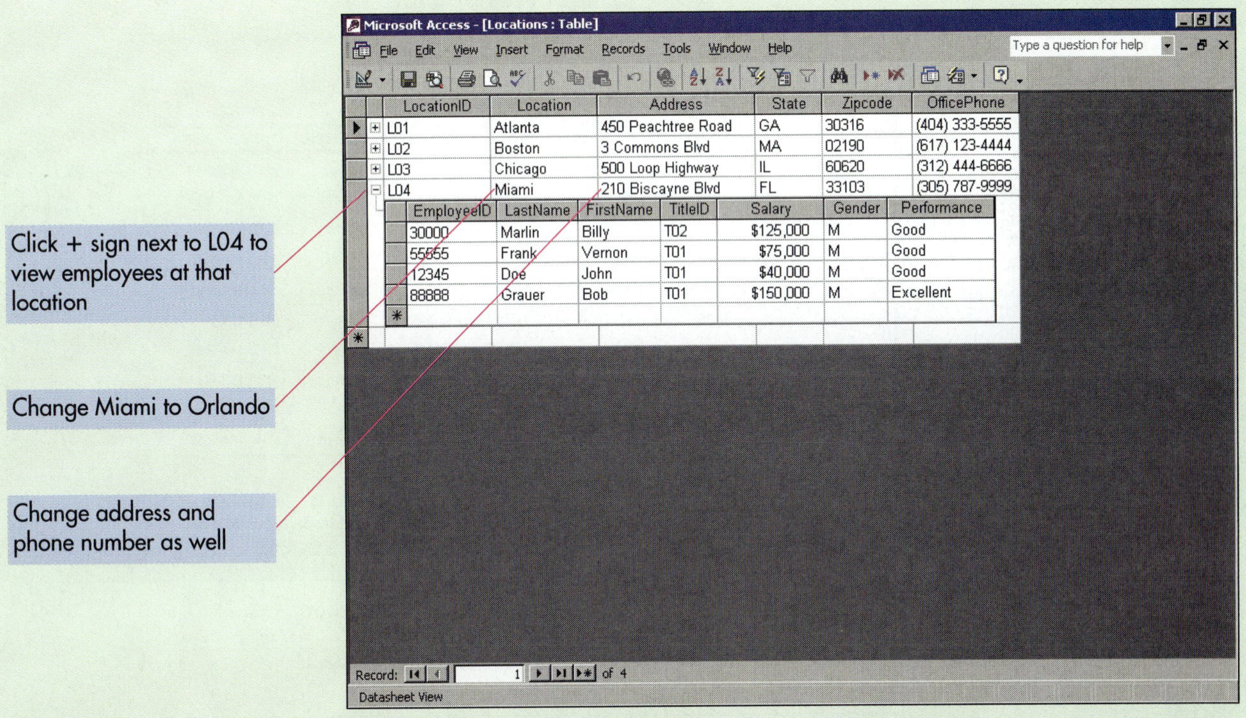

(f) Change the Locations Table (step 6)

FIGURE 1.9 *Hands-on Exercise 3 (continued)*

ADD AND DELETE RELATED RECORDS

Take advantage of the one-to-many relationship between locations and employees (or titles and employees) to add and/or delete records in the Employees table. Open the Locations table, then click the plus sign next to the location where you want to add or delete an employee record. To add a new employee, click the New Record navigation button within the Employees table for that location, then add the new data. To delete a record, click the record, then click the Delete Record button on the Table Datasheet toolbar. Click the minus sign to close the employee list.

Step 7: View the Employees by Title Report

- Click the **Reports button** in the Database window, then double click the **Employees by Title** report to open the report shown in Figure 1.9g.
- This report lists employees by title, rather than alphabetically. Note that you and Bob Grauer are both listed as Account Reps in the Orlando office; that is, the location of the office was changed in the Locations table, and that change is automatically reflected for all employees assigned to that office.
- Click the **Print button** to print the report.
- Close the Report window. Close the Database window. Exit Access. Welcome to the world of relational databases.

Two new employees are listed as Account Reps

Change to Orlando is reflected in report

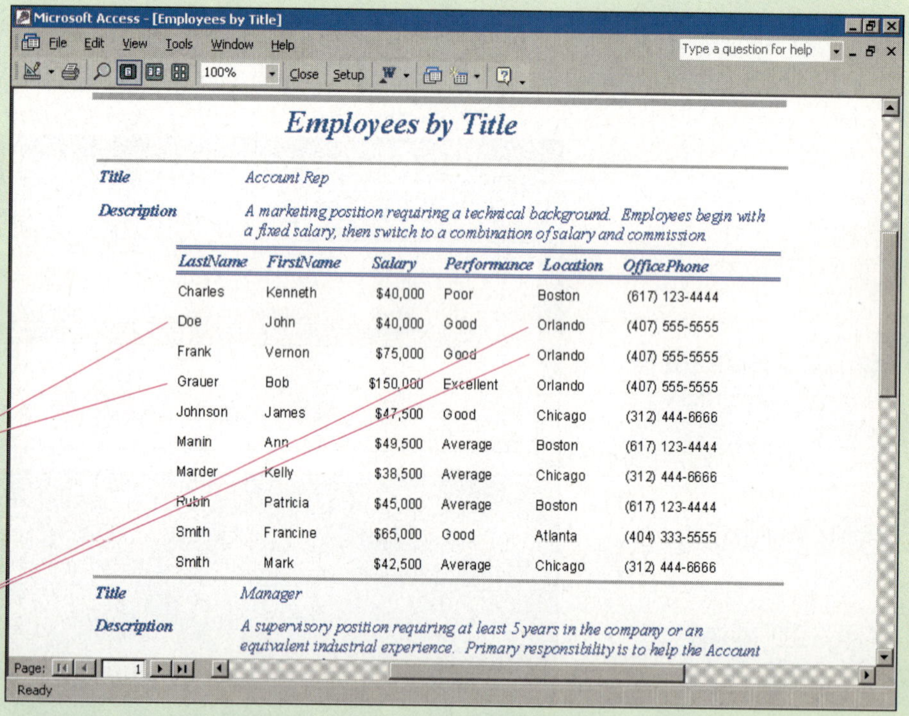

(g) View the Employees by Title Report (step 7)

FIGURE 1.9 *Hands-on Exercise 3 (continued)*

THE WHAT'S THIS COMMAND

Use the What's This command to obtain a detailed explanation for any toolbar button. Pull down the Help menu and click the What's This command (or press the Shift+F1 key) to change the mouse pointer to an arrow with a question mark. Now click any toolbar button for an explanation of that button. Press the Esc key to return the mouse pointer to normal and continue working.

SUMMARY

An Access database has seven types of objects—tables, forms, queries, reports, pages, macros, and modules. The database window displays these objects and enables you to open an existing object or create a new object.

Each table in the database is composed of records, and each record is in turn composed of fields. Every record in a given table has the same fields in the same order. The primary key is the field (or combination of fields) that makes every record in a table unique.

A table is displayed in multiple views. The Design view is used to define the table initially and to specify the fields it will contain. The Datasheet view is the view you use to add, edit, or delete records. The PivotTable view is similar in concept to an Excel pivot table and provides a convenient way to summarize data about groups of records. The PivotChart view creates a chart from the associated PivotTable view.

A record selector symbol is displayed next to the current record in Datasheet view and signifies the status of that record. A triangle indicates that the record has been saved. A pencil indicates that the record has not been saved and that you are in the process of entering (or changing) the data. An asterisk appears next to the blank record present at the end of every table, where you add a new record to the table.

Access automatically saves any changes in the current record as soon as you move to the next record or when you close the table. The Undo Current Record command cancels (undoes) the changes to the previously saved record.

No system, no matter how sophisticated, can produce valid output from invalid input. Data validation is thus a critical part of any system. Access automatically imposes certain types of data validation during data entry. Additional checks can be implemented by the user.

A filter is a set of criteria that is applied to a table in order to display a subset of the records in that table. Microsoft Access lets you filter by selection or filter by form. The application of a filter does not remove the records from the table, but simply suppresses them from view. The records in a table can be displayed in ascending or descending sequence by clicking the appropriate button on the Database toolbar.

A relational database contains multiple tables and enables you to extract information from those tables in a single query. The tables must be consistent with one another, a concept known as referential integrity. Thus, Access automatically implements certain types of data validation to prevent such errors from occurring.

KEY TERMS

AutoCorrect (p. 13)
Current record (p. 10)
Data validation (p. 15)
Database (p. 2)
Database window (p. 3)
Datasheet view (p. 4)
Design view (p. 4)
Field (p. 2)
Filter (p. 19)
Filter by Form (p. 19)
Filter by Selection (p. 19)
Filter Excluding Selection (p. 24)
Find command (p. 12)
Form (p. 5)
GIGO (garbage in, garbage out) (p. 2)
Microsoft Access (p. 3, 9)
One-to-many relationship (p. 31)
Pivot chart (p. 21)
Pivot table (p. 21)
PivotChart view (p. 4)
PivotTable view (p. 4)
Primary key (p. 4)
Query (p. 5)
Record (p. 2)
Referential Integrity (p. 34)
Relational database (p. 30)
Remove filter (p. 19)
Replace command (p. 12)
Report (p. 5)
Sort (p. 19)
Sort Ascending (p. 19)
Sort Descending (p. 19)
Table (p. 2)
Undo command (p. 13)

MULTIPLE CHOICE

1. Which sequence represents the hierarchy of terms, from smallest to largest?
   (a) Database, table, record, field
   (b) Field, record, table, database
   (c) Record, field, table, database
   (d) Field, record, database, table
2. Which of the following is true regarding movement within a record (assuming you are not in the first or last field of that record)?
   (a) Press Tab or the right arrow key to move to the next field
   (b) Press Shift+Tab or the left arrow key to return to the previous field
   (c) Both (a) and (b)
   (d) Neither (a) nor (b)
3. You're performing routine maintenance on a table within an Access database. When should you execute the Save command?
   (a) Immediately after you add, edit, or delete a record
   (b) Periodically during a session—for example, after every fifth change
   (c) Once at the end of a session
   (d) None of the above since Access automatically saves the changes as they are made
4. Which of the following objects are contained within an Access database?
   (a) Tables and forms
   (b) Queries and reports
   (c) Macros and modules
   (d) All of the above
5. Which of the following is true about the views associated with a table?
   (a) The Design view is used to create or modify a table
   (b) The Datasheet view is used to add, edit, or delete records
   (c) The PivotTable and/or PivotChart view is used to display summary information about the table
   (d) All of the above
6. Which of the following is true of an Access database?
   (a) Every record in a table has the same fields as every other record
   (b) Every table contains the same number of records as every other table
   (c) Both (a) and (b)
   (d) Neither (a) nor (b)
7. Which of the following is *false* about the Open Database command?
   (a) It can be executed from the File menu
   (b) It can be executed by clicking the Open button on the Database toolbar
   (c) It loads a database from disk into memory
   (d) It opens the selected table from the Database window
8. Which of the following is true regarding the record selector symbol?
   (a) A pencil indicates that the current record has already been saved
   (b) A triangle indicates that the current record has not changed
   (c) An asterisk indicates the first record in the table
   (d) All of the above

9. Which view is used to add, edit, and delete records in a table?
   (a) The Design view
   (b) The Datasheet view
   (c) Either (a) or (b)
   (d) Neither (a) nor (b)

10. What does GIGO stand for?
   (a) Gee, I Goofed, OK
   (b) Global Input, Global Output
   (c) Garbage In, Garbage Out
   (d) Gospel In, Gospel Out

11. Which of the following will be accepted as valid during data entry?
   (a) Adding a record with a duplicate primary key
   (b) Entering text into a numeric field
   (c) Entering numbers into a text field
   (d) Omitting a required field

12. The find and replace values in a Replace command must be:
   (a) The same length
   (b) The same case
   (c) Both (a) and (b)
   (d) Neither (a) nor (b)

13. An Access table containing 10 records, and 10 fields per record, requires two pages for printing. What, if anything, can be done to print the table on one page?
   (a) Print in Landscape rather than Portrait mode
   (b) Decrease the left and right margins
   (c) Both (a) and (b)
   (d) Neither (a) nor (b)

14. Which of the following capabilities is available through Filter by Selection?
   (a) The imposition of a relational condition
   (b) The imposition of an alternate (OR) condition
   (c) Both (a) and (b)
   (d) Neither (a) nor (b)

15. Which of the following best describes the relationship between locations and employees as implemented in the Look Ahead database within the chapter?
   (a) One to one
   (b) One to many
   (c) Many to many
   (d) Impossible to determine

ANSWERS

1. b	**6.** a	**11.** c
2. c	**7.** d	**12.** d
3. d	**8.** b	**13.** c
4. d	**9.** b	**14.** d
5. d	**10.** c	**15.** b

BUILDS ON

HANDS-ON EXERCISE 2
PAGES 23–29

1. The Employee Database: Review and/or complete the second hands-on exercise that introduced the *Employee* database. Be sure to remove any filters that are in effect at the end of the exercise, then implement the following transactions:
   a. Delete the record for Vernon Frank.
   b. Change James Johnson's salary to $50,500.
   c. Use the Replace command to change all occurrences of "Trainee" to "Account Coordinator".
   d. Give each account coordinator a $2,000 raise. Close the table.
   e. Print the Employee Census report as shown in Figure 1.10 after making the changes in parts (a) through (d). Close the report.
   f. Create a cover page with your name and date. Submit the Employee Census report to your instructor.

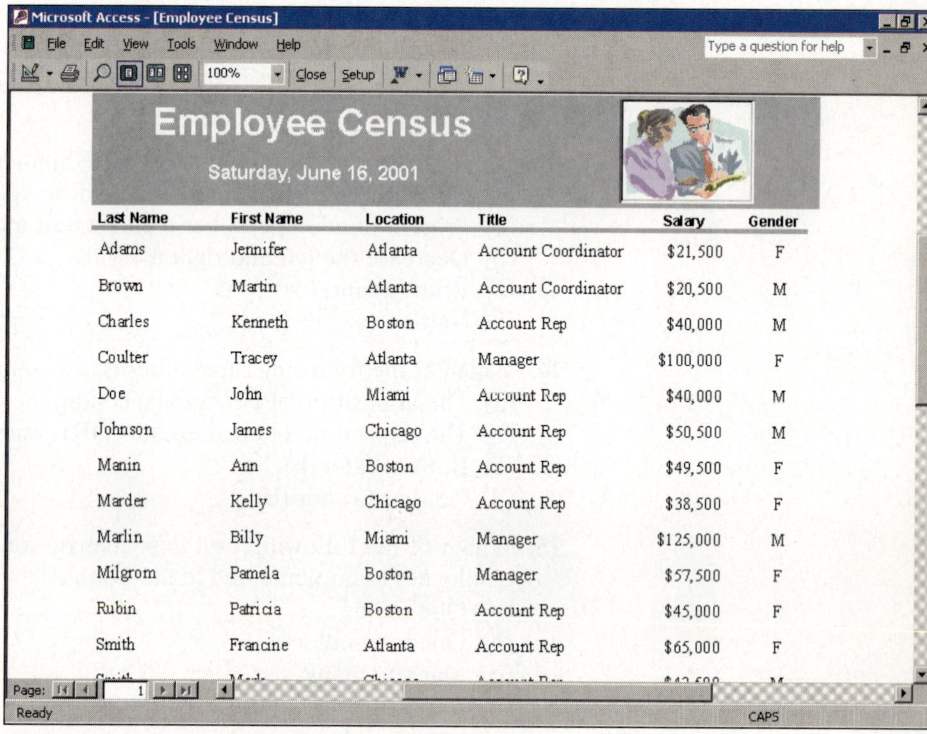

Last Name	First Name	Location	Title	Salary	Gender
Adams	Jennifer	Atlanta	Account Coordinator	$21,500	F
Brown	Martin	Atlanta	Account Coordinator	$20,500	M
Charles	Kenneth	Boston	Account Rep	$40,000	M
Coulter	Tracey	Atlanta	Manager	$100,000	F
Doe	John	Miami	Account Rep	$40,000	M
Johnson	James	Chicago	Account Rep	$50,500	M
Manin	Ann	Boston	Account Rep	$49,500	F
Marder	Kelly	Chicago	Account Rep	$38,500	F
Marlin	Billy	Miami	Manager	$125,000	M
Milgrom	Pamela	Boston	Manager	$57,500	F
Rubin	Patricia	Boston	Account Rep	$45,000	F
Smith	Francine	Atlanta	Account Rep	$65,000	F

FIGURE 1.10 *Employee Database (Exercise 1)*

2. The Oscars: The Academy Awards, also known as the Oscars, are given out each year to honor the best efforts in motion pictures for the previous year. Open the *Oscars* database in the Exploring Access folder, then click the Forms tab (if necessary) and open the Previous Winners form shown in Figure 1.11. Use the navigation bar at the bottom of the form to go to the last record to determine when our database stops.
   a. Click the hyperlink in the form to go to the Oscars site to find out the winners for the years since we published our text. Enter the winners for the six major awards (best picture, best director, best actor and actress, and best supporting actor and actress) into the Oscars database.
   b. Print the form containing the awards for any year that you added.
   c. Return to the Database window, click the Reports tab, then print the report for best picture and best director.
   d. Add a cover sheet, then submit all of the printouts to your instructor.

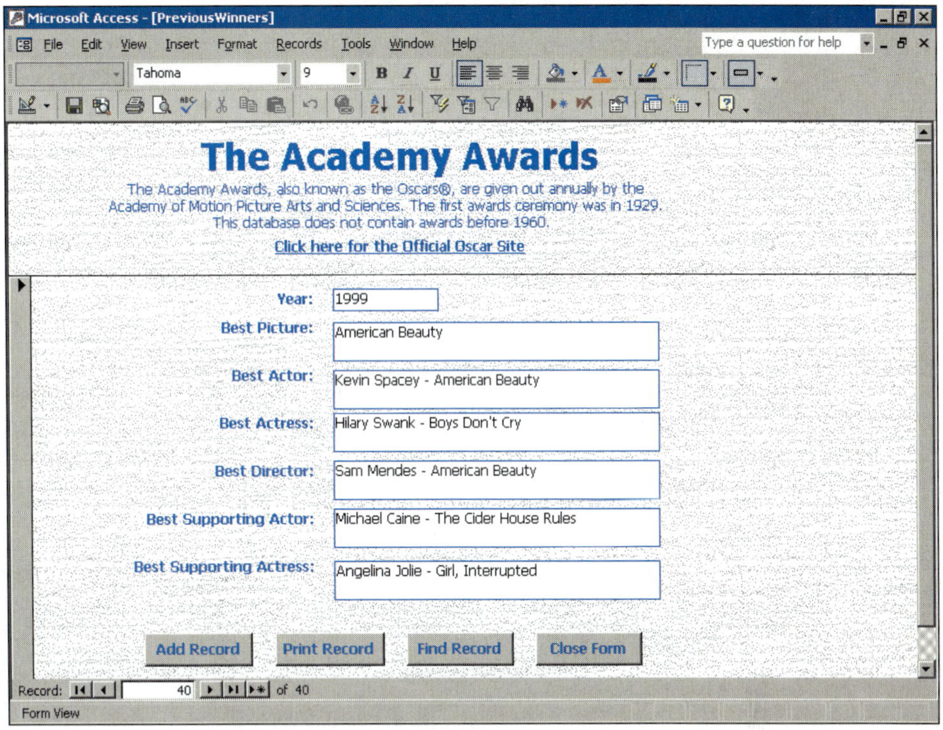

FIGURE 1.11 *The Oscars (Exercise 2)*

3. Large Databases: Figure 1.12 displays a filtered list from the *Large Employee* database that is found in the Exploring Access folder. The database is similar to the Employee database from the chapter, except that it contains more than 300 records. The purpose of this exercise is to give you some experience working with a larger database. The problem also lets you practice with the Format Datasheet command.
   a. Open the *Large Employee* database and add your name as the last record. Assume that you are employed as an Account Rep in Boston. Your salary is $55,000 and your performance has been rated excellent. Use your own name and an EmployeeID of 99999.
   b. Filter the Employee table to display only the employees who are Account Reps in Boston as shown in Figure 1.12. Sort the filtered list by employee number. Your name should appear as the last name in the table.
   c. Pull down the Format menu and click the Datasheet command to display the Format Datasheet dialog box in Figure 1.12. Clear the box to print vertical gridlines, then change the color of the gridlines to dark blue. Click OK to apply the changes to the table. Pull down the Format Datasheet dialog box a second time and make any additional changes.
   d. Click the Print Preview button to be sure that the filtered table will fit on a single sheet of paper. (You may have to use the Page Setup command in the File menu to change to landscape printing.) Print the table.
   e. Remove the existing filter, then impose a new filter to display only those employees who are managers. Sort this filtered list in alphabetical order by last name. Print the list of managers.

4. The United States: Figure 1.13 displays a table from the *United States* database in the Exploring Access folder. The database contains statistical data about all 50 states and enables you to produce various reports.
   a. Open the *United States* database, then open the USStates table, as shown in Figure 1.13. Click anywhere in the Population field, then click the Sort Descending button to list the states in descending order by population. Click and drag to select the first ten records so that you have selected the ten most populous states.

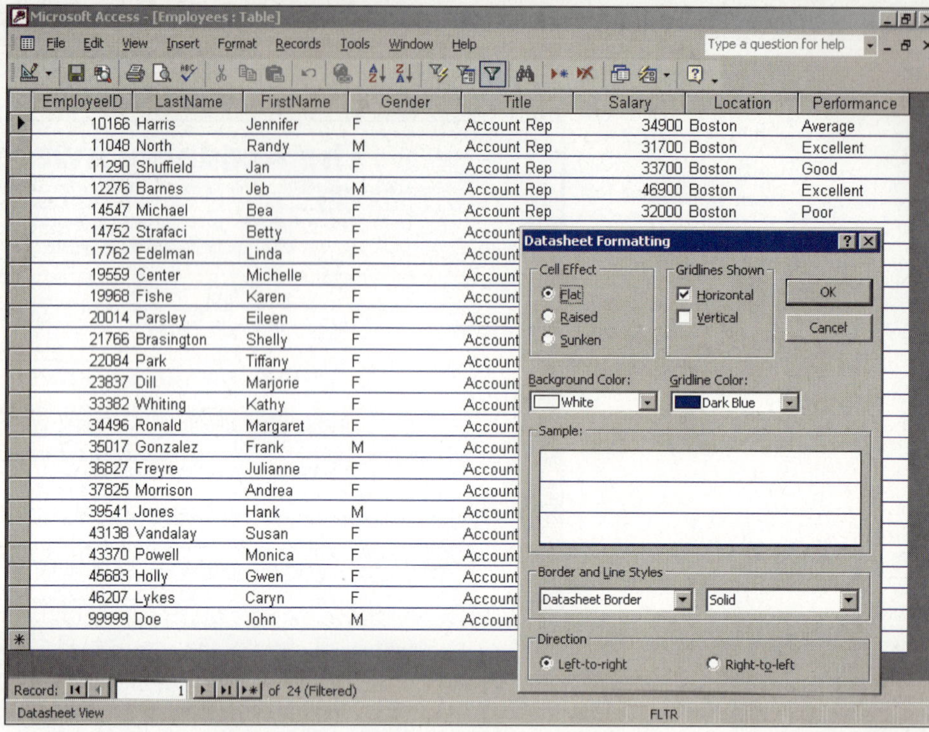

FIGURE 1.12 *Large Databases (Exercise 3)*

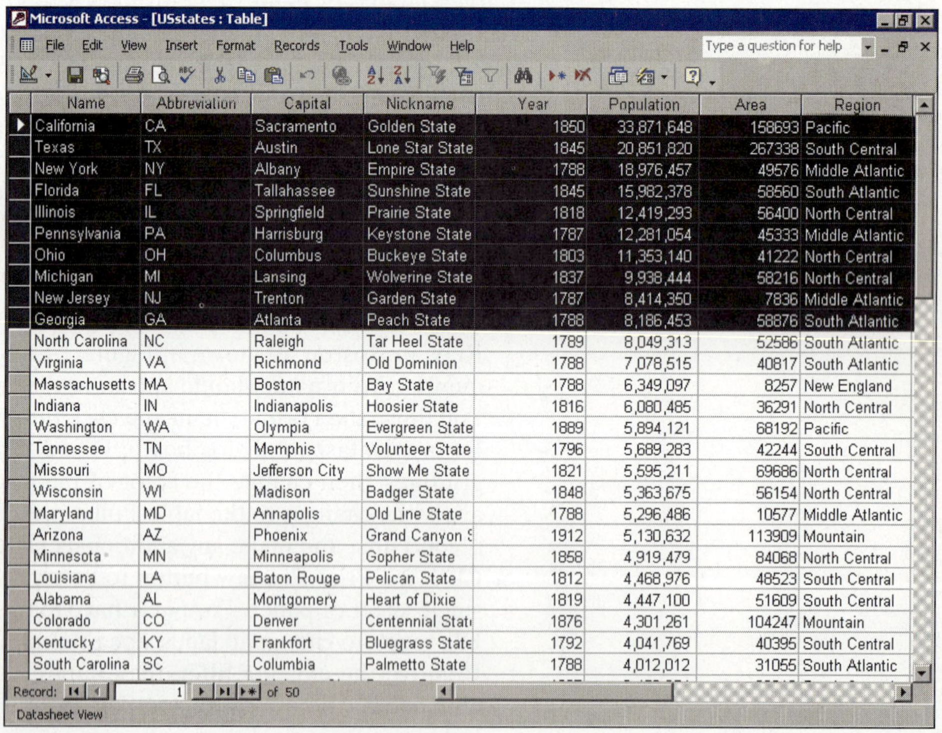

FIGURE 1.13 *The United States (Exercise 4)*

b. Pull down the File menu and click the Page Setup command to display the associated dialog box. Select landscape printing and decrease the left and right margins to one-half an inch. Click the Print Preview button to check that all of the fields for one record fit on one page. If not, return to the Datasheet view and adjust the column widths.
c. Pull down the File menu, click the Print command, then click the option button to print the selected records.
d. Repeat the procedure in steps (a) and (b), but this time print the ten states with the largest area.
e. Repeat the procedure once again to print the first thirteen states admitted to the Union. (You will have to sort in ascending rather than descending sequence.)
f. Submit all three pages, together with a title page, to your instructor.

BUILDS ON

HANDS-ON EXERCISE 4 PAGES 32–38

5. The Look Ahead Database: Review and/or complete the fourth hands-on exercise that pertained to the Look Ahead database. Enter the following additional transactions, then print the Employees by Location report shown in Figure 1.14.
   a. Add a new location to the Locations table. Use L05, Los Angeles, 1000 Rodeo Drive, CA, 90210, and (213) 666-6666 for the LocationID, Location, Address, State, ZipCode, and OfficePhone fields, respectively.
   b. Change the assigned location for Bob Grauer, Francine Smith, and yourself to the Los Angeles Office.
   c. Change Bob's title code to T02 so that Bob becomes the branch manager of the new office.
   d. Delete the record for Kenneth Charles.
   e. Change the title "Manager" to "Supervisor".
   f. Print the Employees by Location report and submit it to your instructor as proof you did this exercise.

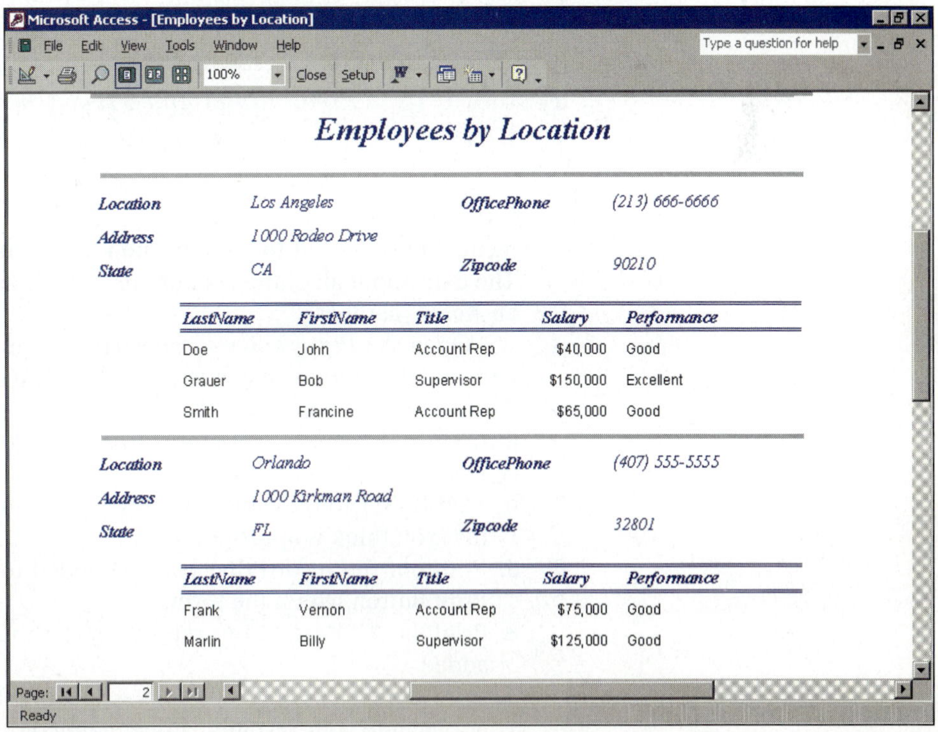

FIGURE 1.14 *The Look Ahead Database (Exercise 5)*

BUILDS ON

PRACTICE EXERCISE 5 PAGE 45

6. Pivot Tables and Pivot Charts: The PivotTable and PivotChart views are available to queries as well as tables. Complete the previous exercise on the Look Ahead database, then open the Employee Information query that exists within the database. Use that query as the basis for the pivot table shown in Figure 1.15. Print the pivot table. Create a pivot chart based on the pivot table. Print the chart for your instructor. Add a cover sheet. Do you see how pivot tables and pivot charts provide summary information?

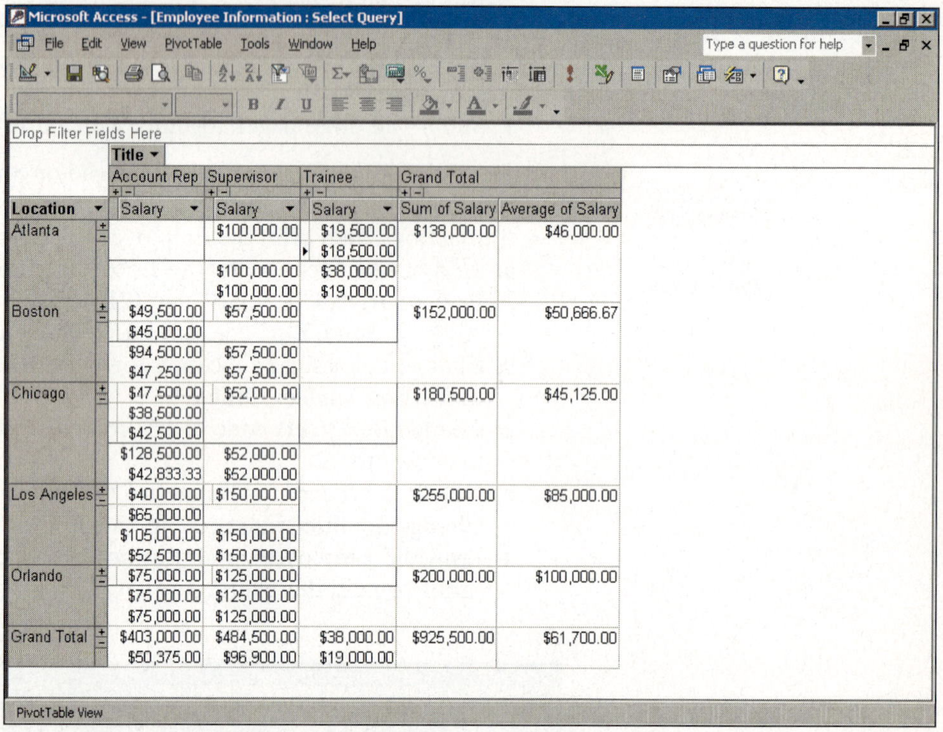

FIGURE 1.15 *Pivot Tables and Pivot Charts (Exercise 6)*

7. Peppy's Restaurants: The Peppy's Restaurant chain is operated by individual franchisees throughout the state of Florida. Each restaurant offers the same menu, but differs in the size of the restaurant and the type of service offered. The data about all of the restaurants is maintained at corporate headquarters in an Access database.

   Open the *Peppy's Restaurants* database in the Exploring Access folder and implement the following changes to the Restaurants table using the associated Restaurants form in Figure 1.16.

   a. Change the annual sales for restaurant R0003 to $1,000,000.
   b. Delete restaurant R0007.
   c. Add R0011 to the table, entering your name as the franchisee. Use any data that you think is appropriate.
   d. Print out the record that you just added for your restaurant by clicking the Print button within the form.
   e. Print the All Restaurants report, which should include the restaurant you just added.
   f. Print the Restaurants With Sales Over $500,000 report, which may or may not include your restaurant, depending on the data you entered.
   g. Submit the printed form for your restaurant, together with the two reports to your instructor as proof you did this exercise.

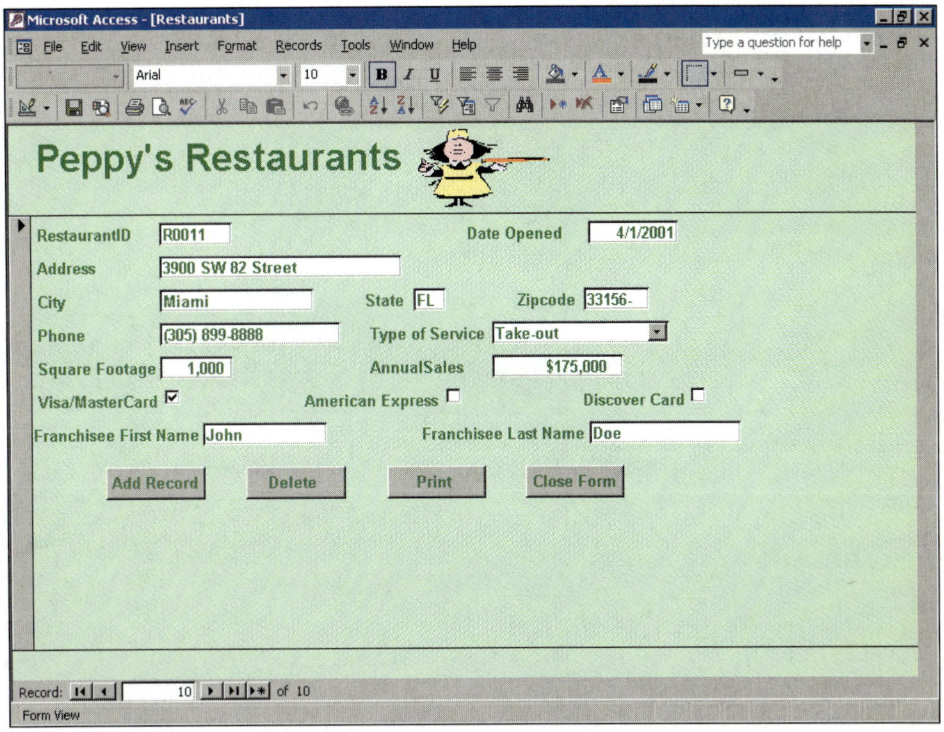

FIGURE 1.16 *Peppy's Restaurant (Exercise 7)*

8. Peppy's Relational Database: The Peppy's chain has outgrown the database from the previous exercise and has replaced it with a relational database that contains separate tables for restaurants and franchisees. We have created a new database for you as opposed to asking you to convert the previous database to a relational format. Nevertheless, there is still work for you to do. Accordingly, open the *Peppy's* relational database and do the following:

a. Create the one-to-many relationship between franchisees (i.e., owners) and restaurants as shown in Figure 1.17. The company encourages individuals to operate more than one restaurant, but a specific restaurant is run by only one franchisee.
b. Open the Franchisees form and add yourself as Franchisee F008. Use any data that you deem appropriate. (You do not have to enter the same information as in the previous problem.)
c. Open the Restaurants form and add restaurant R0011, using any data that you deem appropriate. You must, however, assign yourself (F008) as the franchisee.
d. Change the FranchiseeID in restaurants 9 and 10 to F008 so that you will be associated with these restaurants as well.
e. Print the Master Restaurant report, which displays all restaurants in order of RestaurantID.
f. Print the Restaurant by Franchisee report, which lists the franchisees in order, together with the restaurants they operate.
g. Create a new report for your instructor that displays the relationships within the database. Pull down the Tools menu and click Relationships to open the Relationships window, then pull down the File menu and click the Print Relationships command to display the Print Preview screen of a report that displays the contents of the Relationships window. Print this report for your instructor.
h. Submit all reports to your instructor as proof you did the exercise.

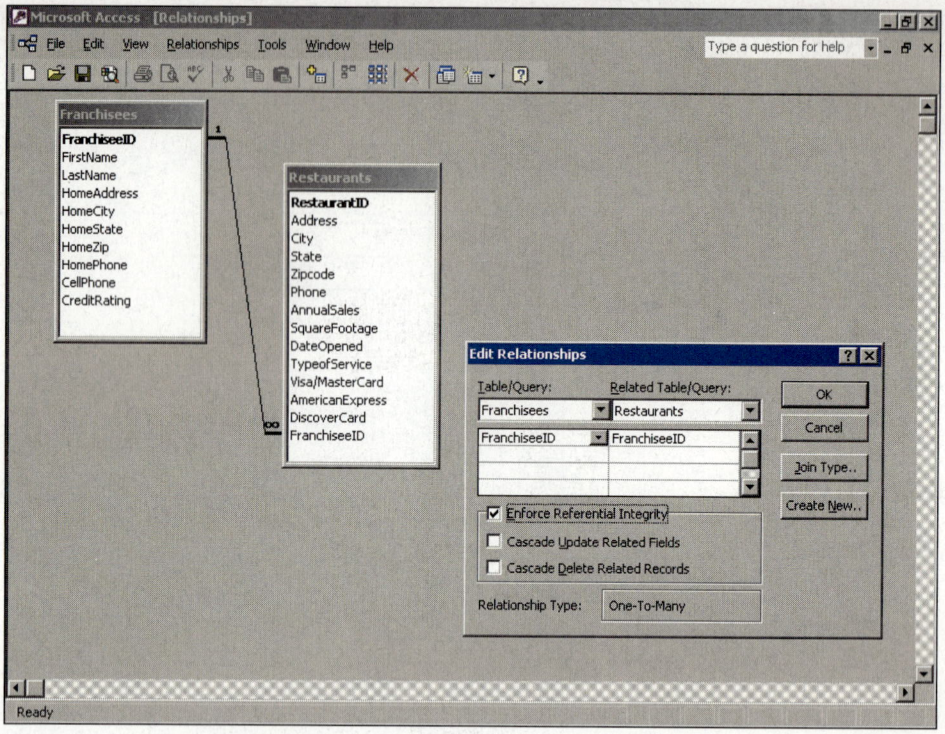

FIGURE 1.17 *Peppy's Relational Database (Exercise 8)*

ON YOUR OWN

The Common User Interface

One of the most significant benefits of the Office environment is the common user interface, which provides a sense of familiarity when you go from one application to another—for example, when you go from Excel to Access. How many similarities can you find between these two applications? Which menus are common to both? Which keyboard shortcuts? Which formatting conventions? Which toolbar icons? Which shortcut menus?

Garbage In, Garbage Out

Your excellent work in this class has earned you an internship in the registrar's office. Your predecessor has created a student database that appears to work well, but in reality has several problems in that many of its reports do not produce the expected information. One problem came to light in conjunction with a report listing business majors: the report contained far fewer majors than were expected. Open the *GIGO database* on the data disk. Find and correct the problem.

The Super Bowl

The *Super Bowl* database in the Exploring Access folder contains a table with data from every game (up to the time of publication). You will find the year the game was played, the two teams that participated, and the score. Open the database and determine the last year for which data has been entered. You can enter additional data by going to the Super Bowl site, www.superbowl.com. Use a combination of the filter and sort commands to show all games in which the NFC won, listing the most recent year first. Print this filtered table, being sure that the table will fit on a single page. Print a second filtered table that shows all years in which the AFC won.

CHAPTER 1

Introduction to Microsoft® PowerPoint®: Presentations Made Easy

OBJECTIVES

AFTER READING THIS CHAPTER YOU WILL BE ABLE TO:

1. Start PowerPoint; open, modify, and view an existing presentation; describe the different ways to print a presentation.
2. List the different views in PowerPoint; describe the unique features of each view.
3. Use the outline to create and edit the text of a presentation; expand and collapse slides within an outline.
4. Add a new slide to a presentation; explain how to change the layout of the objects on an existing slide.
5. Use the Microsoft Media Gallery to add and/or change the clip art on a slide; use the Drawing toolbar to modify existing clip art.
6. Apply a design template to a new presentation; change the template in an existing presentation.
7. Add transition effects to the slides in a presentation; apply custom animation effects to the objects on a slide.
8. Insert user comments into a presentation.
9. Use Microsoft WordArt to insert a WordArt object into a presentation.
10. Distinguish between linking and embedding; link or embed Excel charts and Word tables into a presentation.

OVERVIEW

This chapter introduces you to PowerPoint, one of the four major applications in Microsoft Office (Microsoft Word, Microsoft Excel, and Microsoft Access are the other three). PowerPoint enables you to create a professional presentation without relying on others, then it lets you deliver that presentation in a variety of ways. You can show the presentation on the computer, on the World Wide Web, or via 35mm slides or overhead transparencies.

PowerPoint is easy to learn because it is a Windows application and follows the conventions associated with the common user interface. Thus, if you already know one Windows application, it is that much easier to learn PowerPoint because you can apply what you know. It's even easier if you use Word, Excel, or Access since there are over 100 commands that are common to Microsoft Office.

The chapter begins by showing you an existing PowerPoint presentation so that you can better appreciate what PowerPoint is all about. We discuss the various views within PowerPoint and the advantages of each. We describe how to modify an existing presentation and how to view a presentation on the computer. You are then ready to create your own presentation, a process that requires you to focus on the content and the message you want to deliver. We show you how to enter the text of the presentation, how to add and/or change the format of a slide, and how to apply a design template. We also explain how to animate the presentation to create additional interest. The last portion of the chapter describes how to enhance a presentation through the inclusion of other objects such as a Word table or an Excel chart.

As always, learning is best accomplished by doing, so we include four hands-on exercises that enable you to apply these concepts at the computer. One final point before we begin, is that while PowerPoint can help you create attractive presentations, the content and delivery are still up to you.

A POWERPOINT PRESENTATION

A PowerPoint presentation consists of a series of slides such as those in Figure 1.1. The various slides contain different elements (such as text, clip art, and WordArt), yet the presentation has a consistent look with respect to its overall design and color scheme. You might think that creating this type of presentation is difficult, but it isn't. It is remarkably easy, and that is the beauty of PowerPoint. In essence, PowerPoint allows you to concentrate on the content of a presentation without worrying about its appearance. You supply the text and supporting elements and leave the formatting to PowerPoint.

In addition to helping you create the presentation, PowerPoint provides a variety of ways to deliver it. You can show the presentation on a computer using animated transition effects as you move from one slide to the next. You can include sound and/or video in the presentation, provided your system has a sound card and speakers. You can also automate the presentation and distribute it on a disk for display at a convention booth or kiosk. If you cannot show the presentation on a computer, you can convert it to 35mm slides or overhead transparencies.

PowerPoint also gives you the ability to print the presentation in various ways to distribute to your audience. You can print one slide per page, or you can print miniature versions of each slide and choose among two, three, four, six, or even nine slides per page. You can prepare speaker notes for yourself consisting of a picture of each slide together with notes about the slide. You can also print the text of the presentation in outline form. Giving the audience a copy of the presentation (in any format) enables them to follow it more closely, and to take it home when the session is over.

POLISH YOUR DELIVERY

The speaker is still the most important part of any presentation, and a poor delivery will kill even the best presentation. Look at the audience as you speak to open communication and gain credibility. Don't read from a prepared script. Speak slowly and clearly and try to vary your delivery. Pause to emphasize key points, and be sure the person in the last row can hear you.

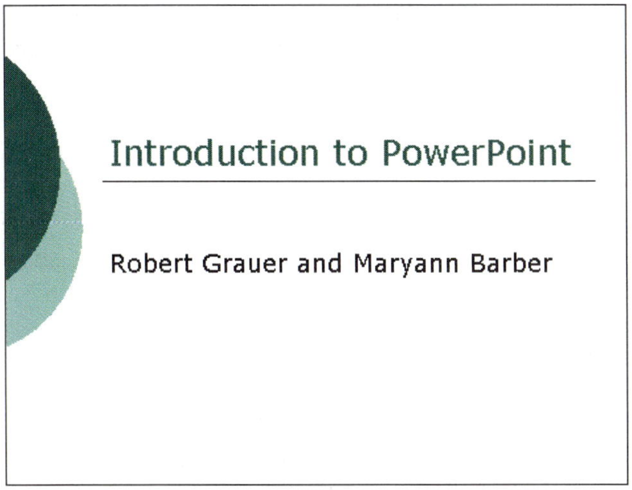

(a) Title Slide

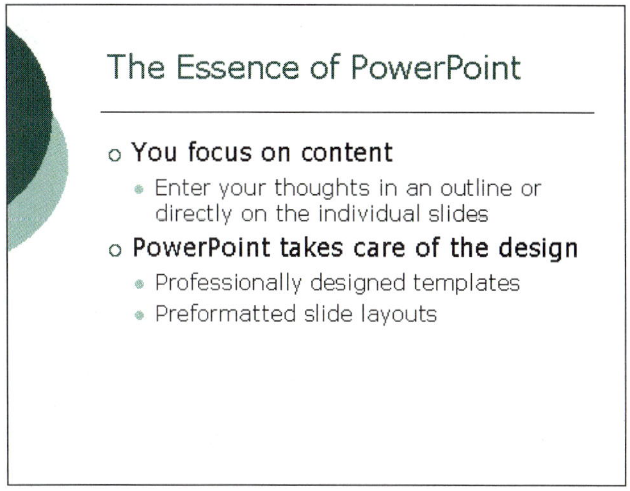

(b) Bullet Slide

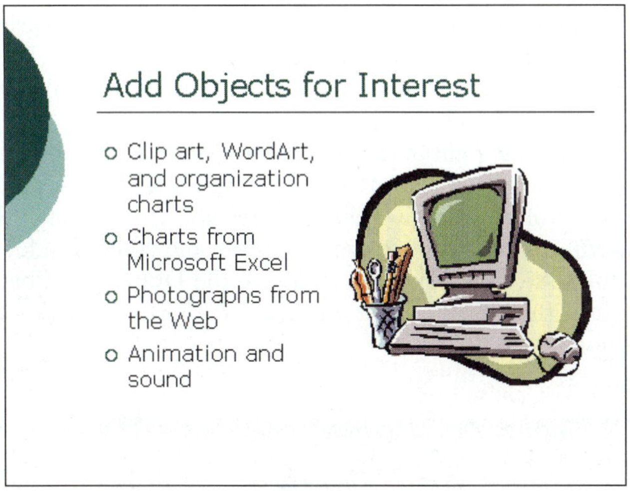

(c) Clip Art

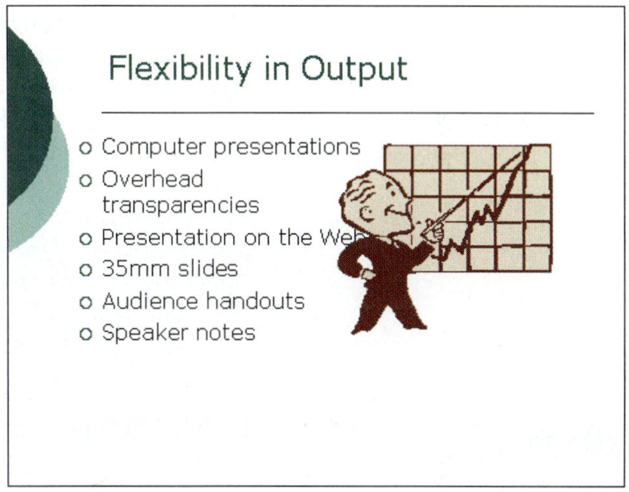

(d) Clip Art

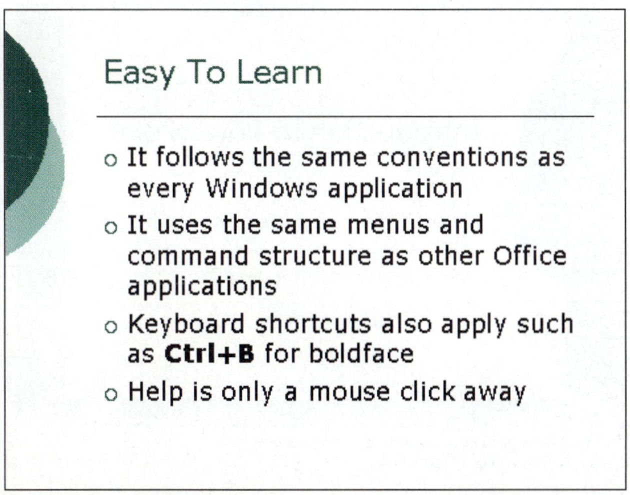

(e) Animated Text

(f) WordArt

FIGURE 1.1 *A PowerPoint Presentation*

The desktop in Figure 1.2 should look somewhat familiar even if you have never used PowerPoint, because PowerPoint shares the common user interface of every Windows application. You should recognize, therefore, the two open windows in Figure 1.2—the application window for PowerPoint and the document window for the current presentation.

The PowerPoint window contains the Minimize, Maximize (or Restore) and Close buttons. The document window, however, contains only a Close button for the current presentation, allowing you to close the presentation, but keep PowerPoint open. The title bar indicates the application (Microsoft PowerPoint) as well as the name of the presentation on which you are working (Introduction to PowerPoint). The ***menu bar*** appears immediately below the title bar and provides access to the pull-down menus within the application. The presentation appears within the document window and shows the outline of the entire presentation, a graphical image of one slide (the title slide in this example), and speaker notes for the selected slide.

The Standard and Formatting toolbars are displayed below the menu bar and are similar to those in Word and Excel. Hence, you may recognize several buttons from those applications. The ***Standard toolbar*** contains buttons for the most basic commands in PowerPoint such as opening, saving, and printing a presentation. The ***Formatting toolbar***, under the Standard toolbar, provides access to formatting operations such as boldface, italics, and underlining.

The vertical ***scroll bar*** is seen at the right of the document window and indicates that the presentation contains additional slides that are not visible. This is consistent with the ***status bar*** at the bottom of the window that indicates you are working on slide 1 of 6. The ***Drawing toolbar*** appears above the status bar and contains additional tools for working on the slide. The view buttons above the Drawing toolbar are used to switch between the different views of a presentation. PowerPoint views are discussed in the next section.

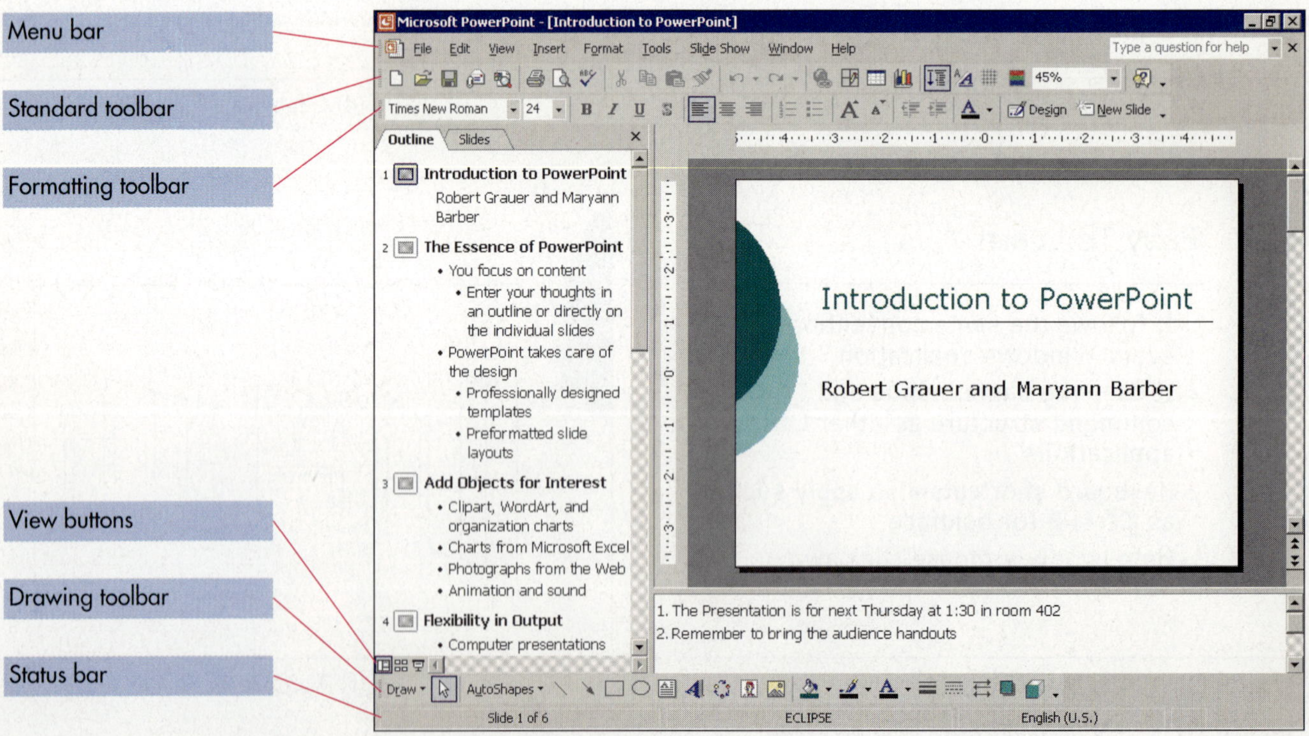

FIGURE 1.2 *Introduction to PowerPoint*

PowerPoint Views

PowerPoint offers multiple views in which to create, modify, and/or deliver a presentation. Each view represents a different way of looking at the presentation and each view has unique capabilities. (There is some redundancy among the views in that certain tasks can be accomplished from multiple views.) The View menu and/or the View buttons at the bottom of the presentation enable you to switch from one view to another.

The ***Normal view*** in Figure 1.3a divides the screen into three panes containing an outline of the presentation, an enlarged view of one slide, and the associated speaker notes (if any) for the selected slide. The ***outline*** provides the fastest way to enter or edit text for the presentation. You type directly into the outline and can move easily from one slide to the next. The outline can also be used to move and copy text from one slide to another and/or to rearrange the order of the slides within a presentation. The outline is limited, however, in that it does not show graphic elements that may be present on individual slides. Thus, you may want to switch to the Normal view in Figure 1.3b that contains ***thumbnail images*** (slide miniatures) rather than the outline. This view also lets you change the order of the slides by clicking and dragging a slide to a new position. The Outline and Slides tabs in the left pane let you switch back and forth between the two variations of the Normal view.

The Normal view also provides access to the individual slides and/or speaker notes, each of which appears in its own pane. The size of the individual panes in the Normal view can be changed by dragging the border that separates one pane from another. The Normal view is all that you will ever need, but many individuals like to close the left pane completely to see just an individual slide as shown in Figure 1.3c. The individual slide, whether it is in the Normal view or displayed in a window by itself, is where you change text or formatting, add graphical elements or apply various animation effects.

You can also elect to work in the Notes Page and/or Slide Sorter view. The ***Notes Page view*** in Figure 1.3d is redundant in that speaker notes can be entered from the Normal view. It is convenient, however, to print audience handouts of this view, since each page will contain a picture of the slide plus the associated speaker notes. The notes do not appear when the presentation is shown, but are intended for use by the speaker to help him or her remember the key points about each slide.

The ***Slide Sorter view*** in Figure 1.3e offers yet another view in which to reorder the slides within a presentation. It also provides a convenient way to delete one or more slides and/or to set transition effects for multiple slides simultaneously. Anything that you do in one view is automatically reflected in the other view. If, for example, you change the order of the slides in the Slide Sorter view, the changes will be automatically reflected in the outline or thumbnail images within the Normal view.

The ***Slide Show view*** in Figure 1.3f is used to deliver the completed presentation to an audience, one slide at a time, as an electronic presentation on the computer. The show may be presented manually where the speaker clicks the mouse to move from one slide to the next. The presentation can also be shown automatically, where each slide stays on the screen for a predetermined amount of time, after which the next slide appears automatically. Either way, the slide show may contain various transition effects from one slide to the next.

THE TASK PANE

All views in PowerPoint 2002 provide access to a ***task pane***, which facilitates the execution of subsequent commands. The task pane serves many functions. It can be used to open an existing presentation, apply clip art to a slide, change the layout of the elements on a slide, apply transition and animation effects, or change the template of the entire presentation.

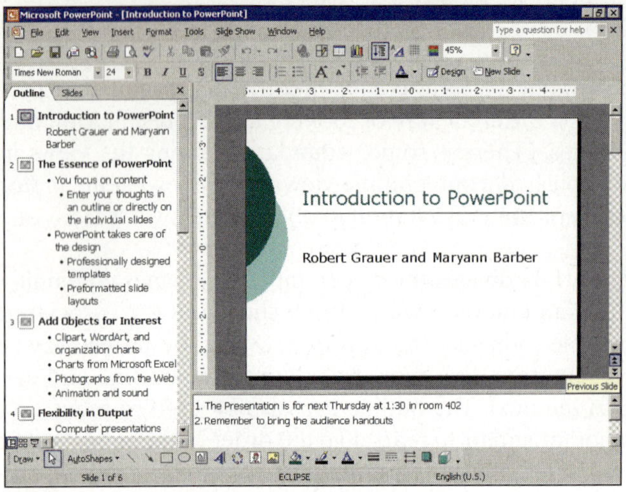

(a) Normal View with Outline

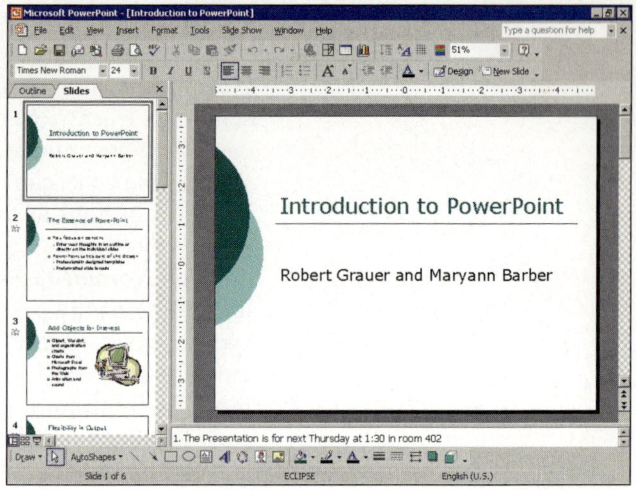

(b) Normal View with Thumbnail Images

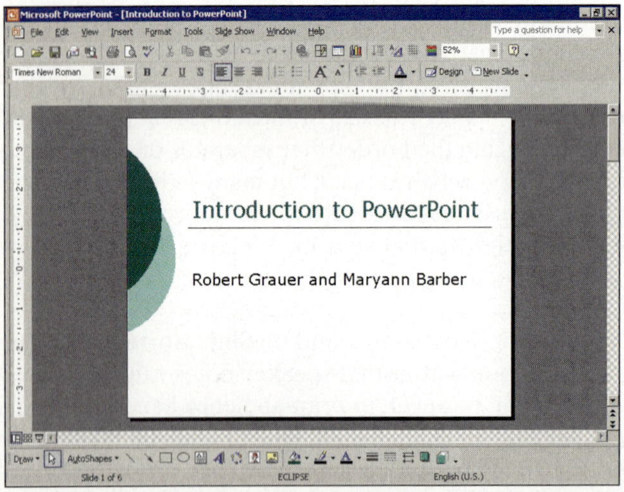

(c) Individual Slide

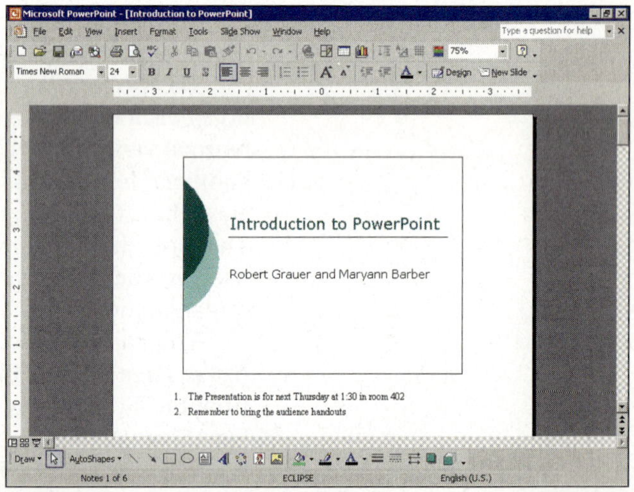

(d) Notes Pages View

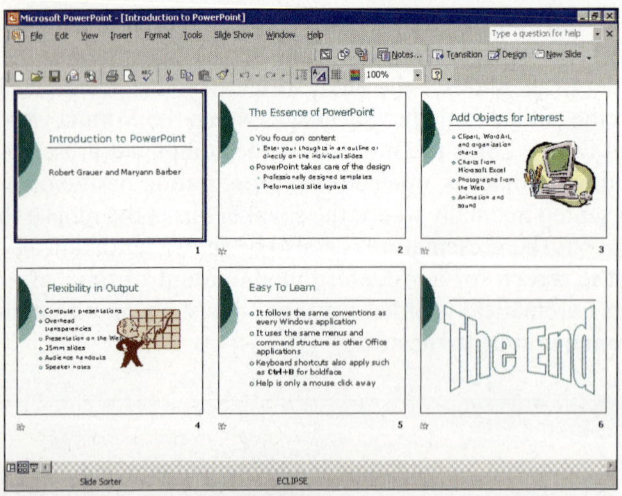

(e) Slide Sorter View

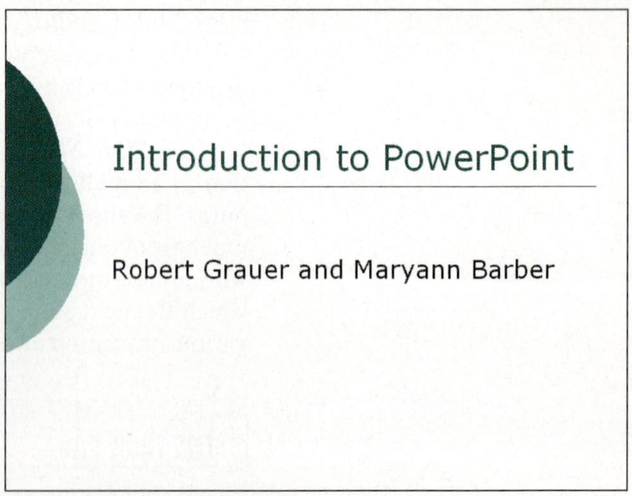

(f) Slide Show View

FIGURE 1.3 *Multiple Views*

The File Menu

The ***File menu*** is a critically important menu in virtually every Windows application. It contains the Save and Open commands to save a presentation on disk, then subsequently retrieve (open) that presentation at a later time. The File menu also contains the ***Print command*** to print a presentation, the ***Close command*** to close the current presentation but continue working in the application, and the ***Exit command*** to quit the application altogether.

The ***Save command*** copies the presentation that you are working on (i.e., the presentation that is currently in memory) to disk. The command functions differently the first time it is executed for a new presentation, in that it displays the Save As dialog box as shown in Figure 1.4a. The dialog box requires you to specify the name of the presentation, the drive (and an optional folder) in which the presentation is to be stored, and its file type. All subsequent executions of the command save the presentation under the assigned name, replacing the previously saved version with the new version.

The ***file name*** (e.g., My First Presentation) can contain up to 255 characters including spaces, commas, and/or periods. (Periods are discouraged, however, since they are too easily confused with DOS extensions.) The Save In list box is used to select the drive (which is not visible in Figure 1.4a) and the folder (e.g., Exploring PowerPoint) in which the file will be saved. The ***Places bar*** provides shortcuts to frequently used folders without having to search through the Save In list box. Click the Desktop icon, for example, and the file is saved on the Windows desktop. The ***file type*** defaults to a PowerPoint 2002 presentation. You can, however, choose a different format, such as an RTF (Rich Text Format) outline that can be imported into Microsoft Word. You can also save any PowerPoint presentation as a Web page (or HTML document).

The ***Open command*** is the opposite of the Save command as it brings a copy of an existing presentation into memory, enabling you to work with that presentation. The Open command displays the Open dialog box in which you specify the file name, the drive (and optionally the folder) that contains the file, and the file type. PowerPoint will then list all files of that type on the designated drive (and folder), enabling you to open the file you want. The Save and Open commands work in conjunction with one another. The Save As dialog box in Figure 1.4a, for example, saves the file My First Presentation in the Exploring PowerPoint folder. The Open dialog box in Figure 1.4b loads that file into memory so that you can work with the file, after which you can save the revised file for use at a later time.

The toolbars in the Save As and Open dialog boxes have several buttons in common that facilitate the execution of either command. The Views button lets you display the files in different views. The Details view (in Figure 1.4a) shows the file size as well as the date and time that the file was last modified. The Preview view (in Figure 1.4b) shows the first slide in a presentation, without having to open the presentation. The List view displays only the file names, and thus lets you see more files at one time. The Properties view shows information about the presentation, including the date of creation and number of revisions.

SORT BY NAME, DATE, OR FILE SIZE

The files in the Save As and Open dialog boxes can be displayed in ascending or descending sequence by name, date modified, or size. Change to the Details view, then click the heading of the desired column; for example, click the Modified column to list the files according to the date they were last changed. Click the column heading a second time to reverse the sequence—that is, to switch from ascending to descending, and vice versa.

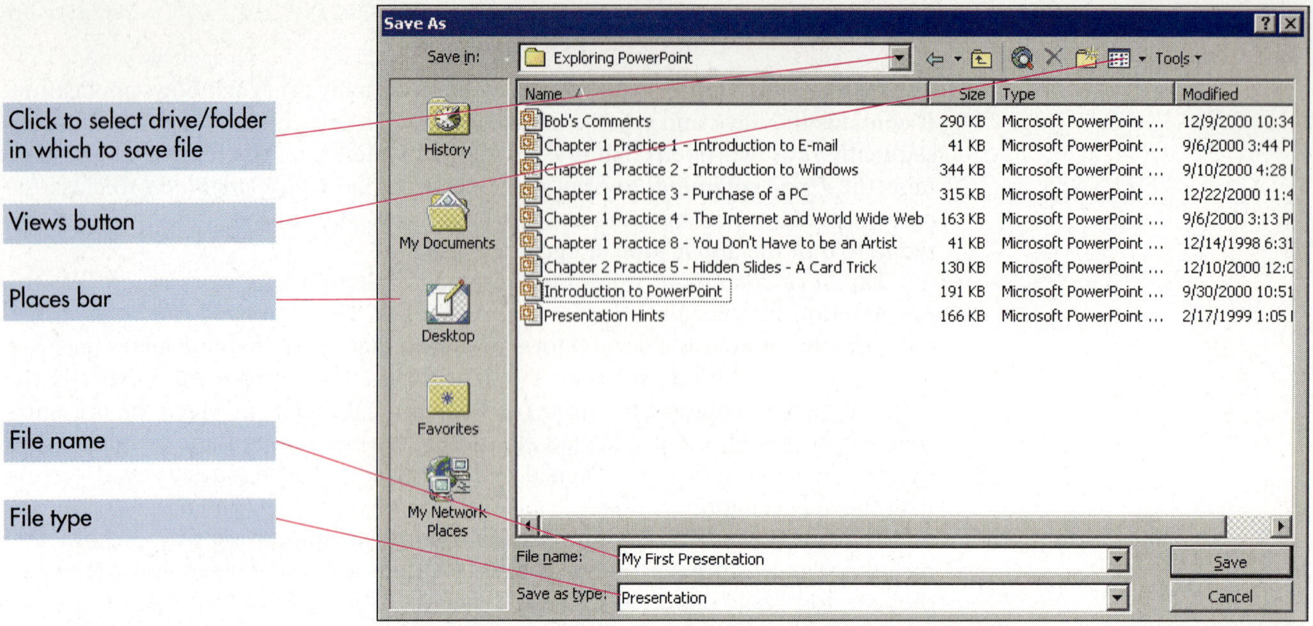

(a) Save As Dialog Box (Details View)

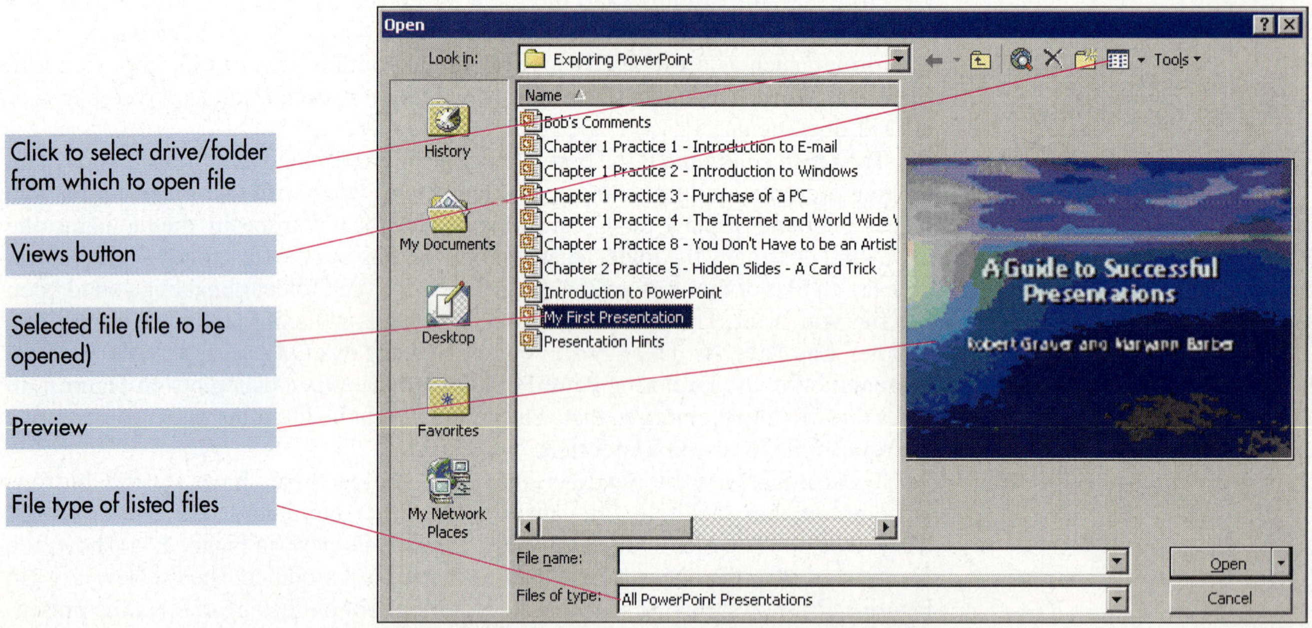

(b) Open Dialog Box (Preview View)

FIGURE 1.4 *The Save and Open Commands*

Hands-on Exercise 1

Introduction to PowerPoint

Objective To start PowerPoint, open an existing presentation, and modify the text on an existing slide; to show an existing presentation and print handouts of its slides. Use Figure 1.5 as a guide in the exercise.

Step 1: **Welcome to Windows**

- Turn on the computer and all of its peripherals. The floppy drive should be empty prior to starting your machine. This ensures that the system starts by reading from the hard disk, which contains the Windows files, as opposed to a floppy disk, which does not.
- Your system will take a minute or so to get started, after which you should see the desktop in Figure 1.5a. Do not be concerned if the appearance of your desktop is different from ours.
- You may also see a Welcome to Windows dialog box with commands to take a tour of the operating system. If so, click the appropriate button(s) or close the dialog box.
- You should be familiar with basic file management and should be very comfortable moving and copying files from one folder to another. If not, you may want to review the material in the Essentials of Microsoft Windows section of this text.

(a) Welcome to Windows (step 1)

FIGURE 1.5 *Hands-on Exercise 1*

Step 2: Download the Data Disk

- We have created a series of practice files (also called a "data disk") for you to use throughout the text. Your instructor will make these files available to you in a variety of ways:
  - The files may be on a network drive, in which case you use Windows Explorer to copy the files from the network to a floppy disk.
  - There may be an actual "data disk" that you are to check out from the lab in order to use the Copy Disk command to duplicate the disk.
- You can also download the files from our Web site, provided you have an Internet connection. Start Internet Explorer, then go to the Exploring Windows home page at **www.prenhall.com/grauer**.
  - Click the book for **Office XP**, which takes you to the Office XP home page. Click the **Student Resources tab** (at the top of the window) to go to the Student Resources page as shown in Figure 1.5b.
  - Click the link to **Student Data Disk** (in the left frame), then scroll down the page until you can select PowerPoint 2002. Click the link to download the student data disk.
  - You will see the File Download dialog box asking what you want to do. The option button to save this program to disk is selected. Click **OK**. The Save As dialog box appears.
  - Click the down arrow in the Save In list box to enter the drive and folder where you want to save the file. It's best to save the file to the Windows desktop or to a temporary folder on drive C..
  - Double click the file after it has been downloaded to your PC, then follow the onscreen instructions.
- Check with your instructor for additional information.

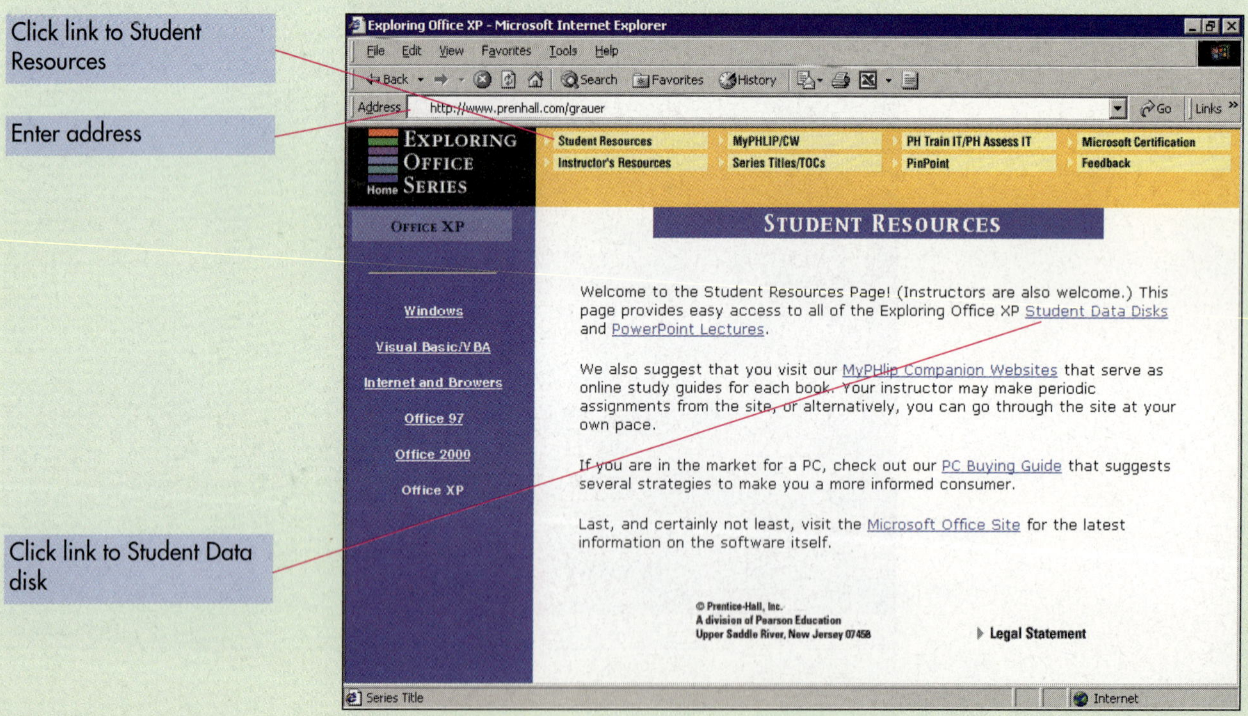

(b) Download the Data Disk (step 2)

FIGURE 1.5 *Hands-on Exercise 1 (continued)*

Step 3: **Start PowerPoint**

- Click the **Start button** to display the Start menu. Slide the mouse pointer over the various menu options and notice that each time you point to a menu item, its submenu (if any) is displayed.
- Point to (or click) the **Programs menu**, then click **Microsoft PowerPoint 2002** to start the program and display a screen similar to Figure 1.5c. Right click the Office Assistant if it appears, then click the command to hide it. We return to the Assistant in step seven.
- If you see the task pane, click the link to **More Presentations**, which in turn will display the Open dialog box. If you do not see the task pane, pull down the **File menu** and click the **Open command** or click the **Open button** on the Standard toolbar.

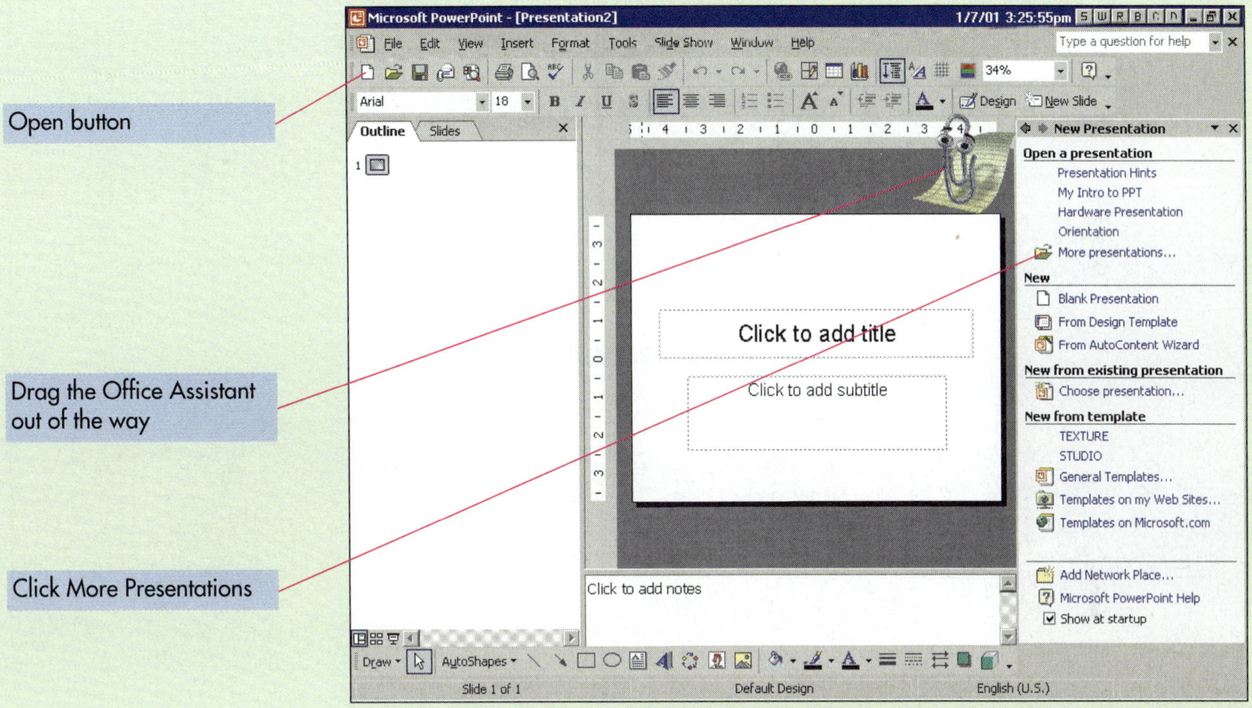

(c) Start PowerPoint (step 3)

FIGURE 1.5 *Hands-on Exercise 1 (continued)*

ABOUT THE ASSISTANT

The Assistant is very powerful and hence you want to experiment with various ways to use it. To ask a question, click the Assistant's icon to toggle its balloon on or off. To change the way in which the Assistant works, click the Options button within this balloon and experiment with the various check boxes to see their effects. If you find the Assistant distracting, click and drag the character out of the way or hide it altogether by pulling down the Help menu and clicking the Hide the Office Assistant command. Pull down the Help menu and click the Show the Office Assistant command to return to the Assistant.

Step 4: Open a Presentation

- You should see an Open dialog box similar to the one in Figure 1.5d. Click the **drop-down arrow** on the Look In list box. Click the appropriate drive, drive C or drive A, depending on the location of your data.
- Double click the **Exploring PowerPoint folder** within the Look In box to make it the active folder. This is the folder from which you will retrieve and into which you will save the presentation.
- Click the **Views button** repeatedly to cycle through the different views. We selected the Preview view in Figure 1.5d.
- Double click **Introduction to PowerPoint** to open the presentation and begin the exercise.

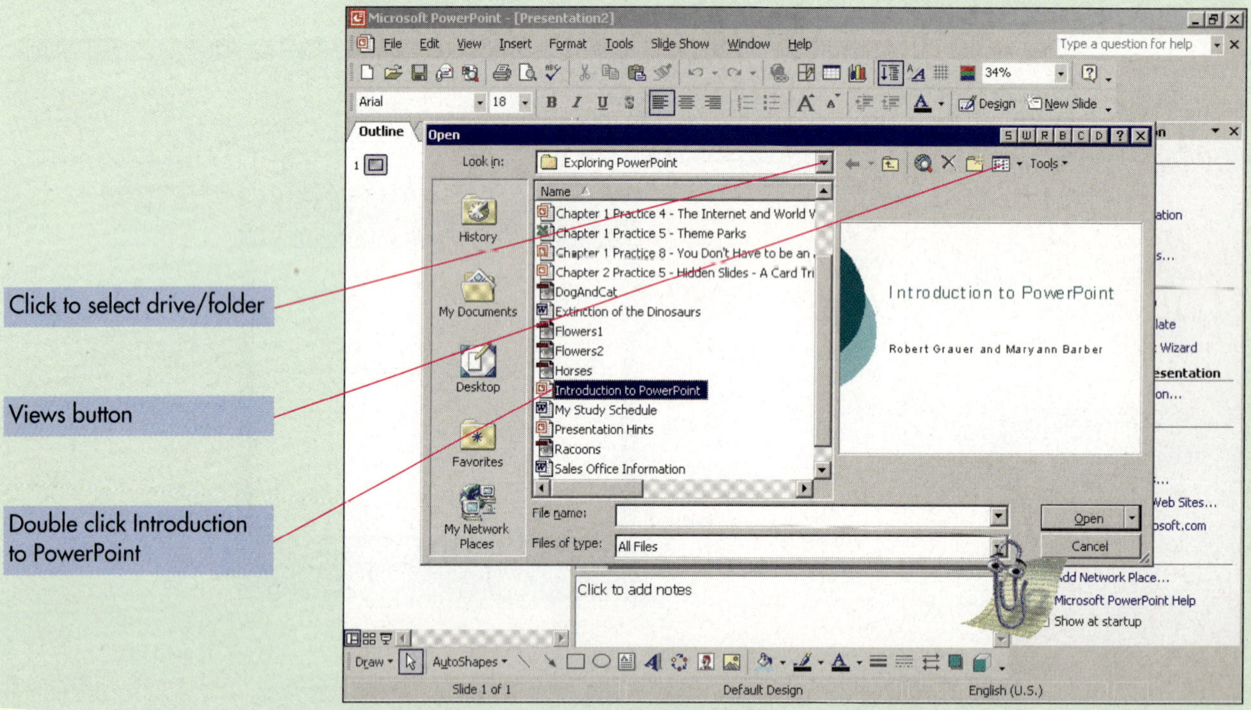

(d) Open a Presentation (step 4)

FIGURE 1.5 *Hands-on Exercise 1 (continued)*

SEPARATE THE TOOLBARS

You may see the Standard and Formatting toolbars displayed on one row to save space within the application window. If so, we suggest you separate the toolbars, so that you see all of the buttons on each. The easiest way to do this is to click the down arrow at the end of any toolbar, then click the option to show the buttons on two rows. You can click the down arrow a second time to show the buttons on one row if you want to return to the other configuration.

Step 5: The Save As Command

- If necessary, click the **Maximize button** in the application window so that PowerPoint takes the entire desktop.
- Click the **Maximize button** in the document window (if necessary) so that the document window is as large as possible.
- Pull down the **File menu**. Click **Save As** to display the dialog box shown in Figure 1.5e. Enter **Finished Introduction** as the name of the new presentation. Click the **Save button**.
- There are now two identical copies of the file on disk, "Introduction to PowerPoint", which is the original presentation that we supplied, and "Finished Introduction", which you just created. The title bar shows the latter name, as it is the presentation currently in memory.

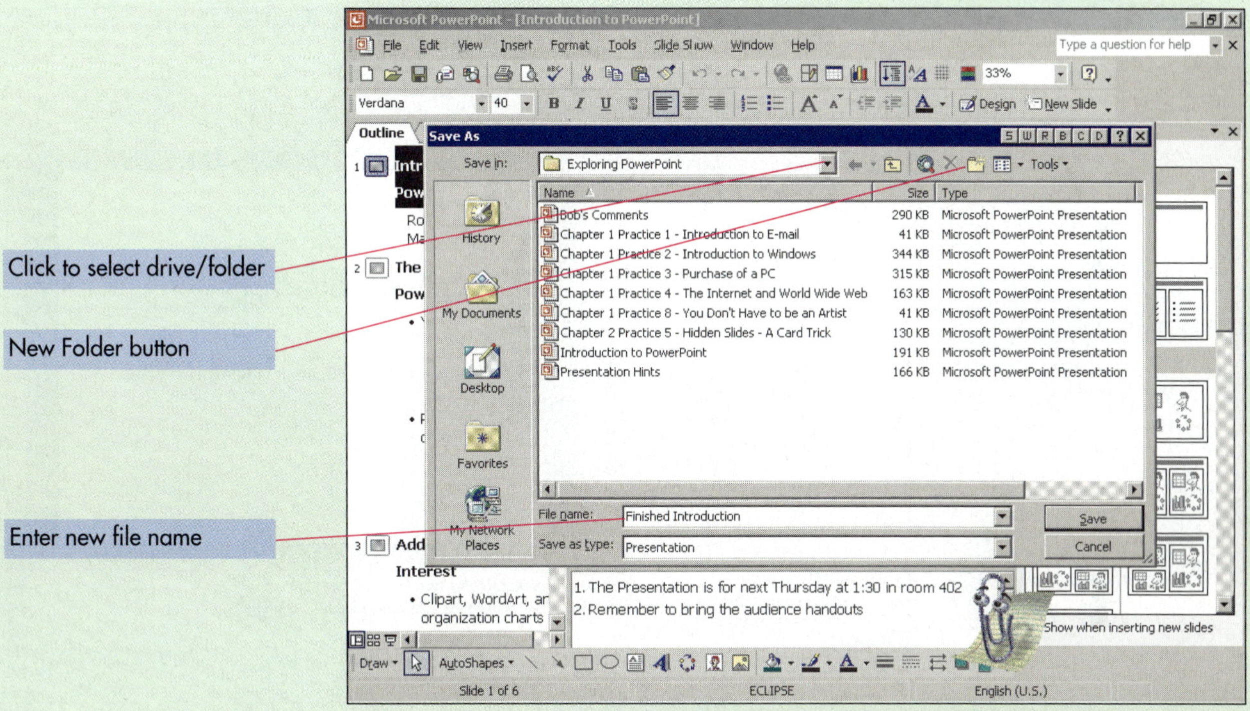

(e) The Save As Command (step 5)

FIGURE 1.5 *Hands-on Exercise 1 (continued)*

CREATE A NEW FOLDER

All Office documents are stored in the My Documents folder by default. It's helpful, however, to create additional folders, especially if you work with a large number of different documents. You can create one folder for school and another for work, and/or you can create different folders for different applications. To create a folder, pull down the File menu, click the Save As command, then click the Create New Folder button to display the New Folder dialog box. Enter the name of the folder, then click OK to create the folder. Once the folder has been created, use the Look In box to change to that folder the next time you open or save a presentation. See practice exercise 11 at the end of the chapter.

Step 6: Modify a Slide

- Press and hold the left mouse button as you drag the mouse over the presenters' names, **Robert Grauer and Maryann Barber**. You can select the text in either the outline or the slide pane.
- Release the mouse. The names should be highlighted (selected) as shown in Figure 1.5f. The selected text is affected by the next command.
- Type your name, which automatically replaces the selected text in both the outline and the slide pane. Press **enter**.
- Type your class on the next line and note that the entry is made in both the slide and the outline pane.
- Pull down the **File menu** and click **Save** (or click the **Save button** on the Standard toolbar).

Save button

Click and drag to select presenters' names

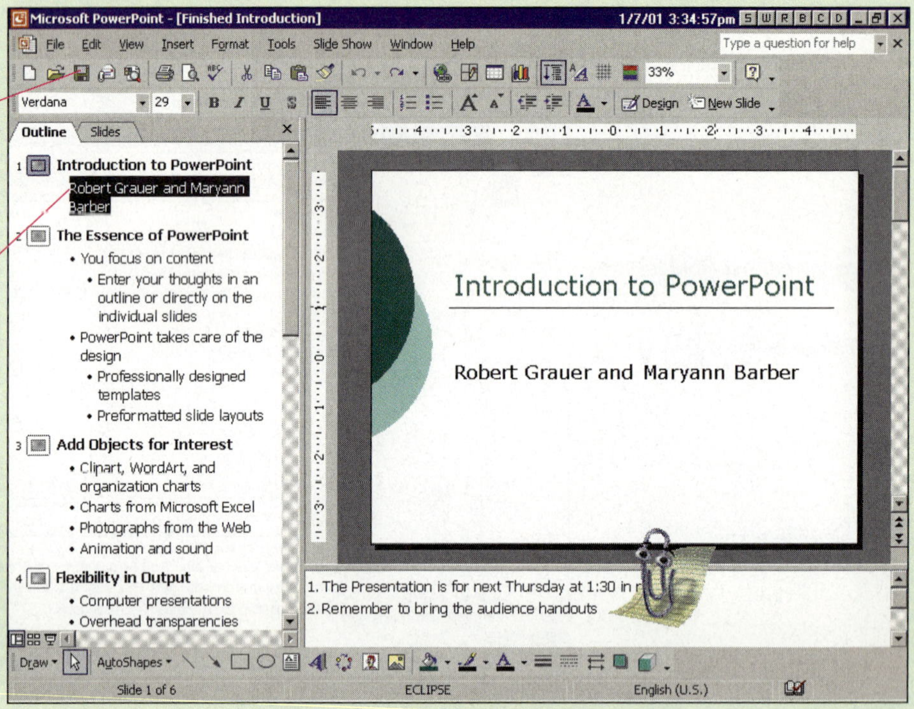

(f) Modify a Slide (step 6)

FIGURE 1.5 *Hands-on Exercise 1 (continued)*

THE AUTOMATIC SPELL CHECK

A red wavy line under a word indicates that the word is misspelled, or in the case of a proper name, that the word is spelled correctly, but that it is not in the dictionary. In either event, point to the underlined word and click the right mouse button to display a shortcut menu. Select the appropriate spelling from the list of suggestions or add the word to the supplementary dictionary. To enable (disable) the automatic spell check, pull down the Tools menu, click the Options command, click the Spelling and Style tab, then check (clear) the option to check spelling as you type.

Step 7: **The Office Assistant**

- You can display the Assistant in one of three ways—press the **F1 key**, click the **Microsoft PowerPoint Help button** on the Standard toolbar, or pull down the **Help menu** and click the **Show the Office Assistant command**.
- If necessary, click the **Office Assistant** to display a balloon, then enter your question, for example, **How do I check spelling?** Click the **Search button** within the balloon.
- The Assistant will return a list of topics that it considers potential answers to your question. Click the second topic, **Show or hide spelling errors**, to display the Help window in Figure 1.5g.
- Click other topics to display additional information about spelling. You can print the contents by clicking the **Print button** in the Help window.
- Close the Help window.

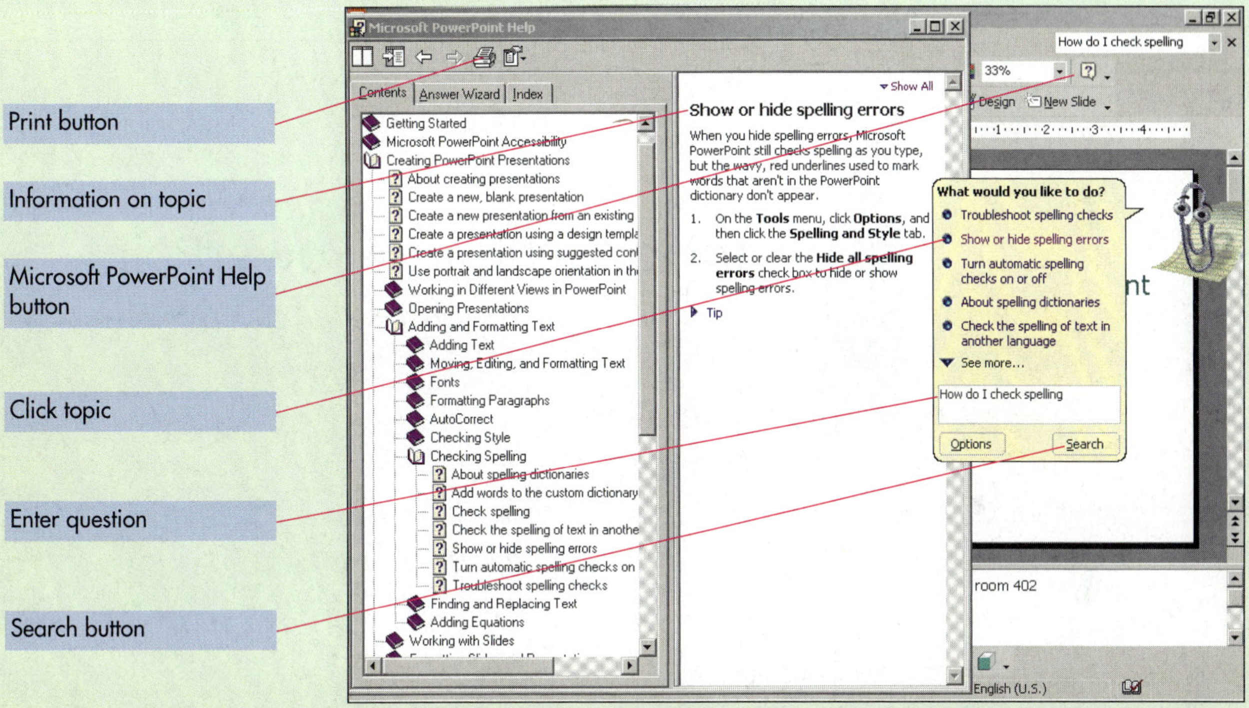

(g) The Office Assistant (step 7)

FIGURE 1.5 *Hands-on Exercise 1 (continued)*

CHOOSE YOUR OWN ASSISTANT

You can choose your own personal assistant from one of several available candidates. If necessary, press the F1 key to display the Assistant, click the Options button to display the Office Assistant dialog box, then click the Gallery tab, where you choose your character. (The Office XP CD is required in order to select some of the other characters.) Some assistants are more animated (distracting) than others. The Office logo is the most passive, while Rocky is quite animated. Experiment with the various check boxes on the Options tab to see the effects on the Assistant.

Step 8: **Show the Presentation**

- Click the **Slide Show button** above the status bar, or pull down the **View menu** and click **Slide Show**. The presentation will begin with the first slide as shown in Figure 1.5h. You should see your name on the slide because of the modification you made in the previous step.
- Click the mouse to move to the second slide, which comes into the presentation from the right side of your monitor. (This is one of several transition effects used to add interest to a presentation.)
- Click the mouse to go to the next (third) slide, which illustrates an animation effect. This requires you to click the mouse to display each succeeding bullet.
- Continue to view the show until you come to the end of the presentation. (You can press the **Esc key** at any time to cancel the show and return to the PowerPoint window.) Note the transition effects and the use of sound (provided you have speakers on your system) to enhance the presentation.

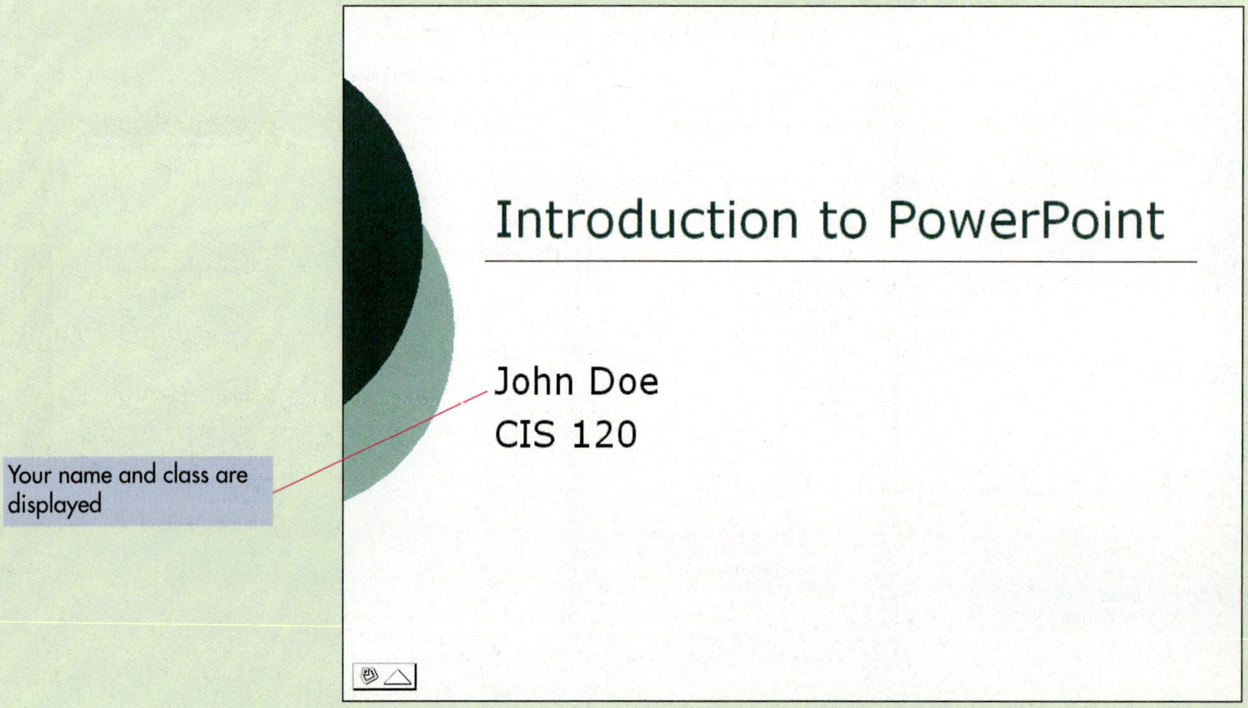

(h) Show the Presentation (step 8)

FIGURE 1.5 *Hands-on Exercise 1 (continued)*

TIP OF THE DAY

You can set the Office Assistant to greet you with a "tip of the day" each time you start PowerPoint. Click the Microsoft PowerPoint Help button (or press the F1 key) to display the Assistant, then click the Options button to display the Office Assistant dialog box. Click the Options tab, check the Show the Tip of the Day at Startup box, then click OK. The next time you start PowerPoint, you will be greeted by the Assistant, who will offer you the tip of the day.

Step 9: **Print the Presentation**

- Pull down the **File menu**. Click **Print** to display the Print dialog box in Figure 1.5i. (Clicking the Print button on the Standard toolbar does not display the Print dialog box.)
- Click the **down arrow** in the **Print What** drop-down list box, click **Handouts**, and specify 6 slides per page as shown in Figure 1.5i.
- Check the box to **Frame Slides**. Check that the **All option button** is selected under Print range. Click the **OK command button** to print the handouts for the presentation.
- Pull down the **File menu**. Click **Close** to close the presentation but remain in PowerPoint. Click **Yes** when asked whether to save the changes.
- Pull down the **File menu**. Click **Exit** to exit PowerPoint if you do not want to continue with the next exercise at this time.

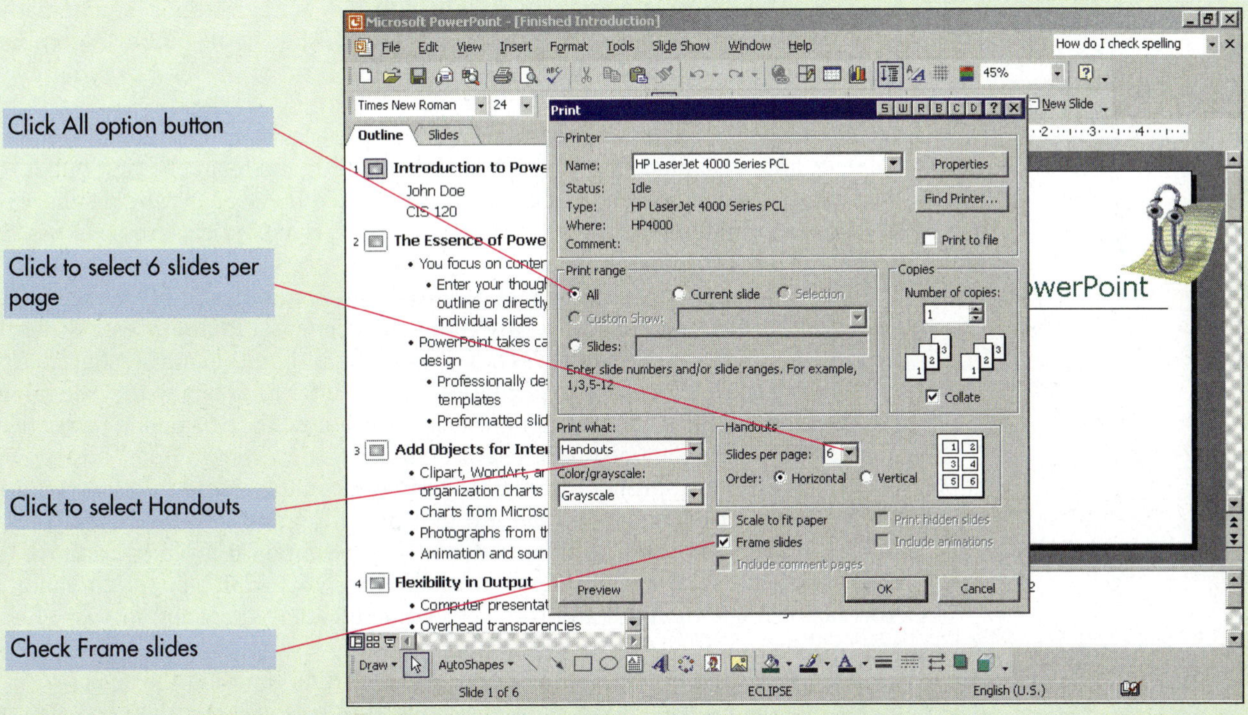

(i) Print the Presentation (step 9)

FIGURE 1.5 *Hands-on Exercise 1 (continued)*

SHOW THE KEYBOARD SHORTCUT IN A SCREENTIP

You can expand the ScreenTip associated with any toolbar button to include the equivalent keyboard shortcut. Pull down the View menu, click Toolbars, then click Customize to display the Customize dialog box. Click the Options tab and check the box to show the shortcut keys in the ScreenTips. Close the dialog box, then point to any toolbar button, and you should see the name of the button as well as the equivalent keyboard shortcut. There is no need to memorize the shortcuts, but they are useful.

You are ready to create your own presentation, a process that requires you to develop its content and apply the formatting through the use of a template or design specification. You can do the steps in either order, but we suggest you start with the content. Both steps are iterative in nature and you are likely to go back and forth many times before you are finished.

You will also find yourself switching from one view to another as you develop the presentation. It doesn't matter which view you use, as long as you can accomplish what you set out to do. You can, for example, enter text one slide at a time in the Slide Normal view. You can also use the outline as shown in Figure 1.6, to view the text of many slides at the same time and thus gain a better sense of the overall presentation.

Each slide in the outline contains a title, followed by bulleted items, which are indented one to five levels, corresponding to the importance of the item. The main points appear on level one. Subsidiary items are indented below the main point to which they apply. Any item can be ***promoted*** to a higher level or ***demoted*** to a lower level, either before or after the text is entered. Each slide in the outline is numbered and the numbers adjust automatically for the insertion or deletion of slides as you edit the presentation.

Consider, for example, slide 4 in Figure 1.6a. The title of the slide, *Develop the Content*, appears immediately after the slide number and icon. The first bullet, *Use the outline*, is indented one level under the title, and it in turn has two subsidiary bullets. The next main bullet, *Review the flow of ideas*, is moved back to level one, and it, too, has two subsidiary bullets.

The outline is (to us) the ideal way to create and edit the presentation. The ***insertion point*** marks the place where new text is entered and is established by clicking anywhere in the outline. (The insertion point is automatically placed at the title of the first slide in a new presentation.) Press enter after typing the title or after entering the text of a bulleted item, which starts a new slide or bullet, respectively. The new item may then be promoted or demoted as necessary.

Editing is accomplished through the same techniques used in other Windows applications. For example, you can use the Cut, Copy, and Paste commands in the Edit menu (or the corresponding buttons on the Standard toolbar) to move and copy selected text or you can simply drag and drop text from one place to another. You can also use the Find and Replace commands that are found in every Office application.

Note, too, that you can format text in the outline by using the ***select-then-do*** approach common to all Office applications; that is, you select the text, then you execute the appropriate command or click the appropriate button. The selected text remains highlighted and is affected by all subsequent commands until you click elsewhere in the outline.

Figure 1.6b displays a collapsed view of the outline, which displays only the title of each slide. The advantage to this view is that you see more slides on the screen at the same time, making it easier to move slides within the presentation. The slides are expanded or collapsed using tools on the ***Outlining toolbar***.

CRYSTALLIZE YOUR MESSAGE

Every presentation exists to deliver a message, whether it's to sell a product, present an idea, or provide instruction. Decide on the message you want to deliver, then write the text for the presentation. Edit the text to be sure it is consistent with your objective. Then, and only then, should you think about formatting, but always keep the message foremost in your mind.

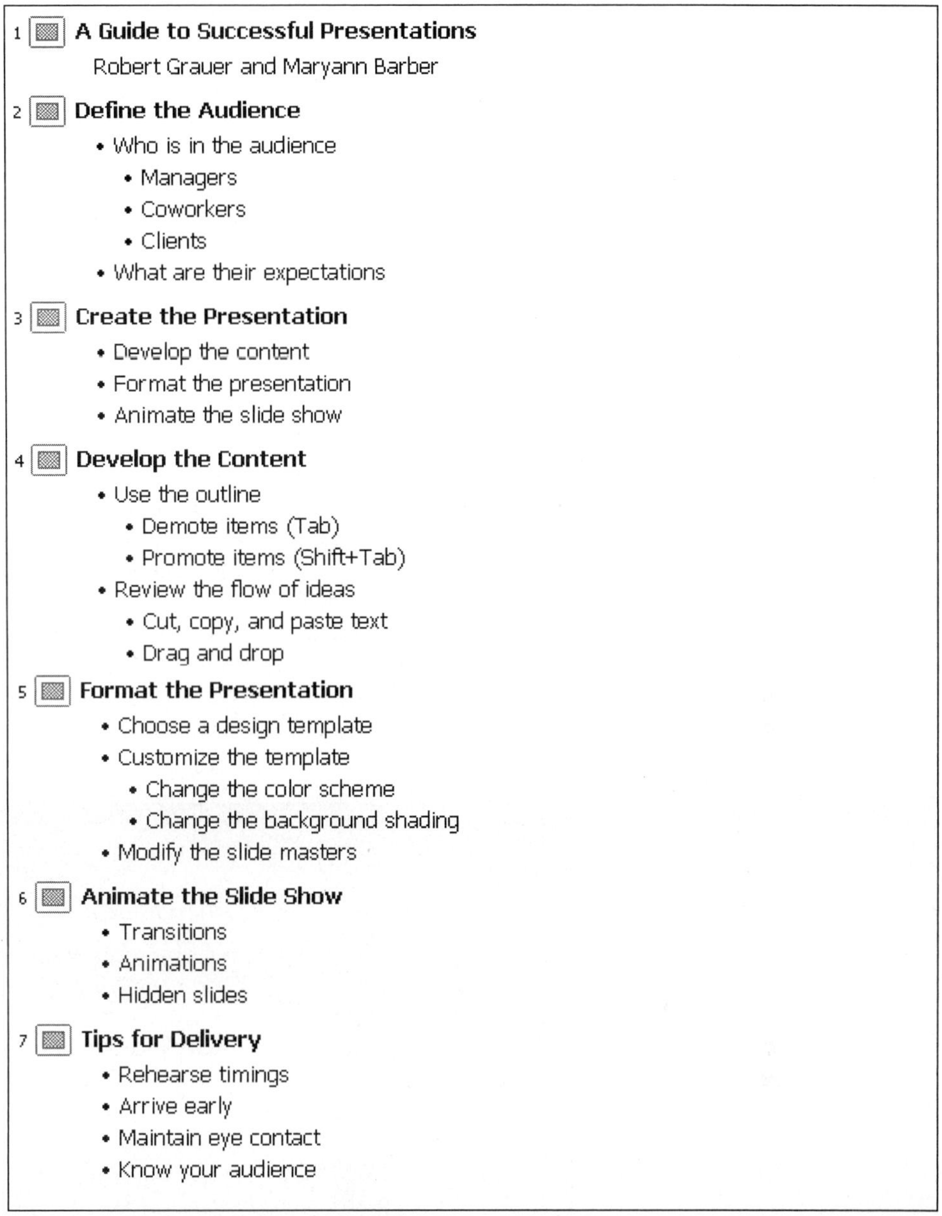

(a) The Expanded Outline

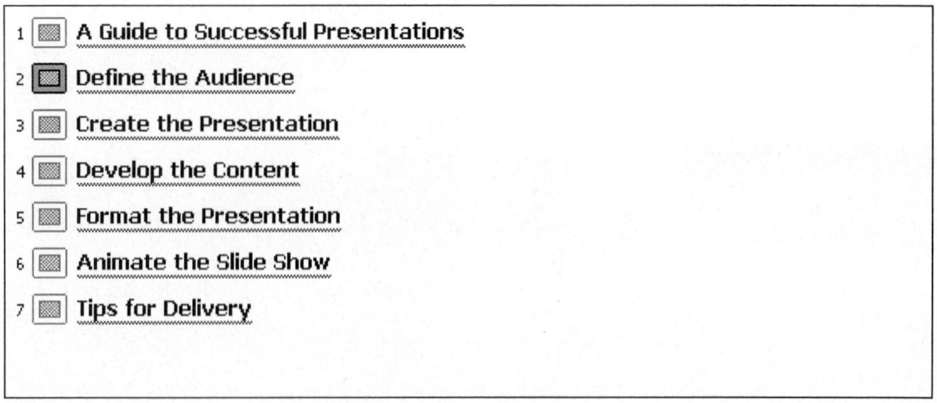

(b) The Collapsed Outline

FIGURE 1.6 *The Presentation Outline*

Slide Layouts

New slides are typically created as text slides, consisting of a slide title and a single column of bullets. The layout of a text (or any other) slide can be changed, however, to include clip art or other objects, and/or to display a double column of bullets. The new elements can be added manually by using the various tools on the Drawing toolbar or by letting PowerPoint change the layout for you.

PowerPoint provides a set of predefined ***slide layouts*** that determine the nature and position of the objects on a slide. The layouts are displayed by default within the task pane whenever the Insert menu is used to add a slide. Just insert the slide, then select the desired layout from the task pane. You can also change the layout of an existing slide by selecting the slide and choosing a different layout from the task pane. (Use the View menu to toggle the task pane open, then click the down arrow within the task pane to display the slide layouts.)

Figure 1.7 illustrates the creation of a two-column text slide, which in turn has three ***placeholders*** that determine the position of each object. Once the layout has been selected, you simply click the appropriate placeholder to add the title or text. Thus, you would click on the placeholder for the title and enter the text of the title as indicated. In similar fashion, you click the placeholder for either column of bullets and enter the associated text. Other layouts include clip art, organization charts, and other objects. (You can change the size and/or position of the placeholders by moving and sizing the placeholders just as you would any other object.) It's easy, as you will see in the exercise, which follows shortly.

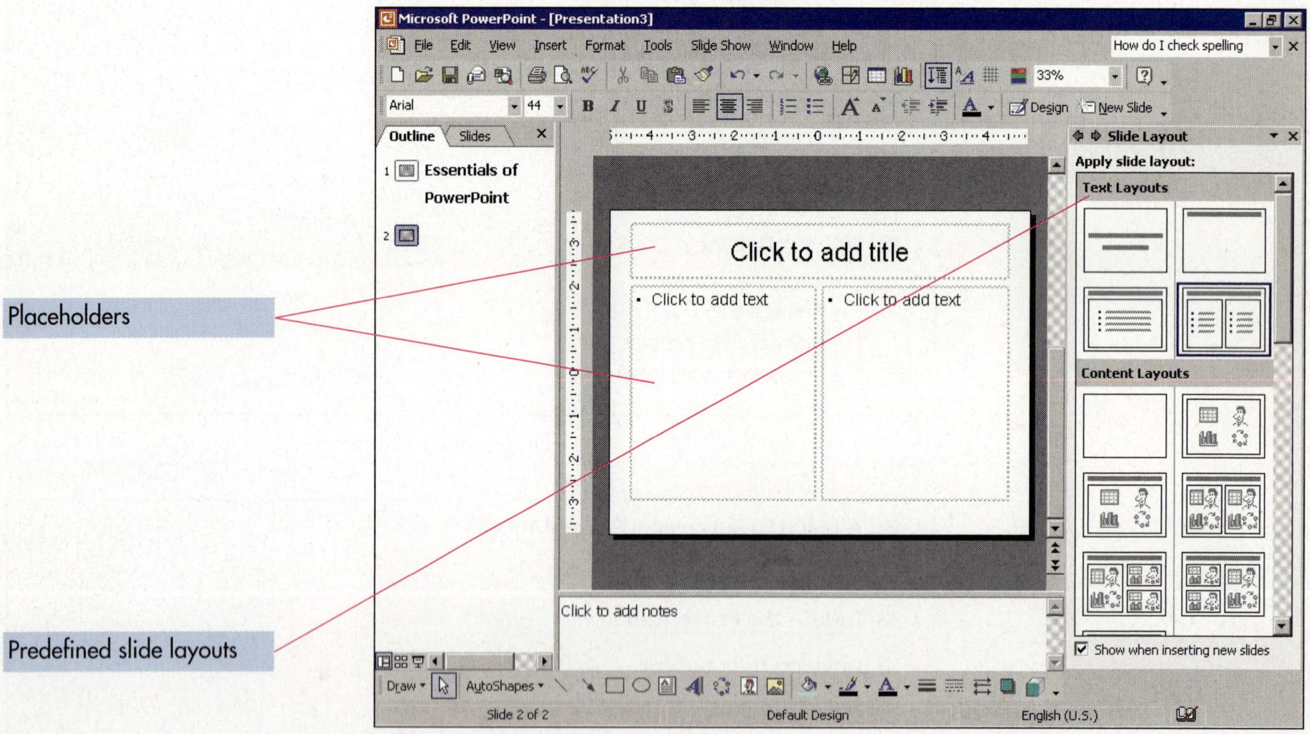

FIGURE 1.7 *Slide Layouts*

PowerPoint enables you to concentrate on the content of a presentation without concern for its appearance. You focus on what you are going to say, and trust in PowerPoint to format the presentation attractively. The formatting is implemented automatically by selecting one of the many templates that are supplied with PowerPoint.

A ***template*** is a design specification that controls every element in a presentation. It specifies the color scheme for the slides and the arrangement of the different elements (placeholders) on each slide. It determines the formatting of the text, the fonts that are used, and the size and placement of the bulleted text.

Figure 1.8 displays the title slide of a presentation in four different templates. Just choose the template you like, and PowerPoint formats the entire presentation according to that template. And don't be afraid to change your mind. You can use the Slide Design command at any time to select a different template and change the look of your presentation.

(a) Cliff

(b) Fireworks

(c) Maple

(d) Ocean

FIGURE 1.8 *Templates*

HANDS-ON EXERCISE 2

CREATING A PRESENTATION

Objective To create a new presentation; to apply a design template to a presentation. Use Figure 1.9 as a guide.

Step 1: **Create a New Presentation**

- Click the **Start button**, click **Programs**, then click **Microsoft PowerPoint** to start PowerPoint. PowerPoint opens with a new blank presentation.
- If necessary, pull down the **View menu** and switch to the **Normal view** and click the **Outline tab** as shown in Figure 1.9a.
- Hide the Office Assistant if it appears. (You can display the Assistant at any time by clicking its button on the Standard toolbar. You can also get help without the Assistant by using the Ask a Question.) Close the task pane.

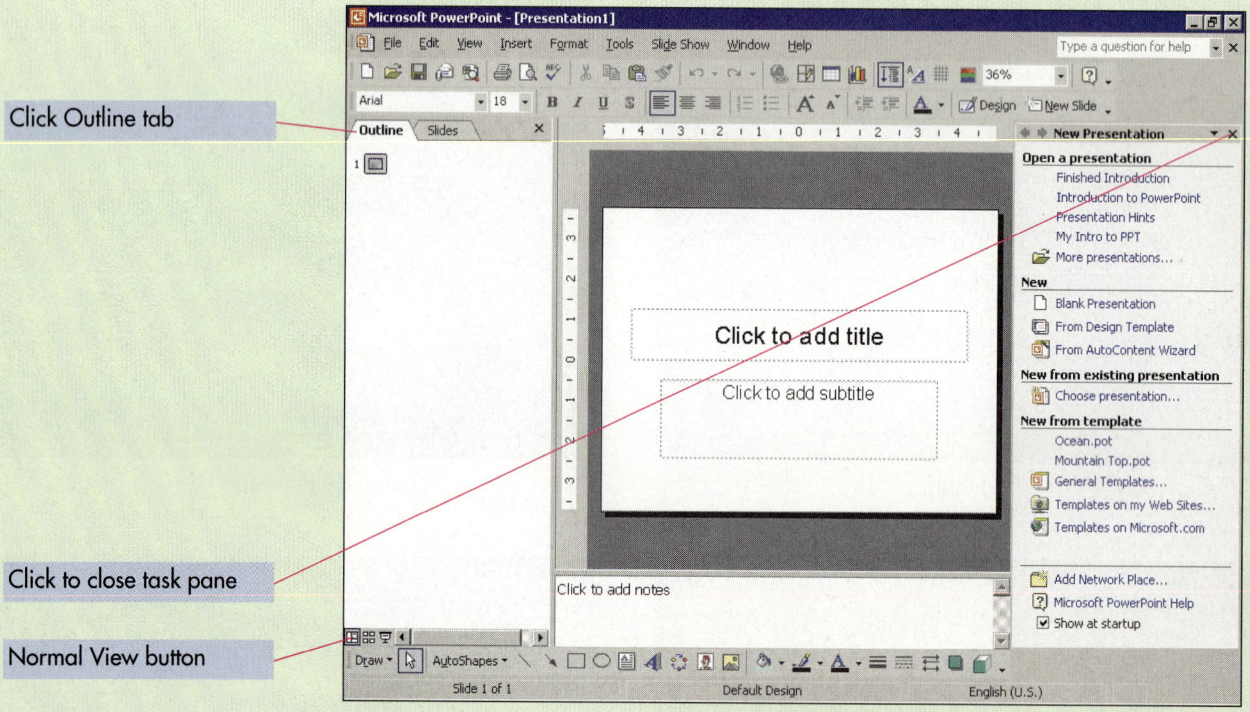

(a) Create a New Presentation (step 1)

FIGURE 1.9 *Hands-on Exercise 2*

> **ASK A QUESTION**
>
> Click in the "Ask a Question" list box that appears at the right of the document window, enter the text of a question such as "What are Speaker Notes?", press enter, and PowerPoint returns a list of potential help topics. Click any topic that appears promising to open the Help window with detailed information. You can ask multiple questions during a PowerPoint session, then click the down arrow in the list box to return to an earlier question, which will return you to the help topics.

Step 2: **Create the Title Slide**

- Click anywhere in the box containing **Click to add title**, then type the title, **A Guide to Successful Presentations** as shown in Figure 1.9b. The title will automatically wrap to a second line.
- Click anywhere in the box containing **Click to add subtitle** and enter your name. Click outside the subtitle placeholder when you have entered your name on the slide.
- The outline now contains the title of the presentation as well as your name. You can use the outline to change either element.
- Click in the Notes pane and enter a speaker's note that pertains to the title slide—for example, the date and time that the presentation is scheduled. The notes are for the speaker, but not for the audience.

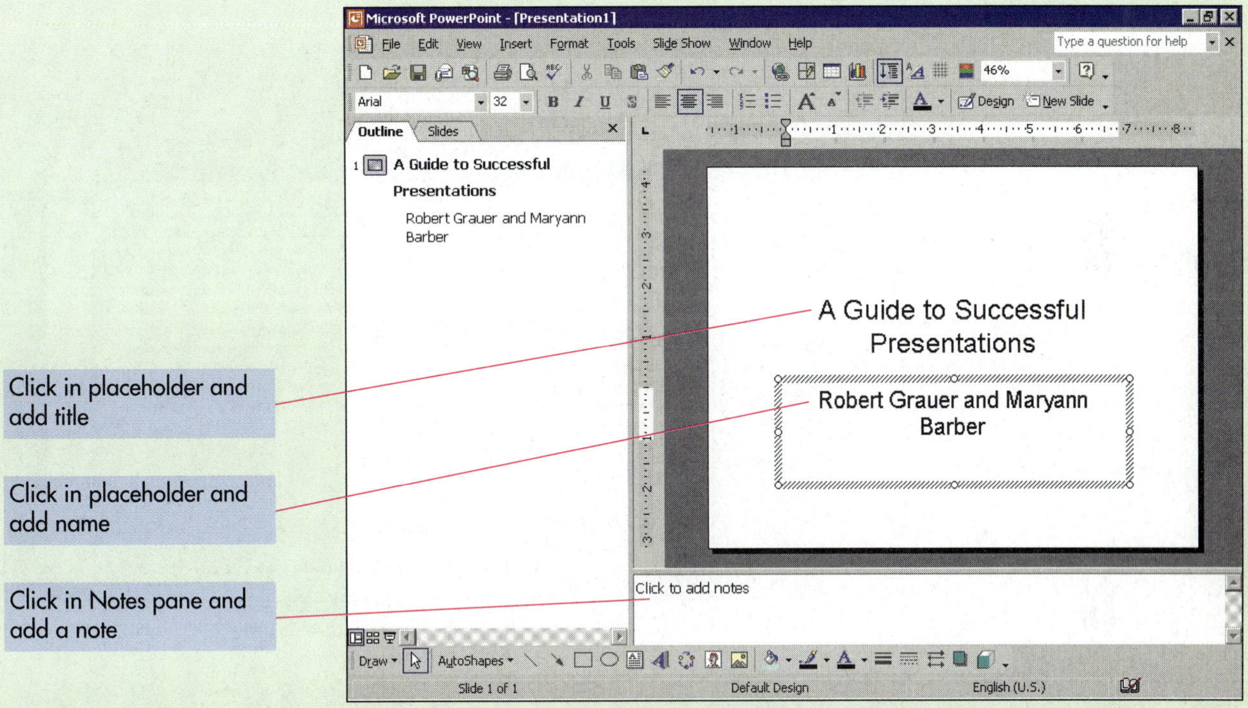

(b) Create the Title Slide (step 2)

FIGURE 1.9 *Hands-on Exercise 2 (continued)*

CONTENT, CONTENT, AND CONTENT

It is much more important to focus on the content of the presentation than to worry about how it will look. Start with the AutoContent Wizard (described later in the chapter) or with a blank presentation in the Outline. Save the formatting for last. Otherwise you will spend too much time changing templates and too little time developing the text.

Step 3: Save the Presentation

- Pull down the **File menu** and click **Save** (or click the **Save button** on the Standard toolbar). You should see the Save As dialog box in Figure 1.9c. If necessary, click the **down arrow** on the **Views button** and click **Details**.
- To save the file:
  - Click the **drop-down arrow** on the Save In list box.
  - Click the appropriate drive, drive C or drive A, depending on whether or not you installed the data disk on your hard drive.
  - Double click the **Exploring PowerPoint folder** to make it the active folder (the folder in which you will save the document).
  - Enter **My First Presentation** as the name of the presentation.
- Click **Save** or press the **enter key**. The title bar changes to reflect the name of the presentation.

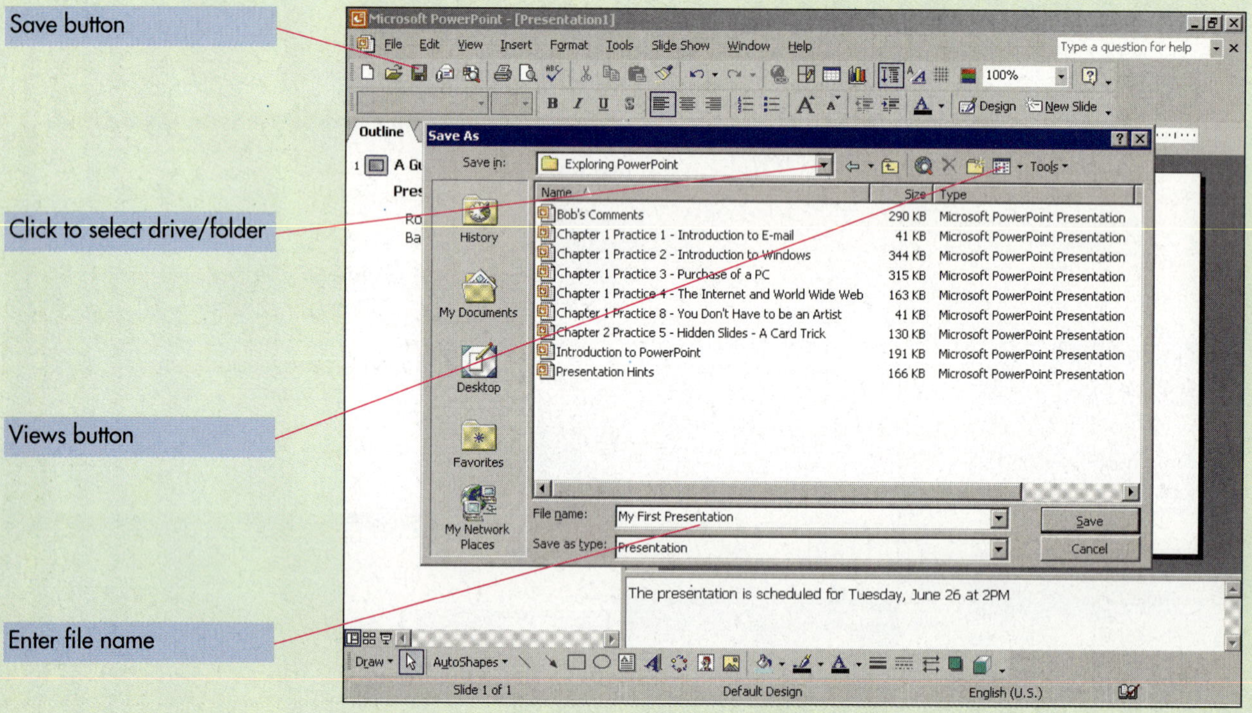

(c) Save the Presentation (step 3)

FIGURE 1.9 *Hands-on Exercise 2 (continued)*

> **CHANGE THE DEFAULT FOLDER**
>
> The default folder is where PowerPoint goes initially to open an existing presentation or to save a new presentation. If you have your own machine, however, you may find it useful to change the default folder. Pull down the Tools menu, click the Options command, then click the Save tab within the Options dialog box. Click in the text box that contains the default file location, enter a new folder, and click OK. The next time you open or save a file, PowerPoint will go automatically to that location.

Step 4: Enter the Text

- Check that the Outlining toolbar is displayed. If not, pull down the **View menu**, click the **Toolbars command**, then click **Outlining** to show the toolbar.
- Click and drag the border between the Outline pane and the Slide pane to enlarge the Outline pane.
- Click after your name in the Outline pane. Press **enter** to begin a new item, then press **Shift+Tab** to promote the item and create slide 2. Type **Define the Audience**. Press **enter**.
- Press the **Tab key** (or click the **Demote button** on the Outline toolbar) to enter the first bullet. Type **Who is in the audience** and press **enter**.
- Press the **Tab key** to enter the second-level bullets. Type **Managers**. Press **enter**. Type **Coworkers**. Press **enter**. Type **Clients**. Press **enter**.
- Press **Shift+Tab** (or click the **Promote button** on the Outline toolbar) to return to the first-level bullets. Type **What are their expectations**. Press **enter**.
- Press **Shift+Tab** to enter the title of the third slide. Type **Tips for Delivery**. Press **enter**, then press **Tab key** to create the first bullet.
- Add the remaining text for this slide and for slide 4 as shown in Figure 1.9d.

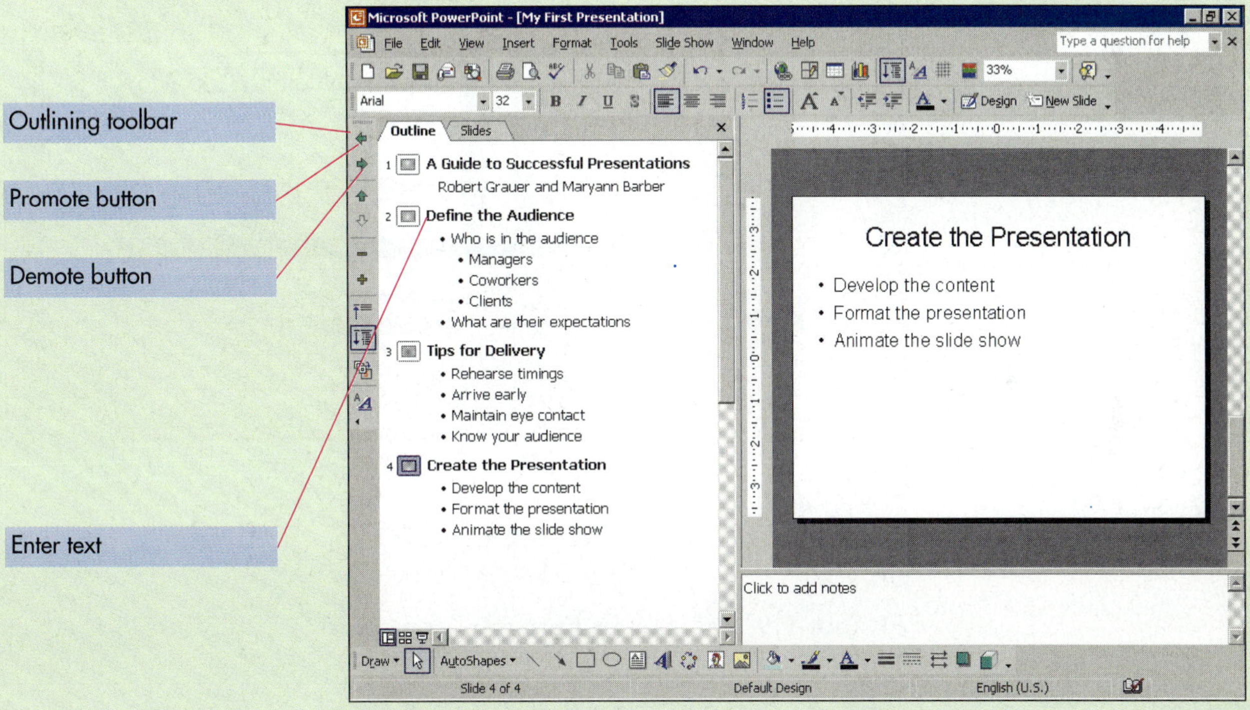

(d) Enter the Text (step 4)

FIGURE 1.9 *Hands-on Exercise 2 (continued)*

JUST KEEP TYPING

The easiest way to enter the text for a presentation is to type continually in the outline. Just type an item, then press enter to move to the next item. You will be automatically positioned at the next item on the same level, where you can type the next entry. Continue to enter text in this manner. Press the Tab key as necessary to demote an item (move it to the next lower level). Press Shift+Tab to promote an item (move it to the next higher level).

Step 5: The Spell Check

- Enter the text of the remaining slides as shown in Figure 1.9e. Do *not* press enter after entering the last bullet on the last slide or else you will add a blank bullet.
- Click the **Spelling button** on the Standard toolbar to check the presentation for spelling:
  - The result of the spell check depends on how accurately you entered the text of the presentation. We deliberately misspelled the word *Transitions* in the last slide.
  - Continue to check the document for spelling errors. Click **OK** when PowerPoint indicates it has checked the entire presentation.
- Click the **Save button** on the Standard toolbar to save the presentation.

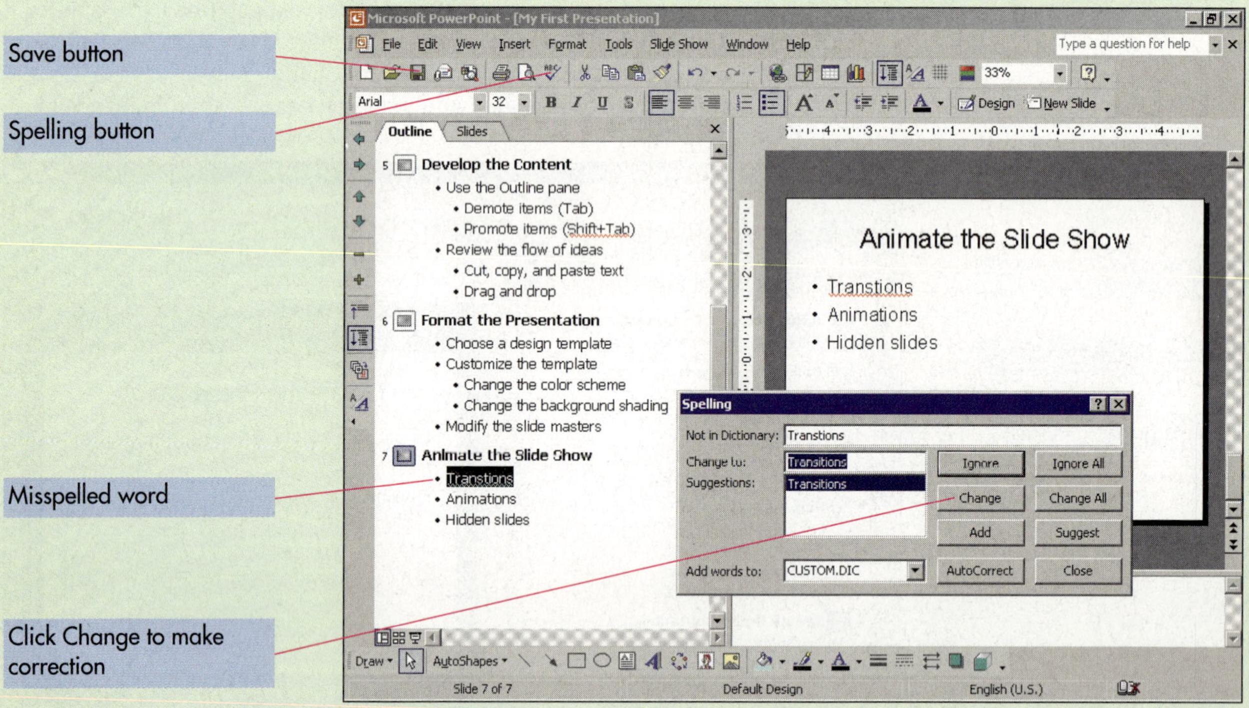

(e) The Spell Check (step 5)

FIGURE 1.9 *Hands-on Exercise 2 (continued)*

CREATE YOUR OWN SHORTHAND

Use the AutoCorrect feature, which is common to all Office applications, to expand abbreviations such as "usa" for United States of America. Pull down the Tools menu, click AutoCorrect Options, then type the abbreviation in the Replace text box and the expanded entry in the With text box. Click the Add command button, then click OK to exit the dialog box and return to the document. The next time you type usa in a presentation, it will automatically be expanded to United States of America.

Step 6: **Drag and Drop**

- Press **Ctrl+Home** to move to the beginning of the presentation. If you don't see the Outlining toolbar, pull down the **View menu**, click the **Toolbars command**, and check **Outlining** to display the toolbar.
- Click the **Collapse All button** on the Outlining toolbar to collapse the outline as shown in Figure 1.9f.
- Click the **icon** for **slide 3** (Tips for Delivery) to select the slide. Point to the **slide icon** (the mouse pointer changes to a four-headed arrow), then click and drag to move the slide to the end of the presentation.
- All of the slides have been renumbered. The slide titled Tips for Delivery has been moved to the end of the presentation and appears as slide 7. Click the **Expand All button** to display the contents of each slide. Click anywhere in the presentation to deselect the last slide.

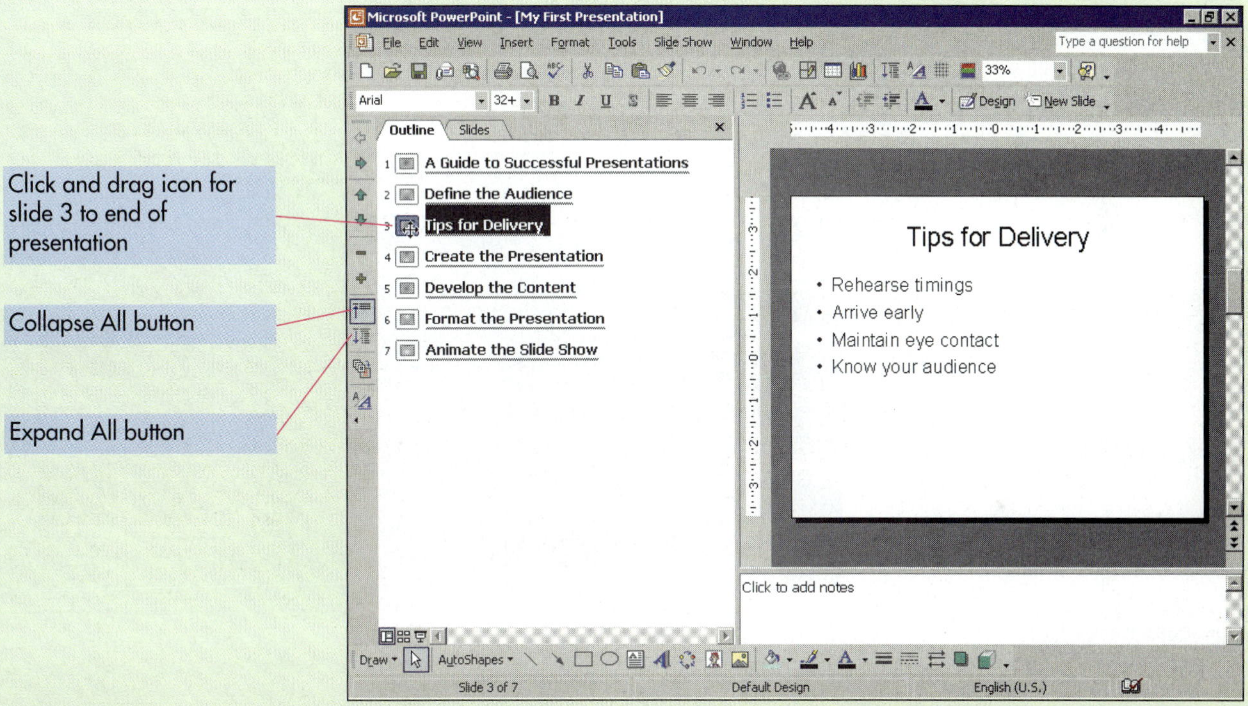

(f) Drag and Drop (step 6)

FIGURE 1.9 *Hands-on Exercise 2 (continued)*

SELECTING SLIDES IN THE OUTLINE

Click the slide icon or the slide number next to the slide title to select the slide. PowerPoint will select the entire slide (including its title, text, and any other objects that are not visible in the outline). Click the first slide, then press and hold the Shift key as you click the ending slide to select a group of sequential slides. Press Ctrl+A to select the entire outline. You can use these techniques to select multiple slides regardless of whether the outline is collapsed or expanded. The selected slides can be copied, moved, expanded, collapsed, or deleted as a unit.

Step 7: Choose a Design Template

- Pull down the **Format menu** and click the **Slide Design command** to open the task pane as shown in Figure 1.9g. (This command will change the contents of the task pane if the task pane is already open.)
- Click the **down arrow** on the scroll bar within the task pane to scroll through the available designs until you find one that you like. (We chose the Ocean design.) Click the selected design in the task pane to apply this template to your presentation.
- Select a different design to see how your presentation looks when set in another template.
- Click the **Undo button** to cancel the last command and return to the previous design. Click the **Redo button** to reverse the undo operation.
- Spend a few minutes until you have the design you like. Save the presentation.

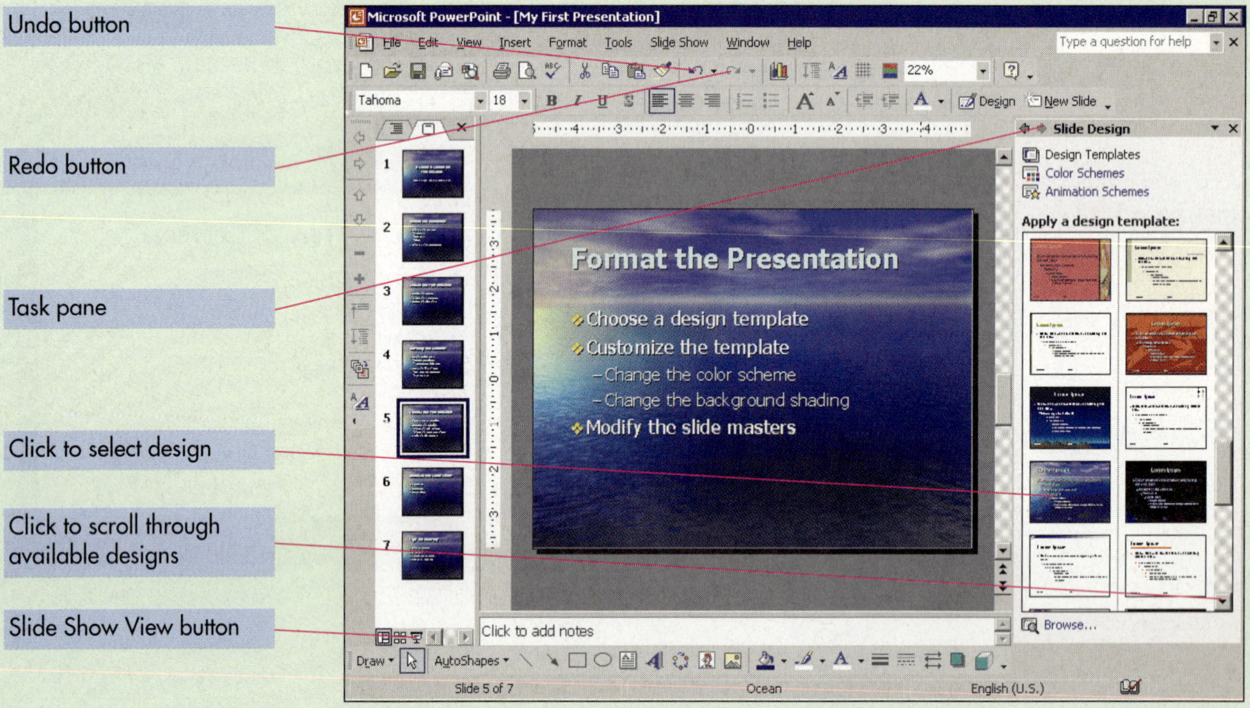

(g) Choose a Design Template (step 7)

FIGURE 1.9 *Hands-on Exercise 2 (continued)*

THE UNDO AND REDO COMMANDS

Click the drop-down arrow next to the Undo button to display a list of your previous actions, then click the action you want to undo, which also undoes all of the preceding commands. Undoing the fifth command in the list, for example, will also undo the preceding four commands. The Redo command works in reverse and cancels the last Undo command.

Step 8: **View the Presentation**

- Press **Ctrl+Home** to move to the beginning of the presentation. Click the **Slide Show button** on the status bar to view the presentation as shown in Figure 1.9h.
  - To move to the next slide: Click the **left mouse button**, type the letter **N**, or press the **PgDn key**.
  - To move to the previous slide: Type the letter **P** or press the **PgUp key**.
- Continue to move from one slide to the next until you come to the end of the presentation and are returned to the Normal view.
- Save the presentation. Exit PowerPoint if you do not want to continue with the next exercise at this time.

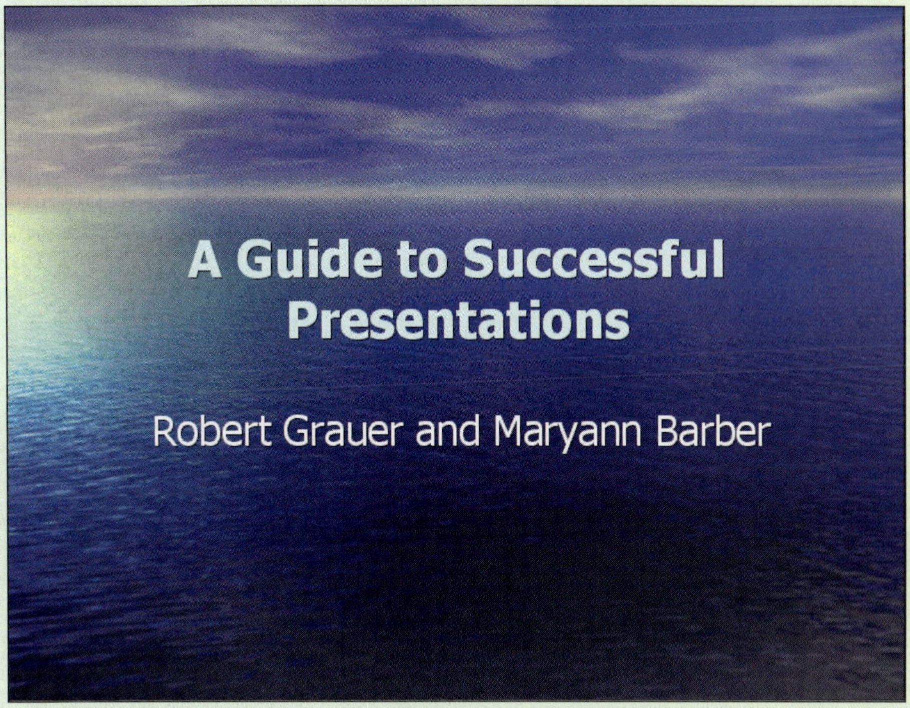

(h) View the Presentation (step 8)

FIGURE 1.9 *Hands-on Exercise 2 (continued)*

ADVICE FROM THE OFFICE ASSISTANT

The Office Assistant indicates it has a suggestion by displaying a lightbulb. Click the lightbulb to display the tip, then click the OK button to close the balloon and continue working. The Assistant will not, however, repeat a tip from an earlier session unless you reset it at the start of a new session. This is especially important in a laboratory situation where you are sharing a computer with many students. To reset the tips, click the Assistant to display the balloon, click the Options button in the balloon, click the Options tab, then click the Reset My Tips button.

You have successfully created a PowerPoint presentation, but the most important step is yet to come—the delivery of the presentation to an audience. This is best accomplished through a computerized slide show (as opposed to using overhead transparencies or 35mm slides). The computer becomes the equivalent of a slide projector and the presentation is called a slide show.

PowerPoint can help you add interest to the slide show in two ways, transitions and animations. ***Transitions*** apply to the slide as a whole and control the way a slide moves on and off the screen. ***Animations*** control the appearance of individual elements on a single slide. Transitions and animations are applied from the task pane within the Normal view as shown in Figure 1.10. (Pull down the Slide Show menu and select the Slide Transition or Custom Animation command to open the task pane with the appropriate options.)

The task pane in Figure 1.10a contains a list box with the available ***transition effects***. Slides may move on to the screen from the left or right, be uncovered by horizontal or vertical blinds, fade, dissolve, and so on. You select a slide, choose the effect, select a speed and sound, then indicate when you want to advance the slide (either on a mouse click or after a specified number of seconds). Click the Play button at the bottom of the pane to preview the transition, or click the Slide Show button to move directly to a complete show. (Transition effects can also be applied from the Slide Sorter view, where you can apply the same transition to multiple slides by selecting the slides prior to applying the effect.)

Figure 1.10b shows the application of animation effects to a specific slide. You can select a predefined animation scheme for the slide as a whole, or you can animate each object individually. The animation schemes are divided into subtle, moderate, and exciting, and it is fun to experiment with the various effects. ***Custom animation*** requires you to select an animation effect for each object on the slide, then specify the order in which the objects are to appear. The slide in Figure 1.10b, for example, displays the title, the four bullets in succession, and the clip art in that order. Look closely at the icons in the task pane and you will see that different effects are chosen for the various objects.

Delivering the Presentation

PowerPoint can help you to create attractive presentations, but the content and delivery are still up to you. You have worked hard to gain the opportunity to present your ideas and you want to be well prepared for the session. Practice aloud several times, preferably under the same conditions as the actual presentation. Time your delivery to be sure that you do not exceed your allotted time. Everyone is nervous, but the more you practice, the more confident you will be.

Arrive early. You need time to gather your thoughts as well as to set up the presentation. Start PowerPoint and open your presentation prior to addressing the audience. Be sure that your notes are with you and check that water is available for you during the presentation. Look at the audience to open communication and gain credibility. Speak clearly and vary your delivery. Try to relax. You'll be great!

QUESTIONS AND ANSWERS (Q & A)

Indicate at the beginning of your talk whether you will take questions during the presentation or collectively at the end. Announce the length of time that will be allocated to questions. Rephrase all questions so the audience can hear. If you do receive a hostile question, rephrase it in a neutral way and try to disarm the challenger by paying a compliment. If you don't know the answer, say so.

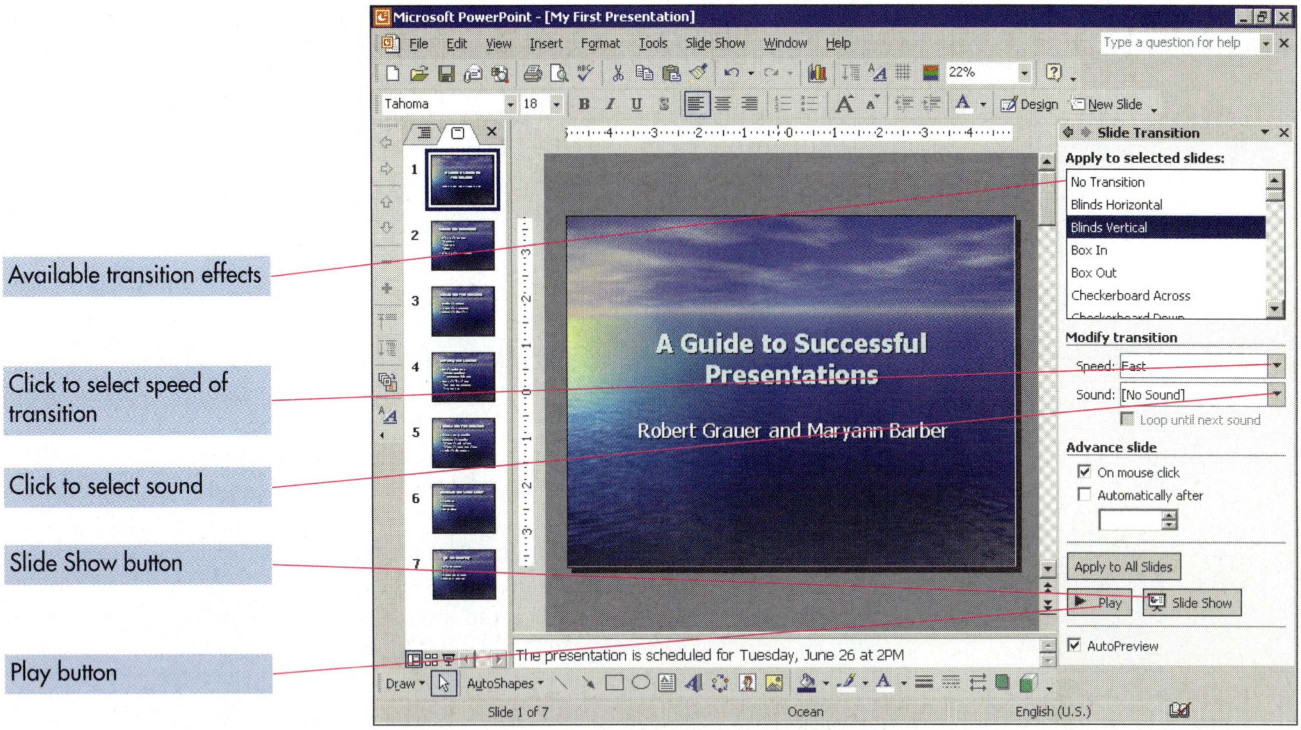

(a) Slide Transition

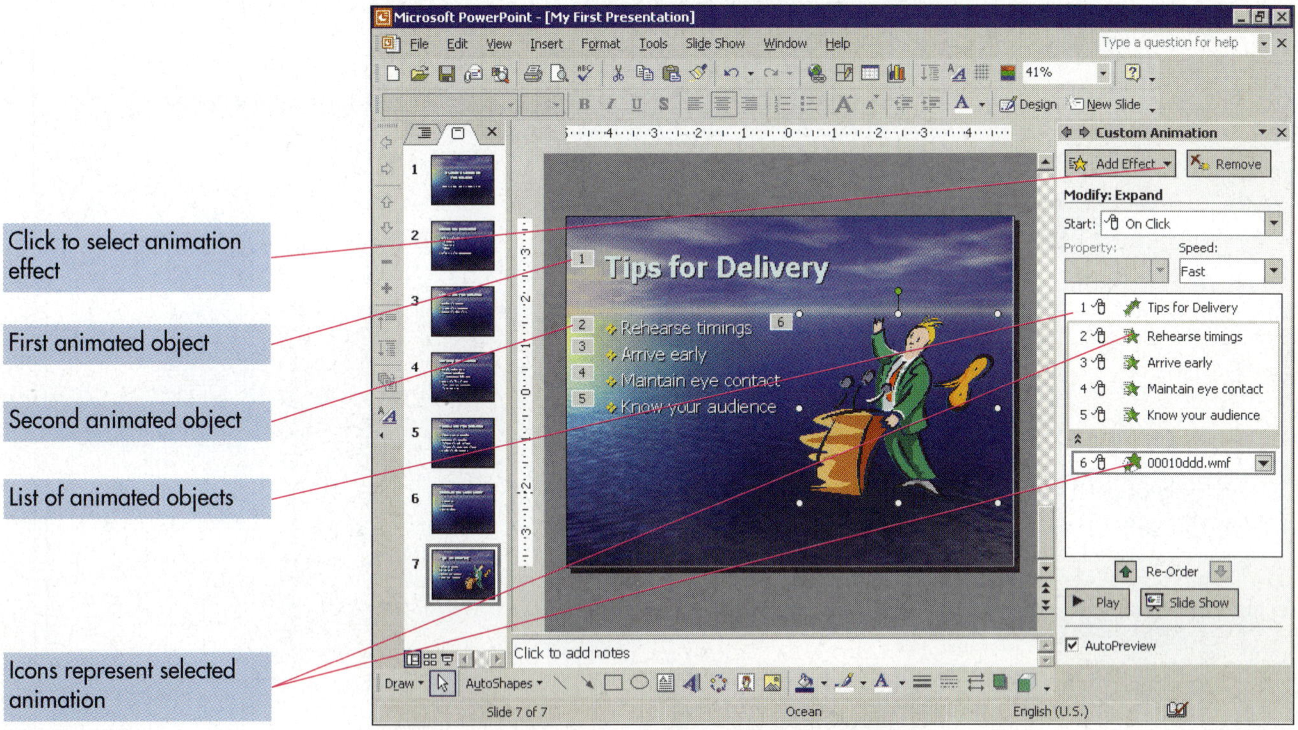

(b) Custom Animation

FIGURE 1.10 *Transition and Animation Effects*

HANDS-ON EXERCISE 3

ANIMATING THE PRESENTATION

Objective To change the layout of an existing slide; to establish transition and animation effects. Use Figure 1.11 as a guide in the exercise.

Step 1: **Change the Slide Layout**

- Start PowerPoint. There are two basic ways to open an existing presentation. You can use the Open command in the File menu, or you can open the presentation from the task pane.
- Pull down the **View menu** and click the **Task pane command** to display the task pane, then (if necessary) click the **down arrow** in the task pane to select **New from Existing Presentation**.
- You should see My First Presentation from the previous exercise since the most recently used presentations are listed automatically.
- Click **My First Presentation**. (Click the link to **More Presentations** if the presentation is not listed, to display the Open dialog box, where you can select the drive and folder to locate your presentation.)
- Click the **Outline tab**, then scroll in the left pane until you can select the **Tips for Delivery slide**.
- Click the **down arrow** on the task pane to select **Slide Layout** as shown in Figure 1.11a. Now scroll in the task pane until you can select the **Text & Clip Art layout** as shown in Figure 1.11a. Click the layout to apply it to the current slide.

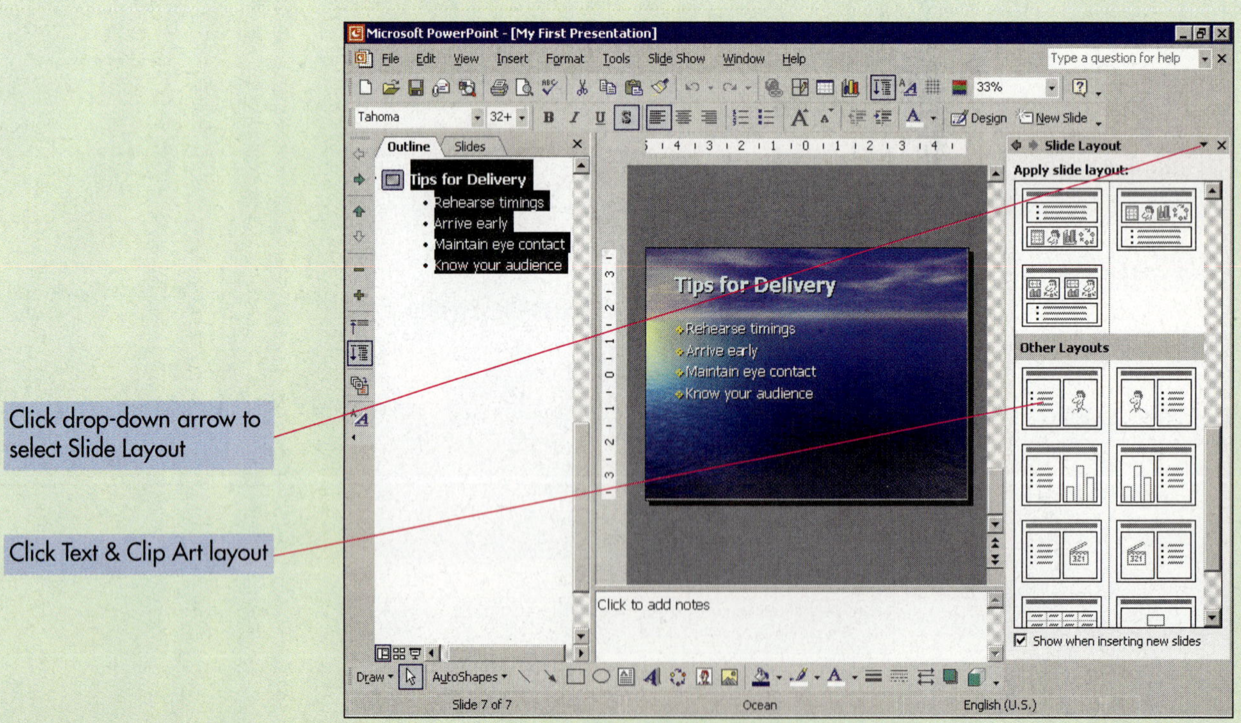

(a) Change the Slide Layout (step 1)

FIGURE 1.11 *Hands-on Exercise 3*

Step 2: **Add the Clip Art**

- Double click the **placeholder** on the slide to add the clip art. You will see the Select Picture dialog box as shown in Figure 1.11b, although the size, position, and content will be different on your screen.
- Click in the **Search** text box and enter the key word **education**, then click the **Search button** to look for clip art that is described by this term.
- Select (click) the clip art you want and click **OK**. The clip art should appear on the slide.
- The clip art is sized automatically to fit the existing placeholder. You can, however, move and size the clip art just like any other Windows object.
- Save the presentation.

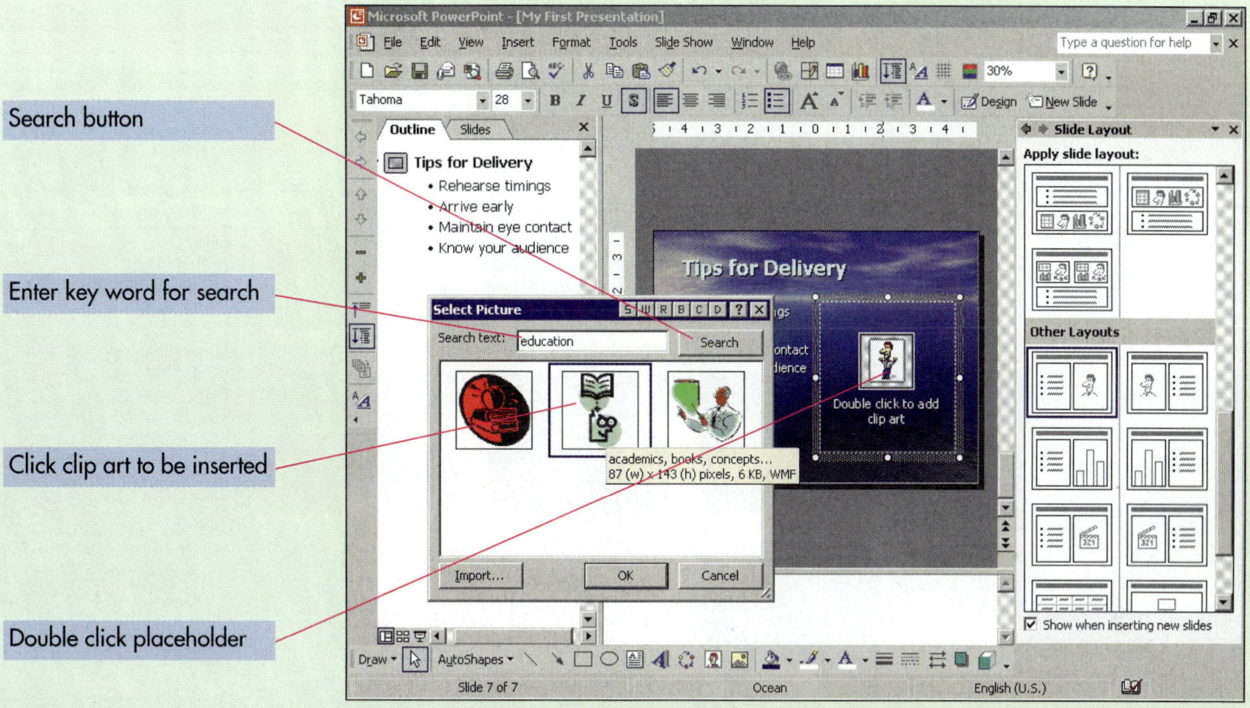

(b) Add the Clip Art (step 2)

FIGURE 1.11 *Hands-on Exercise 3 (continued)*

SEARCH BY COLLECTION

The Media Gallery organizes its contents by collections and provides another way to select clip art. Pull down the Insert menu, click (or point to) the Picture command, then click Clip Art to open the task pane, where you can enter a key word to search for clip art. Instead of searching, however, click the link to Media Gallery at the bottom of the task pane to display the Media Gallery dialog box. Close the My Collections folder if it is open, then open the Office Collections folder where you can explore the available images by collection.

Step 3: Add Transition Effects

- You can apply transitions in either the Normal view (with the thumbnail images) or in the Slide Sorter view. We chose the latter. Thus, click the **Slide Sorter View button** above the status bar to change to this view.
- Select (click) the first slide. Click the **Transition button** on the Slide Sorter toolbar to display the transition effects in the task pane.
- Click in the list box to select the **Blinds Vertical** transition effect (a preview plays automatically) as shown in Figure 1.11c. A transition icon appears under the slide after the effect has been applied. Change the speed to medium.
- Select (click) slide two and apply the **Checkerboard Across** transition effect to this slide. Change the speed to medium.
- Apply different transition effects to the other slides in the presentation. Save the presentation.

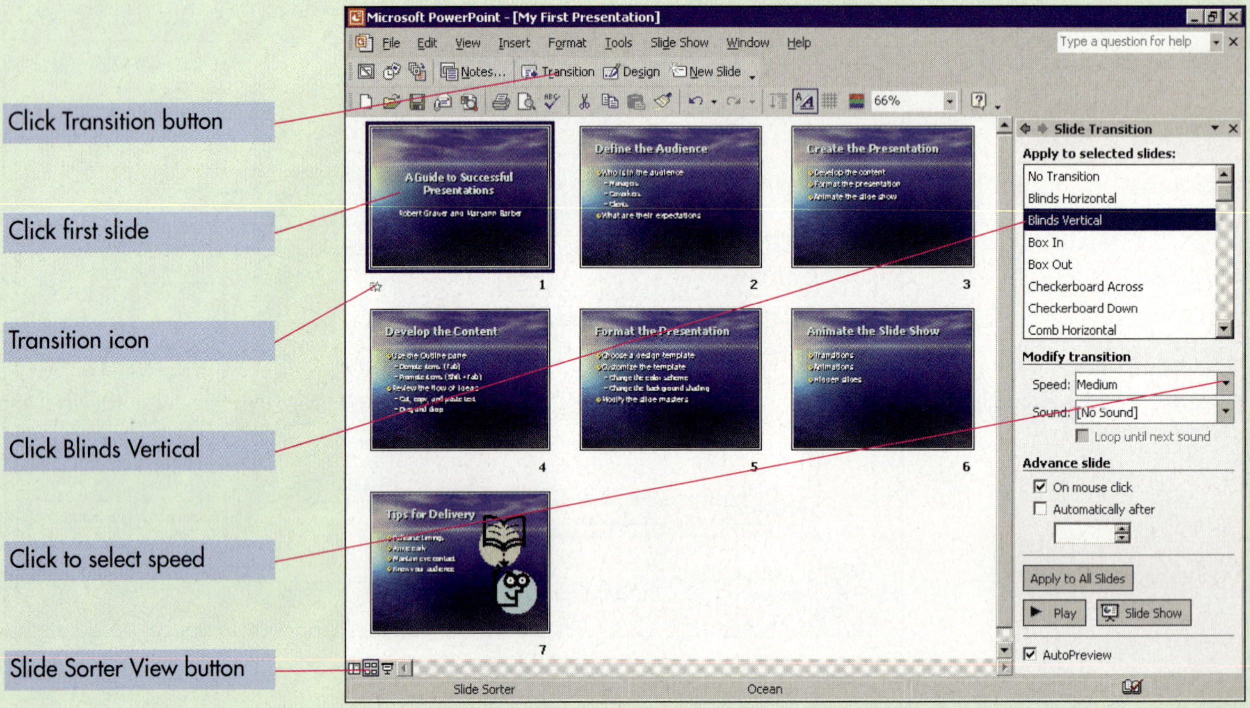

(c) Add Transition Effects (step 3)

FIGURE 1.11 *Hands-on Exercise 3 (continued)*

> **CHANGE THE MAGNIFICATION**
>
> Click the down arrow on the Zoom box to change the display magnification, which in turn controls the size of individual slides. The higher the magnification, the easier it is to read the text of an individual slide, but the fewer slides you see at one time. Conversely, changing to a smaller magnification decreases the size of the individual slides, but enables you to see more of the presentation.

Step 4: **Create a Summary Slide**

- Pull down the **Edit menu** and press **Select All** to select every slide in the presentation. (You can also press **Ctrl+A** or press and hold the **Shift key** as you click each slide in succession.)
- Click the **Summary Slide button** on the Slide Sorter toolbar to create a summary slide containing a bullet with the title of each selected slide. The new slide appears at the beginning of the presentation as shown in Figure 1.11d.
- Click and drag the **summary slide** to the end of the presentation. (As you drag the slide, the mouse pointer changes to include the outline of a miniature slide, and a vertical line appears to indicate the new position of the slide.)
- Release the mouse. The summary slide has been moved to the end of the presentation, and the slides are renumbered automatically.
- Save the presentation.

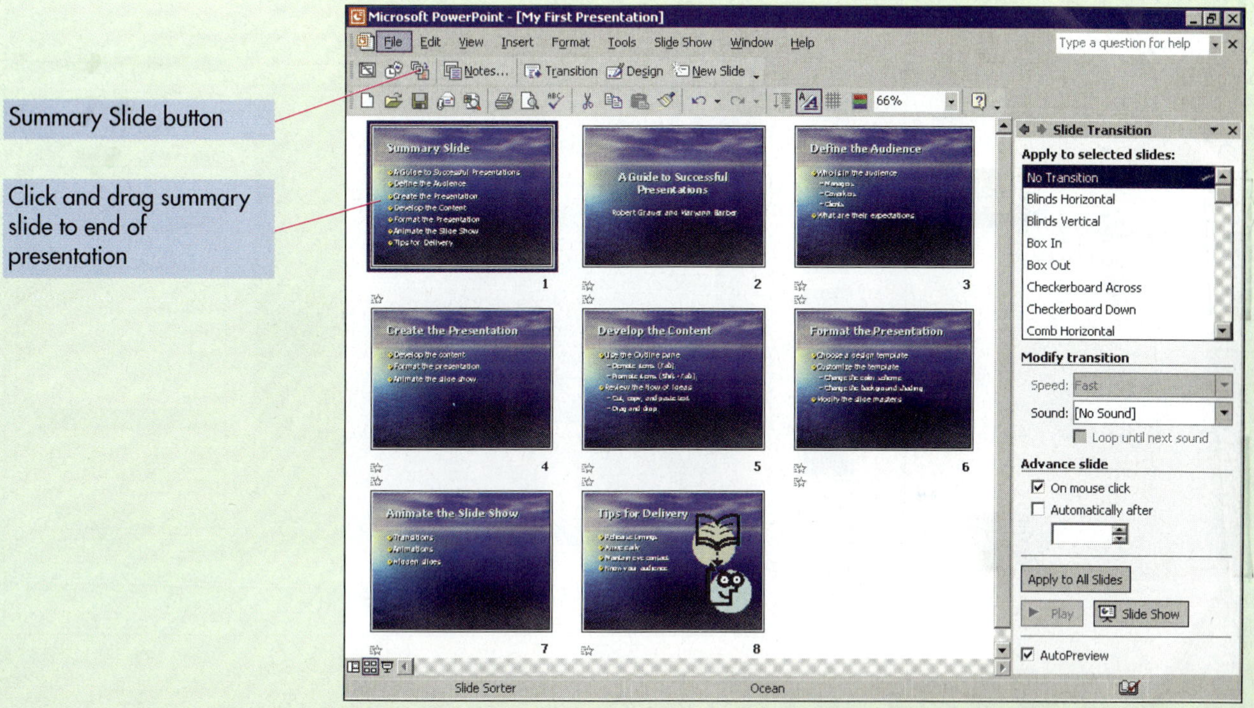

(d) Create a Summary Slide (step 4)

FIGURE 1.11 *Hands-on Exercise 3 (continued)*

SELECTING MULTIPLE SLIDES

You can apply the same transition or animation effect to multiple slides with a single command. Change to the Slide Sorter view, then select the slides by pressing and holding the Shift key as you click the slides. Use the task pane or the Slide Sorter toolbar to choose the desired transition when all the slides have been selected. Click anywhere in the Slide Sorter view to deselect the slides and continue working.

Step 5: **Create Animation Effects**

- Double click the **summary slide** to change to the Normal view. The task pane should still be open. Click the **down arrow** on the task pane to choose **Slide Design—Animation Schemes**.
- Scroll in the Open list box to the **Moderate category**, and choose **Spin** as shown in Figure 1.11e. You will automatically see a preview of the effect.
- Scroll in the Open list box to the Exciting category and choose a different effect. (We're not sure who rates the effects and why one is deemed to be exciting, while the other is only moderate.) Click the **Undo button** if you prefer the original scheme.
- Save the presentation.

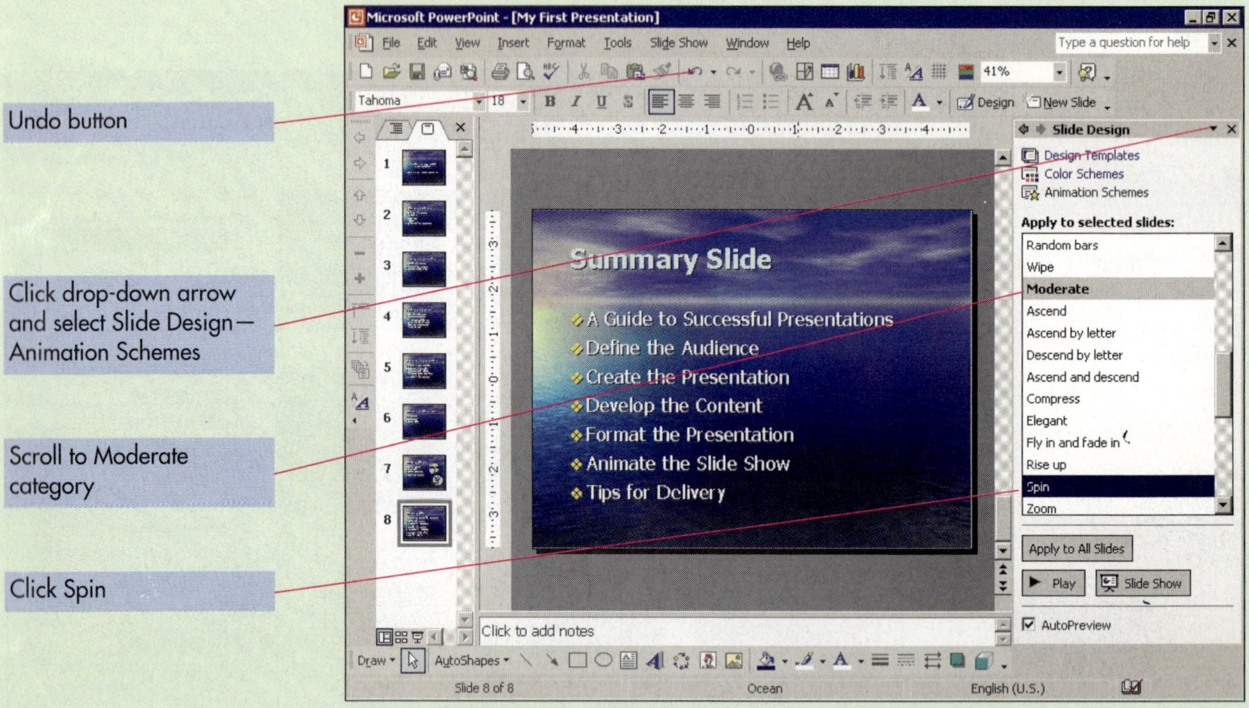

(e) Create Animation Effects (step 5)

FIGURE 1.11 *Hands-on Exercise 3 (continued)*

> **CUSTOMIZE THE ANIMATION**
>
> You can modify the effects of a predefined animation scheme for selected slides and/or objects on those slides. Click the down arrow in the task pane and choose Custom Animation. Select the slide, select the object on the slide that is to receive special treatment, click the Add Effect button to display a menu, and choose the effect, which will preview automatically. (Click the Remove button if you do not like the result.) Set a time limit because PowerPoint gives you virtually unlimited flexibility.

Step 6: **Show the Presentation**

- Press **Ctrl+Home** to return to the first slide, then click the **Slide Show button** above the status bar to view the presentation. You should see the opening slide in Figure 1.11f.
- Click the **left mouse button** to move to the next slide (or to the next bullet on the current slide when animation is in effect).
- Click the **right mouse button** to display the Shortcut menu and return to the previous slide (or to the previous bullet on the current slide when an animation is in effect).
- Continue to view the presentation until you come to the end. Click the **left mouse button** a final time to return to the regular PowerPoint window.
- Close the presentation. Exit PowerPoint if you do not want to continue with the next exercise at this time.

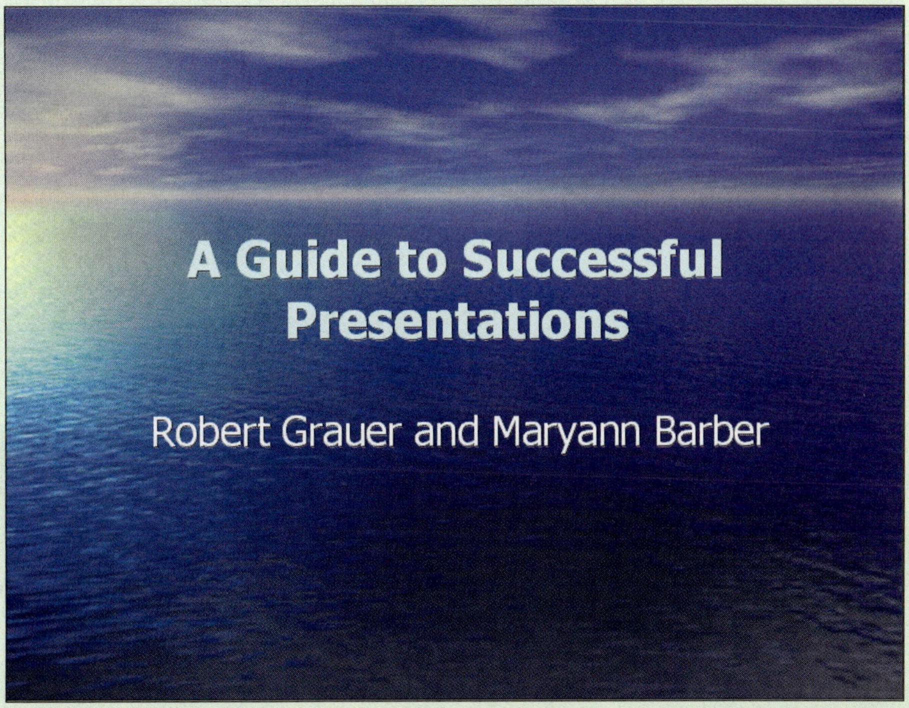

(f) Show the Presentation

FIGURE 1.11 *Hands-on Exercise 3 (continued)*

ANNOTATE A SLIDE

You can annotate a slide just like the sports announcers on television. Click the Slide Show button to begin your presentation, press Ctrl+P to change the mouse pointer to a pen, then click and drag to draw on the slide. The annotation is temporary and lasts only while the slide is on the screen. Use the PgDn and PgUp keys to move forward and back in the presentation when the drawing tool is in effect. Press Ctrl+A at any time to change the mouse pointer back to an arrow.

Thus far we have focused on presentations that consisted largely of text. PowerPoint also enables you to include a variety of visual elements that add impact to a presentation as can be seen in Figure 1.12. (This is the presentation that we will create in the next hands-on exercise.) You can add clip art, sound, or animated clips through the ***Microsoft Media Gallery***, and/or you can obtain the elements from other sources. You can use the supplement applications that are included with Microsoft Office to add organization charts and WordArt. You can also insert objects that were created in other applications, such as a chart from Microsoft Excel or a table from Microsoft Word.

A chart or table is inserted into a presentation through linking or embedding. The essential difference between the two techniques is that embedding places the object into the presentation, whereas linking does not. In other words, an ***embedded object*** is stored within the presentation. A ***linked object***, on the other hand, is stored in its own file, and the presentation is one of many potential documents that are linked to that object. The advantage of linking over embedding is that the presentation is updated automatically if the original object is changed.

Linking is also preferable if the same object is referenced in many documents, so that any change to the object has to be made in only one place (the source document). An Excel chart, for example, may be linked to a Word document and a PowerPoint presentation. You can subsequently change the chart, and both the document and presentation are updated automatically.

You can also add ***comments*** to any presentation to explain your thoughts to colleagues who may review the presentation prior to delivery. The comments appear on a slide during editing, but not during delivery as you will see in the hands-on exercise that follows shortly.

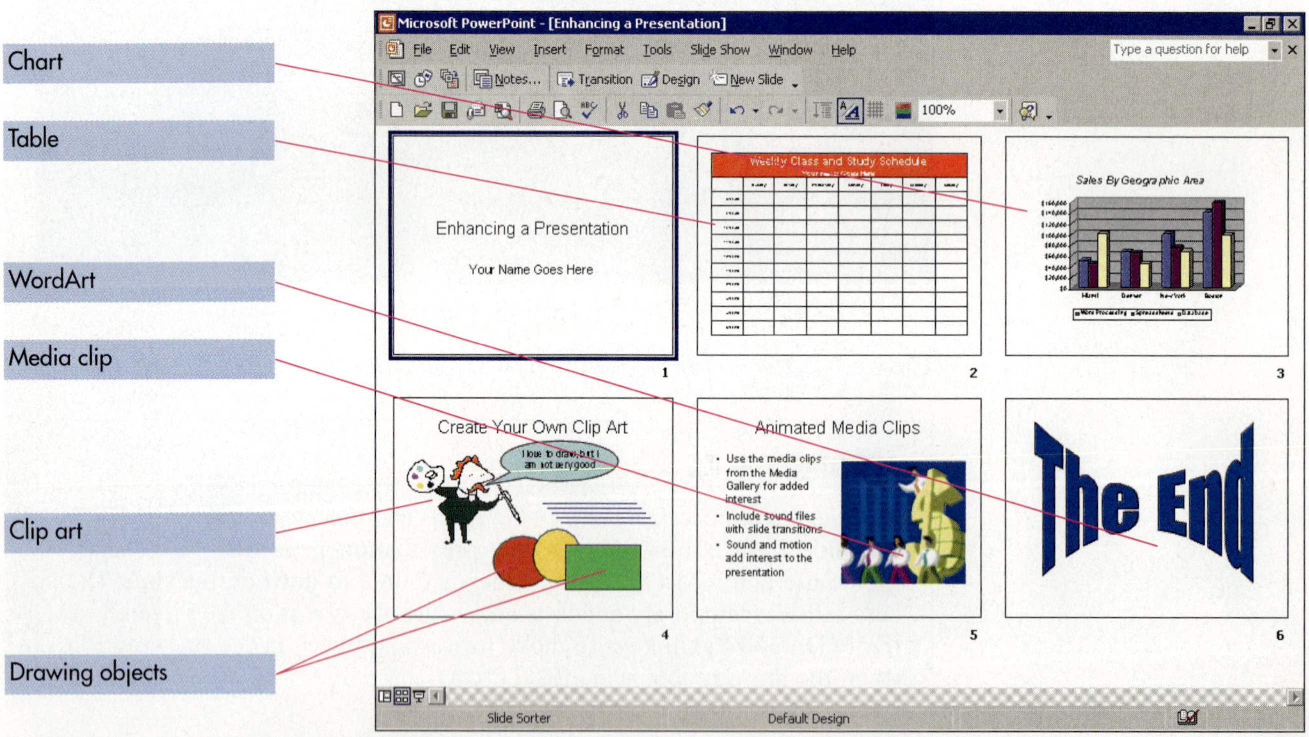

FIGURE 1.12 *Enhancing a Presentation*

Office Art

Everyone likes ***clip art***, but relatively few individuals think in terms of enhancing it. It takes a lot of talent to create original clip art, but it takes only a little imagination to create a drawing from existing clip art as shown in Figure 1.13. There is no way that we could have drawn the artist, but it was very easy to copy the artist and create the slide, given the original clip art.

Any piece of clip art is an object that can be copied, moved, and sized like any other Windows object. Thus, we clicked on the original clip art (the artist in the upper left of the slide) to display the sizing handles, clicked the copy and paste buttons to duplicate the object, then moved and sized the copied image to the bottom of the slide. We then copied the smaller artist across the bottom of the slide.

Next we used various tools on the Drawing toolbar to complete the slide. Select the Line tool, for example, then click and drag to create a line. Once the line has been created, you can select it and change its properties (such as thickness, style, or color) by using other tools on the Drawing toolbar. The oval and rectangle tools work the same way. The AutoShapes button on the Drawing toolbar provides access to the balloon and other callouts in which you enter the text.

There are other techniques you can use as well. You can, for example, select multiple objects simultaneously and group them together in order to move and/or size those objects with a single mouse click. Press and hold the Shift key to select multiple objects (e.g., the large artist, the balloon, and the three circles), click the Draw button, then click the Group command. The five objects have been combined into one larger object with a single set of sizing handles.

All it takes is a little imagination and a sense of what you can do. Use different clip art images on the same slide and you get something entirely different. It is fun and it is easy. Just be flexible and willing to experiment. We think you will be pleased with the results.

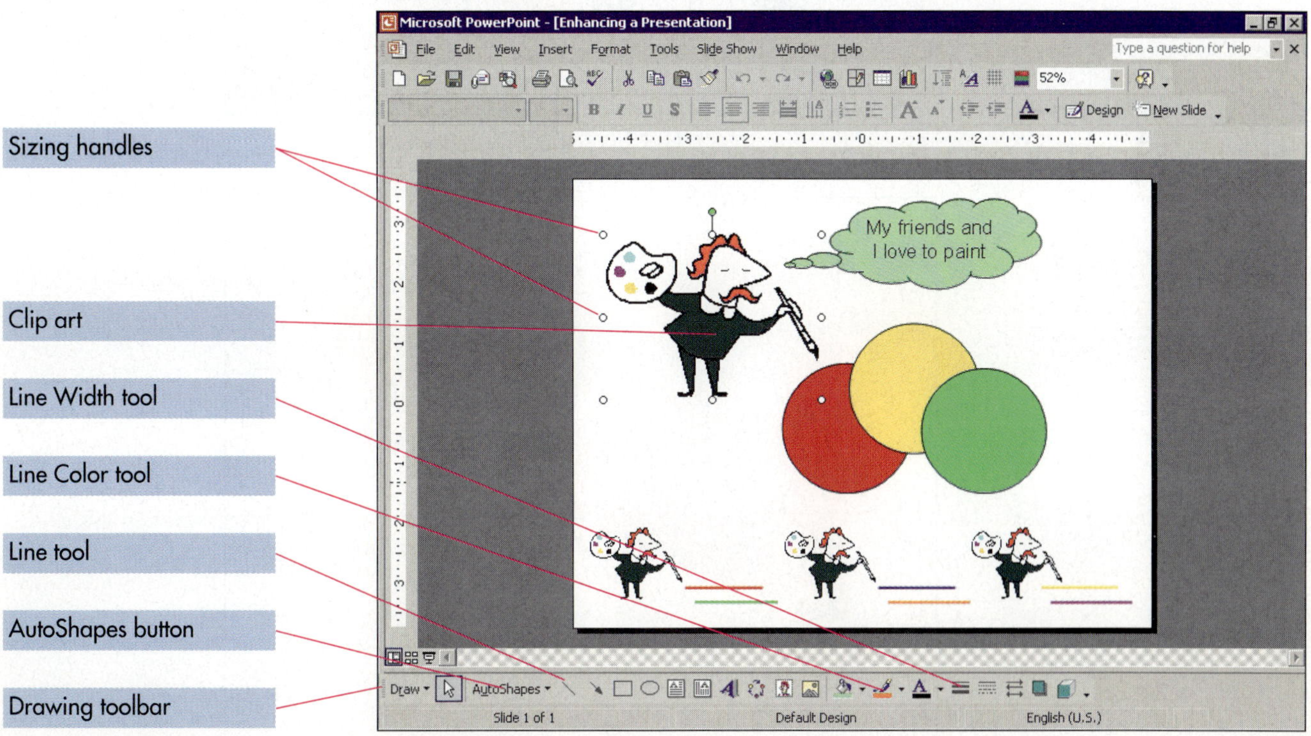

FIGURE 1.13 *Office Art*

Microsoft WordArt

Microsoft WordArt is an application within Microsoft Office that creates decorative text that can be used to add interest to a document. You can use WordArt in addition to clip art within a document, or in place of clip art if the right image is not available. You can rotate text in any direction, add three-dimensional effects, display the text vertically down the page, slant it, arch it, or even print it upside down. In short, you are limited only by your imagination.

WordArt is intuitive and easy to use. In essence, you choose a style for the text from among the selections in Figure 1.14a. Then you enter the specific text in a subsequent dialog box, after which the result is displayed in Figure 1.14b. The finished WordArt is an object that can be moved and sized within a presentation.

(a) Choose the Style

(b) Completed Entry

FIGURE 1.14 *Microsoft WordArt*

HANDS-ON EXERCISE 4

ENHANCING A PRESENTATION

Objective To include a Word table and Excel chart in a presentation; to modify existing clip art and create a WordArt object. Use Figure 1.15 as a guide.

Step 1: **Insert a Comment**

- Start PowerPoint. Click the **New button** on the Standard toolbar to begin a new presentation. Close the task pane. Enter the title of the presentation and your name on the title slide. Save the presentation as **Enhancing a Presentation** in the **Exploring PowerPoint folder**.
- Click the **Normal View button** above the status bar if you are not in the Normal view. Click the **Slides tab** to display the slides in the left pane.
- Pull down the **Insert menu** and click the **Comment command** to insert a comment onto the slide as shown in Figure 1.15a.
- You will see an empty balloon that contains the name of the person who has registered this copy of Office, together with today's date. Enter any text at all as a comment.
- Click anywhere outside the comment. The balloon closes, and you see a comment marker. Click the marker, and the comment reappears.
- The Reviewing toolbar appears automatically whenever you are working with comments. The Comments and Changes buttons at the extreme left of the toolbar toggles the comment markers on and off.
- Click the **New Slide button** on the Formatting toolbar. (This will open the task pane if it is not already open.) Click the **down arrow** in the task pane until you can select a **blank layout**.

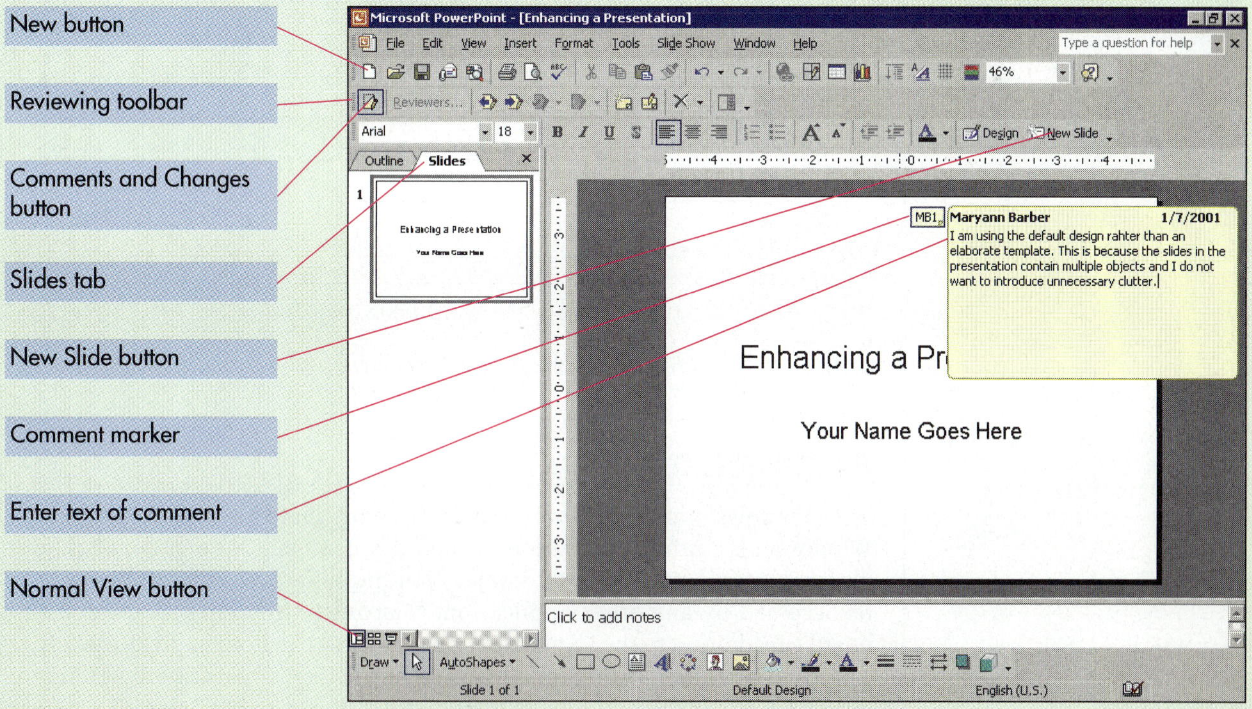

(a) Insert a Comment (step 1)

FIGURE 1.15 *Hands-on Exercise 4*

Step 2: **Copy the Word Table**

- Start Word. Open the **My Study Schedule** Word document in the **Exploring PowerPoint folder** as shown in Figure 1.15b. The document consists entirely of a Word table.
- Click and drag to select the text **Your Name Goes Here** that appears at the top of the table. Type your first and last name, which automatically replaces the selected text.
- You can click in any cell and enter an activity. The text will automatically flow from one line to the next within the cell. Limit the entry to two lines, however, or else the table may not fit on one page (or one slide). Save the document.
- Click the tiny square at the upper left of the table to select the entire table. Be sure that every cell is highlighted, or else the table will not be copied successfully. Click the **Copy button** to copy the table to the clipboard.
- Exit Word. The copied text remains in the clipboard even though Microsoft Word is no longer open.

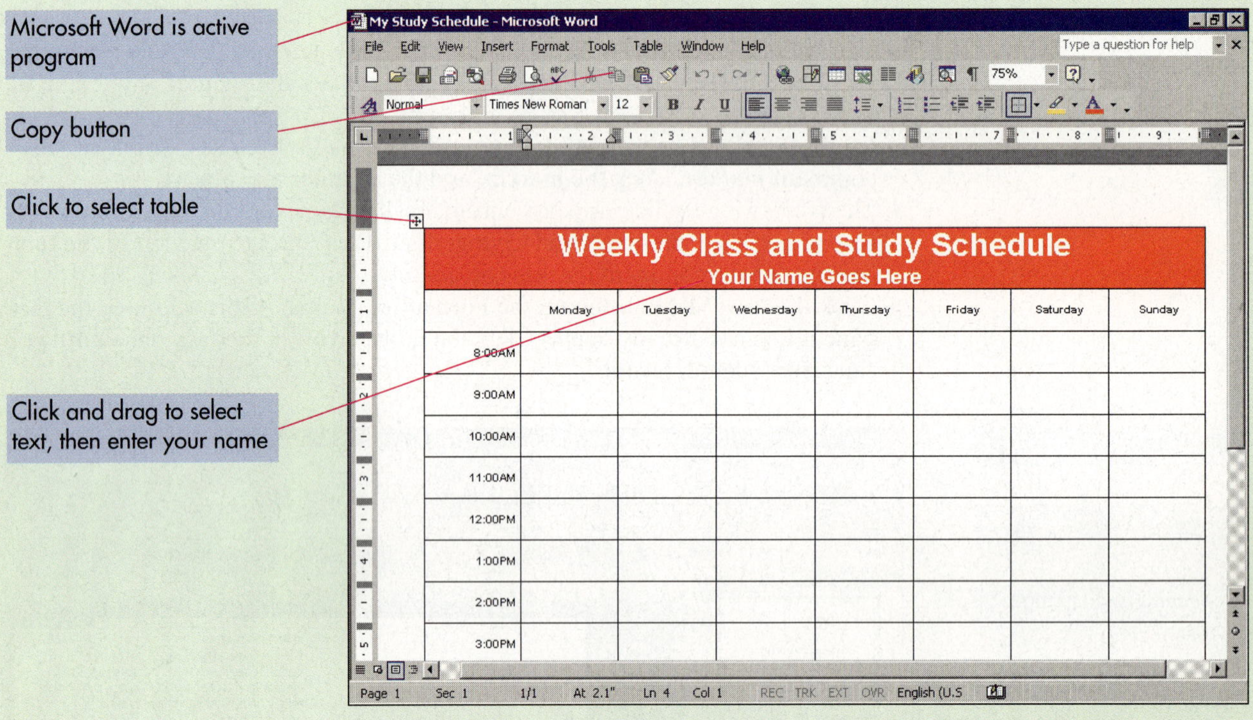

(b) Copy the Word Table (step 2)

FIGURE 1.15 *Hands-on Exercise 4 (continued)*

THE WINDOWS CLIPBOARD

The Windows clipboard is an area of memory that is available to every Windows application. Execution of the copy command in one application places the copied text (or other object) on the clipboard from where it can be accessed by any other application. Microsoft Office has its own clipboard (in addition to the Windows clipboard) that can hold up to 24 objects. You can open the Office clipboard from any Office application by pulling down the Edit menu and selecting the Office Clipboard command.

Step 3: **Insert the Table**

- You should be back in PowerPoint as shown in Figure 1.15c. (If not, click the **PowerPoint button** on the Windows taskbar.)
- Click anywhere on the second slide to select this slide. Click the **Paste button** on the Standard toolbar to paste (embed) the Word table onto this slide.
- Do not be concerned if the table is slightly larger than the slide. Click anywhere in the table to select the table and display the sizing handles.
- Click and drag a corner handle to proportionately shrink the table so that it fits on the slide. Click and drag any hashed border to center the table on the slide.
- Pull down the **Insert menu** and click the **Comment command**. Enter the text of the comment shown in the figure, which indicates that the table has been embedded (rather than linked) into the presentation. Click anywhere outside the comment after you have finished.
- Click the **Previous Item button** on the Reviewing toolbar to move to the previous comment. Click the **Next Item button** to return to this comment.
- Save the presentation.

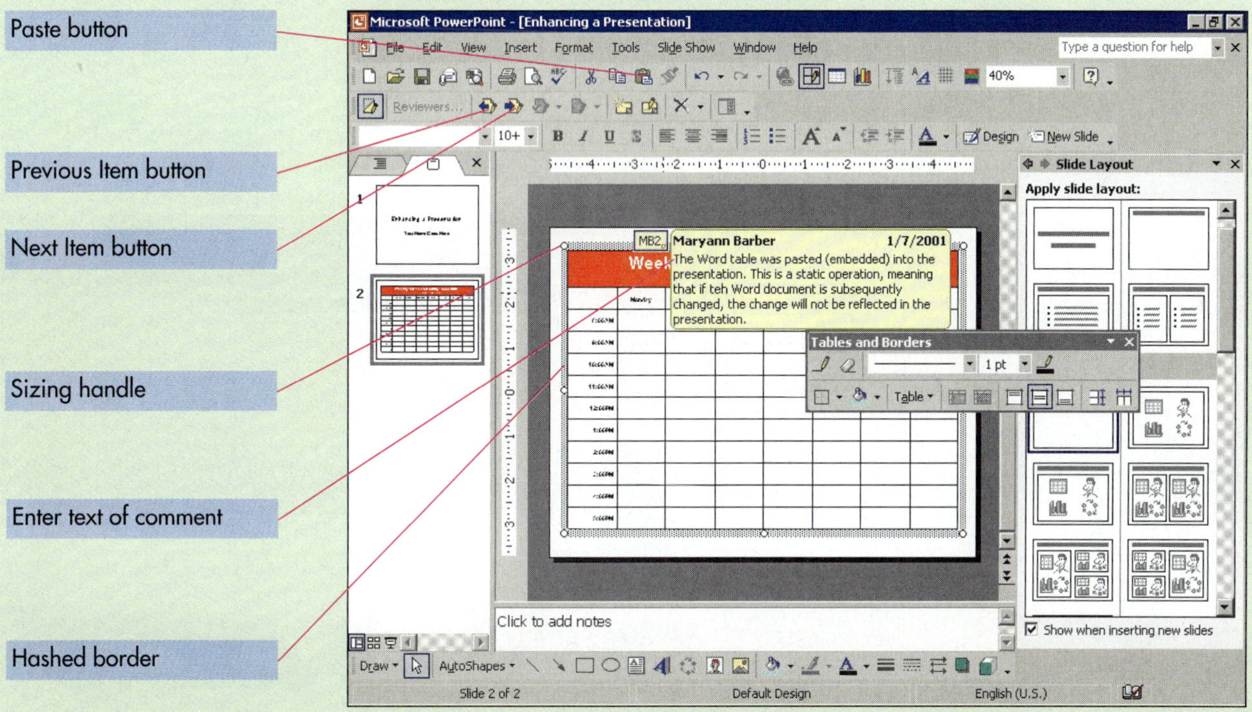

(c) Insert the Table (step 3)

FIGURE 1.15 *Hands-on Exercise 4 (continued)*

SEND SLIDES TO A WORD DOCUMENT

You can embed and/or link Word documents and PowerPoint presentations in either direction; that is, you can insert a Word document into a PowerPoint presentation as was done here, and/or you can send PowerPoint slides to a Word document. Pull down the File menu and click the Send To command, then choose Microsoft Word to display the associated dialog box. You will be given the choice of how to arrange the PowerPoint slides in the resulting Word document. See exercise 10 at the end of the chapter.

Step 4: **Insert the Excel Chart**

- Start Excel. Open the **Software Sales** workbook in the **Exploring PowerPoint folder**. The workbook consists of a single sheet that contains data and a chart.
- Click anywhere in the chart background to select the entire chart. You should see sizing handles around the white border of the chart. Click the **Copy button** on the Standard toolbar to copy the chart to the clipboard. Do not close the workbook as we will return to it momentarily.
- Click the **PowerPoint button** on the Windows taskbar to return to the PowerPoint presentation. Click the **New slide button** and use the Slide Layout task pane to insert a blank slide into the presentation. Close the task pane.
- Pull down the **Edit menu** and click the **Paste Special command** to display the Paste Special dialog box in Figure 1.15d. Click the **Paste Link Option button**. Click **OK** to insert the chart onto the slide. Do not be concerned about the size or position of the chart at this time.
- Save the presentation.

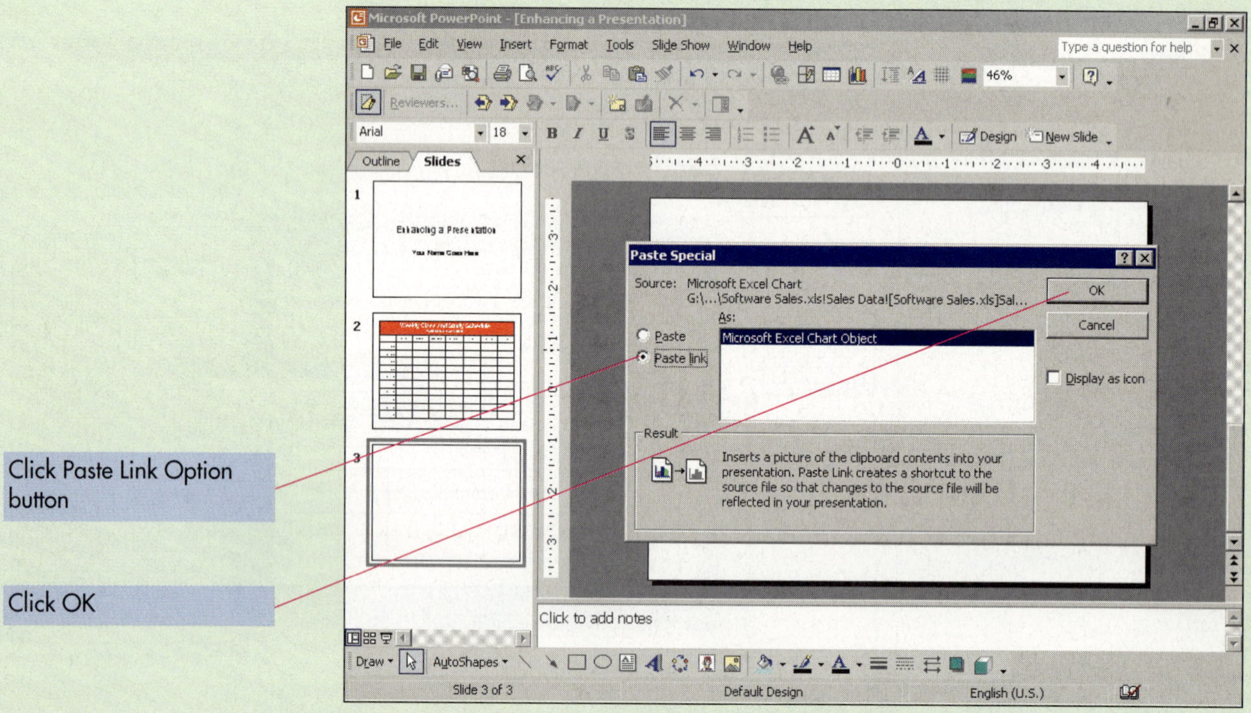

(d) Insert the Excel Chart (step 4)

FIGURE 1.15 *Hands-on Exercise 4 (continued)*

LINKING VERSUS EMBEDDING

Linking is very different from embedding as it provides a dynamic connection to the source document. A linked object, such as an Excel chart, is tied to its source, so that any changes to the source file are reflected in the PowerPoint presentation. Linking is especially useful when the same object is inserted into multiple documents, as changes to the object are made in only one place (in the source file). A linked object must always be saved in its file.

Step 5: **Update the Chart**

- You should see the chart as shown in Figure 1.15e. The sizing handles indicate that the chart is currently selected and can be moved and sized like any other Windows object.
- Click and drag a corner handle (the pointer changes to a two-headed arrow) to proportionally increase (decrease) the size of the chart. Point to any border (the pointer changes to a four-headed arrow) to move the chart on the slide.
- Note that the database sales for Miami are very low ($12,000). Double click the chart to return to Excel (or click the **Excel button** on the Windows taskbar). Click in cell **B4** and change the database sales for Miami to **$100,000**. Save the workbook. Exit Excel.
- Return to PowerPoint. The chart may automatically reflect the change in database sales. If not, right click the chart and select the **Update Link command**.
- Pull down the **Insert menu** and click the **Comment command** to insert an appropriate comment indicating that the chart in the presentation is linked to an Excel workbook. Save the presentation.

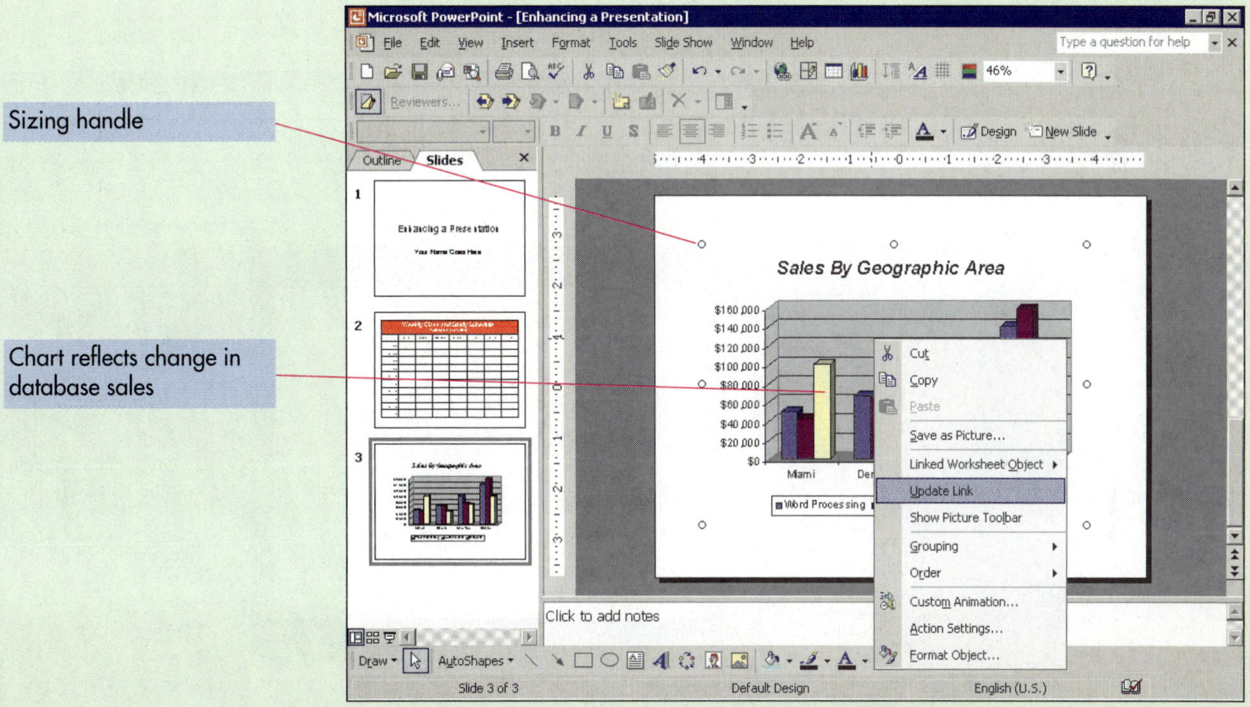

(e) Update the Chart (step 5)

FIGURE 1.15 *Hands-on Exercise 4 (continued)*

> **MULTITASKING**
>
> Multitasking, the ability to run multiple applications at the same time, is one of the primary advantages of the Windows environment. Switching from one application to another is easy—just click the appropriate button on the Windows taskbar. You can also use the classic Alt+Tab shortcut. Press and hold the Alt key as you click the Tab key repeatedly to display and select icons for the open applications, then release the Tab key when the desired application icon is selected.

Step 6: **Insert the Clip Art**

- ➤ Click the **New Slide button** and select the **Title Only** layout. Click in the title placeholder and type **Create Your Own Clip Art**.
- ➤ Pull down the **Insert menu**, click **Picture**, and then click **Clip Art** (or click the **Insert Clip Art button** on the Drawing toolbar). The contents of the task pane change automatically.
- ➤ Type **Artist** in the Search text box. Be sure the list boxes show you are searching all collections and are looking for all media types. Click the **Search button** to initiate the search.
- ➤ The system pauses, then starts to return all objects in the Media Gallery that satisfy the search criteria. The objects are stored on a Web server and hence you need an Internet connection in order to retrieve all of the objects.
- ➤ Click the **down arrow** in the task pane to scroll through the images until you find the one that you want. Point to the right side of the image, then click the **down arrow** that appears to display a menu. Click **Insert**.
- ➤ Choose an appropriate clip art image. Click **Insert**, then move and size the clip art so that it is positioned as shown in Figure 1.15f. Close the task pane. Save the presentation.

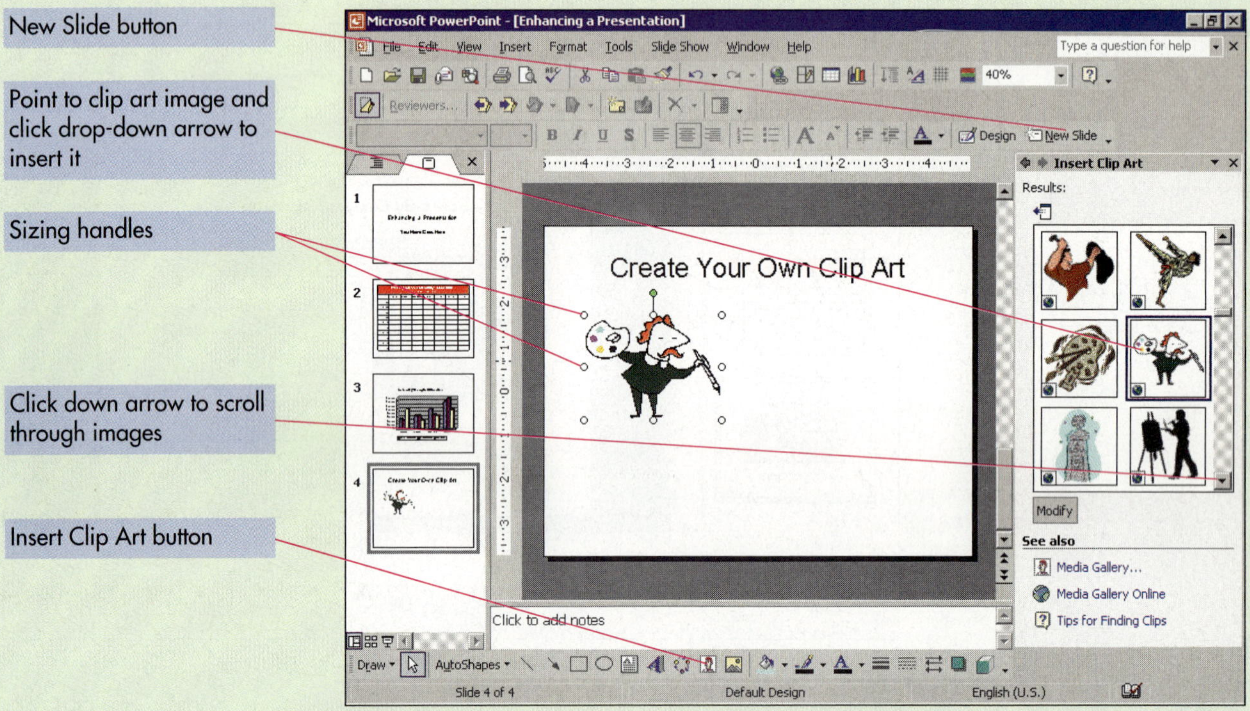

(f) Insert the Clip Art (step 6)

FIGURE 1.15 *Hands-on Exercise 4 (continued)*

> **THE SHIFT KEY**
>
> The Shift key has special significance when used in conjunction with the Line, Rectangle, and Oval tools. Press and hold the Shift key as you drag the line tool horizontally or vertically to create a perfectly straight line in either direction. Press and hold the Shift key as you drag the Rectangle and Oval tool to create a square or circle, respectively.

Step 7: Use the Drawing Toolbar

- Click the **AutoShapes button** on the Drawing toolbar, click **Callouts**, then click the desired balloon. The mouse pointer changes to a tiny crosshair.
- Click and drag on the slide where you want the balloon to go. Release the mouse. The balloon is selected automatically, and the sizing handles are displayed. If necessary, click and drag the balloon to adjust its size or position.
- Type the phrase shown in the figure. You can select the text, then change its font, size, or alignment. Click elsewhere on the slide to deselect the balloon.
- Click the **Line tool** on the Drawing toolbar, then click and drag to draw a line on the slide. To change the color or thickness, select the line (the sizing handles appear), click the appropriate tool on the Drawing toolbar, then select a new color or thickness.
- Select the completed line, click the **Copy button**, then click the **Paste button** several times to copy the line. Use the **Oval** or **Rectangle tools** to draw additional shapes, then use the **Fill Color tool** to change their color.
- Move and size the objects as necessary. Save the presentation.

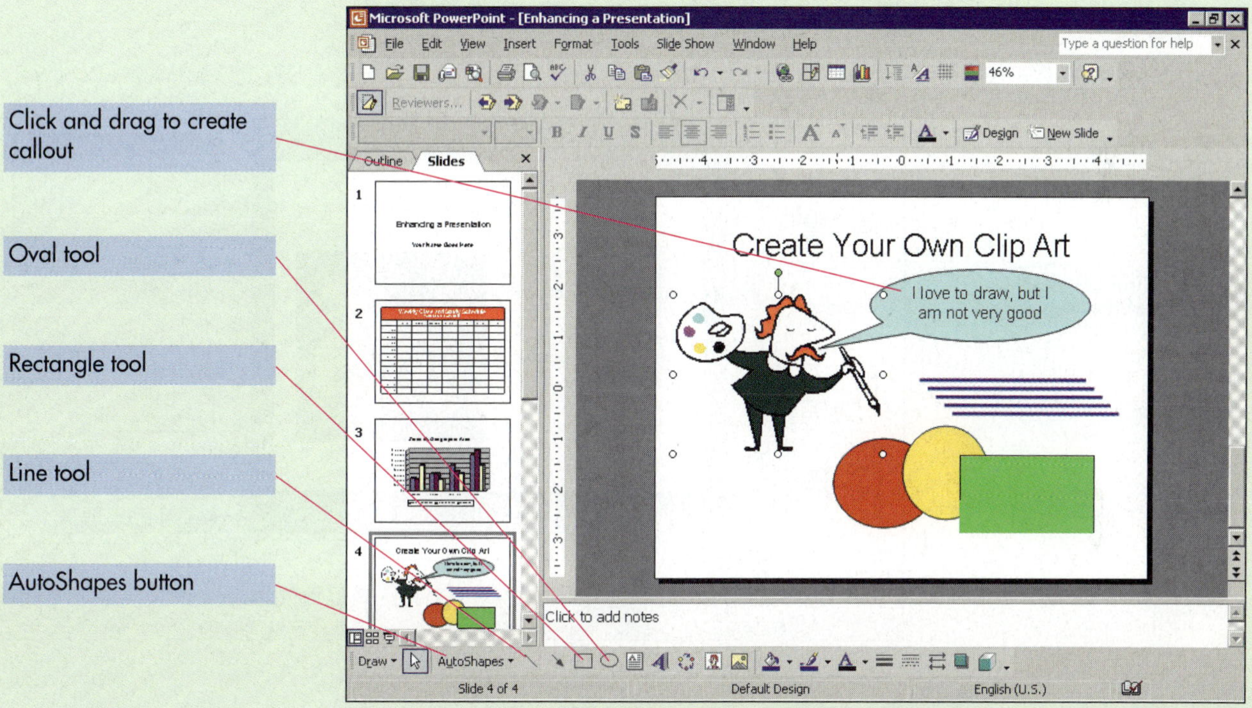

(g) Use the Drawing Toolbar (step 7)

FIGURE 1.15 *Hands-on Exercise 4 (continued)*

AUTOSHAPES

An AutoShape is a predefined shape that is drawn automatically when you select its icon from the AutoShapes toolbar, then click and drag in the slide. (To display the AutoShapes toolbar, click the AutoShape button on the Drawing toolbar.) To place text inside an AutoShape, select the shape and start typing. You can also change the fill color or line thickness by selecting the shape, then clicking the appropriate button on the Drawing toolbar. See exercise 9 at the end of the chapter.

Step 8: Add a Media Clip

- Click the **New Slide button** and select the **Test & Media Clip** layout. Enter **Animated Media Clips** as the title of the slide. Enter the bulleted text as shown in Figure 1.15h.
- Double click the Media placeholder to add the media clip, which in turn displays the Media Clip dialog box. Select the clip that appears in Figure 1.15h and click the **OK button** to insert the clip onto the slide.
- Pull down the **Slide Show menu** and click **Slide Transition** to display these options in the task pane. Click the **down arrow** in the Sound list box and select **Cash Register**.
- Click the **Play button** to preview the effect. You should see the man passing an object to the sound of a cash register. (You need a sound card and speakers to hear the sound.)
- Save the presentation.

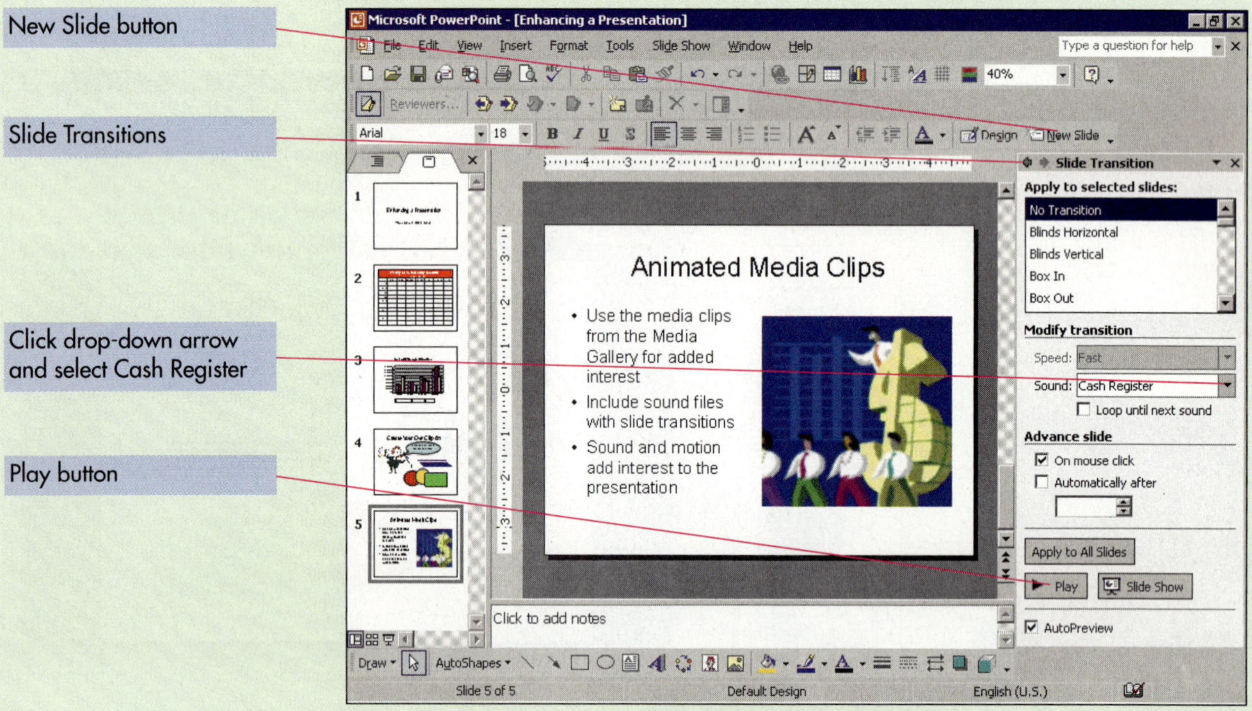

(h) Add a Media Clip (step 8)

FIGURE 1.15 *Hands-on Exercise 4 (continued)*

INSERT SLIDES FROM OTHER PRESENTATIONS

You work hard to develop individual slides and thus you may find it useful to reuse a slide from one presentation to the next. Pull down the Insert menu, click the Slides from Files command to display the Slide Finder dialog box, and click the Browse button to locate the presentation that contains the slides you want. Press and hold the Shift key to select multiple slides from this presentation, then click the Insert button to bring the selected slides into the current presentation.

Step 9: **Add the WordArt**

- We're ready to add the sixth and final slide. Click the **New Slide button** and add another blank slide. Close the task pane.
- Click the **Insert WordArt button** on the Drawing toolbar to display the WordArt Gallery dialog box as shown in Figure 1.15i. Choose any style you like (we took the fourth style from the left in the first row). Click **OK.**
- You should see the Edit WordArt text box. Enter **The End** as the text for your WordArt object. Click **OK** to close the Edit WordArt text box and insert the WordArt into your presentation.
- Move and size the WordArt object just as you would any other Windows object. Click and drag a corner sizing handle to increase the size of the WordArt until it takes the entire slide.
- Point to the middle of the WordArt object (the mouse pointer changes to a four-headed arrow), then click and drag to position the WordArt in the middle of the slide.
- Save the presentation.

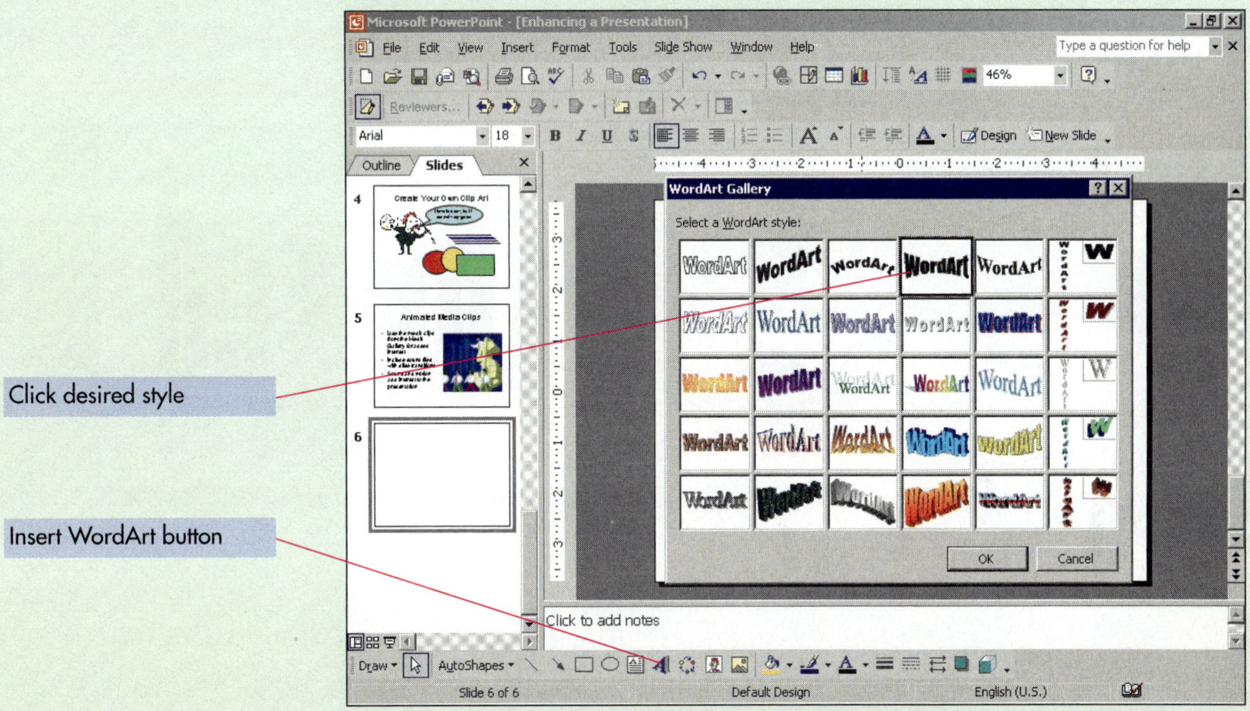

(i) Add the WordArt (step 9)

FIGURE 1.15 *Hands-on Exercise 4 (continued)*

THE WORDART TOOLBAR

The WordArt toolbar is the easiest way to change an existing WordArt object. It is displayed automatically when a WordArt object is selected and is suppressed otherwise. As with any other toolbar, you can point to a button to display a ScreenTip containing the name of the button, which is indicative of its function. You will find buttons to display the text vertically, change the style or shape, and/or edit the text.

Step 10: **Complete the WordArt**

- You should see the WordArt as shown in Figure 1.15j. You can click and drag the yellow diamond to change the slope of the text and/or you can click and drag the green circle to rotate the text.
- Click the **down arrow** for the **Fill Color tool** on the Drawing toolbar to display the available fill colors. Select (click) **blue** to change the color of the WordArt object. Experiment with other tools on the Drawing and/or WordArt toolbars to enhance the WordArt image.
- Pull down the **Slide Show menu** and click **Slide Transition** to display these options in the task pane. Click the **down arrow** in the Sound list box and select **Applause**. Click the **Play button** to preview the effect. (You will need a sound card and speakers to hear the sound.)
- Close the task pane. Save the presentation.

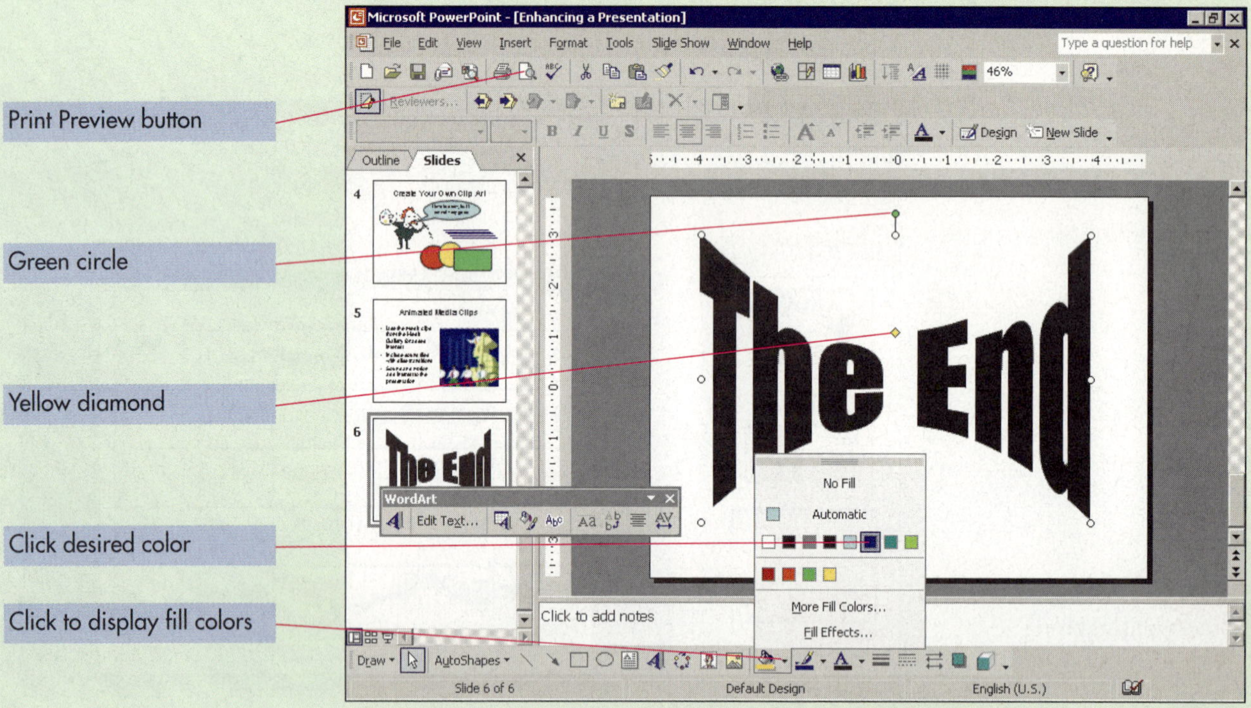

(j) Complete the WordArt (step 10)

FIGURE 1.15 *Hands-on Exercise 4 (continued)*

THE THIRD DIMENSION

You can make your WordArt images even more dramatic by adding 3-D effects. You can tilt the text up or down, right or left, increase or decrease the depth, and change the shading. Pull down the View menu, click Toolbars, click Customize to display the complete list of available toolbars, then check the box to display the 3-D Settings toolbar. Select the WordArt object, then experiment with various tools and special effects. The results are even better if you have a color printer.

Step 11: Print the Comments Pages

- Click the **Print Preview button** to preview the presentation. Click the **down arrow** on the Print What list box to select **Handouts (6 per page)**.
- Click the **down arrow** on the Options list box and toggle **Include Comments Pages** on, as shown in Figure 1.15k.
- The status bar indicates that you are on the first of two pages. Page 1 contains the six handouts. Page 2 contains the comments you entered earlier. Press the **PgDn key** to move to the second page, then scroll to the top of the page to see the comments.
- Click the **Print button** to display the Print dialog box, which contains the same information as the Print Preview screen; that is, you are printing audience handouts and will include comments. Click **OK** to print the presentation. Close the Print Preview window.
- Press **Ctrl+Home** to move to the first slide in the presentation, then click the **Slide Show button** to view the presentation.
- Save the presentation a final time. Exit PowerPoint. Well done!

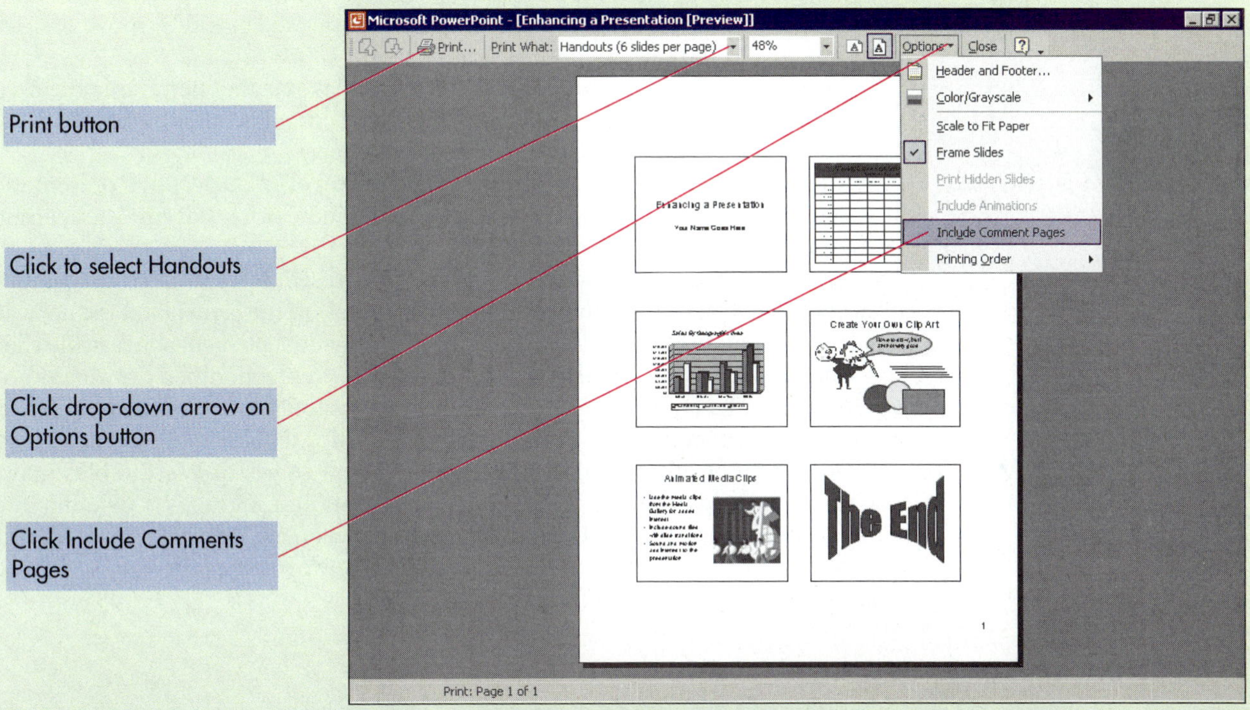

(k) Print the Comments Pages (step 11)

FIGURE 1.15 *Hands-on Exercise 4 (continued)*

UPDATING LINKS

The next time you open this presentation you will see a message indicating that links are present and further, that the links can be updated. You should respond by clicking the Update Links command button, which in turn will bring in the most current version of the chart to the presentation. This assumes that the Excel workbook is still in the same folder where it was created initially. If there is a problem, perhaps because the workbook has been moved or renamed, pull down the Edit menu and click the Links command to modify the link.

SUMMARY

Microsoft PowerPoint enables you to focus on the content of a presentation without worrying about its appearance. You supply the text and supporting elements and leave the formatting to PowerPoint. The resulting presentation consists of a series of slides with a consistent design and color scheme. The presentation can be delivered in a variety of ways, such as a computer slide show, via the Web, or using overhead transparencies. It can also be printed in a variety of formats.

PowerPoint has different views, each with unique capabilities. The Normal view displays the Slide, Outline or Thumbnail images, and Notes Page views in a single window. The Slide Sorter view displays multiple slides on one screen (each slide is in miniature) and lets you see the overall flow of the presentation. The Notes Page view is best suited to printing audience handouts that display the slide and the associated speaker notes. The Slide Show view displays one slide at a time with transition and animation effects.

The outline is the easiest way to enter the text of a presentation. Text is entered continually in the outline, then promoted or demoted so that it appears on the proper level in the slide. The outline can be collapsed to show multiple slides on one screen, thus enabling you to change the order of the slides and/or move text from one slide to another.

PowerPoint provides a set of predefined slide layouts that determine the nature and position of the objects on a slide. Each layout contains one or more placeholders to determine the position of the associated object.

A template is a design specification that controls every aspect of a presentation. It specifies the formatting of the text, the fonts and colors that are used, and the design, size, and placement of the bullets.

Transitions and animations can be added to a presentation for additional interest. Transitions control the way in which one slide moves off the screen and the next slide appears. Animations control the appearance of individual elements on a single slide.

Clip art may be copied, moved, and/or sized to create modified drawings known as Office Art. The Drawing toolbar contains various tools to further enhance the clip art. WordArt is an application within Microsoft Office that creates decorative text.

Objects from other applications such as Excel charts or Word tables may be linked or embedded into a PowerPoint presentation. Linking is a dynamic technique, which means that if the underlying object changes, that change is automatically reflected in the presentation. Embedding, however, is static, and subsequent changes are not reflected in the presentation.

KEY TERMS

Animation (p. 30)
Clip art (p. 33)
Close command (p. 7)
Comments (p. 38)
Drawing toolbar (p. 4)
Embedded object (p. 38)
Exit command (p. 7)
File menu (p. 7)
File name (p. 7)
File type (p. 7)
Formatting toolbar (p. 4)
Insertion point (p. 18)
Linked object (p. 38)
Menu bar (p. 4)
Microsoft Media Gallery (p. 33)
Microsoft WordArt (p. 40)
Normal view (p. 5)
Notes Page view (p. 5)
Open command (p. 7)
Outline (p. 5)
Outlining toolbar (p. 18)
Placeholders (p. 20)
Places bar (p. 7)
Print Command (p. 7)
Save As command (p. 13)
Save command (p. 7)
Scroll bar (p. 4)
Select-then-do (p. 18)
Slide Layout (p. 20)
Slide Show view (p. 5)
Slide Sorter view (p. 5)
Spell check (p. 14)
Standard toolbar (p. 4)
Status bar (p. 4)
Task pane (p. 5)
Template (p. 21)
Thumbnail image (p. 5)
Transition effects (p. 30)

MULTIPLE CHOICE

1. How do you save changes to a PowerPoint presentation?
   (a) Pull down the File menu and click the Save command
   (b) Click the Save button on the Standard toolbar
   (c) Either (a) and (b)
   (d) Neither (a) nor (b)

2. Which of the following can be printed in support of a PowerPoint presentation?
   (a) Audience handouts
   (b) Speaker's notes
   (c) An outline
   (d) All of the above

3. Which menu contains the Undo command?
   (a) File menu
   (b) Edit menu
   (c) Tools menu
   (d) Format menu

4. Ctrl+Home and Ctrl+End are keyboard shortcuts that move to the beginning or end of the presentation in the:
   (a) Outline
   (b) Slide Sorter view
   (c) Either (a) or (b)
   (d) Neither (a) nor (b)

5. The predefined slide formats in PowerPoint are known as:
   (a) View
   (b) Slide layouts
   (c) Audience handouts
   (d) Speaker notes

6. Which menu contains the commands to save the current presentation, or to open a previously saved presentation?
   (a) The Tools menu
   (b) The File menu
   (c) The View menu
   (d) The Edit menu

7. The Open command:
   (a) Brings a presentation from disk into memory
   (b) Brings a presentation from disk into memory, then erases the presentation on disk
   (c) Stores the presentation in memory on disk
   (d) Stores the presentation in memory on disk, then erases the presentation from memory

8. The Save command:
   (a) Brings a presentation from disk into memory
   (b) Brings a presentation from disk into memory, then erases the presentation on disk
   (c) Stores the presentation in memory on disk
   (d) Stores the presentation in memory on disk, then erases the presentation from memory

9. Which of the following can be displayed in the task pane?
   (a) Animation and transition effects
   (b) Design templates and slide layouts
   (c) Both (a) and (b)
   (d) Neither (a) nor (b)

10. Where will the insertion point be after you complete the text for a bullet in the outline and press the enter key?
   (a) On the next bullet at the same level of indentation
   (b) On the next bullet at a higher level of indentation
   (c) On the next bullet at a lower level of indentation
   (d) It is impossible to determine

11. Which of the following is true about an Excel chart that is linked to both a Word document and a PowerPoint presentation?
   (a) The chart cannot be linked to any other presentations or Word documents
   (b) The chart cannot be modified since it is already linked to two documents
   (c) The chart can be modified, but any changes have to be made in two places, once in the Word document and once in the PowerPoint presentation
   (d) Any changes to the chart will be reflected automatically in both the Word document and the PowerPoint presentation.

12. What advantage, if any, is there to collapsing the outline so that only the slide titles are visible?
   (a) More slides are displayed at one time, making it easier to rearrange the slides in the presentation
   (b) Transition and build effects can be added
   (c) Graphic objects become visible
   (d) All of the above

13. Which of the following is true regarding transition and build effects?
   (a) Every slide must have the same transition effect
   (b) Every bullet must have the same build effect
   (c) Both (a) and (b)
   (d) Neither (a) nor (b)

14. Which of the following is true?
   (a) Slides can be added to a presentation after a template has been chosen
   (b) The template can be changed after all of the slides have been created
   (c) Both (a) and (b)
   (d) Neither (a) nor (b)

15. Which of the following can be changed after a slide has been created?
   (a) Its layout and transition effect
   (b) Its position within the presentation
   (c) Both (a) and (b)
   (d) Neither (a) nor (b)

ANSWERS

1. c	**6.** b	**11.** d
2. d	**7.** a	**12.** a
3. b	**8.** c	**13.** d
4. d	**9.** c	**14.** c
5. b	**10.** a	**15.** c

1. Introduction to E-Mail: The presentation in Figure 1.16 is intended to review the basics of e-mail and provide practice with modifying an existing PowerPoint presentation. Open the partially completed presentation in *Chapter 1 Practice 1* within the Exploring PowerPoint folder and do the following:
    a. Modify the title slide to include your name and e-mail address.
    b. Select the fifth slide (Mail Folders). Boldface and italicize the name of each folder on the slide.
    c. Move the last two slides (Obtaining an E-mail Account and Privacy and Terms of Agreement) before the Mail Folders slide.
    d. Apply a suitable template to the completed presentation. Add transition effects as you see fit from one slide to the next.
    e. Print the presentation in multiple ways. Print the title slide as a slide (full page) to serve as a cover page. Print audience handouts for the entire presentation (six per page). Be sure to frame the individual slides. And finally, print the presentation in outline form.

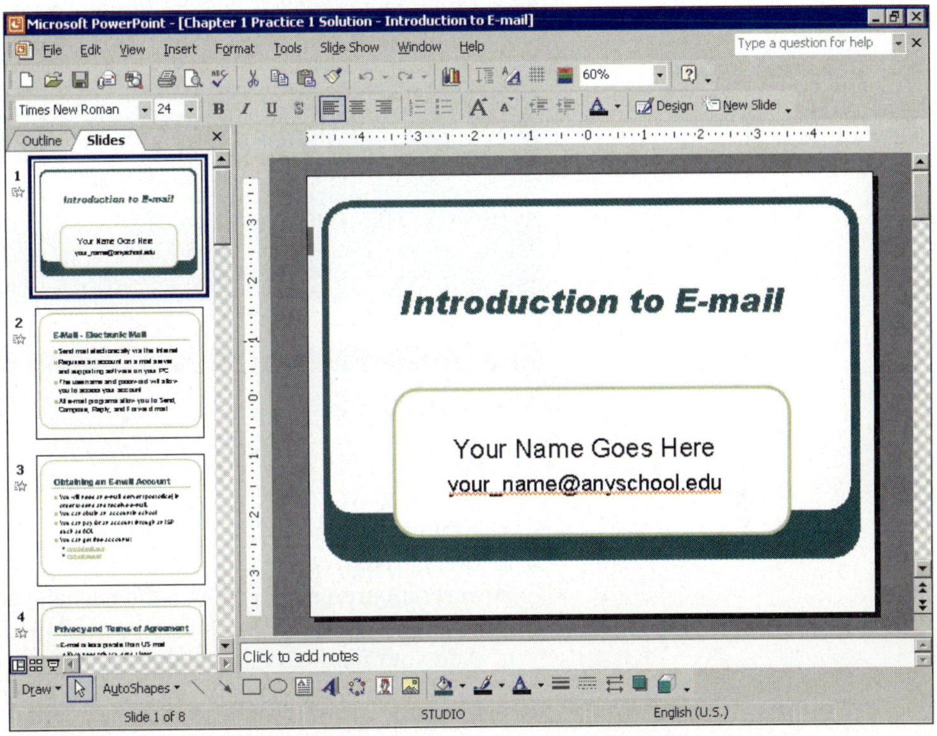

FIGURE 1.16 *Introduction to E-mail (Exercise 1)*

2. Introduction to Windows: The presentation in Figure 1.17 is intended to review the basics of Windows and provide practice with modifying an existing PowerPoint presentation. Open the partially completed presentation in *Chapter 1 Practice 2* within the Exploring PowerPoint folder and do the following:
    a. Add your name to the title page as indicated.
    b. Use the Insert Symbol command to insert the Windows logo ⊞ on the title slide. Click in the title slide at the end of the title to position the insertion point. Pull down the Insert menu, click the Symbol command, and click the Symbols tab if necessary. Select the Wingdings font, scroll until you come to the last character, then press the Insert button. Click and drag to select the newly inserted symbol, and then increase the font size as appropriate.

c. Insert a new slide after slide six (The Devices on a System) that describes the system you have at home or the system you are using at school. Add a final bullet that specifies the version of Windows under which you are running.
d. Apply a suitable template to the completed presentation. Add transition effects as you see fit from one slide to the next.
e. Print the presentation in multiple ways. Print the title slide as a slide (full page) to serve as a cover page. Print audience handouts for the entire presentation (six per page). And finally, print the presentation in outline form.

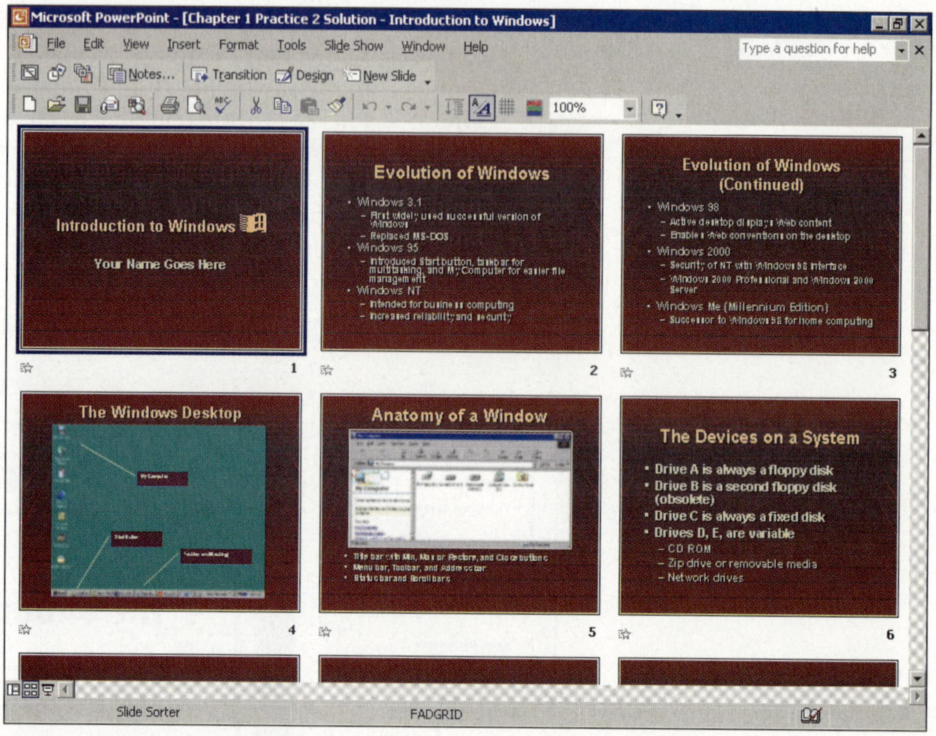

FIGURE 1.17 *Introduction to Windows (Exercise 2)*

3. The Purchase of a PC: The presentation in Figure 1.18 describes considerations in the purchase of a PC and provide practice with modifying an existing PowerPoint presentation. Open the partially completed presentation in *Chapter 1 Practice 3* within the Exploring PowerPoint folder and do the following:
   a. Add your name to the title page as indicated.
   b. Boldface and italicize the terms byte, kilobyte, megabyte, and gigabyte on the fourth slide.
   c. Apply a suitable template to the completed presentation. Add transition effects as you see fit from one slide to the next.
   d. Add a two-column bulleted slide at the end of the current presentation that describes your ideal PC in today's environment. Include the specifications for the microprocessor, RAM, fixed disk, and removable mass storage. Include additional information on the monitor, graphics card, speakers, sound card, and any other devices that you will include in the purchase.
   e. Add an additional slide (after the two-column bulleted slide) that includes hyperlinks to at least three vendors. (Pull down the Insert menu and click the Hyperlink command to display the Insert Hyperlink dialog box, where you enter the text that is to appear and the associated URL.) The title of this slide should be "Purchasing on the Web".
   f. Print the presentation in multiple ways. Print the title slide as a slide (full page) to serve as a cover page. Print audience handouts for the entire presentation (six per page). Finally, print the presentation in outline form.

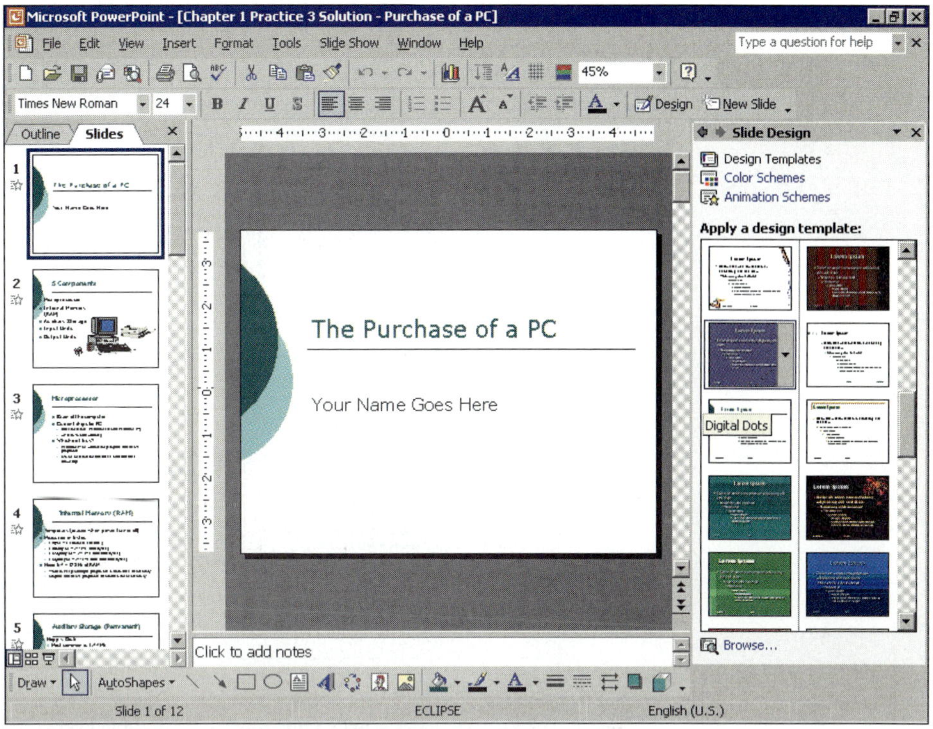

FIGURE 1.18 *The Purchase of a PC (Exercise 3)*

4. Introduction to the Internet: The presentation in Figure 1.19 is intended to review the basics of the Internet and provide practice with modifying an existing PowerPoint presentation. Open the presentation in *Chapter 1 Practice 4* within the Exploring PowerPoint folder and do the following:
   a. Add your name to the title page as indicated.
   b. Boldface and italicize the four acronyms on the fifth slide.
   c. Delete the clip art on the "Connecting to the Internet" slide. Change the layout of this slide to a two-column bulleted slide, and then describe your Internet connection(s) in the second column.
   d. Add a bulleted slide after the slide on "URL Format" that lists five specific Web sites. The first bullet should reference your school or professor. The second bullet should reference the Exploring Windows Web site. Each bullet should name the site followed by its URL—for example, The Exploring Windows Web site at www.prenhall.com/grauer.
   e. Apply a suitable template to the completed presentation. Add transition effects as you see fit from one slide to the next.
   f. Print the presentation in multiple ways. Print the title slide as a slide (full page) to serve as a cover page. Print audience handouts for the entire presentation (six per page). Be sure to frame the individual slides. And finally, print the presentation in outline form.
   g. Go through the presentation one slide at a time to learn and/or review the material. Did you learn anything new? What additional material (if any) would you include in the presentation? Summarize your thoughts in a brief note to your instructor.
   h. Use the Help command to learn how to save a presentation as a Web page for display within an Internet browser. Print one or two Help screens for your instructor to show you understand the procedure.

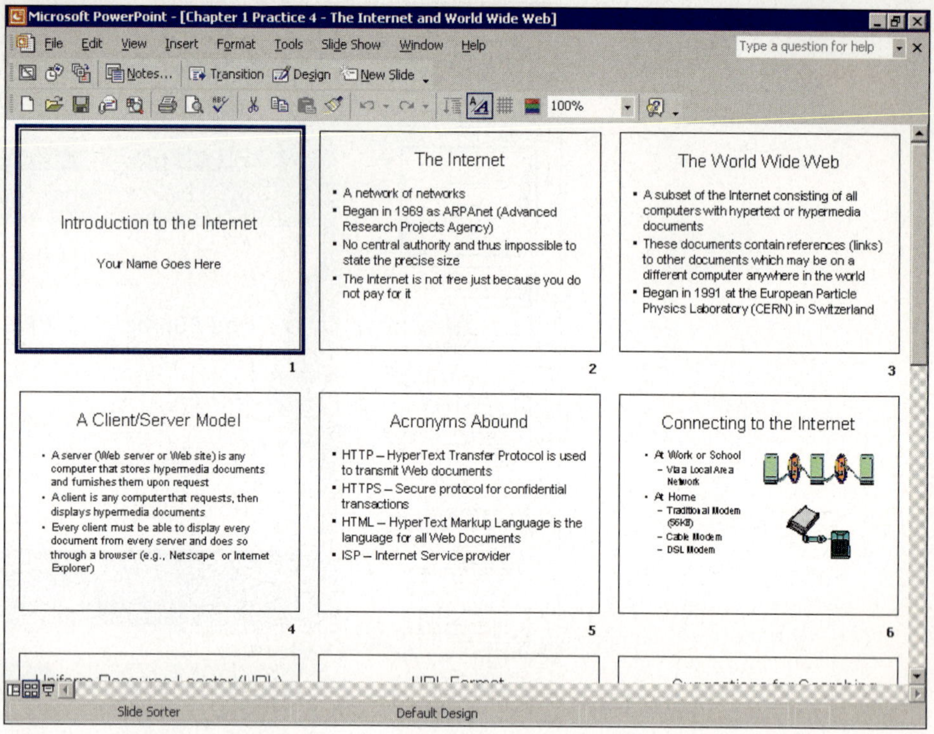

FIGURE 1.19 *Introduction to the Internet (Exercise 4)*

5. Theme Park Admissions: The presentation in Figure 1.20 is based on the Excel workbook in the file *Chapter 1 Practice 5* within the Exploring PowerPoint folder. The workbook contains two worksheets, one with tabular data, and one with a side-by-side column chart. The presentation should contain a title slide with your name (not visible in the figure), the Admissions Summary slide, a slide containing the side-by-side column chart, and a concluding slide that contains a congratulatory message. The tabular data and chart should be linked to the underlying workbook. Print the completed presentation as audience handouts, two slides per page, for your instructor.

6. My Favorite Presidents: Create a presentation similar to the one in Figure 1.21. The presentation consists of three slides—a title slide and two slides containing text and a photograph that was downloaded from the Internet. The title slide includes your name and a reference to the White House Web site (www.whitehouse.gov) as the source of your photographs.

a. Start Internet Explorer and go to the White House Web site. Click the link to White House History and then click the link to the Presidents of the United States. Select a president, point to the picture of the president, click the right mouse button to display a shortcut menu and save the picture. Be sure you remember the location of the file when you save it on your local machine.

b. Switch to PowerPoint. Insert a new slide and select the Text layout. Click in the title area of this slide and add the president's name and years in office. Click in the text area and press the backspace key to delete the bullet that appears automatically, then enter the text describing this president.

c. Click and drag the sizing handles that surround the text to make the box narrower in order to allow room for the president's picture. Click outside the text area. Pull down the Insert menu, click the Picture command, then click From File to display the Insert Picture dialog box. Select the folder where you saved the file in step (a). Select the picture, then click the Insert button to insert the picture onto the slide. Move and size the picture as appropriate.

d. Repeat these steps for a second president. Print all three slides and submit them to your instructor as proof you did this exercise.

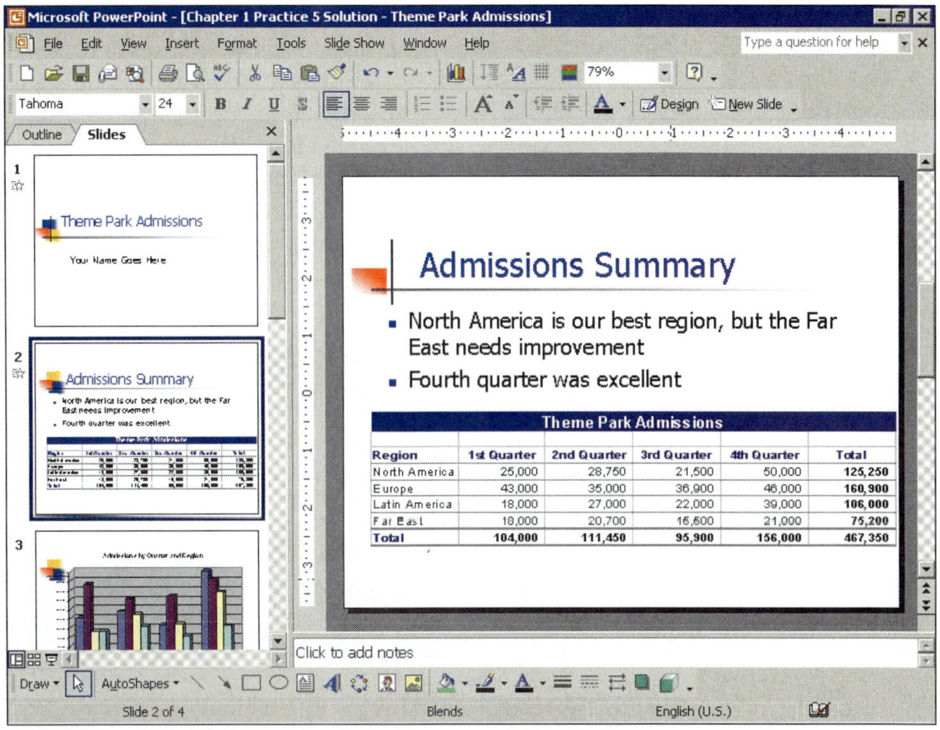

FIGURE 1.20 *Theme Park Admissions (Exercise 5)*

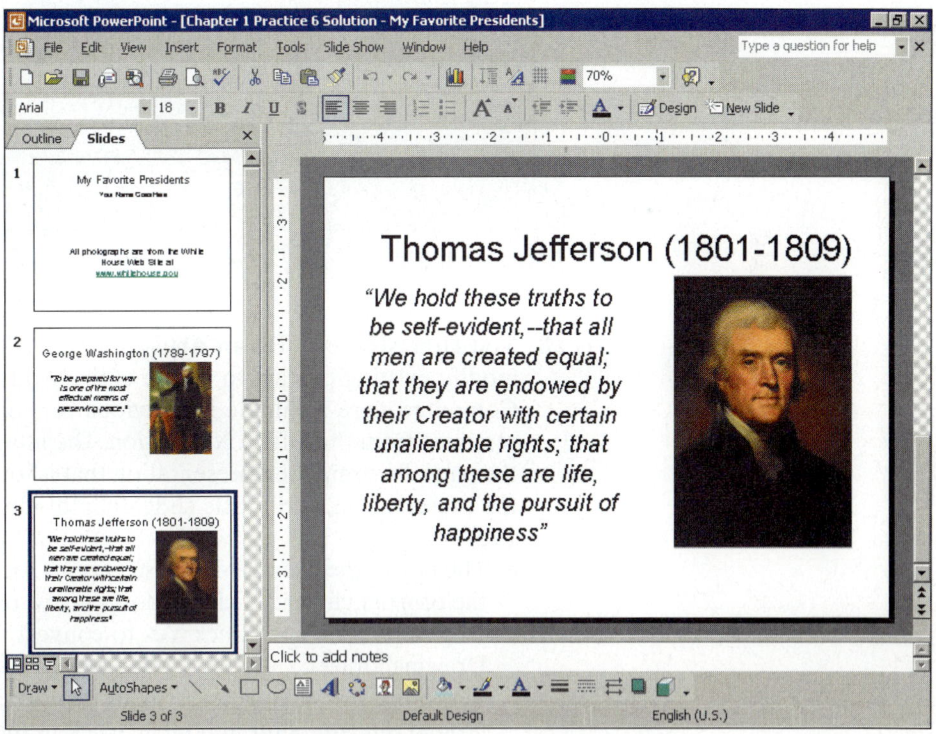

FIGURE 1.21 *My Favorite Presidents (Exercise 6)*

7. Your Favorite Performer: The subject of a PowerPoint presentation is limited only by your imagination. Use any Internet search engine to locate information about your favorite singer or recording group, then download information about that person or group to create a presentation such as the one in Figure 1.22. Use the technique described in the previous problem to download a picture and insert the picture into the presentation.

   Print the presentation in multiple ways. Print the title slide as a full slide to serve as a cover page. Print the entire presentation as audience handouts, six per page. (Frame the slides.) Print the entire presentation as an outline.

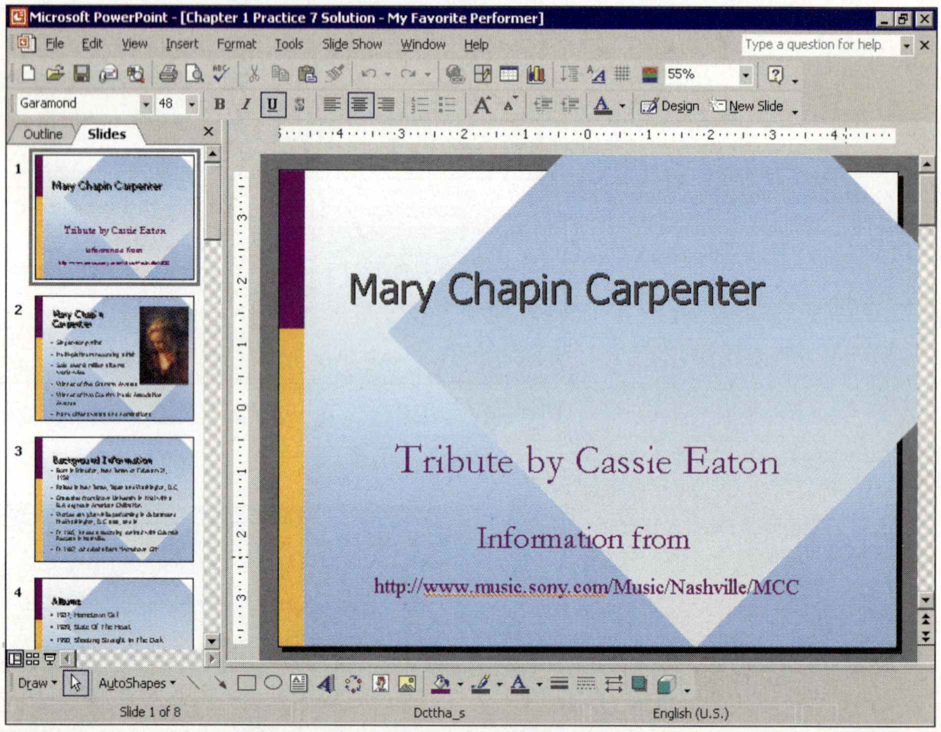

FIGURE 1.22 *Your Favorite Performer (Exercise 7)*

8. You Don't Have to Be an Artist: Figure 1.23 further illustrates how you can modify existing clip art to create entirely different images. The Duck and the Computer were available in previous versions of Microsoft Office, but were removed from the Office XP version. The image is, however, available to you in the partially completed presentation that is found in *Chapter 1 Exercise 8*. Open the presentation, add a title slide, then modify the clip art as shown in Figure 1.23.
   a. The key to the exercise is to use various tools on the Drawing toolbar. Select the original clip art, click the down arrow on the Draw button, then click the Ungroup command. Click Yes to convert the picture to a Microsoft Office Drawing Object.
   b. There are now two sets of sizing handles, one around the duck, and one around the computer and table. Click in the background area of the slide to deselect both objects.
   c. Click on the duck and experiment with the various tools to flip the image horizontally or vertically. Add a title to the slide.
   d. Copy the modified slide several times, then use the appropriate tools on the Drawing toolbar to create the presentation in Figure 1.23. Add your name to the first slide, then print the completed presentation, in the form of audience handouts (six per page), for your instructor.

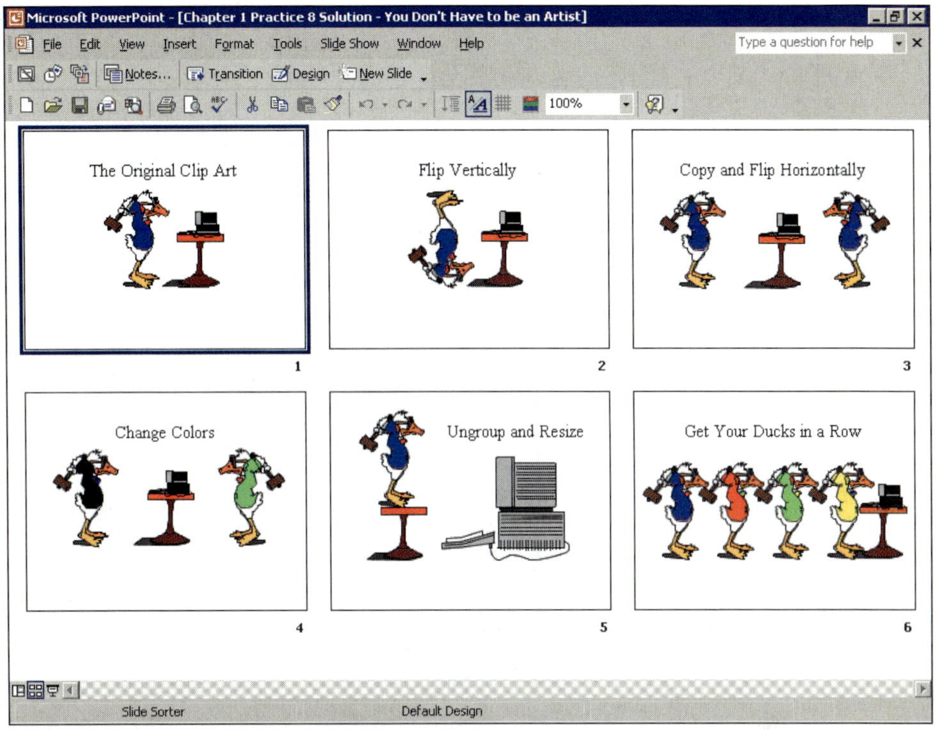

FIGURE 1.23 *You Don't Have to Be an Artist (Exercise 8)*

BUILDS ON

HANDS-ON EXERCISE 4 PAGES 41–51

9. Exploring AutoShapes: Figure 1.24 displays a single slide containing a variety of AutoShapes. Open the presentation created in the fourth hands-on exercise.
   a. Add a blank slide immediately before the last slide.
   b. Click the AutoShapes tool on the Drawing toolbar to display the AutoShapes toolbar. Click and drag the top of the menu to make it a floating toolbar.
   c. Point to an AutoShape, then click and drag in the slide to create the shape on the slide. (You can press and hold the Shift key as you drag for special effects; for example, press and hold the Shift key as you drag the ellipse or rectangle tool to draw a circle or square, respectively. You can also use the Shift key in conjunction with the Line tool to draw a perfectly horizontal or vertical line, or a line at a 45-degree angle.)
   d. To place text inside a shape, select the shape and start typing.
   e. To change the fill color or line thickness, select the shape, then click the appropriate button on the Drawing toolbar.
   f. Use these techniques to duplicate Figure 1.24, or better yet, create your own design. Add your name to the completed slide.

10. Export an Outline to Word: The Send To command enables you to export a presentation to Microsoft Word as shown in Figure 1.25. You can send just the outline. You can also send slide miniatures to display several slides on one page with notes for each.
   a. Choose any presentation that you have created in this chapter.
   b. Pull down the File menu, click the Send To command, and choose Microsoft Word to display the Send to Microsoft Word dialog box. Click the option button to send the Outline only.
   c. Change to the Outline view in Microsoft Word and print the outline.
   d. Return to PowerPoint, click the Send To command, choose Microsoft Word, and choose the option to send Notes next to slides.
   e. Change to the Page Layout view in Word. Click in the cell next to each slide (the Word document is a table) and enter an appropriate comment.
   f. Submit the finished document to your instructor.

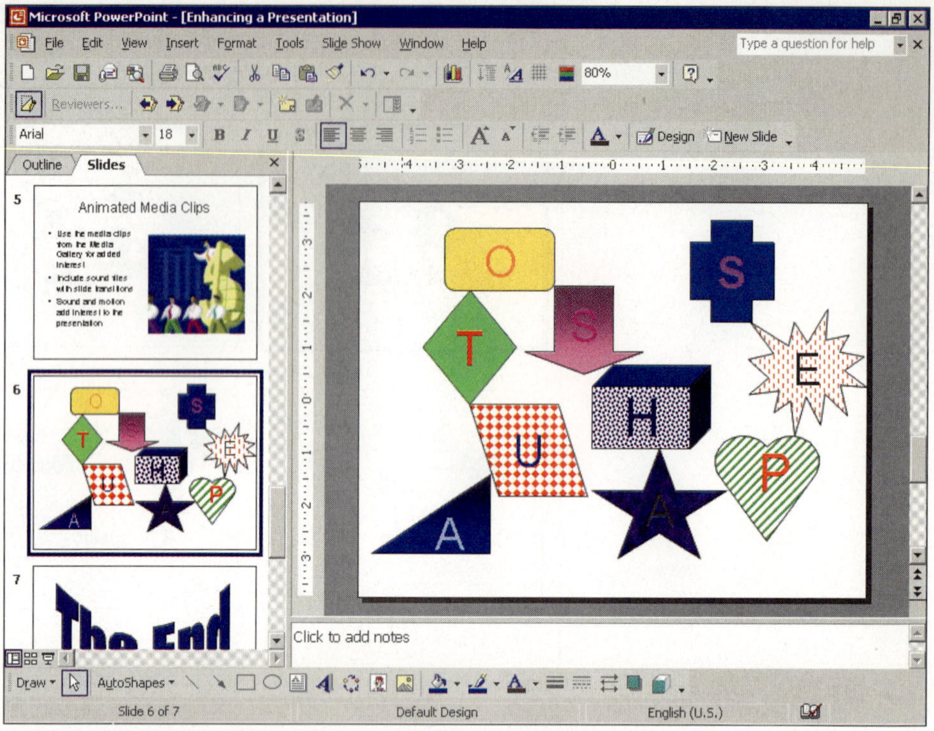

FIGURE 1.24 *Exploring AutoShapes (Exercise 9)*

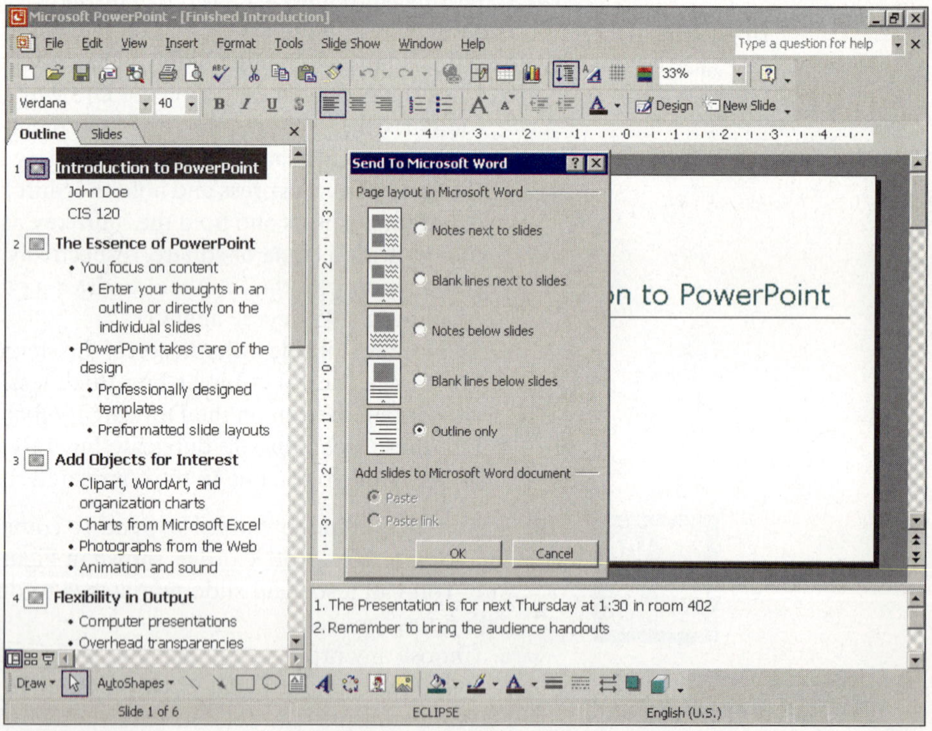

FIGURE 1.25 *Export an Outline to Word (Exercise 10)*

11. Create a New Folder: Open any presentation, pull down the File menu, and click the Save As command to display the dialog box in Figure 1.26a. Change to the Exploring PowerPoint folder, click the New Folder button, then create a new folder within this folder. Save the presentation in this folder, then close the presentation. Now click the Open button and reopen the presentation from the new folder as shown in Figure 1.26b. Creating additional folders in this fashion is very useful as you work with a large number of documents.

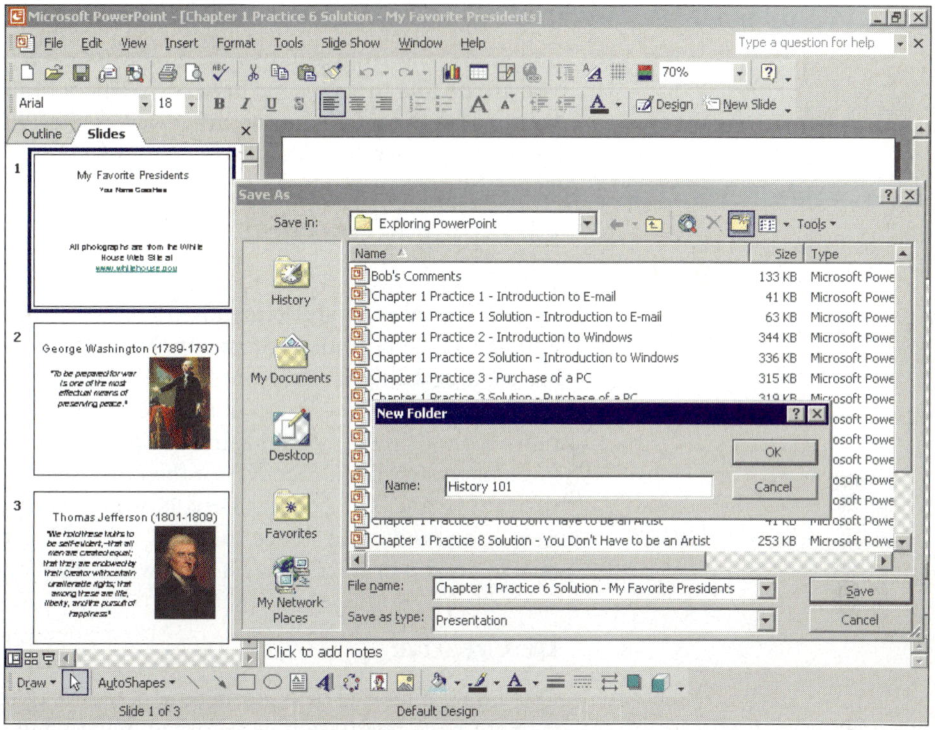

(a) Create a New Folder

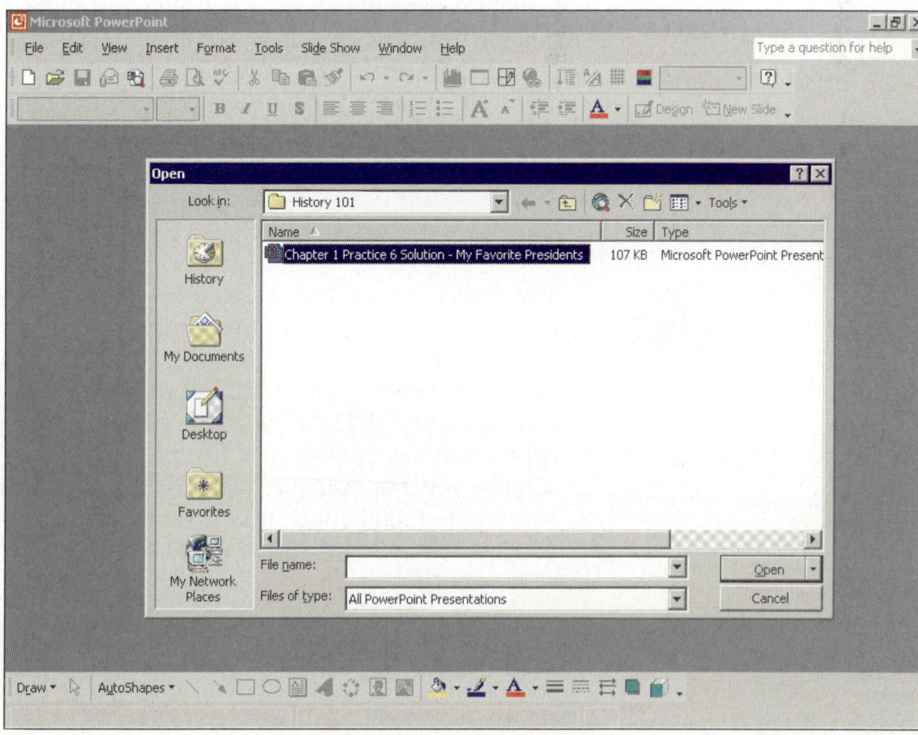

(b) Open the Presentation

FIGURE 1.26 *Create a New Folder (Exercise 11)*

Planning for Disaster

This case has nothing to do with presentations per se, but it is perhaps the most important case of all, as it deals with the question of backup. Do you have a backup strategy? Do you even know what a backup strategy is? This is a good time to learn, because sooner or later you will need to recover a file. The problem always seems to occur the night before an assignment is due. You accidentally erased a file, are unable to read from a floppy disk, or worse yet, suffer a hardware failure in which you are unable to access the hard drive. The ultimate disaster is the disappearance of your computer, by theft or natural disaster. Describe in 250 words or less the backup strategy you plan to implement in conjunction with your work in this class.

Changing Menus and Toolbars

Office XP lets you switch to a series of short menus that contain only basic commands. The additional commands are made visible by clicking the double arrow that appears at the bottom of the menu. New commands are added to the menu as they are used, and conversely, other commands are removed if they are not used. A similar strategy is followed for the Standard and Formatting toolbars, which are displayed on a single row, and thus do not show all of the buttons at one time. The intent is to simplify Office XP for the new user by limiting the number of commands that are visible. The consequence, however, is that the individual is not exposed to new commands, and hence may not use Office to its full potential. Which set of menus do you prefer? How do you switch from one set to the other?

Be Creative

One interesting way of exploring the potential of presentation graphics is to imagine it might have been used by historical figures had it been available. Choose any historical figure or current personality and create at least a six-slide presentation. You could, for example, show how Columbus might have used PowerPoint to request funding from Queen Isabella, or how Elvis Presley might have pleaded for his first recording contract. The content of your presentation should be reasonable, but you don't have to spend an inordinate amount of time on research. Just be creative and use your imagination. Use clip art as appropriate, but don't overdo it. Place your name on the title slide as technical adviser.

The National Debt

The deficit is gone, but the national debt is staggering—more than $5 trillion, or approximately $20,000 for every man, woman, and child in the United States. The annual budget is approximately $2 trillion. Use the Internet to obtain exact figures for the current year, then use this information to create a presentation on income and expenditures. Do some additional research and obtain data on the budget, the deficit, and the national debt for the years 1945, 1967, and 1980. The numbers may surprise you. For example, how does the interest expense for the current year compare to the total budget in 1967 (at the height of the Viet Nam War)? To the total budget in 1945 (at the end of World War II)?

The Internet and World Wide Web: Welcome to Cyberspace

OBJECTIVES

AFTER READING THIS CHAPTER YOU WILL BE ABLE TO:

1. Define the Internet and give a brief overview of its history; explain how the World Wide Web differs from the Internet.
2. Describe the various buttons on the Internet Explorer toolbar; explain how to enter a Web address in Internet Explorer.
3. Explain how to save the address of a favorite Web site and return to it later; distinguish between the History and Favorites lists.
4. Name three different search engines; explain why it is often necessary to use multiple search engines with a single query.
5. Distinguish between the Boolean operations And, Or, and Not.
6. Describe the structure of a Web address; explain why backing up within the address may lead to other relevant documents.
7. Download a graphic from the Web.
8. Draw several parallels between e-commerce and traditional commerce; describe several capabilities that are available through e-commerce that are not found in traditional commerce.
9. Distinguish between the http and https protocols; define a cookie.
10. Use the Save As Web Page command to convert a Word document to HTML; use the Insert Hyperlink command to include hyperlinks.

OVERVIEW

The Internet. It has transformed the world and is arguably the most important invention of the twentieth century. You can download music or software, view movie clips, do research, and shop for virtually anything. You can post your résumé, bank electronically, get the score of any sporting event as it happens, or check the price of a stock. You may start or end your day with e-mail.

If you are doing these things, you already know how to use the Internet, but do you really understand it? Do you know how to search for information efficiently, as opposed to casually browsing? Do you know the difference between an Internet Service Provider and a browser or between a modem and a cable modem? Are you truly comfortable with privacy and security issues that permeate the news? Do you know how to create a Web page? This introduction will answer these and other questions as you begin your journey through ***cyberspace***, the term used to describe the invisible realm of the Internet.

We begin with a brief history of the Internet and World Wide Web, describe how Web documents are accessed on a server, and define basic terms such as HTTP (HyperText Transfer Protocol). We show you how to organize your favorite sites into folders. We also describe the History folder, which provides an easy way to return to sites that you viewed previously. We define a search engine and present several tips to search efficiently. We describe the lure of e-commerce and discuss issues of privacy and security. We also show you how to create a Web page. As always, learning is best accomplished by doing, and so we include four hands-on exercises that let you apply the concepts in the chapter.

THE INTERNET

The ***Internet*** is a network of networks that connects computers across the country and around the world. It grew out of a U.S. Department of Defense (DOD) experimental project begun in 1969 to test the feasibility of a wide area (long distance) computer network over which scientists and military personnel could share messages and data. The country was in the midst of the Cold War, and the military imposed the additional requirement that the network be able to function with partial outages in times of national emergency (e.g., a nuclear disaster), when one or more computers in the network might be down.

The proposed solution was to create a network with no central authority. Each ***node*** (computer attached to the network) would be equal to every other node, with the ability to originate, pass, and receive messages. The path that a particular message took in getting to its destination would be insignificant. Only the final result was important, as the message would be passed from node to node until it arrived at its destination.

The experiment was (to say the least) enormously successful. Known originally as the ARPANet (Advanced Research Projects Agency Network), the original network of four computers has grown exponentially to include tens of millions of computers. To say that the Internet is large is a gross understatement, but by its very nature, it's impossible to determine just how large it really is. How many networks there are, and how many users are connected to those networks, is of no importance as long as you yourself have access.

The Internet is a network of networks, but if that were all it was, there would hardly be so much commotion. It's what you can do on the Internet, coupled with the ease of access, that makes the Internet so exciting. In essence, the Internet provides two basic capabilities, information retrieval and worldwide communication, functions that are already provided by libraries and print media, the postal system and the telephone, television, and other types of long distance media. The difference, however, is that the Internet is interactive in nature, and more importantly, it is both global and immediate.

The Internet enables you to request a document from virtually anywhere in the world, and to begin to receive that document almost instantly. No other medium lets you do that. Television, for example, has the capability to send information globally and in real time (while events are unfolding), but it is not interactive in that you cannot request a specific program. Federal Express promises overnight delivery, but that is hardly immediate. The stacks in your university library provide access to the information that is physically in that library, but that is not global access. Indeed, the Internet, and in particular the World Wide Web, is truly unique.

The original language of the Internet was uninviting and difficult to use. The potential was exciting, but you had to use a variety of esoteric programs (such as Archie and Gopher) to locate and download data. The programs were based on the Unix operating system, and you had to know the precise syntax of the commands within each program. There was no common user interface to speed learning. And, even if you were able to find what you wanted, everything was communicated in plain text, as graphics and sound were not available. All of this changed in 1991 with the introduction of the World Wide Web.

The ***World Wide Web*** (***WWW***, or simply the Web) is a very large subset of the Internet, consisting of documents with links to one another. Each document contains a ***hyperlink*** (reference) to another document, which may be on the same computer, or even on a different computer, with the latter located anywhere in the world. Hyperlinks may reference graphic, sound, and video files in addition to text files.

Hyperlinks enable you to move effortlessly from one document (or computer) to another. And therein lies the fascination of the Web, in that you simply click on link after link to go effortlessly from one document to the next. You can start your journey at your professor's home page in New York, for example, which may link to a document in the Library of Congress, which in turn may take you to a different document, and so on. So, off you go to Washington, DC, and from there to a reference across the country or perhaps around the world.

Any computer that stores a hypermedia document anywhere on the Web, and further, makes that document available to other computers, is known as a ***server*** (or ***Web server***). Any computer that is connected to the Web, and requests a document from a server, is known as a ***client***. In other words, you work on a client computer (e.g., a node on a local area network or your PC at home) and by clicking a link in a hypermedia document, you are requesting a document from a Web server.

In order for the Web to work, every client (be it a PC or a Mac) must be able to display every document from every server. This is accomplished by imposing a set of standards known as a protocol to govern the way data is transmitted across the Web. Thus, data travels from client to server, and back, through a protocol known as the ***HyperText Transfer Protocol*** (or http for short). In addition, in order to access the documents that are transmitted through this protocol, you need a special type of program known as a ***browser***. Indeed, a browser is aptly named because it enables you visit the Web in a leisurely and casual way (the dictionary definition of the word "browse"). ***Internet Explorer*** is the browser we use throughout the text, but the concepts apply equally well to ***Netscape Navigator***, the other browser that is popular in today's environment.

Internet Explorer is easy to use because it shares the common user interface and consistent command structure that are present in every Windows application. Every screen contains several familiar elements that include the title bar, and the Minimize, Maximize (or Restore), and Close buttons. Commands are executed from pull-down menus or from command buttons that appear on a toolbar under the menu bar. A vertical and/or horizontal scroll bar appears if the entire document is not visible at one time. The title bar displays the name of the document you are currently viewing.

Figure 1 depicts the use of Internet Explorer during a typical session in which we "surf the Web" to visit various Web sites. Our journey begins through a ***portal***, or gateway into the Internet. A portal is a very general site that contains a series of links to a variety of topics. We have chosen to visit **about.com**, but there are many such sites on the Web (Yahoo.com and Excite.com are other examples). The developers of these sites make them as interesting and as comprehensive as possible in order to entice visitors to the site.

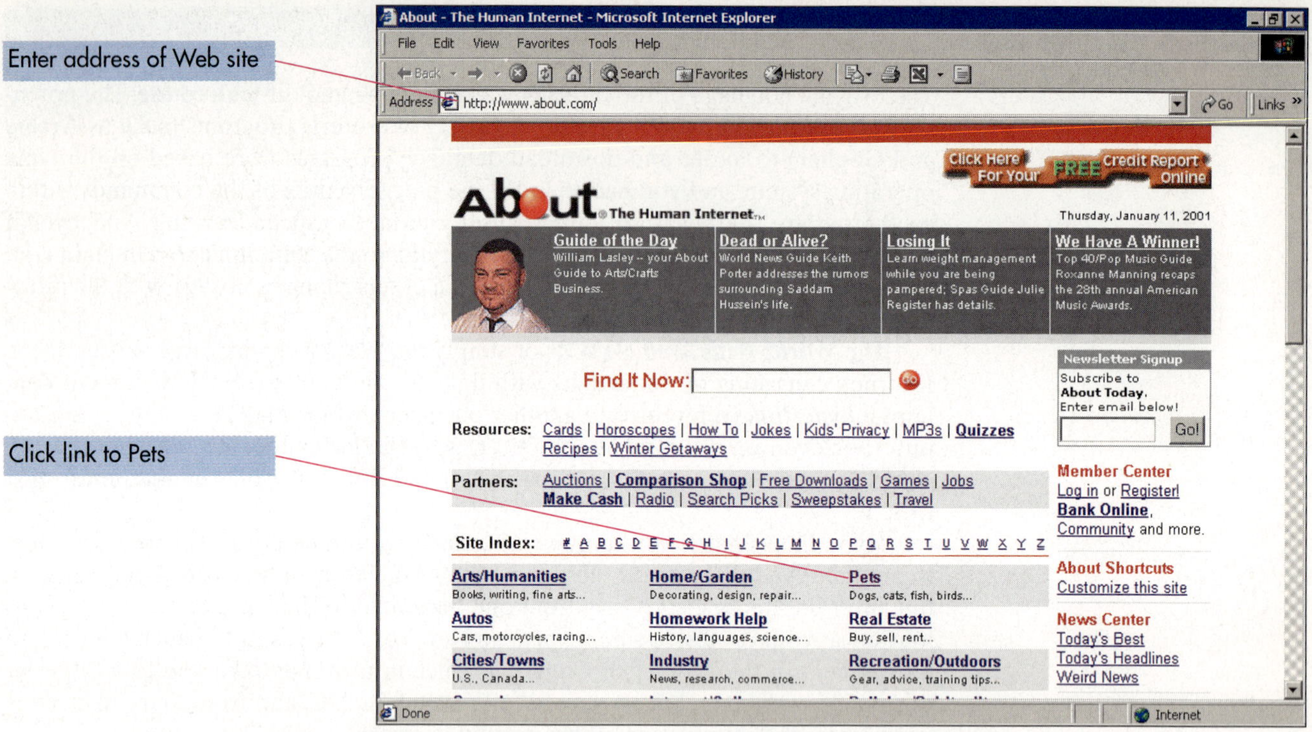

(a) About.com Home Page

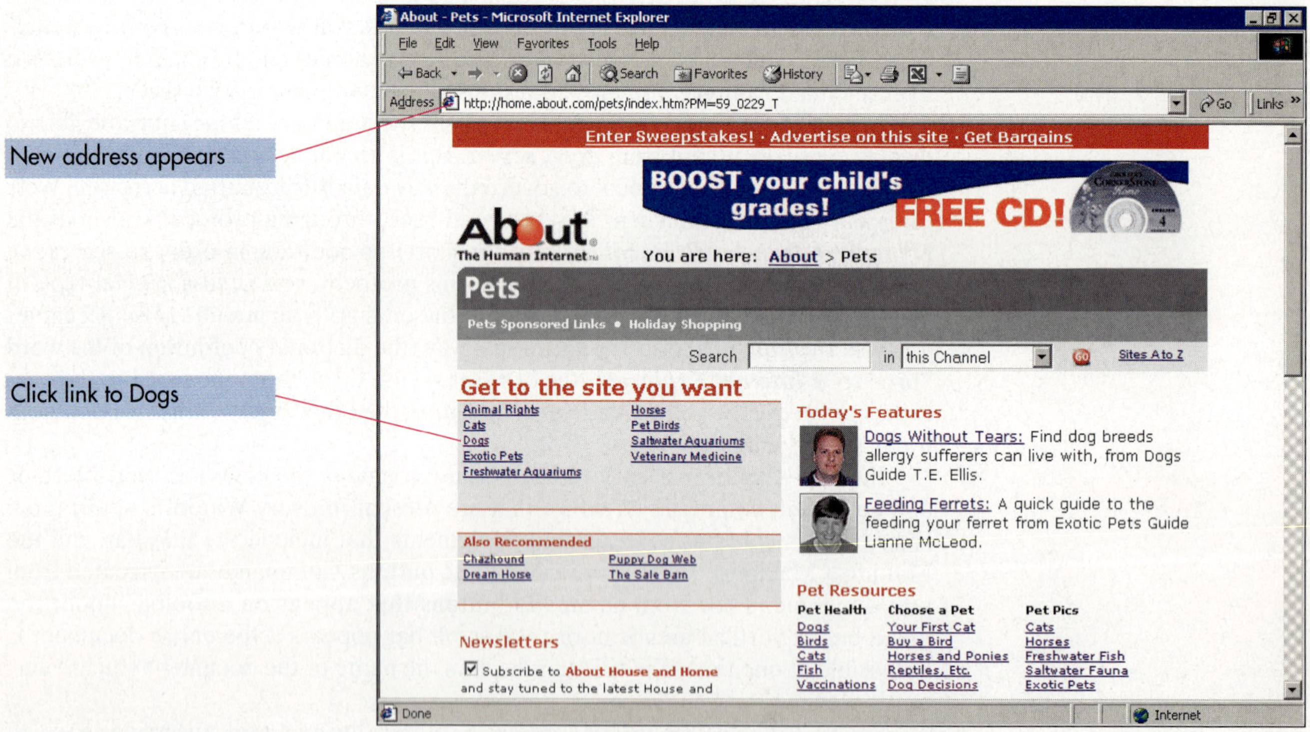

(b) The Pets Page

FIGURE 1 *The World Wide Web*

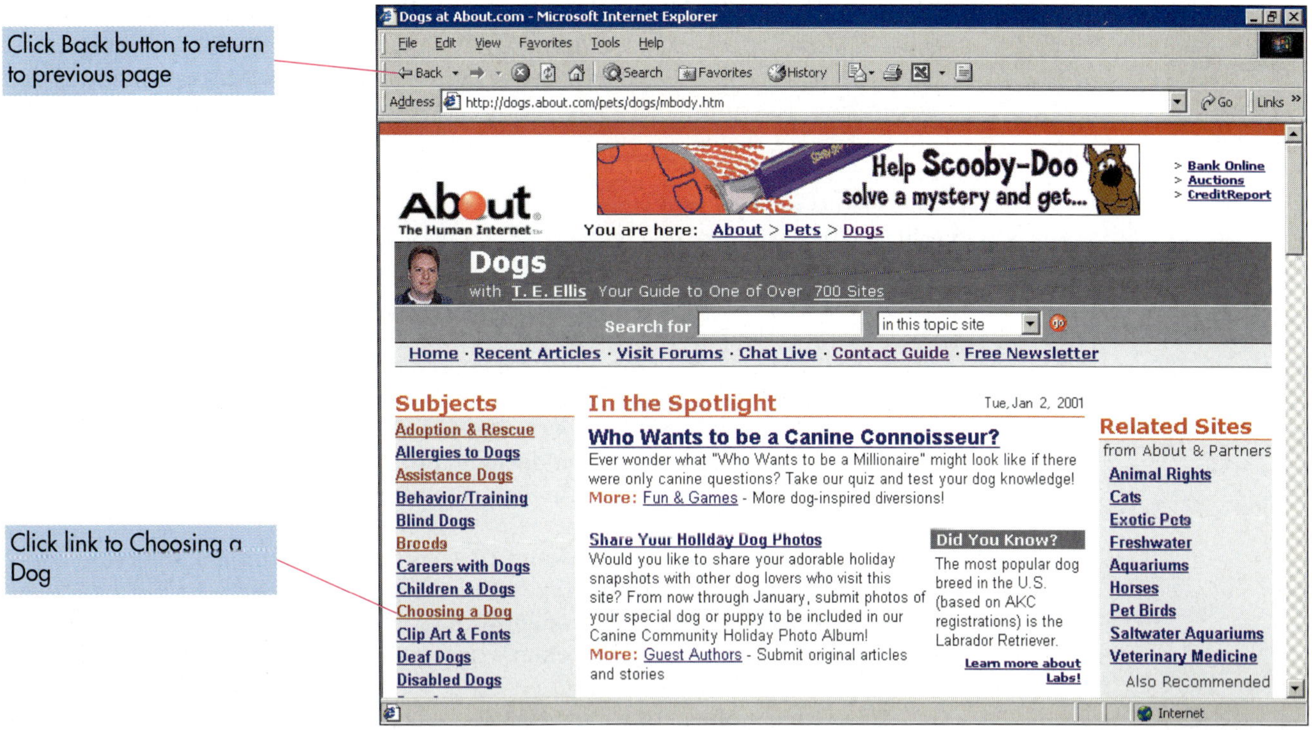

(c) The Dogs Page

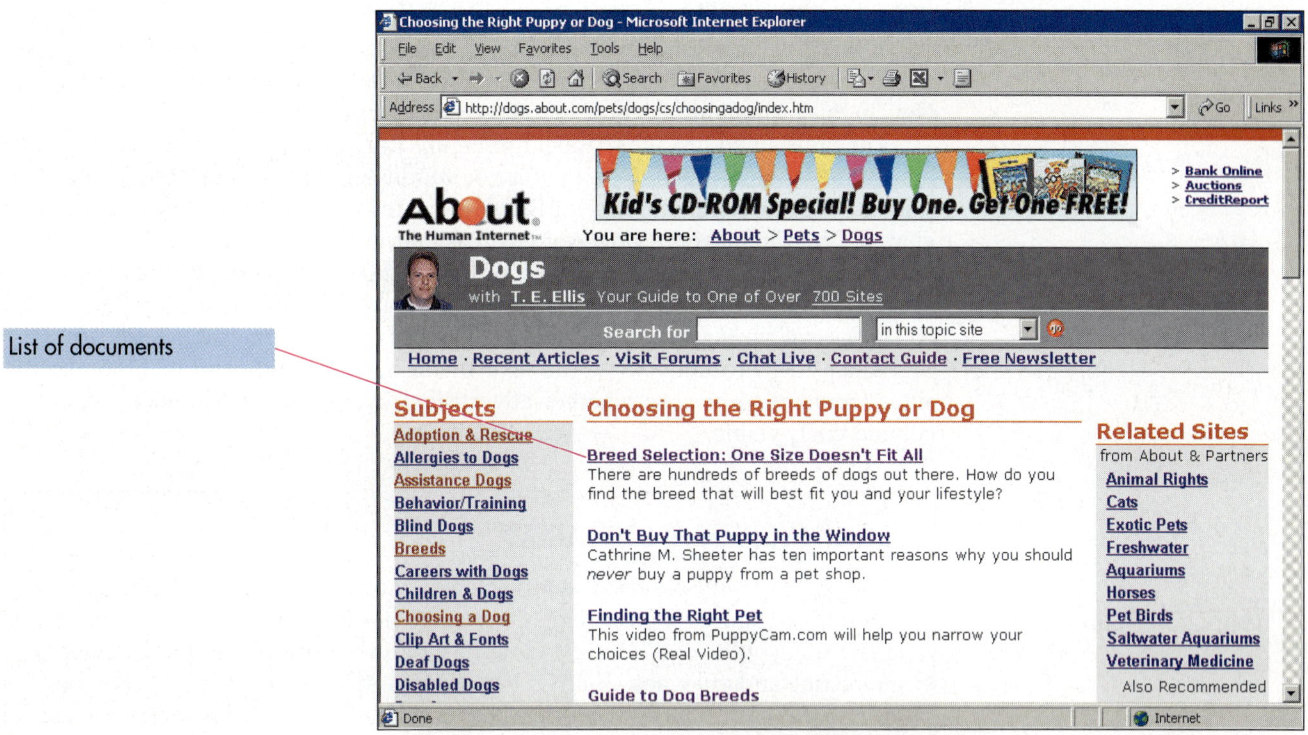

(d) Choosing a Dog Page

FIGURE 1 *The World Wide Web (continued)*

There is no charge to you to visit a portal, but the developers have an ulterior motive. Most sites contain one or more advertisements, as can be seen in Figure 1a. The developer sells advertising just as commercial billboards on a highway sell advertising. The more visitors to the site, the more the developer can charge for advertising on the site. Nevertheless, portals perform an invaluable service and enable you to browse the Web in leisurely fashion. Once you arrive at the portal (by entering its address into your browser), you can click any link that interests you, which in turn will take you to other links and other sites.

Let's assume, for example, that we are interested in a acquiring a golden retriever puppy and we want to find a breeder in our hometown from whom to purchase our pet. That is a very specific request, but it's easy to find the information we need. We start by going to the about.com portal in Figure 1a, where we click the link to Pets, which in turn displays the document in Figure 1b. (Note how the address changes automatically in the Address bar. Indeed, that is what the Web is all about as you move effortlessly from one document to another.) We then click the link to Dogs, which takes us to the page in Figure 1c, where we click the link to Choosing a Dog.

This takes us to the page in Figure 1d, where we scroll through the list of documents to learn more about the type of dog that will best suit our life style (e.g., choosing between dogs for apartment dwellers versus home owners). Eventually, you will find sites where you can enter a zip code to locate specific breeders in your area.

Think for a moment of what we have just accomplished. We started with a general reference page and in a matter of minutes were in the process of contacting a breeder in our hometown. There is no beginning (other than the starting point or Web portal) and no end. You simply read the various Web documents in any way that makes sense to you, jumping to explore whatever topic you want to see next. All of this is accomplished with a graphical browser, such as Internet Explorer, and a connection between your computer and the Internet. The process of "surfing the Net" in this fashion has become an integral part of our culture.

The underlined links that appear in Figure 1 are displayed in one of two colors, blue or magenta, depending on whether or not the link has been previously selected. Any link in blue (the majority of links) indicates the document has not yet been viewed. Links in magenta, however (such as Pets in Figure 1a), imply the associated document has been retrieved earlier in that session or in a previous session. Note, too, the presence of advertising in several screens of Figure 1, such as "Kids CD-ROM Special" in Figure 1d. The vendor pays the owner of the site for the advertising, which helps to underwrite the investment in developing and maintaining the site. It remains to be seen whether advertising revenue alone will make such sites commercially viable.

SEARCH ENGINES—A LOOK AHEAD

There are two very general ways to navigate through the Web. You can start by entering the address of a specific site, such as about.com, then once you arrive at the site, you can go leisurely from link to link. Browsing in this manner is interesting and enjoyable, but it is not always efficient. Hence when searching for specific information, you often need a special tool called a search engine, with which you conduct a key word search of the Web, much as you search a card catalog or online database in the library. Search engines are discussed later in the chapter.

The Uniform Resource Locator (URL)

The address (or location) of a document appears in the ***Address bar*** and is known as a ***Uniform Resource Locator*** (URL), or more simply as a Web address. The URL is the primary means of navigating the Web, as it indicates the address of the Web server (computer) from which you have requested a document. Change the URL (e.g., by clicking a link or by entering a new address in the Address bar) and you jump to a different document, and possibly a different server.

A URL consists of several parts: the method of access, the Internet address of the Web server, an optional path in the directory (folder) structure on the Web server to the document, and finally the document name. (Some URLs do not include the document name, in which case the browser displays a default document, typically called index.html). Each time you click a link within a document, you are effectively entering a new address with which to connect. Note, for example, how the contents of the Address bar change within Figure 1 as you access the different pages. The address is transparent to you because it changes automatically. The general format of a Web address is as follows:

http://dogs.about.com/pets/dogs/msub13.htm

- Document
- Path (directories or folders)
- Web site (address of Web server)
- Means of access (HyperText Transfer Protocol)

The components in the address can be read from right to left. In other words, the preceding address references the document msub13.htm (the document name is case sensitive) in the dogs folder (within the pets folder) on the Web server dogs.about.com according to the http protocol.

You can guess the address of a company or organization by using the general format, www.company.com—for example, www.microsoft.com. The ending letters ("com" in this example) are the domain name. Other common domains are "gov" and "edu", for government and education, respectively. Thus, www.irs.gov and www.miami.edu will take you to the Web sites of the Internal Revenue Service and the University of Miami, respectively.

To go to a particular site, enter its address through the ***Open command*** in the File menu or type the address directly in the Address bar, press the enter key, and off you go. Once you arrive at a site, click the ***hyperlinks*** (underlined items or graphical icons) that interest you, which in turn will take you to other documents at that site or even at a different site. The resources on the Web are connected in such a way that you need not be concerned with where (on which computer) the linked document is located. Indeed, that is the beauty of the Web, because you move from one document to the next simply by clicking the links that interest you.

WHAT IS HTML?

Web documents are written in HTML (HyperText Markup Language) and display the extension html (or htm) at the end of the document name in the Web address. HTML documents can be created through specialized programs, such as FrontPage, or more easily through Microsoft Word, as you will see later in this chapter.

CONNECTING TO THE INTERNET

There are two basic ways to connect to the Internet—from a ***local area network (LAN)*** or by dialing in. It's much easier if you connect from a LAN (typically at school or work) since the installation and setup have been done for you, and all you have to do is follow the instructions provided by your professor. If you connect from home, you will need a modem, cable modem, or DSL modem, and an ***Internet Service Provider*** (or ***ISP***).

A ***modem*** is the hardware interface between your computer and the telephone system. In essence, you instruct the modem, via the appropriate software, to dial the phone number of your ISP, which in turn lets you access the Internet. A ***cable modem*** provides high-speed access (20 to 30 times that of an ordinary modem) through the same cable as used for cable TV. A ***DSL modem*** also provides high-speed access through a special type of phone line.

An Internet Service Provider is a company or organization that maintains a computer with permanent access to the Internet. Typically, you have to pay for this service, but you may be able to dial into your school or university at no charge. If not, you need to sign up with a commercial vendor such as America Online (AOL). Not only does AOL provide access to the Internet, but it also offers a proprietary interface and other services such as local chat rooms. The Microsoft Network (MSN) is a direct competitor to AOL, and it, too, offers Internet access as well as a proprietary interface and extra services. Alternatively, you can choose from a host of other vendors who provide Internet access without the proprietary interface of AOL or MSN.

Regardless of whom you choose as an ISP, be sure you understand the fee structure. The monthly fee may entitle you to a set number of hours per month (after which you pay an additional fee), or it may give you unlimited access. The terms vary widely, and we suggest you shop around for the best possible deal. In addition, be sure you are given a local access number (i.e., that you are not making a long distance call), or else your telephone bill will be outrageous. Check that the facilities of your provider are adequate and that you can obtain access whenever you want. Few things are more frustrating than to receive continual busy signals when you are trying to log on.

DISABLE CALL WAITING

Your friend may understand if you excuse yourself in the middle of a conversation to answer another incoming call. A computer, however, is not so tolerant and will often break the current connection if another call comes in. Accordingly, check the settings of your communications program to disable call waiting prior to connecting to the Internet (typically by entering *70 in front of the access number). Your friends may complain of a busy signal, but you will be able to work without interruption.

LEARNING BY DOING

The Web cannot be appreciated until you experience it for yourself, and so we come to our first hands-on exercise. We suggest a specific starting point, a portal known as the Reference Desk (at refdesk.com), then browse leisurely through a series of documents. The exercise will illustrate the concept of browsing as well as basic commands in Internet Explorer. Remember, too, that the World Wide Web is a "living document" that changes continually, so don't be surprised if you cannot duplicate the hands-on exercise exactly. It doesn't matter, because you want current information, not "yesterday's headlines."

Hands-on Exercise 1

Introduction to the World Wide Web

Objective To access the Internet and World Wide Web and to practice basic commands in Internet Explorer. Use Figure 2 as a guide in the exercise.

Step 1: **Start Internet Explorer**

- Click the **Start button**, click (or point to) **Programs**, click or point to **Internet Explorer** (or click **Internet Access** to display a cascaded menu, then click **Internet Explorer**).
- It does not matter which page you see initially as long as you are able to start Internet Explorer and connect to the Internet. If necessary, click the **Maximize button** so that Internet Explorer takes the entire desktop.
- Enter the address of the Reference Desk, the portal we shall use for this exercise:
  - Pull down the **File** menu and click the **Open command** to display the Open dialog box in Figure 2a. Enter the address of the Web site you want to explore; in this case, **www.refdesk.com** (you don't have to enter http:// as it is assumed). Click **OK**.
  - *Or,* click in the **Address bar**, which automatically selects the current address. Enter **www.refdesk.com** (the http:// is assumed). Press **enter**.
- Be sure you enter the address correctly, or else you will not be able to get to the site. If necessary, pull down the **View menu**, click the **Toolbars command**, and check the **Standard Buttons**, **Address Bar**, and **Links commands** so that your toolbars match ours.

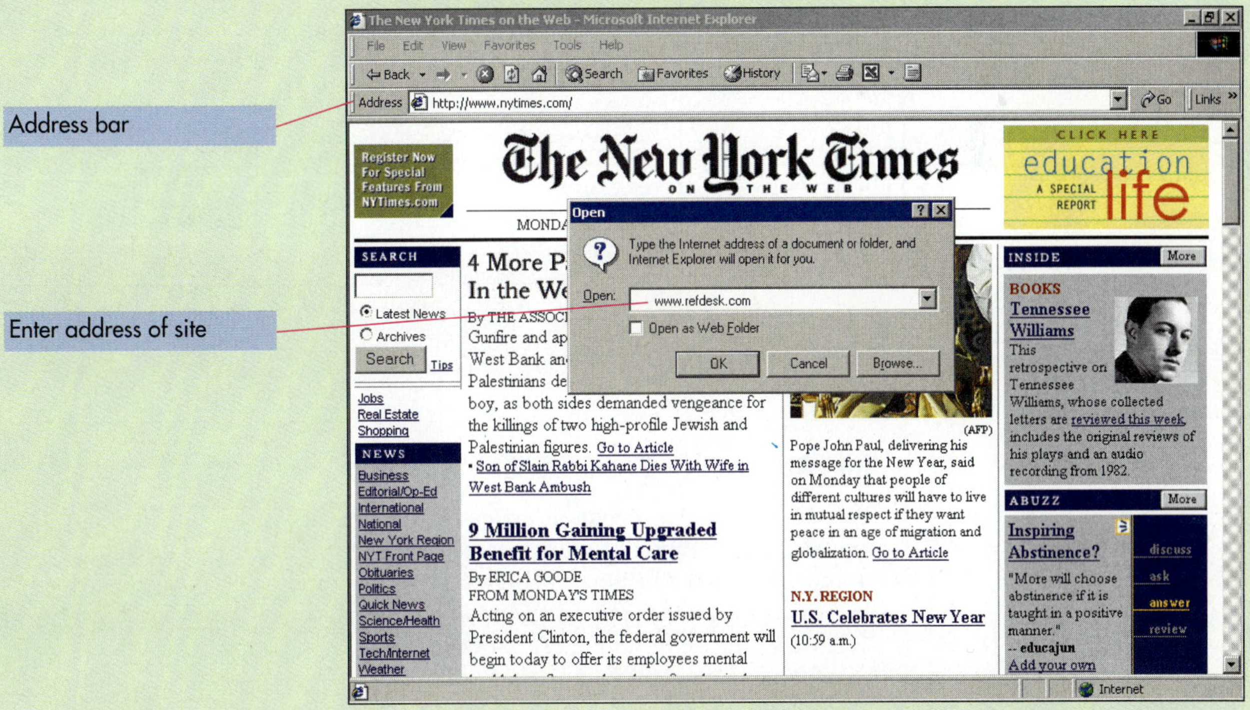

(a) Start Internet Explorer (step 1)

Figure 2 *Hands-on Exercise 1*

Step 2: **The Reference Desk**

- ➤ You should see the home page of the Reference Desk, as shown in Figure 2b, although the content will surely be different.
- ➤ Look in the Facts-of-the-Day section for the link to Word-of-the-Day. You cannot click this text per se.
- ➤ Select one of the three associated links in the Word-of-the-Day area: OED for Oxford English Dictionary, MW for Merriam Webster, or RH for Random House. We chose **MW** for the Merriam Webster dictionary.
- ➤ If you are unable to get to the Reference Desk, pull down the **File menu**, click the **Open command**, and re-enter the address shown in the Address bar in Figure 2b. Press **enter**.
- ➤ If you are still unable to get to the site, enter the address of any other site you wish to explore. You will not be able to duplicate the exercise exactly, but you will be able to practice with commands in Internet Explorer.

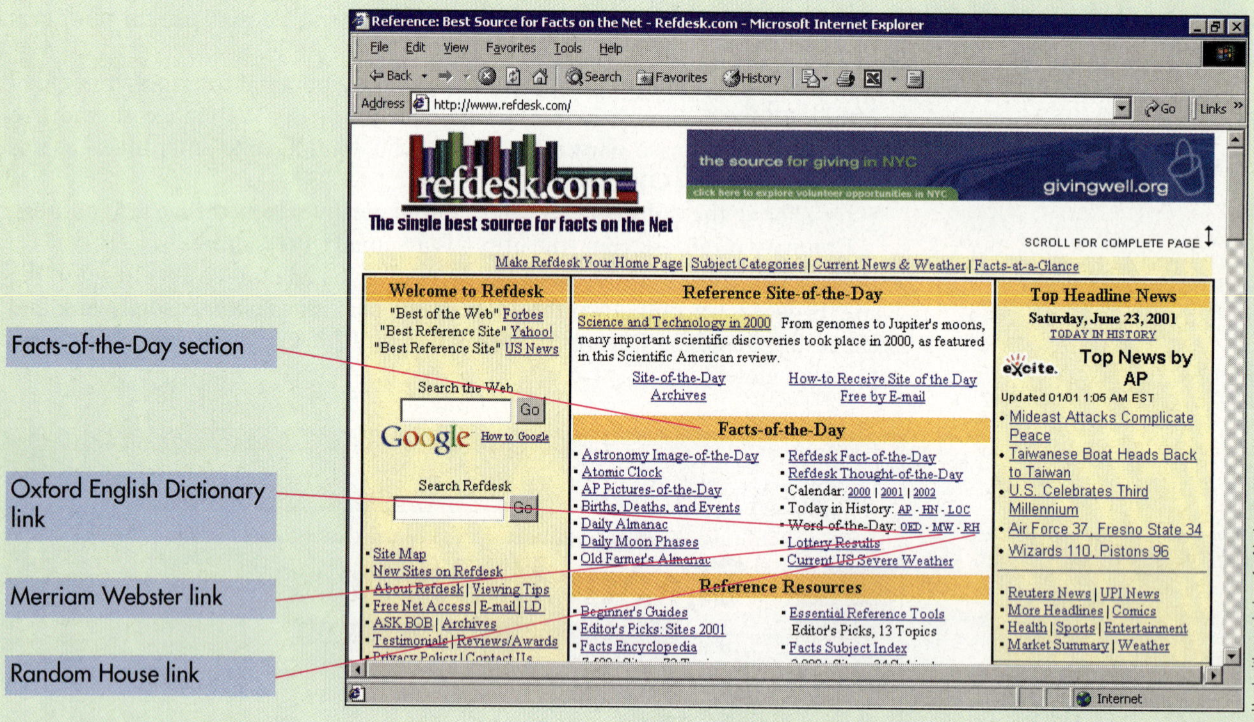

(b) The Reference Desk (step 2)

FIGURE 2 *Hands-on Exercise 1 (continued)*

THE PAGE CANNOT BE DISPLAYED

Two things have to occur in order for Internet Explorer to display the requested document—it must locate the server on which the document is stored, and it must be able to connect to that computer. The exact wording of the error messages may vary, but look carefully at the text for an indication of what went wrong. A message such as "The Page Cannot Be Displayed" generally means that you entered some part of the address incorrectly. Click the Address bar, and re-enter the address and try again.

Step 3: **The Word of the Day**

- You should see the word of the day as shown in Figure 2c, but the word you see will be different from ours. Click the **Print button** on the Standard Buttons toolbar to print this page for your instructor.
- Click the **Back button** on the Standard Buttons toolbar to return to the main page for the Reference Desk. Note that the link to the Merriam Webster dictionary has changed color (from blue to magenta on our page) to indicate that you have viewed the associated page.
- Click the **Forward button** from the Reference Desk home page to return to the Merriam Webster dictionary. The left pane on the Merriam Webster page provides several additional links that are related to building your vocabulary.
- Click the link to the **Thesaurus**, then search for synonyms for the word of the day. Print this page for your instructor as well.

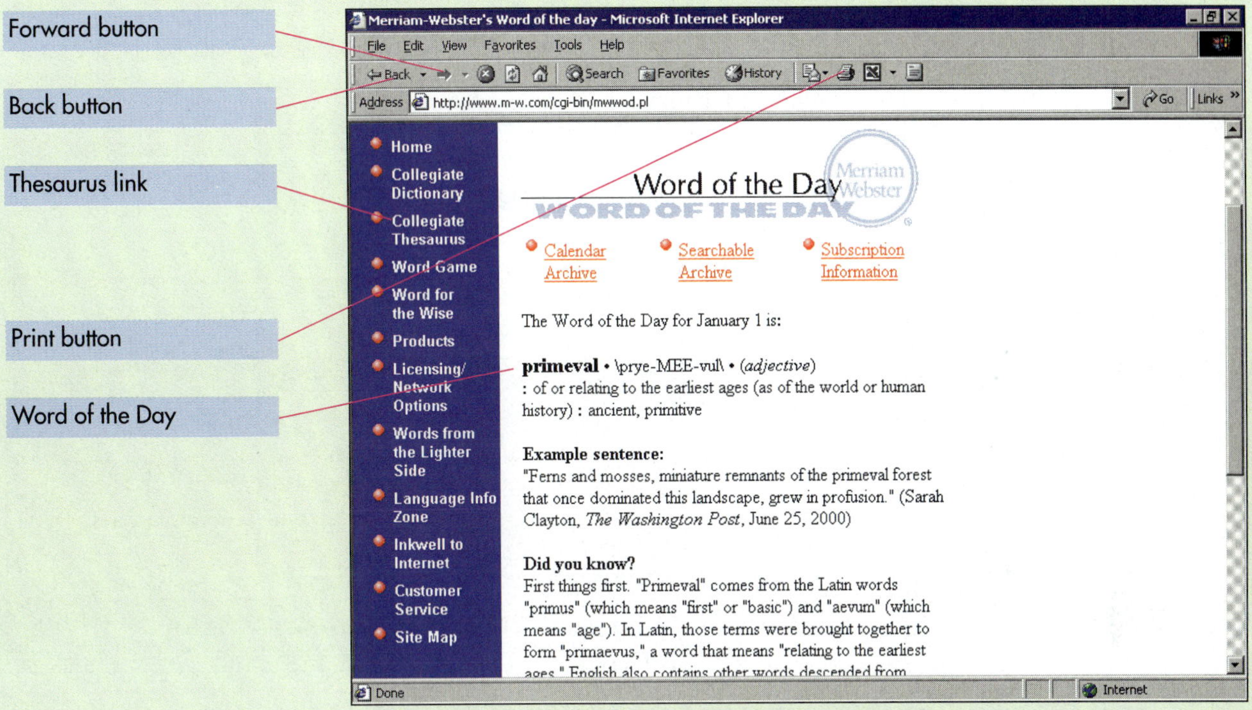

(c) The Word of the Day (step 3)

FIGURE 2 *Hands-on Exercise 1 (continued)*

THE FAVORITES LIST

The easiest way to return to a page is to add it to the Favorites list. Once you arrive at a page that you consider special, pull down the Favorites menu and click the Add to Favorites command to display the Add Favorites dialog box. Internet Explorer provides a default name for the page, but you can enter a more descriptive name if you prefer. Click OK to add the site and close the dialog box. To return to the page in the future, pull down the Favorites menu and click the indicated link.

Step 4: The Page Setup Command

- Click the **down arrow** next to the Back button to display a list of the sites you have visited, then click the link to the Reference Desk to return to that page. Go to the Facts-of-the-Day section and look for the link to Today in History.
- Once again, you have your choice of three different links. Click the **AP link** to display a page similar to the one in Figure 2d.
- Pull down the **File menu** and click the **Page Setup command** to display the Page Setup dialog box. You do not have to change any of these options at this time, just be aware that they exist (see the boxed tip below). Click **OK** to close the dialog box.
- Click the **Print button** on the Standard Buttons toolbar to print this page for your instructor.

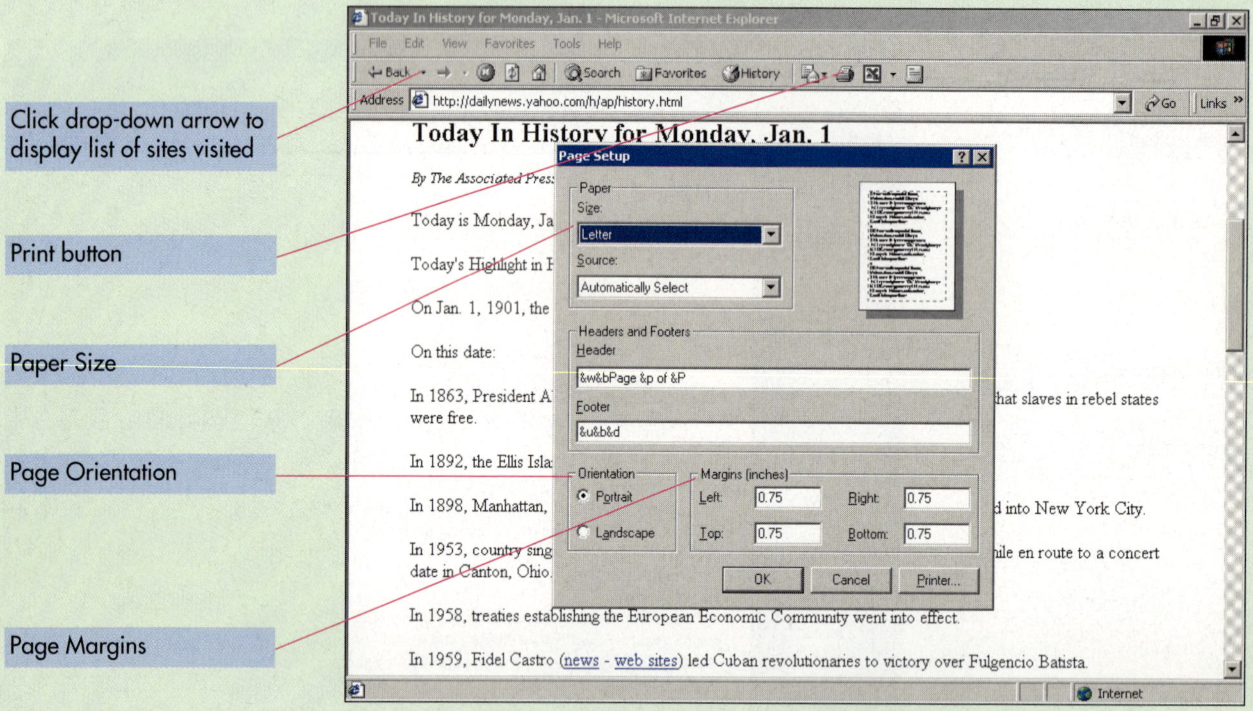

(d) The Page Setup Command (step 4)

FIGURE 2 *Hands-on Exercise 1 (continued)*

THE PAGE SETUP COMMAND

The header and/or footer in Web pages printed by Internet Explorer typically contain the address of the page and the date it was printed. Pull down the File menu and click the Page Setup command to display the Page Setup dialog box. Click the question mark in the title bar of the Page Setup dialog box, then click the header or footer text box to see the meaning of the various codes. Right click within the list of codes and click the Print Topic command to obtain hard copy, then modify the header and/or footer text boxes to display the information you want.

Step 5: **The Help Command**

- Pull down the **Help menu** and click the **Contents and Index command** to display the Help window. If necessary, click the **Contents tab** to see a list of major help topics, each of which is represented by a book. Maximize the window.
- Click the **book icon** next to **Finding the Web Pages You Want**, then click the topic **Change your home page** to display this information in the right pane as shown in Figure 2e.
- Right click anywhere in the left pane, click **Options**, then click **Print** to display the Print Topics dialog box. Click the option button to print the selected topic, click **OK**, then click **Print** to print this topic.
- Click the **Close button** to exit Help.

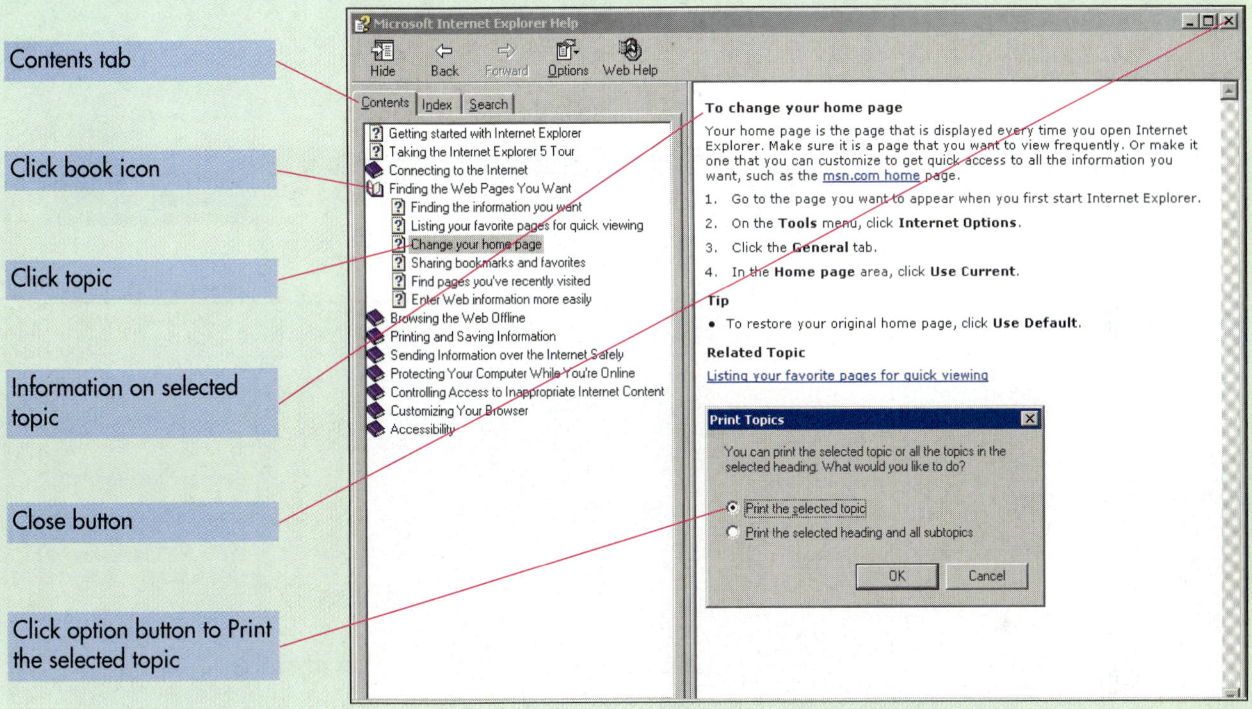

(e) The Help Command (step 5)

FIGURE 2 *Hands-on Exercise 1 (continued)*

ABOUT INTERNET EXPLORER

There are many versions of Internet Explorer, each with subtle differences in the features it supports. To find out which version you have, pull down the Help menu and click About Internet Explorer to display a screen with the version and release number. You will need this information if you are having trouble with your browser and are seeking help from technical support. The About command is present in the Help menu of every Windows application.

Step 6: Change the Start Page

- ➤ Do this step only if you are working on your own machine and you want to change your start (home) page. Click the **Back button** repeatedly (or click the **down arrow** next to the Back button to display a list of all sites visited) until you return to the home page for the Reference desk.
- ➤ Follow the instructions that you printed out in the previous step. Pull down the **Tools menu** and click the **Internet Options command** to display the Internet Options dialog box as shown in Figure 2f.
- ➤ Click the **General tab**, then click the **Use Current command button** in the Home Page area. Click **OK** to accept the settings and close the dialog box. The next time you start Internet Explorer, you will go immediately to the Reference Desk.

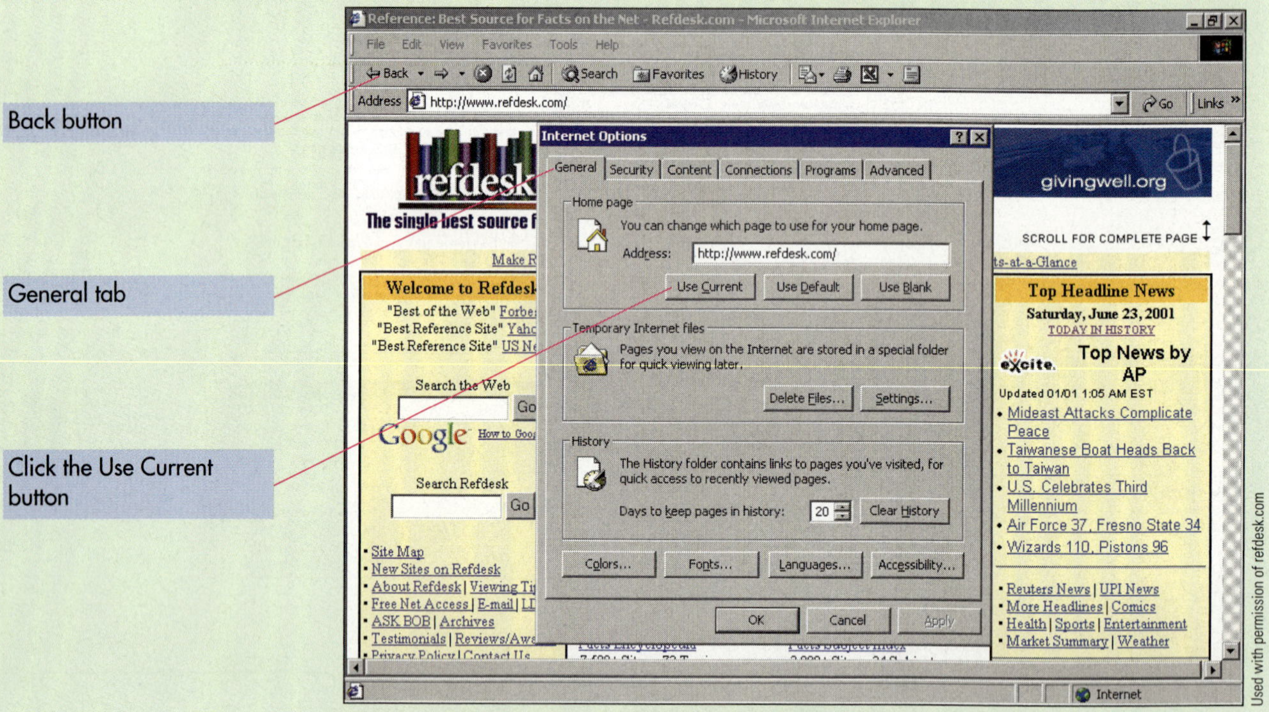

(f) Change the Start Page (step 6)

FIGURE 2 *Hands-on Exercise 1 (continued)*

THE HISTORY LIST

The History list contains links to all pages that you have recently visited for easy access to those sites. It also makes it possible for anyone looking at your computer (e.g. your instructor or employer) to see all of the sites that you have visited. Click the History button on the Standard Buttons toolbar to display the list of sites, click the down arrow next to the View button under History to sort by date, then click any day to view the sites you visited that day. Use the Internet Options command in the Tools menu to clear the History list if you want to erase this information.

Step 7: **Surf the Web**

- You've done what we have asked and have gotten a taste of the World Wide Web. Now it's time to explore on your own by going to new and different sites.
- Return to the Reference Desk and try any of the myriad links that are on this page. Click any link that interests you, and off you go. Use the **Print command** to print an additional page from a second site to prove to your instructor that you did the exercise.
- You can also guess at the address of a site you might want to visit according to the boxed tip below. Type **www.nba.com**, for example, and you will go to the home page of the National Basketball Association as shown in Figure 2g.
- Set a time limit for yourself, as the Web is addicting and you have other work to do. Close Internet Explorer when you are finished exploring. Shut down your computer if you do not wish to do the next exercise at this time.

Enter address

(g) Surf the Web (step 7)

FIGURE 2 *Hands-on Exercise 1 (continued)*

> **GUESS THE URL**
>
> You can often guess the address of a site according to the addressing scheme, www.company.com, such as www.microsoft.com, www.yahoo.com, or www.cnn.com for the home page of Microsoft, Yahoo!, and CNN, respectively. It also works for sports; for example, try www.nfl.com or www.nba.com to go to the home pages of the National Football League or National Basketball Association, the "com" ending takes you to the commercial domain of the Internet, whereas the "edu" ending takes you to the educational domain. Try www.yourschool.edu, for example, to find the home page of your school or university.

The Internet contains a wealth of information that is readily available. That is the good news. The bad news is that the Internet contains so much information that it is often difficult to find what you are looking for. A leisurely stroll from site to site may be interesting and enjoyable, but it is not an efficient means of locating specific information. There is a better way.

A ***search engine*** is a program that systematically searches the Web for documents in response to a specific request (***query***) for information. All search engines work essentially the same way. You enter a key word or phrase into a ***search form*** and then the engine looks for documents that are related to the key words you entered. The engine returns the titles and/or abstracts of the documents it finds (if any), together with a link to each document.

There are many different search engines available, each of which can return different results to the same query, as can be seen in Figure 3. All four engines were instructed to search for information on Albert Einstein. The results of the search are displayed as a series of links underneath the list box. You can click any link in the left pane to display the corresponding document in the right pane; for example, we clicked the first link, Einstein Honored in Figure 3a to see the associated document in the right pane.

Each engine has a slightly different feature set as can be seen by taking a closer look at the left pane in each figure. The MSN Search in Figure 3a, for example, has a check box that lets you display document summaries to quickly see more information about each document. The AltaVista engine in Figure 3b lets you specify the language of the document. Remember the Web is international in scope, and a document in French or Spanish will not do you any good unless you speak the language. The Excite engine in Figure 3c provides immediate access to a Help screen that lets you enter additional parameters to expand or limit the scope of the search. The Yahoo! engine in Figure 3d returns categories (such as "physicists", where you can expect links to physicists other than Einstein) as well as individual documents.

The most significant difference between the engines, however, is the list of documents that appear in response to a given query. Every engine maintains its own database through a program known as a ***spider,*** which continually searches the Web for new pages. Each time the spider finds a new document, it extracts information about that document, such as the URL (Web address), key words that describe the document, and selected information from the document. It's obvious, therefore, that each engine will return a different set of documents to a given query because each engine searches through its own database. Moreover, some search engines store only the document's title, others contain the first few lines of text, and still others contain every word in the document. This, too, affects the results of a search.

Search engines also differ with respect to the algorithm (or process) used to go through the database and the way in which the documents are ranked with respect to their relevancy or likelihood that the document matches the query. Look again at the documents that were returned by the various search engines in Figure 3. Some documents, such as "Albert Einstein online", are listed by more than one engine, as you would expect, although the rank of the document varies from one engine to the next. "Albert Einstein online", for example, was listed first (after the featured sites) for the MSN Search in Figure 3a, but second for the Excite engine in Figure 3c. Suffice it to say, therefore, that *the single most important guideline for a successful search is to use multiple search engines*, because as we have seen, the same query will return different results with different search engines. That said, you can run into two distinct problems—you have either too few documents or too many.

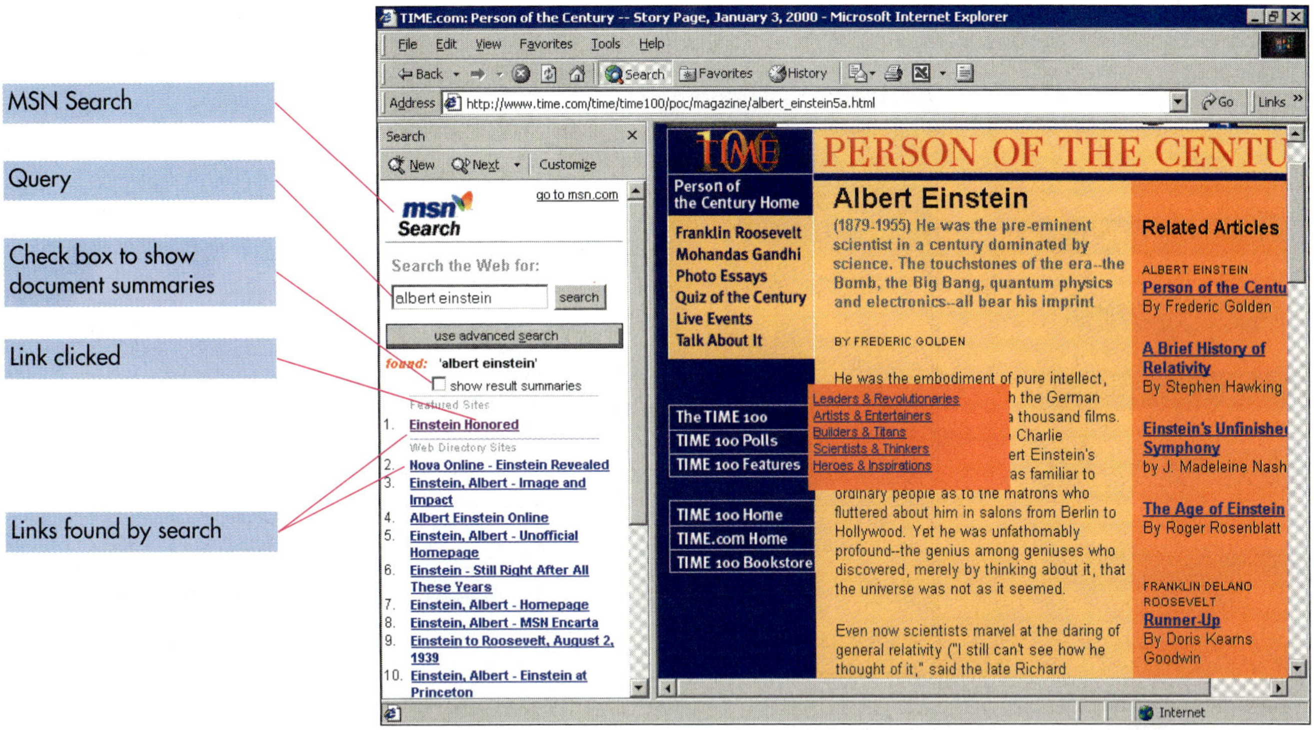

(a) MSN Search Engine

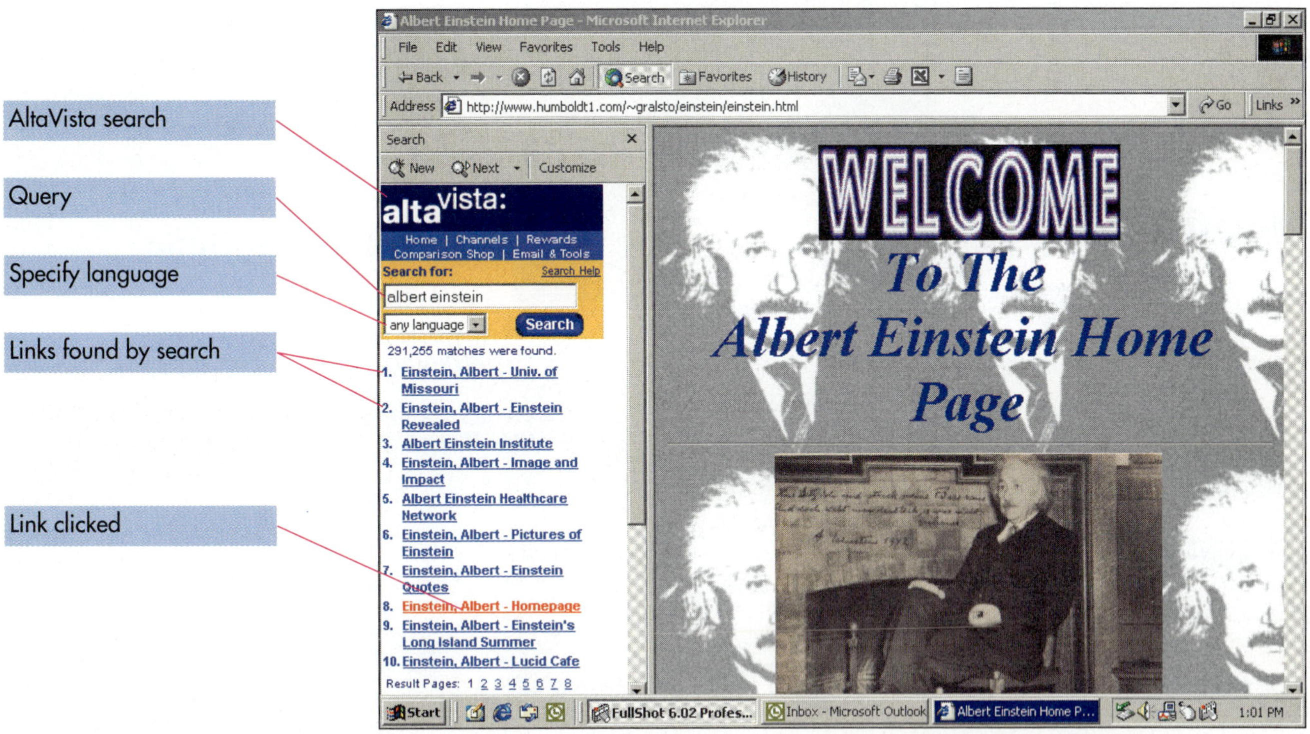

(b) Alta Vista Search Engine

FIGURE 3 *Search Engines*

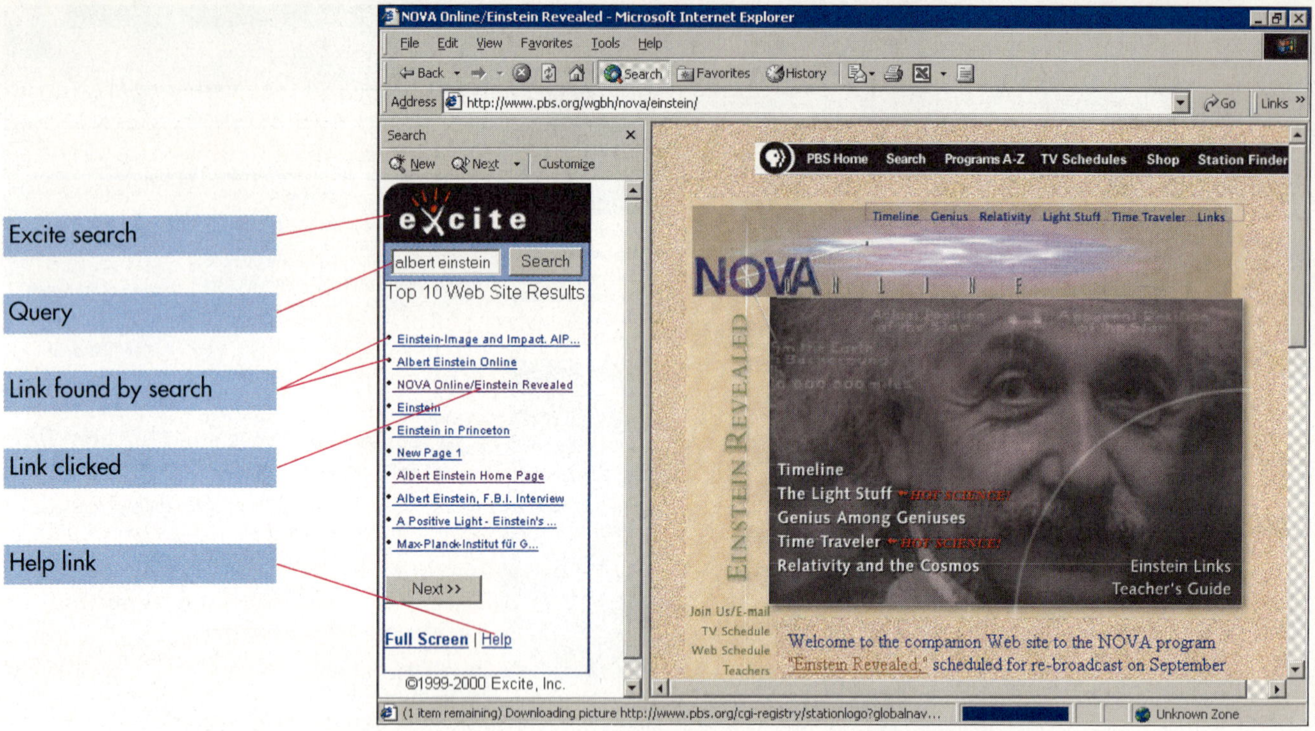

(c) Excite Search Engine

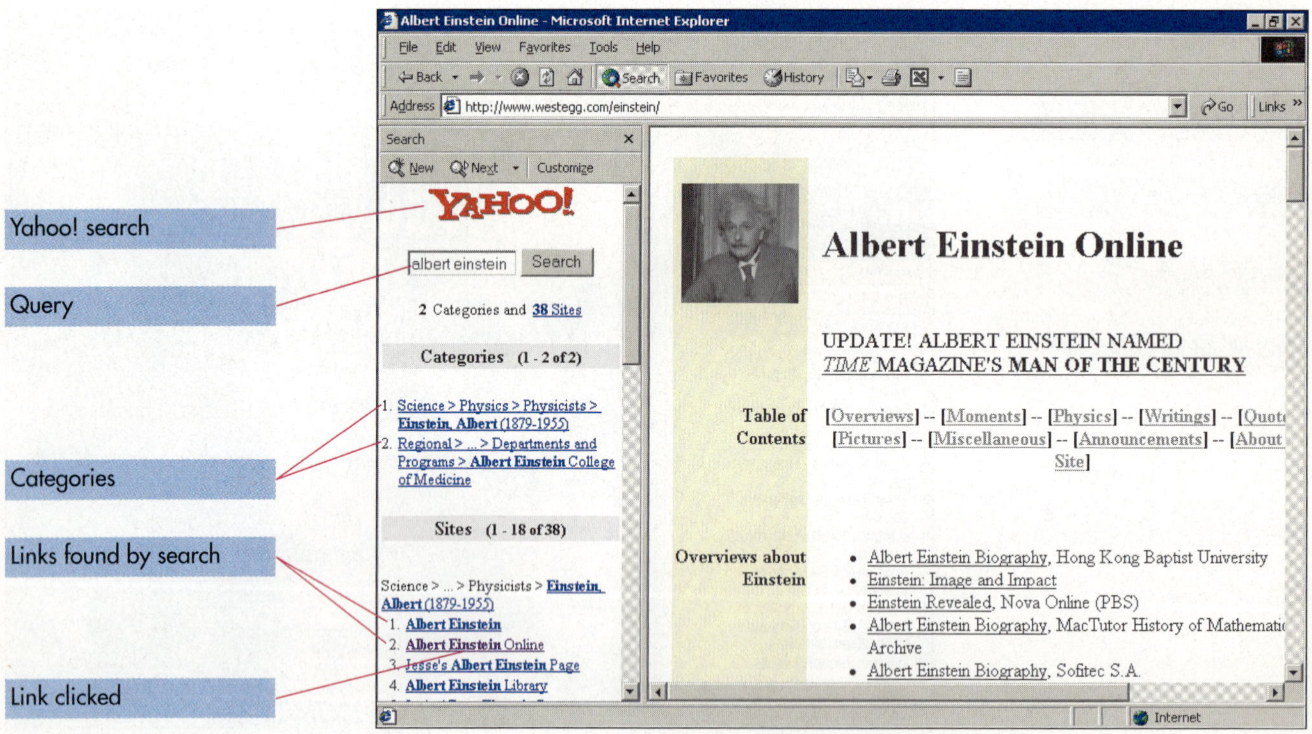

(d) Yahoo! Search Engine

FIGURE 3 *Search Engines (continued)*

Logical (Boolean) Operators

The Web continues to grow exponentially, and as it does, the number of ***hits*** (documents matching your query) that will be returned by a search also increases. A large number of hits does not necessarily guarantee a successful search, however, because you also need to be concerned with the relevancy of those hits. The AltaVista search in Figure 3b returned more than 200,000 potential documents, far too many to review individually. All of those documents contained the key words "Albert Einstein" but many of the documents referred to various hospitals named for the scientist. If you are looking for information about Einstein's life, you are not interested in these documents and would be better served if they were omitted from the list.

You can limit the documents that are returned by a search through a combination of the logical (***Boolean***) ***operators And***, ***Or***, and ***Not***. The And operator requires that every key word must be present. Searching for "American" and "Airlines", for example, will return documents that contain both words such as documents that deal with American Airlines (the airline). The Or operator, however, requires that only one of the terms be present, so that searching for "American" or "Airlines" will return documents containing "American" (anything American) or "Airlines" (any airline). Some search engines also enable you to use Not. Searching for "American Airlines" and not "Arena" will return documents about "American Airlines", but not the American Airlines Arena (in Miami). The way in which you specify the Boolean operators depends on the search engine and is described in its online help.

Explore the URL

We're almost ready for our next hands-on exercise, but first we wanted to share one lesser known technique that we have found to be truly invaluable, and that is to fully explore the URL of a relevant document. The document in Figure 4 is the result of a search on the Sistine Chapel and the works of Michelangelo. The address looks complicated, but it is easily broken down, which in turn can lead to other relevant documents in ways that you might not expect.

The URL of any Web document is composed of several components in the following sequence: the means of access (typically http), the server on which the document is located, the path on that computer (if any) to get to the document, and finally the document itself. Thus the URL in Figure 4 is divided as follows:

http://metalab.unc.edu/wm/paint/auth/michelangelo/michelangelo.creation.jpg

Document

Path (directories)

Server (computer)

Means of access (HyperText Transfer Protocol)

In other words, we found a specific server (whose address is metalab.unc.edu) that contained a picture of a fragment from the ceiling of the Sistine Chapel by Michelangelo. It's logical to think that the same computer may contain other pictures or information in which we would be interested. You can get to that information by backing up one level at a time in the address, starting from the right and moving to the left. Thus you can click in the Address bar and delete the last portion of the address, up to and including the forward slash so that the URL ends simply in "Michelangelo". This will take you to a folder containing information and other works about the artist.

FIGURE 4 *Explore the URL*

Go back one or two levels so that you end on "paint", and you have a listing of all painters on the site, and so on. Continue to backtrack in this way until you get to the Web site itself. Aside from being a wonderful way to browse, it may also be a boon to your research, because you are often searching for a concept rather than a specific term. You might, for example, be interested in Renaissance artists in general, rather than just Michelangelo. If so, you have just discovered an invaluable resource.

Copyright Protection

A ***copyright*** provides legal protection to a written or artistic work, giving the author exclusive rights to its use and reproduction, except as governed under the ***fair use exclusion*** as explained below. Anything on the Internet or World Wide Web should be considered copyrighted unless the document specifically says it is in the ***public domain***, in which case the author is giving everyone the right to freely reproduce and distribute the material.

Does this mean you cannot quote statistics and other facts that you found on the Web in your term papers? Does it mean you cannot download an image to include in your report? The answer to both questions depends on the amount of the material and on your intended use of the information. It is considered fair use, and thus not an infringement of copyright, to use a portion of the work for educational or nonprofit purposes, or for the purpose of critical review or commentary. In other words, you can use a quote, downloaded image, or other information from the Web, provided you cite the original work in your footnotes and/or bibliography. Facts themselves are not covered by copyright, so you can use statistical and other data without fear of infringement. *Be sure, however, to always cite the original source in your document.*

HANDS-ON EXERCISE 2

SEARCHING THE WEB

Objective To search the Web for specific information; to download a photograph and include it in a Word document; to locate an audio file. Use Figure 5 as a guide in the exercise.

Step 1: **Search the Web**

- Start Internet Explorer. It does not matter which page you see initially, as long as you are able to connect to the Internet and start Internet Explorer. Click the **Maximize button** so that Internet Explorer takes the entire screen.
- Click the **Search button** on the Standard Buttons toolbar to display the Search pane in the Explorer bar at the left of the Internet Explorer window. The option button to find a Web page is selected by default.
- Enter **Apollo 11** in the Find a Web page text box, then click the **Search button**. The results of the search are displayed in the left pane as shown in Figure 5a. The results you obtain will be different from ours.
- Check to see which search engine you used, and if necessary click the **down arrow** to the right of the Next button to select **Lycos** (the engine we used). The search will be repeated with this engine. Your results can still be different from ours, because new pages are continually added to the Web.
- Select (click) the link to **Apollo 11 Home**. (Enter the URL www.nasm.edu/apollo/AS11 manually if your search engine does not display this link.)
- Click the **Close button** to close the Search pane, so that your selected document takes the entire screen.

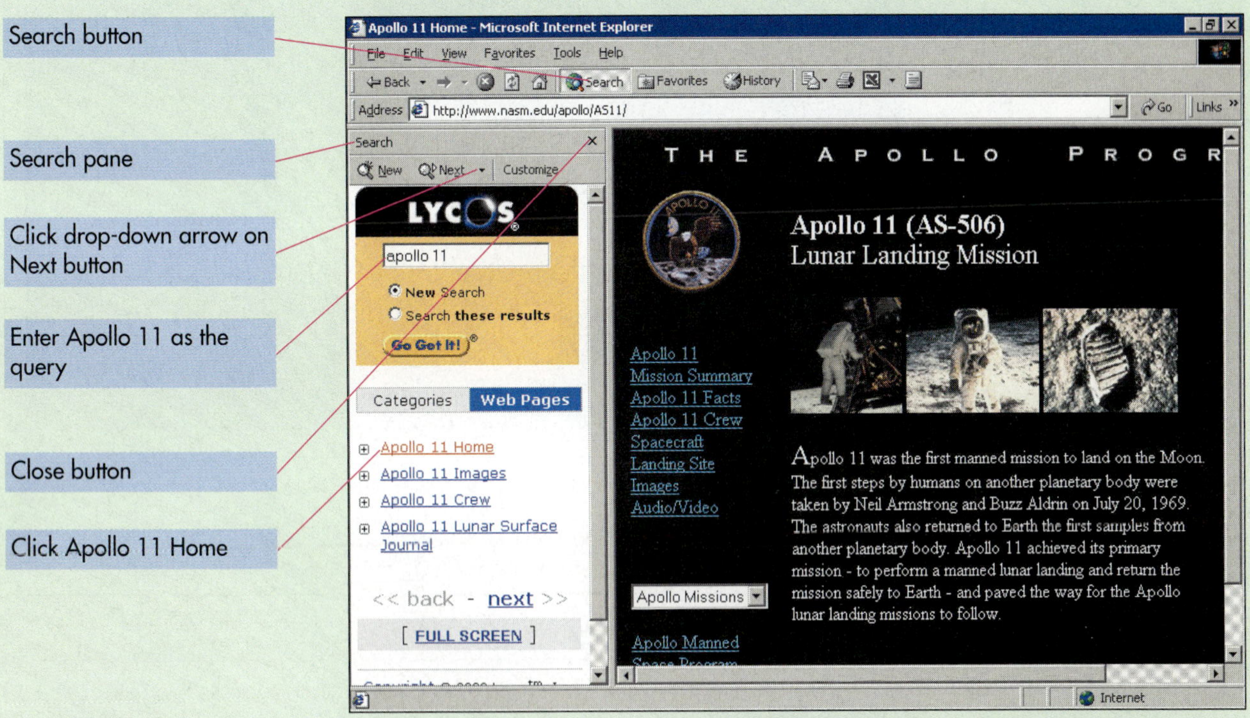

(a) Search the Web (step 1)

FIGURE 5 *Hands-on Exercise 2*

Step 2: **Choose a Picture**

- Click the link to **Images** from the Apollo 11 home page to display multiple images from the Apollo 11 mission as shown in Figure 5b. Choose any image you like. Scroll to the bottom of the page and click the link to **Page 2** to see more images.
- You should download the full picture, rather than the thumbnail image, to avoid distortion when you subsequently include the picture in a document. Thus, click the link under the picture (75K jpeg) to expand the picture.
- Point to the picture you have chosen, click the **right mouse button** to display a shortcut menu, then click the **Save Picture As command** to display the Save As dialog box.
  - Click the **drop-down arrow** in the Save In list box to specify the drive and folder in which to save the graphic (e.g., in the **My Documents folder**).
  - Internet Explorer supplies the file name and file type for you. You may change the name, but you cannot change the file type.
  - Click the **Save button** to download the image. Remember the file name and location, as you will need to access the file in the next step.
- The Save As dialog box will close automatically after the picture has been downloaded. Click the **Minimize button** in the Internet Explorer window.

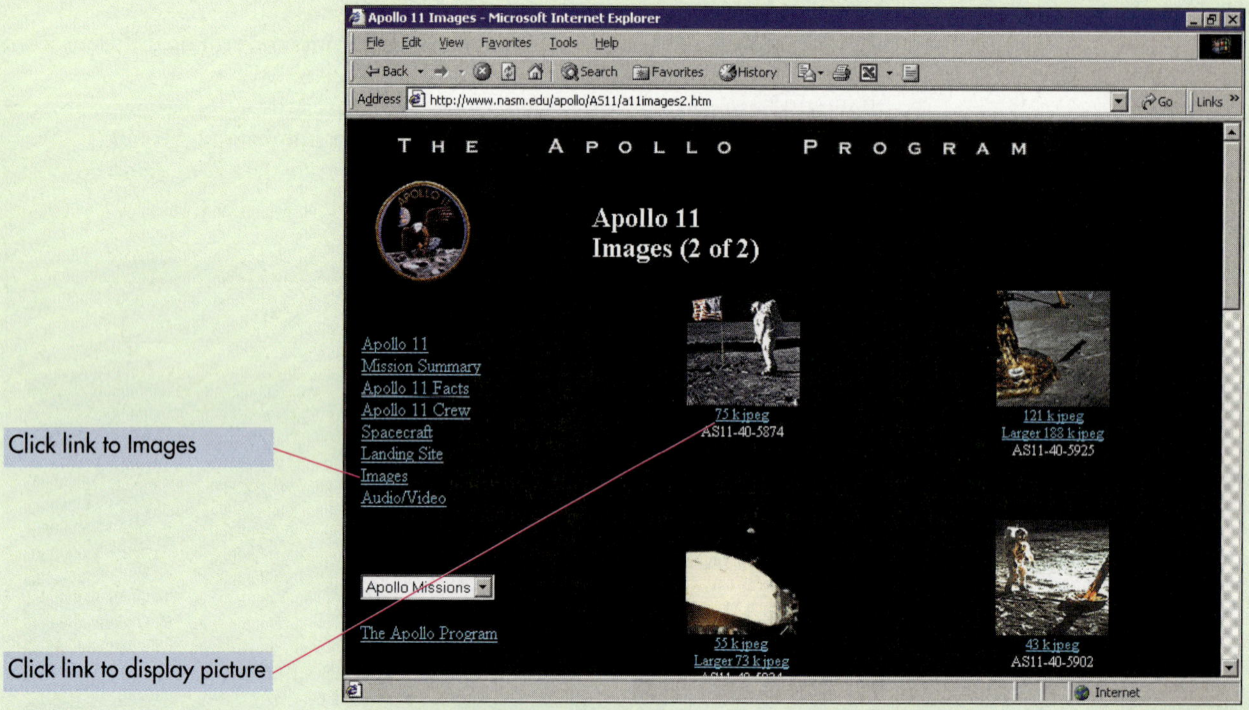

(b) Choose a Picture (step 2)

FIGURE 5 *Hands-on Exercise 2 (continued)*

THE AUTOSEARCH FEATURE

The fastest way to initiate a search is to click in the Address box, enter the key word "go" followed by the topic (e.g., go University of Miami), then press the enter key. Internet Explorer automatically invokes the MSN search engine and returns the relevant documents. Remember, too, that you can guess a Web address by typing, www.company.com.

Step 3: Insert the Picture

- Start Word, and if necessary, maximize the application window. Close the task pane. Pull down the **View menu** to be sure that you are in the **Print Layout view** (or else you will not see the picture after it is inserted into the document).
- Enter the title and quotation in an appropriate font and point size as shown in Figure 5c. (The Insert Picture dialog box is not yet visible.) Type your name under the quotation, press **enter**, then enter any additional information required by your instructor. Center the text. Press **enter** to begin a new line.
- Pull down the **Insert menu**, click **Picture**, then click **From File** to display the Insert Picture dialog box. Select the drive and folder in which you saved the picture (e.g., My Documents on drive C). Click the **down arrow** on the Files of type list box and specify **All files**.
- Select (click) the picture (e.g., **AS11_40-5874**), then click **Insert**, and the picture is inserted into the Word document. Do not worry about its size or position at this time.
- Save the document as **Apollo 11**.

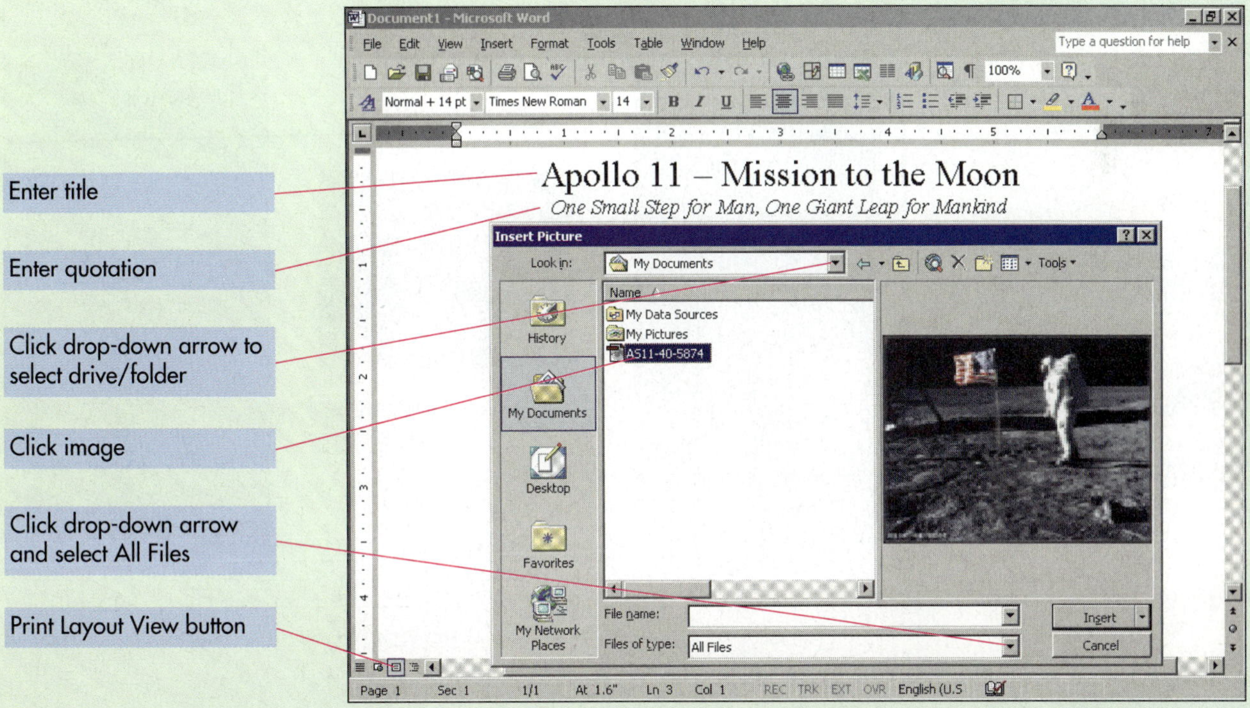

(c) Insert the Picture (step 3)

FIGURE 5 *Hands-on Exercise 2 (continued)*

MULTITASKING

Multitasking, the ability to run multiple applications at the same time, is one of the primary advantages of the Windows environment. Switching from one application to another is easy—just click the appropriate button on the Windows taskbar. You can also use the classic Alt+Tab shortcut. Press and hold the Alt key as you click the Tab key repeatedly to display and select icons for the open applications, then release the Tab key when the desired application icon is selected.

Step 4: **Move and Size the Picture**

- Pull down the **View menu**, click **Zoom**, then click the option button to zoom to **Whole Page**. Click **OK**. Right click the picture to display a context-sensitive menu, then click the **Format Picture command** to display the Format Picture dialog box.
- Click the **Layout tab**, then choose any wrapping style other than In line with text. You will now be able to move and size the picture as shown in Figure 5d.
  - To size the picture, drag a corner handle (the mouse pointer changes to a double arrow) to keep the object in proportion.
  - To move the picture, point to any part of the picture except a sizing handle (the mouse pointer changes to a four-sided arrow) and click and drag the picture elsewhere in the document.
- Save the document.

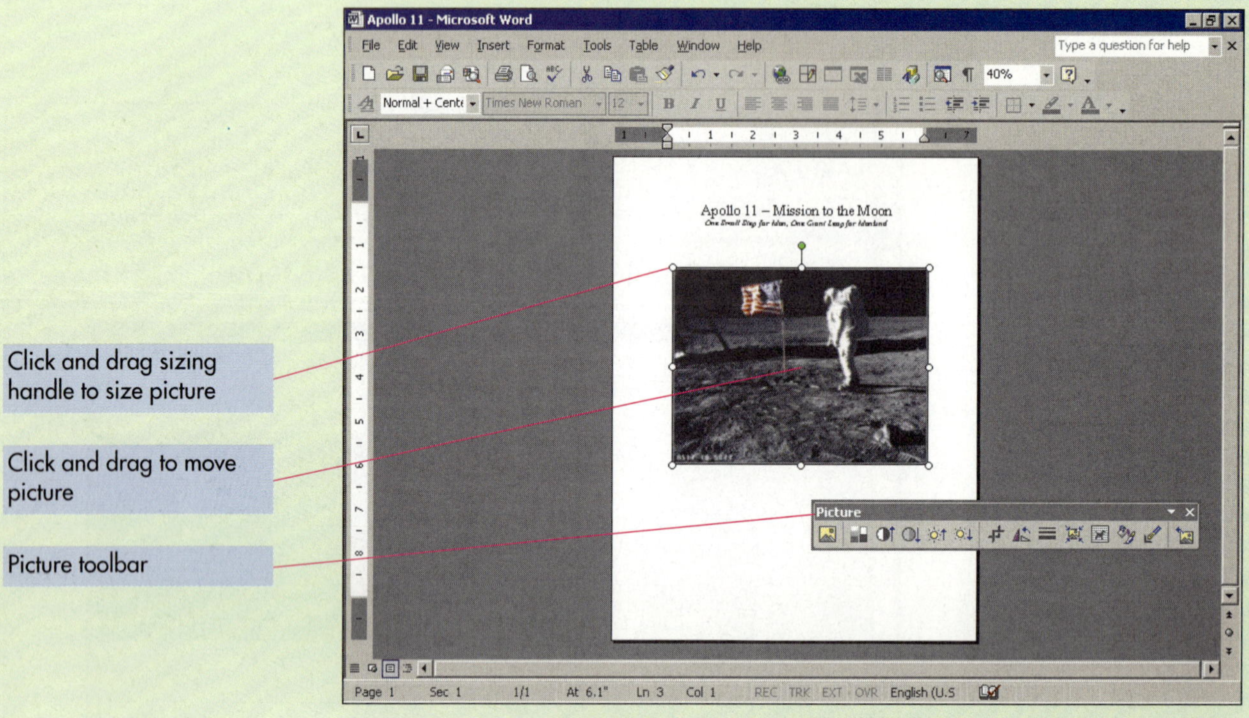

(d) Move and Size the Picture (step 4)

FIGURE 5 *Hands-on Exercise 2 (continued)*

CROPPING A PICTURE

The Crop tool is one of the most useful tools when dealing with a photograph as it let you eliminate (crop) part of a picture. Select (click) the picture to display the Picture toolbar and sizing handles. (If you do not see the Picture toolbar, right click the picture to display a context-sensitive menu, then click the Show Picture Toolbar command. Click the Crop tool (the ScreenTip will display the name of the tool), then click and drag a sizing handle to crop the part of the picture you want to eliminate. Click the Crop button a second time to turn the feature off.

Step 5: **Insert a Footnote**

- Click after the words Apollo 11 (the point at which you will insert the footnote) in the title of the document. Pull down the **Insert menu**. Click **Reference**, then click **Footnote** to display the Footnote and Endnote dialog box in Figure 5e.
- Check that the option button for Footnotes is selected and that the Numbering drop-down list is set to Continuous. Click **Insert**.
- Word inserts a new footnote and simultaneously moves the insertion point to the bottom of the page to add the actual note. Zoom to **Page Width**.
- Enter the address of the Web page from where you took the picture, together with an appropriate reference.
- Click at the end of the quotation, and insert a second footnote indicating that these are the words of Neil Armstrong as he became the first person to set foot on the moon.
- Save the document. Print the cover page for your instructor as proof you did this exercise. Close Word.

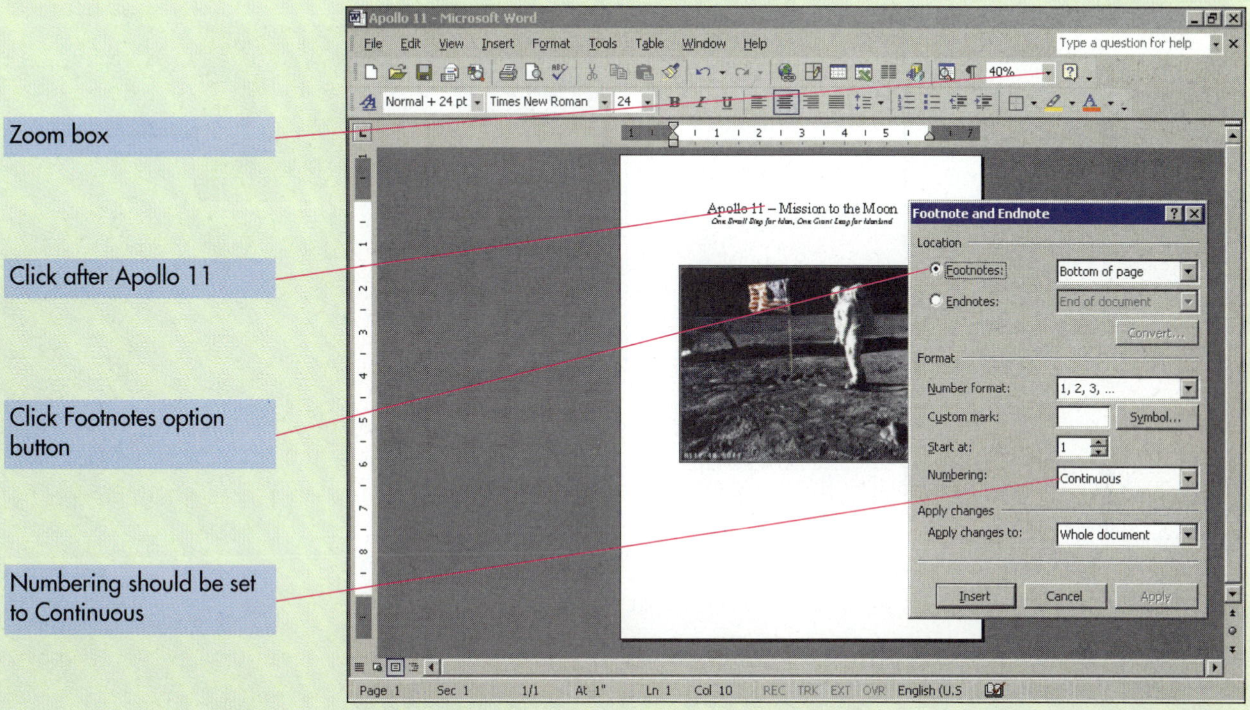

(e) Insert a Footnote (step 5)

FIGURE 5 *Hands-on Exercise 2 (continued)*

ENTER THE URL AUTOMATICALLY

Use the Copy command to enter the URL into a footnote. Not only do you save time by not having to type the address yourself, but you also ensure that it is entered correctly. Click in the Address bar of Internet Explorer to select the URL, then pull down the Edit menu and click the Copy command (or use the Ctrl+C Windows shortcut). Switch to the Word document, click at the place in the document where you want to insert the URL, then pull down the Edit menu and click Paste (or press Ctrl+V).

Step 6: **Use Multiple Search Engines**

- If necessary, point to the bottom of the screen to display the taskbar, then click the button for **Internet Explorer**. Click the **Search button** on the toolbar to reopen the Search pane.
- You do not need to initiate a new search if you still see the previous query for Apollo 11. Just click the **down arrow** to the right of the Next button and select **Yahoo!** from the list of available search engines. (If the previous query is no longer there, click the **New button** to reenter the search parameters, then click the Next button to select Yahoo! as the search engine.)
- The results of our search are shown in Figure 5f, but you will most likely see a different set of documents from ours. Select any document in the right pane, then print the selected document for your instructor.

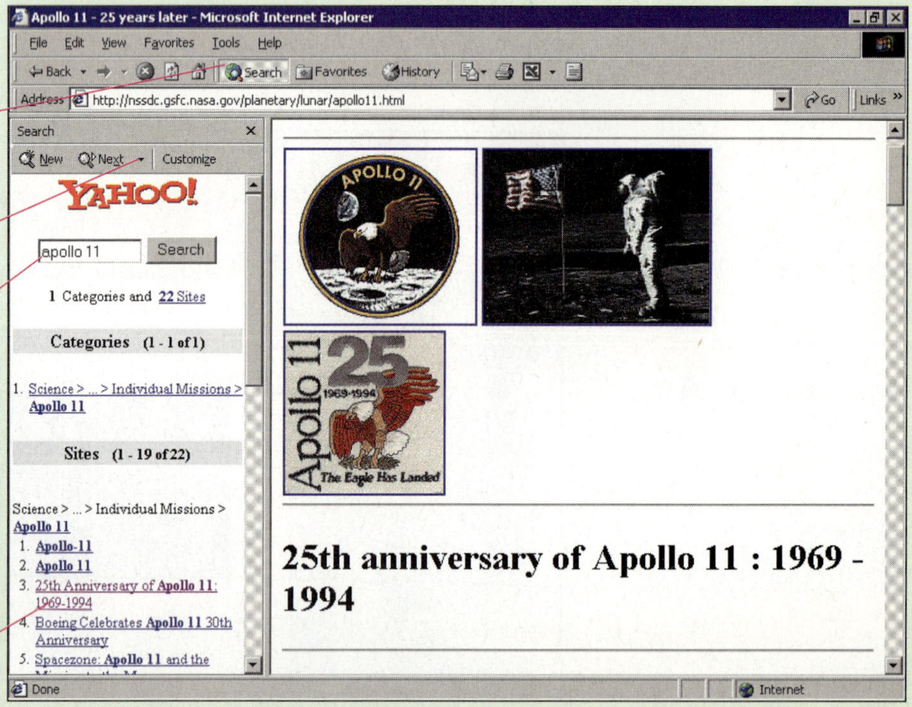

(f) Use Multiple Search Engines (step 6)

FIGURE 5 *Hands-on Exercise 2 (continued)*

ABOUT YAHOO!—CATEGORIES VERSUS DOCUMENTS

Yahoo! (www.yahoo.com) is one of the oldest and best-known search tools on the Web. It provides a search engine in which you can enter the text of a specific query. It also organizes its database into categories (a list of sites) that let you search in a more leisurely way. Click any category and you are taken to a list of subcategories, which in turn take you to other categories, which lead eventually to specific documents. You can browse leisurely through the listed categories that often suggest related sites that you might not have considered initially.

Step 7: Advanced Search

- Click the **down arrow** to the right of the Next button to select the **MSN** search engine. (Choose any other engine if you do not see this engine.)
- Click the **Use Advanced Search** link to display the form shown in Figure 5g. Check the **Audio** box, then click the **Search button** to look for documents that contain audio files pertaining to the Apollo 11 mission.
- Choose any document that seems appropriate, then click the link to play the sound file, in this case, Neil Armstrong's words as he set foot on the moon. Sound and video are an integral part of the Web.
- The bottom line—searching the Web is a trial-and-error process in which you continually try new searches until you locate the information you need.
- Close Internet Explorer if you do not want to continue with the next exercise at this time.

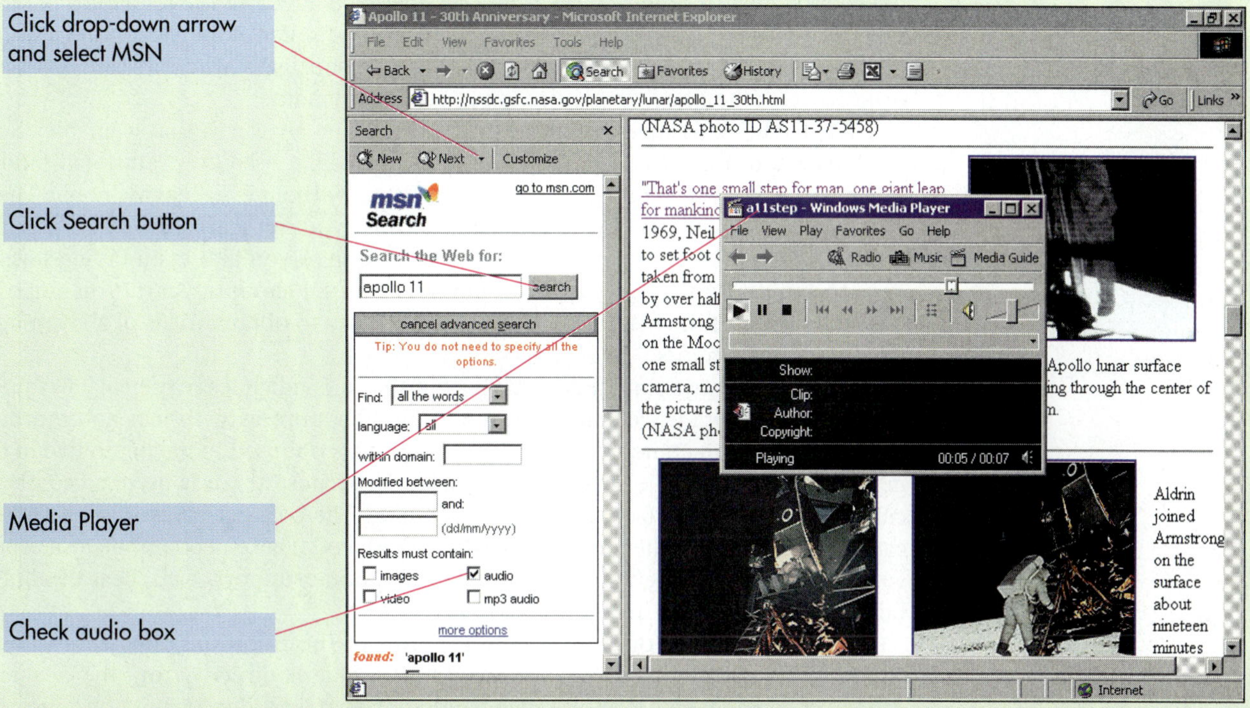

(g) Advanced Search (step 7)

FIGURE 5 *Hands-on Exercise 2 (continued)*

ASK JEEVES

"Ask Jeeves" is a natural search engine in which you type your request in the form of a question. Jeeves will search through its own database, and in addition, display the hits it obtains using other search engines. You cannot access Jeeves directly from the Internet Explorer Search button, and have to enter its URL (www.askjeeves.com) directly in the Address bar. See exercise 3 at the end of the chapter.

It's difficult to think of the Internet as existing without any type of commercial enterprise. The Internet began, however, as a project of the United States government with a strict prohibition against commercial activity. It was not until 1991, some twenty years after its inception, that the National Science Foundation lifted the prohibition on commercial use. The subsequent growth has been both unprecedented and exponential, as companies of every size, from multinational corporations to "mom and pop" shops, maintain sites and conduct business on the Web.

The world has truly changed, and you cannot escape (nor do you want to) the excitement and potential of the new economy. The best way to appreciate the impact of ***e-commerce*** is to step back and think of commerce in the traditional sense, which is nothing more than the exchange of goods and services. The same elements are present, regardless of whether you go to a mall or shop on the Web. Commerce of either type involves buyers and sellers, products and services, and suppliers or producers of the products and services. The buyer and seller need a place to meet in order for the transaction to take place. The seller employs various marketing strategies to attract the buyer to the place of business, where it can accept an order, deliver the goods or services, then accept payment.

What then is so special about e-commerce? The answer is that it enables both the buyer and seller to do things that are not possible with the traditional model. The buyer can shop 24 hours a day, 7 days a week, without ever leaving home. There is no need to walk up and down the aisles, because you can search the entire product line with the click of a mouse. You can shop as long as you like, even taking several days to build an order as you add items to a virtual shopping cart. You can also assure yourself of the best price because it is so easy to obtain prices of a given item from multiple vendors.

The seller enjoys similar advantages because it is much less expensive to implement and maintain a Web site than it is to build a store with "bricks and mortar." The customers can come from all over the world, as opposed to having to live in the neighborhood. The seller can stock more items because there is no need to physically display products or even to print a catalog. The cost per transaction is significantly lower because the personnel costs are reduced. There need not be a salesperson although many Web sites do provide telephone support. And, best of all, the business remains open around the clock.

We tend to think of e-commerce in terms of the traditional business-to-consumer or retail model, where the consumer purchases directly from the business. Money does not even have to change hands, however, in order for both business and consumer to reap benefits through e-commerce or more generally, through e-business. For example, a business can provide information electronically over the Web and save the cost of printing and distribution. Consumers benefit as well by having instant access to their accounts 24 hours a day, as opposed to having to wait for a monthly statement. The Web also makes it possible to build consumer-to-consumer sites such as eBay.com (the online auction site). And all of this activity pales before the potential of the ***business-to-business (B2B)*** model in which businesses interact electronically to exchange goods and services.

THE MALL WILL NOT GO AWAY

It's convenient to shop on the Web, especially if you know exactly what you want and/or you are pressed for time. It's not as much fun, however, as going to the mall, meeting your friends, trying on clothes, seeing and touching a real product, or having a snack at the "Food Court." In short, shopping is a social experience, and the mall is not going to disappear.

Security

The advent of commercial activity brought about a fundamental rethinking of the way data is transmitted across the Internet. ***Security*** was suddenly essential, but this contradicted the original vision of the Internet as an open network that allowed all users open access to resources on remote computers. The Internet was built on data traveling freely from one computer to another, as it is routed through multiple networks to reach its destination. Each computer along the way has access to that data, which is a potential problem if the information is confidential (e.g., a credit card number).

E-commerce, however, depends entirely on the availability of secure transactions. The buyer and seller must both be assured that data is safe and cannot be compromised. This is accomplished through ***encryption***, the process of encoding data so that it is no longer in its original form when it is sent across the Internet. The precise way in which data is encrypted prior to being sent, then decrypted on the receiving end, is beyond the scope of our description. Just realize that encryption is built into Internet Explorer and that it takes place automatically when you communicate with a secure site.

Figures 6a and 6b illustrate a nonsecure and a secure connection, respectively. Any information that is transmitted in connection with Figure 6a (e.g., clicking on any of the links on the page) is of a nonconfidential nature and need not be encrypted. You can tell that the transmission is not secure in two ways—the transmission protocol is http, and the status bar does not contain a padlock icon. The form in Figure 6b, however, contains confidential data (a Login ID and password) and thus it needs to be encrypted before it is sent. You can tell that the connection is secure because a different protocol, ***https*** rather than http, is in effect, and further because the status bar in Internet Explorer displays a padlock icon. If you intend to participate in e-commerce in any way, you should be aware of the different ways to transmit data (encrypted versus unencrypted) and the implications of each. You can feel comfortable, for example, transmitting data of a nonpersonal nature via the http (nonsecure) protocol. Anything of a confidential nature, however, such as a credit card or account number, should be sent only with the secure protocol.

A SIMPLE ENCRYPTION ALGORITHM

Julius Caesar is given credit for developing one of the oldest encryption schemes. Caesar used a simple substitution algorithm in which each letter in the original text was replaced by the letter three positions further in the alphabet. The letter "a" was replaced by the letter "d," the letter "b" by the letter "e," and so on. The word "cat," for example, would be encrypted as "fdw." It was simple, but it worked as long as the recipient knew the key, the number of letters to jump in the alphabet.

Privacy

You can't have it both ways. The convenience of returning to a site and having the site know your likes and dislikes in order to steer you to the goods or information you are most likely to request, is offset by the thought that the site knows all about you. How much it knows, and what it will do with that information, are growing concerns. It is all a function of ***cookies***—the small files that are written to your hard drive each time you visit a site. There is nothing harmful about a cookie per se. It is not a virus, and it will not erase or alter the programs on your computer. It is simply a text file that contains information about your visit to a site, and therein lies the problem.

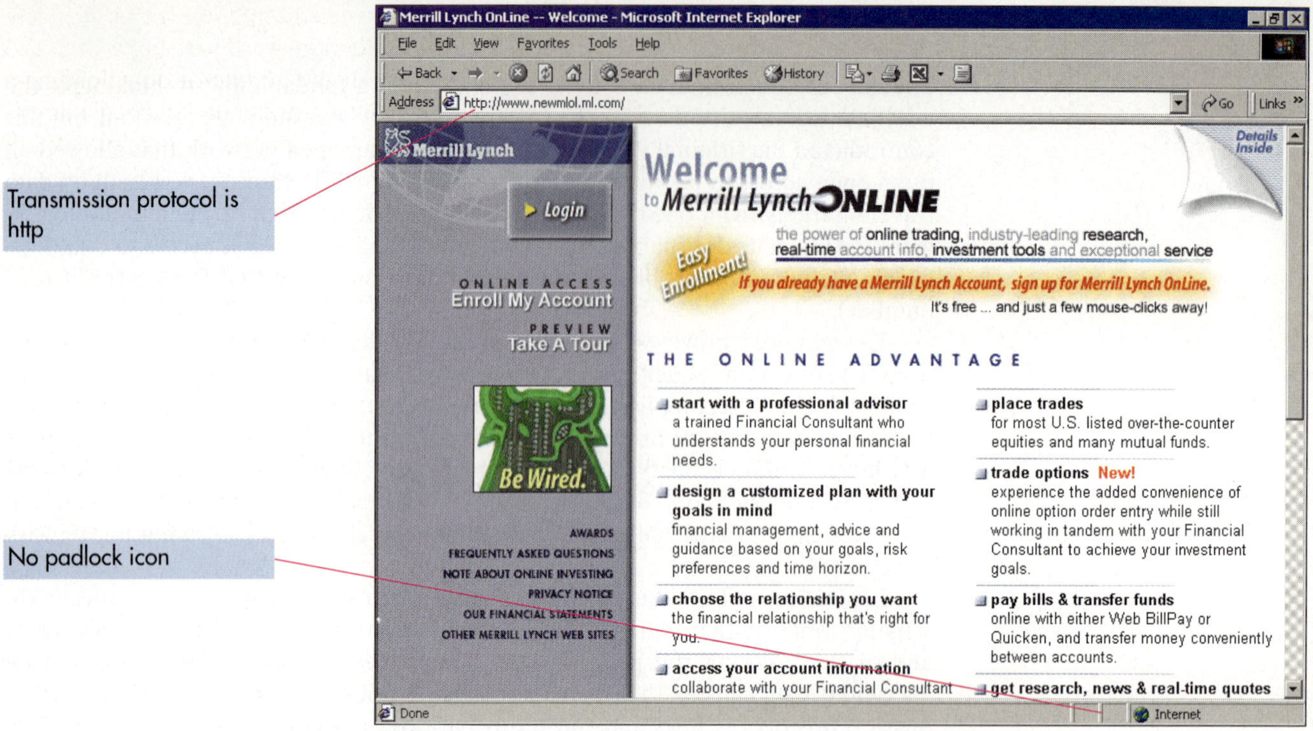

(a) Nonsecure Connection (http protocol)

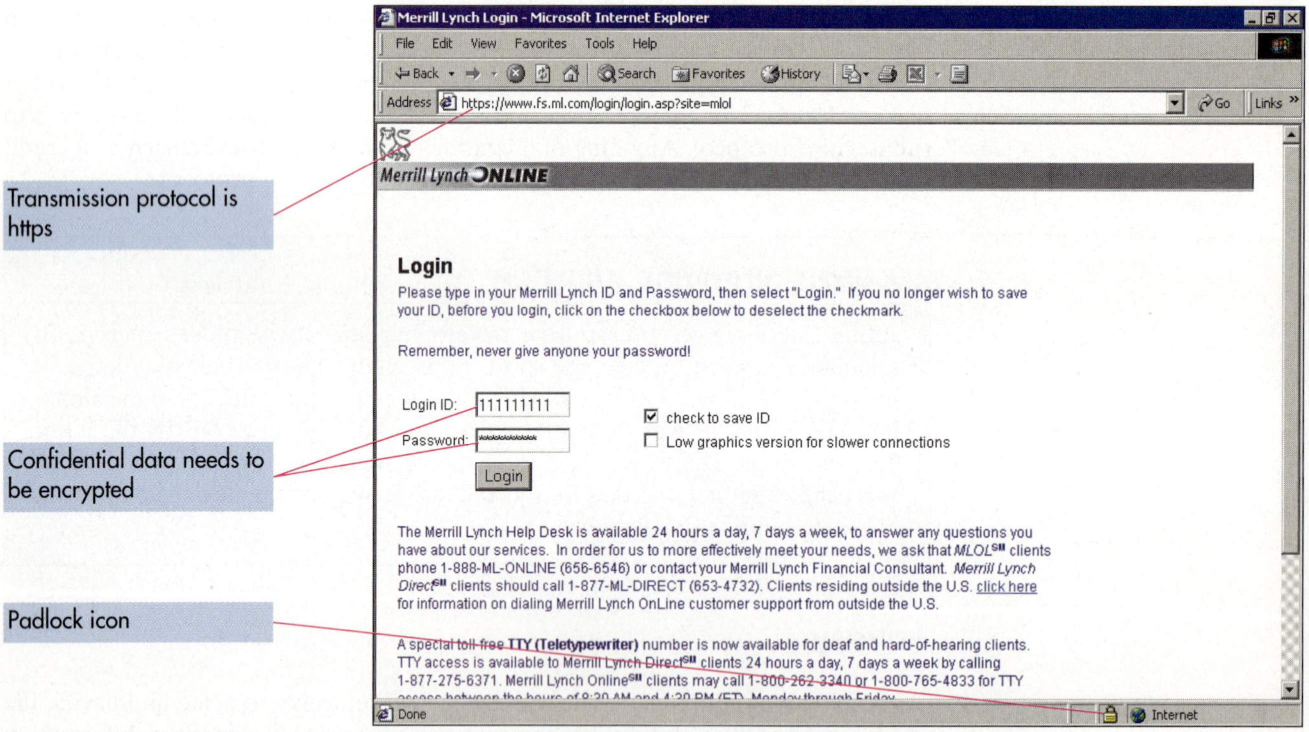

(b) Secure Connection (https protocol)

FIGURE 6 *Security on the Web*

In essence, cookies enable you to personalize your interaction with a Web site and thus offer a tremendous convenience while simultaneously raising a threat to your privacy. If, for example, you are interrupted in the middle of downloading a large file, a cookie makes it possible for you to reconnect to the site and begin downloading at the point where you were disconnected. Most people would agree that's good, but it is possible only because the site wrote a cookie to your computer with information about your progress. Cookies also make it possible for a retail site to send you information about the types of products you are likely to buy. Many people would think that's good, but it also means that the site knows your shopping habits, which it learned by recording the types of links you selected and the purchases you made. Cookies also let you customize various sites so that you see immediately the news or stock prices of interest to you. That can be good, but it means that the site can make inferences about stocks you own.

Cookies have always been present, but it is only recently that they have raised a furor. Most people would agree that individual cookies are not harmful. If, for example, you purchase CDs online, it is convenient for the site to know the type of music and/or artists that you like in order to notify you of new releases. One cookie from one site is not likely to invade your ***privacy***. Nor are several cookies from several sites because a site can read only the cookie it created.

But what if one site could read the cookies from several sites? That is precisely what a company called DoubleClick.com has accomplished. DoubleClick is in the business of placing ads on multiple Web sites, enabling it to write cookies to a machine from multiple places, and thereby track the movements of that machine across many sites. It can tell not only what was purchased, but also which sites were visited along the way, and even the identity of the person on the machine. Some people are indifferent, whereas others are incensed at the invasion of privacy. Our objective is simply to make you aware of what is technically possible.

Returning to a Previous Site

Internet Explorer enables you to move effortlessly from one Web document to another. As you browse through the Web, it's all too easy to forget how you arrived at a particular site, making it difficult to return to that site. You could click the ***Back button*** repeatedly, but that is somewhat tedious, and further, it works only for the particular session. What if you wanted to return to a site you visited last Monday? Internet Explorer anticipates the problem and provides two different sets of links, the Favorites list and the History list.

The ***Favorites list*** in Figure 7a consists of sites that you save with the expectation of returning to those sites at a future time. (Favorites are not restricted to Web sites and can include folders and/or documents on your machine.) Once you arrive at a site that you consider special, just pull down the Favorites menu and click the Add to Favorites command. Internet Explorer then creates a link to that site within the Favorites list. The links can be stored individually, or they can be stored with related links in a folder. The typical user starts by creating individual links, then eventually opts for folders to organize the links more efficiently.

The ***History list*** in Figure 7b is even easier to use in that the links are created automatically and consist of all sites that were visited during a specified time span. (The default is 20 days.) The links in the History list are organized automatically into subfolders, one for each day of the current week, then a separate folder for previous weeks. The links are further divided to show the site, then the various pages at that site.

Either list can be displayed by clicking the appropriate button on the Internet Explorer toolbar. The buttons function as toggle switches; that is, click the Favorites button, and the Favorites list is displayed in a separate pane. Click the Favorites button a second time and the list disappears.

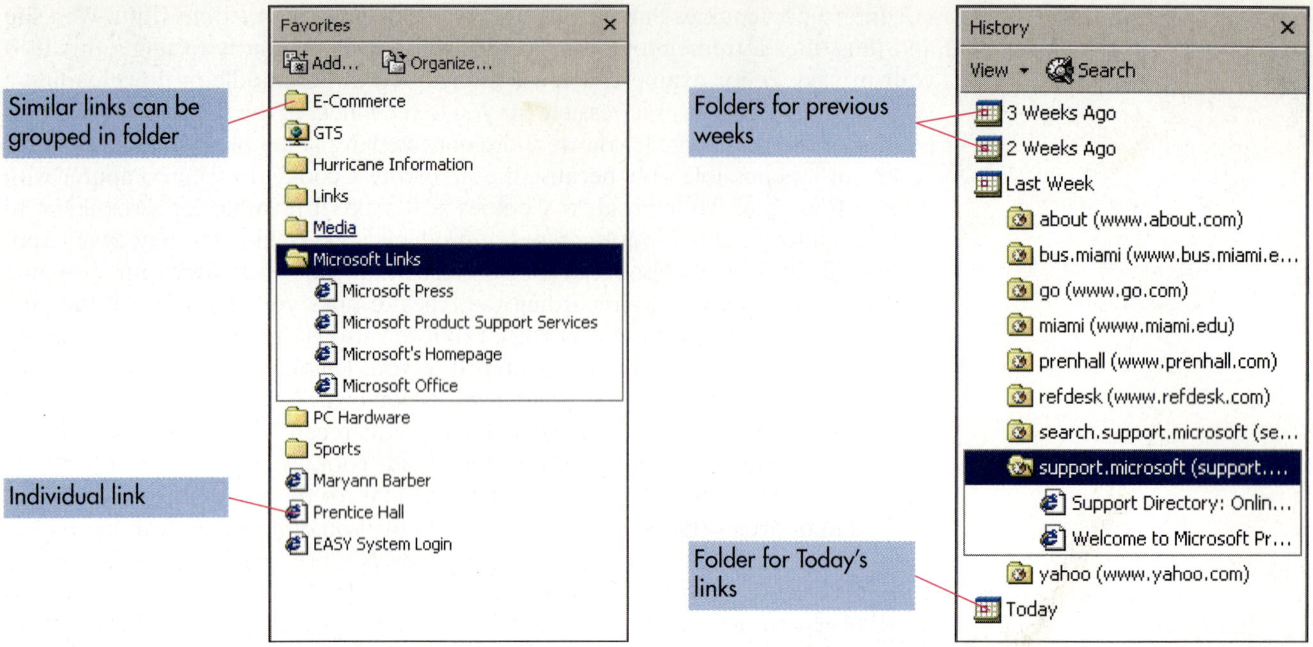

(a) Favorites Folder (b) History Folder

FIGURE 7 *Returning to a Previous Site*

OUR NEXT EXERCISE

Our next exercise takes you on a virtual shopping spree in which you visit several well-known commercial sites. Window shopping is perfectly acceptable, and there is no requirement to buy anything. Our objective is to show you the potential of shopping on the Web, to illustrate the security protocols we have been discussing, and to demonstrate the creation of a cookie. We also illustrate the Favorites list and the History list.

Our exercise focuses on the Barnes & Noble Web site, which is "traditional" in the sense that you browse through a well-defined inventory and purchase items at a specified price. We deliberately limited our shopping spree, but you might want to include additional stops. Start with eBay (www.ebay.com), where buyers and sellers are brought together in an online auction. As exciting as the concept of an auction may be, there is another class of buyers that wants a bargain, knows exactly what they want, but simply does not have the patience to wait for bidding to be completed. If that describes your shopping preference, visit www.half.com, where you can obtain previously owned items at no more than one half of their original price. The price is posted and there is no waiting for the auction to be complete. And finally, you can visit www.priceline.com, where you name your price for airline tickets, hotel rooms, and rental cars.

SET A TIME LIMIT

The exercise you are about to do has you browse continually, looking for interesting sites on which to hone your skills. We warn you that the Web is addictive, and that once you start surfing, it is difficult to stop. We suggest, therefore, that you set a time limit before you begin, and that you stick to it when the time has expired. Tomorrow is another day, with new places to explore.

Hands-on Exercise 3

Shopping in Cyberspace

Objective To explore shopping on the Web and to illustrate the use of the https protocol; to organize favorites more efficiently through creation of a folder. Use Figure 8 as a guide in the exercise.

Step 1: **Visit Barnes & Noble**

- Start Internet Explorer. Click in the Address bar and type **www.barnes&noble.com** or **www.bn.com** (either address will work). Press **enter**.
- You should see the home page of Barnes & Noble. Click the **Favorites button** on the Standard Buttons toolbar to display the Favorites list.
- The Favorites button functions as a toggle switch; that is, click the button, and the Favorites list is displayed. Click the button a second time and the list is closed.
- The contents of your Favorites list will be different from ours, but it should not yet include the Barnes & Noble site. Pull down the **Favorites menu** and click the **Add to Favorites command** to display the Add Favorite dialog box in Figure 8a.
- Click **OK** to add the site to your list of favorites and close the Add Favorite dialog box. The Barnes & Noble site should appear within the Favorites list. Click the **Favorites button** to see if it's there.

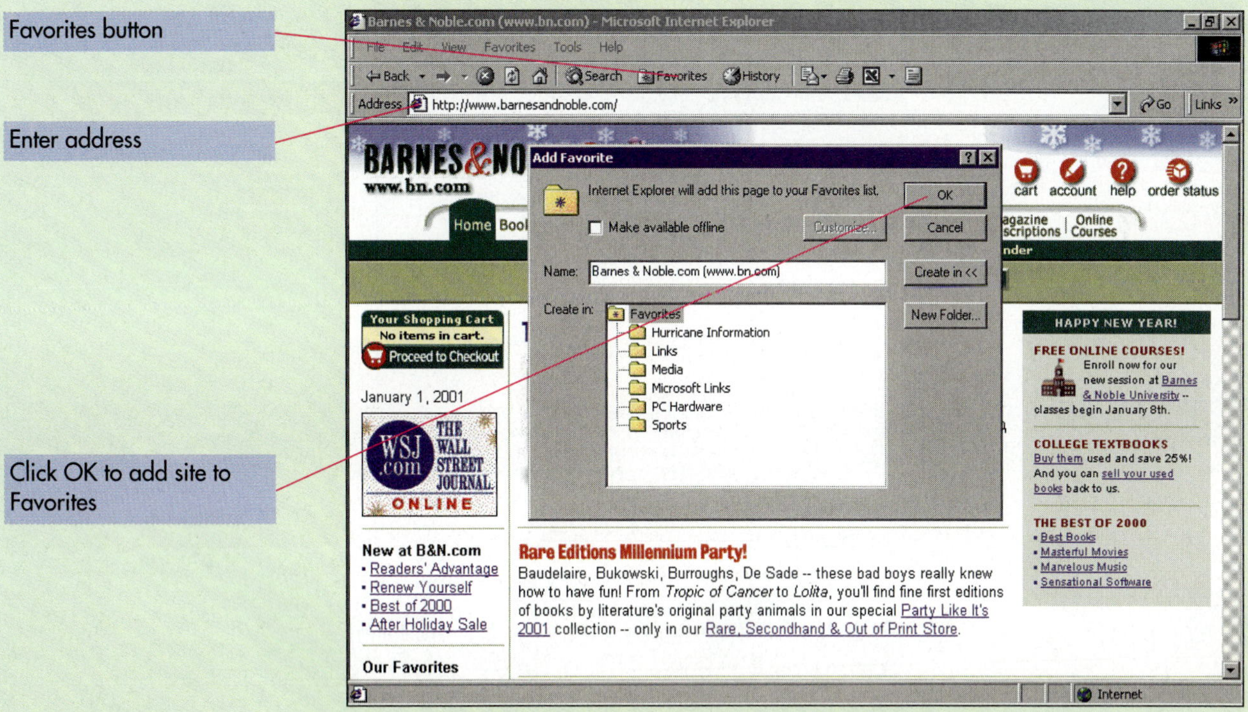

(a) Visit Barnes & Noble (step 1)

Figure 8 *Hands-on Exercise 3*

Step 2: Create the E-Commerce Folder

- ➤ It's more efficient to store related links in a folder, as opposed to a single list of favorites. Pull down the **Favorites menu** and click the **Organize Favorites command** (or click the **Organize button** from within the Favorites pane) to display the Organize Favorites dialog box.
- ➤ Click the **Create Folder button**. A new folder appears within the dialog box, with the default name of the folder (New Folder). Type **E-Commerce** as the name of the folder and press **enter**.
- ➤ Select (click) the link to Barnes & Noble that you added in the previous step. Click the **Move to Folder** button within the Organize Favorites dialog box as shown in Figure 8b. Select the newly created E-Commerce folder and click **OK**.
- ➤ The Barnes & Noble link disappears from within the Organize Favorites dialog box because it has been moved to the E-commerce folder. Click the folder to open it, and you will see the Barnes & Noble link within the folder. Close the Organize Favorites dialog box.
- ➤ Click the **Favorites button** on the Standard Buttons toolbar to open the Favorites pane, which now contains the E-commerce folder. Click the **Favorites button** a second time to close the Favorites pane.

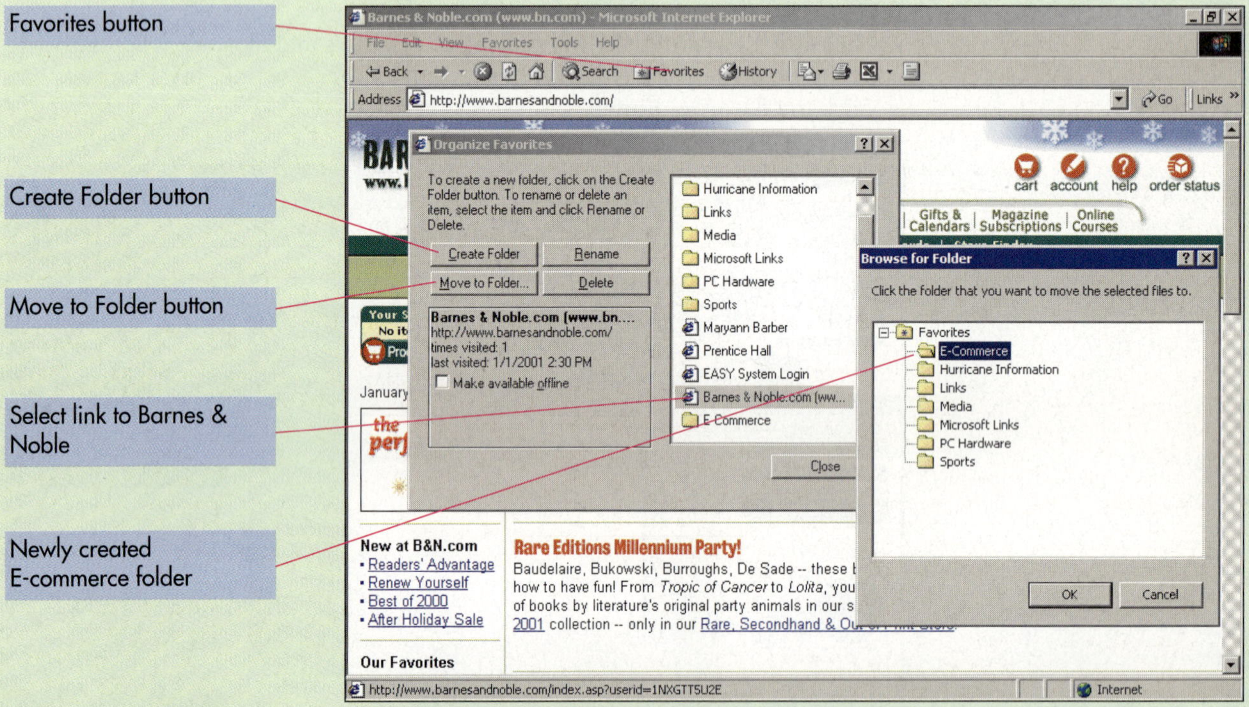

(b) Create the E-Commerce Folder (step 2)

FIGURE 8 *Hands-on Exercise 3 (continued)*

THE RIGHT MOUSE BUTTON

The right mouse button is one of the best-kept secrets in Windows, but it is one of the most powerful techniques you can use. Point to any object in a standard Windows application and click the right mouse button to display a context-sensitive menu with commands. Use the technique within the Favorites list to delete, rename, or copy any folder or individual link.

Step 3: **Search for a Book**

- Click the **Bookstore tab** at the top of the Barnes & Noble site. Click the **down arrow** in the Key word list box (near the top of the screen) and select **Title**.
- Type **Harry Potter** in the Search text box, then click the **Search button** at the top of the page. You should see a list of all titles that contain Harry Potter as shown in Figure 8c. (The large number of titles is attributed to the many different editions that exist for each book in the series.)
- You can add any title to your shopping cart immediately by clicking the **Add to Cart button**. Alternatively, you can select the link to any title to read more about a selection, then decide if you want to purchase the book.
- Add at least one item to your shopping cart, click the **Proceed to Checkout button** to initiate the actual purchase, then click the link to **Checkout Now**.
- Enter your e-mail address and click **Continue Checkout**. We will *not* ask you to purchase a book, but we want you to see the beginning of the checkout process.
- Click **OK** if you see a security alert indicating that you are about to view a secure page.

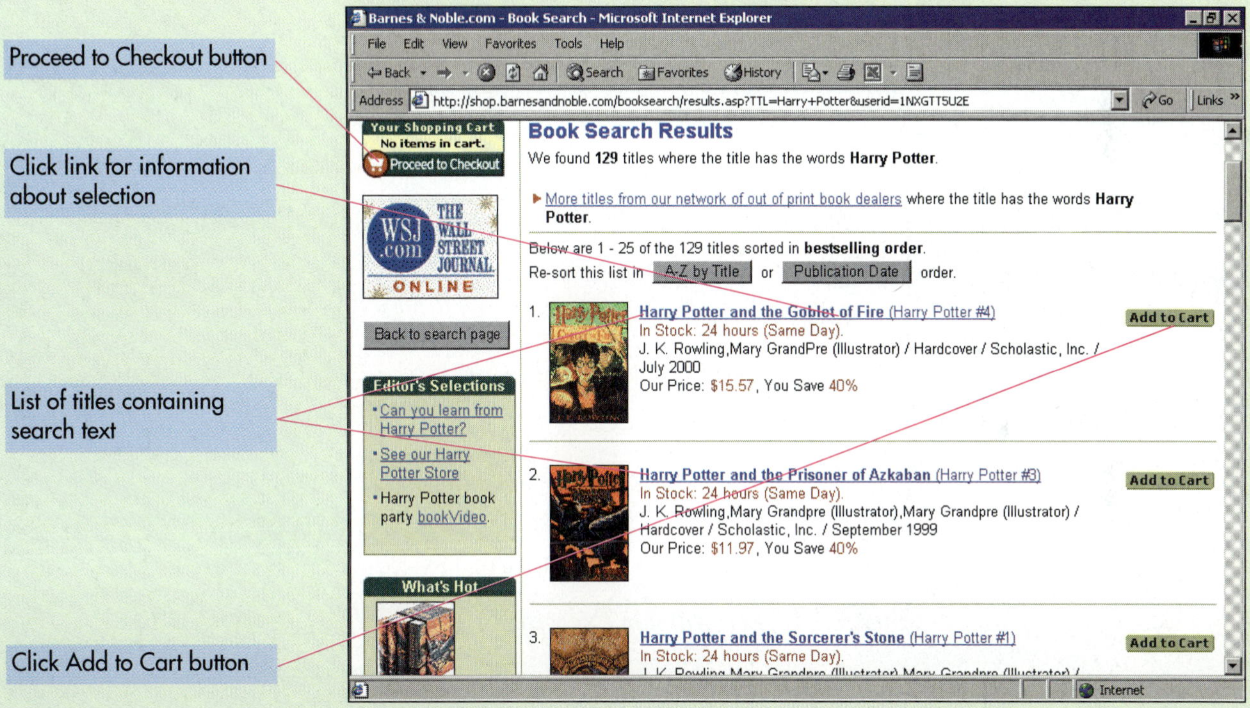

(c) Search for a Book (step 3)

FIGURE 8 *Hands-on Exercise 3 (continued)*

CHANGE THE FONT

The Web designer selects the font size he or she deems most appropriate. You can, however, change the font size of the displayed page to display more or less information as you see fit. Pull down the View menu and click the Text Size command to display a menu with five different sizes. The sizes are relative (from smallest to largest), as opposed to a specific point size. Click the size you prefer, and the display changes automatically. This command affects only the monitor and not the printed output.

Step 4: Check Out Now

- You should see a screen similar to the Checkout screen in Figure 8d. This is a secure screen as can be seen by the https protocol in the Address bar and padlock icon in the status bar.
- There is no need for you to complete the form at this time, since you will not be making an actual purchase. Note, however, some fields are asterisked (e.g., last name), whereas others (address 2 or 3) are not, indicating required and optional fields, respectively.
- Click the **Back button** to return to the previous screen and cancel the checkout process. You may see the Security Alert in Figure 8d, indicating that you are leaving a secure site. Click **Yes** to confirm that you want to leave.

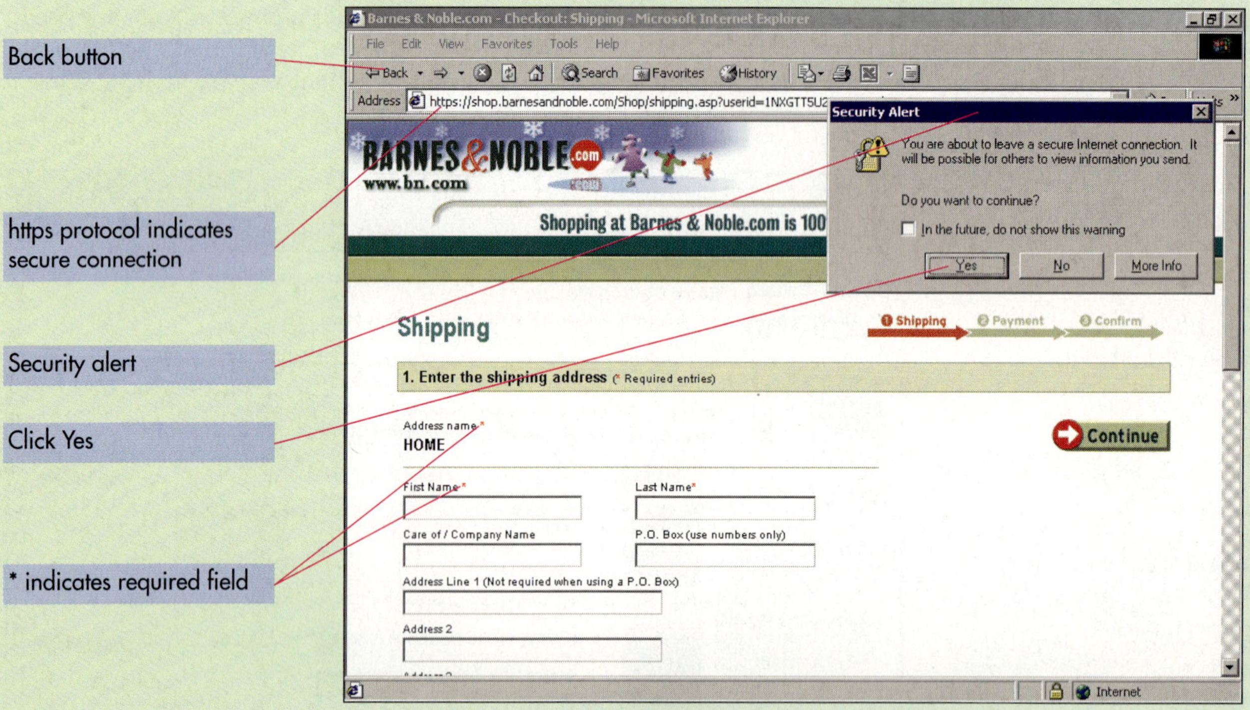

(d) Check Out Now (step 4)

FIGURE 8 *Hands-on Exercise 3 (continued)*

COMMON SENSE IS THE BEST SECURITY

You can complete your purchase over the Web and transmit confidential information, including your credit card number, in safety, provided you have a secure connection as indicated by the lock on the IE status bar. Even so, the best security protocol is common sense. Do not submit your credit card number over a computer that is not your own as the information may be stored permanently on that computer. Nor should you release confidential information to a company or Web site that you do not know. Forewarned is forearmed. And never give a password to anyone, no matter how innocent the request.

Step 5: Add Sites to the E-Commerce Folder

- Click in the **Address bar**, type **www.gateway.com**, and press **enter** to go to the Gateway 2000 Web site.
- Pull down the **Favorites menu** and click the **Add to Favorites command** to display the Add Favorites dialog box in Figure 8e.
- Click the **Create in command button** if you do not see the set of Favorites folders, then click the **E-Commerce folder** to open the folder and save the current site within this folder. Click **OK**.
- Add at least two additional sites to the E-commerce folder. We added Dell Computer (**www.dell.com**), the E-bay auction site (**www.ebay.com**), and Microsoft's CarPoint (**carpoint.msn.com**).

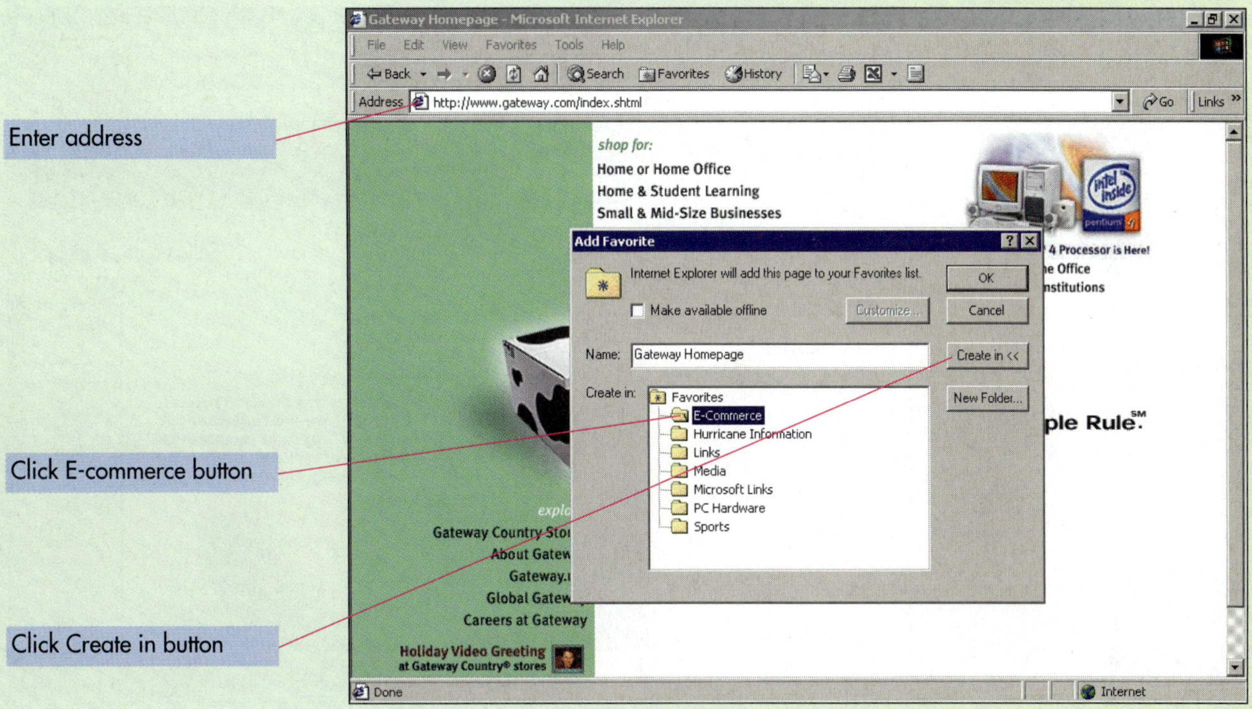

(e) Add Sites to the E-Commerce Folder (step 5)

FIGURE 8 *Hands-on Exercise 3 (continued)*

INSIST ON 30-DAY PRICE PROTECTION

Computer prices are always falling, but that doesn't mean you should wait for a better price to buy a computer. Any reputable vendor will provide a 30-day price-protection policy, which credits your account with any price reductions during the first 30 days you own your system. It is incumbent on you, however, to contact the vendor within the allotted time frame to request a refund. Don't forget to do so (and send us an e-mail message if we save you some money).

Step 6: **Return to a Favorite**

- Click the **Favorites button** on the Standard Buttons toolbar to display the Favorites list, then if necessary, click the **E-Commerce folder** to open the folder and display its contents as shown in Figure 8f.
- You should see the various sites that were added to this folder in the previous step. Click any link within the E-commerce folder to return to a previous site.
- You can also click and drag a link from one folder to another (or you can click the **Organize button** to move the links from one folder to another).
- Click the **E-Commerce folder** a second time to close the folder. (Each time you click a folder, you toggle the folder open or closed.)
- Close the Favorites pane.

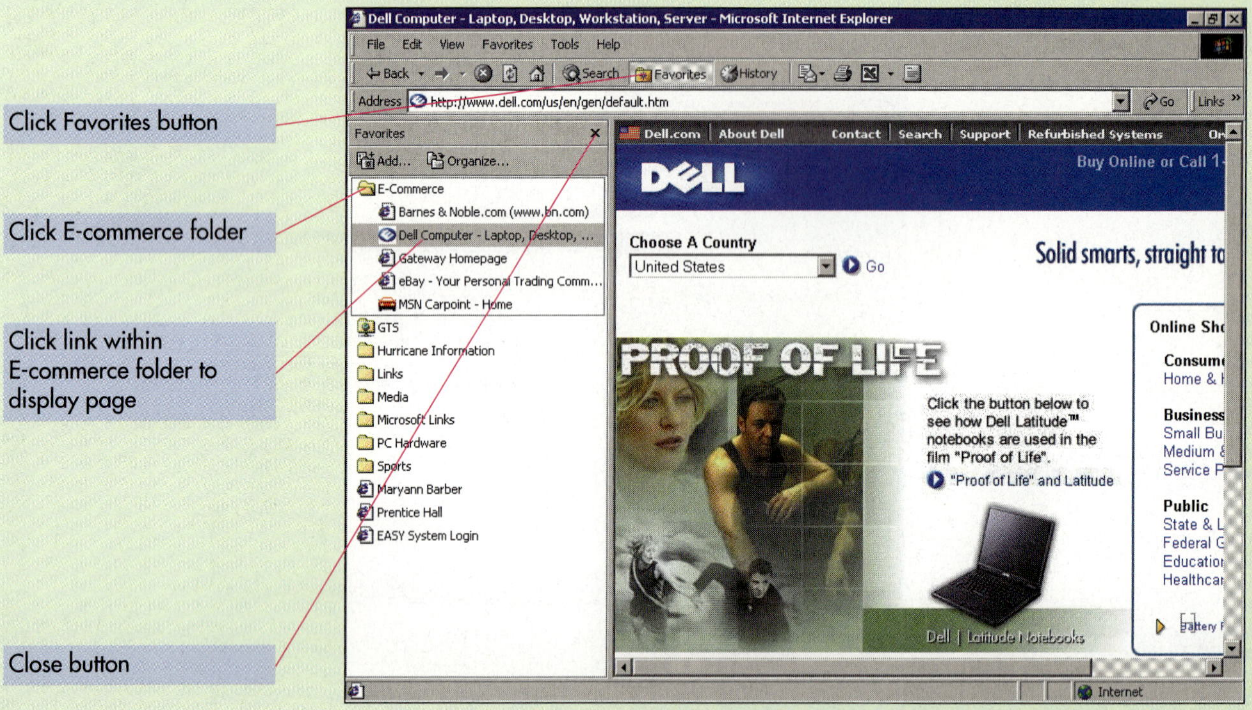

(f) Return to a Favorite (step 6)

FIGURE 8 *Hands-on Exercise 3 (continued)*

> **DOUBLE THE WARRANTY**
>
> You can double the warranty of any purchase (up to one additional year) by using a major credit card that offers a "buyer's protection" policy. Check with your credit card company to see whether it has this feature, and if it doesn't, consider getting a different credit card. The extended warranty is free, and it goes into effect automatically when you charge the purchase. It is applicable to any item except an automobile.

Step 7: **Internet Options**

- Pull down the **Tools menu** and click the **Internet Options command** to display the Internet Options dialog box, and (if necessary) click the **General Tab** as shown in Figure 8g.
- Click the **Settings button** in the Temporary Internet Files area to display the Settings dialog box, then click the **View Files button** to open an Explorer window showing the files in this folder. Be patient. It may take a few seconds for the folder to open.
- Click the **Last Modified column heading** to sort the files in order according to the date the files were last modified. Click the column heading once and the dates are in ascending order. Click the column heading a second time and the dates are in descending order.
- Arrange the files in descending order, then notice that the first few files are cookies that were created during this exercise. You do not need to open a cookie (you would be unable to read it anyway). The point is simply that multiple cookies were created as you visited the various sites in this exercise.
- Close the Temporary Internet Files window. Click **Cancel** to close the Settings dialog box, then click **Cancel** a second time to close the Options dialog box.

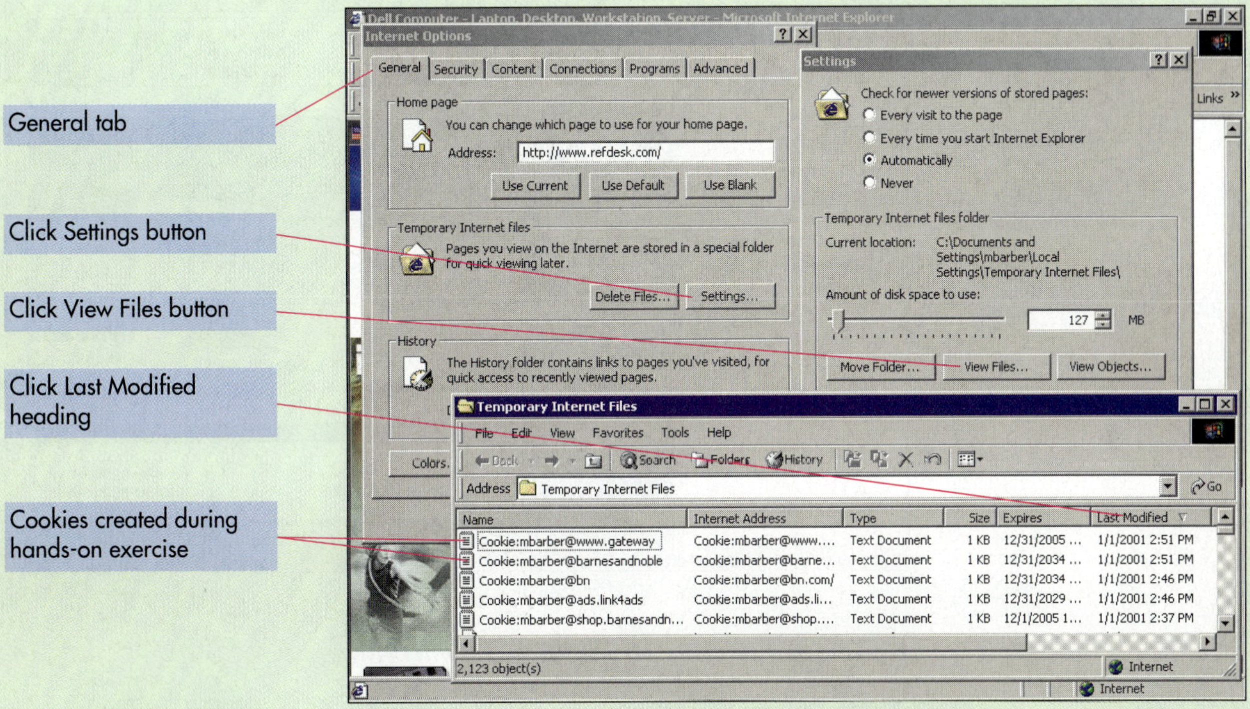

(g) Internet Options (step 7)

FIGURE 8 *Hands-on Exercise 3 (continued)*

COOKIE CENTRAL

Visit www.cookiecentral.com to learn more about cookies, the small files that are written to your computer each time you visit a Web site. Cookies are at the heart of the privacy controversy. They make it possible to customize a Web site so that you see the products and information that you are interested in, but at the expense of storing information about you in a file.

Step 8: The History List

- Click the **History button** on the Standard Buttons toolbar to open the History list as shown in Figure 8h. The History button functions as a toggle switch; click the button, and the History list is displayed. Click the button a second time and the pane is closed.
- Click the **down arrow** next to the View button to see the different ways in which the contents of the folder can be displayed. If necessary, click **By Date**, so that the contents of the folder are displayed in chronological order.
- Click the **Today folder** to toggle this folder open or closed. Leave the folder open as shown in Figure 8h, so that you can see the sites that you visited in this exercise. Click any link within the Today folder to return to that link.
- The History list provides a complete log of your session. It is very useful in the context of shopping and/or searching the Web for information.
- Close Internet Explorer.

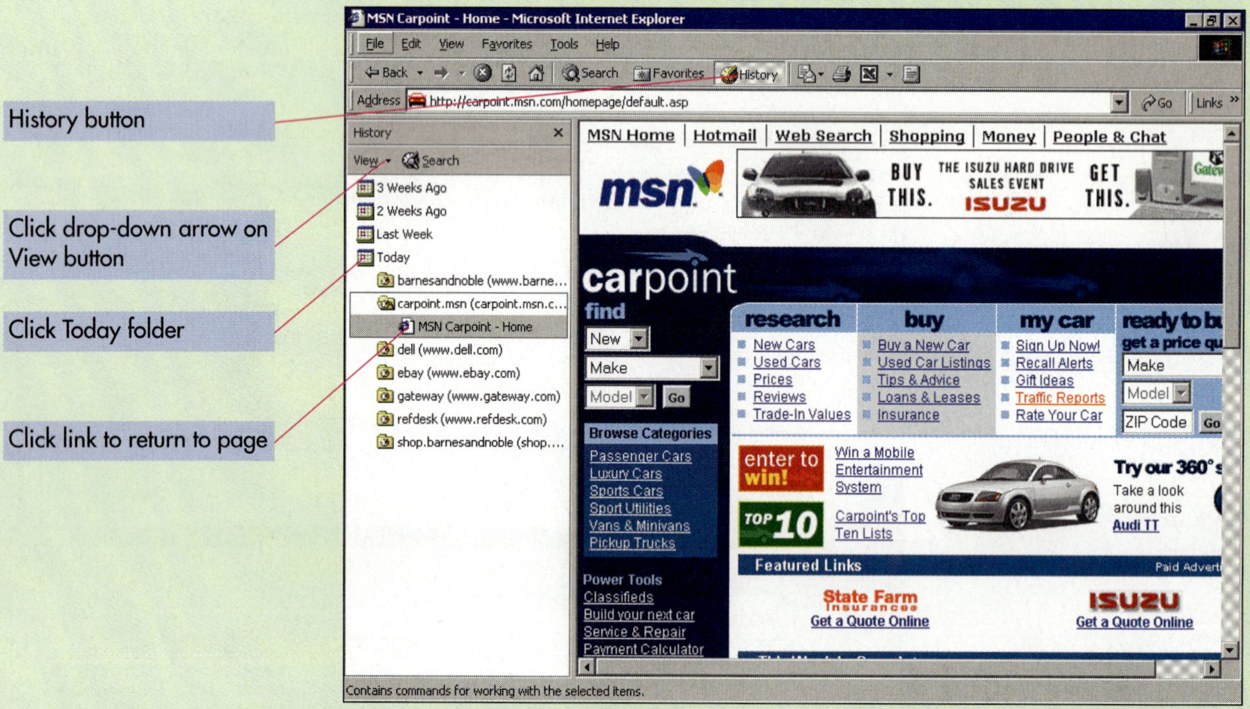

(h) The History List (step 8)

FIGURE 8 *Hands-on Exercise 3 (continued)*

> **WHAT IS CACHE?**
>
> A cache stores the Web pages you have accessed on your PC in an attempt to improve performance. The pages are stored in two places—in RAM and on the hard drive. The first time you request a page, it is downloaded from a Web server, which, depending on the size of the page and the traffic on the Internet, can take considerable time. The next time you request the page, Internet Explorer checks to see if it is already in cache (first memory, then disk), and if so, displays it from there. This explains why it takes several seconds (or longer) to display a page initially, and why the same page appears almost instantly if you return to it later in the session.

It's only a matter of time before you will want to create a home page and/or a Web site of your own. That, in turn, requires an appreciation for ***Hypertext Markup Language*** (***HTML***), the language in which all Web pages are written. A Web page (HTML document) consists of text and graphics, together with a set of codes (or ***tags***) that describe how the document is to appear when viewed in a Web browser such as Internet Explorer.

Initially, anyone who wanted to create a Web document had to learn each of these codes and enter them explicitly. Today, it's much easier as you can create a Web document directly in any application in Microsoft Office. In essence, you enter the text of a document, apply basic formatting—such as boldface or italics—then simply save the file as a Web document. There are, of course, other commands that you will need to learn, but all commands are executed from within the Office application, through pull-down menus, toolbars, or keyboard shortcuts. You can create a single document (called a ***home page***), or you can create multiple documents to build a simple Web site. Either way, the document(s) can be viewed locally within a Web browser—such as Internet Explorer—and/or they can be placed on a Web server, where they can be accessed by anyone with an Internet connection.

The procedure to place a document on the Web is straightforward, but it requires you to have an account on a Web server, a username, and a password. You can obtain the account from your professor and/or your ISP. You then upload the document from your machine to the server using a program known as FTP (File Transfer Protocol). Once the page has been loaded onto the Web server, it is part of the Web and can be viewed by anyone with Internet access, provided they know the address of your page.

Figure 9 displays a simple Web page that includes different types of formatting, a bulleted list, underlined links, and a heading displayed in a larger font. All of these elements are associated with specific HTML codes that identify the appearance and characteristics of the item. Figure 9a displays the document as it would appear when viewed in Internet Explorer. Figure 9b shows the underlying HTML codes (tags) that are necessary to format the page.

Fortunately, however, it is not necessary to memorize the HTML tags since you can usually determine their meaning from the codes themselves. Nor is it even necessary for you to enter the tags, as Word will create the HTML tags for you based on the formatting in the document. Nevertheless, we think it worthwhile for you to gain an appreciation for HTML by comparing the two views of the document.

HTML codes become less intimidating when you realize that they are enclosed in angle brackets and are used consistently from document to document. Most tags occur in pairs, at the beginning and end of the text to be formatted, with the ending code preceded by a slash, such as <p> and </p> to indicate the beginning and end of a paragraph. Links to other pages (which are known as hyperlinks) are enclosed within a pair of anchor tags <A> and </A> in which you specify the URL address of the document through the HREF parameter.

THE INTRANET

The ability to create links to local documents and to view those pages through a Web browser has created an entirely new way to disseminate information. Many organizations take advantage of this capability to develop an Intranet in which Web pages are placed on a local area network for use within an organization. The documents on an Intranet are available only to individuals with access to the LAN on which the documents are stored. This is in contrast to loading the pages onto a Web server, where they can be viewed by anyone with Internet access.

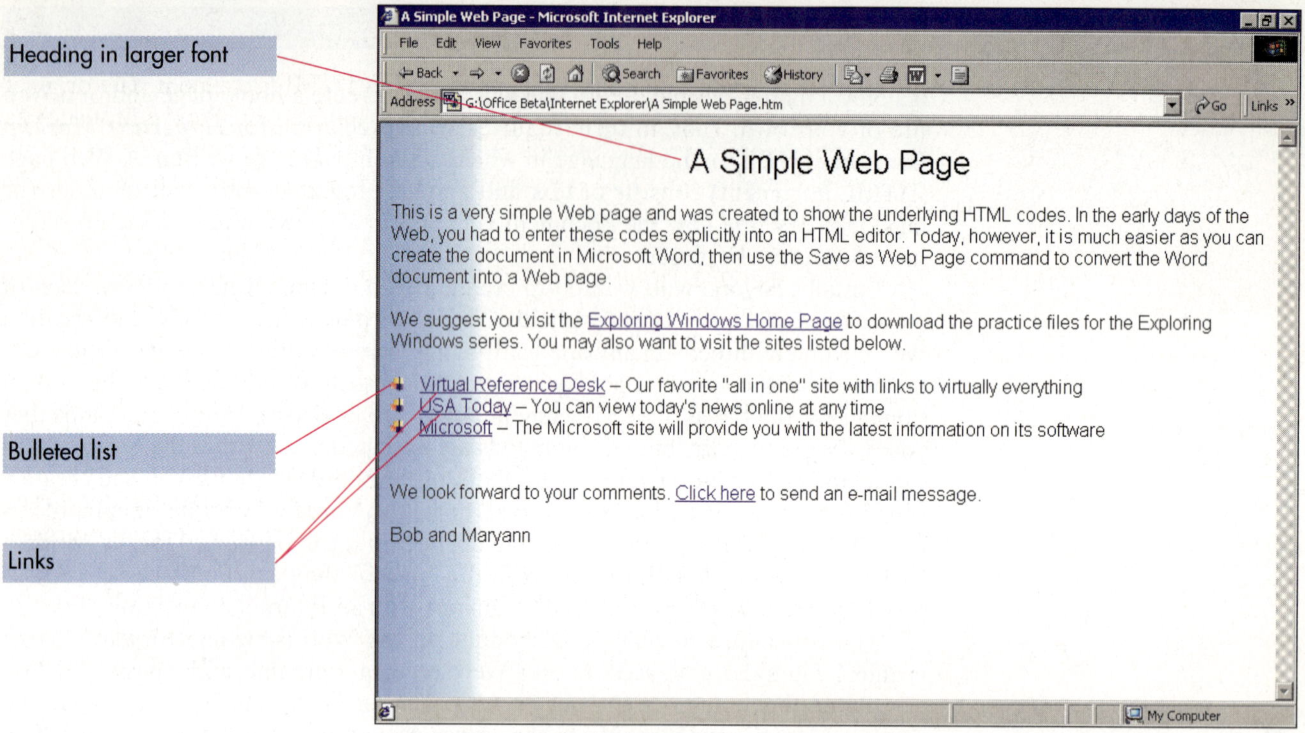

(a) Internet Explorer

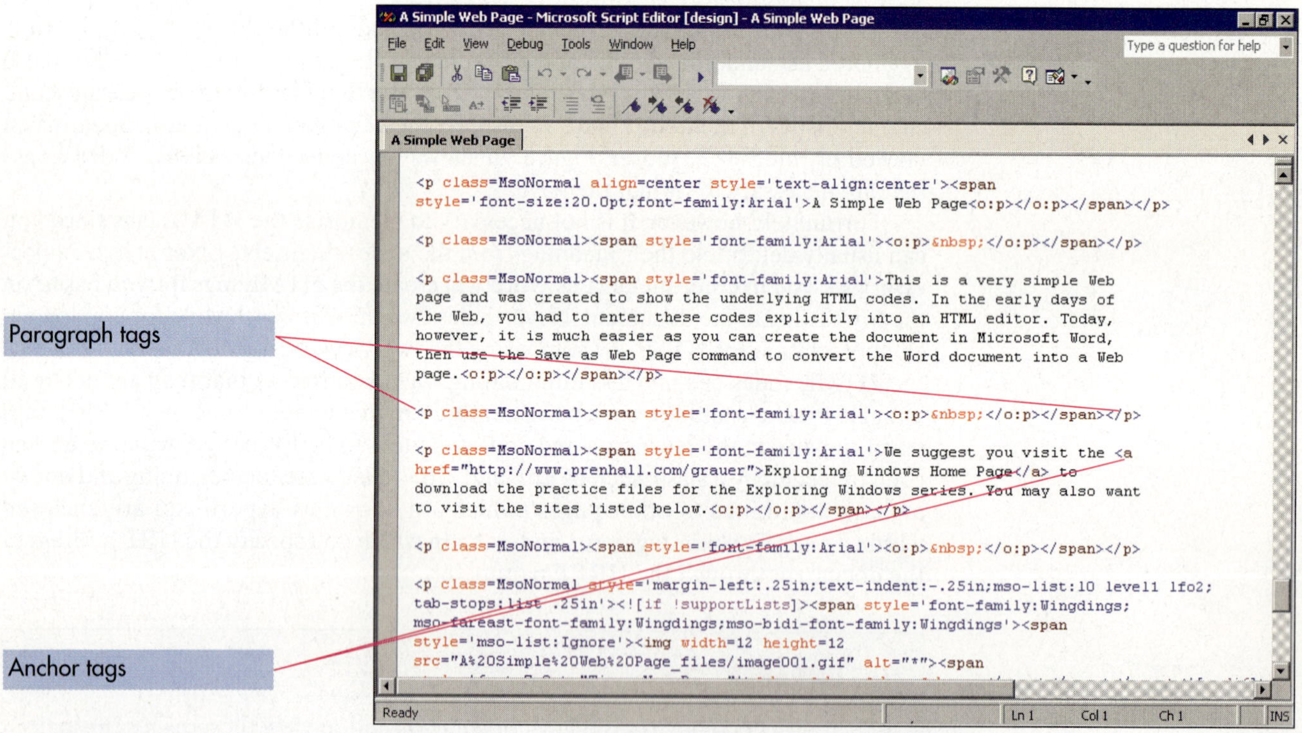

(b) HTML Source Code

FIGURE 9 *Introduction to HTML*

Microsoft Word

As indicated, there are different ways to create an HTML document. The original (and more difficult) method was to enter the codes explicitly in a text editor such as the Notepad accessory that is built into Windows. An easier way (and the only method you need to consider) is to use Microsoft Word (or a specialized Web editor) to create the document for you, without having to enter the HTML codes at all.

Figure 10 displays the home page of a hypothetical computer super store as it might be created in Microsoft Word. You can create a similar page using Word by entering and formatting the text just as you would enter the text of an ordinary document. The only difference is that instead of saving the document in the default format (as a Word document), you use the ***Save As Web Page command*** to specify the HTML format. Microsoft Word does the rest, generating the HTML codes needed to create the document.

You can enter text and/or change the formatting of existing text just as you would with an ordinary Word document. Hyperlinks are entered through the Insert Hyperlink button on the Standard toolbar or through the corresponding command in the Insert menu. You can format the elements of the document (the heading, bullets, text, and so on) individually, or you can select a ***theme*** from those provided by Microsoft Word. A theme (or template) is a set of unified design elements and color schemes that will save you time while making your document more attractive.

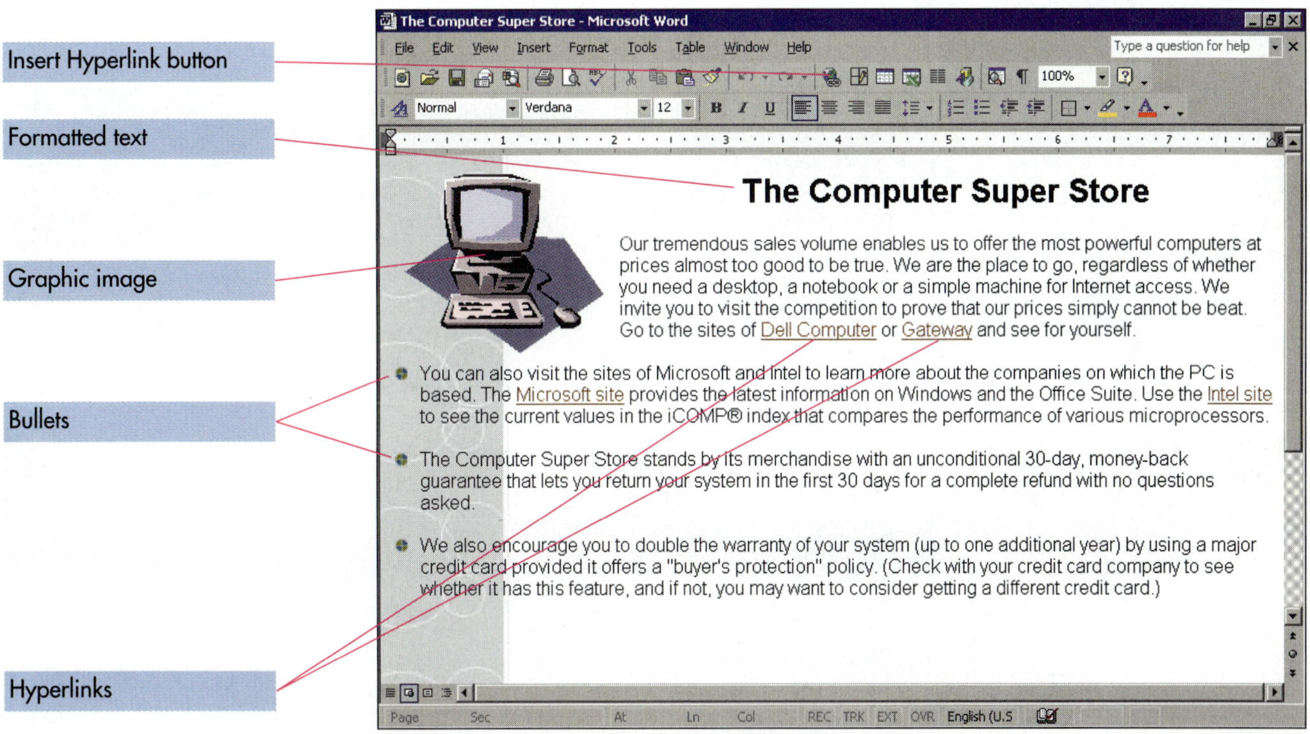

FIGURE 10 *A Web Page in Microsoft Word*

> **REGISTER YOUR SITE**
>
> You can apply for a domain name (Web address) through any of a number of independent companies. The company will verify that the name has not been previously taken, then register that name with InterNIC, the government agency that actually assigns the name. The cost is approximately $35 a year for the domain name. See practice exercise 5 at the end of the chapter.

HANDS-ON EXERCISE 4

INTRODUCTION TO HTML

Objective To use Microsoft Word to create a simple Web page with clip art and multiple hyperlinks. Use Figure 11 as a guide in the exercise.

Step 1: **Enter the Text**

- Start Microsoft Word. Pull down the **View menu** and click the **Web Layout command**. Enter the text of the document as shown in Figure 11a.
- Click and drag to select the second, third, and fourth paragraphs, then click the **Bullets button** to precede each paragraph with a bullet. If necessary, click the **Decrease Indent button** to move the bullets to the left margin.
- Click the **Spelling and Grammar button** to check the document for spelling. You should accept iCOMP® as it is spelled.

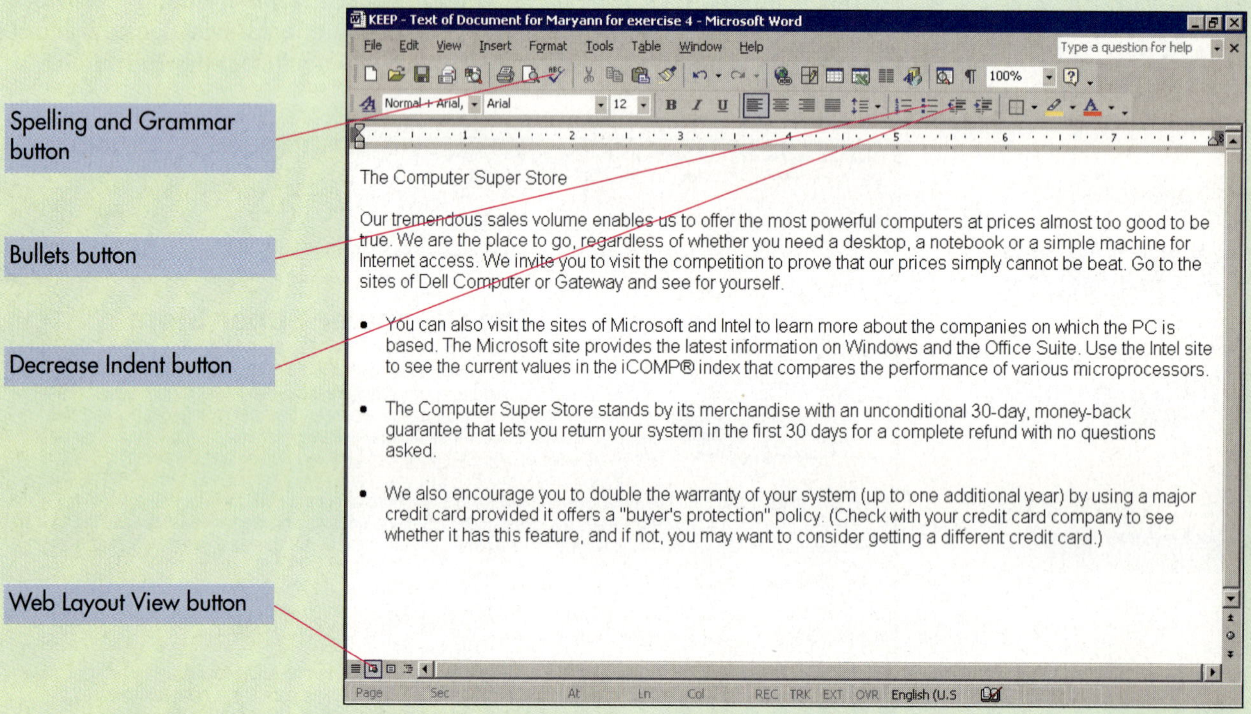

(a) Enter the Text (step 1)

FIGURE 11 *Hands-on Exercise 4*

THE WEB PAGE WIZARD

This hands-on exercise focuses on the creation of a single page or "home page." You might also explore the Web Page Wizard that creates a Web site (or set of pages) with horizontal or vertical frames for ease of navigation. Pull down the File menu, click the New command, and click General Templates in the task pane to display the Templates dialog box. Click the Web Pages tab, then select the Web Page Wizard.

Step 2: Save the Document

- Pull down the **File menu** and click the **Save As Web Page command** to display the Save As dialog box in Figure 11b.
- Click the **drop-down arrow** in the Save In list box to select the appropriate drive, drive C or drive A. If necessary, click the **Up One Level button** on the Save As toolbar continually until you come to the drive itself, then click the **Create New Folder button** and create the **Exploring the Internet folder**.
- Check that the name of the document is **The Computer Super Store**. Click the **Change Title button** if you want to change the title of the Web page as it will appear in the title bar of the Web browser.
- Click the **Save button**. The title bar reflects the name of the Web page (The Computer Super Store), but the screen does not change in any other way. In other words, you can continue to work in Microsoft Word, and enhance your page through ordinary Word commands.

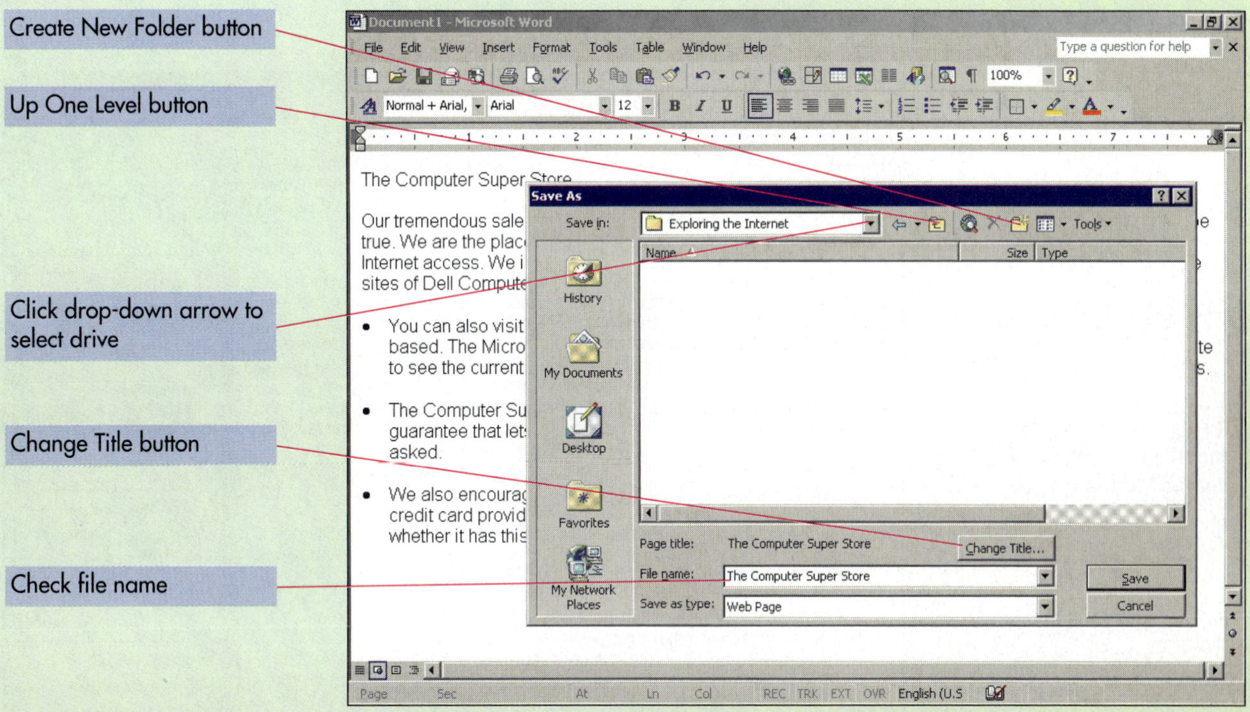

(b) Save the Document (step 2)

FIGURE 11 *Hands-on Exercise 4 (continued)*

> **THE FILE TYPES ARE DIFFERENT**
>
> Click the Start button, click (or point to) the Programs command, click Accessories, then start Windows Explorer. Select the drive and folder where you saved the Web document. If necessary, pull down the View menu and change to the Details view. Look for the Web document you just created, and note that it is displayed with the icon of a Web browser (Internet Explorer or Netscape Navigator) to indicate that it is an HTML document, rather than a Word document.

Step 3: Add the Clip Art

- Pull down the **Insert menu**, click (or point to) **Picture**, then click **Clip Art**. The task pane opens (if it is not already open) and displays the Media Gallery Search pane as shown in Figure 11c.
- Click in the **Search text box**. Type **computer** to search for any clip art image that is indexed with this key word, then click the **Search button** or press **enter**.
- The images are displayed in the Results box. Point to an image to display a drop-down arrow to its right. Click the arrow to display a context menu. Click **Insert** to insert the image into the document. Close the task pane.
- Point to the picture, click the **right mouse** button to display the context-sensitive menu, then click the **Format Picture command** to display the Format Picture dialog box.
- Click the **Layout tab**, choose the **Square layout**, then click the option button for **Left alignment**. Click **OK** to close the dialog box. Click and drag the sizing handles on the picture as appropriate, then drag the picture to the left of the first paragraph. Save the document.

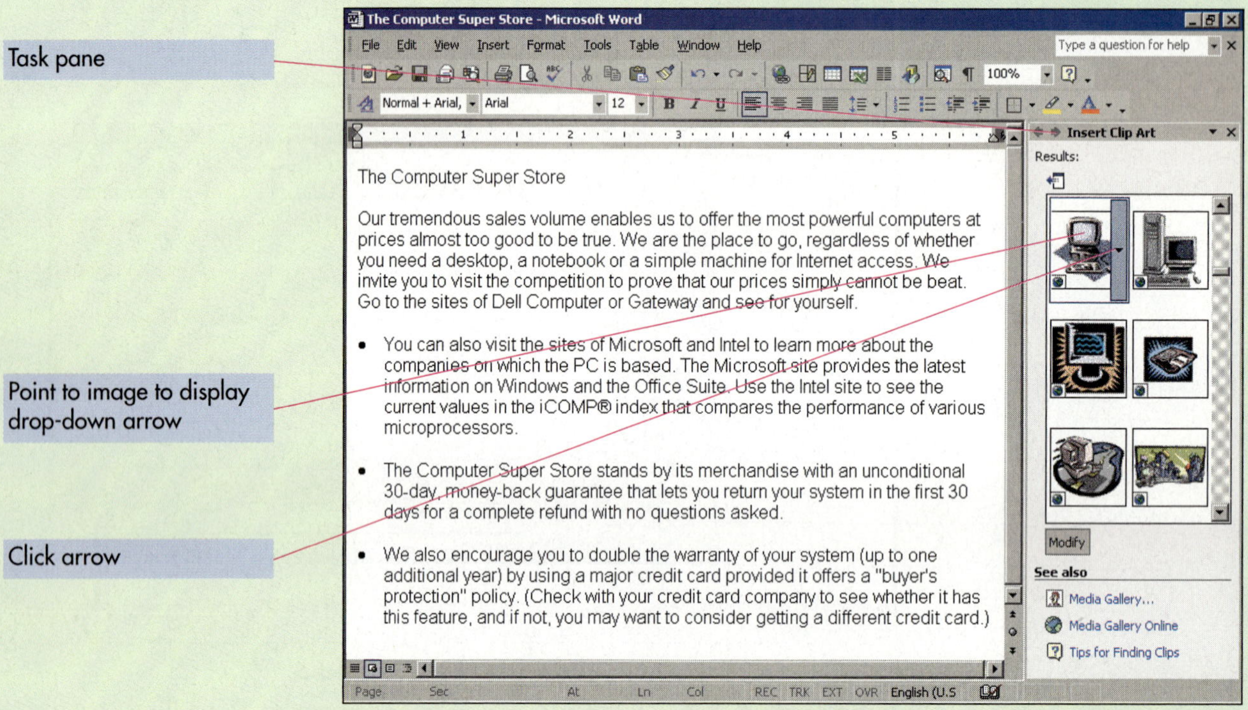

(c) Insert the Clip Art (step 3)

FIGURE 11 *Hands-on Exercise 4 (continued)*

SEARCH THE MEDIA GALLERY

The Media Gallery organizes its contents by category and provides another way to select clip art. Pull down the Insert menu, click (or point to) the Picture command, then click Clip Art to open the task pane, where you can enter a key word to search for clip art. Instead of searching, however, click the link to Media Gallery at the bottom of the task pane to display the Media Gallery dialog box. Close the My Collections folder if it is open, then open the Office Collections folder, where you can explore the available images by category.

Step 4: Add the Hyperlinks

- Select **Dell Computer** (the text for the first hyperlink). Pull down the **Insert menu** and click **Hyperlink** (or click the **Insert Hyperlink button** on the Standard toolbar) to display the Insert Hyperlink dialog box in Figure 11d.
- The text to display (Dell Computer) is already entered because the text was selected prior to executing the Insert Hyperlink command. If necessary, click the icon for **Existing File or Web Page**.
- Click in the **Address text box** and enter the desired Web address **www.dell.com** (the http is assumed).
- Click **OK** to accept the settings and close the dialog box. The hyperlink should appear as an underlined entry in the document.
- Add the additional links in similar fashion. The addresses in our document are **www.gateway.com**, **www.microsoft.com**, and **www.intel.com**.
- Save the document.

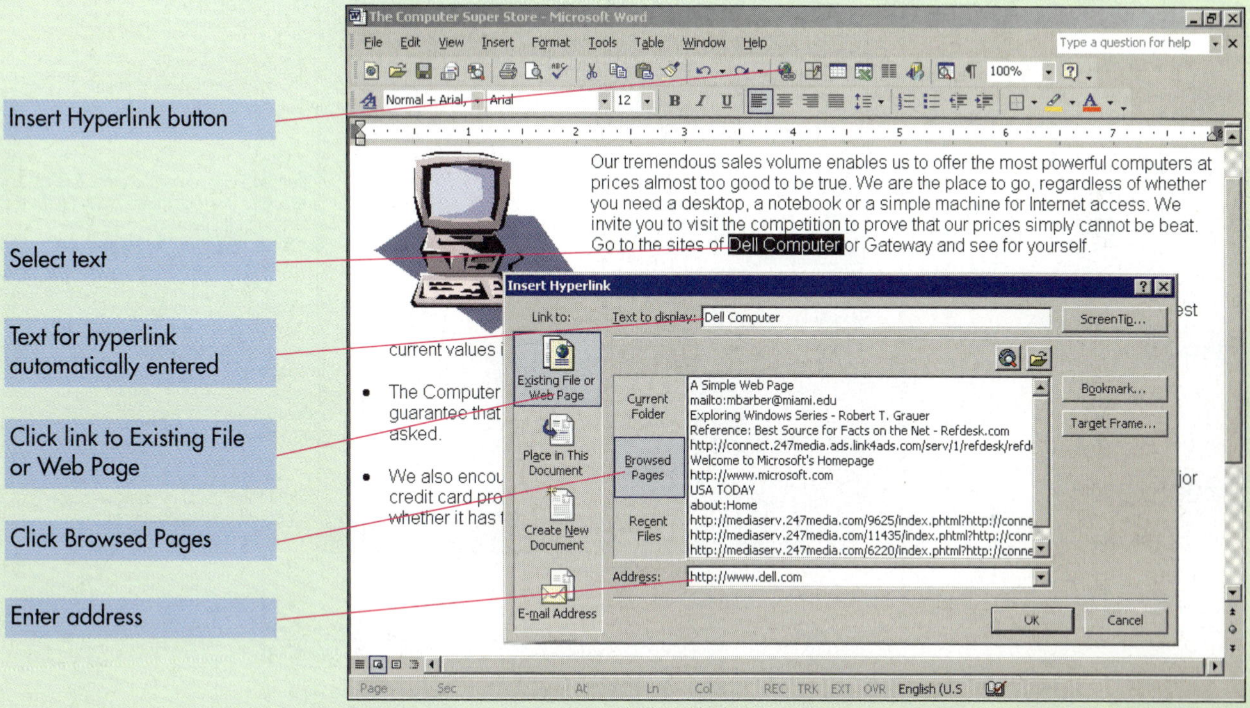

(d) Add the Hyperlinks (step 4)

FIGURE 11 *Hands-on Exercise 4 (continued)*

CLICK TO EDIT, CTRL+CLICK TO VIEW THE PAGE

Point to a hyperlink within a Word document and you see a ToolTip indicating that you need to press and hold the Ctrl key as you click the link (Ctrl + Click) to follow the link. This is a different convention because you normally just click the link to follow it. This time, however, clicking the link enables you to edit the link. Alternatively, you can right click the hyperlink to display a context-sensitive menu from where you can make the appropriate choice.

Step 5: **Apply a Theme**

- You should see underlined hyperlinks in your document. Pull down the **Format menu** and click the **Theme command** to display the Theme dialog box as shown in Figure 11e.
- Select (click) a theme (we chose the Radius theme) from the list box on the left, and a sample of the design appears in the right. Click **OK**. (Only a limited number of the listed themes are installed by default, however, and thus you may be prompted for the Microsoft Office CD, depending on your selection.)
- You can go from one theme to the next by clicking the new theme. There are approximately 65 themes to choose from, and they are all visually appealing. Every theme offers a professionally designed set of formatting specifications for the various headings, horizontal lines, bullets, and links.
- Save the document.

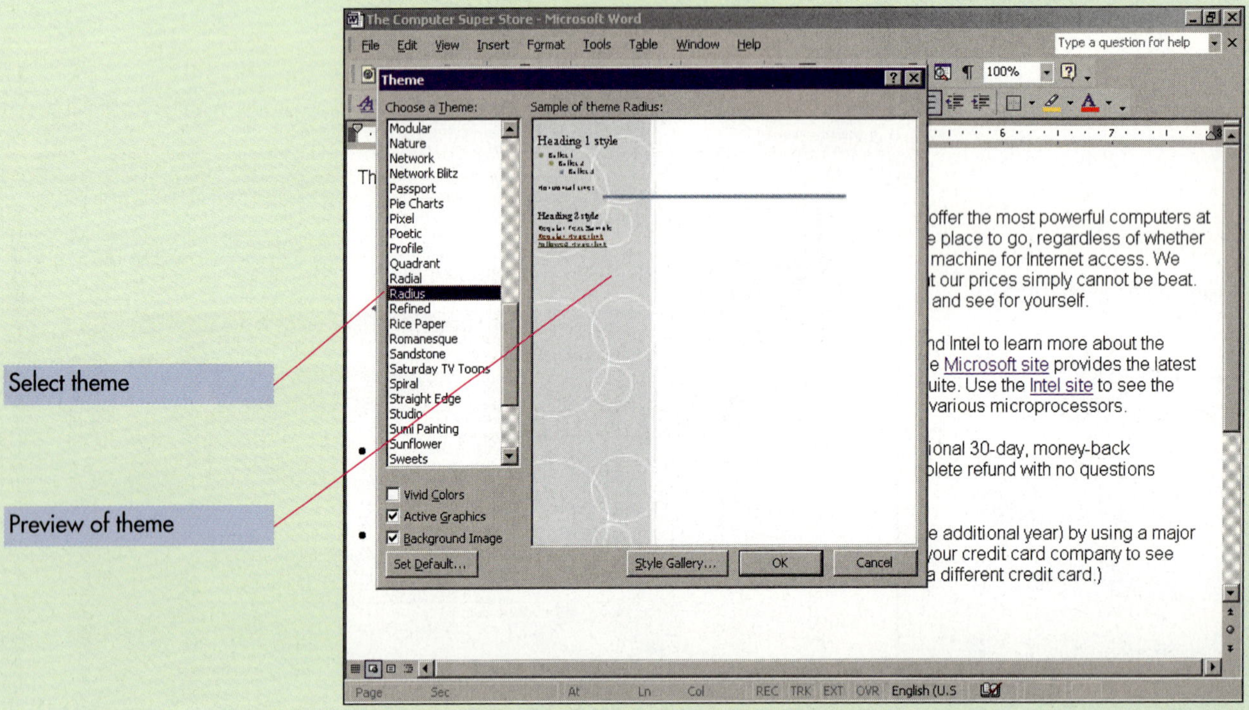

(e) Apply a Theme (step 5)

FIGURE 11 *Hands-on Exercise 4 (continued)*

> **KEEP IT SIMPLE**
>
> Too many would-be designers clutter a page unnecessarily by importing a complex background, which tends to obscure the text. The best design is a simple design—either no background or a very simple pattern. We also prefer light backgrounds with dark text (e.g., black or dark blue text on a white background), as opposed to the other way around. Design, however, is subjective, and there is no consensus as to what makes an attractive page. Variety is indeed the spice of life.

Step 6: The Finishing Touches

- Your document should be similar to the one in Figure 11f. It should contain clip art, a theme, and three bulleted paragraphs.
- Make any final adjustments to the size and position of the clip art. You can position the image at the left or right of the paragraph, but not in the middle.
- Increase the size of the title, then bold and center the title as shown. Make any additional adjustments that you see fit. The final appearance of the document is left to you.
- Save the document a final time.

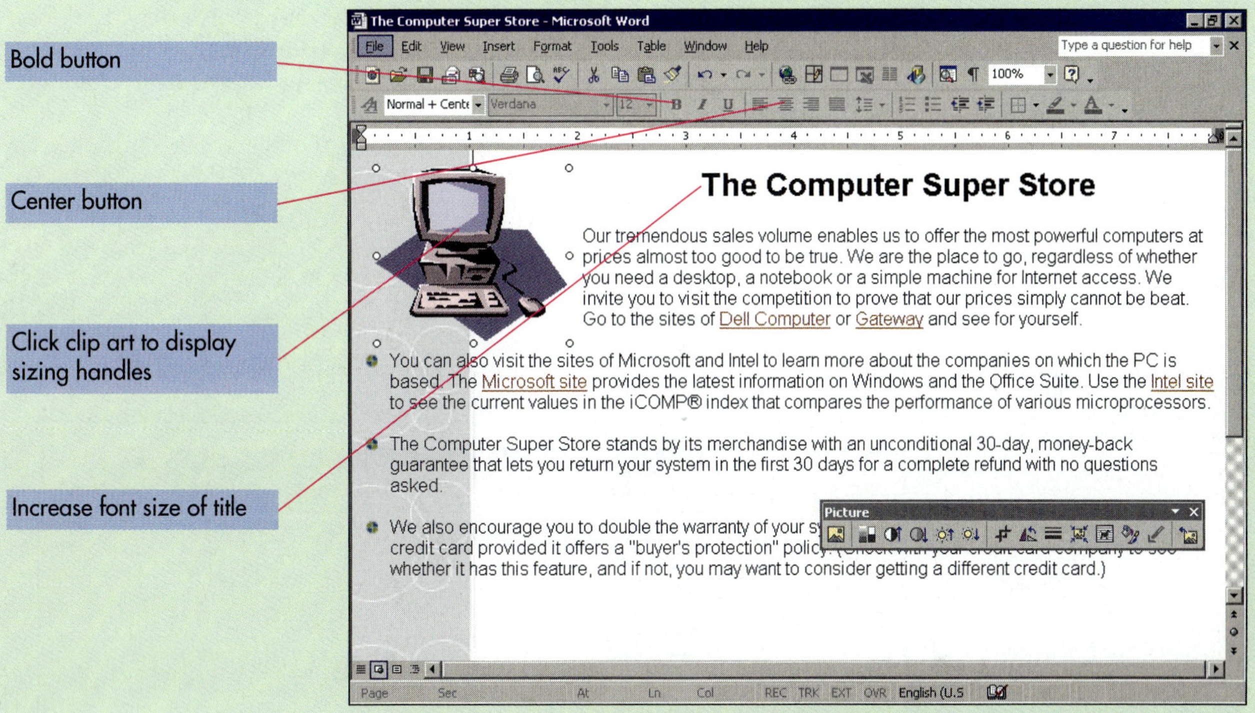

(f) The Finishing Touches (step 6)

FIGURE 11 *Hands-on Exercise 4 (continued)*

ROUND TRIP HTML

The concept of "round trip HTML" enables you to open a Web document in both Internet Explorer and Microsoft Word. You start with a Word document and use the Save As Web Page command to convert the document to a Web page. You then use Internet Explorer to view the page, but you can return to Word to edit the document by clicking the Edit button on the Standard Buttons toolbar. You can also right click the html document in Windows Explorer, then choose Open or Edit to view or edit the document in Internet Explorer or Word, respectively.

Step 7: Open the Web Page

- Start your Web browser. Pull down the **File menu** and click the **Open command** to display the Open dialog box in Figure 11g.
- Click the **Browse button**, click the **drop-down arrow** in the Look In box, and select the drive and folder (e.g., Exploring Internet on drive C) where you saved the Web page.
- Select (click) the **Computer Super Store document**, click **Open**, then click **OK** to open the document. You should see the Web page that was just created except that you are viewing it in a browser rather than in Microsoft Word.
- The Address bar shows the local address (C:\Exploring Internet\The Computer Super Store.htm) of the document. (You can also open the document from the Address bar, by clicking in the **Address bar**, then typing the address of the document; for example, C:\Exploring Internet\The Computer Super Store.htm)
- Click the **Print button** on the Internet Explorer toolbar to print this page for your instructor.

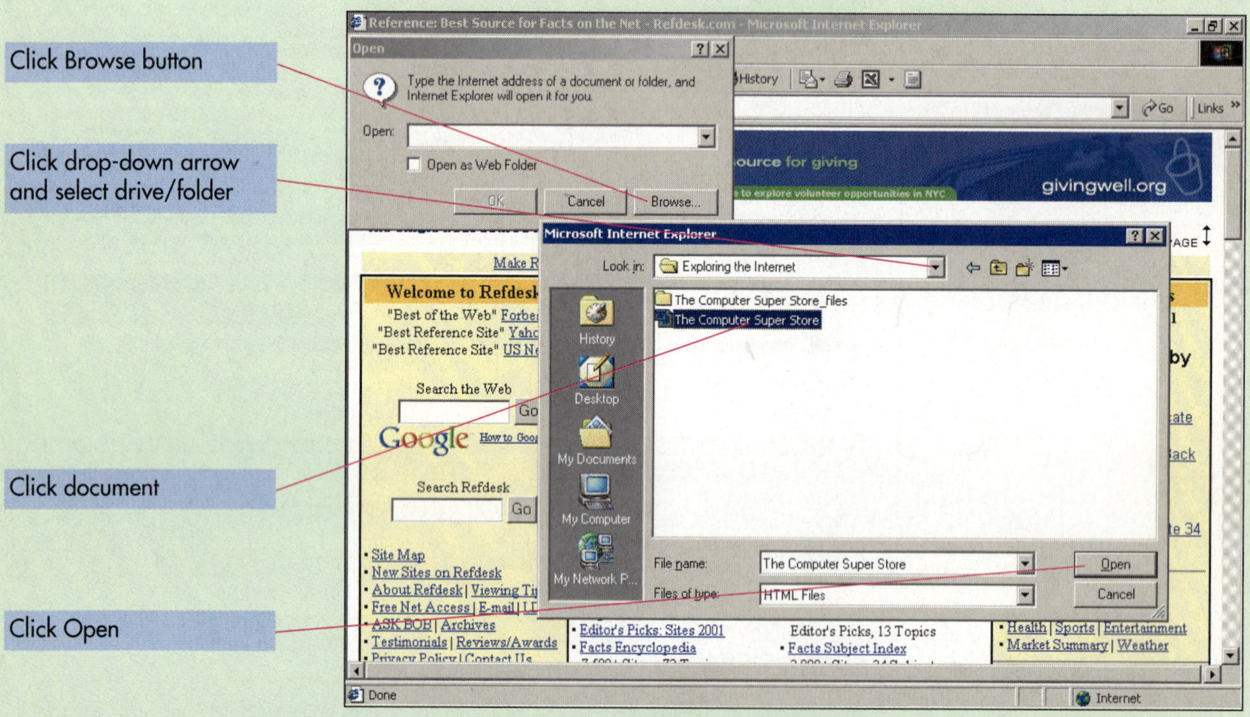

(g) Open the Web Page (step 7)

FIGURE 11 *Hands-on Exercise 4 (continued)*

> **AN EXTRA FOLDER**
>
> Look carefully at the contents of the Exploring Internet folder within the Open dialog box. You see the HTML document you just created as well as a folder that was created automatically by the Save As Web Page command. The latter folder contains the various objects that are referenced by the Web page. Be sure to copy the contents of this folder to the Web server in addition to your Web page if you decide to post the page.

Step 8: Test the Web Page

- This step requires an Internet connection because you will be verifying the addresses you entered earlier.
- Click the hyperlink to the **Microsoft** site to display the Web page in Figure 11h. You can explore this site, or you can click the **Back button** to return to your Web page and test another link.
- If you are unable to connect to the Microsoft site, click the **Back button** to return to your Web page, then click a second hyperlink to see if you can connect to that site. If you connect to one site, but not the other, you should return to your original document to correct the URL.
  - Click the **Word button** on the taskbar to return to the Web page, **right click** the hyperlink to display a context-sensitive menu, click **Edit Hyperlink**, and make the necessary correction. Save the corrected document.
  - Click the **Browser button** on the Windows taskbar to return to the browser, click the **Refresh button** to load the corrected page, then try the hyperlink a second time.
- Exit Word and Internet Explorer.

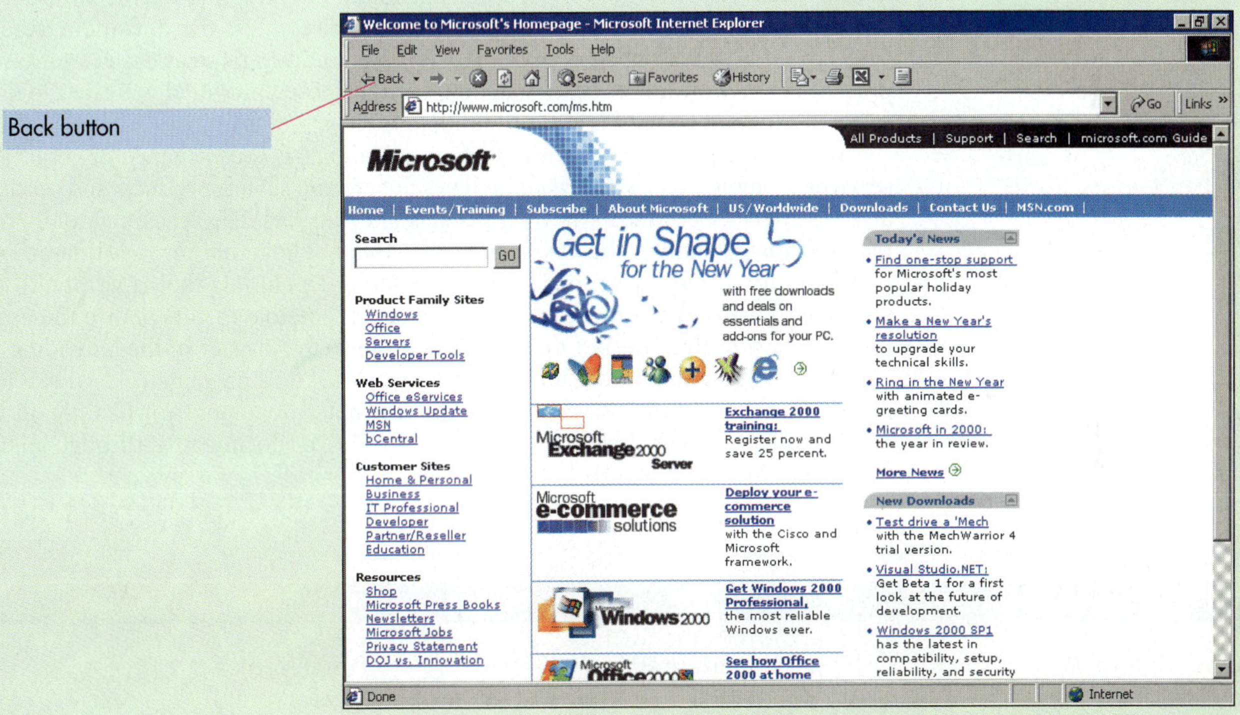

(h) Test the Web Page (step 8)

FIGURE 11 *Hands-on Exercise 4 (continued)*

> **VIEW THE HTML SOURCE CODE**
>
> Pull down the View menu in Internet Explorer and click the Source command to view the HTML statements that comprise the Web page. The statements are displayed in their own window, which is typically the Notepad accessory. Pull down the File menu in Notepad and click the Print command to print the HTML code. Do you see any relationship between the HTML statements and the Web page?

SUMMARY

The Internet is a network of networks. The World Wide Web (or simply the Web) is a very large subset of the Internet, consisting of hypertext and/or hypermedia documents. A program known as a browser is required to view documents that are stored on the Web. Internet Explorer and Netscape Navigator are competing browsers. The location (or address) of the Web page appears in the Address bar and is known as a Uniform Resource Locator (URL).

Search engines provide an efficient way to look for information. You enter a query consisting of the key words you are searching for, and the search engine responds with a number of "hits," or Web documents that meet the search criteria.

Many different search engines are available, each of which uses a different database and different search algorithm. Each database stores information about its set of Web documents (running into the millions) and consists of the document's URL (i.e., its Web address) and information (key words) about what is contained in each document. It is important, therefore, to try different engines with the same query, and further, to continually refine a query during the course of a search.

A copyright provides legal protection to a written or artistic work, giving the author exclusive rights to its use and reproduction. Anything on the Internet or World Wide Web should be considered copyrighted unless the document specifically says it is in the public domain. The fair use exclusion, however, lets you use a portion of the work for educational, nonprofit purposes, provided you cite the original work in your footnotes and/or bibliography.

Commerce, whether it is electronic or traditional, is the exchange of goods and services. Commerce of either type involves buyers and sellers, products and services, and suppliers or producers of the products and services. The advantage of e-commerce is that it enables the buyer and seller to come together in ways that are not possible with a traditional storefront. A cookie is a small file that is written to the user's hard drive by a specific site, which makes it possible to personalize the user's interaction with that site, but may also compromise the privacy of the individual.

Web documents are written in HyperText Markup Language (HTML), a language that consists of codes (or tags) that format a document for display on the World Wide Web. The easiest way to create an HTML document is through an editor such as Microsoft Word.

KEY TERMS

Address bar (p. 7)
And (p. 19)
Back button (p. 31)
Boolean operator (p. 19)
Browser (p. 3)
Business-to-business (B2B) (p. 28)
Cable modem (p. 8)
Cache (p. 40)
Client (p. 3)
Cookie (p. 29)
Copyright (p. 20)
Cyberspace (p. 2)
DSL modem (p. 8)
E-commerce (p. 28)
Encryption (p. 29)
Fair use exclusion (p. 20)
Favorites list (p. 31)
History list (p. 31)
Hit (p. 19)
Home page (p. 41)
HTML (p. 41)
HTTP protocol (p. 3)
HTTPS protocol (p. 29)
Hyperlink (p. 3, 7)
Internet (p. 2)
Internet Explorer (p. 3)
Internet Service Provider (p. 8)
Local Area Network (p. 8)
Modem (p. 8)
Netscape Navigator (p. 3)
Node (p. 2)
Not (p. 19)
Open command (p. 7)
Or (p. 19)
Portal (p. 3)
Privacy (p. 29)
Public domain (p. 20)
Query (p. 16)
Save As Web Page command (p. 43)
Search engine (p. 16)
Search form (p. 16)
Security (p. 29)
Server (p. 3)
Spider (p. 16)
Tags (p. 41)
Theme (p. 43)
Uniform Resource Locator (p. 7)
Web server (p. 3)
World Wide Web (WWW) (p. 3)

MULTIPLE CHOICE

1. Which of the following statements about the Internet is true?
   (a) The Internet is less than 10 years old
   (b) The Internet is accessed by millions of people, the exact number of which is impossible to determine
   (c) The Internet is maintained and administered by the federal government
   (d) All of the above
2. Web documents are created in
   (a) HyperText Transfer Protocol (HTTP)
   (b) HyperText Markup Language (HTML)
   (c) Transmission Control Protocol (TCP)
   (d) Internet Protocol (IP)
3. Which of the following is true about the hyperlinks that appear as text within a Web document?
   (a) They are shown in different colors, depending on whether or not the links have been previously accessed
   (b) They appear as underlined text to indicate that they are hyperlinks
   (c) They may access documents on different computers
   (d) All of the above
4. What is the likely address of IBM's home page?
   (a) ibm@internet.com
   (b) www.ibm.com
   (c) www.ibm.edu
   (d) internet.ibm.com
5. Which of the following is a true statement regarding search engines?
   (a) Different search engines can return different results for the same query
   (b) The same search engine can return different results for the same query at different times (e.g., a month apart)
   (c) Both (a) and (b)
   (d) Neither (a) nor (b)
6. The Favorites list is currently displayed in the left pane of the Internet Explorer window. What will happen if you click the Favorites button on the Standard Buttons toolbar?
   (a) An error message is displayed to indicate that the list is already open
   (b) The Favorites list remains open and all folders within the Favorites list are open as well
   (c) There is no visible change in the display because the list is already open
   (d) The Favorites list disappears and the left pane is closed
7. Which of the following is considered the best search engine, and thus the only engine you need to use?
   (a) Yahoo!
   (b) Lycos
   (c) Excite
   (d) There is no agreement on the best search engine
8. Which of the following will return the largest number of documents regardless of the search engine in use?
   (a) "Tiger" or "Woods"
   (b) "Tiger" and "Woods"
   (c) "Tiger" not "Woods"
   (d) Impossible to determine

9. A spider is a program that:
  (a) Prevents cookies from being stored on a PC
  (b) Automatically crawls through the Web searching for new pages to add to the database of a search engine
  (c) Searches the Web for documents in response to a specific query
  (d) Protects a computer against infection from viruses

10. Which of the following appear together within Internet Explorer to indicate that the transmission of information will be secure?
  (a) The https protocol with a padlock icon on the status bar
  (b) The http protocol with a padlock icon on the status bar
  (c) The https protocol with the word "secure" on the status bar
  (d) The http protocol with the word "secure" on the status bar

11. Which part of the URL http://www.prenhall.com/grauer/win2000/index.html identifies the Internet address of the Web site (server)?
  (a) http://
  (b) www.prenhall.com
  (c) win2000
  (d) index.html

12. What is the general rule regarding the use of information that was downloaded from the Internet?
  (a) It should be assumed that the material is under copyright protection unless the author states that the document is in the public domain
  (b) Factual material may be cited even if the material has been copyrighted
  (c) A limited portion of copyrighted material may be used for noncommercial purposes under the fair use exclusion, provided the source is cited
  (d) All of the above

13. What is the easiest way to switch back and forth between Word and Internet Explorer, given that both are open?
  (a) Click the appropriate button on the Windows taskbar
  (b) Click the Start button, click Programs, then choose the appropriate program
  (c) Minimize all applications to display the Windows desktop, then double click the icon for the appropriate application
  (d) All of the above are equally convenient

14. How do you save a Word document as a Web page?
  (a) Pull down the Tools menu and click the Convert to Web Page command
  (b) Pull down the File menu and click the Save As Web Page command
  (c) Both (a) and (b)
  (d) Neither (a) nor (b)

15. Internet Explorer can display an HTML page that is stored on:
  (a) A local area network
  (b) A Web server
  (c) Drive A or drive C of a standalone PC
  (d) All of the above

ANSWERS

1. b	**6.** d	**11.** b
2. b	**7.** d	**12.** d
3. d	**8.** a	**13.** a
4. b	**9.** b	**14.** b
5. c	**10.** a	**15.** d

1. The History List: The History list makes it easy to return to a site that was recently visited, as can be seen by Figure 12. All you do is click the History button on the Standard Buttons toolbar to display the History list in the left pane, click the day when you last visited the site, then click the shortcut to return to the site.
   a. How long does Internet Explorer retain the contents of the History list? How do you change the number of days that pages are kept in history?
   b. Is it possible to erase the contents of the History list? If so, how? Why would you want to do this?
   c. Do you think the History list is a convenience or an invasion of your privacy, in that it enables anyone with access to your machine to see your activity on the Web? Summarize your thoughts in a brief note to your instructor.

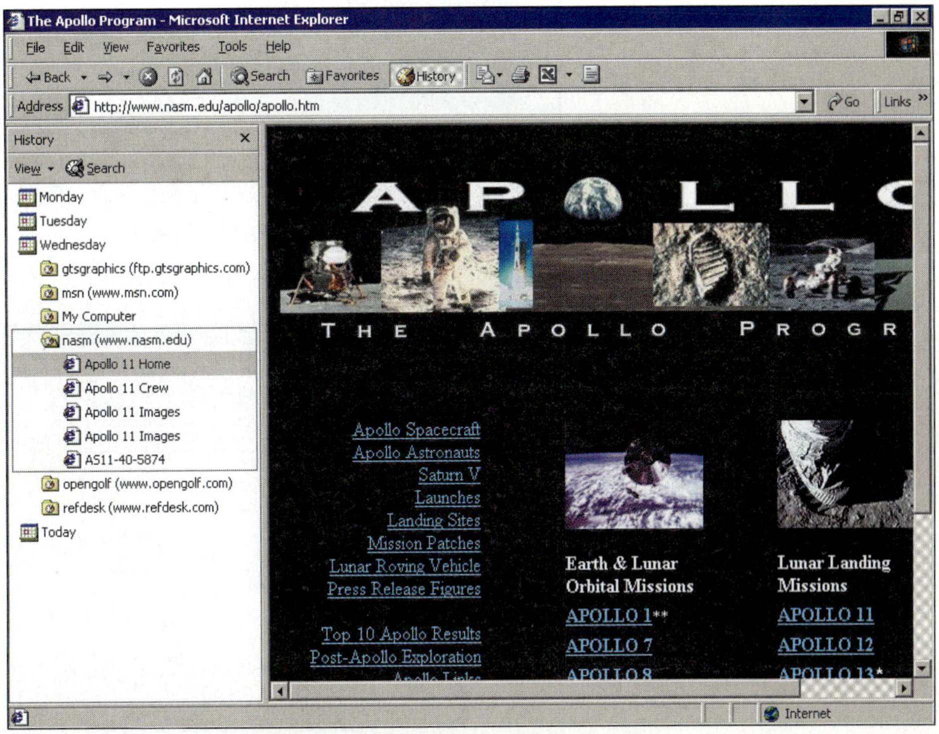

FIGURE 12 *The History List (Exercise 1)*

2. Mia Hamm: Mia Hamm is the most prolific goal scorer in U.S. soccer history, and considered by many to be the best all-around woman player in the world. Use your favorite search engine to locate two different Web pages with information on her accomplishments. (We removed the URL in Figure 13, or else this assignment would be too easy.) Print the pages you find, add a cover page with your name, class, and today's date and submit the material to your instructor.

3. Ask Jeeves: Ask Jeeves is a "natural language" search engine, which means that you can ask a question in English, as opposed to using a traditional query. Jeeves not only gives you several avenues to explore as can be seen by the screen in Figure 14, but he also polls several search engines to arrive at his results. Go to www.askjeeves.com and enter our question about the Oscars, then explore the information that you get back. Compare the results supplied by Jeeves to those of your favorite search engine. Which do you prefer, Jeeves, or your favorite engine? Summarize your findings for your instructor.

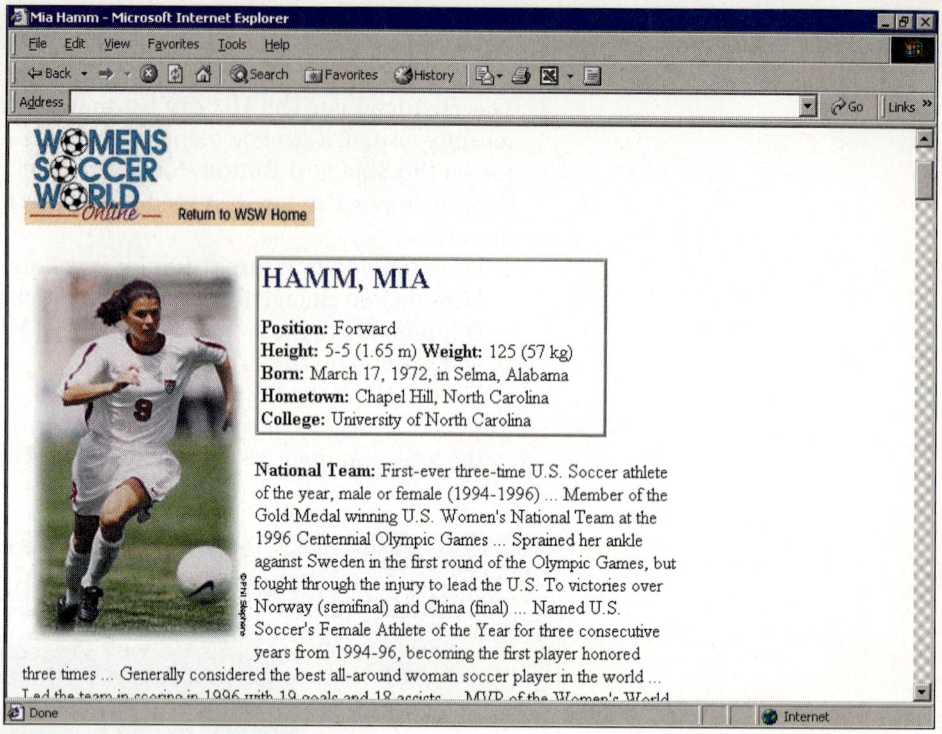

FIGURE 13 *Mia Hamm (Exercise 2)*

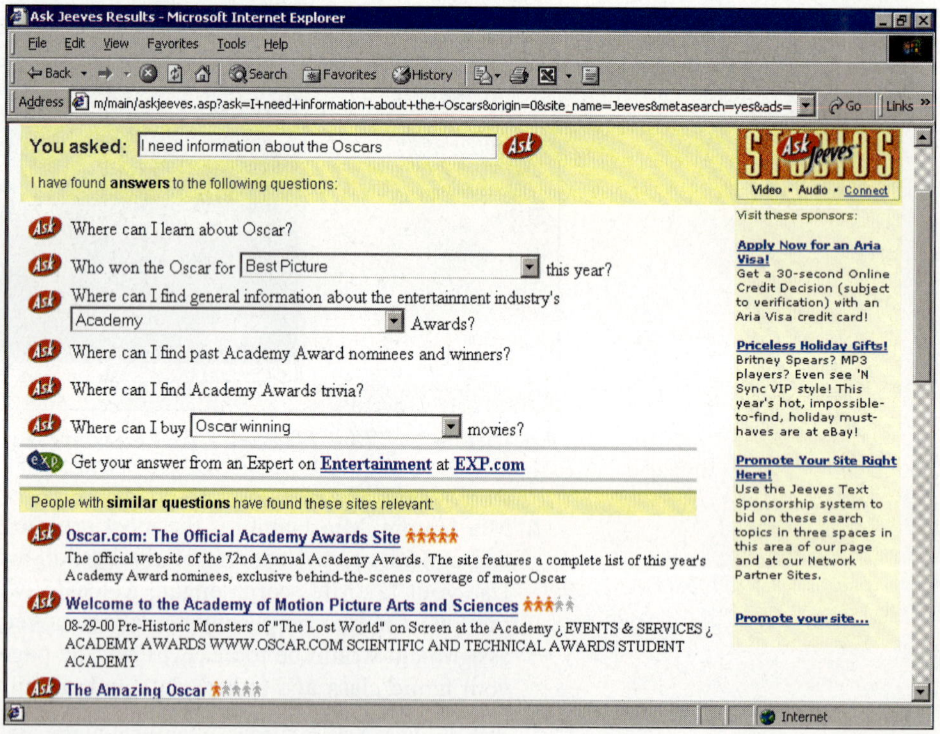

FIGURE 14 *Ask Jeeves (Exercise 3)*

4. The Congressional Web Site: Do you know the names of your elected representatives, such as your congressional representative and your two state senators? There is no excuse for not knowing because the information is readily available. There are many sites with this information, but "Thomas," the Congressional Website, is special since it also has information on all legislation that is currently before Congress.
   a. Go to the Congressional Web site as shown in Figure 15. What are the names of your congressional representative and two state senators?
   b. List at least three bills that are currently under discussion. Just give the name and number of each bill, together with a one-sentence summary of the proposed legislation.
   c. Add a cover sheet, then print all of the information for your instructor.

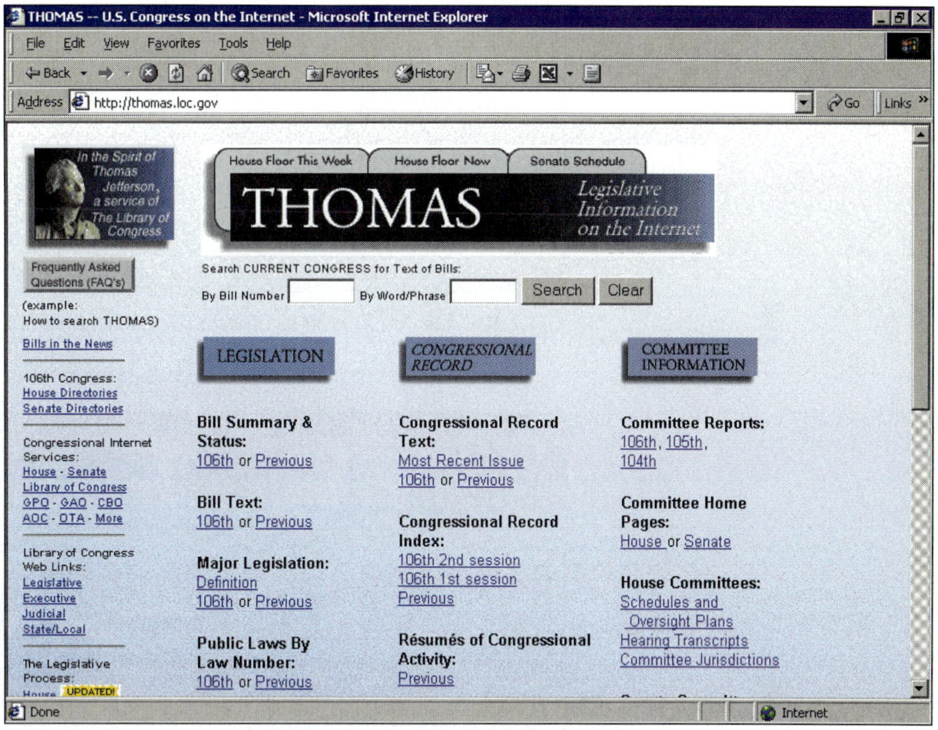

FIGURE 15 *The Congressional Web Site (Exercise 4)*

5. Domain Name Registration: Use any search engine to locate the home page of InterNIC, the government agency that is responsible for assigning domain names. Once you arrive at the site, search on the name computersuperstore.com as shown in Figure 16. The name is already taken, and the first part of your assignment is to find out who owns the name and when it was registered. Next, use your imagination to look for a suitable domain name for the hypothetical computer store described in the third hands-on exercise. Submit your findings in a brief note to your instructor.

6. News on the Net: The *USA Today* site in Figure 17 is typical of virtually every major newspaper in that you can read today's edition online at no cost, as opposed to purchasing it at the newsstand. Choose any newspaper, find it on the Web, print today's front page, then answer each of the following in a sentence or short paragraph:
   a. Which version do you prefer—the printed version its online equivalent?
   b. Why would a publishing company "give away" something that they sell?
   c. How do you make the paper's Web site the start page for your browser?
   d. Add a cover page, then submit the completed assignment to your instructor.

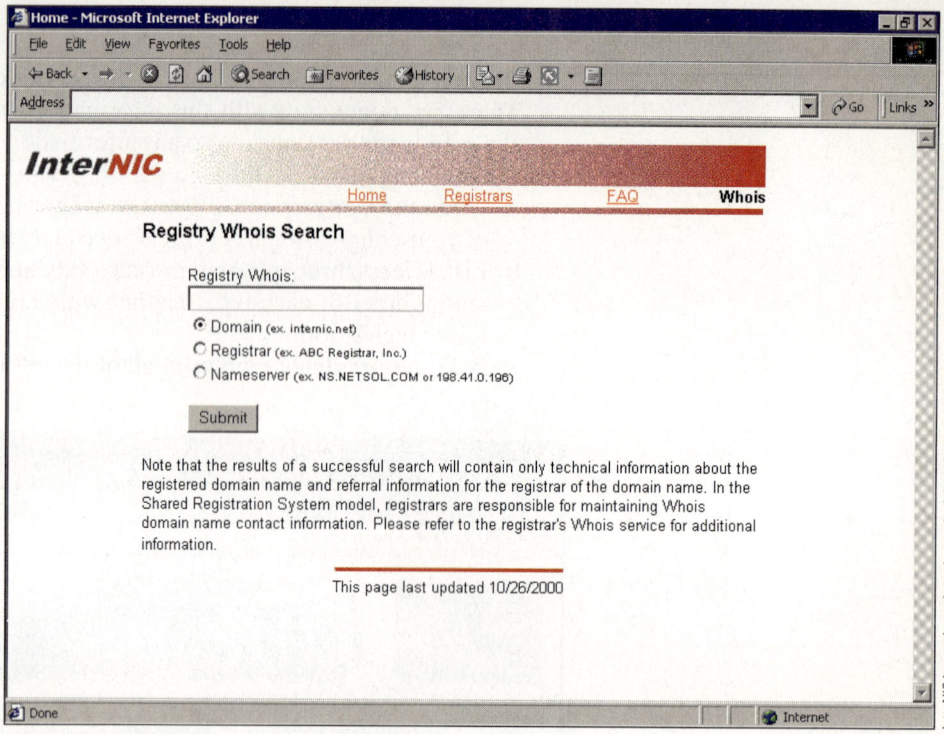

FIGURE 16 *Domain Name Registration (Exercise 5)*

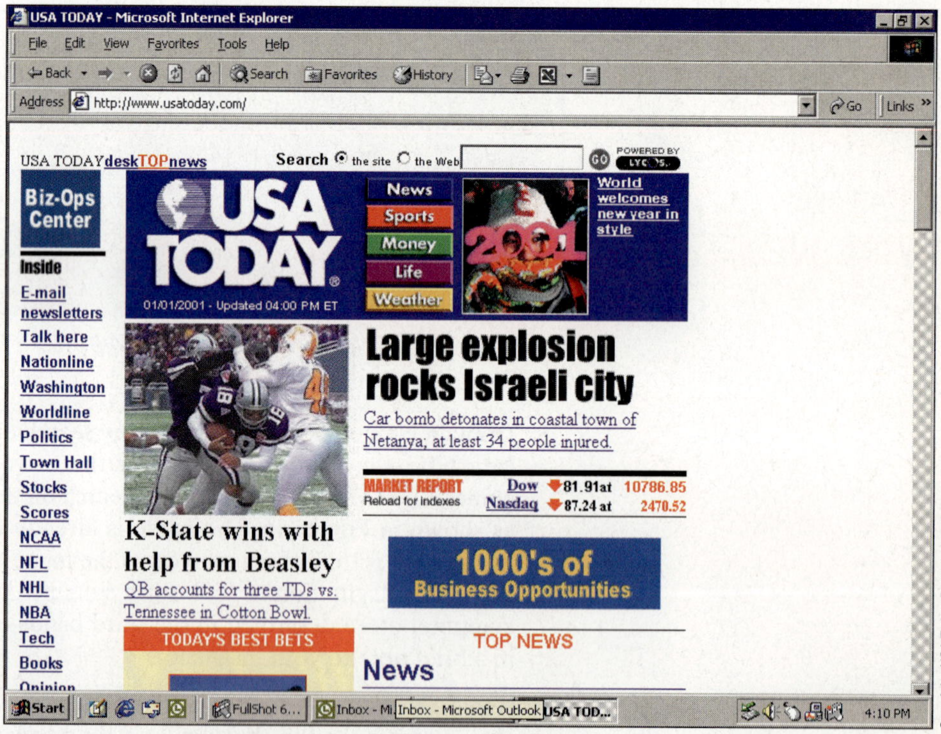

FIGURE 17 *News on the Net (Exercise 6)*

7. How Stuff Works: The How Stuff Works Web site in Figure 18 is a personal favorite that provides easily understood explanations to basic technology. Go to the site, enter any topic that interests you, then read through the various articles that are returned by the site. Is the information useful? Is it too basic, just about right, or too complex? Can you locate another site on the Web that has comparable information? Summarize your thoughts in a brief note to your instructor.

FIGURE 18 *How Stuff Works (Exercise 7)*

8. Search the URL: The classic painting in Figure 19 is by the Dutch master, Rembrandt, and was located through a search on the artist's name. The html in the Address bar looks intimidating, but it can lead you to other interesting pages. Try to enter the address as it appears in the figure. If you can't type it all in, look for the Web museum, then explore the museum until you arrive at the painting. (There are multiple servers, so you may connect to a server other than the one in our figure.) Do the following once you get to the Night Watch painting:
   a. Back up one level by deleting the last part of the address, rembrandt.nightwatch.jpg. What do you find?
   b. Back up another level to 1640. What do you find in this folder?
   c. Continue to back up one level at a time, making a note of what you find each step along the way.
   d. Submit the results to your instructor. Do you see how backing up within the URL can lead to interesting related documents?

9. The Travel Agent: The Web is the best place to check for airline connections as typified by the document in Figure 20. Choose a hypothetical flight for yourself and a traveling companion, then search to find a site where you can check the schedules of multiple airlines. What is the best fare you can get? What are the best connections? Do you feel comfortable ordering the ticket online, or would you prefer to order through a conventional travel agent? Submit the results to your instructor as proof that you did this exercise.

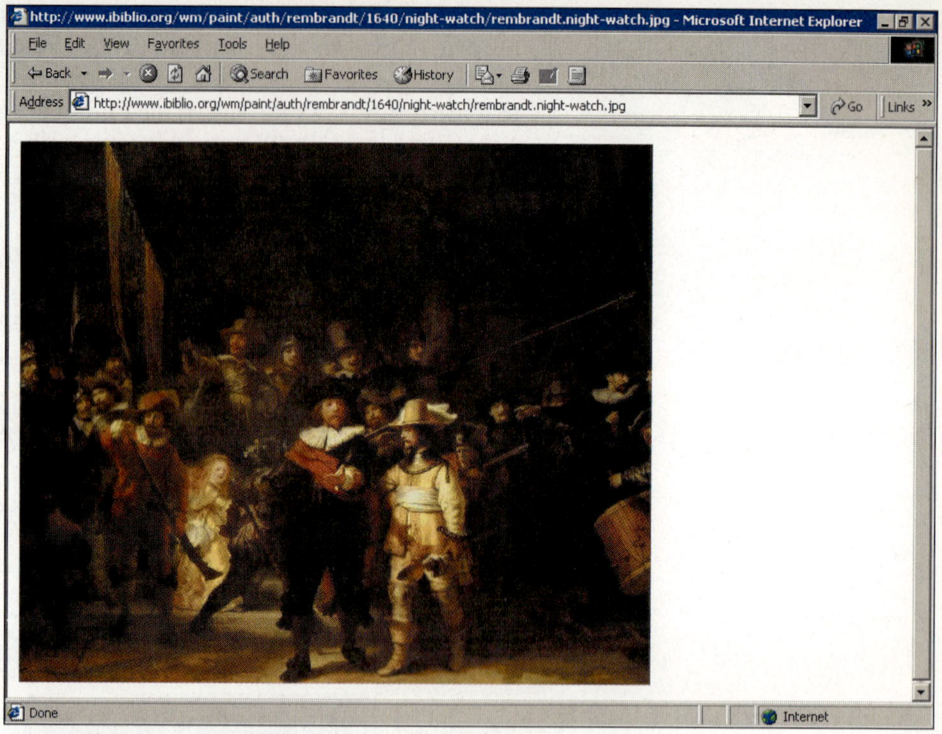

FIGURE 19 *Search the URL (Exercise 8)*

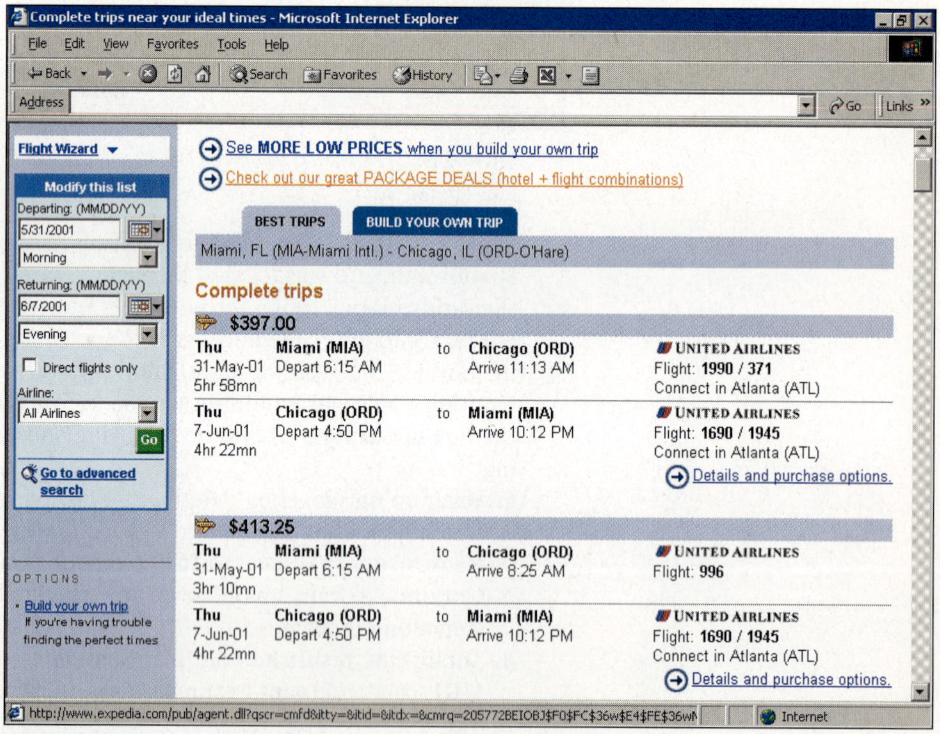

FIGURE 20 *The Travel Agent (Exercise 9)*

10. Federal Agencies: What is the current population of the United States? You can find the answer to this and many other questions at the official Web site of the U.S. Census Bureau as shown in Figure 21. Go to this site, answer our question, then explore the site to see what additional information is available.
    a. Stay connected to the site for at least five minutes, then hit the Refresh button on the Standard Buttons toolbar. Has the population of the country changed in the time that you were connected?
    b. Why is it necessary to use the Refresh button to get the most current version of a page? Give examples of other pages where you would find yourself continually using the refresh button.
    c. What is the national debt? Use any search engine to locate a site that contains the national debt as of today. The size of the debt may surprise you.
    d. What is the national debt per person? Divide the amount of the debt in part (c) by the number of people in part (a). This answer may also surprise you.

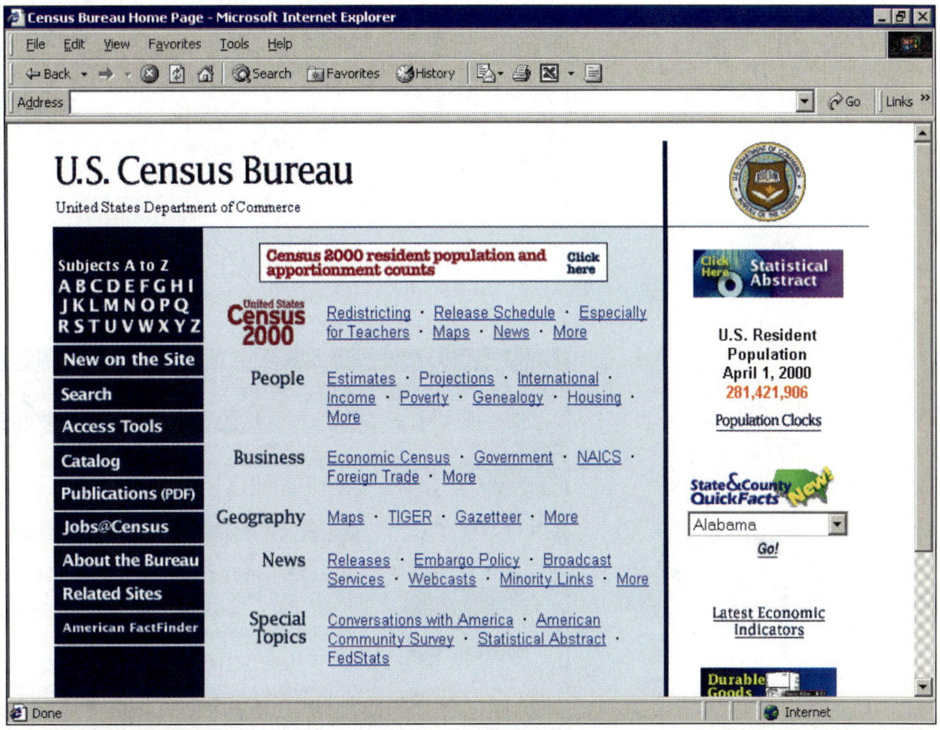

FIGURE 21 *Federal Agencies (Exercise 10)*

11. Found Money: Our favorite database is the Found Money database shown in Figure 22. It's not a gag, and you really do have a chance at finding money in your name, or the name of a relative. In essence, the site stores public records of abandoned money—bank accounts, utility deposits, tax refunds, and so on. There is no charge to search the database to see whether there is an account in your name; there is, however, a charge for detailed information on any hits that you receive if you elect to pursue that information. Try it, and let us know if you find any money.

12. Driving Directions: Your family is planning a vacation and you need driving directions. You can obtain detailed information with a map and printed directions that are not visible in Figure 23. Choose your home or school as a starting point and a favorite vacation spot as the destination, then search the Web for directions. Try starting with the Reference Desk (www.refdesk.com), then see if you can find a link to a map and driving directions directly on this page. Compare your results to those of your classmates.

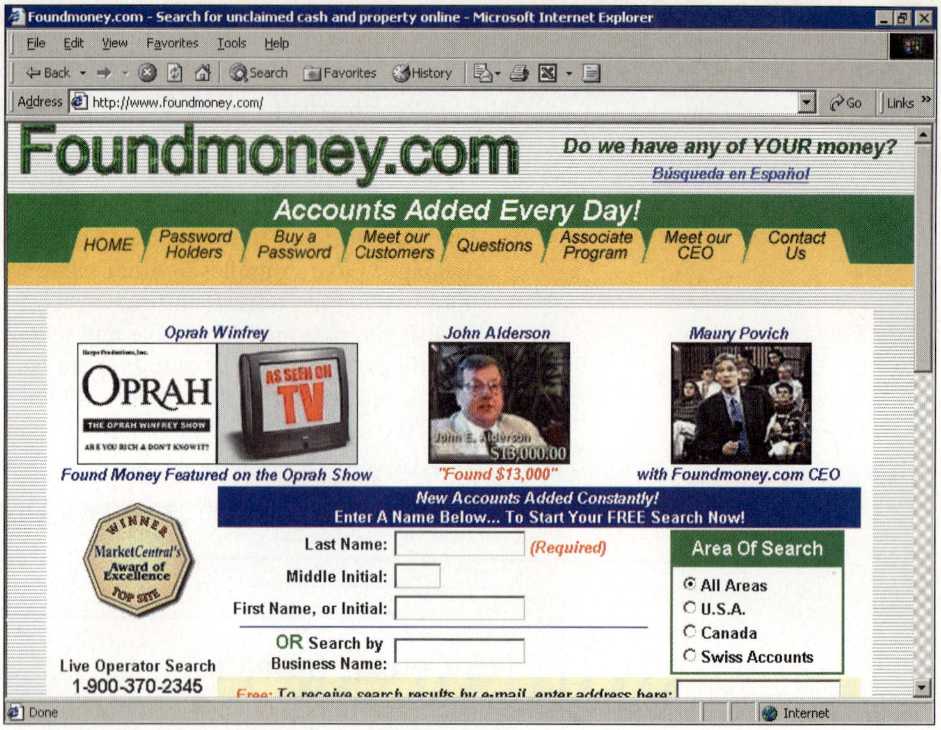

FIGURE 22 *Found Money (Exercise 11)*

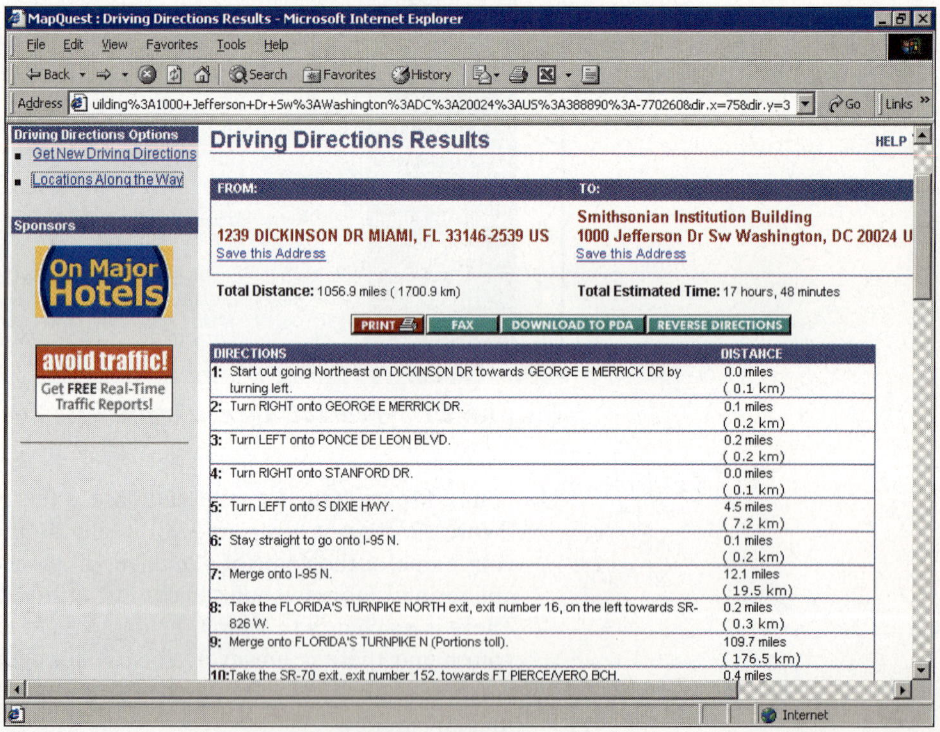

FIGURE 23 *Driving Directions (Exercise 12)*

Campus Access to the Internet

The easiest way to access the Internet is from a local area network on campus. But which students are given access, and what—if anything—do you have to do to open an account? Does the university provide an e-mail account? If so, what is your username and password? What is your e-mail address? Does your e-mail account expire at the end of the semester, or does it continue throughout your stay at the university? You don't have to put your answers in writing, but you will need to know this information if you are to be successful in this class.

The Internet Service Provider

You can use at least three different technologies to connect to the Internet from home: a regular modem, a cable modem, or a DSL line. What is the rated speed of each technology? How reliable is the technology? What are the installation cost (if any) and the monthly service charge? Contact at least two different Internet Service Providers in your area to compare prices. Summarize the results in a short note to your instructor.

It's the URL, Not the Browser

Our text focuses on Internet Explorer, but the concepts apply equally well to any other browser. Choose a different browser (Netscape Navigator) and use it to display several pages that were referenced in this chapter. What difference (if any) do you see in a given page when it is viewed in Netscape rather than Internet Explorer? Which browser is better from a developer's point of view? Which is better from a user's point of view?

Employment on the Web

Graduation is fast approaching and you need a job. How can the Web help you in your search for full-time employment? Is it also useful to secure an internship or part-time job? Use your favorite search engine to locate at least two sites where you can post a résumé and/or search through a job bank. Do you think you have a realistic expectation for success by using the Web?

A Collection of Trivia

This exercise asks you to find the answer to a variety of unrelated questions. Some of the answers are contained in a specialized directory, whereas others may require a general search. Good luck. What is the toll-free number for UPS? What is the zip code for the address 10000 Sample Road in Coral Springs, Florida? What is today's price of Intel stock? What is the value of $1 in British pounds? What does PCMCIA (associated with notebook computers) stand for?

On Your Own

This loosely structured exercise asks you to experiment with different search engines and search parameters. Select any topic in which you are interested, then choose a search engine, construct an initial query, then record the number of hits the engine returns. Choose a different engine, enter the identical query, and record the number of hits you get with that engine. Select the more promising result, then submit a new query that limits your search through inclusion of additional key words or other logical operators. Summarize the results in a one- or two-page Word document that you will submit to the instructor. The document should contain all the information you recorded manually in the preceding steps.

Going Abroad

Congratulations! You have just won a scholarship to spend your junior year abroad. You need a passport, and you need it quickly. Search the Web to learn how to apply for a passport. You should be able to find a site that enables you to download an actual passport application with specific instructions on where to apply; that is, an address in the city in which you live or attend school. What additional software, if any, do you need to print the application?

Tax Time

April 15 is just around the corner and you have yet to file your income tax. Search the Web to download the necessary tax forms to file your federal income tax. What other information regarding your income taxes is available from this site? What additional software, if any, do you need to print the form on your PC? Extend your search to the necessary forms for state income taxes if you live in a state that has an income tax.

The Contest

Almost everyone enjoys some form of competition. Ask your instructor to choose a theme for a Web site such as a school club, and to declare a contest in the class to produce the "best" document. Submit your entry, but write your name on the back of the document so that it can be judged anonymously. Your instructor may want to select a set of semi-finalists, then distribute copies of those documents so that the class can vote on the winner.

The Web Page Wizard

The Web Page Wizard is built into Microsoft Office to facilitate the creation of a Web site as opposed to a single Web page. It provides a suggested template that includes navigation through specification of horizontal or vertical frames. You can also select a theme so that your pages have a consistent and professional look. Use the Wizard to create a simple site, consisting of 3 to 6 Web pages for a hypothetical business.

Front Page

Microsoft Word is an excellent way to begin creating Web documents. It is only a beginning, however, and there are many specialty programs that offer significantly more capability. One such product is Front Page, a product aimed at creating a Web site, as opposed to isolated documents. Search the Microsoft Web site for information on Front Page, then summarize your findings in a short note to your instructor. Be sure to include information on capabilities that are included in Front Page, which are not found in Word.

Getting Started: Essential Computing Concepts

OBJECTIVES

AFTER READING THIS MODULE YOU WILL BE ABLE TO:

1. Describe components of a computer system; define the terms used to measure the capacity and speed of a microprocessor, memory, and auxiliary storage.
2. Describe the contribution of IBM, Microsoft, and Intel in the evolution of the PC; discuss several considerations in the purchase of a computer system.
3. Distinguish between system software and application software; describe the evolution of Microsoft Windows®; list the major applications in Microsoft Office®.
4. Describe how to safeguard a system through acquisition of an antivirus program and through systematic backup.
5. Define a local area network; distinguish between a server and a workstation.
6. Define the Internet and the World Wide Web; explain how to access the Internet via a local area network or by dialing in through an Internet Service Provider.
7. Draw several parallels between e-commerce and traditional commerce; describe several capabilities that are available through e-commerce that are not found in traditional commerce.
8. Describe e-mail; distinguish between a mail server and a mail client. Explain the use of an address book, distribution list, and mailing list.

OVERVIEW

Computer literacy is the absolute requirement of the new millennium. Corporations require their employees to be computer literate, parents expect their children to be computer literate, and you are taking this course in order to fulfill the computer literacy requirement at your school or university. We hope, therefore, that when you finish reading this section, you will feel comfortable with the computer and be able to use it effectively in a world of rapidly changing technology. This module introduces you to the essential computing concepts you will need.

A ***computer*** is an electronic device that accepts data (input), then manipulates or processes that data to produce information (output). It operates under the control of a ***program*** (or set of instructions) that is stored internally within the computer's memory. A computer system consists of the computer and its memory, peripheral devices such as a keyboard, disk, monitor, and printer, and the various programs that enable it to perform its intended function.

The idea of a general-purpose machine to solve mathematical problems was first proposed over 150 years ago by an Englishman named Charles Babbage. Babbage's machine would have been the world's first computer, but the technology of his day was incapable of producing the mechanical components to the required precision. Babbage died alone and penniless, having lost a personal fortune in a vain attempt to build his computer.

As happens so often with geniuses who are ahead of their time, Babbage's theory was validated a century after his death, since all modern computers are designed along the lines he proposed. Thus, every computer system, from Babbage's dream (called the Analytical Engine) to today's PC, includes the following components:

- The ***central processing unit*** (***CPU***) is the "brain" of the computer and performs the actual calculations.
- ***Memory*** (which is also known as ***r***andom ***a***ccess ***m***emory or ***RAM***) temporarily stores any program being executed by the computer, as well as the data on which the program operates.
- ***Auxiliary storage*** (also called secondary storage or external storage) provides a place where data can be permanently stored, and then transferred to and from main memory. A floppy disk, hard disk, CD-ROM, DVD, high-capacity removable media, and tape backup unit are the primary types of auxiliary storage used with a PC.
- ***Input devices*** accept data from an external source and convert it to electric signals, which are sent to the CPU. Virtually every PC is configured with a keyboard and mouse as its input devices. A joystick, scanner, and microphone are other common input devices. Auxiliary storage is also considered an input device.
- ***Output devices*** accept electric signals from the CPU and convert them to a form suitable for output. The monitor and printer are common output devices. Speakers are also considered an output device and are necessary in order to hear sound from a PC. Auxiliary storage is also considered an output device.

Charles Babbage

AHEAD OF THEIR TIME

Charles Babbage (1792–1871) went broke trying to build a general-purpose computing device he called the Analytical Engine. Babbage worked closely with Ada Lovelace (Lord Byron's daughter), who realized the potential of the machine and formulated basic programming principles. She is credited with being history's first programmer.

The relationship between the components in a computer system is shown graphically in Figure 1. In essence, the CPU accepts data from an input device or auxiliary storage, stores it temporarily in memory while it computes an answer, then sends the results to an output device or auxiliary storage. All of this happens under the control of the ***operating system***, a computer program (actually many programs) that links the various hardware components to one another. The operating system is stored on the hard disk, and it is loaded into memory when the computer is turned on. Once in memory, the operating system takes over, and it manages the system throughout the session.

Think for a moment about what happens when you sit down at the PC. You turn on the computer, which automatically loads the operating system from the hard disk (auxiliary storage) into memory (RAM) from where the instructions are processed by the CPU. The initial commands in the operating system direct the monitor (an output device) to display the Windows desktop. You react to the output displayed on the screen by using the mouse (an input device) to click an icon such as the Start

FIGURE 1 *Components of a Computer System*

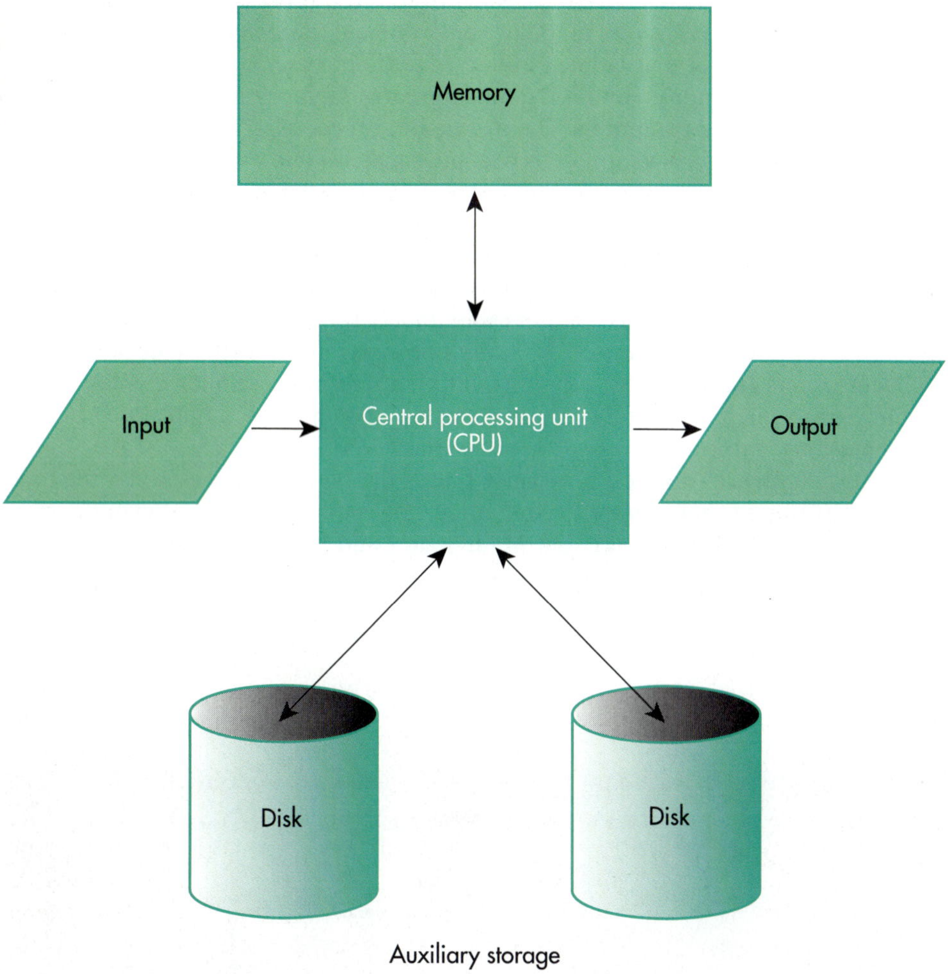

WHAT IS AN OPERATING SYSTEM?

Every computer functions the same way. The CPU accepts data from an input device or auxiliary storage, stores it temporarily in memory while it computes an answer, then sends the result to an output device or auxiliary storage. All of this happens under the control of an operating system, a computer program (actually many programs) that links the various components of a computer to one another.

button, and then follow with subsequent clicks to start a program. The operating system processes your commands, then determines it needs to load an application program (such as Microsoft Word or Microsoft Excel) from auxiliary storage (the hard disk) into memory.

Now you are ready to go to work. You type at the keyboard (an input device) and enter the text of your document, which is stored in the computer's memory and simultaneously displayed on the monitor (an output device). When you're finished with the document, you execute a Print command to transfer the contents of memory to the printer (an alternate output device). And, of course, you will save the document, which copies the contents of memory to a disk (auxiliary storage). The next time you want to access the document, you execute the Open command, which copies the document from disk into memory, at which point you can further edit the document. You make the necessary changes, save the corrected document to disk, then print the revised document. The cycle continues indefinitely.

As you gain proficiency, you will take these operations for granted. It helps, however, if you reflect on the components of a computer system and how they interact with one another. And remember these principles apply to every computer system, from a PC to a massive mainframe.

From Micro to Mainframe

Traditionally, computers have been divided into three broad classes—***mainframes***, ***minicomputers*** (called ***servers*** in today's environment), and ***microcomputers*** (PCs). The classification is primarily one of scale. Mainframes are much larger, faster, cost significantly more money, and have much greater memory and auxiliary storage capacities than other computers. The distinction is becoming increasingly difficult, however, as mainframes continue to become smaller while PCs grow more powerful. Indeed, the machine on your desk has more processing power and storage capability than the mainframe of a decade ago.

Another way to distinguish between the different types of computers is by the number of users who can access the machine at one time. A mainframe supports hundreds (or even thousands) of users simultaneously and is at the core of national and global networks supported by large corporations and other organizations. Minicomputers (servers) also support multiple users, but a smaller number than a mainframe. A microcomputer or PC is restricted to one user at a time. Price is also a distinguishing factor.

Our text focuses on the PC because that is the type of computer you see most frequently. There is much more to computing, however, than the PC on your desk or the notebook computer you carry. Mainframes and servers are the backbone of information systems in corporations, universities, and other organizations. Figure 2 illustrates an IBM mainframe.

FIGURE 2 *IBM Mainframe*

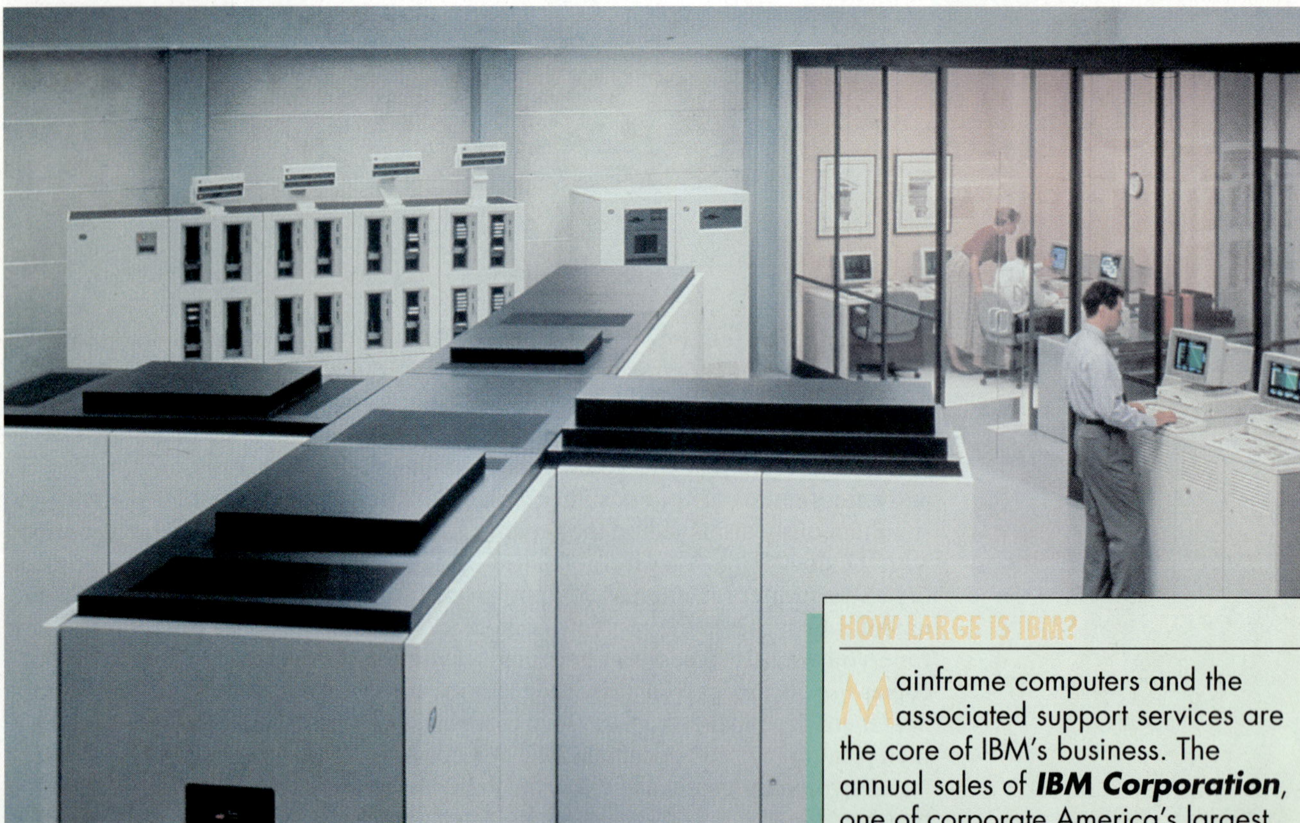

HOW LARGE IS IBM?

Mainframe computers and the associated support services are the core of IBM's business. The annual sales of ***IBM Corporation***, one of corporate America's largest companies, are approximately $90 billion, or almost twice the combined sales of Microsoft and Intel.

Bits and Bytes

A computer is first and foremost a numerical machine. It is designed to perform mathematical calculations and it does so very efficiently. It also works with text, graphics, and multimedia files such as sound and video, all of which are converted to a numeric equivalent. You need not be concerned with precisely how this is accomplished. What is important is that you realize that computers work exclusively with numerical data.

In addition, computers use binary numbers (zeros and ones) rather than decimal numbers. Why binary, and not decimal? The answer is that a binary machine is easy to build, as only two values are required. A current may be on or off, or a switch may be up or down. A decimal computer would be far more difficult.

The binary system is described in terms of bits and bytes. A ***bit*** (binary digit) has two values, zero and one. Individual bits do not, however, convey meaningful information, and so computer storage is divided into bytes, where one ***byte*** consists of eight bits. In other words, a byte is the smallest addressable unit of memory, and any reference to the size of a computer's memory or to the capacity of its disk drive is in terms of bytes.

As indicated, a byte consists of eight bits, each of which can be either a zero or a one. Thus, there are 2^8 (or 256) possible combinations of zeros and ones that can be stored in a byte. We need, however, a way to make sense of the bits and bytes that are processed by the computer. Accordingly, a code was developed in which each combination of eight bits (one byte) represents a different character. It is known as the American Standard Code for Information Interchange (***ASCII*** for short and pronounced as "as key").

The ASCII code provides for 256 different characters, which is more than enough to represent the 26 letters of the alphabet (both upper- and lowercase), the digits, 0 through 9, the punctuation marks, and various special keys you find on the typical keyboard. The ASCII codes for the uppercase letters are shown in Figure 3a. Can you see how those representations are used to create the message in Figure 3b, which represents the contents of five contiguous (adjacent) bytes in memory?

FIGURE 3 *ASCII*

ASCII CODES

Character	ASCII Code
A	01000001
B	01000010
C	01000011
D	01000100
E	01000101
F	01000110
G	01000111
H	01001000
I	01001001
J	01001010
K	01001011
L	01001100
M	01001101
N	01001110
O	01001111
P	01010000
Q	01010001
R	01010010
S	01010011
T	01010100
U	01010101
V	01010110
W	01010111
X	01011000
Y	01011001
Z	01011010
space	00000000

(a) ASCII Codes

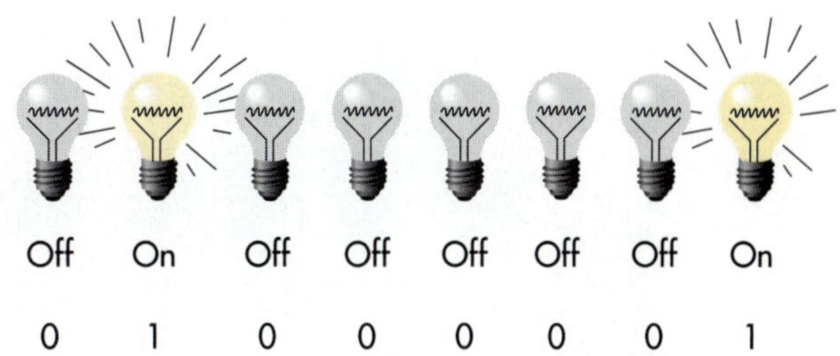

This Pattern of Electrical Circuits Represents the Capital Letter A

01001000 01000101 01001100 01001100 01001111

H E L L O

(b) "Hello" in ASCII

IBM announced its version of the personal computer (PC) in 1981 and broke a longstanding corporate tradition by going to external sources for supporting hardware and software. ***Intel Corporation*** designed the microprocessor. ***Microsoft Corporation*** developed the operating system. The decision to go outside the corporation was motivated in part because IBM was playing "catch up." The Apple II and the Radio Shack TRS-80 had each been available for three years. More to the point, IBM was a mainframe company and simply did not believe in the future of the PC, a decision that the company would regret.

The IBM PC was an instant success, in large part because of its open design that let independent vendors offer supporting products to enhance the functionality of the machine. This was accomplished by creating ***expansion slots*** on the ***motherboard*** (the main system board inside the PC) that could accommodate ***adapter cards*** from sources outside IBM. The motherboard contains the circuitry that connects the components of the PC to one another, and thus plugging in an adapter card is the equivalent of adding another device to the machine. IBM made public the necessary technical information to create the adapter cards, enabling other companies to build peripheral devices for the PC and enhance its overall capability.

The open design of the PC was a mixed blessing for IBM, in that ***PC-compatibles*** based on the same microprocessor and able to run the same software began to appear as early as 1982 and offered superior performance for less money. Companies and individuals that were once willing to pay a premium for the IBM name began ordering the "same" machine from other vendors. IBM today has less than ten percent of the market it was so instrumental in creating, as the personal computer has become a commodity. "PC" is a generic term for any computer based on Intel-compatible microprocessors that are capable of running Microsoft Windows.

Figure 4 illustrates a typical Windows workstation, as it exists today. We view the system from the front (Figure 4a), the rear (Figure 4b), and from inside the system unit (Figure 4c). Your system will be different from ours, but you should be able to recognize the various components regardless of whether you use a desktop, tower, or notebook computer. We continue with a discussion of each component.

FIGURE 4 *A Windows Workstation*

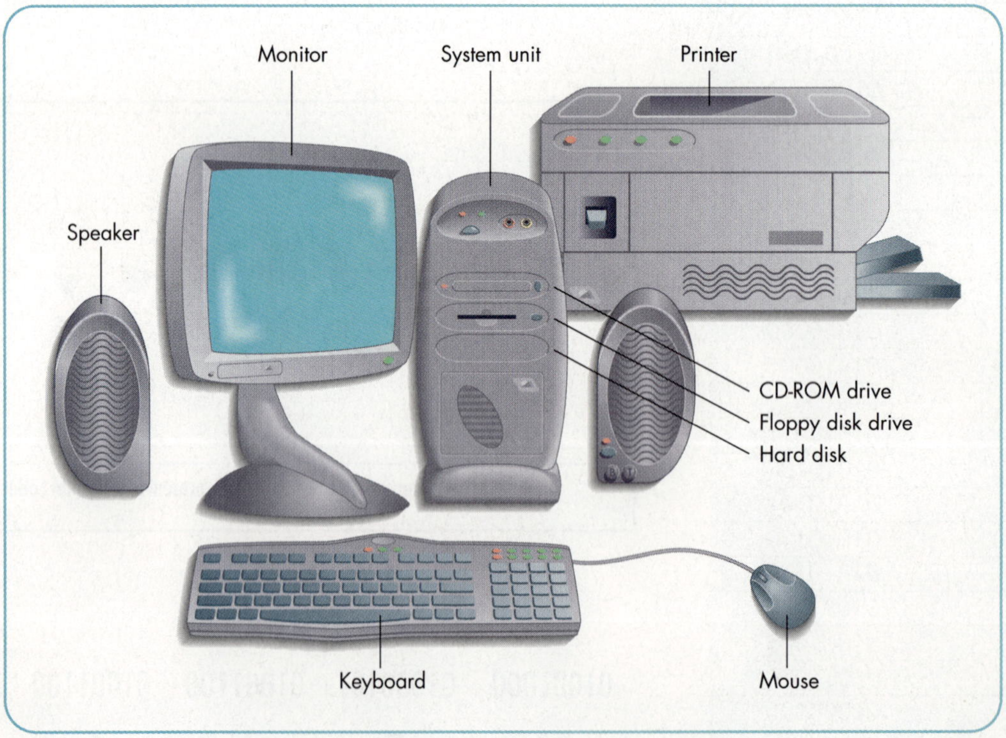

(a) Front View

FIGURE 4 *A Windows Workstation (continued)*

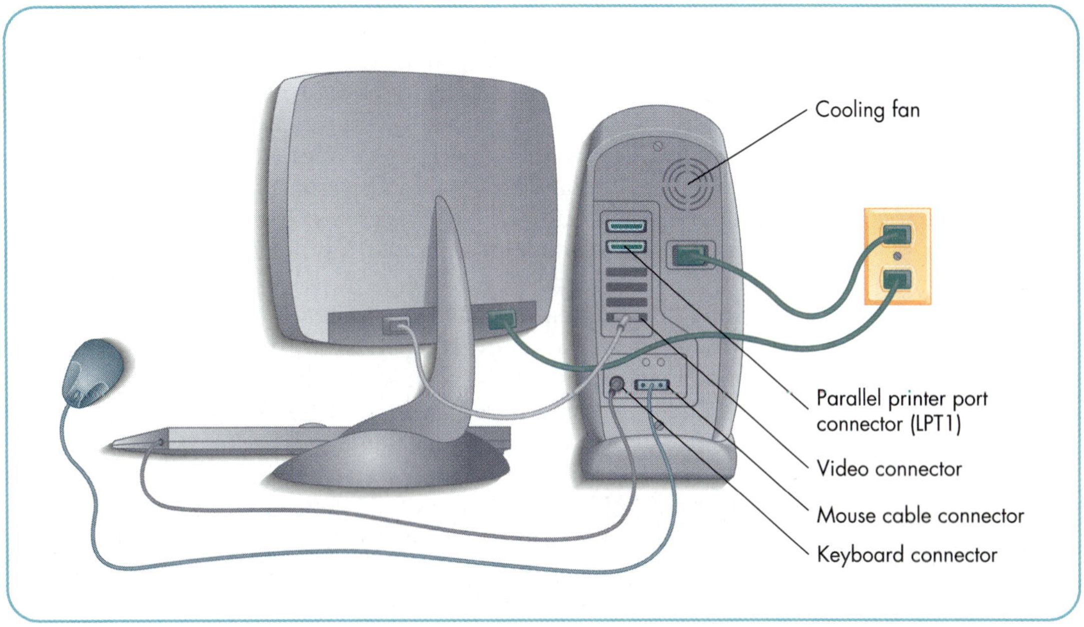

(b) Rear View

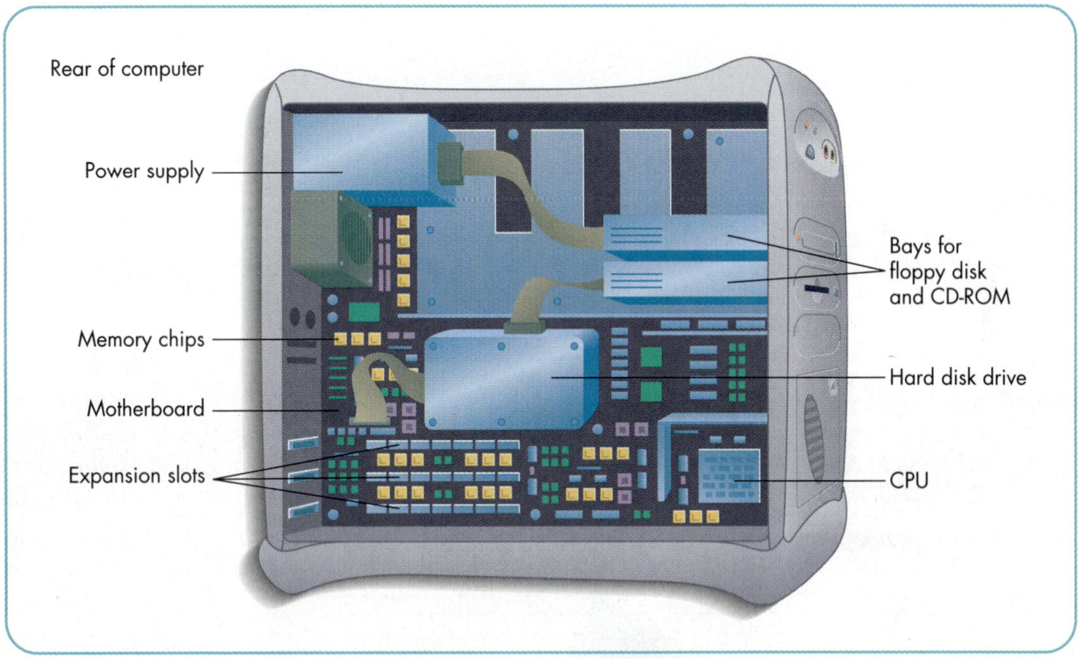

(c) Inside the Computer

The Microprocessor

The PC, like any other microcomputer, is characterized by the fact that its entire CPU is contained on a single silicon chip known as a ***microprocessor***. Intel microprocessors were known originally by a number, but other vendors such as AMD and Cyrix were producing functionally equivalent chips using the same numbering scheme. Then, in a stroke of marketing genius, Intel trademarked the ***Pentium*** name to differentiate its chips from the competition, and followed up with the Pentium II, Pentium III, and soon-to-arrive Pentium IV. You can still purchase Intel-compatible chips from other vendors, but only Intel has the Pentium, which has become a highly recognized brand name.

Not all Pentiums are created equal because the chips are further differentiated by ***clock speed***, an indication of how fast instructions are executed. Clock speed is measured in ***megahertz*** (***MHz*** or millions of cycles) or ***gigahertz*** (***GHz*** or billions of cycles). The higher the clock speed the faster the microprocessor. Thus, a Pentium III running at 1GHz is faster than a Pentium III running at 700MHz. To facilitate the comparison of one microprocessor to another, Intel has created the ***Intel CPU performance (iCOMP) index*** as shown in Figure 5.

The index consists of a single number to indicate the relative performance of a microprocessor—the higher the number the faster the processor. (You can obtain a current version of the index by going to the Intel Web site at www.intel.com.) There is a relatively small increase in the iCOMP number between the chips at the top of the chart, whereas the difference in cost can be significant. We suggest, therefore, that you buy one or two chips from the top in order to get the "biggest bang for the buck."

FIGURE 5 *The Microprocessor*

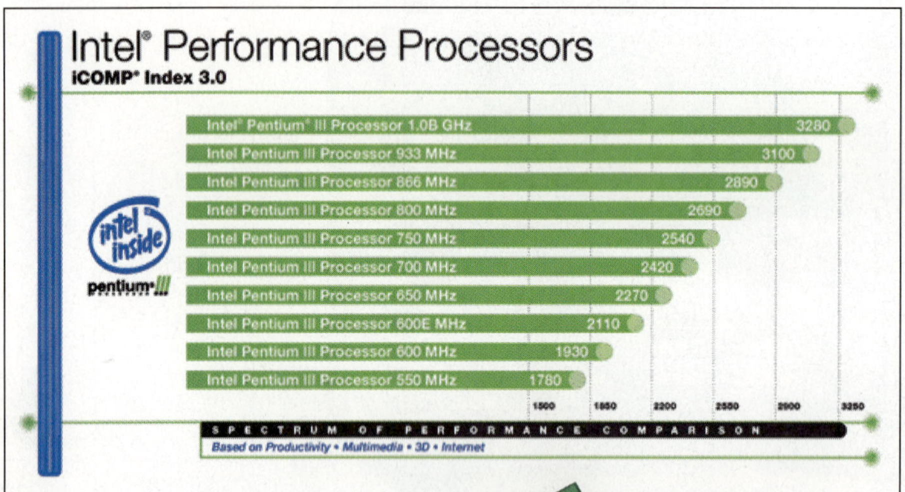

MOORE'S LAW

The fundamental unit of the microprocessor is the transistor—the on/off, zero/one switch that is at the heart of the digital computer. The key to improving the performance of a microprocessor is to increase the number of transistors; the more transistors, the more powerful the microprocessor. In 1965 Gordon Moore, the founder of Intel, predicted that transistor densities would continue to double every 18 months, a prediction that has held, and that accounts for the incredible increase in computer power.

Memory

The microprocessor is the brain of the PC, but it needs instructions that tell it what to do, data on which to work, and a place to store the result of its calculations. All of this takes place in memory, a temporary storage area that holds data, instructions, and results, and passes everything back and forth to the CPU. The amount of memory a system has is important because the larger the memory, the more sophisticated the programs are that the computer is capable of executing, and further, the more programs and data that can remain in memory at the same time. Increasing the memory of a computer also increases the speed at which those programs are executed.

As depicted in Figure 6, the memory of a computer (also known as random access memory or RAM) is divided into individual storage locations, each of which holds one byte. In the early days of the PC, memory was measured in ***kilobytes*** (***Kb***). Today RAM is measured in ***megabytes*** (***Mb***). One Kb and Mb are equal to approximately one thousand and one million characters, respectively. In actuality 1Kb equals 1,024 (or 2^{10}) bytes, whereas 1Mb is 1,048,576 (or 2^{20}) bytes. A Windows workstation typically has 128Mb of memory in today's environment. This is truly a fantastic amount, especially when you consider that mainframes that once cost millions of dollars had memories of 128Kb and less.

The microprocessor also reads data from a second type of memory known as ***read-only memory*** (***ROM***). Read-only memory is accessed only when the computer is first turned on, as it contains the instructions telling the computer to check itself, and then to load the essential portion of the operating system into memory. The contents of ROM are established at the factory and cannot be altered by application programs, hence the name "read only."

The size of a computer's memory refers only to the amount of RAM available. The contents of RAM, however, are volatile and change constantly as different programs are executed, or every time the same program is executed with different data. RAM is also transient, which means that shutting off (or losing) the power to the system erases the contents of memory. Auxiliary storage devices, however, retain their contents even when there is no power.

HOW LARGE IS 128MB?

Imagine that you have been assigned the task of checking the contents of each byte of a computer with 128Mb of RAM, and that it takes you one second per byte. At that rate, it would take approximately four years to view the contents of every location. In other words, you could spend your entire college career reviewing the contents of memory, using only one second for each byte.

FIGURE 6 *Memory*

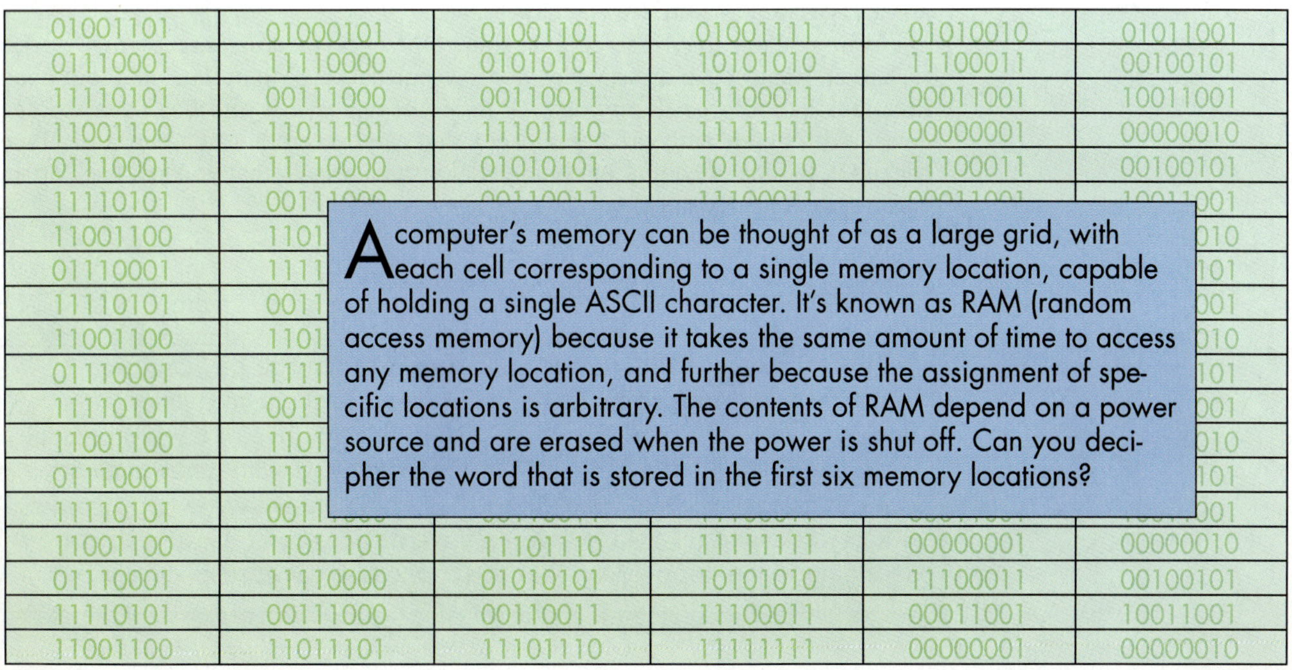

A computer's memory can be thought of as a large grid, with each cell corresponding to a single memory location, capable of holding a single ASCII character. It's known as RAM (random access memory) because it takes the same amount of time to access any memory location, and further because the assignment of specific locations is arbitrary. The contents of RAM depend on a power source and are erased when the power is shut off. Can you decipher the word that is stored in the first six memory locations?

Auxiliary Storage

A disk drive is the most common type of auxiliary storage. The ***floppy disk*** gets its name because it is made of a flexible plastic (although it is enclosed in a hard plastic case). A ***hard disk*** uses rigid metal platters. A hard disk is also called a ***fixed disk*** because it remains permanently inside the system unit. A hard disk holds significantly more data than a floppy disk, and it accesses that data much faster.

The PC of today has standardized on the 3½-inch high-density floppy disk with a capacity of 1.44Mb. (The 5¼-inch floppy disk is obsolete, as is the double-density 3½-inch floppy disk, which had a capacity of 720Kb. Thus, all references to a floppy disk will be to the 3½-inch high-density disk.) The capacity of a hard disk is much greater and is measured in ***gigabytes*** (Gb), where 1Gb is approximately one billion (or 2^{30}) bytes. There is no such item as a standard hard disk as each system is configured independently, but disks with 20 to 40Gb and more are typical in today's environment.

All disks are also characterized by ***access time***, which is the average time required to locate a specific item on the disk. Access time is measured in milliseconds (ms), where one millisecond equals one thousandth of a second. The shorter the access time, the faster the disk. The floppy disk has an average time of 175 ms, whereas the typical fixed disk has an access time of less than ten ms.

There are many other types of auxiliary storage. The ***CD-ROM***, once a high-priced optional device, has become a standard on today's PC. CD-ROM stands for Compact Disk, Read-Only Memory, meaning that you can read from the CD but you cannot write to the CD. The standard CD has a storage capacity of 650Mb (compared to 1.44Mb on a floppy disk). The large capacity, coupled with the relatively modest cost of duplicating a CD ($1.00 or less in large quantities), makes the CD an ideal way to distribute software. We take for granted the single CD as opposed to multiple floppy disks of years past. Reference material, such as an encyclopedia, is also distributed via a CD. ***DVD*** is a new standard with significantly greater capacity, up to 17Gb (as opposed to 650Mb for CD-ROM) that will gain increasing acceptance in coming years.

A CD-ROM is the perfect medium to distribute a program, but what if you are seeking a way to copy data from your fixed disk to a removable medium as a means of backup? You would do well to consider a recordable CD drive that lets you burn new CDs as well as read existing CDs.

Your system should also contain some type of ***removable mass storage*** device such as an Iomega Zip drive, which holds as much as 250Mb of data, and looks and functions like a large floppy disk. A ***tape backup unit*** is another mass storage device, with significantly greater capacity that can exceed that of a hard disk. Tape backup is an ideal medium for commercial installations in that you can back up an entire system on one tape.

WHAT IS DRIVE C?

The CPU needs to differentiate one auxiliary storage device from another and does so by designating each device with a letter. The floppy drive is always drive A. (A second floppy drive, if it were present, would be drive B.) The hard disk is always drive C with other auxiliary devices assigned letters from D on. Thus, a system with one floppy drive, a hard disk, and a CD-ROM would have devices as A, C, and D, corresponding to the floppy disk, hard disk, and CD-ROM, respectively.

FIGURE 7 *Auxiliary Storage*

HOW DISK STORAGE WORKS

Computer disks—both floppy and hard—are flat dishes coated on both sides with a magnetic film. When a disk is formatted, magnetic codes are embedded in the film to divide the surface of the disk into sectors (pie-slice wedges) and tracks (concentric circles). They organize the disk so that the data can be recorded in a logical manner and accessed quickly by the read/write heads that move back and forth over the disk as it spins. The number of sectors and tracks that fit on a disk determine its capacity.

(a) Floppy Disks

(b) Hard Disk

(c) CD-ROM

(d) Zip Disk

BACK UP YOUR DATA

How much would you pay to have another copy of your term paper or company project that just disappeared from your hard drive? It can happen very easily because hard disks do fail, whether it is a hardware problem, virus infection, or software error. We urge you, therefore, to take time at the end of every session to back up the files you cannot afford to lose. You need not copy every file, only the data files that were changed during that session. It takes only a few minutes, but one day you will thank us.

Input Devices

The ***keyboard*** and the ***mouse*** are the primary input devices for the PC. The keys on the keyboard are arranged much like those of a typewriter, in the standard QWERTY pattern (named for the first six characters in the third row). In addition, there are several special keys that are unique to the PC as shown in Figure 8.

The Caps Lock key eliminates the need to continually press the shift key to enter uppercase letters. The Caps Lock key functions as a toggle switch; that is, pressing it once causes all uppercase letters to be entered, pressing it a second time returns to lowercase, pressing it again returns to uppercase, and so on. The Num Lock key is similar in concept and activates the numeric keypad at the right side of the keyboard.

Function keys (F1 through F12) are special-purpose keys, used by various application programs to execute specific commands and/or save keystrokes. The exact purpose of a particular function key varies from program to program. The Ctrl and Alt keys work in similar fashion and are used with other keys to execute a specific command.

Cursor keys [the four arrow keys, up (↑), down (↓), right (→), and left (←)] control movement of the cursor (the blinking line or box), which shows where on the monitor the data will be entered. The Home, End, PgUp, and PgDn keys also serve to move the cursor.

The Enter (Return) key signals the completion of an entry and correspondingly causes the characters typed on the keyboard to be transmitted to the CPU. Other special keys include the Insert (Ins) and Delete (Del) keys that insert and/or delete characters, respectively. The Escape (Esc) key is used by many programs to cancel (or escape from) current actions. The Print Screen key copies the image on the monitor into memory from where it can be inserted into a document. The Windows key (found only on newer keyboards) is equivalent to clicking the Start button in Microsoft Windows.

The standard mouse has two buttons and recognizes four basic operations with which you must become familiar:

- To point to an object, move the mouse pointer onto the object.
- To click an object, point to it, then press and release the left mouse button; to right click an object, point to the object, then press and release the right mouse button.
- To double click an object, point to it, then quickly click the left button twice in succession.
- To drag an object, move the pointer to the object, then press and hold the left button while you move the mouse to place the object in a new position.

The keyboard and mouse are the primary input devices for the PC, but there are others. A ***microphone*** is required to record your own sound files, which can then be played through the soundboard and speakers. A ***scanner*** enables you to convert a graphic image into its digital equivalent for subsequent inclusion in a document. A scanner also enables you to convert text into a form suitable for word processing. And don't forget a ***joystick***, which is an essential component on many computer games.

THE WINDOWS ⊞ KEY

Use the Windows ⊞ key in conjunction with various other letters as valuable keyboard shortcuts. Press and hold the Windows key with the letter "D", for example, to minimize or restore all open applications. ⊞ + E will open My Computer and ⊞ + F opens the Search window to look for a file or folder. ⊞ by itself displays the start menu.

FIGURE 8 *Input Devices*

THE MOUSE OR THE KEYBOARD

Almost every command in Windows can be executed in different ways, using either the mouse or the keyboard. Most people start with the mouse and add keyboard shortcuts as they become more proficient. There is no right or wrong technique, just different techniques, and the one you choose depends entirely on personal preference in a specific situation. If, for example, your hands are already on the keyboard, it is faster to use the keyboard shortcut. Other times, your hand will be on the mouse and that will be the fastest way.

Joystick

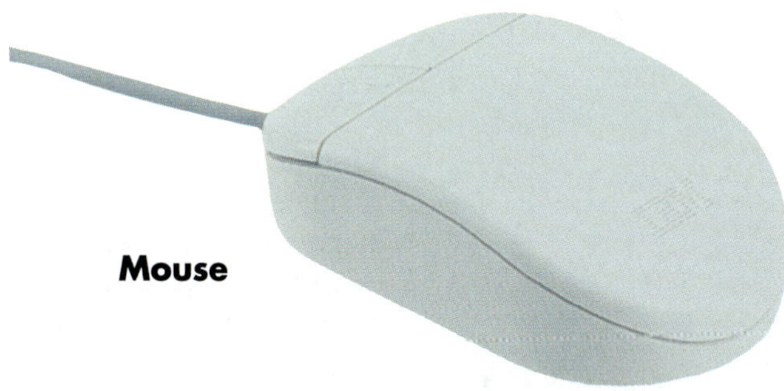

Mouse

Keyboard

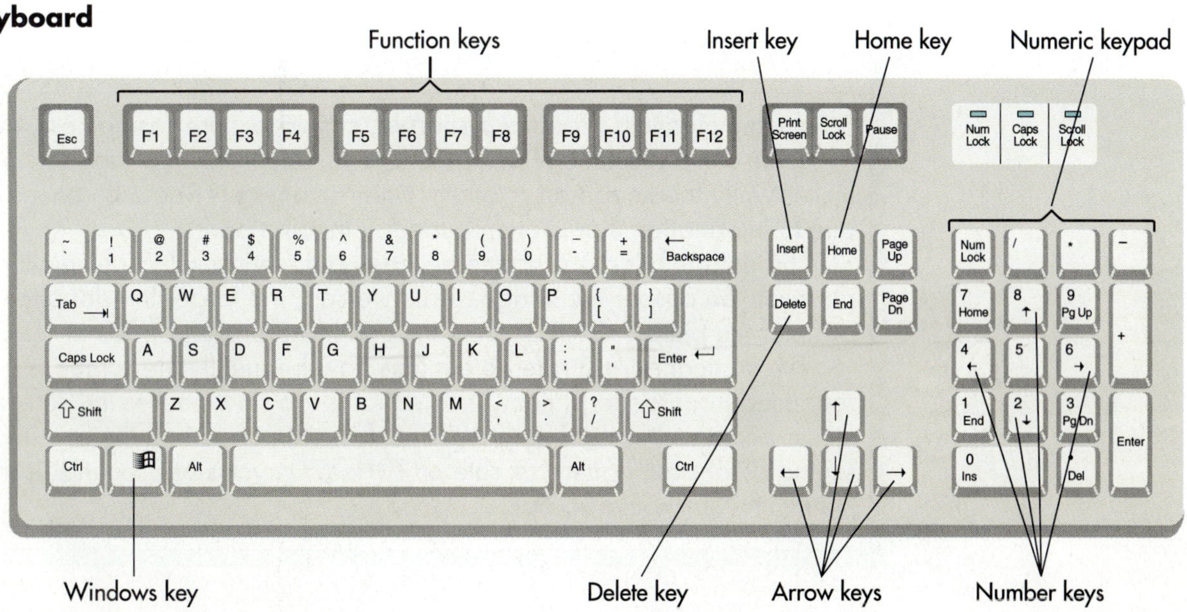

The Monitor

The ***monitor*** (or video display) is an output device. The monitor of a typical desktop configuration uses CRT (cathode ray tube) technology, the same technology that is used for television. Notebook computers, however, use a flat-panel display known as a liquid crystal display (LCD). Either way, the image that is displayed consists of ***pixels*** (the tiny dots or *pic*ture *el*ements).

The ***resolution*** of a monitor is the number of pixels that are displayed at one time. Several resolutions are possible, but you are most likely to see either *800 × 600* (800 pixels across by 600 pixels down) or *1,024 × 768* (1,024 pixels across by 768 down). An earlier standard of 640 × 480 has passed into obsolescence. The advantage of the higher resolution is that more pixels are displayed on the screen and hence you see more of the document—for example, more columns in a spreadsheet or more pages in a word processing document. The disadvantage is that the size of the text is smaller at the higher resolutions. Thus, the higher the resolution, the larger the monitor should be.

Figure 9 illustrates the effect of increasing the resolution on a screen of fixed size. The 640 × 480 screen in Figure 9a displays rows 1 to 17 and columns A to G. Moving to 800 × 600, as in Figure 9b, enables us to see rows 1 to 24 and columns A to J. We see more data, but the text is smaller. Figures 9c and 9d further increase the resolution with similar effects. You choose the resolution in conjunction with the size of the monitor. A 17-inch monitor, for example, works well with a resolution of 800 × 600, or depending on your vision, even 1,024 × 768. Higher resolutions, such as 1,280 × 1,024 or even 1,600 × 1,200, require larger and (considerably) more expensive monitors.

The processing requirements imposed on the system at higher resolutions are enormous. At 800 × 600, for example, the CPU has to send 480,000 bytes to display a single screen (given that each pixel requires only one byte), and that is only the beginning. The screen has to be refreshed approximately 70 times a second, and each pixel typically takes two or three bytes, rather than one. The requirements become even more demanding at higher resolutions. To speed processing, a PC is equipped with a video (display) adapter (or graphics card). You can think of the video adapter as an assistant to the CPU in that the task of displaying and refreshing a screen is shifted from the microprocessor to the graphics card. A graphics card also has its own memory, which is known as video memory.

CHOOSING A MONITOR

Do some monitors produce a sharper, crisper picture than others, even at the same resolution? Does the image on one monitor appear to flicker while the image on another remains constant? The differences are due to information that is often buried in the fine print.

The dot pitch is the distance between adjacent pixels. The smaller the dot pitch the crisper the image, or conversely, the larger the dot pitch the grainier the picture. Choose a monitor with a dot pitch of .28 or less.

The vertical refresh rate determines how frequently the screen is repainted from top to bottom. A rate that is too slow causes the screen to flicker because it is not being redrawn fast enough to fool the eye into seeing a constant pattern. A rate of 70Hz (70 cycles per second) is the minimum you should accept.

FIGURE 9 *Monitor Size and Resolution*

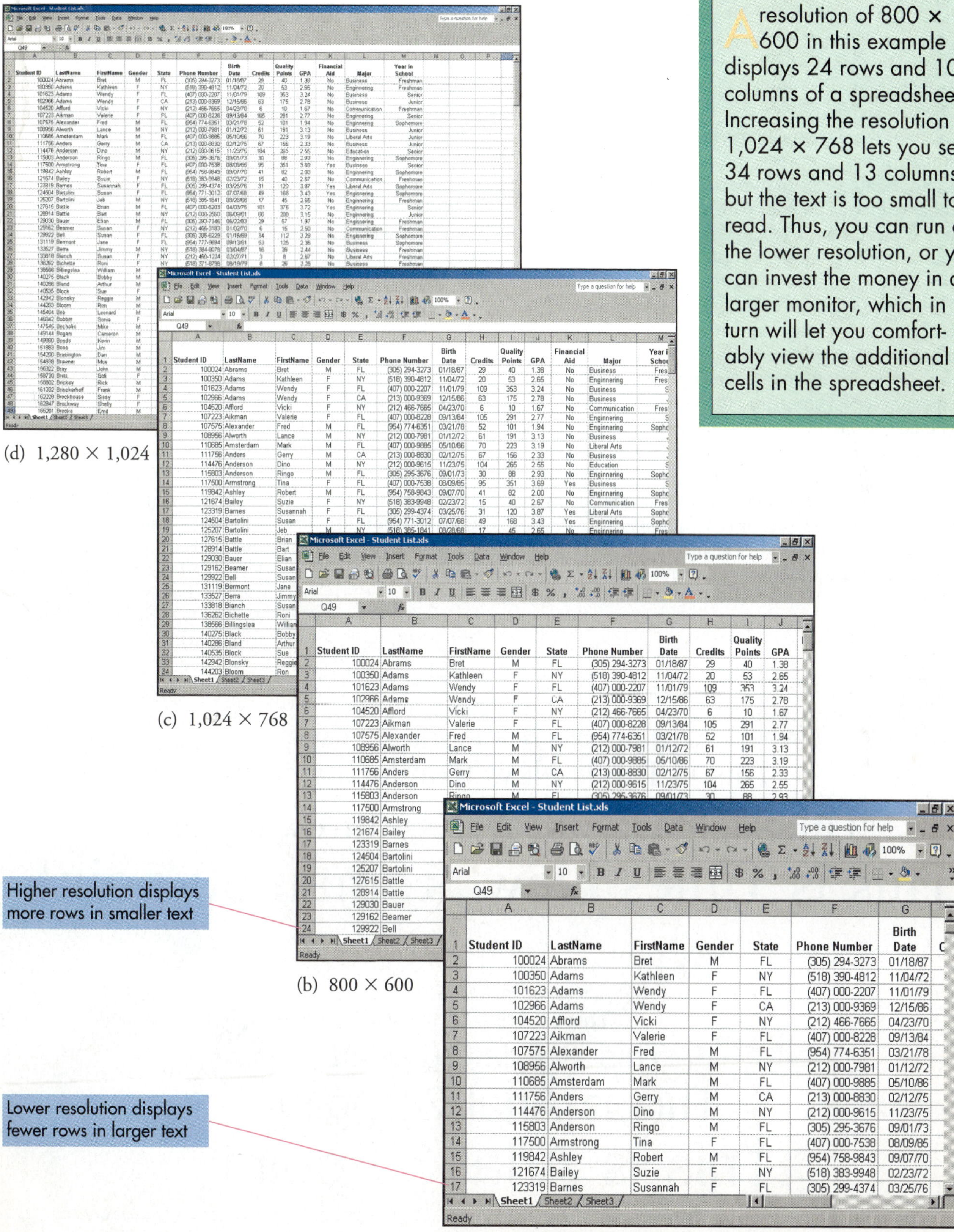

(d) 1,280 × 1,024

(c) 1,024 × 768

(b) 800 × 600

(a) 640 × 480

RESOLUTION AND MONITOR SIZE

A resolution of 800 × 600 in this example displays 24 rows and 10 columns of a spreadsheet. Increasing the resolution to 1,024 × 768 lets you see 34 rows and 13 columns, but the text is too small to read. Thus, you can run at the lower resolution, or you can invest the money in a larger monitor, which in turn will let you comfortably view the additional cells in the spreadsheet.

The Printer

A printer produces output on paper or acetate transparencies. The output is referred to as ***hard copy*** because it is more tangible than the files written to a disk or other electronic devices. Printers vary greatly in terms of design, price, and capability as can be seen in Figure 10.

The dot matrix printer was the entry-level printer of choice for many years. It was inexpensive and versatile, but suffered from two major drawbacks—it was noisy and it had a less-than-perfect print quality, since each character was created with a pattern of dots. The dot matrix printer has become virtually obsolete, due to the emergence of the ink jet printer. It is still used occasionally, however, for multipart forms.

The ***ink jet printer*** is today's entry-level printer. It is quieter than a dot matrix printer, its print quality is much better, and it prints in color. The downside is that supplies (replacement cartridges for the colored ink) are expensive when compared to the cost of the printer.

The ***laser printer*** is the top-of-the-line device, and it offers speed and quality superior to that of an ink jet. A personal laser printer is only slightly more expensive than an ink jet, and it prints considerably faster, albeit in black and white. The resolution (quality) of a laser printer is measured in dots per inch (e.g., 1,200 dpi), and its speed is measured in pages per minute (e.g., 8 ppm).

Regardless of the printer you choose, you will need to learn about typography when you begin to create your own documents. ***Typography*** is the process of selecting typefaces, type styles, and type sizes. It is a critical, often subtle element in the success of a document. Good typography goes almost unnoticed, whereas poor typography calls attention to itself and detracts from a document.

A typeface (or font) is a complete set of characters (upper- and lowercase letters, numbers, punctuation marks, and special symbols). Typefaces are divided into two general categories, serif and sans serif. A serif typeface (e.g., Times New Roman) has tiny cross lines at the ends of the characters to help the eye connect one letter with the next. A sans serif typeface (e.g., Arial) does not have these lines. A commonly accepted practice is to use serif typefaces with larger amounts of text and sans serif typefaces for smaller amounts.

Type size is a vertical measurement and is specified in points. One point is equal to $1/72$ of an inch. The text in most documents is set in 10- or 12-point type. (The text you are reading is set in a 10-point serif typeface.) Different elements in the same document are often set in different type sizes to provide suitable emphasis.

This is Times New Roman 10 point

This is Times New Roman 12 point

This is Times New Roman 18 point

This is Times New Roman 24 point

This is Times New Roman 30 point

This is Arial 10 point

This is Arial 12 point

This is Arial 18 point

This is Arial 24 point

This is Arial 30 point

Basics of Typography—Typefaces and Point Sizes

FIGURE 10 *Printers*

(a) Network Printer

(b) Inkjet Printer

(c) Laser Printer

Are you confused about all the ads for personal computers? You can buy from hundreds of companies, retail or through the mail, with no such thing as a standard configuration. The PC has, in effect, become a commodity where the consumer is able to select each component. We suggest you approach the purchase of a PC just as you would the purchase of any big-ticket item, with research and planning. Be sure you know your hardware requirements before you walk into a computer store, or else you will spend too much money or buy the wrong system. Stick to your requirements and don't be swayed to a different item if the vendor is out of stock. You've waited this long to buy a computer, and another week or two won't matter.

FIGURE 11 *Working in Comfort*

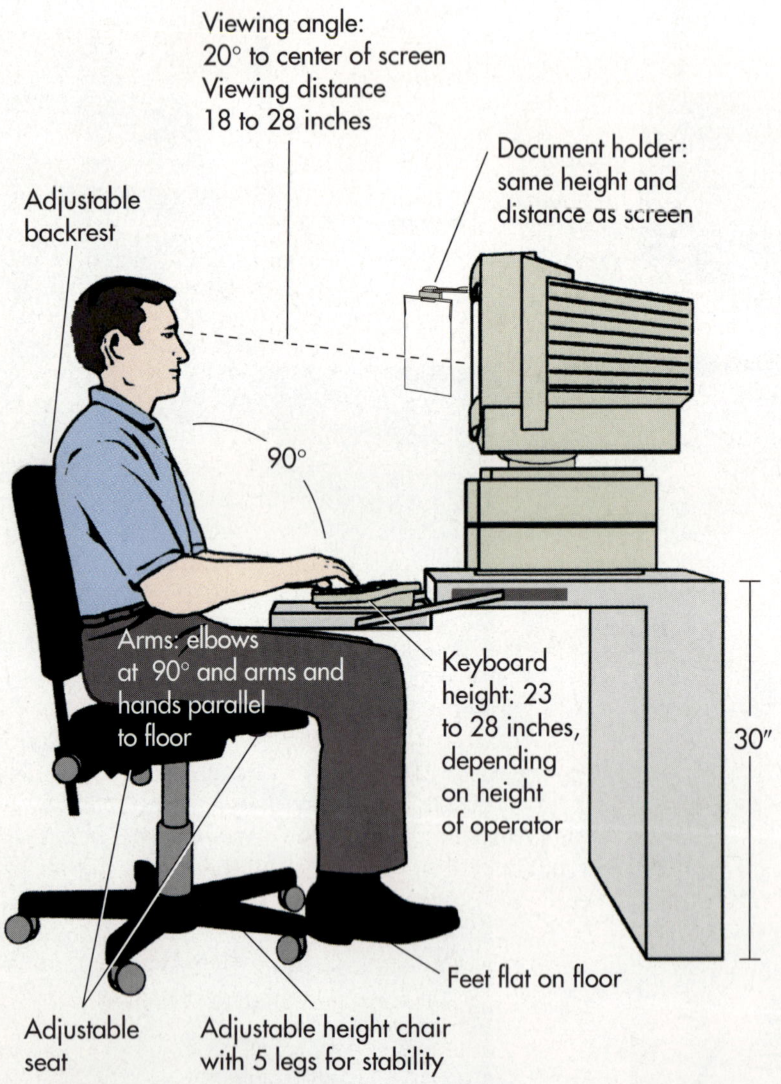

BE KIND TO YOURSELF

Are you the type of person who will spend thousands on a new computer, only to set it up on your regular desk and sit on a $10 bridge chair? Don't. A conventional desk (or the dining room table) is 30 inches high, but the recommended typing height is 27 inches. The difference accounts for the stiff neck, tight shoulders, and aching backs reported by many people who sit at a computer over an extended period of time. Be kind to yourself and include a computer table with lots of room as well as a comfortable chair in your budget.

Mail order will almost always offer better prices than a retail establishment, but price should not be the sole consideration. Local service and support are also important, especially if you are a nontechnical new user. A little research, however, and you can purchase through the mail with confidence, and save yourself money in the process. If you do purchase by mail, confirm the order in writing, stating exactly what you are expecting to receive and when. Include the specific brands and/or model numbers and the agreed-upon price, including shipping and handling, to have documentation in the event of a dispute.

The vast majority of dealers, both retail and mail order, are reputable, but as with any purchase, *caveat emptor*. Good luck, good shopping, and keep the following in mind.

Don't forget the software. Any machine you buy will come with some version of the Windows operating system, but that is only the beginning since you must also purchase the application software you intend to run. Many first-time buyers are surprised that they have to pay extra for software, but you had better allow for software in your budget. Ideally, ***Microsoft Office*** will be bundled with your machine, but if not, the university bookstore is generally your best bet as it offers a substantial educational discount.

Don't skimp on memory. The more memory a system has the better its overall performance. The Office suite is very powerful, but it requires adequate resources to run efficiently. 64Mb of RAM is recommended as the absolute minimum you should consider, but 128Mb is preferable. Either way, be sure your system can accommodate additional memory easily and inexpensively.

Buy more disk space than you think you need. We purchased our first hard disk as an upgrade to the original PC in 1984. It was a "whopping" 10Mb, and our biggest concern was that we would never fill it all. The storage requirements of application programs have increased significantly. Today's version of Microsoft Office requires several hundred megabytes for a complete installation. A 10Gb drive is the minimum you should consider, but for an additional $100 (or less) you can add significantly more storage. It is money well spent.

Let your fingers do the walking. A single issue of a computer magazine contains advertisements from many vendors making it possible to comparison shop from multiple mail-order vendors from the convenience of home. You can also shop online and can visit a vendor's Web site to obtain the latest information. Go to the Exploring Windows home page, www.prenhall.com/grauer, click the link to additional resources, then click the link to a PC Buying Guide to visit some suggested sites.

Look for 30-day price protection. An unconditional 30-day money-back guarantee is an industry standard. Insist on this guarantee and be sure you have it in writing. A reputable vendor will also refund the amount of any price reduction that occurs during the first 30 days, but it is incumbent on you to contact the vendor and request a refund. Don't forget to do so.

Use a credit card. You can double the warranty of any system (up to one additional year) by using a major credit card provided it offers a "buyer's protection" policy. (Check with your credit card company to see whether it has this feature, and if not, you may want to consider getting a different credit card.) The extended warranty is free, and it goes into effect automatically when you charge your computer. The use of a credit card also gives you additional leverage if you are dissatisfied with an item.

Don't forget the extras. The standard PC does not include a network card or removable mass storage device. You need a network card if you plan to connect to the Internet via a cable modem, DSL, or through a local area network in your dorm. A mass storage device such as an Iomega Zip drive is essential for backup. Speakers may also be extra. Any vendor will gladly sell you these components. Just remember to ask.

Don't be frustrated when prices drop. The system you buy today will invariably cost less tomorrow, and further, tomorrow's machine will run circles around today's most powerful system. The IBM/XT, for example, sold for approximately $5,000 and was configured with an 8088 microprocessor, a 10Mb hard disk, 128Kb of RAM, and monochrome monitor, but it was the best system you could buy in 1983. The point of this example is that you enjoy the machine you buy today without concern for future technology. Indeed, if you wait until prices come down, you will never buy anything, because there will always be something better and less expensive.

The ***IBM PC*** was introduced in 1981, literally a lifetime ago, because it predates today's college generation. IBM was neither first (the Apple II, TRS-80, and Commodore 64 all preceded the PC) nor technologically innovative, but its announcement put the personal computer on the desks of American business, just as Apple had put the computer in the home. By 1985 IBM had manufactured its three millionth PC, and had spawned an entire industry in the process. To appreciate how far we've come, consider this subjective list of innovative computers.

Altair 8800 (1975): The January 1975 issue of *Popular Electronics* featured the Altair 8800 on its cover: The world's first PC had to be built from a kit that cost $439. It had no keyboard or monitor, no software, and was programmed by switches on the front panel.

Apple II (1977): The Apple II was a fully assembled home computer in an attractive case, complete with keyboard, connection to a TV screen, color, memory to 64Kb, and the BASIC programming language. The machine was to launch the personal computer revolution and vault its founders, Steve Wozniak and Steve Jobs, from garage to glory.

Apple Macintosh (1984): The Macintosh was far from an instant success, but once Apple got the bugs out and added an internal hard disk, laser printer, and expanded memory, the machine took off. Its ease of use and graphical interface offered an entirely different perspective on computing.

Palm Pilot 1000 (1996): The Palm Pilot 1000 began as a hand-held "organizer" intended to make people's lives easier. The original applications of a date book, address book, and "to do" list have evolved into an Internet connectivity device that provides instant access to all types of information, from e-mail to stock quotes, medical data, and corporate-level database information.

Apple iMac (1998): The "i" in iMac is to remind the public of the easy-to-use Internet features that are built into this colorful and innovative computer that restored profitability to Apple. It supports wireless communication and is quieter than a PC because it is built without an internal fan. It's also a powerful computer that intrigues its users with the ability to create movies on the desktop.

The PC Today: The first portable PC was introduced by Compaq Computer in 1983, but at 35 pounds, it was more "luggable" than portable. Today's notebook computer is a marvel of technology and innovation with capabilities that were unthinkable just a few years ago. It weighs in at less than 5 pounds, yet is equipped with 128Mb of RAM, a 10Gb fixed disk, and a 750 MHz processor. These parameters were typical at the time we went to press, but may well have increased as you are reading our text.

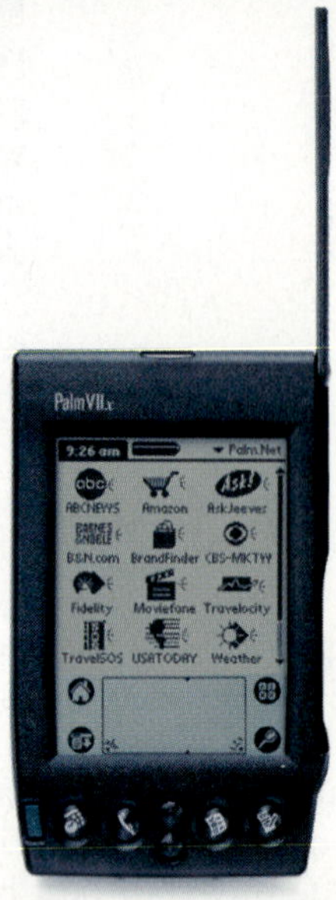

Palm™ VIIx Handheld

iMac

Notebook

The most powerful computer system is useless without appropriate ***software***. Indeed, it is the availability of the software that justifies the purchase of the ***hardware*** and dictates how the computer will be used. Without software, the computer is just an expensive paperweight. Software is divided broadly into two classes, ***system software*** (consisting of the operating system and supporting programs) and ***application software***. The wonderful thing about application software is that replacing one application with another completely changes the personality of the computer. The same computer that is used for word processing can also be used to surf the Internet, prepare long-range financial forecasts, compose music, or play a computer game, merely by changing the application program.

The application programs depend, however, on the ***operating system***, a program (actually many programs) that links the hardware components to one another. Thus, it is the operating system that lets you enter text at a keyboard, have that text displayed on a monitor, stored permanently on disk, then appear as hard copy on the printer. An application program (such as Microsoft Word) simply forwards your commands to the operating system, which does its work unobtrusively behind the scenes. A portion of the operating system is loaded into memory at the time the computer is turned on and it remains there throughout the session, enabling you to do the work that you want to do.

The Evolution of the Desktop

The operating system for the PC has improved continually over time. As new hardware became available, new versions of the operating system were written to take advantage of the increased performance. Each improvement in hardware brought with it a new and better operating system, which in turn demanded faster hardware with more storage capability. Figure 12 displays a screen from three different versions of Windows—Windows 3.1, Windows 95 (the first of the so-called "modern" Windows), and Windows XP—and provides an appreciation of the achievements of the last several years. Before Windows, however, there was MS-DOS.

MS-DOS 1.0 was announced with the PC in 1981. The hardware was primitive by today's standards as a fully loaded PC came with 64Kb of RAM, two 5¼ floppy drives (a hard disk was not yet available), and a monochrome monitor that displayed only text (not graphics). The operating system was equally basic and required only 20Kb of disk storage, but it was perfectly matched to the available hardware.

MS-DOS would improve significantly over the years, but it was always a text-based system. The flashing cursor and cryptic A:\> or C:\> prompt that was displayed on the screen was intimidating to the new user who had to know which commands to enter. The applications were also limited in that they were text-based and totally unrelated to one another. WordPerfect, Lotus, and dBase, for example, were the dominant applications of their day, but each had a completely different interface so that knowledge of one did not help you to learn the other. And even if you knew all three applications, you could run only one application at a time.

All of this changed with the introduction of ***Windows 3.1*** in 1991, which introduced the ***graphical user interface*** (***GUI*** and pronounced "gooey") that let you use a mouse to point and click icons instead of having to enter text-based commands. Windows 3.1 also provided a ***WYSIWYG*** (pronounced "wizzywig" and standing for What You See Is What You Get) interface in which text and graphic elements appeared on the screen exactly as they appeared on the printer. Boldface and italics were displayed in different point sizes and different typefaces. The Windows 3.1 interface looks primitive today, but it was a very big deal at the time. It was slow to catch on initially, but it signaled the beginning of the end for MS-DOS.

FIGURE 12 *Evolution of the Desktop*

WINDOWS 3.1

Windows 3.1 (1991) introduced the graphical user interface as well as a common user interface and consistent command structure for all applications. It also provided multitasking and Object Linking and Embedding.

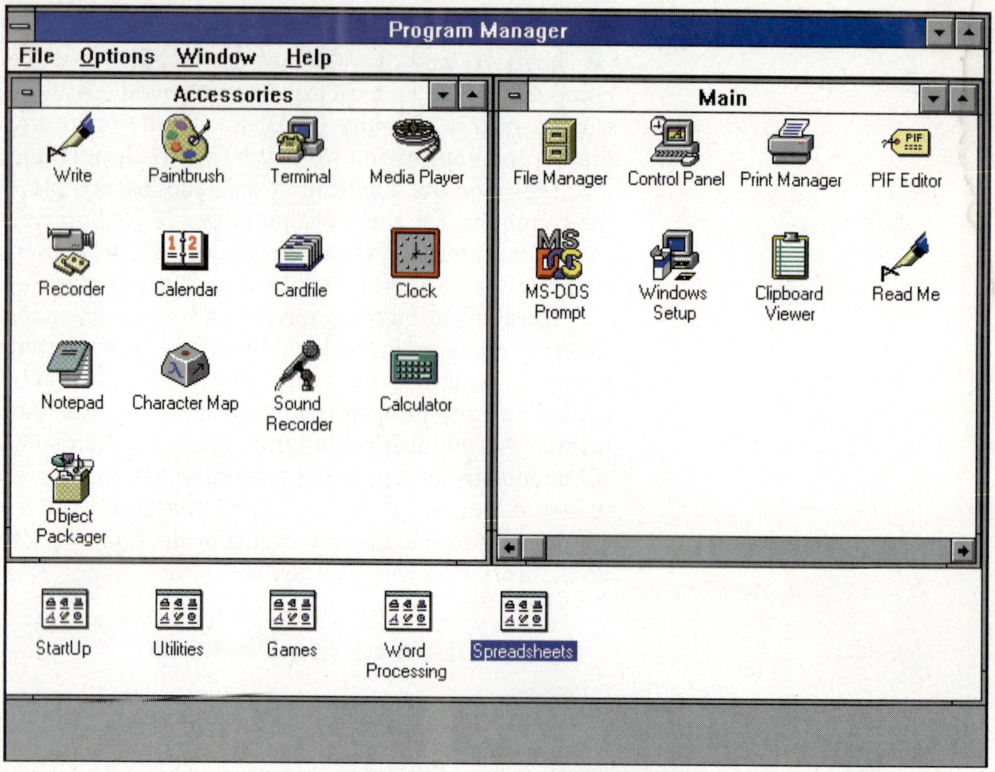

WINDOWS 95

Windows 95 (1995) simplified the desktop by providing a Start button to simplify program execution, as well as a taskbar to facilitate multitasking. File management was made easier through My Computer.

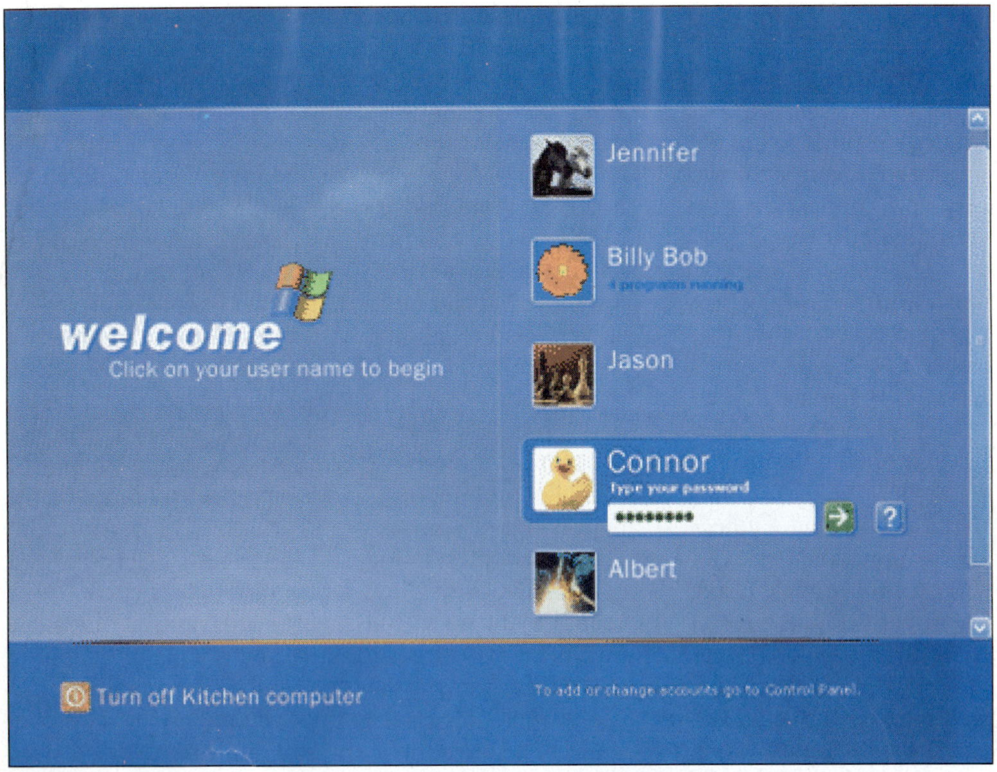

WINDOWS XP

Windows XP is the successor to all current breeds of Windows—Windows 95, 98, Me, NT, and 2000. This desktop is typical of what might appear on a home computer, in which individual accounts are established for everyone who uses the computer.

THE WORKING DESKTOP

The Working Desktop is common to all versions of Windows and shows multiple open windows, each with a different application open. The taskbar is one way to switch from one application to another.

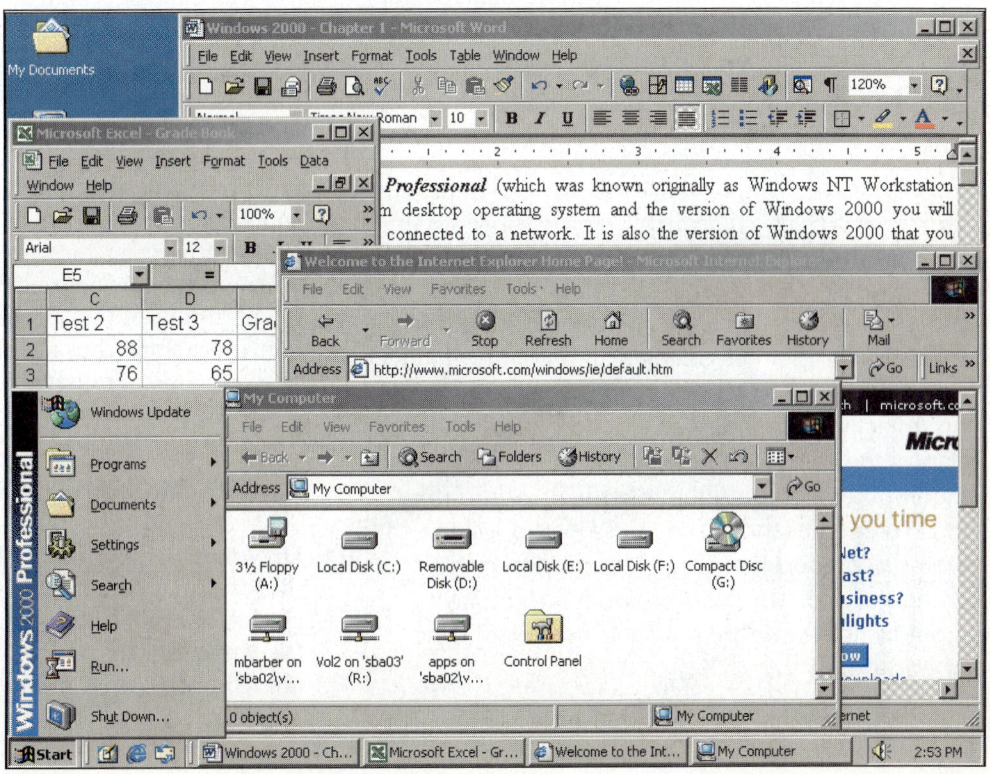

Windows 3.1 was much more than just a pretty facelift because it also introduced three significant innovations. First and foremost is the ***common user interface***, whereby all applications adhere to the same conventions and work basically the same way. This means that once you learn one Windows application, it is that much easier to learn the next because all applications follow a consistent command structure. Think about the significance of this capability. Anyone can sit down at a computer, start an entirely new application with which they are unfamiliar, yet know how to proceed intuitively.

Windows 3.1 also introduced ***multitasking***, which lets you run more than one program at a time. This enables you to go back and forth between tasks, putting down a word processing document, for example, to read an e-mail message. This, too, is tremendously important because you previously had to close one application in order to start another.

The third innovation, ***Object Linking and Embedding*** (abbreviated ***OLE*** and pronounced "olay"), enables you to share data between applications. Using OLE you can create a document with data (objects) from multiple applications—for example, a Word document that contains an Excel spreadsheet and chart.

Windows 95 was announced in 1995 and sought to make the PC even easier to use. The simpler desktop in Windows 95 lets the user click the Start button to begin. Multitasking is implemented by clicking a button on the Windows 95 taskbar (as opposed to having to use the Alt+Tab shortcut in Windows 3.1). File management was made more intuitive through introduction of the My Computer icon on the desktop. Windows 95 also introduced long filenames (up to 255 characters) as opposed to the eight-character filenames that existed under MS-DOS and carried over to Windows 3.1.

Windows 95 was the first of the so-called "modern Windows" and was followed by ***Windows NT***, ***Windows 98***, ***Windows 2000***, and ***Windows Me*** (the Millennium edition). It's difficult to keep track of the different versions and the subtle variations in each, especially since the biggest differences are "behind the scenes." The operating systems are intended for different audiences, however. Windows 98 and Windows Me are geared for the home user and provide extensive support for games and peripheral devices. Windows NT and Windows 2000 are aimed at the business user and provide increased security and reliability. All four operating systems have substantially the same interface as Windows 95 (albeit with minor changes) that is typified by the working desktop in Figure 12d. ***Windows XP*** is the successor to all current breeds of Windows. It is based on the NT/2000 architecture and is significantly more stable than Win95, 98, or Me.

The desktop in Figure 12d has four open windows, each of which displays a program that is currently in use. The ability to run several programs at the same time is known as multitasking, and is a major benefit of the Windows environment. Multitasking enables you to run a word processor in one window, create a spreadsheet in a second window, surf the Internet in a third window, play a game in a fourth window, and so on. You can work in a program as long as you want, then change to a different program by clicking its window.

You can also change from one program to another by using the taskbar at the bottom of the desktop. The taskbar contains a button for each open program, and it enables you to switch back and forth between those programs by clicking the appropriate button. The icons on the desktop are used to access programs or other functions. The My Computer icon is the most basic. It enables you to view the devices on your system, including the drives on a local area network to which you have direct access. The contents of My Computer depend on the hardware of the specific computer system. Our system, for example, has one floppy drive, three local (hard or fixed) disks, a removable disk (an Iomega Zip drive), a CD-ROM, and access to various network drives.

THE FIRST BUG

Software is supposed to be error-free, but all too often it isn't. A mistake in a computer program is known as a bug—hence debugging refers to the process of correcting programming errors. According to legend, the first bug was an unlucky moth that was crushed to death in one of the relays of the electromechanical Mark II computer, bringing the machine's operation to a screeching halt. The cause of the failure was discovered by Grace Hopper, an early computer pioneer, who promptly taped the moth to her logbook, noting "First actual case of bug being found."

Antivirus Software

Do you remember the Melissa or "I Love You" viruses that attacked computers around the world a few years ago? A ***computer virus*** is an actively infectious program that attaches itself to various files and has the ability to alter the way your computer works. Some viruses do nothing more than display an annoying message at an inopportune time. Other viruses are more harmful and corrupt the program and/or data files on a hard disk and in extreme instances can erase every file on a system.

A virus is transmitted in two ways, from an infected floppy disk or via a file that was downloaded from the Internet. Once a system is infected, the typical virus can copy itself onto every floppy disk that is put into your floppy drive, which in turn can infect other computers if the same disk is used elsewhere. In other words, the floppy disk given to you by your well-meaning friend or colleague can transmit the virus to your computer and wreak havoc.

The Internet is even more of a threat because the typical user is online several hours a day. You can download infected files or more commonly receive infected attachments to e-mail messages, which in turn can be sent to other users. You don't even have to write the e-mail yourself, because the most malicious virus will mail itself to everyone in your address book.

Suffice it to say that the threat of a virus is very real. You can, however, protect your system through the installation of an ***antivirus program*** that can automatically detect a virus should it threaten your system. Many such programs are available, but their effectiveness depends on constant updating since new viruses appear all the time. Most vendors maintain a Web site through which the updates are delivered. It takes only a few minutes. Do it!

IS YOUR PROTECTION UP TO DATE?

Try this simple classroom test. Take a show of hands to see how many students have an antivirus program installed on their home computer. Our guess is that the vast majority will respond in the affirmative. Now ask your classmates how many have updated their protection in the last week or two. Our guess is that the number of positive responses will be much less. In other words, most of your classmates are operating under a false sense of security, thinking that their systems are protected, when in fact they are susceptible to the most recent (and often most virulent) computer virus.

Backup

The bulk of your time at the computer will be spent using different applications to create a variety of documents. Take it from us, however, it's not a question of *if* it will happen, but *when*—hard disks die and files are lost, and further, it always seems to happen the day before a major assignment or project is due. We urge you, therefore, to prepare for the inevitable by creating adequate ***backup*** (duplicate copies of important files) before the problem occurs. The essence of a backup strategy is to decide which files to back up, how often to do the backup, and where to keep the backup. Once you decide on a strategy, follow it, and follow it faithfully.

Our strategy is very simple—back up what you can't afford to lose, do so on a daily basis, and store the backup away from your computer. You need not copy every file, every day. Instead copy just the files that changed during the current session. Realize, too, that it is much more important to back up your data files than your program files. You can always reinstall the application from the original CD or floppy disks, or if necessary, go to the vendor for another copy of an application. You, however, are the only one who has a copy of the term paper that is due tomorrow. Do your friends and acquaintances a favor and encourage them to implement a regular backup routine. You will be surprised at how many individuals are lax in this regard.

Application Software

The ultimate goal of computer literacy is the ability to do useful work, which is accomplished through application software. In this section we discuss the major applications of the PC and introduce you to ***Microsoft Office***, the dominant application suite in today's environment.

Word processing was the first major business application of microcomputers. A novelty in the 1970s, it is accepted as commonplace in the 1990s. With a word processor you enter a document into the computer using the keyboard, then save the document on disk. You can return to the document at a later time to insert new text and/or delete superfluous material. A powerful set of editing commands lets you move words, sentences, or even paragraphs from one place to another, and/or alter the appearance of your document by changing margins or line spacing. Additional features check spelling and grammar, provide access to a thesaurus, and prepare form letters. And like all other Windows applications, the WYSIWYG nature of today's word processing software enables you to create the document in a variety of typefaces, sizes, and styles, and/or combine a document with graphical images such as clip art or photographs.

Spreadsheets are the application most widely used by business managers. A spreadsheet is the electronic equivalent of an accountant's ledger. Anything that lends itself to expression in row-and-column format is a potential spreadsheet (for example, a professor's grade book or a financial forecast). The advantages of the spreadsheet are that changes are far easier to make than with pad and pencil, and further, that the necessary recalculations are made instantly, accurately, and automatically.

Data management software allows you to maintain records electronically, be they student records in a university, customer records in a business, or inventory records in a warehouse. Data management software provides for the addition of new records as well as the modification or deletion of existing data. You can retrieve your data in any order that you like, for example alphabetically or by identification number. You can display all the information or only a selected portion. For example, you could see only those students who are on the dean's list, only those customers with delinquent accounts, or only those inventory items that need reordering.

Presentation software helps you to communicate your ideas to others in an effective way. It lets you focus on the content of your presentation without concern for its appearance. Then, when you have decided what you want to say, the software takes care of the formatting and creates an attractive presentation based on one of many professionally designed templates. The color scheme and graphic design are applied automatically. You have the option of delivering the presentation in a variety of formats, such as on a computer screen or transparencies displayed on an overhead projector. You can also distribute an outline or handouts of the presentation.

The emergence of the Internet and World Wide Web has created an entirely new type of application known as a ***browser*** that enables you to display pages from the Web on a PC. Internet Explorer and Netscape Navigator are the two dominant browsers in today's environment.

GARBAGE IN, GARBAGE OUT (GIGO)

A computer does exactly what you tell it to do, which is not necessarily what you want it to do. It is critical, therefore, that you validate the data that goes into a system or else the associated information will not be correct. No system, no matter how sophisticated, can produce valid output from invalid input. The financial projections in a spreadsheet, for example, will produce erroneous results if they are based on invalid assumptions. In other words, garbage in—garbage out.

Microsoft Office

Microsoft Office XP was released in 2001 and, like its predecessors, it contains four major applications—***Microsoft Word***, ***Excel***, ***Access***, and ***PowerPoint***. (Other versions of the Office suite contain different sets of applications, which can lead to unpleasant surprises. Not every version contains PowerPoint or Access, whereas other versions contain additional applications such as FrontPage and PhotoDraw.) This section describes the similarities between the various applications in Office XP, where you will find the same commands in the same menus, you will see the same toolbar buttons from one application to the next, and you will be able to take advantage of the same keyboard shortcuts.

Figure 13 displays a screen from each application in the Microsoft Office—Word, Excel, PowerPoint, and Access, in Figures 13a, 13b, 13c, and 13d, respectively. Look closely at Figure 13, and realize that each screen contains both an application window and a document window, and that each document window has been maximized within the application window. The title bars of the application and document windows have been merged into a single title bar that appears at the top of the application window. The title bar displays the application (e.g., Microsoft Word in Figure 13a) as well as the name of the document (Web Enabled) on which you are working.

All four screens in Figure 13 are similar in appearance even though the applications accomplish very different tasks. Each application window has an identifying icon, a menu bar, a title bar, and a minimize, a maximize or restore, and a close button. Each document window has its own identifying icon and its own close button. The Windows taskbar appears at the bottom of each application window and shows the open applications. The status bar appears above the taskbar and displays information relevant to the window or selected object.

The applications in Microsoft Office have a consistent command structure in which the same basic menus (the File, Edit, View, Insert, Tools, Window, and Help menus) are present in each application. In addition, the same commands are found in the same menus. The Save, Open, Print, and Exit commands, for example, are contained in the File menu. The Cut, Copy, Paste, and Undo commands are found in the Edit menu.

The means for accessing the pull-down menus are consistent from one application to the next. Click the menu name on the menu bar, or press the Alt key plus the underlined letter of the menu name; for example, press Alt+F to pull down the File menu. If you already know some keyboard shortcuts in one application, there is a good chance that the shortcuts will work in another application. Ctrl+Home and Ctrl+End, for example, move to the beginning and end of a document, respectively.

All four applications use consistent (and often identical) dialog boxes. The dialog boxes to open and close a file, for example, are identical in every application. All four applications also share a common dictionary that is accessed whenever a spell check is executed.

There are, of course, differences between the applications. Each application has its own unique menus and associated toolbars. Nevertheless, the Standard and Formatting toolbars in all applications contain many of the same tools (especially the first several tools on the left of each toolbar). The ***Standard toolbar*** contains buttons for basic commands such as open, save, or print. It also contains buttons to cut, copy, and paste, and all of these buttons are identical in all four applications. The ***Formatting toolbar*** provides access to common formatting operations such as boldface, italics, or underlining, or changing the font or point size, and again, these buttons are identical in all four applications. ScreenTips that identify the purpose of a tool are present in all applications. Suffice it to say, therefore, that once you know one Office application, you have a tremendous head start in learning another.

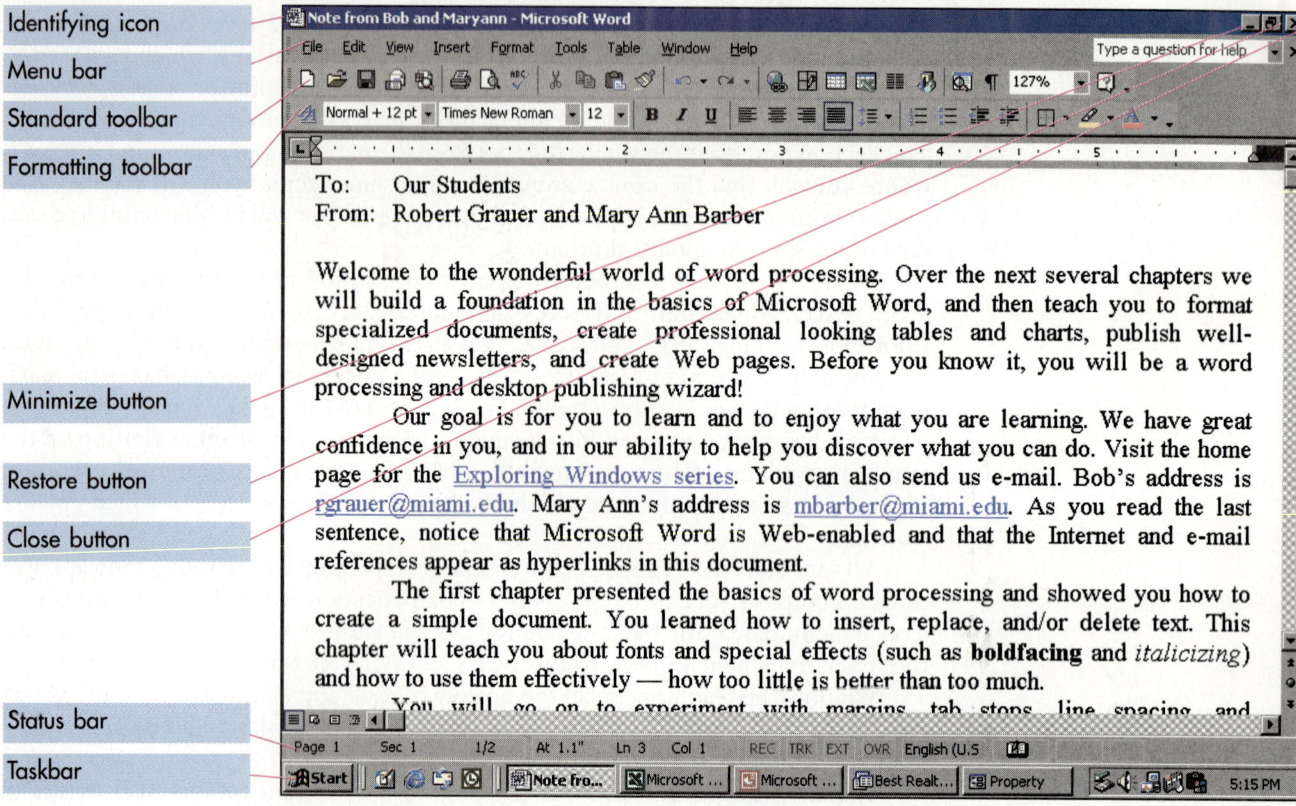

(a) Microsoft Word

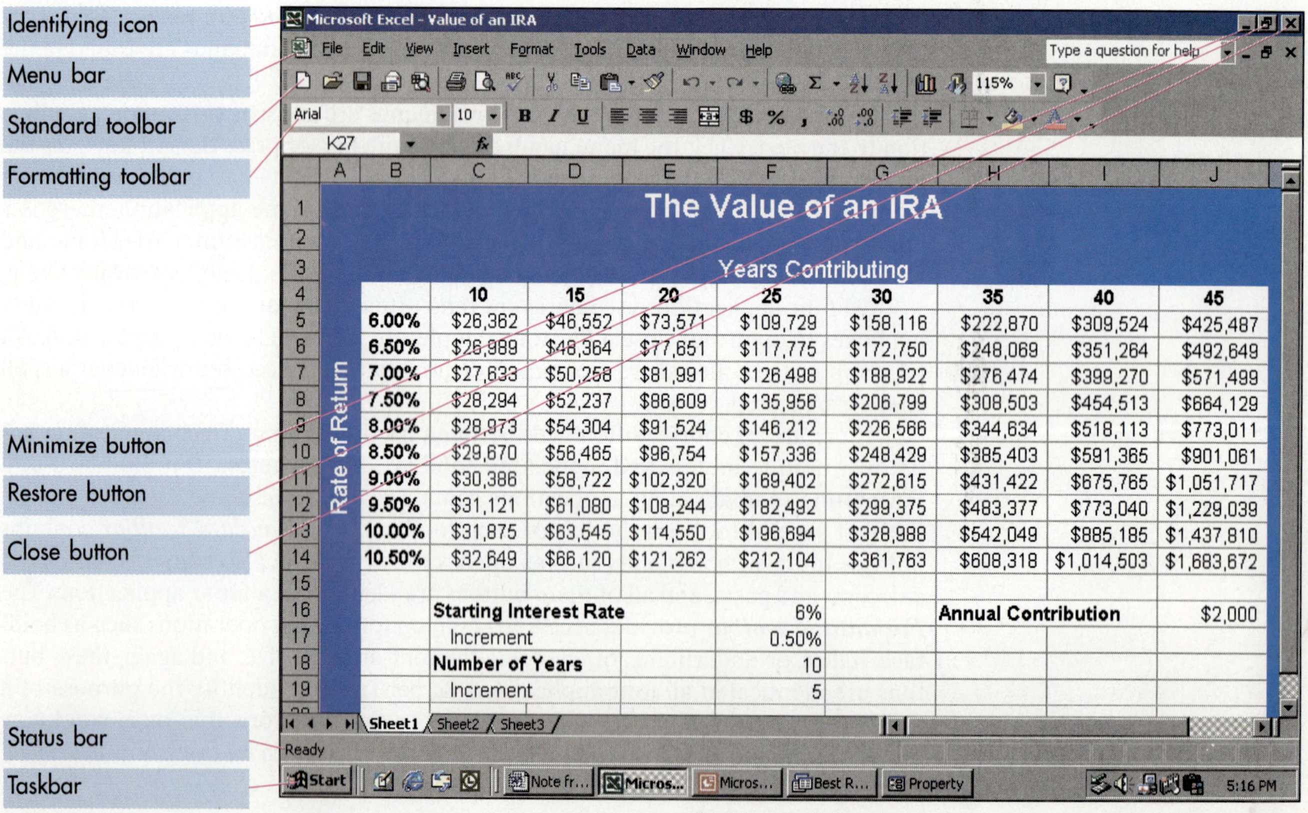

(b) Microsoft Excel

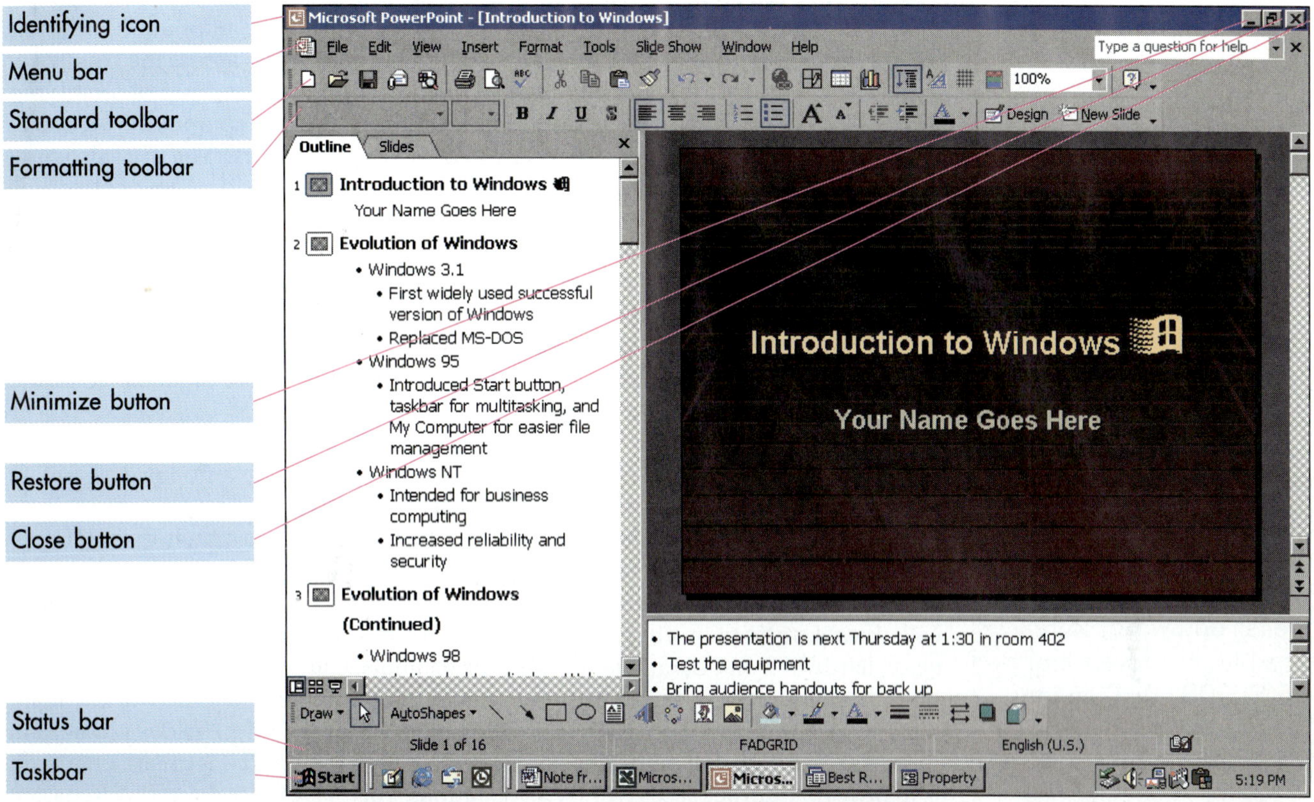

(c) Microsoft PowerPoint

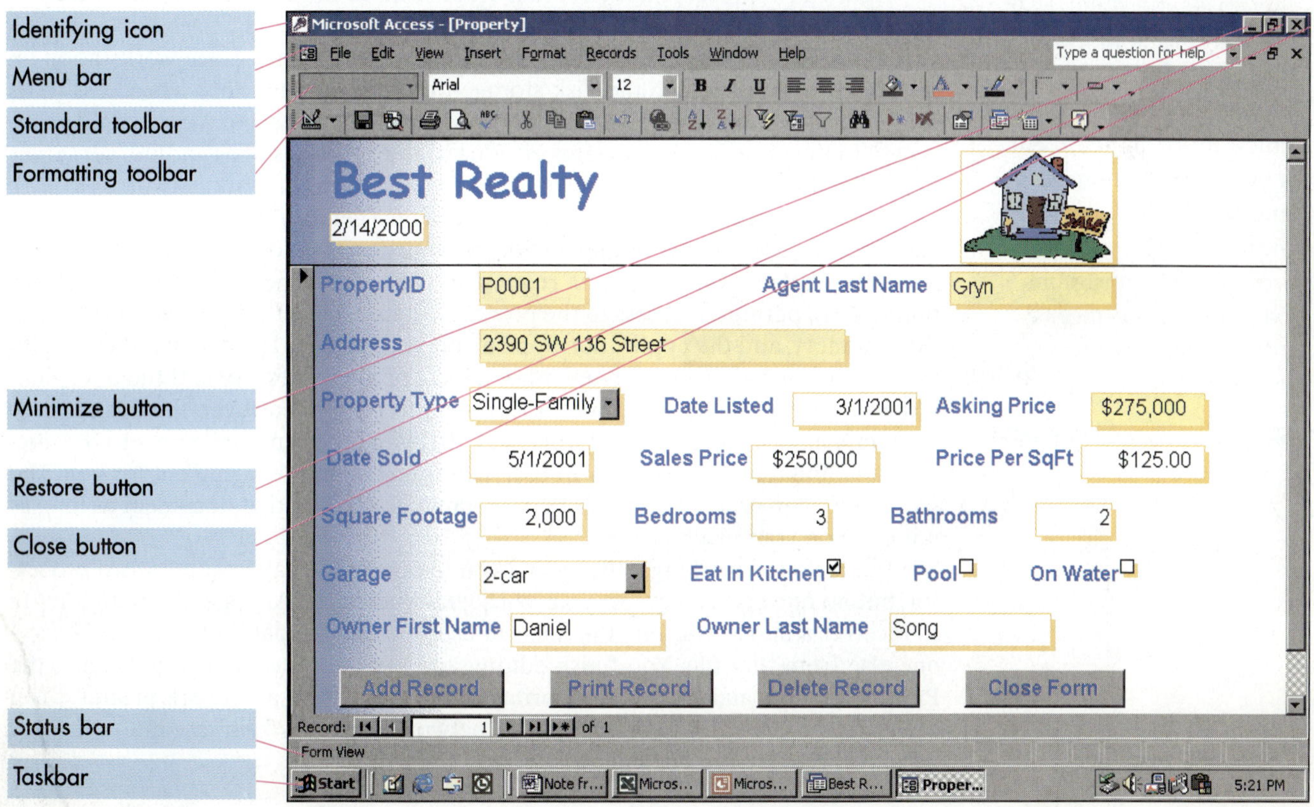

(d) Microsoft Access

A ***network*** is a combination of hardware and software that enables the connected computers to share resources and communicate with one another. It may be a ***wide area network*** or WAN that encompasses computers across the country or around the world, or it may be limited to the computers on one floor of a building. The latter is known as a ***local area network*** or ***LAN***. The computer you use at school or work is most likely connected to a local area network. You may also have multiple computers at home, which can also be connected in a local area network to share resources.

Local area networks are common today, but that was not always true. Without a LAN, you often created a file on one computer, then carried the disk to another machine in order to use the laser printer. Or you might have had to run down the hall to borrow a disk that contained a specific file in order to load the file on your computer. Or you might have left a message for a friend or colleague in his or her in-box, only to have it get lost under a pile of paper.

All of these situations are examples of network applications, implemented informally in a "sneaker net," whereby you transferred a file to a floppy disk, put on your sneakers, and ran down the hall to deliver the disk to someone else. A local area network automates the process, and while sneaker net may not sound very impressive, it does illustrate the concept rather effectively.

The idea behind a LAN is very simple—to enable the connected computers, called ***workstations*** or ***nodes***, to share network resources such as application software, hardware, and data. One printer, for example, can support multiple workstations, because not everyone needs to print at the same time. The network is managed by a more powerful computer called a ***file server*** that provides a common place to store data and programs. Another major function of the local area network is to provide Internet access for its workstations. This is typically done via a separate network computer known as an ***Internet server***.

Figure 14 represents a conceptual view of three different LANs that are connected to one another, which is typical on a university campus. Each network consists of multiple workstations, a file server, and a laser printer. Each workstation on the network has access to the disk storage on the server and thus has access to its programs and/or data. Different types of workstations (PCs and Macs) can be connected to the same local area network. One of the LANs also has an Internet server to provide Internet access to the connected workstations on both networks.

Application programs are typically stored on a server rather than on individual machines. To use a network application on your workstation, you click the icon to load the program, which issues a request to the server. The server in turn verifies that you are permitted access to the program, then it loads the application into your PC's memory, and the application appears on your screen. The document used with the application may be stored on either a local or a network drive. If the document is stored locally, the network does not come into play. If, however, the document is kept on the network, the server will check that you are permitted access to the document and that it is not already in use, then it will open the document for you. The server will then prevent other users from gaining access to that document as long as it is open on your machine.

While you're working, other people on the network may load the word processor, but no one else can access your particular document. Anyone attempting to do so receives a message saying the file is in use, because the network locks out everyone else from that file. You finish editing and save the file. Then you execute the Print command, and the network prints the document on a network printer. (You can also place the document on a shared network drive, in which case multiple users will gain access to the document.)

PROTECT YOUR PASSWORD

Almost all computer break-ins occur because of a poorly chosen password. A four-letter password, for example, has fewer than 500,000 combinations, and can be broken by a hacker in only 30 seconds of computer time. Opting for eight letters increases the number of combinations to more than 200 billion, which makes the intruder's job much more difficult. And if you include numbers in addition to letters, an eight-character password (letters and numbers) has more than 2 trillion combinations. Protect your password!

FIGURE 14 *A Local Area Network*

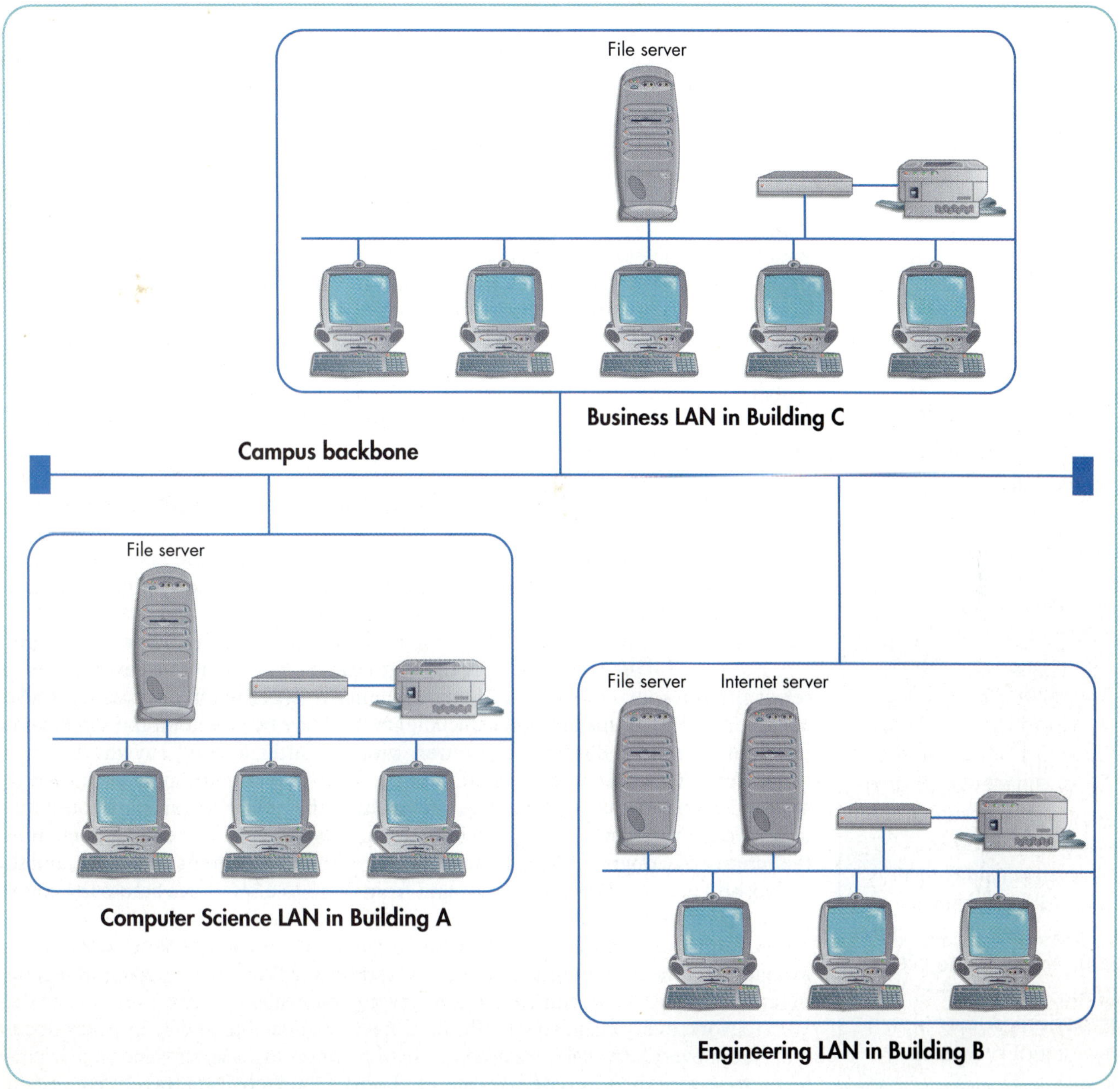

THE HOME NETWORK

The rationale for a home network is identical to that for any other LAN, namely the ability to share files, hardware devices, and/or an Internet connection. Each computer requires a network card, but the required software is built into Windows 98 and its successors. The computers can be connected to one another directly through wiring or linked together through an ordinary telephone line. According to one survey, more than 20 million American homes have more than one computer, making the home network much more common than you might imagine.

The ***Internet*** is a network of networks that spans the globe. It grew out of a government project that began in 1969 to test the feasibility of a network where scientists and military personnel could share messages and data no matter where they were. The original network consisted of only four computers. Today, there are literally millions of computers with an Internet connection (the exact number is impossible to determine) and tens of millions of people with Internet access.

Yes, the Internet is a collection of networks, but if that were all it was, there would hardly be so much commotion. It's what you can do on the Internet, coupled with the ease of access that makes the Internet so exciting. In essence, the Internet provides two basic capabilities, information retrieval and worldwide communication, functions that are already provided by libraries and print media, the postal system and the telephone, television, and other types of long-distance media. The difference is that the Internet is interactive in nature, and more importantly, it is both global and immediate. The Internet enables you to request a document from virtually anywhere in the world, and to begin to receive that document almost instantly. No other medium lets you do that.

The potential of the Internet was exciting from its inception, but you had to use a variety of esoteric programs (such as Archie and Gopher) to locate and download data. The programs were based on the Unix operating system, and you had to know the precise syntax of the commands within each program. There was no common user interface to speed learning. And, even if you were able to find what you wanted, everything was communicated in plain text, as graphics and sound were not available. All of this changed in 1991 with the introduction of the World Wide Web.

The ***World Wide Web*** (or simply the Web) can be thought of as a very large subset of the Internet, consisting of hypertext and/or hypermedia documents. These documents contain links to other documents that may be stored on the same computer, or even on a different computer, with the latter located anywhere in the world. And therein lies the fascination of the Web, in that you simply click on link after link to go effortlessly from one document to the next. You can start your journey at your professor's home page in New York, which may link to a document in the Library of Congress, which in turn may take you to a different document, and so on. So, off you go to Washington DC and from there to a reference across the country or perhaps around the world.

Any computer that stores hypertext documents and makes those documents available to other computers, is known as a ***server*** (or Web server), whereas a computer that requests a document from a server is known as a ***client***. In order for the Web to work, every client (be it a PC or a Mac) must be able to display every document from every server. This is accomplished by imposing a set of standards or protocols to govern the way data is transmitted across the Web. Data travels from client to server and back, through a protocol known as the ***HyperText Transfer Protocol*** (or http for short).

In addition, in order to access the documents that are transmitted through this protocol, you need a special type of program known as a ***browser.*** Indeed, a browser is aptly named because it enables you inspect the Web in a leisurely and casual way (the dictionary definition of the word "browse"). ***Internet Explorer*** is the browser provided by Microsoft. ***Netscape Navigator*** is a competing product. Microsoft and Netscape are constantly trying to outdo one another, but both programs are incredibly good. Figures 15a and 15b display the Exploring Windows home page (www.prenhall.com/grauer) in Netscape Navigator and Internet Explorer, respectively. The toolbars and menu bars are different, but both programs have similar capabilities and share the common user interface common to all Windows applications. Either program will suffice. Your main concern is gaining access to the Internet.

IT'S THE URL, NOT THE BROWSER

Microsoft and Netscape argue vehemently about which is the superior browser. In actuality, however, both products are so feature-rich that it doesn't really matter which one you choose. To see for yourself, try viewing the same Web page in both browsers. What difference (if any) do you see when a page is viewed in Netscape rather than Internet Explorer? Do you agree with our statement that it is the URL (Web address) that is important, rather than the actual browser?

FIGURE 15 *Internet Browsers*

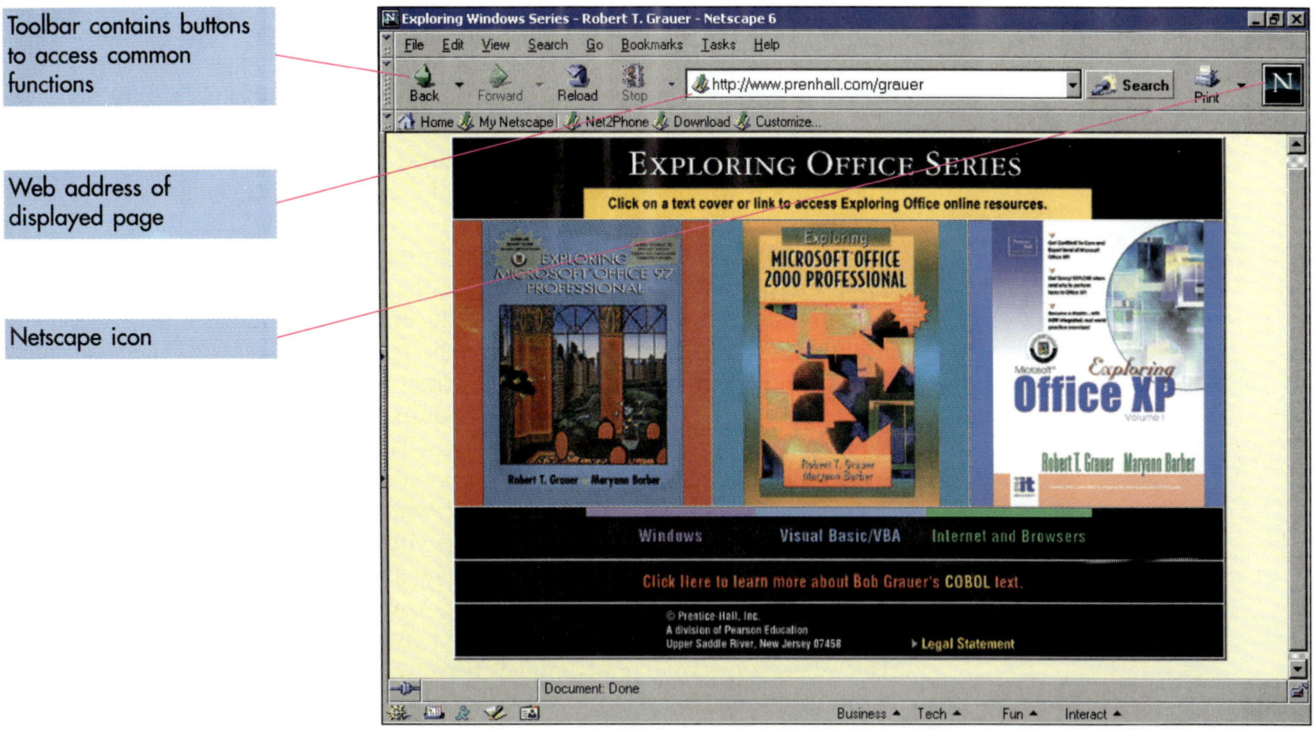

(a) Netscape Navigator

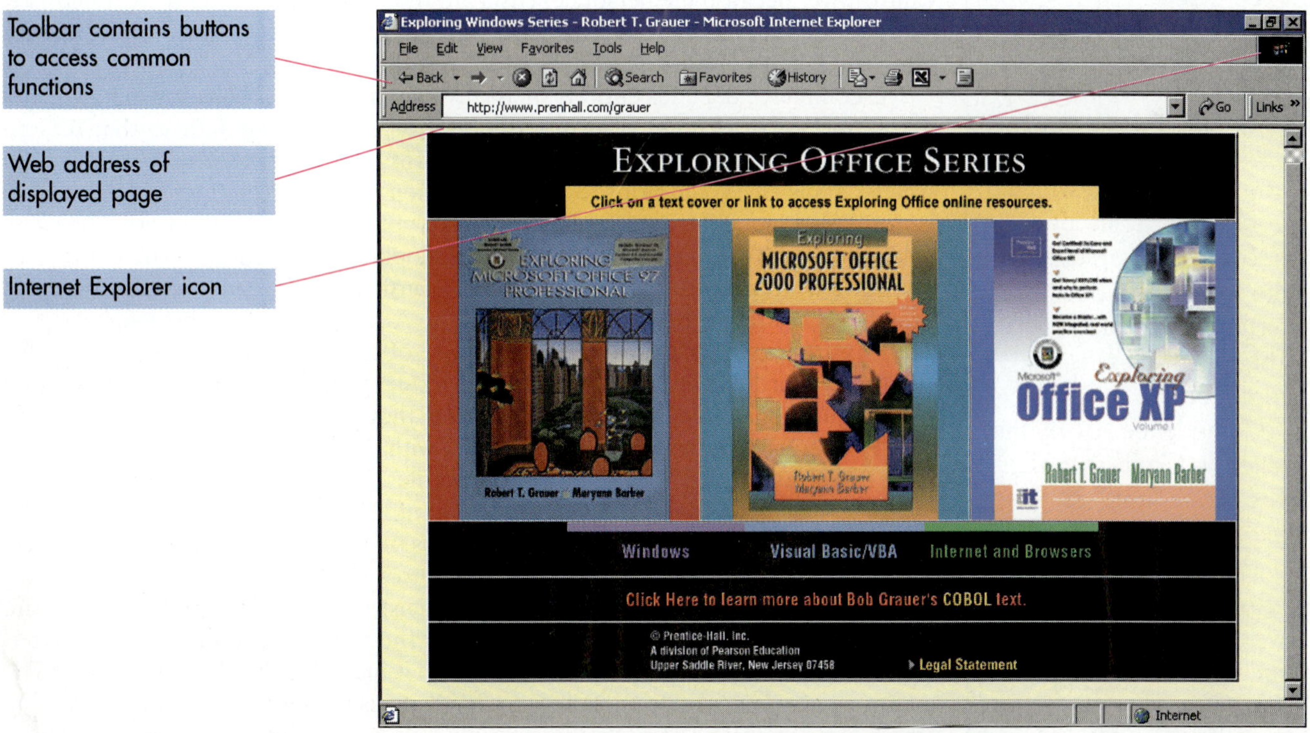

(b) Internet Explorer

The Commercialization of Cyberspace

It's difficult to think of the Internet as existing without any type of commercial enterprise. The Internet began, however, as a project of the United States government with a strict prohibition against commercial activity. It was not until 1991, some twenty years after its inception, that the National Science Foundation lifted the prohibition on commercial use. The subsequent growth has been both unprecedented and exponential, as companies of every size, from multinational corporations to "mom and pop" shops, conduct business on the Web.

The best way to appreciate the impact of ***e-commerce*** is to step back and think of commerce in the traditional sense, which is nothing more than the exchange of goods and services. The same elements are present, regardless of whether you go to a mall or shop on the Web. Commerce of either type involves buyers and sellers, products and services, and suppliers or producers of the products and services. The buyer and seller need a place to meet for the transaction to take place. The seller employs various marketing strategies to attract the buyer to the place of business where it can accept an order, deliver the goods or services, and then accept payment.

What then is so special about e-commerce? The answer is that it enables both the buyer and seller to do things that are not possible with the traditional model. The buyer can shop 24 hours a day, 7 days a week, without ever leaving home. There is no need to walk up and down the aisles, because you can search the entire product line with the click of a mouse. You can shop as long as you like, even taking several days to build an order in a virtual shopping cart. You can also assure yourself the best price because it is so easy to obtain prices of a given item from multiple vendors.

The seller enjoys similar advantages because it is much less expensive to implement and maintain a Web site than it is to build a store with "bricks and mortar." The customers can come from all over the world as opposed to having to live in the neighborhood. The seller can stock more items because there is no need to physically display products or even to print a catalog. The cost per transaction is significantly lower because the personnel costs are reduced. There need not be a salesperson although many Web sites do provide telephone support. And, best of all, the business remains open around the clock.

> **A SIMPLE ENCRYPTION ALGORITHM**
>
> Julius Caesar is given credit for developing one of the oldest encryption schemes. Caesar used a simple substitution algorithm in which each letter in the original text was replaced by the letter three positions further in the alphabet. The letter "a" was replaced by the letter "d," the letter "b" by the letter "e," and so on. The word "cat," for example, would be encrypted as "fdw." It was simple, but it worked as long as the recipient knew the key—the number of letters to jump in the alphabet.

E-commerce depends entirely on the availability of secure transactions, which is accomplished through ***encryption***, the process of encoding data so that it is no longer in its original form when it is sent across the Internet. The precise way in which data is encrypted prior to being sent, then decrypted on the receiving end, is beyond the scope of our description. Encryption is built into both Netscape Navigator and Internet Explorer, and it takes place automatically when you communicate with a secure site. You can tell a transmission is secure when a different protocol, https rather than http, appears in the Address bar of the browser.

Privacy is another issue. The convenience of returning to a site and having the site know your likes and dislikes in order to steer you to the goods or information you are most likely to request, is offset by the thought that the site knows all about you. How much it knows, and what it will do with that information is a growing concern. It is all a function of ***cookies***—the small files that are written to your hard drive each time you visit a site. There is nothing harmful about a cookie per se. It is not a virus and it will not erase or alter the programs on your computer. It is simply a text file that contains information about your visit to a site.

Cookies enable a vendor to personalize a customer's interaction with a Web site by sending only selected information about the types of products a customer is likely to buy. It's good for the vendor because it increases the chance of a sale. The consumer also likes the concept because he or she is not inundated with information that is of no interest. The process is possible only because the site knows your shopping habits, which it learned by recording the types of links you selected and the purchases you made. Is that good, or is it an invasion of privacy? Opinion is divided, to say the least.

IMPLEMENT A FIREWALL

A cable modem or DSL line provides a continuous high speed connection to the Internet. That is the good news. The bad news is that your PC is vulnerable to potential hackers because of the unbroken connection. Hence, you may want to implement a firewall to protect your system from unwanted intrusion. A firewall is a program that blocks and intercepts access to your system from the outside. It is easy to install and available from many vendors, typically the same vendors who supply antivirus software.

Connecting to the Internet

Your connection to the Internet begins with the selection of an ***Internet Service Provider (ISP)***, a company or organization that maintains a computer with permanent access to the Internet. You may already have free Internet access through your school or university, but if not, you will have to sign up with a commercial vendor. America Online (AOL) is perhaps the best known because of its proprietary interface, but there are many other choices.

The next decision is the means of access, whether it is a modem, a cable modem, or a DSL modem from your telephone company. A ***modem*** is the interface between a computer and the telephone. It converts the digital signal from your computer to an analog signal that traverses the phone system, then back again to a digital signal on the other end, as shown conceptually in Figure 16. In essence you instruct the modem to dial the phone number of your ISP, which in turn lets you access the Internet. You should purchase the fastest modem available, which is 56Kbps (Kilobits per second). This speed is adequate to transmit text and limited graphics, but it pales when compared to the new technologies.

A ***cable modem*** attaches a PC to a local TV cable and receives data at about 1.5 Mbps. This is approximately 30 times faster than an ordinary modem, but the service is also more expensive. Whether or not it is worth the extra money depends on your budget and the amount of time you spend online. A cable modem requires a network card in your computer.

DSL (Digital Subscriber Line) is a new technology that lets you transmit voice and digital data simultaneously over a telephone line. In other words, you can be speaking on the phone at the same time you are connected to the Internet. (This is in contrast to an ordinary modem that ties up your phone line.) DSL has a theoretical transmission rate of up to 8.4Mbps, but the typical connection is at 1.5Mbps, which competes directly with a cable modem.

FIGURE 16 *How a Modem Works*

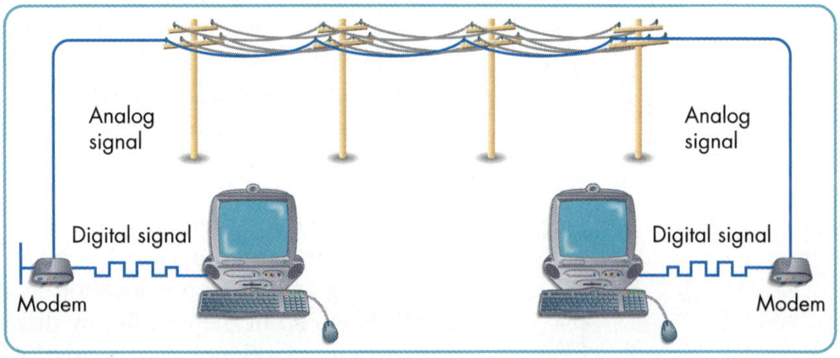

WHEN YOU USE A MODEM

1. The communication software in your computer sends a command to your modem to dial the phone number of the remote computer. The modem dials the number.
2. The remote computer answers the phone and returns a whistling sound. Your modem answers with a sound of its own.
3. The modems exchange information, a process called handshaking, to enable the communication to take place.
4. The sending computer transmits the data to its modem, which converts the data to a sound wave and sends it over the phone line.
5. The receiving modem converts the sound wave to a digital signal for the receiving computer which processes the data and sends a reply.
6. Communications continue back and forth until eventually one of the computers instructs its modem to end the session.

File Compression

The ability to download a file from the Internet is a very significant capability. It enables a vendor to post the latest version of its software on its Web site and to make that material available to its clients or end-users. The cost saving is significant, as the vendor does not have to manufacture disks, CDs, or printed documentation, and further saves on postage and handling costs. The end-user benefits as well, inasmuch as he or she gains immediate access to the file, often at no cost.

Files are often compressed (made smaller) to reduce the file size, when sending a file from one location to another, such as when you are downloading software from the Internet to your PC. The amount of time it takes to download a file is proportional to its size, so that compressing a file reduces the time for downloading. A second advantage is that multiple files can be placed inside a single ***compressed file*** (also called an ***archive***), enabling you to send or receive one file, after which the individual files can be extracted. That is a lot easier than having to download each of the files individually. All of this is accomplished by a ***file compression program*** that reduces the size of the file without losing any of the data in the file.

Compression algorithms are very sophisticated, and the details of how they work are beyond this discussion. What is important is the concept of file compression, the advantage of creating a ***self-extracting file*** as opposed to a simple archive, and the associated software requirements. Figure 17a illustrates a two-stage compression process (the second step is optional). Step 1 uses a file compression program to place three individual files (that total 500Kb in size) into a single compressed file of 100Kb. Step 2 takes the compressed file (archive) that was just created and runs it through the compression program a second time to create a self-extracting file of 125Kb. The latter is slightly larger than the original compressed file, but it is still significantly smaller than the combined size of the individual files.

Figures 17b and 17c illustrate two different ways in which the individual files within the compressed file are extracted. Figure 17b extracts the individual files from the archive, but requires the file compression utility to do so. In other words, if a user is given just the archive, he or she also needs the compression utility to expand it. This is a potential problem because the compression program is *not* built into Windows and requires a separate purchase. Figure 17c, however, shows that the files can be extracted automatically without the need for the compression program if the user was given a self-extracting file.

You can appreciate why you would want to download a self-extracting file but may be wondering when the typical end-user would need to compress a file on his or her PC. As indicated earlier, the need for compression is greatest when you are transferring a file from one location to another—for example, if you wanted to copy a 2Mb PowerPoint file to a floppy disk in order to take the presentation with you. The capacity of a floppy disk is only 1.44Mb, so the only way to transfer the file to a floppy disk is to compress the file. You might also want to compress the file before e-mailing to a colleague, especially if you are connecting to the Internet by modem, because the smaller the file, the less time it takes to send and receive.

DISABLE CALL WAITING

Your friend may understand if you excuse yourself in the middle of a conversation to answer another incoming call. A computer, however, is not so tolerant and will often break the current connection if another call comes in. Accordingly, check the settings of your communications program to disable call waiting prior to connecting to the Internet (typically by entering *70 in front of the access number). Your friends may complain of a busy signal, but you will work without interruption.

FIGURE 17 *File Compression*

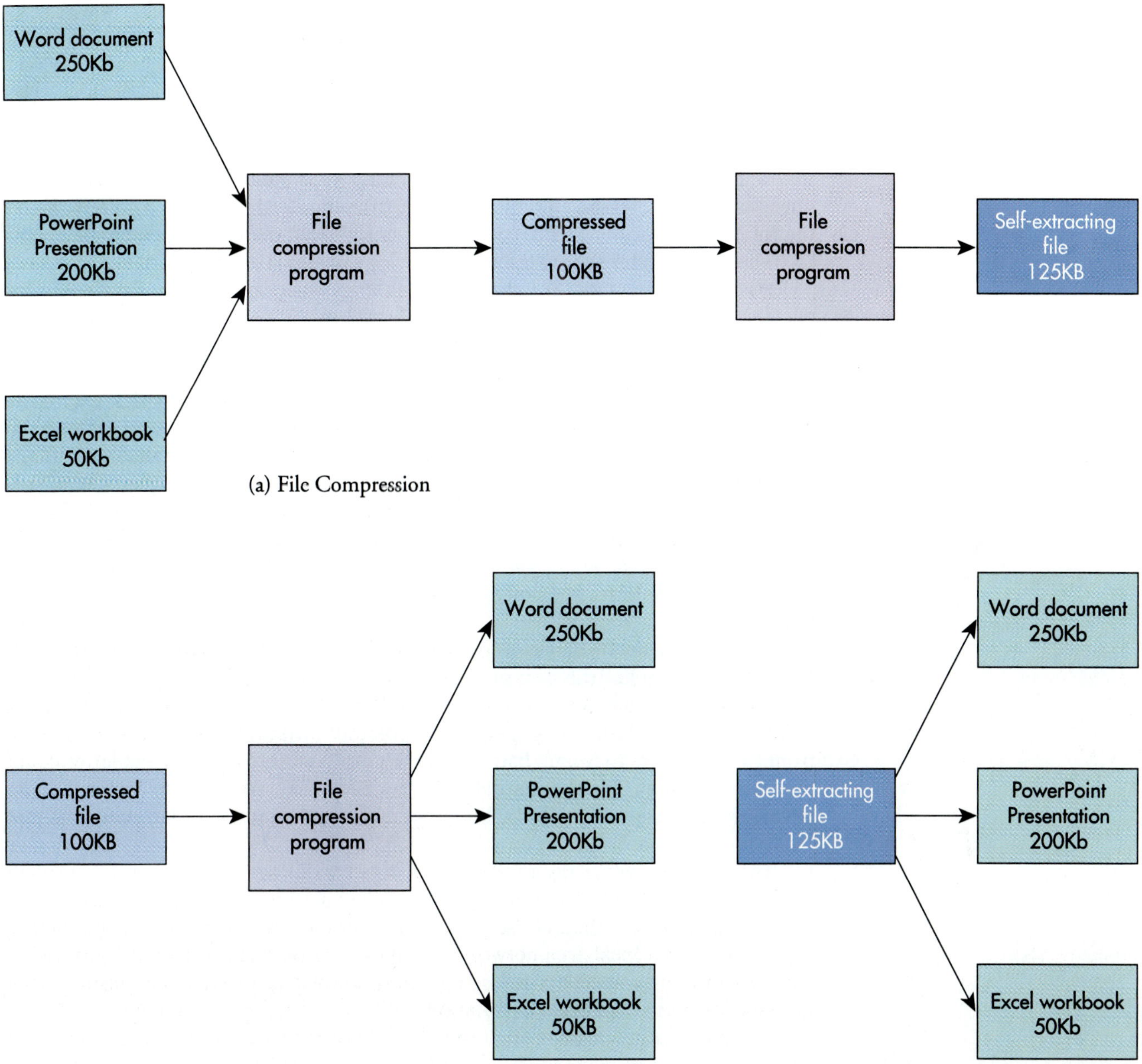

(a) File Compression

(b) Uncompressing a File

(c) Self-Extracting File

ZIP FILES, ZIP DISKS, ZIP DRIVES, AND THE WINZIP COMPRESSION PROGRAM

The WinZip file compression program is the industry leader, and hence a compressed file is often called a "zip" file regardless of the program that was used to create it. Zip® disk and Zip® drive are trademarks of the Iomega Corporation and refer to the removable mass storage medium and associated device (analogous to a floppy disk and floppy drive). The terms Zip disk and Zip drive have nothing to do with file compression.

TCP/IP—How the Internet Works

The Internet works and we take it for granted. Spend a few minutes, however, to learn how it works. Our explanation is not overly technical, and it will give you a better appreciation for the incredible technology at your fingertips.

Data is transmitted across the Internet through a series of protocols known collectively as ***TCP/IP*** (Transmission Control Protocol/Internet Protocol). A ***protocol*** is an agreed-upon set of conventions that define the rules of communication. You follow a protocol in class; for example, you raise your hand and wait to be acknowledged by your professor. In similar fashion, the sending and receiving computers on the Internet follow the TCP/IP protocol to ensure that data is transmitted correctly.

The postal system provides a good analogy of how (but certainly not how fast) TCP/IP is implemented. (The post office analogy was suggested by Ed Krol in his excellent book, *The Whole Internet*, published by O'Reilly and Associates, Inc., Sebastopol, CA, 1992.) When you mail a regular letter, you drop it into a mailbox, where it is picked up along with a lot of other letters and delivered to the local post office. The letters are sorted and sent on their way to a larger post office, where the letters are sorted again, until eventually each letter reaches the post office closest to its destination, where it is delivered to the addressee by the local mail carrier. If, for example, you sent a letter from Coral Springs, Florida, to Upper Saddle River, New Jersey, the letter would not travel directly from Coral Springs to Upper Saddle River. Instead, the Postal Service would forward the letter from one substation to the next, making a new decision at each substation as to the best (most efficient) route—for example, from Coral Springs, to Miami, to Newark, and finally, to Upper Saddle River.

Each postal substation considers all of the routes it has available to the next substation and makes the best possible decision according to the prevailing conditions. This means that the next time you mail a letter from Coral Springs to Upper Saddle River, the letter may travel a completely different path. If the mail truck from Coral Springs to Miami had already left or was full to capacity, the letter could be routed through Fort Lauderdale to New York City, and then to Upper Saddle River. The actual route taken by the letter is not important. All that matters is that the letter arrives at its destination.

The Internet works the same way, as data travels across the Internet through several levels of networks until it gets to its destination. E-mail messages arrive at the local post office (the mail server) from a remote PC connected by modem, or from a node on a local area network. The messages then leave the local post office and pass through a special-purpose computer known as a router that ensures each message is sent to its correct destination.

A message may pass through several networks to get to its destination. Each network has its own router that determines how best to move the message closer to its destination, taking into account the traffic on the network. A message passes from one network to the next, until it arrives at the destination network, from where it can be sent to the recipient, who has a mailbox on that network. The process is depicted graphically in Figure 18.

In actuality, the TCP/IP protocol is slightly more complicated than what we have been portraying, and it applies to all types of data, not just e-mail. To continue with the post office analogy, let's assume that you are sending a book, rather than a letter, and that the post office (for whatever reason) does not accept large packages. One alternative would be to rip the pages out of the book, mail each page individually by placing it into its own envelope, then trust that all of the envelopes arrive at the destination, and finally, that the person on the other end would be able to reassemble the individual pages. That may sound awkward, but it is a truer picture of how the Internet works.

Data (whether it is an e-mail message or a Web page) is sent across the Internet in ***packets***, with each packet limited in size. The rules for creating, addressing, and sending the packets are specified by TCP/IP, which is actually two separate protocols. The TCP portion divides the file that you want to send into packets, then numbers each packet so that the message can be reconstructed at the other end. The IP portion sends each packet on its way by specifying the addresses of the sending and receiving computers so that the routers will be able to do their job.

The TCP/IP protocol may seem unnecessarily complicated, but it is actually very clever. Dividing large files into smaller pieces ensures that no single file monopolizes the network. A second advantage has to do with ensuring that the data arrives correctly. Static or noise on a telephone line is merely annoying to people having a conversation, but devastating when a file (especially a computer program) is transmitted and a byte or two is lost or corrupted. The larger the file being sent, the greater the chance that noise will be introduced and that the file will be corrupted. Sending the data in smaller pieces (packets), and verifying that the packets were received correctly, helps ensure the integrity of the data. If one packet is received incorrectly, the entire file does not have to be sent again, only the corrupted pocket.

FIGURE 18 *A Message Travels the Internet*

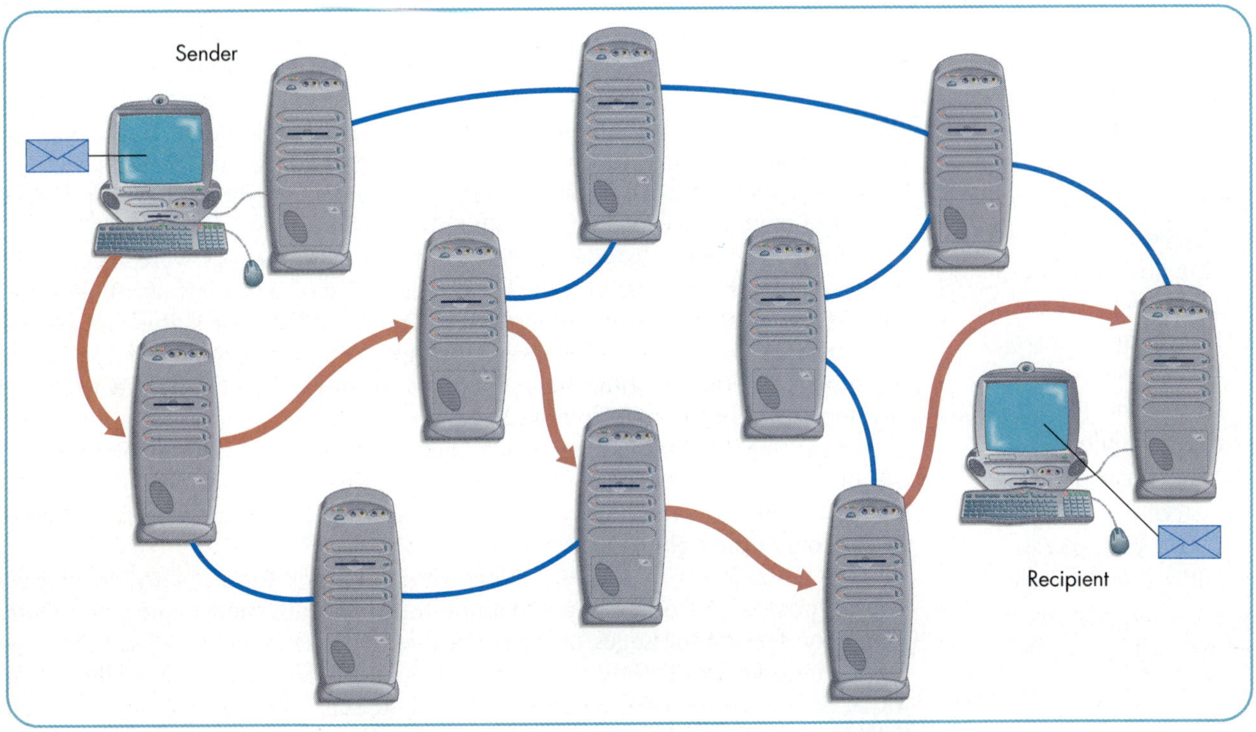

ONLY THE DESTINATION MATTERS

Data is sent across the Internet in "packets," with each packet passing through several networks to get to its destination. The only thing that matters is a packet's eventual destination. Each network has its own router that determines how best to move the message forward, taking into account the traffic on the network. This means that the next time a message is sent from "point A to point B," it could travel an entirely different path. The entire process is governed by the TCP/IP protocol that sends data across the globe in seconds.

Electronic mail, or ***e-mail***, is conceptually the same as writing a letter and sending it through the US Postal Service with one very significant advantage—e-mail messages are delivered almost instantly as opposed to regular (snail) mail, which requires several days. E-mail was unknown to the general public only a few years ago, but it has become an integral part of American culture.

All Windows-based e-mail systems work basically the same way. You need access to a ***mail server*** (a computer with a network connection) to receive your incoming messages and to deliver the messages you send. You also need an e-mail program such as ***Microsoft Outlook***, in order to read and compose e-mail messages, and to transfer mail back and forth to the server.

The mail server functions as a central post office and provides private mailboxes to persons authorized to use its services. It receives mail around the clock and holds it until you sign on to retrieve it. You gain access to your mailbox via a ***username*** and a ***password***. The username identifies you to the server. The password protects your account from unauthorized use by others. Once you log on successfully, you can read your mail. It can be downloaded (sent from the server and stored locally), or it can be left on the server, in which case you can access it from another computer at another time. Outgoing mail is uploaded (sent from your PC) to the server, where it is sent on its way across a local area network to another person within your organization or across the Internet to the world at large.

Figure 19 displays a typical screen in Outlook. The various mail folders are shown in the left pane. Only one folder can be selected at a time, for example, the *Inbox folder* in Figure 19a, and its contents are displayed in the right pane. The inbox displays a list of all incoming messages, the person who sent the message, the subject of the message, and the date and time the message was received.

The messages are listed in order according to when they were received (the most recent message is listed at the bottom of the list). Look carefully at the appearance of the messages in the inbox to learn more about their status and contents. Four messages have not yet been read and appear with a sealed envelope icon and the subject in bold. All other messages have been read and appear with an open envelope icon and in regular type. Several of the messages also have a paper clip icon indicating that they contain an attached file. A red exclamation point (!) next to one of the messages indicates the sender labeled it as a high-priority message. One message is selected within the inbox, and the content of that message is displayed at the bottom of the right pane.

The inbox is one of several folders within Outlook for use with Internet mail. The purpose of the other folders can be inferred from their names. The *Outbox folder* contains all messages that have not yet been sent (uploaded) to the server. Once a message is sent, however, it is moved automatically to the *Sent Items folder*. Messages remain indefinitely in the Inbox and Sent Items folders unless they are moved to another folder or deleted, in which case they are moved to the *Deleted Items folder*. Messages that you close before completing and sending them are stored in the *Drafts folder*.

NO MORE TELEPHONE TAG

E-mail has changed the way we communicate and in many ways is superior to the telephone. You send a message when it is convenient for you. The recipient reads the message when it is convenient to do so. Neither person has to be online for the other to access his or her e-mail system. You can send the same message to many people as opposed to having to call them individually. And best of all, e-mail is a lot cheaper than a long distance phone call.

An Internet Address

All Internet addresses follow the general format, username@mailserver. The combination of the username and mail server is unique. Bob Grauer, for example, is the only individual in the world with the e-mail address rgrauer@miami.edu. There can be many individuals who go by the username "rgrauer", and there are many more individuals who use the miami.edu mail server. But Bob is the only person who has the e-mail address rgrauer@miami.edu.

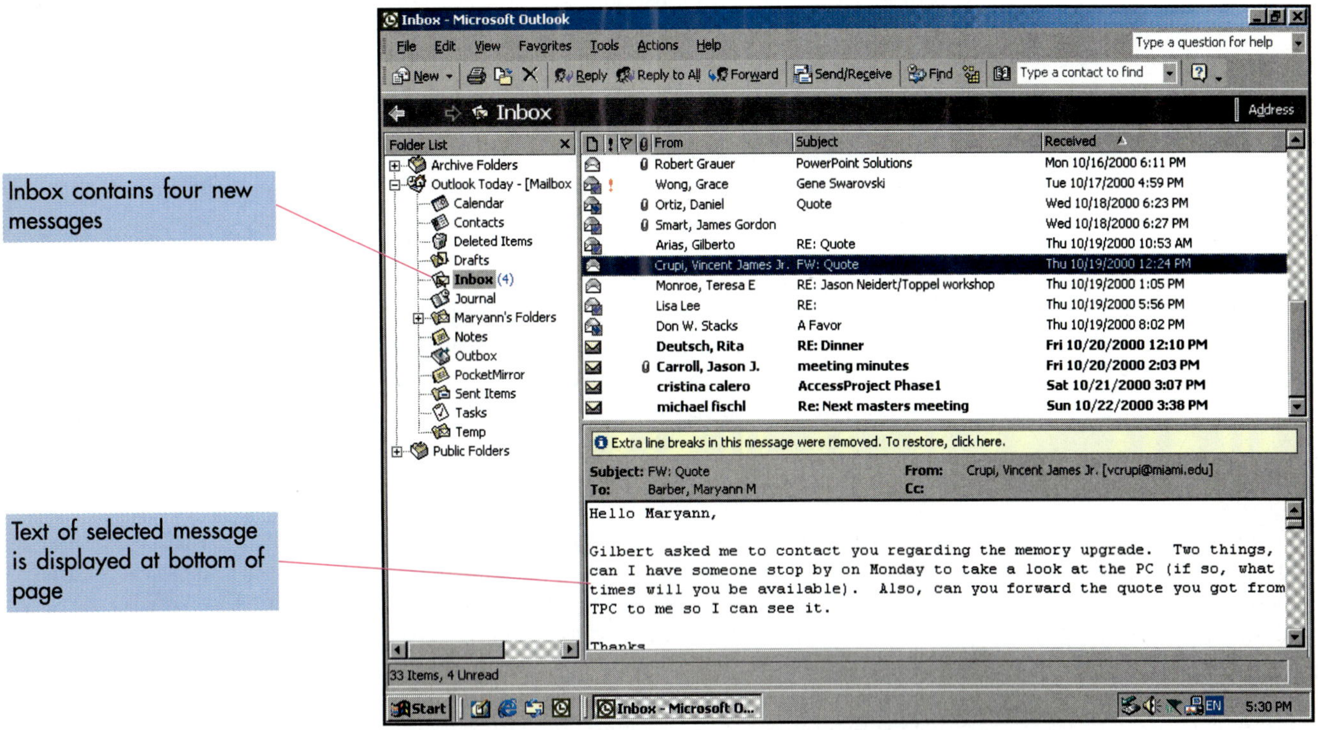

(a) The Inbox

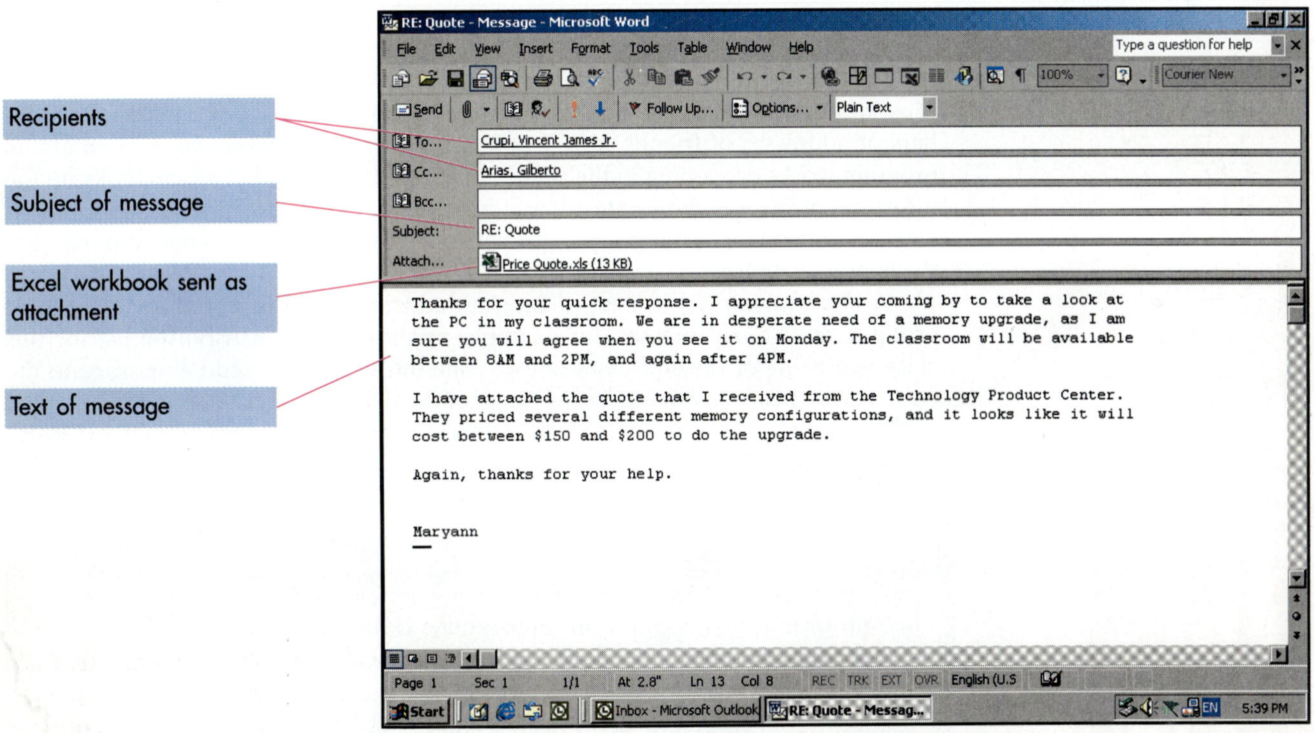

(b) Composing a Message

Anatomy of an E-Mail Message

All e-mail systems provide the same basic commands to compose, send, reply, and forward e-mail. You start by composing (or creating) a new message on your PC, then you execute the Send command to upload the message from your PC to the mail server, where it goes out to the Internet. You reply to messages that appear in your inbox, and/or you can forward messages you receive to others. Figure 19b displays the Outlook window in which you compose a new message.

The function of the text boxes at the top of the message is apparent from their names. The To text box contains the address of the recipient(s). The Cc (courtesy or carbon copy) text box indicates the names of other people who are to receive copies of the message. The text of the message appears in the message area below the subject line. You can also attach one or more files to the e-mail message such as a Word document or Excel workbook. The recipient reads the message as usual, and then has the ability to view and/or edit the attached file (provided that the associated application is installed on his or her machine). To mail the message, click the Send button when you have finished. That's all there is to it.

Replying to an existing message is similar in concept to creating a new message, except that Outlook automatically enters the addressee for you. You open a message from the inbox to read it, click the Reply button to open a window similar to Figure 19b, then enter the text of your message. You can enter additional recipients to your reply and/or forward the original message to someone else.

The ability to forward an e-mail message to a third party is quite useful. Select the message in any folder, click the Forward Message button on the Outlook toolbar to open the editing window, then enter the recipient's e-mail address in the To box. The subject is entered automatically and begins with the letters FW to indicate the message has been forwarded. The text of the original message and any attached files appear in the editing window. You can edit the message and/or add additional comments of your own. Click the Send button to send the message.

The Address Book

Most of us use some type of personal address book to look up the telephone numbers or addresses of friends, family, and colleagues. The ***address book*** in an e-mail program works conceptually the same way, except the e-mail program looks up the information for you. You enter the addressee's name in the To field and Outlook will look up and insert the address for you. It's a lot easier than having to remember the complete address.

A ***distribution list*** is a set of Internet addresses that is stored under a single group name. Your professor, for example, might create a distribution list for this class, consisting of the addresses of everyone in the class. To send a message to the entire class, the professor enters the name of the distribution list (e.g., CIS120) in the To field (or selects the group from the address book). The mail program then locates the list and automatically retrieves the e-mail addresses of all recipients in the list.

PRIVACY ISSUES

One of the most significant differences between e-mail and regular mail is privacy or the lack thereof. The network administrator has the ability to read the messages in your inbox, and indeed, many employers maintain they have the legal right to read their employees' e-mail—and the courts have agreed. Sending private e-mail on company time is potential grounds for dismissal. Send e-mail on your own time, and think twice about putting anything of a personal nature in an e-mail message, regardless of whether the message is personal or professional.

SUMMARY

A computer is an electronic device that accepts data (input), then manipulates or processes that data to produce information (output). A computer system consists of the computer and its memory, peripheral devices such as a disk, monitor, and printer, and the various programs that enable it to perform its intended functions.

IBM announced its version of the personal computer (PC) in 1981 and broke a longstanding corporate tradition by going to external sources for supporting hardware and software. Intel designed the microprocessor. Microsoft developed the operating system. Today, PC is a generic term for any computer that is based on Intel-compatible hardware and that runs Microsoft software.

Computer memory and storage capacity is described in bytes. Each byte holds 8 bits (binary digits) or one ASCII character. A kilobyte, megabyte, and gigabyte are approximately one thousand, one million, and one billion bytes, respectively.

There are several types of auxiliary storage devices. A 1.44Mb floppy drive is present on virtually every computer system. A hard (fixed) disk is the primary auxiliary storage device with a typical capacity of several gigabytes. The CD-ROM is also standard, but the newer DVD standard is gaining popularity. A removable mass storage device (such as an Iomega Zip drive) is recommended for backup.

The keyboard and the mouse are the primary input devices for the PC. The standard mouse has two buttons and recognizes four basic operations: point, click (with either button), double click, and drag.

The monitor (or video display) is an output device. The resolution of a monitor is defined as the number of pixels (picture elements) that are displayed at one time—for example, 800 × 600 or 1,024 × 768. Higher resolutions require larger monitors. The quality of a monitor is measured by its dot pitch; the smaller the dot pitch the crisper the image.

A printer produces output on paper or acetate transparencies. The output is referred to as hard copy because it is more tangible than the files written to a disk or other electronic device. Printers vary greatly in terms of design, price, and capability.

Software is divided broadly into two classes—system software (referred to as the operating system) and application software. The operating system determines the types of applications the system can run. Windows 95 was the first of the "modern" Windows operating systems. Windows 98 and its successor, Windows Me, are intended for the home user and provide extensive support for games and peripheral devices. Windows NT and its successor, Windows 2000, are aimed at the business user and provide increased security and reliability. All four operating systems have substantially the same interface as Windows 95.

Microsoft Office XP contains four major applications—Microsoft Word, Excel, Access, and PowerPoint—for word processing, spreadsheets, database, and presentations, respectively. The applications share a common user interface and similar command structure. Adequate backup should also be created for all essential documents on a regular basis and stored offsite.

A computer virus is an actively infectious program that alters and/or erases the files on a system. A computer is at potential risk to virus attack every time it reads a floppy drive, receives an e-mail message, or downloads a file from the Internet. The acquisition of antivirus software (with continual updates) is essential.

A network is a combination of hardware and software that enables the connected computers to share resources and communicate with one another. It may be large enough to encompass computers across the country and around the world, or it may be limited to the computers on one floor of a building. The latter is known as a local area network or LAN.

The Internet is a network of networks. The World Wide Web (or simply the Web) is a very large subset of the Internet, consisting of those computers that store hypertext and hypermedia documents. A browser such as Internet Explorer or Netscape Navigator is required to view documents from the Web. A connection to the Internet is established through a local area network (LAN) or by connecting to an Internet Service Provider (ISP) via a modem, cable modem, or DSL line.

E-commerce involves many of the same concepts as traditional commerce, namely the exchange of goods and services between buyers and sellers. E-commerce also enables both buyer and seller to conduct business in ways that are not possible with traditional bricks and mortar. A cookie is a small file that a Web site writes to a PC each time the site is visited, enabling a vendor to customize a user's interaction with a Web site.

Electronic mail, or e-mail, is the most widely used Internet service. An e-mail address follows the general format username@mailserver. All e-mail systems provide the same basic commands to compose, send, reply, and forward e-mail.

KEY TERMS

MULTIPLE CHOICE

1. How many bytes are in 1Kb?
   (a) 1,000
   (b) 1,024
   (c) 1,000,000
   (d) 1,024,000

2. The size of a computer's memory refers to:
   (a) The capacity of its hard disk
   (b) The capacity of its floppy disk
   (c) The amount of ROM available
   (d) The amount of RAM available

3. Hard copy refers to:
   (a) The difficulty of duplicating disk
   (b) Information stored on a hard drive
   (c) Written material that is difficult to read
   (d) None of the above

4. Which of the following is an *invalid* drive designation?
   (a) Drive A for a floppy disk
   (b) Drive B for a CD-ROM
   (c) Drive C for a fixed disk
   (d) Drive D for a removable mass storage device

5. Which of the following is best suited as a backup device?
   (a) A floppy disk
   (b) A hard (fixed) disk
   (c) A CD-ROM
   (d) An Iomega Zip Drive (or its equivalent)

6. Which of the following displays capacities from largest to smallest?
   (a) Kb, Mb, Gb
   (b) Gb, Mb, Kb
   (c) Gb, Kb, Mb
   (d) Mb, Kb, Gb

7. Which of the following best describes the memory and fixed disk in a PC you would buy today?
   (a) The capacity of RAM is measured in megabytes, the capacity of a fixed disk is measured in gigabytes
   (b) The capacity of RAM is measured in gigabytes, the capacity of a fixed disk is measured in megabytes
   (c) The capacities of RAM and a fixed disk are both measured in gigabytes
   (d) The capacities of RAM and a fixed disk are both measured in megabytes

8. A local area network is intended to:
   (a) Share data among connected computers
   (b) Share peripheral devices among computers
   (c) Share programs among connected computers
   (d) All of the above

9. A virus can be transmitted when you:
   (a) Download files from the Internet
   (b) Copy files from a floppy disk to your hard drive
   (c) Both (a) and (b)
   (d) Neither (a) nor (b)

10. Which of the following was the first "modern" Windows operating system?
   (a) Windows 95
   (b) Windows 98
   (c) Windows 2000
   (d) Windows NT

11. Which version of Windows is (was) not intended for the typical home user?
   (a) Windows 98
   (b) Windows 95
   (c) Windows NT
   (d) Windows Me

12. When is a file compression program *not* necessary?
   (a) To compress individual files into a compressed (zip) file
   (b) To create a self-extracting file from a compressed file
   (c) To expand a compressed (zip) file
   (d) To expand a self-extracting file

13. Which of the following capabilities is built into the Microsoft Windows?
   (a) File compression
   (b) Antivirus software
   (c) Both (a) and (b)
   (d) Neither (a) nor (b)

14. Which of the following means of Internet access will tie up your telephone line and prevent you from speaking when the Internet connection is in effect?
   (a) A regular modem
   (b) A cable modem
   (c) A DSL line from your local telephone company
   (d) All of the above

15. What is a cookie?
   (a) A computer virus
   (b) A small file that is written to a PC by a Web site
   (c) A self-extracting file
   (d) A file compression program

16. Which of the following is true about Microsoft Office XP?
   (a) It is bundled with Microsoft Windows at no additional cost
   (b) It is available in different versions, with different applications in each version
   (c) It includes a file compression program for efficient storage of Office documents
   (d) It includes an antivirus program

ANSWERS

1. b	**5.** d	**9.** c	**13.** d
2. d	**6.** a	**10.** a	**14.** a
3. d	**7.** a	**11.** c	**15.** b
4. b	**8.** d	**12.** d	**16.** b

History of Computers

Use your favorite search engine to locate at least two computer museums and describe the current exhibits in a note to your instructor. You will learn about computers such as the ENIAC (Electronic Numerical Integrator and Calculator), which is recognized as the first operational electronic computer. The ENIAC was built in 1946, weighed 30 tons, and required 1,500 square feet of floor space, yet its computational capability was a fraction of today's entry-level PC.

Microsoft Office

Does Microsoft Office include both Microsoft PowerPoint and Microsoft Access? The answer depends on which version of Microsoft Office you are referring to. Go to the Office site, www.microsoft.com/office, to see which versions of Office are available, then create a table that summarizes the different versions and the software that is included in each version. What is the best (cheapest) price you can find for Office Professional? Summarize your findings in a brief note to your instructor.

Best of the Web

There are so many excellent sites on the Web that it's hard to know where to begin. Use your favorite search engine to find one or more "Best of the Web" lists, then check out the lists to see what is available. Create your own list of five outstanding Web sites and submit the list to your instructor. Compare your sites to those submitted by your classmates. Which sites were suggested by multiple students? Can you create a "Best of the Web" list as suggested by your class?

Antivirus Software

Use your favorite search engine to locate at least two companies that offer antivirus software, and then compare their offerings. How much do the products cost? How frequently are the products updated with respect to protection for new viruses? Do the vendors also offer a firewall? What other information (if any) is available at the site? Survey your class to determine the percent of students who employ some type of antivirus software, and further, how often the software is updated. Summarize your information in a brief note to your instructor.

Buying a PC

What configuration would you suggest for an entry-level PC? Visit the Web sites of at least two vendors to learn about their current offerings and the cost of your configuration. Does the vendor include 30-day price protection? What type of warranty is provided? Summarize your findings in a brief note to your instructor. In addition, explain why it is important to use a credit card in your purchase.

File Compression

Go to the WinZip Web site at www.winzip.com to learn more about file compression. Is it possible to download an evaluation copy of the WinZip file compression program? How much does it cost? What competing programs are available? Is the WinZip software capable of creating a self-extracting file, or is additional software required? Summarize your findings in a brief note to your instructor.

Campus Access to the Internet

The easiest way to access the Internet is from a local area network on campus. But which students are given access, and what (if anything) do you have to do to open an account? Does the university provide an e-mail account? If so, what is your user-name and password? What is your e-mail address? Does your e-mail account expire at the end of the semester, or does it continue throughout your stay at the university? You don't have to put your answers in writing, but you will need to know this information if you are to be successful in this class.

The Internet Service Provider

You can use at least three different technologies to connect to the Internet from home: a regular modem, a cable modem, or a DSL modem. What is the rated speed of each technology? How reliable is the technology? What is the installation cost (if any) and the monthly service charge? Contact at least two different Internet Service Providers in your area to compare prices. Summarize the results in a short note to your instructor.

Employment on the Web

How can the Web help you in a search for full-time employment? Is the Web useful to secure an internship or part-time job? Use your favorite search engine to locate at least two sites where you can post a résumé and/or search through a job bank. Survey your classmates to find out if they have been successful in a Web search for employment. Do you think you have a realistic expectation for success by using the Web?

Photo Credits

Page 2 Stock Montage, Inc.

Page 4 Courtesy of International Business Machines Corporation. Unauthorized use not permitted.

Page 8 Courtesy of Intel® Corporation/© 2001.

Page 11 (a) Courtesy of International Business Machines Corporation. Unauthorized use not permitted. (b) Courtesy of Seagate Technology/C & I Photography. (c) Courtesy of Imation Corporation/CD-RW. (d) Courtesy of Iomega Corporation.

Page 13 Joystick: Courtesy of Microsoft Corporation; Mouse: Courtesy of International Business Machines Corporation. Unauthorized use not permitted.

Page 17 (a) Courtesy of International Business Machines Corporation. Unauthorized use not permitted. (b) Courtesy of Epson America, Inc. (c) Courtesy of Hewlett-Packard Company.

Page 20 Palm™ VIIx handheld: copyright © 2001. ACME, Inc. All rights reserved. Acme is a registered trademark; and Palm and Palm.net are trademarks of Palm, Inc. iMac: Courtesy of Mark Laita. Notebook: Courtesy of Dell Computer Corporation.

INDEX

A = Access   C = Concepts   E = Excel   I = Internet   P = PowerPoint   PR = Windows Prerequisites   W = Word

A

B

C

D

E

F

G

H

I

J

K

L

M

N

O

P

Q

R

S

T

U

V

W

Z